Understanding
Social Problems

Understanding Social Problems

Linda A. Mooney
David Knox
Caroline Schacht

East Carolina University

West Publishing Company

Minneapolis/St. Paul   New York   Los Angeles   San Francisco

Copyediting:	Patricia A. Lewis
Text Design:	Michelle Webb, Hespenheide Design
Composition and Artwork:	Carlisle Communications
Index:	Schroeder Indexing
Cover Image:	*The Fight between Carnival and Lent* by Pieter Brueghel the Elder, Kunsthistorisches Museum, Vienna/ ©SuperStock, Inc.

British Library Cataloging-in-Publication Data. A catalogue record for this book is available from the British Library.

COPYRIGHT © 1997 By WEST PUBLISHING COMPANY
   610 Opperman Drive
   P.O. Box 64526
   St. Paul, MN 55164-0526

Library of Congress Cataloging-in-Publication Data

Mooney, Linda A.
 Understanding social problems / Linda A. Mooney, David Knox, Caroline Schacht.
  p. cm.
 Includes bibliographical references and index.
 ISBN 0-314-06717-5 (soft : alk. paper)
 1. Social problems—United States. 2. United States—Social conditions—1980- I. Knox, David, 1943- . II. Schacht, Caroline. III. Title.
HN59.2.M66 1997
361.1′0973—dc20   96-2132
           CIP

WEST'S COMMITMENT TO THE ENVIRONMENT

In 1906, West Publishing Company began recycling materials left over from the production of books. This began a tradition of efficient and responsible use of resources. Today, 100% of our legal bound volume are printed on acid-free, recycled paper consisting of 50% new paper pulp and 50% paper that has undergone a de-inking process. We also use vegetable-based inks to print all of our books. West recycles nearly 27,700,000 pounds of scrap paper annually—the equivalent of 229,300 trees. Since the 1960s, West has devised ways to capture and recycle waste inks, solvents, oils, and vapors created in the printing process. We also recycle plastics of all kinds, wood, glass, corrugated cardboard, and batteries, and have eliminated the use of polystyrene book packaging. We at West are proud of the longevity and the scope of our commitment to the environment.

West pocket parts and advance sheets are printed on recyclable paper and can be collected and recycled with newspapers. Staples do not have to be removed. Bound volumes can be recycled after removing the cover.

Production, Prepress, Printing and Binding by West Publishing Company.

Printed with Printwise ∞
Environmentally Advanced Water Washable Ink

Photo Credits

(continued after index)

To Our Parents

Thomas and Margaret Mooney
Dave and Jeannette Knox
Herb and Emily Schacht

Contents

Illness and Health Care 35

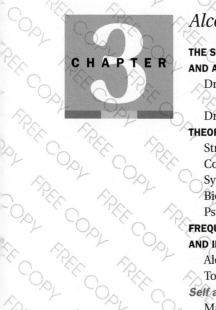

Alcohol and Other Drugs 63

Crime and Violence   93

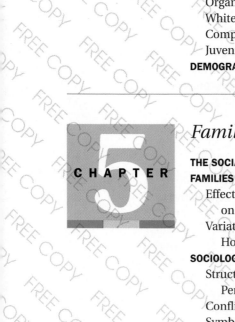

Family Problems   125

Section Two: Problems of Human Diversity   158

Youth and Aging   *161*

CHAPTER 6

Sexual Orientation 191

Gender Inequality 221

Racial and Ethnic Relations — 247

Section Three: Problems of Inequality and Power — 278

Work — 281

Wealth and Poverty 311

Urban Decline and Growth 341

Crisis in Education   367

Section Four: Problems of Modernization   398

CHAPTER 14

Science and Technology   401

CHAPTER 15

Population and the Environment   429

Global Conflict   *463*

CHAPTER 16

Preface

Crime, violence, homelessness, illiteracy, divorce, and inadequate health care are some of the "high visibility" social problems in the United States. This text emphasizes that understanding social problems—their causes, consequences, and solutions—requires an understanding of the social structure and culture of the society in which they exist. In addition, the text reflects an integrative theoretical approach, i.e., an approach that utilizes various theoretical perspectives to best understand the respective social problem under consideration.

Academic Features

Specific academic features of the text include the following:

- *Strong theoretical foundation.* The three major sociological approaches, structural functionalism, symbolic interactionism, and conflict theory, are introduced in the first chapter and discussed, where appropriate, throughout the text. Specific theories of social problems, as well as feminist approaches, are also presented where appropriate.
- *Emphasis on the structure and culture of society.* As noted above, the text emphasizes how the social structure and culture of society contribute to and maintain social problems, as well as providing the basis for alternative solutions.
- *Review of basic sociological terms.* An overview of basic sociological terms and concepts is presented in the first chapter. This overview is essential for students who have not taken an introductory course and is helpful, as a review, for those who have.
- *Unique organization.* The sixteen chapters are organized around four major areas of social problems today: problems of individual well-being, problems of human diversity, problems of inequality and power, and problems of modernization. The order of topic presentation reflects a progression from a micro to a macro level of analysis, focusing first on problems of health care, drug use, and crime and then broadening to the wider concerns of science and technology, population and the environment, and global conflict.

  Two chapters merit special mention: Sexual Orientation (Chapter 7) and Science and Technology (Chapter 14). Whereas traditional texts discuss sexual orientation under the rubric of "deviance," this topic is examined in the section on problems of human diversity along with the related issues of age, gender, and racial and ethnic inequality.

The chapter on Science and Technology includes such topics as biotechnology, the computer revolution, and the information highway. This chapter emphasizes the transformation of society through scientific and technological innovations, the societal costs of such innovations, and issues of social responsibility.

- *Unique chapter format.* Each chapter follows a similar format: the social problem is defined, the theoretical explanations are discussed, the consequences of the social problem are explored, and the alternative solutions and policies are examined. A concluding section assesses the current state of knowledge for each problem.
- *Standard and cutting edge topics.* In addition to problems that are typically addressed in social problems courses and texts, new and emerging topics are examined. These include affirmative action and welfare reform, multicultural education, the economic conversion of excess military production, diversity training in the workplace, information warfare, and the militia movement.

Pedagogy

In addition to the various academic features of the text, we have tried to present the material in a "user friendly" format. Pedagogical features include the following:

- *National and international data.* Official statistics and research data from nationally representative samples are presented in marginal inserts called "National Data." Similar inserts called "International Data" present national data from other countries around the world.
- *Consideration sections.* Sections labeled "Consideration" provide unique examples, insights, implications, explanations, and applications of material presented in the text. These sections are designed to illuminate a previous point in a thought-provoking way.
- *Self and Society.* Each chapter includes a social survey designed to help students assess their own attitudes, beliefs, knowledge, or behavior regarding some aspect of a social problem. Students may also compare their responses with those from a larger sample. Examples include a Criminal Activities Survey, an Abusive Behavior Inventory, and an AIDS Knowledge Scale.
- *The Human Side.* To personalize the information being discussed, each chapter includes a feature entitled "The Human Side." These features illustrate how individuals experience the social problem under discussion. Examples include personal experience with homelessness, racism, drug abuse, and mental illness.
- *In Focus.* Offset boxes called "In Focus" contain expanded discussions of some aspect of the social problem under consideration. For

example, "Female Genital Mutilation" is highlighted in Chapter 8 (Gender Inequality), and "Indoor Air Pollution" is the *In Focus* topic in Chapter 15 (Population and the Environment).

- *Is It True?* Each chapter begins with five true-false items to stimulate student interest and thinking.
- *Critical Thinking.* Each chapter ends with a brief section called "Critical Thinking" that raises several questions related to the chapter topic. These questions invite the student to use critical thinking skills in applying the information discussed in the chapter.
- *Worldwide Web Home Page.* As an additional pedagogical tool, *Understanding Social Problems* has its own home page on the Worldwide Web! Students and faculty can access relevant research studies, statistics, and theoretical links conveniently listed by chapter topic. For example, under Crime and Violence (Chapter 4), students can enter the Federal Bureau of Investigation and the U.S. Department of Justice Home Pages. Students and faculty can also send questions, comments, or suggestions directly to the authors and contact West Publishing Company concerning book adoption. *Understanding Social Problem's* Home Page is located on the Web at http://ecuvax.cis.ecu.edu/~somooney/undersp.html.

Acknowledgments

This text reflects the work of many people. Peter Marshall, as executive editor, provided information from teachers about the qualities of a textbook they would like for their social problems courses. Jane Bass, as developmental editor, provided quick turnaround on five sets of reviews. Pat Lewis copyedited the manuscript. Angela Musey secured permissions and Kara ZumBahlen served as production editor. All were superb in their respective roles.

We would also like to acknowledge the support and assistance of Blair Carr, Betty Petteway, Richard Caston, Jim Mitchell, Emily Boyce, Ruth Katz, Ken Wilson, Christa Reiser, Bob Hummer, Jasper Register, Sarah Brabant, Bob Gramling, Pat Seitz, Brian Crisp, Kim Harris, Laurin Gipson, Tracie Gardner, and Joe Reid. To each we are grateful.

Additionally, we are indebted to those who read the manuscript in its various drafts and provided valuable insights and suggestions, many of which have been incorporated into the final manuscript:

David Allen
University of New Orleans

Patricia Atchison
Colorado State University

Roland Chilton
University of Massachusetts

Barbara Costello
Mississippi State University

Robert Gliner
San Jose State University

Millie Harmon
Chemeketa Community College

Sylvia Jones
Jefferson Community College

Judith Mayo
Arizona State University

Madonna Harrington-Meyer
University of Illinois

John Stratton
University of Iowa

Clifford Mottaz
University of Wisconsin—
River Falls

Joseph Trumino
St. Vincent's College of St. John's
 University

Ed Ponczek
William Rainey Harper College

Joseph Vielbig
Arizona Western University

Rita Sakitt
Suffolk County Community College

Oscar Williams
Diablo Valley College

Lawrence Stern
Collin County Community College

Finally, we are interested in ways to improve the text and invite your feedback and suggestions for new ideas and material to be included in subsequent editions.

Linda A. Mooney
David Knox
Caroline Schacht
 Department of Sociology
 East Carolina University
 Greenville, NC 27858

E-mail addresses:
SOMOONEY@ECUVM.CIS.ECU.EDU
SOKNOX@ECUVM.CIS.ECU.EDU
SOSCHACHT@ECUVM.CIS.ECU.EDU

1

CHAPTER

Thinking about Social Problems

IS IT TRUE?

An annual study of social well-being in America revealed that since 1970 social conditions have steadily improved in our society (p. 2).

Prior to the nineteenth century, it was considered a husband's legal right and marital obligation to discipline and control his wife through the use of physical force (p. 4).

In seventeenth- and eighteenth-century England, tea drinking was considered a social problem (p. 4).

Questions involving values, religion, and morality can only be answered through scientific research (p. 20).

In a national survey of first-year college students in the United States, most students agreed with the statement: "Realistically, an individual person can do little to bring about changes in our society" (p. 27).

ANS: 1. F 2. T 3. T 4. F 5. F

> Ours is a time of uneasiness and indifference—not yet formulated in such ways as to permit the work of reason and the play of sensibility. Instead of troubles—defined in terms of values and threats—there is often the misery of vague uneasiness; instead of explicit issues there is merely the beat feeling that all is somehow not right.
>
> C. Wright Mills, Sociologist

It is easy to find things in the real world that are not perfect and to say that something should be done to correct the problems. However, for every ten people who see the same problem, there will be ten different ideal solutions.
—Randall G. Holcombe Chairman of the Research Advisory Council of the James Madison Institute for Public Policy Studies

Researchers at Fordham University conduct an annual study called "The Index of Social Health." This study evaluates the cumulative effect on Americans of sixteen major social problems, including crime, unemployment, drug abuse, suicide rates, homicide rates, and child abuse. According to a report in the *New York Times,* this study found that the level of social well-being in the United States in the early 1990s was the lowest since the study began in the 1970s (Steinberg 1993). Teenage pregnancy, AIDS, inadequate health care, crime, racial conflict, drug abuse, and other social issues have become national and international concerns. Such problems present both a threat and a challenge to our society.

The primary goal of this text is to provide an increased awareness and understanding of social conditions that are considered problematic in our society and throughout the world. Although the topics covered in this text vary widely, all chapters have similar objectives: to explain how social problems are created and maintained; to indicate how they affect individuals, social groups, and society as a whole; and to examine the difficulties involved in selecting and implementing the best policies for change. We begin by looking at the nature of social problems.

What Is a Social Problem?

It is reasonable to begin a course in social problems by asking, "What is a social problem? How does a social condition become defined as a social problem?" The answers to these questions are not as simple as they might seem at first glance. There is no universal, constant, or absolute definition of what constitutes a social problem. Rather, social problems are defined by a combination of objective and subjective criteria that vary across societies, among individuals and groups within a society, and across historical time periods.

OBJECTIVE AND SUBJECTIVE ELEMENTS OF SOCIAL PROBLEMS

Although social problems take many forms, they all share two important elements: an objective social condition and a subjective interpretation of that social condition. Both elements are essential to the definition.

Objective Element of Social Problems The objective element of a social problem refers to the existence of a social condition. We become aware of social

We become aware of the existence of domestic violence and other social problems in various ways, but society must view these conditions as harmful and in need of remedy before they fit the definition of a social problem.

conditions through our own life experience and through reports in the media. We see the homeless, hear gunfire in the streets, and see battered women in hospital emergency rooms. We hear unemployment figures reported in the media and know people who have lost their jobs and the difficulties unemployment causes for them and their families.

Subjective Element of Social Problems The subjective element of a social problem refers to the belief that a particular social condition is harmful to society, or to a segment of society, and that it should and can be changed. We know that crime, drug addiction, poverty, racism, violence, and pollution exist. These social conditions are not considered social problems, however, unless at least a segment of society believes that these conditions diminish the quality of human life.

By combining these objective and subjective elements, we arrive at the following definition: A **social problem** is a social condition that a segment of society views as harmful to members of society and in need of remedy. Notice that how society subjectively views a condition is as important to the definition as the condition itself.

Social problems are fundamentally products of collective definition. . . . A social problem does not exist for society unless it is recognized by that society to exist.
—Herbert Blumer
Sociologist

> **Consideration** *Between 1933 and 1945, more than 12 million Jews, homosexuals, people with mental and physical disabilities, and gypsies were exterminated in death camps by Hitler's Nazi regime. Hitler's goal was to rid German society of "inferior" people so he could build a "master Aryan race." Why did the German population accept what Hitler was doing? Why didn't they view the extermination of millions of people as a social problem?*
>
> *One reason is that, to some degree, Hitler kept the existence of the extermination camps hidden from the German population. Thus, to some extent, the objective condition was unknown. In addition, Hitler worked hard to influence how those Germans who were aware of the camps subjectively interpreted this social condition. Hitler's propaganda suggested that these*

were labor camps—not death camps. Germans who were aware of what was actually happening in the camps were encouraged to view the mass extermination as important and necessary for the future of Aryan society, rather than as a harmful social condition that should be stopped.

VARIABILITY IN DEFINITIONS OF SOCIAL PROBLEMS

Individuals and groups frequently disagree about what constitutes a social problem. For example, some Americans view the availability of abortion as a social problem, while others view restrictions on abortion as a social problem. Similarly, some Americans view homosexuality as a social problem, while others view prejudice and discrimination against homosexuals as a social problem. Such variations in what is considered a social problem are due to several factors, including the different political climates in which individuals and groups exist and differences in values, beliefs, and life experiences.

Definitions of social problems vary not only within societies, but across societies and historical time periods as well. For example, prior to the nineteenth century, it was a husband's legal right and marital obligation to discipline and control his wife through the use of physical force. Today, as people have become increasingly concerned about the devastating consequences of domestic violence, the use of physical force is regarded as a social problem rather than as a marital right.

Tea drinking is another example of how what is considered a social problem can change over time. In seventeenth- and eighteenth-century England, tea drinking was regarded as a "base Indian practice" that was "pernicious to health, obscuring industry, and impoverishing the nation" (Ukers 1935, cited in Troyer and Markle 1984). Today, the English are known for their tradition of drinking tea in the afternoon. Similarly, marijuana and cocaine were once legally available in the United States. Today, consumers and sellers of these drugs are the target of federal agents.

Because social problems can be highly complex, it is helpful to have a framework within which to view them. Sociology provides such a framework.

While some Americans view the availability of abortion as a social problem, others view restrictions on abortion as a social problem. The disagreement can lead to violence or destruction. Arson is suspected in the burning of this abortion clinic.

Using a sociological perspective to examine social problems requires a knowledge of the basic concepts and tools of sociology. In the remainder of this chapter, we discuss some of these concepts and tools: social structure, culture, the "sociological imagination," major theoretical perspectives, and types of research methods.

Elements of Social Structure and Culture

Human beings are social creatures; we influence and are influenced by the social world in which we live. Although society surrounds us and permeates our lives, it is difficult to "see" society. By thinking of society in terms of a picture or image, however, we can visualize society and therefore better understand it. Imagine that society is a coin with two sides: on one side is the structure of society, and on the other is the culture of society. Although each "side" is distinct, both are inseparable from the whole. By looking at the various elements of social structure and culture, we can better understand the root causes of social problems.

ELEMENTS OF SOCIAL STRUCTURE

The *structure* of a society refers to the way society is organized. Society is organized into different parts: institutions, social groups, statuses, and roles.

Institutions The largest elements of the structure of society are its social institutions. An **institution** is an established and enduring pattern of social relationships. The five traditional institutions are family, religion, politics, economics, and education, but some sociologists argue that other social institutions, such as science and technology, mass media, medicine, sport, and the military, are also playing important roles in modern society.

Many social problems are generated by inadequacies in various institutions. For example, unemployment may be influenced by the educational institution's failure to prepare individuals for the job market and by alterations in the structure of the economic institution. Further, poverty is exacerbated by all three conditions: unemployment, inferior education, and changes in the economy.

Social Groups Institutions are made up of social groups. A **social group** is defined as two or more people who have a common identity, interact, and form a social relationship. The family in which you were reared is a social group that is part of the family institution. The religious association to which you may belong is a social group that is part of the religious institution. Your co-workers at your place of employment and the employees at the store where you buy your groceries comprise social groups that are part of the economic institution. The city or town council where you live is a social group that represents the political institution. Lastly, the members of your social problems class form a social group that is part of the educational institution.

Social groups may be categorized as primary or secondary. *Primary groups,* which tend to involve small numbers of individuals, are characterized by intimate and informal interaction. Families and friends are examples of primary groups. *Secondary groups,* which may involve small or large numbers of individuals, are task-oriented and characterized by impersonal and formal interaction. Examples of secondary groups include employers and their employees, clerks and their customers, and members of the local PTA.

Statuses Just as institutions consist of social groups, social groups consist of statuses. A **status** is a position a person occupies within a social group and thus within the structure of society. The statuses we occupy largely define our social identity. The statuses in a family may consist of mother, father, stepmother, stepfather, wife, husband, child, and so on. Discussions of social problems may involve such statuses as juvenile delinquent, pregnant teenager, and drug addict.

Statuses may be either ascribed or achieved. An **ascribed status** is one that society assigns to an individual on the basis of factors over which the individual has no control. For example, we have no control over the sex, race, ethnic background, and socioeconomic status into which we are born. Similarly, we are assigned the status of "child," "teenager," "adult," or "senior citizen" on the basis of our age—something we do not choose or control.

An **achieved status** is assigned on the basis of some characteristic or behavior over which the individual has some control. Whether or not you achieve the status of college graduate, spouse, parent, bank president, or prison inmate depends largely on your own efforts, behavior, and choices. One's ascribed statuses may affect the likelihood of achieving other statuses, however. For example, if you are born into a poor socioeconomic status, you may find it more difficult to achieve the status of "college graduate" because of the high cost of a college education.

Every individual has numerous statuses simultaneously. You may be a student, parent, tutor, volunteer fundraiser, female, and Hispanic. A person's *master status* is the status that is considered the most significant in a person's social identity. Typically, a person's occupational status is regarded as his or her master status. If you are a full-time student, your master status is likely to be "student."

Roles Every status is associated with many **roles,** or the set of rights, obligations, and expectations associated with a status. Our social statuses identify who we are; our roles identify the behaviors we are expected to engage in. Roles guide our behavior and allow us to predict the behavior of others. As a student, you are expected to attend class, listen and take notes, study for tests, and complete assignments. Because you know what the role of teacher involves, you can predict that your teacher will lecture, give exams, and assign grades based on your performance on tests.

A single status involves more than one role. For example, the status of prison inmate includes one role for interacting with prison guards and parole boards and another role for interacting with other prison inmates. Similarly, the status of nurse involves different roles for interacting with physicians and with patients.

ELEMENTS OF CULTURE

Whereas social structure refers to the organization of society, *culture* refers to the meanings and ways of life that characterize a society. The elements of culture include beliefs, values, norms, sanctions, and symbols. Together, these elements comprise the symbolic and expressive aspects of society (Wuthnow 1987).

When I fulfill my obligations as a brother, husband, or citizen, when I execute contracts, I perform duties that are defined externally to myself. . . Even if I conform in my own sentiments and feel their reality subjectively, such reality is still objective, for I did not create them; I merely inherited them.
—Emile Durkheim
Sociologist

Beliefs **Beliefs** refer to definitions and explanations about what is assumed to be true. The beliefs of an individual or group influence whether that individual or group views a particular social condition as a social problem. Does secondhand smoke harm nonsmokers? Are nuclear power plants safe? Does violence in movies and on television lead to increased aggression in children? Our beliefs regarding these issues influence whether we view the issues as social problems.

> **Consideration** *Beliefs not only influence how a social condition is interpreted, they also influence the existence of the condition itself. For example, men who believe that when a woman says "no," she really means "yes" or "maybe" are more likely to commit rape and sexual assault than men who do not have these beliefs (Frank 1991).*

Values **Values** are social agreements about what is considered good and bad, right and wrong, desirable and undesirable. Frequently, social conditions are viewed as social problems when the conditions are incompatible with or contradict closely held values. For example, poverty and homelessness violate the value of human welfare; crime contradicts the values of honesty, private property, and non-violence; racism, sexism, and heterosexism violate the values of equality and fairness.

Values play an important role not only in the interpretation of a condition as a social problem, but also in the development of the social condition itself. Sylvia Ann Hewlett (1992) explains how the American values of freedom and individualism are at the root of many of our social problems:

> *There are two sides to the coin of freedom. On the one hand, there is enormous potential for prosperity and personal fulfillment; on the other are all the hazards of untrammeled opportunity and unfettered choice. Free markets can produce grinding poverty as well as spectacular wealth; unregulated industry can create dangerous levels of pollution as well as rapid rates of growth; and an uncluttered drive for personal fulfillment can have disastrous effects on families and children. Rampant individualism does not bring with it sweet freedom; rather, it explodes in our faces and limits life's potential. (pp. 350–51)*

Absent or weak values may contribute to some social problems. For example, many industries do not value protection of the environment and thus contribute to environmental pollution. The fact that many teenagers do not value sexual abstinence may contribute to the high rate of teenage pregnancy in the United States.

Norms and Sanctions **Norms** are socially defined rules of behavior. A norm is "an idea in the minds of the members of a group, an idea that can be put in the form of a statement specifying what the members or other [people] should do, ought to do, are expected to do, under given circumstances" (Homans 1974, 2). Norms serve as guidelines for our behavior and for our expectations of the behavior of others.

All norms are associated with **sanctions,** or social consequences for conforming to or violating norms. When we conform to a social norm, we may be rewarded by a *positive sanction*. These may range from an approving smile to

When people cherish some set of values and do not feel any threat to them, they experience well-being. When they cherish values but do feel them to be threatened, they experience a crisis—either as a personal trouble or as a public issue.
—C. Wright Mills
Sociologist

National Data: A survey of 237,777 first-year students at 461 colleges and universities in 1994 revealed that their three top values were being well-off financially (74 percent), raising a family (71 percent), and becoming an authority in one's field (65 percent).

SOURCE: American Council on Education and University of California 1994.

a public ceremony in our honor. When we violate a social norm, we may be punished by a *negative sanction*, which may range from a disapproving look to the death penalty or life in prison. Most sanctions are spontaneous expressions of approval or disapproval by groups or individuals—these are referred to as *informal sanctions*. Sanctions that are carried out according to some recognized or formal procedure are referred to as *formal sanctions*. The various types of sanctions, then, include positive informal sanctions, positive formal sanctions, negative informal sanctions, and negative formal sanctions. Table 1.1 provides examples of each type of sanction.

Sociologists have identified three types of norms: folkways, laws, and mores. *Folkways* refer to the customs and manners of society. In many segments of our society, it is customary to shake hands when being introduced to a new acquaintance, to say "excuse me" after sneezing, and to give presents to family and friends on their birthdays. Although no laws require us to do these things, we are expected to do them because they are part of the cultural traditions, or folkways, of the society in which we live.

Laws are norms that are formalized and backed by political authority. A person who eats food out of a public garbage container is violating a folkway; no law prohibits this behavior. However, throwing trash onto a public street is considered littering and is against the law.

Some norms, called *mores*, have a moral basis. Violations of mores may produce shock, horror, and moral indignation. Both littering and child sexual abuse are violations of law, but child sexual abuse is also a violation of our mores because we view such behavior as immoral.

Symbols A symbol is something that represents something else. The social nature of human interaction depends on the unique ability of humans to use symbols. Without symbols, we could not communicate with each other or live as social beings.

The symbols of a culture include language, gestures, and objects whose meaning is commonly understood by the members of a society. In our society, a red ribbon tied around a car antenna symbolizes Mothers Against Drunk Driving, a peace sign symbolizes the value of nonviolence, and a white hooded robe symbolizes the Ku Klux Klan.

For the most part we do not first see then define; we define and then see.
—Walter Lippman
Social critic

TABLE 1.1		
TYPES AND EXAMPLES OF SANCTIONS		
	POSITIVE	**NEGATIVE**
INFORMAL	Being praised by one's neighbors for organizing a neighborhood recycling program	Being criticized by one's neighbors for refusing to participate in the neighborhood recycling program
FORMAL	Being granted a citizen's award for organizing a neighborhood recycling program	Being fined by the city for failure to dispose of trash properly

Consideration *Sometimes people attach different meanings to the same symbol. The Confederate flag is a symbol of Southern pride to some, a symbol of racial bigotry to others. Feelings about symbols may be intense. Four teens in Guthrie, Kentucky, the birthplace of the president of the Confederacy, were accused of shooting a passing motorist. Officials at the scene said that the Confederate flag that flew from the back of the motorist's pickup truck led to his death (Castaneda 1995).*

The elements of the social structure and culture just discussed play a central role in the creation, maintenance, and social response to various social problems. One of the goals of taking a course in social problems is to develop an awareness of how the elements of social structure and culture contribute to social problems. Sociologists refer to this awareness as the "sociological imagination."

The Sociological Imagination

The **sociological imagination,** a term developed by C. Wright Mills (1959), refers to the ability to see the connections between our personal lives and the social world in which we live. When we use our sociological imagination, we are able to distinguish between "private troubles" and "public issues" and to see connections between the events and conditions of our lives and the social and historical context in which we live.

For example, that one man is unemployed constitutes a private trouble. That millions of people are unemployed in the United States constitutes a public issue. Once we understand that personal troubles such as mental illness, criminal victimization, and poverty are shared by other segments of society, we can look for the elements of social structure and culture that contribute to these public issues and private troubles.

Rather than viewing the private trouble of being unemployed as being due to an individual's faulty character or lack of job skills, we may understand unemployment as a public issue that results from the failure of the economic and political institutions of society to provide job opportunities to all citizens. Technological innovations emerging from the Industrial Revolution led to individual workers being replaced by machines. During the economic recession of the 1980s, employers fired employees so the firm could stay in business. Thus, in both these cases, social forces rather than individual skills largely determined whether a person was employed or not.

Divorce is a social problem that is experienced as a private trouble by more than two million men and women annually (National Center for Health Statistics 1994). Divorced individuals may try to understand their situation by examining their childhood, personality characteristics, and marital relationship. Alternatively, using the sociological imagination and the concepts of social structure and culture, we can view divorce rates as a consequence of social factors. For example, structural changes in society, such as technological innovations in birth control and increased life expectancy, led to changes in beliefs and values about marriage and monogamy. One change was that sexual intercourse and marriage were no longer necessarily linked. As these and other beliefs and values about marriage changed, so did laws regarding divorce—"no-fault divorce" laws made it easier to get divorced.

In addition, when the political institution sent men to fight in World War II, American women entered the workforce in unprecedented numbers. Since World War II, women have remained in the workforce; this new financial independence makes it more feasible for wives to divorce their husbands. Divorce rates may also be linked to the rise in the cultural value of individualism over familism. Unhappy spouses contemplating divorce may be more likely to ask themselves, "Will I be happier?" rather than "Will my family be happier?" Finally, religious groups, which once applied negative sanctions to members who divorced, have become more accepting of divorce as a solution to an unhappy marriage.

If the various elements of social structure and culture contribute to private troubles and public issues, then society's social structure and culture must be changed if these concerns are to be resolved. Persons who share similar private troubles often unite to create such social change. For example, single-parent mothers who did not receive child support from their ex-husbands formed groups to lobby for changes in child support laws (Coltrane and Hickman 1993). Their efforts were successful; the Family Support Act of 1994 allows individual states to withhold court-ordered child support payments from the noncustodial parent's paycheck.

Theoretical Perspectives

The most incomprehensible thing about the world is the fact that it is comprehensible.
—Albert Einstein
Scientist

In the movie *Dead Poets' Society*, actor Robin Williams plays an English teacher in a private boys' school. In one scene he asks his students to get out of their seats and, one by one, climb onto his desk at the front of the classroom, look around, and then return to their seats. The students were perplexed; why did their teacher want them to stand on top of his desk and look around the room? The teacher told them that he wanted them to view the world, beginning with the classroom, from a new and different perspective.

Similarly, theories in sociology provide us with different perspectives with which to view our social world. A *perspective* is simply a way of looking at the world. A *theory* is a set of interrelated propositions or principles designed to answer a question or explain a particular phenomenon; it provides us with a perspective. Sociological theories help us to explain and predict the social world in which we live.

Sociology includes three major theoretical perspectives: the structural-functionalist perspective, the conflict perspective, and the symbolic interactionist perspective. Each perspective offers a variety of explanations about the causes of and possible solutions for social problems. The next paragraphs examine these major perspectives and discuss their relevance to the study of social problems (the following discussion is indebted to Rubington and Weinberg 1995).

STRUCTURAL-FUNCTIONALIST PERSPECTIVE

The structural-functionalist perspective is largely based on the works of Herbert Spencer, Emile Durkheim, Talcott Parsons, and Robert Merton.

According to **structural-functionalism,** society is a system of interconnected parts that work together in harmony to maintain a state of balance and social equilibrium for the whole. For example, each of the social institutions contributes important functions for society: family provides a context for reproducing, nurturing, and socializing children; education offers a way to transmit a society's skills, knowledge, and culture to its youth; politics provides a means of governing members of society; economics provides for the production, distribution, and consumption of goods and services; and religion provides moral guidance and an outlet for worship of a higher power.

The structural-functionalist perspective emphasizes the interconnectedness of society by focusing on how each part influences and is influenced by other parts. For example, the increase in single-parent and dual-earner families has contributed to the number of children who are failing in school because parents have become less available to supervise their children's homework. Due to changes in technology, colleges are offering more technical programs, and many adults are returning to school to learn new skills that are required in the workplace. The increasing number of women in the workforce has contributed to the formulation of policies against sexual harassment and job discrimination.

Consideration *In viewing society as a set of interrelated parts, structural-functionalists also note that proposed solutions to a social problem may cause additional social problems. For example, racial imbalance in public schools led to forced integration, which in turn generated violence and increased hostility between the races. The use of plea bargaining was adopted as a means of dealing with overcrowded court dockets but resulted in "the revolving door of justice." Urban renewal projects often displaced residents and broke up community cohesion.*

Structural-functionalists use the terms "functional" and "dysfunctional" to describe the effects of social elements on society. Elements of society are *functional* if they contribute to social stability and *dysfunctional* if they disrupt social stability. Some aspects of society may be both functional and dysfunctional for society. For example, crime is dysfunctional in that it is associated with physical violence, loss of property, and fear. But, according to Durkheim and other functionalists, crime is also functional for society because it leads to heightened awareness of shared moral bonds and increased social cohesion.

Consideration *Functional does not necessarily mean "good," and dysfunctional does not necessarily mean "bad." For example, the civil rights movement in the 1950s was dysfunctional in that it disrupted social stability, but many Americans would consider this disruption necessary and "good" for our nation. The statement that something is functional for society invites the question "functional for whom?"*

Sociologists have identified two types of functions: manifest and latent (Merton 1968). **Manifest functions** are consequences that are intended and commonly recognized. **Latent functions** are consequences that are unintended and often hidden. For example, the manifest function of education is to transmit knowledge and skills to society's youth. But public elementary schools also serve as baby-sitters for employed parents, and colleges offer a place for young adults to meet potential mates. The baby-sitting and mate selection functions are not the intended or commonly recognized functions of education—hence, they are latent functions.

STRUCTURAL-FUNCTIONALIST THEORIES OF SOCIAL PROBLEMS

Two dominant theories of social problems grew out of the structural-functionalist perspective: social pathology and social disorganization. Both are indebted to Durkheim's writings.

Social Pathology According to the social pathology model, social problems result from some "sickness" in society. Just as the human body becomes ill when our systems, organs, and cells do not function normally, society becomes "ill" when its parts (i.e., elements of the structure and culture) no longer perform properly. For example, such problems as crime, violence, poverty, and juvenile delinquency are often attributed to the breakdown of the family institution, the decline of the religious institution, and inadequacies in our economic, educational, and political institutions.

Social "illness" also results when members of a society are not adequately socialized to adopt its norms and values. Persons who do not value honesty, for example, are prone to dishonesties of all sorts. Early theorists attributed the failure in socialization to "sick" people who could not be socialized. Later theorists recognized that failure in the socialization process stemmed from "sick" social conditions, not "sick" people. To prevent or solve social problems, members of society must receive proper socialization and moral education, which may be accomplished in the family, schools, churches, workplace and/or through the media.

Social Disorganization According to the social disorganization view of social problems, rapid social change disrupts the norms in a society. When norms become weak or are in conflict with each other, society is in a state of **anomie** or normlessness. Hence, people may steal, physically abuse their spouse or children, abuse drugs, rape, or engage in other deviant behavior because the norms regarding these behaviors are weak or conflicting. According to this view, the solution to social problems lies in slowing the pace of social change and strengthening social norms.

For example, although the use of alcohol by teenagers is considered a violation of a social norm in our society, this norm is weak. The media portray young people drinking alcohol, teenagers teach each other to drink alcohol and buy fake identification cards to purchase alcohol, and parents model drinking behavior by having a few drinks after work or at a social event. Solutions to teenage drinking may involve strengthening norms against it through public education, restricting media depictions of youth and alcohol, imposing stronger sanctions against the use of fake IDs to purchase alcohol, and educating parents to model moderate and responsible drinking behavior.

CONFLICT PERSPECTIVE

Whereas the structural-functionalist perspective views society as comprised of different parts working together, the **conflict perspective** views society as comprised of different groups and interests competing for power and resources. The conflict perspective explains various aspects of our social world by looking at which groups have power and benefit from a particular social arrangement.

The origins of the conflict perspective can be traced to the classic works of Karl Marx (1818–1883). Marx suggested that all societies go through stages of economic development. As societies evolve from agricultural to industrial, concern over meeting survival needs is replaced by concern over making a profit, the hallmark of a capitalist system. Industrialization also leads to the development of two classes of people: the bourgeoisie, or the owners of the means of production (e.g., factories, farms, businesses), and the proletariat, or the workers who earn wages.

The division of society into two broad classes of people—the "haves" and the "have-nots"—is beneficial to the owners of the means of production. The workers, who may earn only subsistence wages, are denied access to the many resources available to the wealthy owners. According to Marx, the bourgeoisie use their power to control the institutions of society to their advantage. For example, Marx suggested that religion serves as an "opiate of the masses" in that it soothes the distress and suffering associated with the working-class lifestyle and focuses the workers' attention on spirituality, God, and the afterlife rather than on such worldly concerns as living conditions. In essence, religion diverts the workers so that they concentrate on being rewarded in heaven for living a moral life rather than on questioning their exploitation.

CONFLICT THEORIES OF SOCIAL PROBLEMS

Today, the conflict perspective provides the basis for two general types of theories of social problems: Marxist and non-Marxist. Marxist theories focus on social conflict that results from economic inequalities; non-Marxist theories focus on social conflict that results from competing values and interests among social groups.

Marxist Conflict Theories According to contemporary Marxist theorists, social problems result from class inequality inherent in a capitalistic system. A system

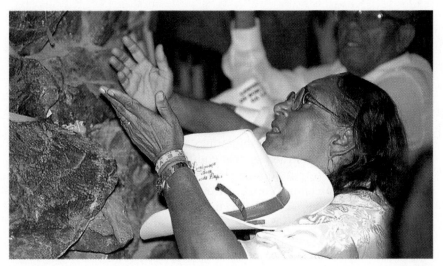

According to Marxist theory, religion is a tool of the bourgeoisie, in that it focuses the attention of the workers on the next life, keeping them from asking why they are being exploited by their bosses in this life. This photo reflects a woman focused on a religious ritual.

of "haves" and "have-nots" may be beneficial to the "haves," but often translates into poverty for the "have-nots." As we shall explore later in this text, many social problems, including physical and mental illness, low educational achievement, and crime, are linked to poverty.

In addition to creating an impoverished class of people, capitalism also encourages "corporate violence." Corporate violence may be defined as actual harm and/or risk of harm inflicted on consumers, workers, and the general public as a result of decisions by corporate executives or managers. Corporate violence may also result from corporate negligence, the quest for profits at any cost, and willful violations of health, safety, and environmental laws (Hills 1987). Our profit-motivated economy encourages individuals who are otherwise good, kind, and law-abiding to knowingly participate in the manufacturing and marketing of defective brakes on American jets, fuel tanks on automobiles, and contraceptive devices (IUDs). The profit motive has also caused individuals to sell defective medical devices, toxic pesticides, and contaminated foods to developing countries. Blumberg (1989) suggests that "in an economic system based exclusively on motives of self-interest and profit, such behavior is inevitable" (p. 106).

Marxist conflict theories also focus on the problem of **alienation,** or powerlessness and meaninglessness in people's lives. In industrialized societies, workers often have little power or control over their jobs, which fosters a sense of powerlessness in their lives. The specialized nature of work requires workers to perform limited and repetitive tasks; as a result, the workers may come to feel that their lives are meaningless.

Alienation is bred not only in the workplace, but also in the classroom. Students have little power over their education and often find the curriculum is not meaningful to their lives. Like poverty, alienation is linked to other social problems, such as low educational achievement, violence, and suicide.

Marxist explanations of social problems imply that the solution lies in eliminating inequality among classes of people by creating a classless society. The nature of work must also change to avoid alienation. Finally, stronger controls must be applied to corporations to ensure that corporate decisions and practices are based on safety rather than profit considerations.

Non-Marxist Conflict Theories Non-Marxist conflict theorists such as Ralf Dahrendorf are concerned with conflict that arises when groups have opposing values and interests. For example, anti-abortion activists value the life of unborn embryos and fetuses; pro-choice activists value the right of women to control their own body and reproductive decisions. These different value positions reflect different subjective interpretations of what constitutes a social problem. For anti-abortionists, the availability of abortion is the social problem; for pro-choice advocates, restrictions on abortion are the social problem. Sometimes the social problem is not the conflict itself, but rather the way that conflict is expressed. Even most pro-life advocates agree that shooting doctors who perform abortions and blowing up abortion clinics constitute unnecessary violence and lack of respect for life. Value conflicts may occur between diverse categories of people including nonwhites versus whites, heterosexuals versus homosexuals, young versus old, Democrats versus Republicans, and environmentalists versus industrialists.

Solutions to the problems that are generated by competing values may involve ensuring that conflicting groups understand each other's views, resolving differences through negotiation or mediation, or agreeing to disagree. Ideally, solutions should be win-win; both conflicting groups are satisfied with the solution. However, outcomes of value conflicts are often influenced by power; the group with the most power may use its position to influence the outcome of value conflicts. For example, when Congress could not get all states to voluntarily increase the legal drinking age to twenty-one, it threatened to withdraw federal highway funds from those that would not comply.

SYMBOLIC INTERACTIONIST PERSPECTIVE

Both the structural-functionalist and the conflict perspective are concerned with how large aspects of society, such as institutions and large social groups, influence the social world. This level of sociological analysis is called *macrosociology:* it looks at the "big picture" of society and suggests how social problems are affected at the institutional level.

Microsociology, another level of sociological analysis, is concerned with the social psychological dynamics of individuals interacting in small groups. Symbolic interactionism reflects the microsociological perspective and was largely influenced by the work of early sociologists and philosophers such as Max Weber, Georg Simmel, Charles Horton Cooley, G. H. Mead, W. I. Thomas, Erving Goffman, and Howard Becker. **Symbolic interactionism** emphasizes that human behavior is influenced by definitions and meanings that are created and maintained through symbolic interaction with others. While structural-functionalists argue that meanings and definitions are learned through the socialization process, symbolic interactionists suggest that definitions are socially constructed anew in each interactive setting.

Sociologist W. I. Thomas ([1931] 1966) emphasized the importance of definitions and meanings in social behavior and its consequences. He suggested that humans respond to their definition of a situation rather than to the objective situation itself. Hence, Thomas noted that situations we define as real become real in their consequences.

Symbolic interactionism also suggests that our identity or sense of self is shaped by social interaction. We develop our self-concept by observing how others interact with us and label us. By observing how others view us, we see a reflection of ourselves that Cooley calls the "looking glass self."

Lastly, the symbolic interaction perspective has important implications for how social scientists conduct research. The German sociologist Max Weber (1864–1920) argued that in order to understand individual and group behavior, social scientists must see the world from the eyes of that individual or group. Weber called this approach *Verstehen,* which in German means "empathy." *Verstehen* implies that in conducting research, social scientists must try to understand others' view of reality and the subjective aspects of their experiences, including their symbols, values, attitudes, and beliefs.

Each to each a looking glass, Reflects the other that doth pass.
—Charles Horton Cooley
Sociologist

SYMBOLIC INTERACTIONIST THEORIES OF SOCIAL PROBLEMS

A basic premise of symbolic interactionist theories of social problems is that a condition must be defined or recognized as a social problem in order for it to be a social problem. Based on this premise, Herbert Blumer (1971) suggests that social problems develop in stages. First, social problems pass through the stage of "societal recognition"—the process by which a social problem, for example, drunk driving, is "born." Second, "social legitimation" takes place when the social problem achieves recognition by the larger community, including the media, schools, and churches. As the visibility of traffic fatalities associated with alcohol increased, so did the legitimation of drunk driving as a social problem. The next stage in the development of a social problem involves "mobilization for action," which occurs when individuals and groups, such as Mothers Against Drunk Driving, become concerned about how to respond to the social condition. This mobilization leads to the "development and implementation of an official plan" for dealing with the problem involving, for example, highway checkpoints, lower legal blood alcohol levels, and tougher drunk driving regulations.

Blumer's stage development view of social problems is helpful in tracing the development of social problems. For example, although sexual harassment and date rape have occurred throughout this century, these issues did not begin to receive recognition as social problems until the 1970s. Social legitimation of these problems was achieved when high schools, colleges, churches, employers, and the media recognized their existence. Organized social groups mobilized to develop and implement plans to deal with these problems. For example, groups successfully lobbied for the enactment of laws against sexual harassment and the enforcement of sanctions against violators of these laws. Groups also mobilized to provide educational seminars on date rape for high school and college students and to offer support services to victims of date rape. Some disagree with the symbolic interactionist view that social problems exist only if they are recognized. According to this view, individuals who were victims of date rape in the 1960s may be considered victims of a problem, even though date rape was not recognized at that time as a social problem.

Labeling theory, a major symbolic interactionist theory of social problems, suggests that a social condition or group is viewed as problematic if it is labeled as such. According to labeling theory, resolving social problems sometimes involves changing the meanings and definitions that are attributed to people and situations. For example, as long as teenagers define drinking alcohol as "cool" and "fun," they will continue to abuse alcohol. As long as our society defines providing sex education and contraceptives to teenagers as inappropriate or immoral, the teenage pregnancy rate in our country will continue to be higher than in other industrialized nations.

> **Consideration** *When mainstream America viewed AIDS as a "gay problem," nonhomosexuals believed they were immune from the disease and, therefore, did not practice safer sex techniques. This furthered the spread of HIV infection. According to the Centers for Disease Control (1994), heterosexually transmitted HIV cases are growing faster than any other category of HIV cases.*

Gusfield (1989) notes the influence of labels in defining and dealing with social problems. He states:

[W]e use words like "welfare" and "helping" and "social problem" to emphasize the temporary and uncommitted nature of benevolence or control,

rather than using the language of rights, which creates a different meaning. To use the language of "social problem" is to portray its subjects as "sick" or "troublesome." We do not use a language of personal deficiencies to talk about economic concerns or to describe recession as the problem of sick businessmen, nor do we describe investment counselors as "market therapists." The income of the client affects the language of the profession. Subsidies to the auto industry are not called "aid to dependent factories." (p. 435)

Gill and Maynard (1995) point out how physicians are very careful in labeling a malady for a patient. For example, a physician does not tell a mother that her son has autism but that he is "well within the criteria" for an autistic diagnosis (p. 24). Such care reflects an awareness that labels have outcomes in both interpersonal and societal contexts.

The group who controls the definition of an issue as a social problem can also control who may be identified as the group to treat the problem. Psychiatrists and gynecologists fought over whether PMS was a mental or biologically based issue in the hope of being identified as the group who would provide a remedy and reap the profits from doing so (Figert 1995).

Table 1.2 summarizes and compares the major theoretical perspectives, their criticisms, and social policy recommendations as they relate to social problems. The study of social problems is based on research as well as theory, however. Indeed, research and theory are intricately related. As Wilson (1983) states,

Most of us think of theorizing as quite divorced from the business of gathering facts. It seems to require an abstractness of thought remote from the practical activity of empirical research. But theory building is not a separate activity within sociology. Without theory, the empirical researcher would find it impossible to decide what to observe, how to observe it, or what to make of the observations. . . . (p. 1)

Social Problems Research

Most students taking a course in social problems will not become researchers or conduct research on social problems. Nevertheless, we are all consumers of research that is reported in the media. Politicians, social activist groups, and organizations attempt to justify their decisions, actions, and positions by citing research results. As consumers of research, it is important to understand that our personal experience and casual observations are less reliable than generalizations based on systematic research. The following are some examples of claims based on personal beliefs versus the findings of empirical research:

- "Capital punishment acts as a deterrent and prevents some people from committing murder" versus "Capital punishment does not deter people from committing murder."
- "High school students should not have access to condoms because it increases the number of sexually active students" versus "Providing condoms to high school students reduces teenage pregnancy and the spread of HIV and other sexually transmitted diseases."

TABLE 1.2

COMPARISON OF THEORETICAL PERSPECTIVES

	STRUCTURAL-FUNCTIONALISM	CONFLICT THEORY	SYMBOLIC INTERACTIONISM
Representative Theorists	Emile Durkheim Talcott Parsons Robert Merton	Karl Marx Ralf Dahrendorf	George H. Mead Charles Cooley Erving Goffman
Society	Society is a set of interrelated parts; cultural consensus exists and leads to social order; natural state of society—balance and harmony.	Society is marked by power struggles over scarce resources; inequities result in conflict; social change is inevitable; natural state of society—imbalance.	Society is a network of interlocking roles; social order is constructed through interaction as individuals, through shared meaning, make sense out of their social world.
Individuals	Individuals are socialized by society's institutions; socialization is the process by which social control is exerted; people need society and its institutions.	People are inherently good but are corrupted by society and its economic structure; institutions are controlled by groups with power; "order" is part of the illusion.	Humans are interpretative and interactive; they are constantly changing as their "social beings" emerge and are molded by changing circumstances.
Cause of Social Problems?	Rapid social change: social disorganization that disrupts the harmony and balance; inadequate socialization and/or weak institutions.	Inequality; the dominance of groups of people over other groups of people; oppression and exploitation; competition between groups.	Different interpretations of roles; labeling of individuals, groups, or behaviors as deviant; definition of an objective condition as a social problem.
Social Policy/Solutions	Repair weak institutions; assure proper socialization; cultivate a strong collective sense of right and wrong.	Minimize competition; create an equitable system for the distribution of resources.	Reduce impact of labeling and associated stigmatization; alter definitions of what is defined as a social problem.
Criticisms	Called "sunshine sociology"; supports the maintenance of the status quo; needs to ask "functional for whom?" Does not deal with issues of power and conflict; incorrectly assumes a consensus.	Utopian model; Marxist states have failed; denies existence of cooperation and equitable exchange. Can't explain cohesion and harmony.	Concentrates on micro issues only; fails to link micro issues to macro-level concerns; too psychological in its approach; assumes label amplifies problem.

- "Maternal employment is associated with negative effects on the well-being of children" versus "Maternal employment is not associated with negative effects on the well-being of children."
- "Divorce is harmful to children and should be avoided at all costs" versus "It is better for a child to grow up in a divorced home than a home where the parents are unhappy and in conflict."

The remainder of this section discusses the stages of conducting a research study and the various methods of research used by sociologists.

STAGES OF CONDUCTING A RESEARCH STUDY

Ideally, sociologists progress through various stages in conducting research on a social problem. This section describes the first four stages: formulating a question, reviewing the literature, defining variables, and formulating a hypothesis.

Formulating a Research Question An empirical study usually begins with a research question. When the Kinsey Institute decided to explore the issue of homosexuality, the researchers formulated a number of questions they wanted to answer (Klassen, Williams, and Levitt 1989, 293):

- What perceptions and information about homosexuality are held among the public? How widely are these perceptions held?
- To what extent, and in what ways, is homosexuality seen as a threat to the social order?
- What are the correlates (e.g., age, sex, education) of negative views toward homosexuality?

Where do research questions originate? How does a particular researcher come to ask a particular research question? In some cases, researchers have a personal interest in a specific topic because of their own life experience. For example, a researcher who has experienced spouse abuse may wish to do research on such questions as "What factors are associated with domestic violence?" and "How helpful are battered women's shelters in helping abused women break the cycle of abuse in their lives?" Other researchers may ask a particular research question because of their personal values—their concern for humanity and the desire to improve human life. Researchers who are concerned about the spread of HIV infection and AIDS may conduct research on such questions as "What are people's beliefs about how HIV is transmitted?" "How does the use of alcohol influence condom use?" and "What educational strategies are effective for increasing safer sex behavior?" Researchers may also want to test a particular sociological theory, or some aspect of it, in order to establish its validity.

Not all research questions stem from the researcher's personal interests or values, life experience, humanitarian concerns, or desire to test theory. Government, industry, and other organizations hire researchers to investigate certain issues. After several commuter airline crashes in late 1994, the government ordered a series of tests in which the implicated models were flown in freezing rain to determine how ice on the wings affected the pilot's ability to control the aircraft. This research project represents only a small portion of federal funding for research.

> **National Data:** In 1994, the federal government spent more than $62 billion in research and development.
>
> SOURCE: Statistical Abstract of the United States: 1995, Table 980.

> *Consideration* Many questions cannot be answered through scientific research. Questions involving values, religion, and morality are almost always outside the domain of science. For example, scientific research cannot determine whether the death penalty or anything else is moral or immoral. Scientific research can, however, reveal information that may support or cause us to question our own moral judgments. Research can tell us how various segments of the population view capital punishment and what social and personal factors are associated with the different views. Research may also identify some of the social and economic consequences of allowing versus prohibiting capital punishment.

> *Science is meaningless because it gives no answer to the question, the only question of importance for us: "What shall we do and how shall we live?"*
> —Leo Tolstoy
> Novelist

Reviewing the Literature After a research question is formulated, the researcher reviews the published material on the topic to find out what is already known about it. Reviewing the literature involves reading professional journal articles, books, and research reports related to the research topic to find out whether other researchers have already asked (and perhaps answered) the researcher's question. Reviewing the literature also provides researchers with ideas about how to conduct their research and helps them formulate new research questions. A literature review also serves as an evaluation tool, allowing a comparison of research findings and other sources of information, such as expert opinions, political claims, and journalistic reports.

Defining Variables A **variable** is any measurable event, characteristic, or property that varies or is subject to change. Researchers must operationally define the variables they study. An **operational definition** specifies how a variable is to be measured. For example, an operational definition of the variable "religiosity" might be the number of times the respondent reports going to church or synagogue. Another operational definition of "religiosity" might be the respondent's answer to the question, "How important is religion in your life?" (1 = not important, 2 = somewhat important, 3 = very important).

Operational definitions are particularly important for defining variables that cannot be directly observed. For example, researchers cannot directly observe concepts such as "mental illness," "sexual harassment," "child neglect," "job satisfaction," and "drug abuse." Nor can researchers directly observe perceptions, values, and attitudes.

Formulating a Hypothesis After defining the research variables, researchers may formulate a **hypothesis,** which is a prediction or educated guess about how one variable is related to another variable. The **dependent variable** is the variable that the researcher wants to explain; that is, it is the variable of interest. The **independent variable** is the variable that is expected to explain change in the dependent variable. In formulating a hypothesis, the researcher predicts how the independent variable affects the dependent variable. For example, Peterson and Krivo (1993) hypothesized that residential segregation, and the associated social isolation, affects the probability of homicide victimization of African Americans. Their research found that as racial segregation increases, the probability of homicide victimization of blacks also increases. In this example, the independent variable is residential segregation; the dependent variable is homicide victimization. Table 1.3 identifies the independent and dependent variables of several research hypotheses.

> **Consideration**   Some social problems act as independent variables in the production of other social problems. Social problems that produce many other social problems are called "primary social problems" (Manis 1974). For example, poverty is a social problem that leads to the secondary social problem of slum neighborhoods, which, in turn, lead to the social problems of juvenile delinquency and addiction. In this example, "slum neighborhoods" act as both an independent and a dependent variable.

In studying social problems, researchers often assess the effects of several independent variables on one or more dependent variables. For example, Kishor (1993) found that increased female infant mortality in India (the dependent variable) is associated with several independent variables, including (1) low rates of female labor force participation, (2) low rates of rice cultivation (which decrease the need for women, who traditionally worked in the rice fields), and (3) the dominant role of men in the Indian family system. Each of

TABLE 1.3

INDEPENDENT AND DEPENDENT VARIABLES

HYPOTHESIS	INDEPENDENT VARIABLE	DEPENDENT VARIABLE
Teenage pregnancy rates are higher among non-whites than among whites.	Race	Teenage pregnancy rates
Conservative Protestants have more favorable attitudes toward capital punishment than do other non-conservative Protestants.	Religious affiliation	Attitudes toward capital punishment
Divorce is more likely to occur among couples who marry at an early age (i.e. teens) compared to couples who marry in their twenties or thirties.	Age	Divorce

these three factors helps to explain why female infants in India are more likely than male infants to be denied food and medical care.

METHODS OF DATA COLLECTION

After identifying a research topic, reviewing the literature, and developing hypotheses, researchers decide which method of data collection to use. Alternatives include experiments, surveys, field research, and secondary data.

Kishor found several independent variables operating in combination to help explain why female infants and young children in India, like the child on the left in the photo, are more likely than males to be denied food and medical care.

Experiments **Experiments** involve manipulating the independent variable in order to determine how it affects the dependent variable. Experiments require one or more experimental groups that are exposed to the experimental treatment(s) and a control group that is not exposed. Research participants are randomly assigned to either an experimental or a control group. *Randomization* allows the researcher to assume that the experimental groups and the control group are theoretically the same in terms of members' characteristics. Thus, randomization allows the researcher to compare the experimental groups with the control group and assume that any differences between the two groups are due to the experimental treatment(s).

After the researcher randomly assigns participants to either an experimental or a control group, she or he measures the dependent variable. After the experimental groups(s) are exposed to the treatment, the research measures the dependent variable again. If participants have been randomly assigned to the different groups, the researcher may conclude that any difference in the dependent variable between the groups is due to the effect of the independent variable.

An example of a "social problems" experiment on poverty would be to provide welfare payments to one group of unemployed single mothers (experimental group) and no such payments to another group of unemployed single mothers (control group). The independent variable would be welfare payments; the dependent variable would be employment. The researcher's hypothesis would be that mothers in the experimental group would be less likely to be have a job after 12 months than mothers in the control group.

The major strength of the experimental method is that it provides evidence for causal relationships; that is, how one variable affects another. A primary weakness is that experiments are often conducted on small samples, usually in artificial laboratory settings; thus, the findings may not be generalized to other people in natural settings.

My latest survey shows that people don't believe in surveys.
—Laurence Peter
Humorist

Surveys Experiments represent only a small portion of the research on social problems; most of the research is based on surveys. **Survey research** involves eliciting information from respondents through questions. An important part of survey research is selecting a sample of those to be questioned. A **sample** is a portion of the population, selected to be representative so that the information from the sample can be generalized to a larger population. For example, instead of asking all abused spouses about their experience, you could ask a representative sample of them and assume those you did not question would give similar responses. After selecting a representative sample, survey researchers either interview people or ask them to complete written questionnaires.

1. *Interviews.* In interview survey research, trained interviewers ask respondents a series of questions and make written notes about or tape-record the respondents' answers. Interviews may be conducted over the telephone or face-to-face. A major social problem is substance abuse. Researcher Barr (1993) and her colleagues studied the relationship between education, race, and substance abuse by interviewing a representative sample of 6,364 adults living in New York State. The results indicated that ". . . black and white male college graduates differed little in alcohol and drug use" (p. 325). As educa-

tion level declined, however, use increased to the point that black males with less than a high school education drank and used drugs more than three times as much as white males.

One advantage of interview research is that researchers are able to clarify questions for the respondent and follow up on answers to particular questions. Researchers often conduct face-to-face interviews with groups of individuals who might otherwise be inaccessible. For example, some AIDS-related research attempts to assess the degree to which individuals engage in behavior that places them at high risk for transmitting or contracting HIV. Street youth and intravenous drug users, both high-risk groups for HIV infection, may not have a telephone or address due to their transient lifestyle (Catania et al. 1990). These groups may be accessible, however, if the researcher locates their hangouts and conducts face-to-face interviews. Research on homeless individuals may also require a face-to-face interview survey design.

The most serious disadvantages of interview reasearch are cost and the lack of privacy and anonymity. Respondents may feel embarrassed or threatened when asked questions that relate to personal issues such as drug use, domestic violence, and sexual behavior. As a result, some respondents may choose not to participate in interview research on sensitive topics. Those who do participate may conceal or alter information or give socially desirable answers to the interviewer's questions (e.g., "No, I have never used any drug. . . well, maybe once").

2. *Questionnaires.* Instead of conducting personal or phone interviews, researchers may develop questionnaires that they either mail or give to a sample of respondents. Most large-scale survey research on social problems involves mailing a questionnaire to the research sample. Questionnaire research offers the advantages of being less expensive and time-consuming than face-to-face or telephone surveys. In addition, questionnaire research provides privacy and anonymity to the research participants. This reduces the likelihood that they will feel threatened or embarrassed when asked personal questions and increases the likelihood that they will provide answers that are not intentionally inaccurate or distorted.

The major disadvantage of mail questionnaires is that it is difficult to obtain an adequate response rate. The typical response rate for a mail questionnaire is between 20 and 40 percent. In contrast, the response rate for a personal interview is usually about 95 percent (Nachmias and Nachmias 1987). Many people do not want to take the time or make the effort to complete and mail a questionnaire. Others may be unable to read and understand the questionnaire.

The problem with having a low response rate is that nonrespondents are usually different from those people who do respond. In general, questionnaire nonrespondents are often poorly educated or elderly and may be unable to read or understand the questions (Nachmias and Nachmias 1987). Because respondents may not constitute a representative sample, the researcher may not be able to generalize the findings to the larger population.

When I was younger I could remember anything—whether it happened or not.
—Mark Twain
American humorist
and writer

Field Research **Field research** involves observing and studying social behavior in settings in which it occurs naturally. Two types of field research are participant observation and nonparticipant observation. In each case, the researcher observes the phenomenon being studied and records these observations.

In *participant observation research,* the researcher participates in the phenomenon being studied in order to obtain an insider's perspective of the people and/or behavior being observed. Coleman (1990), a middle-class white male, changed clothes to live on the streets of New York as a homeless person for ten days. In *nonparticipant observation research,* the researcher observes the phenomenon being studied without actively participating in the group or the activity. For example, Adler and Adler (1988) studied a drug smuggling community in southwestern California by gaining the trust of members in the community, observing their behavior and interactions, and conducting personal interviews with group members. However, they did not participate in smuggling drugs.

Sometimes sociologists conduct in-depth detailed analyses or *case studies* of an individual, group, or event. For example, Skeen (1991) conducted case studies of a prostitute and her adjustment to leaving the profession, an incest survivor, and a person with AIDS.

The main advantage of field research on social problems is that it provides qualitative data. Thus, field research may yield detailed information about the values, rituals, norms, behaviors, symbols, beliefs, and emotions of those being studied. A potential problem with field research is that the researcher's observations may be biased (e.g., the researcher becomes too involved in the group to be objective). In addition, because field research is usually based on small samples, the findings may not be generalizable.

Secondary Data Research Sometimes researchers analyze *secondary data,* which are data that have already been collected by other researchers or government agencies or that exist in forms such as historical documents, police reports, hospital records, and official records of marriages, births, and deaths. For example, Roberts (1993) used nationally representative data from the 1989 National Opinion Research Center (NORC) General Social Survey to examine the effect of "unhealthy" and "dangerous" workplaces on such psychosocial variables as depression and trust. Results indicated that working in unhealthy conditions was related to higher levels of unhappiness and depression and lower levels of trust and confidence in big business, corporations, government, and science.

A major advantage of using secondary data in studying social problems is that the data are readily accessible, so researchers avoid the time and expense of collecting their own data. Secondary data are also often based on large representative samples. The disadvantage of secondary data is that the researcher is limited to the data already collected.

Further information on research methods including data analysis and ethical considerations involved in social problems research can be found in Appendix A.

Goals of the Text

Understanding social problems requires a thorough understanding of the elements of the social structure and culture, theoretical perspectives, and methods of research. Without these tools, we tend to rely on our own experiences as a basis for knowledge. It is difficult to see the world around us from an objective viewpoint, however, particularly when we are in the midst of such volatile political issues as sexism, racism, crime, violence, and poverty. Due to this difficulty, this text approaches the study of social problems with several goals in mind.

PROVIDE AN INTEGRATED THEORETICAL BACKGROUND FOR UNDERSTANDING SOCIAL PROBLEMS

This text reflects an integrative theoretical approach to the study of social problems. More than one theoretical perspective can be used to explain a social problem because social problems usually have multiple causes. For example, youth crime is linked to (1) an increased number of youth living in inner-city neighborhoods with little or no parental supervision (social disorganization), (2) young people having no legitimate means of acquiring material wealth (anomie theory), (3) youth being angry and frustrated at the inequality and racism in our society (conflict theory), and (4) teachers regarding youth as "no good" and treating them accordingly (labeling theory).

More than one theoretical perspective can also be used to explain different aspects of the same social problem. For example, mental illness as a social problem manifests itself in a variety of ways. Depression may best be explained by labeling theory, whereas schizophrenia may be more appropriately explained by sociobiological theory.

Finally, different theories may be more useful in explaining different social problems. For example, structural functionalism may help explain criminal behavior but be of less value in explaining homosexuality. Symbolic interactionism may be particularly helpful in explaining school dropouts but less helpful in explaining problems in health care delivery.

PROVIDE RESEARCH SUPPORT AND DOCUMENTATION FOR THEORIES OF SOCIAL PROBLEMS

Understanding social problems requires the ability to critically evaluate various theoretical explanations of social problems on the basis of research evidence. This text presents the findings of classic studies and current research on the causes and consequences of social problems. Research findings are also important in evaluating the effectiveness of interventions designed to alleviate social problems.

ENCOURAGE THE DEVELOPMENT OF A SOCIOLOGICAL IMAGINATION

Each chapter emphasizes how elements of the structure and culture of society may cause or contribute to various social problems. This emphasis encourages you to develop your sociological imagination by recognizing how structural and cultural factors influence private troubles and public issues.

EMPHASIZE THE HUMAN SIDE OF SOCIAL PROBLEMS

Subsequent chapters in this text contain a feature called "*The Human Side.*" These are personal stories of how social problems have affected individual lives. This feature illustrates the private pain and personal triumphs associated

Everybody should live a good and productive life. When there are impediments to that, we as a society have a responsibility to help.
—Tipper Gore
Social activist

Personal Beliefs about Various Social Problems

Indicate whether you agree or disagree with each of the following statements:

Statement	Agree	Disagree
1. The federal government is not doing enough to promote disarmament.	____	____
2. A national health care plan is needed to cover everybody's medical costs.	____	____
3. The federal government is not doing enough to control environmental pollution.	____	____
4. Wealthy people should pay a larger share of taxes than they do now.	____	____
5. The death penalty should be abolished.	____	____
6. Busing is all right if it helps to achieve racial balance in the schools.	____	____
7. The federal government should raise taxes to reduce the deficit.	____	____
8. Abortion should be legal.	____	____
9. College officials have the right to ban persons with extreme views from speaking on campus.	____	____
10. Marijuana should be legalized.	____	____
11. Women should receive the same salaries and opportunities for advancement as men in comparable positions.	____	____
12. Just because a man feels a woman has "led him on" does not entitle him to have sex with her.	____	____
13. The activities of married women are best confined to the home and family.	____	____

with social problems. For example, *The Human Side* feature in Chapter 2 describes the experience of people who have been labeled mentally ill.

Activism pays the rent on being alive and being here on the planet. . . . If I weren't active politically, I would feel as if I were sitting back eating at the banquet without washing the dishes or preparing the food. It wouldn't feel right.
—Alice Walker
Novelist

PROVIDE STUDENTS AN OPPORTUNITY TO ASSESS PERSONAL BELIEFS AND ATTITUDES

Each chapter contains a section called "*Self and Society*," which offers you an opportunity to assess your attitudes and beliefs regarding some aspect of the social problem discussed. In this chapter's *Self and Society* self-assessment, you may assess your own beliefs about a number of social problems and compare your beliefs with a national sample of first-year college students.

ENCOURAGE INDIVIDUALS TO TAKE PROSOCIAL ACTION

Individuals who understand the factors that contribute to social problems may be better able to formulate interventions to remediate those problems.

Statement	Agree	Disagree
14. The chief benefit of a college education is that it increases one's earning power.	___	___
15. Realistically, an individual person can do little to bring about changes in our society.	___	___

You may compare your answers with those obtained in a national survey of first-year college students by looking at Table SS1.1. Notice that the percentage agreeing with each statement differed in 1985 and 1989.

TABLE SS1.1 PERCENTAGE OF FIRST-YEAR COLLEGE STUDENTS AGREEING WITH BELIEF STATEMENTS

STATEMENT NUMBER	PERCENTAGE AGREEING IN:	
	1985	1989
1. Disarmament	66.3	64.8
2. National health care	56.9	65.7
3. Pollution control	79.0	87.4
4. Tax wealthy	72.2	71.5
5. Death penalty	27.9	25.2
6. Busing	50.7	46.5
7. Reduce deficit	24.2	29.3
8. Abortion	55.1	72.7
9. Ban speakers	78.7	82.9
10. Marijuana	20.5	19.5
11. Women's salaries	92.2	95.9
12. "Led him on"	83.8	94.3
13. Women remain at home	80.1	88.5
14. College increases salary	64.9	47.9
15. Individuals do little	32.8	31.1

SOURCE: Alexander W. Astin, 1993. *What Matters in College? Four Critical Years Revisited.* San Francisco: Jossey Bass Publishers. Used by permission.

Recognizing the personal pain and public costs associated with social problems encourages some to initiate social intervention. Most college students feel that they can make a difference.

Of course, the action one takes depends on one's perspective. For example, in Nazi Germany the social problem from the perspective of the Nazis was the proliferation of "inferior Jews." But from the point of view of the Jews, the social problem was Hitler's regime gone mad.

Individuals can make a difference by the choices they make. Individuals may choose to vote for one candidate over another, demand the right to reproductive choice or protest government policies that permit it, drive drunk or stop a friend from driving drunk, repeat a racist or sexist joke or chastise the person who tells it, and practice safe sex or risk the transmission of sexually transmitted diseases.

Although individual choices make an important impact, collective social action often has a more pervasive effect. For example, while individual parents emphasized alcohol control in their own children, Mothers Against Drunk Driving

National Data: In a study of more than 200,000 first-year students in more than 450 colleges and universities, less than a third (32.6 percent) agreed with the statement, "Realistically, an individual can do little to bring about changes in our society."

SOURCE: American Council on Education and University of California 1994.

contributed to the enactment of national legislation that potentially will influence every U.S. citizen's decision about whether to use alcohol while driving.

UNDERSTANDING
SOCIAL PROBLEMS

At the end of each chapter to follow, we offer a section on "Understanding" in which we attempt to re-emphasize the social origin of the problem being discussed, the consequences, and the alternative social solutions. It is our hope that the reader will end each chapter with a "sociological imagination" view of the problem and how, as a society, we might approach a solution.

Sociologists have been studying social problems since the Industrial Revolution at the turn of the twentieth century. Industrialization brought about massive social changes: the influence of religion declined; families became smaller and moved from traditional, rural communities to urban settings. These and other changes have been associated with increases in crime, pollution, divorce, and juvenile delinquency. As these social problems became more widespread, the need to understand their origins and possible solutions became more urgent. The field of sociology developed in response to this urgency. Social problems provided the initial impetus for the development of the field of sociology and continue to be a major focus of sociology.

There is no single agreed upon definition of what constitutes a social problem. Most sociologists agree, however, that all social problems share two important elements: an objective social condition and a subjective interpretation of that condition. Three major theoretical perspectives in sociology—structural-functionalist, conflict, and symbolic interactionist—each has its own notion of the causes, consequences, and solutions of social problems. These theoretical perspectives also focus on different research questions concerning social problems and offer different interpretations of research findings.

CRITICAL THINKING

1. Can a social problem exist if no one is aware of it?
2. What role does the media play in our awareness of social problems?
3. What social condition that is now widely accepted might be viewed as a social problem in the future?
4. To what degree are the lives of individuals influenced by social factors? To what degree are individuals responsible for their life circumstances?
5. How does the expression "The person who pays the piper calls the tune" relate to social problems research?

KEY TERMS

social problem	norm	symbolic interactionism
institution	sanction	variable
social group	sociological imagination	operational definition
status	structural-functionalism	hypothesis
ascribed status	manifest function	dependent variable
achieved status	latent function	independent variable
role	anomie	experiment
beliefs	conflict perspective	survey research
values	alienation	sample
		field research

REFERENCES

Adler, Patricia A., and Peter Adler. 1988. "Shifts and Oscillations in Deviant Careers: The Case of Upper Level Drug Dealers and Smugglers." *Social Problems* 31: 195–207.

American Council on Education and University of California. 1994. "The American Freshman: National Norms for Fall, 1994." Los Angeles: Los Angeles Higher Education Research Institute.

Astin, Alexander W. 1993. *What Matters in College? Four Critical Years Revisited.* San Francisco: Jossey Bass.

Barr, Kellie, Michael Farrell, Grace Barnes, and John Welte. 1993. "Race, Class, and Gender Differences in Substance Abuse: Evidence of Middle-Class/Under-Class Polarization among Black Males." *Social Problems* 40: 314–27.

Blumberg, Paul. 1989. *The Predatory Society: Deception in the American Market Place.* New York: Oxford University Press.

Blumer, Herbert. 1971. "Social Problems as Collective Behavior." *Social Problems* 8 (3): 298–306.

Castaneda, Carol J. 1995. "In Kentucky, Confederate Flag Is Fatal." *USA Today,* January 30, A-2.

Catania, Joseph A., David. R. Gibson, Dale. D. Chitwook, and Thomas J. Coates. 1990. "Methodological Problems in AIDS Behavioral Research: Influences on Measurement Error and Participation Bias in Studies of Sexual Behavior." *Psychological Bulletin* 108: 339–62.

Centers for Disease Control and Prevention. 1994. "HIV/AIDS Surveillance Report." 6 (2): 1–39. U.S. Department of Health and Human Services, Atlanta, Georgia 30333.

Coleman, John R. 1990. "Diary of a Homeless Man." In *Social Problems,* edited by James M. Henslin. Englewood Cliffs, NJ: Prentice Hall, pp. 160–169.

Coltrane, Scott, and Neal Hickman. 1993. "The Rhetoric of Rights and Needs: Moral Discourse in the Reform of Child Custody and Child Support Laws." *Social Problems* 39 (4): 400–420.

Figert, Anne E. 1995. "The Three Faces of PMS: The Professional, Gendered, and Scientific Structuring of a Psychiatric Disorder." *Social Problems* 42: 56–73.

Frank, James G. 1991. "Risk Factors for Rape: Empirical Confirmation and Preventive Implications." Poster session presented at the 99th annual convention of the American Psychological Association, August 16, at San Francisco.

Gill, Virginia T., and Douglas W. Maynard. 1995. "On Labeling in Actual Interaction: Delivering and Receiving Diagnoses of Developmental Disabilities." *Social Problems* 42: 11–37

Gusfield, Joseph R. 1989. "Constructing the Ownership of Social Problems: Fun and Profit in the Welfare State." *Social Problems* 36: 431–41.

Hewlett, Sylvia Ann. 1992. *When the Bough Breaks: The Cost of Neglecting Our Children.* New York: Harper Perennial.

Hills, Stuart L. 1987. *Corporate Violence—Injury and Death for Profit,* edited by Stuart L. Mills. Lanham, M.: Rowman & Littlefield.

Homans, George C. 1974. *Social Structure in Its Elementary Forms.* New York: Harcourt Brace Jovanovich.

Kishor, Sunita. 1993. "May God Give Sons to All." *American Sociological Review* 58: 247–65.

Klassen, Albert D., Colin J. Williams, and Eugene E. Levitt. 1989. *Sex and Morality in the U.S.* Middletown, Conn.: Wesleyan University Press.

Manis, Jerome G. 1974. "Assessing the Seriousness of Social Problems." *Social Problems* 22: 1–15.

Merton, Robert K. 1968. *Social Theory and Social Structure.* New York: Free Press.

Mills, C. Wright. 1959. *The Sociological Imagination.* London: Oxford University Press.

Nachmias, David, and Chava Nachmias. 1987. *Research Methods in the Social Sciences,* 3d ed. New York: St. Martin's Press.

National Center for Health Statistics. 1994. Births, Marriages, Divorces, and Deaths for August 1994. Monthly vital statistics report 42 (8). Hyattsville, Md.: Public Health Service.

Peterson, Ruth, and Lauren J. Krivo. 1993. "Racial Segregation and Black Urban Homicide." *Social Forces* 59: 131–41.

Roberts, J. Timmons. 1993. "Psychosocial Effects of Workplace Hazardous Exposures: Theoretical Synthesis and Preliminary Findings." *Social Problems* 40: 74–89.

Rubington, Earl, and Martin S. Weinberg. 1995. *The Study of Social Problems,* 5th ed. New York: Oxford University Press.

Skeen, Dick. 1991. *Different Sexual Worlds: Contemporary Case Studies of Sexuality.* Lexington, Mass.: Lexington Books.

Statistical Abstract of the United States: 1995, 115th ed. Washington, D.C.: U.S. Bureau of the Census, 1995.

Steinberg, Jaques. 1993. "U.S. Social Well-Being Is Rated Lowest since Study Began in 1970." *New York Times: Themes of the Times (Sociology)* (Fall), 4.

Thomas, W. I. [1931] 1966. "The Relation of Research to the Social Process." In *W. I. Thomas on Social Organization and Social Personality,* edited by Morris Janowitz. Chicago: University of Chicago Press, pp. 289–305.

Troyer, Ronald J., and Gerald E. Markle. 1984. "Coffee Drinking: An Emerging Social Problem." *Social Problems* 31: 403–16.

Ukers, William H. 1935. *All about Tea,* vol. 1. The Tea and Coffee Trade Journal Co.

Wilson, John. 1983. *Social Theory.* Englewood Cliffs, N.J.: Prentice-Hall.

Wuthnow, Robert. 1987. *Meaning and Moral Order: Explorations in Cultural Analysis.* Berkeley: University of California Press.

Problems of Individual Well-Being

SECTION 1

Section 1 deals with problems that are often regarded as private rather than public issues; that is, they are viewed as internally caused or as a function of individual free will. People often respond to these problems by assuming that the problem is the victims' fault—that in some way they have freely chosen their plight. In this set of problems, blame is most often attached to the individuals themselves. Thus, the physically and mentally ill (Chapter 2), the drunk and the drug addict (Chapter 3), the criminal and the delinquent (Chapter 4), and the divorced person and the child abuser (Chapter 5) are thought to be bad, or weak, or immoral, or somehow different from the average person. Consider the following scenarios:

1. A man on a fixed income without health insurance decides not to go to a doctor in order to save money to pay the rent and buy food for his children. When he becomes sick, his illness is blamed on his decision not to go to the doctor. As sociologists, we would say that the man did not want to be sick, but rather chose what he perceived as the lesser of several unfortunate alternatives. In this case, factors that underlie his illness include poverty, the structure of medical care in the United States, the rising cost of health insurance, and the value system that stresses parental responsibility and sacrifice.

2. A teenager from an urban lower-class neighborhood decides to sell drugs rather than stay in school or get a regular

job. Such a teenager is generally viewed as being "weak" or having "low" morals. Sociologists view such a person as a lower-class, poorly educated individual with few alternatives in a society that values success. Raised in an environment where the most successful role models are often criminals, legitimate opportunities are few, traditional norms and values are weak, and peer pressure to use and sell drugs is strong, what are his choices? He can pump gas or serve fast food for minimum wage, or he can sell drugs for a possible $7,000 a week.

3. A mother comes home from work and finds her children playing and messing up the house. She had told the children to clean the house while she was gone. She decides they need to be whipped with a belt because of their disobedience. The physical abuse she engages in is viewed as a reflection of her mental instability and her inability to control her temper. Research indicates, however, that fewer than 10 percent of identified child abusers are severely psychologically impaired.

   If being mentally unstable, does not explain the majority of child abuse cases, what does explain it? A history of being abused as a child is the strongest independent predictor of who will be a child abuser as an adult. Additionally, the culture of society includes a myriad of beliefs that contribute to child abuse: acceptance of corporal punishment of children and the ambiguity surrounding what constitutes appropriate discipline, the belief that parental control is an inalienable right, and the historical and lingering belief that children (as well as women) are property.

4. A college student drinks alcohol daily and often cuts classes. While the general public views such behavior as a personal weakness, sociologists emphasize the role of the individual's socialization and society. For example, a disproportionate number of individuals with drinking problems were reared in homes where one or both parents drank heavily. In the general culture, media portrayals of drinking as desirable, fun, glamorous, and a source of status further promote drinking. College culture itself often emphasizes bars and drinking parties as primary sources of recreation and affiliation.

These examples illustrate that many behaviors result more from social factors than from individual choice. To the degree that individuals do make choices, these choices are socially determined in that the structure and culture of society limit and influence individual choices. For example, customers in a restaurant cannot choose anything they want to eat; they are limited to what is on the menu. Sociologically, one's social status—black, white, male, female, young, old, rich, poor—determines one's menu of life choices.

In each of the above examples, the alternatives were limited by the individual's position in the social structure of society and by the cultural and subcultural definitions of appropriate behavior. While conflict theorists, structural-functionalists, and symbolic interactionists may disagree as to the relative importance and mechanisms of the shared structure and culture of society in determining the problems identified, all would agree that society, not the individual, is the primary source of the solutions. In this and the following sections, we emphasize the importance of the social structure and culture of society as both the sources and solutions to social problems.

2

Illness and Health Care

IS IT TRUE?

1. Due to a new cultural emphasis on physical fitness, the proportion of Americans who lead essentially sedentary lifestyles has declined (p. 45).

2. Compared to other industrialized countries, the United States has the lowest infant mortality rate (p. 39).

3. Married people tend to be physically healthier and to experience less depression and suicide than single people (p. 53).

4. Men have higher rates of personality disorders than women (p. 53).

5. About twenty-five cents of every dollar spent on medical care goes for medical administration (p. 54).

ANS: 1.F 2.F 3.T 4.T 5.T

> Health is a crossroads. It is where biological and social factors, the individual and the community, the social and the economic policy all converge. . . . Health is a means to personal and collective advancement. It is, therefore, an indicator of success achieved by a society and its institutions of government in promoting well-being, which is the ultimate meaning of development.
>
> Julio Frenk

It is tragic enough that 1.5 million children died as a result of wars over the past decade. But it is far more unforgivable that, in the same period, 40 million children died from diseases completely preventable with simple vaccines or medicine.
—Bill Clinton
U.S. President

Sexual health is the integration of the somatic, emotional, intellectual and social aspects of sexual beings in ways that are positively enriching and that enhance personality, communication and love.
—World Health Organization

Presidential and congressional attention to health care, skyrocketing health care costs, and large numbers of uninsured individuals point to a crisis of health care in our society. Indeed, illness and health care are central concerns of all societies. The economic institution cannot perform the work of society efficiently when workers are ill; the educational institution cannot educate children who are too sick to learn; and, parents cannot promote family well-being if they are emotionally and financially stressed by caring for ailing relatives.

In spite of the importance of good health, more than 1.3 billion women, men, and children—20 percent of the world population—suffer from serious illness or malnourishment. Most of these people are in South and East Asia where more than 500 million suffer from malnutrition and diseases such as malaria, measles, diarrhea, and respiratory problems. Health problems are also severe in sub-Saharan Africa where malnutrition and disease, including AIDS, are believed to affect 30 percent of the population, or 160 million individuals (Okie 1993). Health problems also include mental as well as physical illness. Almost half of all Americans will experience mental illness at some point during their lifetime.

In this chapter, we review physical and mental health concerns in the United States and throughout the world. The World Health Organization (1946) defines health as "a state of complete physical, mental, and social well-being" (p. 3). Health is affected by lifestyle and genetics, as well as by environmental, social, and economic factors (Fielding and Halfon 1994). Throughout this chapter we emphasize the social dimensions of health, that is, how social conditions affect health and how health affects social conditions. We also look at the U.S. health care system and its inadequacies, as well as at alternative solutions to help remedy health care problems. We begin by looking at one of the major global social concerns associated with health—reproductive and sexual health problems.

The Social Context: Global Health Concerns

Reproductive and sexual health problems include complications associated with pregnancy and childbirth, low birthweight and other problems of infants, and AIDS and other sexually transmissible diseases. Table 2.1 provides a summary of selected reproductive and sexual health problems and indicates their impact on the world population.

REPRODUCTIVE AND SEXUAL HEALTH PROBLEMS AND THEIR IMPACT ON THE WORLD'S POPULATION

	HEALTH PROBLEM	ESTIMATED WORLDWIDE MORTALITY	ANNUAL IMPACT MORBIDITY
Women and Men:	Unsafe abortion	110,000	25 million
	Maternal anemia	40,000	58 million
	HIV	(a)	1.9 million
	AIDS	1 million	1 million
	Gonorrhea	(a)	20 million
	Chlamydia	(a)	50 million
	Syphilis	(a)	4 million
Children:	Low birthweight	3.5 million	24 million
	Perinatal infection	1.4 million	(a)

(a) Data not available.

SOURCE: Adapted from Iain Aitken and Laura Reichenbach. 1994. "Reproductive and Sexual Health Services: Expanding Access and Enhancing Quality." In *Population Policies Reconsidered: Health, Empowerment, and Rights*, ed. G. Sen, A. Germain, and L. C. Chen, pp. 177–92. Boston: Harvard School of Public Health. Table 1, p. 179. Used by permission.

International Data: More than 18 million adults and over 1.5 million children have been infected with HIV since the late 1970s/ early 1980s. From the start of the pandemic until mid-1994, about 4 million individuals worldwide had developed AIDS.

SOURCE: World Health Organization 1994; Cooper 1995.

AIDS AND OTHER SEXUALLY TRANSMISSIBLE DISEASES

One of the most urgent public health concerns around the globe is the spread of the human immunodeficiency virus (HIV) and AIDS. As Figure 2.1 illustrates, Africa has suffered the highest incidence of AIDS cases since the start of the pandemic.

HIV is transmitted through sexual contact with infected individuals, intravenous drug use with contaminated needles, blood transfusions (prior to 1985, donor blood was not screened for HIV), organ or tissue transplants, and donor semen. Pregnant mothers infected with HIV may also transmit the virus through the placenta to their unborn children. This chapter's *Self and Society* allows you to assess your knowledge of AIDS.

In the United States, only 4 percent of HIV infection cases have been officially attributed exclusively to heterosexual transmission (Centers for Disease

Some students have a hard time understanding that the consequences of one unprotected sexual encounter may not be reversible.
—American College Health Association

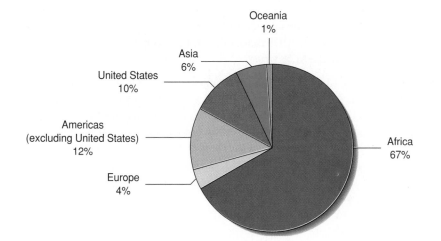

FIGURE 2.1 Percentage of Estimated AIDS Cases in Adults and Children from Late 1970s/Early 1980s until Mid-1994

SOURCE: Based on World Health Organization. 1994. "AIDS Cases Soar in Past Year." *Global AIDS News* (No. 3). Internet: The Newsletter of the W.H.O. Geneva, Switzerland: Global Program on AIDS.

AIDS Knowledge Scale

Indicate whether you think the following items are true or false.   **True**   **False**

1. Hemophiliacs can get AIDS.   _____   _____
2. AIDS is an epidemic.   _____   _____
3. Only homosexuals get AIDS.   _____   _____
4. The virus that causes AIDS is called human immunodeficiency virus (HIV).   _____   _____
5. The AIDS virus can remain infectious outside the body for up to ten days
    if it is at room temperature.   _____   _____
6. One can get AIDS by sharing a meal with a person who has AIDS.   _____   _____
7. People who have AIDS do not develop cancer.   _____   _____
8. Today the blood supply in hospitals and blood donation centers
    is screened for the AIDS virus.   _____   _____
9. Impaired memory and concentration and motor deficits may occur
    in some AIDS patients.   _____   _____
10. One can get AIDS by sharing drug needles.   _____   _____
11. The AIDS virus may live in the human body for years before symptoms appear.   _____   _____
12. One can get AIDS from receiving blood or sperm from a donor who has AIDS.   _____   _____
13. By using a condom when having sex, one is always safe from contracting AIDS.   _____   _____
14. The HIV test is a blood test that can tell if a person has AIDS.   _____   _____
15. There is a cure for AIDS.   _____   _____
16. AIDS victims may show extreme tiredness, night sweats, fever,
    weight loss, diarrhea, etc.   _____   _____
17. One can get AIDS by having sexual intercourse with an infected person.   _____   _____
18. AIDS is spread by sneezing, coughing, or touching.   _____   _____
19. AZT is the only drug approved by the U.S. Food and Drug Administration
    for the treatment of AIDS.   _____   _____
20. One can get AIDS by having sex with someone who uses intravenous drugs.   _____   _____
21. AIDS can be spread by having contact with towels or bed linens
    used by a person with AIDS.   _____   _____
22. An infected mother can give the AIDS virus to the baby during
    pregnancy and/or through breast feeding.   _____   _____
23. About 400,000 people in the United States are infected with the HIV virus.   _____   _____
24. Blacks and Hispanics show higher incidence rates of AIDS than other ethnic groups.   _____   _____
25. More women than men have been infected by the AIDS virus.   _____   _____

Scoring: The following items are true: 1, 2, 4, 8, 9, 10, 11, 12, 16, 17, 20, 22, and 24. The following items are false: 3, 5, 6, 7, 13, 14, 15, 18, 19, 21, 23, 25. The scale is scored by totaling the number of items answered correctly. Possible scores range from 0 to 25. The higher the score, the higher the degree of knowledge of HIV/AIDS.

Comparison: The average score of 68 undergraduate men at a large urban public university on the East Coast was 17.41; the average score of 98 undergraduate women at the same university was 17.87.

SOURCE: David S. Goh. 1993. "The Development and Reliability of the Attitudes Toward AIDS Scale." *College Student Journal*, 27: 208–14. The scale is on p. 214. Permission granted by *College Student Journal*.

Control and Prevention 1994). However, HIV infections attributed to heterosexual transmission are growing faster than any other category of HIV cases in the United States. Worldwide, AIDS is primarily a heterosexual disease.

AIDS and other sexually transmitted diseases are more prevalent in developing countries where access to and cultural acceptance of condoms are limited. However, sexually transmissible diseases are also common in developed countries, including the United States.

MATERNAL MORTALITY

Maternal mortality refers to deaths that result from complications associated with pregnancy or childbirth. Ninety-nine percent of maternal deaths take place in developing countries. The major causes of maternal deaths include hemorrhage, induced abortion, hypertension, obstructed labor, and infection (Freedman and Maine 1993).

INFANT MORTALITY AND LOW-BIRTHWEIGHT BABIES

Globally, expectation of life at birth has increased by nearly twenty years in the last half century. This increase in life expectancy is largely due to the decrease in infant mortality. **Infant mortality rates,** or the number of deaths of infants under one year of age per 1,000 live births, provide one measure of the health of a society. Worldwide, infant mortality rates have declined from 92 in the 1970s to about 62 in the 1990s. In developed regions, the infant mortality rate declined from 22 to 12, and in developing regions from 105 to 69 (Johnson 1994). In poorer countries, inadequate nutrition, impoverished living conditions, and lack of medical care contribute to high infant mortality rates. For example, the infant mortality rate is 109 in Ethiopia and Bangladesh, 110 in Haiti, and 159 in Afghanistan.

In the United States, the infant mortality rate has steadily declined from 20 deaths per 1,000 in 1970 to 8.4 in 1994 (National Center for Health Statistics 1994). Nevertheless, America lags behind other industrialized countries in infant health. The infant mortality rate in Belgium, France, Denmark, and Spain is seven; in Japan, it is only four.

Hewlett (1992) reports that about half of all U.S. children who die before their first birthday do so as a direct result of their mother's receiving little or no prenatal care. Women who do not receive adequate prenatal care are three times as likely to have premature, low-birthweight babies. Infants who weigh less than 5.5 pounds at birth often need expensive medical attention and are much more likely than full-term babies to suffer lifelong disabilities such as cerebral palsy, seizure disorders, blindness, and mental retardation. The main reason why more than one-third of U.S. pregnant women receive insufficient prenatal care is financial—they have no private health insurance and they fail to qualify for Medicaid.

REPRODUCTIVE AND SEXUAL HEALTH INTERVENTIONS

When compared with other health interventions through cost-effective analyses, reproductive health interventions are among the "best buys" in terms of health returns for each dollar invested (World Bank 1993). Therefore, reproductive

International Data: According to the World Health Organization, by the year 2000 more than 40 million people will be infected with HIV; up to 90 percent of HIV infections will have been contracted through heterosexual transmission.
SOURCE: Aral and Holmes 1991; Cowley 1994.

National Data: In 1994, an estimated 12 million Americans were diagnosed as having a sexually transmitted disease.
SOURCE: Pinkney 1994.

International Data: The World Health Organization estimates that every year about 500,000 women die in pregnancy and childbirth. In Bangladesh, Egypt, India, and Indonesia, more than one out of every five deaths among women in their childbearing years is related to pregnancy. By contrast, in the United States, only one out of every two hundred deaths among women of reproductive age is related to pregnancy.
SOURCE: Reported in Freedman and Maine 1993.

An AIDS prevention poster from Lagos, Nigeria, produced by the Society for Women and AIDS in Africa.

health services, including sex education programs and family planning clinics that provide birth control services and access to safe abortion services, should have high priority in all societies (Aitken and Reichenbach 1994). Other interventions include screening for and treating HIV and other sexually transmissible diseases and preventing the transmission of these diseases by advocating sexual abstinence, sexual monogamy, and condom use (see also Chapter 15).

Consideration *In Africa, where the spread of AIDS is most catastrophic, women are powerless to get their husbands to use condoms (Health Is a Right 1992). Bandura (1989) suggests that cultural norms, values, and roles make it difficult for women to insist that their partners use condoms:*

It is difficult for women to press the issue in the face of emotional and economic dependence, coercive threat, and subcultural prescription of compliant roles for them. Women who are enmeshed in relationships of imbalanced power need to be taught how to negotiate protected sex non-confrontationally. At the broader societal level, attitudes and social norms must be altered to increase men's sense of responsibility for the consequences of their sexuality. (p. 137)

Due to the controversies surrounding sexuality, the availability and funding of reproductive health services in the United States are restricted. Many health insurance companies do not pay for contraceptives, and abortion may not be covered by health care reform plans. Yet, Klerman and Klerman (1994) report that most studies show that in states with higher expenditures for family planning, including education, birth control, and abortion, pregnant women are more likely to get prenatal care, fewer low-birthweight and premature infants are born, and mothers and infants are healthier. The authors suggest that preventing unwanted pregnancies and births results in healthier children, perhaps because parents take better care of children that are wanted.

Prenatal care represents a vital part of overall reproductive services. One aspect of prenatal care involves ensuring that pregnant women receive adequate nutrition. In the United States, the Special Supplemental Food Program for Women, Infants, and Children (WIC) is a federally funded health promotion program aimed at improving the nutritional status of low-income pregnant, breast feeding, and postpartum women and their infants and children up to age five. By reducing the incidence of low-birthweight infants, WIC saves Medicaid costs for federal and state governments and saves money for insurers, hospitals, and private payers as well. According to Avruch and Cackley (1995), "WIC returns $1.36 for every dollar invested" (p. 33), due to the medical savings associated with reducing the number of low-birthweight babies.

Countries can reduce their rates of maternal mortality by providing access to medical facilities and trained medical professionals. Maternal mortality may also be decreased by raising the legal minimum age for marriage. This would eliminate some high-risk deliveries by decreasing the incidence of pregnancy among girls whose pelvises are not yet mature (Freedman and Maine 1993). Lastly, because poor nutritional status affects maternal mortality, ensuring that pregnant women receive adequate nutrition would reduce maternal mortality rates (Merchant and Kurz 1993).

National Data: Of 208 countries surveyed, 25 countries had lower infant mortality rates than the U.S. rate of 8 per 1,000.

SOURCE: Cherner 1995.

International Data: In developed countries, virtually all births are attended by trained medical personnel. In Asian and African countries, less than half of all births are attended by trained medical personnel.

SOURCE: World Health Organization 1989.

Sociological Theories of Illness and Health Care

As the preceding section described, illness and health care are significant social problems throughout the world. Three major theoretical perspectives—structural-functionalism, conflict theory, and symbolic interactionism—are useful in understanding and interpreting the issues surrounding these problems.

STRUCTURAL-FUNCTIONALIST PERSPECTIVE

According to the structural-functionalist perspective, medicine comprises a social institution that functions to maintain the well-being of societal members and, consequently, of the social system as a whole. Illness is dysfunctional in that it interferes with people performing needed social roles. To cope with non-functioning members and to control the negative effects of illness, society assigns a temporary and unique role to those who are ill—the sick role (Parsons 1951). This role assures that societal members receive needed care and compassion, yet at the same time, it carries with it an expectation that the person who is ill will seek competent medical advice, adhere to the prescribed regime, and return as soon as possible to normal role obligations.

Structural-functionalists explain the high cost of medical care by arguing that society must entice people into the medical profession by offering high salaries. Without such an incentive, individuals would not be motivated to endure the rigors of medical training or the stress of being a physician. Further, because medical care in the United States is treated as a commodity rather than an entitlement, competition among health care providers, insurance companies, pharmaceutical manufacturers, and medical technologies assures the highest quality care. Thus, although expensive, the structure of medical care in the United States is functional for society.

CONFLICT PERSPECTIVE

Conflict theorists examine how wealth and power, or the lack thereof, influence illness and health care. Worldwide, the have-nots not only experience the adverse health effects of poverty, they also have less access to medical insurance and quality medical care. In the United States, for example, nonwhites suffer higher rates of almost all diseases, are more often disabled, are less likely to have medical insurance, and have lower life expectancies.

The conflict perspective also focuses on how the profit motive influences health problems and health care. The profit motive underlies much of the illness, injury, and death that occurs from hazardous working conditions and dangerous consumer products. While stricter adherence to health and safety regulations and a government ban on such products as alcohol and tobacco would significantly increase the health status of millions of Americans, many corporations continue to resist such policies.

> **Consideration** *The profit motive sometimes results in corporate action that promotes health. For example, after a Cleveland employee of AmeriTrust gave birth to a premature infant, costing the company $1.4 million for medical care, the company started holding free "Perfectly Pregnant" seminars at*

lunchtime for employees. These seminars gave pregnant employees advice on everything from medical care to company maternity benefits. The program reduced the incidence of premature infants born to employees, which resulted in monetary savings for the company. For every week an expectant mother remains pregnant (that is, does not give birth to a premature infant), the company saves as much as $10,000 in health insurance costs (reported in Hewlett 1992).

Conflict theorists also argue that the high cost of medical care in the United States is a consequence of restrictions on the number of professionals entering the field. For example, by granting or withholding accreditation of medical schools and restricting the number of persons admitted, the American Medical Association limits the supply of doctors and keeps physicians' incomes high. Further, the practice of third-party billing accommodated the escalating costs of health care as insurance companies paid what families and individuals could not. Medical costs began to soar as more and more services were provided. However, conflict theorists argue that many of the services provided are motivated by greed rather than need: needless and expensive diagnostic tests, unnecessary surgeries, and overmedication primarily benefit physicians and other health care providers, and the corporations that provide health care goods and services. Acting in concert with one another to maximize profits, these components of the medical establishment comprise what is called the **medical-industrial complex** (Relman 1980).

Concern for profit also explains obstacles to health care reform. Insurance companies realize that health care reform translates into federal regulation of the insurance industry. In an effort to buy political influence to maintain profits, the insurance industry has contributed millions of dollars to congressional candidates. Indeed, more than two hundred political action committees representing the medical, pharmaceutical, and insurance industries contributed more than $60 million to congressional candidates between 1980 and 1991 (Kemper and Novak 1994).

SYMBOLIC INTERACTIONIST PERSPECTIVE

Symbolic interactionists focus on how meanings, definitions, and labels influence illness and health care. Before medical research documented the health hazards of tobacco, our society defined cigarette smoking as fashionable. Cigarette advertisements still attempt to associate positive meanings (such as youth, sex, and romance) with smoking to entice people to smoke. Additionally, the cultural meaning "thin is beautiful" helps explain why some women have eating disorders, either starving themselves (anorexia) or eating excessively and then taking laxatives or forcing themselves to disgorge (bulimia).

Psychiatrist Thomas Szasz (1970) argues that what we call "mental illness" is no more than a label conferred on those individuals who are "different," that is, who don't conform to society's definitions of appropriate behavior. The American Psychiatric Association (1994), however, rejects this notion:

Neither deviant behavior (e.g., political, religious, or sexual) nor conflicts that are primarily between the individual and society are mental disorders unless the deviance or conflict is a symptom of a dysfunction in the

In the past, men created witches; now they create mental patients.
—Thomas Szasz
Psychiatrist

individual [that causes distress, disability, or an increased risk of suffering or disability]. . . . (p. xxii)

Symbolic interactionists also focus on the stigmatizing effects of being labeled "ill." Individuals with mental illnesses, drug addictions, physical deformities and disabilities, and HIV and AIDS are particularly prone to being labeled in a way that affects their self-concepts and social identities. Often the social identities of those with stigmatized illnesses are obscured by the master status of being "sick."

> **Consideration** *In an effort to counteract the stigmatizing effects of mental illness, the American Psychiatric Association (1994) classifies disorders that people have, not the people themselves. "Thus, health professionals speak of individuals with schizophrenia rather than 'schizophrenics'." (p. xxi)*

Finally, definitions of health and illness vary over time and from society to society. In some countries, being fat is a sign of health and wellness; in others it is an indication of mental illness or a lack of self-control. Increasingly, in the United States, there is a trend toward **medicalization,** that is, the tendency to define negatively evaluated behaviors and/or conditions as medical problems. Obesity, gambling, criminality, alcoholism, hyperactivity, insomnia, anxiety, sexual addiction, and learning disabilities are examples of phenomena that have recently been redefined in terms of the need for medical intervention.

Health in the United States

Several status indicators provide measures of overall societal health. After examining some of these indicators, we will discuss the impact of the American lifestyle on health and illness.

HEALTH STATUS INDICATORS

Health status indicators include infant mortality rates (discussed earlier in this chapter), life expectancy, and morbidity rates. **Life expectancy,** or the average number of years that a person born in a given year can expect to live, provides one measure of the health of a society. In many impoverished, developing countries, the life expectancy is less than fifty years. In contrast, most U.S. citizens born in 1995 can expect to live into their seventies. As Table 2.2 shows, the life expectancy of U.S. citizens has been steadily increasing.

Morbidity refers to the amount of disease, impairment, and accidents in a population. In 1993, the most common acute conditions among Americans were influenza, the common cold, and injuries. Based on individuals who sought medical treatment or experienced at least one day of restricted activity, estimates suggest that in 1993, more than 50 percent of Americans had influenza and about a quarter of Americans suffered from the common cold or incurred a physical injury (*Statistical Abstract of the United States; 1995,* Table 214). The most common chronic conditions in the United States for all ages combined were sinusitis, arthritis, deformities or orthopedic impairment, and high blood pressure (Table 215).

TABLE 2.2

LIFE EXPECTANCY OF U.S. CITIZENS

YEAR	LIFE EXPECTANCY
1970	70.8
1980	73.7
1985	74.7
1990	75.4
1995	76.3
2000	76.7

SOURCE: *Statistical Abstract of the United States: 1995,* 115th ed., U.S. Bureau of the Census (Washington, D.C.: U.S. Government Printing Office, 1995), Table 114.

TABLE 2.3

TEN LEADING CAUSES OF DEATH IN THE UNITED STATES, 1992

CAUSE OF DEATH	DEATH RATE PER 100,000 POPULATION
Heart disease	281.4
Cancer	204.1
Stroke	56.4
Chronic obstructive pulmonary disease	36.0
Accidents	34.0
Pneumonia	29.7
Diabetes	19.6
Suicide	12.0
HIV infection	13.2
Homicide and legal intervention	10.0

SOURCE: *Statistical Abstract of the United States: 1995,* 115th U.S. Bureau of the Census, (Washington, D.C.: U.S. Government Printing Office, 1995), Table 127.

THE AMERICAN LIFESTYLE

In general, Americans view themselves as healthy. Compared to impoverished and developing countries, people in the United States do have good health. Nevertheless, several aspects of life in the United States have adverse health effects. These include stress, workplace hazards, sedentary lifestyles, poor eating habits, cigarette smoking, drug and alcohol abuse, and environmental pollution. These factors contribute to several of the ten leading causes of death in the United States (see Table 2.3). For example, stress; diets high in saturated fat, salt, and cholesterol; cigarette smoking; and sedentary lifestyles contribute to the number one killer in America—heart disease. Diets high in fat and low in fiber; chemical pollutants in our air, water, and food; and stress also contribute to the second most common cause of death in the United States—cancer.

Other chapters will discuss the health hazards of environmental pollution (Chapter 15) and the use of cigarettes, alcohol, and other drugs (Chapter 3). Here, we examine the physical health hazards associated with stress, the workplace (see also Chapter 10), and sedentary lifestyles.

Stress Stress, commonly experienced as emotional or mental pressure or strain, is a hallmark of American life. Common sources of stress, or stressors, include workplace or school demands; personal, family, and community problems; poverty; job insecurity; competition; and role conflict. Stress contributes to a variety of physical and mental health problems, including heart and cerebrovascular disease, hypertension, peptic ulcers, inflammatory bowel diseases, musculoskeletal problems, and asthma. Evidence also suggests that stress interferes with the immune system, possibly facilitating the development of cancer.

Further, chronic stress contributes to the use of alcohol, drugs, and cigarettes and to anxiety, depression, and mental disorders (Baker and Karasek 1995). Too much stress can also facilitate suicide. In a Connecticut study of 656 eleventh and twelfth graders, 10 percent had attempted suicide. Of these, one-fourth reported that stress ("I couldn't take it anymore") was the motivating factor for the suicide attempt (Patrick 1995).

Workplace Hazards In the workplace, workers are exposed to a wide range of occupational and safety hazards. Technology has increased the speed of production, putting pressure on workers to perform rapid, repetitive motions that are damaging to physical and mental health. Stress associated with workplace demands also leads to physical and mental health problems. Exposure to toxic substances, such as lead, mercury, and solvents, may not only cause physical health problems for workers, but may produce psychiatric syndromes as well (Schottenfeld 1995).

> **Consideration** *Even unpaid household work—the single largest category of work done by women in society—involves health hazards. Products used routinely in the home, such as drain cleaners, chlorine bleaches, scouring powders, ammonia, oven cleaners containing lye, furniture polish, and home pesticides "are potential hazards . . . particularly when used in a confined space, such as an unventilated bathroom or attic . . ." (Quinn, Woskie, and Rosenberg 1995, 630).*

The mining industry has one of the highest rates of workers killed on the job.

Sedentary Lifestyles Just as physical activity and exercise have positive effects on physical and mental health, lack of physical activity or exercise contributes to poor health among many Americans. In spite of the presumed craze for physical fitness, "there has been no decline in the proportion of people who lead essentially sedentary lifestyles" (McGinnis and Lee 1995, 125).

A physically active lifestyle reduces the risk for several chronic diseases, including coronary heart disease, hypertension, diabetes, osteoporosis, and colon cancer. In addition, people who maintain or improve their strength and flexibility through physical activity may be better able to avoid disability as they age. Regular physical activity contributes to better balance, coordination, and agility, which in turn may help prevent falls that often cause injuries in the elderly.

Physical activity also benefits mental health by reducing the risk of anxiety and depression (Pate et al. 1995). The reduction of stress that results from recreational physical activity and exercise reduces stress-induced violence, child abuse, and family discord. This chapter's *In Focus* emphasizes the social and cultural barriers to being physically active.

National Data: Experts estimate that as many as 250,000 deaths per year in the United States, approximately 12 percent of the total, are attributable to a lack of regular exercise.
SOURCE: Pate et al. 1995.

Mental Illness as a Social Problem

Mental illness is related to a number of other social problems. Link, Andrews, and Cullen (1992) observed that psychotics were disproportionately represented among those who had used a weapon, been in a fight, or hit someone. People diagnosed as having a "mental illness" often have difficulty interacting with others, succeeding in school, holding a job, or taking care of themselves and their children. Some mentally ill persons are completely dependent on others for their survival, and those who have no family or financial support may become one of the thousands of Americans who are homeless.

Consideration In the 1950s and 1960s, in part because of the increased use of psychotropic drugs, there was a movement toward **deinstitutionalization.** For example, in 1955 the number of institutionalized

Social and Cultural Barriers to Physical Activity and Exercise

The Centers for Disease Control and Prevention (CDC) and the American College of Sports Medicine (ACSM) recommend that people aged six and older engage regularly, preferably daily, in light to moderate physical activity for at least thirty minutes per day. Experts agree that "if Americans who lead sedentary lives would adopt a more active lifestyle, there would be enormous benefit to the public's health and to individual well-being" (Pate et al. 1995, 406). Yet in a telephone survey of over 87,000 U.S. adults, only about 22 percent reported being active at the recommended level; 24 percent reported that they led a completely sedentary lifestyle (that is, they reported no leisure-time physical activity in the past month) (Pate et al. 1995).

A number of social and cultural factors contribute to the sedentary lifestyle of many Americans. First, the demands of the workplace leave little time for recreational physical activities. Indeed, the most commonly cited barrier to physical activity is a lack of time (Pate et al. 1995). Employed wives and mothers who fulfill traditional gender role expectations of having primary responsibility for domestic chores and child care have even less leisure time to exercise than men.

Outdoor physical activity is also constrained by safety concerns. Women who are worried about their safety are less likely to use parks at certain hours or engage in outdoor activities such as walking, jogging, bicycling, and roller blading in unsafe neighborhoods. Other environmental barriers to physical activity include lack of access to recreational and sports facilities and an absence of bicycle trails and walking paths away from traffic.

The cultural obsession with watching television may also deter persons from being physically active. Adult men and women in the United States spend an average of fifteen hours a week, representing 38 percent of their total leisure time, watching television (Robinson 1990). This may be partly due to the fact that people are too tired from work to engage in more active leisure activities. However, when a national sample of women were asked, "If there were one more hour in the day, how would you

mental patients was nearly 600,000; by 1990, that number had decreased to 110,000 (Mechanic 1990). Deinstitutionalization has been identified as one of the major causes of homelessness in the United States. It should be noted, however, that homelessness may be a cause of mental illness, as well as a result.

Mental health problems among children also constitute a serious social concern. Children with disruptive behavior disorders, including attention deficit hyperactivity disorder (ADHD), conduct disorder, and oppositional defiant disorder, are at high risk for developing antisocial personality disorders as adults, getting into trouble with the law, experiencing divorce, having difficulty holding down a steady job, and staying free of drug and alcohol problems. Girls with disruptive behavior disorders are at higher risk for unplanned pregnancy (Angold 1994).

spend it?" the most common response was "participate in active sports." Only 1 percent reported that they would watch more TV (Robinson 1990).

One way society can improve the health of its members is to facilitate regular participation in physical activity and exercise. While the decision to be physically active is an individual one, cultural and social norms can promote active lifestyles in several ways. The following recommendations are from a committee of experts assembled by the CDC and the ACSM (Pate et al. 1995):

1. Public health agencies should strengthen their efforts to promote physically active lifestyles. These agencies include the CDC, the ACSM, the President's Council on Physical Fitness and Sports, the American Heart Association, state and local health departments, departments of public transportation and planning, and parks and recreation associations. Walk-a-thons, health fairs, and road races are good beginnings.

2. Physicians and other health professionals should routinely counsel patients to adopt

and maintain regular physical activity. These professionals should also provide follow-up to help encourage the maintenance of physical exercise.

3. Special efforts should be directed to target populations where physical inactivity is prevalent. These groups include the socioeconomically disadvantaged, the less educated, persons with disabilities, and older adults.

4. Corporate, government, school, and hospital policies should be restructured to encourage individuals to be active by making time and facilities available to workers and students. Increasingly, these institutions feature on-site health clubs, exercise equipment, and aerobic classes.

SOURCES: Russell R. Pate, Michael Pratt, Steven N. Blair, William L. Haskell, Caroline A. Macera, Claude Bouchard, David Buchner, Walter Ettiger, Gregory W. Health, Abby C. King, Andrea Kriska, Arthur L. Leon, Bess H. Marcus, Jeremy Morris, Ralph S. Paffenbarger, Kevin Patrick, Michael L. Pollock, James M. Rippe, James Sallis, and Jack H. Wilmore. 1995 (Feb. 1). "Physical Activity and Public Health: A Recommendation from the Centers for Disease Control and Prevention and the American College of Sports Medicine." *Journal of the American Medical Association* 273 (5): 402–6; John P. Robinson. 1990. "The Leisure Pie." *American Demographics*, p. 39.

THE NATURE OF MENTAL ILLNESS

Everyone experiences "problems in living" from time to time, and many people seek help from mental health professionals including counseling, chemotherapy, community treatment, and institutionalization. Typical problems that may cause mental distress or impairment in functioning include relationship problems, criminal or domestic victimization, work-related problems, stress, and low self-esteem. However, some conditions, or mental disorders, are more intense, persistent, and debilitating. The American Psychiatric Association (1994) defines a **mental disorder** as a "behavioral or psychological syndrome or pattern that occurs in an individual and that is associated with present distress (e.g., painful symptoms) or disability (i.e., impairment in one or more important areas of functioning) or with a significantly increased risk of suffering death, pain, disability, or an important loss of freedom" (p. xxi).

Consideration The term "mental disorder" implies a distinction between "mental disorders" and "physical disorders." However, health professionals recognize that "there is much 'physical' in 'mental' disorders
and much 'mental' in 'physical disorders'" (American Psychiatric
Association 1994, xxi). For example, poor physical health often leads to depression (Ross 1994), and depression may result in a person abusing
drugs or alcohol, becoming physically inactive, and failing to engage in
health maintenance behaviors.

Social and cultural factors greatly influence definitions of mental health
and illness. For example, the American Psychiatric Association once considered homosexuality to be a mental disorder. As homosexuals gained increased
social support, cultural acceptance, and political power, the association responded by removing homosexuality from the classification system of mental
disorders. How can a behavior be an indication of mental illness one year and
not the next? Symbolic interactionists respond that the symptoms of mental
illness are socially defined and thus change over time, circumstance, and individuals involved.

In a classic study by Rosenhan et al. (1973), sixteen "pseudopatients" feigning such symptoms as hearing loud voices saying "thud" and "hollow" sought
admission to psychiatric facilities. In reality, the pseudopatients were associates of Rosenhan's—three were psychiatrists and one was a psychologist! All
except one were admitted to the hospital. While there, the most normal behaviors were defined as symptomatic of mental illness. For example, as researchers, the pseudopatients took lengthy notes. In the hospital records, their
note taking was described as "bizarre writing behavior." The patients were
eventually released after an average stay of nineteen days and were discharged
with the diagnosis of "schizophrenia in remission."

This study suggests the difficulty in diagnosing mental illness and the questionable reliability of the admissions process. It also documents the effect of
labeling. Once the pseudopatients were labeled mentally ill, the staff never
questioned their sanity but instead interpreted all behaviors in light of what
was thought to be true. Although symbolic interactionists emphasize the importance of the labeling process and the social construction of mental illness,
they do not hold that all mental illness is socially determined. They acknowledge that some disorders are biologically and/or psychologically based (Scheff
1984). The following *Human Side* describes what it is like to suffer from mental illness and experience the impact of the labeling process.

PREVALENCE OF MENTAL ILLNESS IN THE UNITED STATES

Mental illness is a common social phenomenon in the United States, but assessing its exact prevalence is problematic due to the difficulty of defining
mental illness. However, the National Institute of Mental Health estimates that
there are nearly five million mentally ill adults in the United States (National
Center for Health Statistics 1992). No national studies have been conducted to
determine the prevalence of mental disorders among children, but local studies and studies in other countries indicate that between 17 and 22 percent of
children have diagnosable mental disorders. About 3 to 5 percent have severe
emotional or behavioral problems that significantly interfere with daily functioning (Hoagwood and Rupp 1994).

*We now know that we can
not distinguish insanity
from sanity.*
—David Rosenhan
Psychologist

National Data: In a study
of more than 8,000 respondents between the ages of
15 and 54, almost half (48
percent) reported having experienced at least one of
fourteen identified psychiatric disorders at some
time in their lives, and
close to 30 percent re-
ported experiencing at least
one disorder in the past
twelve months. The most
common disorders were de-
pression, alcohol depen-
dence, and social phobias.
SOURCE: Kessler et al. 1994.

THE EXPERIENCE OF MENTAL ILLNESS

Two researchers (Vellenga and Christenson 1994) asked fifteen men with a history of mental illness the following questions: "Tell me about you and your illness?" "What is this illness like for you?" "How do you feel your illness has affected the way you live?" Four themes emerged from the interviews.

STIGMATIZATION AND ALIENATION

The respondents reported feeling shamed because of their illness. They were aware of being viewed as different from other people and felt that people treated them differently. The following excerpts reflect the stigmatization and alienation felt by the respondents:

- I go out with a woman, and when I tell her that I have a mental illness, she acts like I have rabies or something. Things change right after that.

- I feel shunned. . . . How do you tell people that you don't work, but there's nothing physically wrong? I wish I'd have a heart attack or some physical problem. Then people would understand.

- If I don't take the medicine, the voices are so strong that they interfere with my ability to talk to others without them finding out about the voices. When I do take the medicine, I don't have enough energy to go out there with the rest of the people; and if I do, they can tell I'm on the medication.

- I'm paranoid about people finding out about my illness. It's difficult to explain to people why I'm 40 and retired. I avoid it by being a loner.

- I cope by not doing anything, or saying anything, or by not getting close to anybody. It's kind of a sad life. I have a very sad life, though I shouldn't.

LOSS

The men in this study lamented that their mental illness had caused them to lose their self-esteem, jobs, and important relationships:

- If I have even a moderate amount of stress, the voices get worse. What that means to me is a loss of self-esteem.

- When I was going into major highs and major lows, I was in school. I failed at school, and that's a loss I know I'll never regain.

- Having a mental illness is a very lonely life . . . you just give up a lot of things that other people have in their life, like a close relationship.

- My depression decreased my interest in things. I should have been involved with my kids at school. The desire

(continued on the next page)

was there but not the energy. I lost out on a lot as far as being a parent, but they probably lost out on more because of my illness.

DISTRESS

Distress, defined as pain and suffering, was reported by several of the respondents:

- I feel totally alone. I don't think I would equate it with hell. It's more like being in prison inside of myself with no feeling, no happiness, sadness. It is painful, very painful in my mind.

- This illness is a great burden. Day-to-day survival is a big question, and I just feel in a turmoil a lot of the time.

- It's a frightening experience because, like for me personally, most of the time when I get into a state or condition, I hear voices that aren't there usually. And I spend a lot of my waking hours in the midst of this anxiety, trying to decide if what I'm hearing is real or not. I spend a lot of waking energy doing this.

NEED FOR ACCEPTANCE

Subjects spoke of the need to accept themselves and to have others do so:

- I know I have a mental illness, and it would be better if I didn't, but I know what to do to control the voices. And I just have to do that, like taking my medication.

- I have a mental illness and my new wife has a mental illness, and that makes it hard, but it also makes it easier because we understand each other and what we've gone through. I call her the missing piece in my life—the missing puzzle piece.

SOURCE: Barbara A. Vellenga and Janell Christenson, 1994. "Persistent and Severely Mentally Ill Clients' Perceptions of Their Mental Illness." *Issues in Mental Health Nursing* 15: 359–71. Used by permission.

Social Correlates of Physical and Mental Health Problems

Persons of all categories experience physical and mental health problems. Nevertheless, the nature and prevalence of health problems vary according to social class, race and ethnicity, gender, and marital status.

SOCIAL CLASS

For a variety of reasons, people in the lower classes suffer from poorer physical and mental health than individuals who have more economic resources. Persons in the lower socioeconomic classes are more likely to have poor hous-

TABLE 2.4

SELECTED HEALTH INDICATORS: A COMPARISON OF U.S. BLACKS AND WHITES

	WHITES	BLACKS
Life expectancy at birth (born in 1995)	77.0 years	70.3 years
Infant mortality rate (1994)*	6.7	15.6
Percentage of children with up-to-date immunization for polio (1993)	79.8%	73.4%

*Infant mortality rate is number of infant deaths per 1000 live births.

SOURCES: National Center for Health Statistics. 1995 (June 13). "Monthly Vital Statistics Report." Vol. 43 (12). Hyattsville, Md: Public Health Service. Table 5. *Statistical Abstract of the United States: 1995*, 115th ed., U.S. Bureau of the Census (Washington, D.C.: U.S. Government Printing Office, 1995), Tables 114, 210.

ing and nutrition, lack adequate access to medical care, work in jobs that involve occupational hazards (including job stress), and engage in such risk-taking behaviors as smoking and drug use (Charlton 1994; Pappas 1994). The poor also receive less prenatal care and less preventive care (such as immunizations) and are more prone to contract communicable diseases than high-income individuals and families (U.S. Department of Health and Human Services 1991).

Studies consistently show that higher rates of mental disorders occur among persons with low income, education, and occupational status (Williams, Takeuchi, and Adair 1992). Rates of depression and substance abuse are also higher in the lower socioeconomic classes (Kessler et al. 1994). Why do poor people have higher rates of mental illness? One explanation suggests that lower-class individuals experience greater stress due to their deprived and difficult living conditions. Another explanation suggests that individuals with mental health problems may be unable to function in the educational and economic institutions of society, which limits their upward mobility. In this case, socioeconomic status is a consequence of mental problems, not a cause. Finally, some argue that members of the lower class are simply more likely to have their behaviors identified and treated as mental illness. In other words, they are not more likely to *be* mentally ill, but they are more likely to *be labeled* mentally ill.

RACE AND ETHNICITY

In general, racial and ethnic minorities experience more physical and mental health problems than whites. Table 2.4 reveals that blacks have a lower life expectancy, a higher infant mortality rate, and a lower rate of childhood immunizations. In addition, rates of various diseases, including hypertension, pneumonia, influenza, diabetes mellitus, cirrhosis, cerebrovascular disease, and tuberculosis are higher among blacks than whites (Davis et al. 1995).

The poorer health status of minorities is due primarily to the fact that they are overrepresented in the lower classes (Pappas 1994). Compared to the more affluent white majority, minorities tend to have inadequate nutrition, poorer living conditions, and higher stress. Minorities are also more likely than whites to work in hazardous occupations. Lastly, African Americans, as well as other minorities, are less likely than whites to have private medical insurance—

The Constitution of the Republic should make provisions for medical freedom as well as religious freedom. To restrict the art of healing to one class of men and deny equal privilege to others will constitute the Bastille of medical science.
—Benjamin Rush Colonial American physician—signed Declaration of Independence

17 percent versus 61 percent, respectively (Leigh 1994). The percentage of minorities not covered by health insurance is increasing rather than decreasing (McGinnis and Lee 1995). African Americans also have less access to medical care, and when they do receive medical care, it is often inferior to that received by whites.

The association between race and mental illness is also due, in part, to the disproportionate number of poor minorities; members of the lower class have higher rates of mental illness, and they are also disproportionately minorities. Research does indicate, however, that comparing whites and blacks with the same class background does yield variations. For example, blacks are much more likely than whites to report symptoms of depression. This can be explained by the relatively poor living conditions of African Americans (Cockerham 1989), years of oppression, higher levels of stress, and racism.

GENDER

Regardless of race, females live longer than males. According to the U.S. Bureau of the Census, women born in the year 2000 may expect to live about seven years longer than men—80.2 versus 73.2. Black women may expect to live about a year longer than white men (75.1 versus 74.3). In the United States, black males born in the year 2000 have the lowest estimated life expectancy–only 65.3 years (*Statistical Abstract of the United States; 1995*, Table 114).

Women tend to live longer than men for a variety of reasons. The culture of society socializes men to be aggressive and competitive and to engage in risky behaviors. Men are more likely than women to smoke, use alcohol, work under hazardous conditions, incur injury, and die from suicide and homicide. Thus, male gender roles, rather than male biology, largely account for the lower life expectancy of U.S. males. Krieger and Fee (1994) explain:

> *The higher accident rates of younger men are not accidental. They are due to more hazardous occupations, higher rates of illicit drug and alcohol*

Men in our society are more likely than women to be heavy drinkers. As a result, men are nearly twice as likely as women to die of liver disease.

use, firearms injuries, and motor vehicle crashes—hazards related to gen-
der roles and expectations. The fact that men die earlier of heart disease—
the single most common cause of death in both sexes—may also be related
to gender roles. Men have higher rates of cigarette smoking and fewer
sources of social support, suggesting that the masculine ideal of the
Marlboro man is not a healthy one. (p. 273)

Yet, throughout most of life, women report feeling less healthy than men. Among the factors contributing to this finding include lower subjective work rewards, economic hardship, and little leisure time. In contrast, men are more likely to be involved in work they regard as fulfilling, are more likely to exercise, and have more leisure time available because of fewer family responsibilities (Ross and Bird 1994).

Regarding mental illness, men are more likely to abuse drugs and have higher rates of personality disorders. Women are more likely to suffer from mood disorders such as depression, phobias, and anxiety attacks (Cockerham 1989; Kessler et al. 1994). Some research indicates that the labeling of women as mentally ill is closely tied to gender roles. Women who violate traditional definitions of femininity by displaying aggressiveness, independence, and dominance are more likely to be diagnosed as mentally ill.

MARITAL STATUS

In general, married individuals experience better physical and mental health than single or divorced individuals. Married people have a lower incidence of disease, a lower mortality rate, less alcoholism, fewer suicides, fewer psychiatric problems, and higher self-reported happiness than individuals who have never married (Coombs 1991).

Divorced individuals, compared to married and never-married persons, have the highest rates of depression and suicide (Stack 1989; Broman 1988) and report being less happy. Based on a national sample, only 18 percent of divorced men, compared to 36 percent of married men, said that they were "very happy" (Glenn and Weaver 1988). Only 19 percent of divorced women, compared to 40 percent of married women, said that they were "very happy."

One explanation for the better mental health among married persons is that marital relationships provide social and emotional support that helps individuals cope with stress and difficult life situations. An alternative explanation is that individuals with mental or emotional problems are less likely to marry, so the higher level of mental health among marrieds is due to a selection process. In the first case, mental illness is the dependent variable—marital status affects mental health. In the second case, mental illness is the independent variable—the mentally ill are less likely to marry.

The American Health Care System

The United States boasts of having the best physicians, hospitals, and advanced medical technology in the world. Yet, two major factors suggest that the U.S. health care system is experiencing a crisis: the rising cost of medical care and the significant proportion of Americans who have no or limited access to quality medical care.

TABLE 2.5

HEALTH CARE SPENDING IN SEVEN COUNTRIES, 1991

	PERCENTAGE OF GDP	PER CAPITA
Canada	10.0%	$1,917
France	9.1	1,656
Germany	8.4	1,663
Japan	6.8	1,307
Sweden	8.6	1,443
United Kingdom	6.6	1,033
United States	13.4	2,867

SOURCE: *OECD Health Data*. 1993. Organization for Economic Cooperation and Development.

HIGH COST OF MEDICAL CARE

The United States spends more on health care than any other country in the world (see Table 2.5). Health care costs have risen faster than the rate of inflation. In 1950, for example, health care expenditures accounted for 4.4 percent of the gross domestic product; by 1993, they accounted for 13.9 percent (Cherner 1995).

Several factors have contributed to escalating medical costs—technology, malpractice insurance, defensive medicine, administrative expenses, insurance, an aging population, and fraud. Advances in medical technology account for about half of the rise of health care costs over the past several decades (Schwartz 1994). Such advances include the development of CAT scanners, laser surgery, magnetic resonance imaging (MRI), ultrasound, angioplasty, and coronary bypass surgery. Many of these technologies were unavailable just decades ago; today they are routinely prescribed.

The high cost of malpractice insurance also contributes to high medical costs. Annual costs of malpractice insurance for physicians range from $15,000 to $200,000 depending on the medical specialty. These costs are passed on to the patient.

Fear of being sued and the size of financial judgments against physicians and other health care providers also contribute to the practice of defensive medicine. **Defensive medicine** involves giving patients expensive tests and treatments, which may not be necessary, but which help to protect physicians and hospitals against malpractice lawsuits. While adhering to the old adage "better safe than sorry" may protect health care professionals, the cost of overutilizing medical tests and procedures is astronomical.

Administrative expenses, which are higher in the United States than in any other nation, are another reason for high medical care costs. About twenty-five cents of each dollar spent on medical care goes for medical administration (Rasell 1994). A major source of administrative costs is the existence of 1,500 competing insurance plans in the United States. If the United States were to adopt a single-payer health care system as in Canada, $117.7 billion would be saved annually—an amount more than sufficient to fund universal health care (Hellander et al. 1994). In a **single-payer system**, a single tax-financed public insurance program replaces private insurance companies. The insurance industry, not surprisingly, opposes the adoption of such a system because the private health insurance industry would be virtually eliminated.

National Data: In 1991, U.S. physicians spent $5.6 billion and hospitals $9 billion for malpractice insurance.

SOURCE: Shenkin 1994.

Increasing medical costs also stem from the aging of the population. The elderly have more health problems that require both acute and long-term care. In 1989, people over age sixty-five made up 12 percent of the population but were responsible for 36 percent of medical care costs (Shenkin 1994). As the elderly population continues to grow (see Chapter 6), the amount of health care spending will also increase.

High costs of public and private insurance have also contributed to escalating health care expenditures. Medicaid and Medicare are two types of public health insurance. **Medicaid** is a jointly funded, federal-state-local program designed to provide health care for the poor. **Medicare,** a national public insurance program created by Title XVIII of the Social Security Act of 1965, was originally designed to protect people sixty-five years of age and older from the rising costs of health care. In 1972, it was extended to permanently disabled workers and their dependents and persons with end-stage renal disease.

Private insurance costs have also risen over the last few decades. The average cost of group health insurance per year for a family is $5,232 (Rowland et al. 1994, 284). Businesses that provide health insurance benefits bear much of the expense of the insurance for their employees. Small businesses pay premiums 25 to 40 percent higher than large businesses. According to the National Federation of Independent Business, health insurance was listed as the "No. 1 problem" by almost 500,000 small business owners (Kemper and Novak 1994). The high cost of employer-provided health insurance is passed on to the consumers who buy the companies' products or services.

Another contributor to the high cost of public and private medical insurance is insurance fraud, which is estimated to cost between $60 and $80 billion annually (Crenshaw 1993). Insurance fraud occurs when insurance companies are billed for services that were never rendered. For example, "rolling labs" (so named because they do not stay in one place very long so as to avoid prosecution) offer "free" medical checkups or "free therapy" to customers who receive a battery of tests such as electrocardiograms and blood pressure checks. The patients sign a blank insurance form, which the clinic then submits to the patient's insurer for payment for services never rendered. "[A] creative lab can rack up to $10,000 worth of charges from a single visit" (Crenshaw 1993, 233).

> *Consideration* One proposal for controlling the high cost of medical care is to ration health care, or deny certain medical treatments to people in order to save money. For example, the cost of one very low-birthweight baby (1.5 pounds) remaining in intensive care for several months is $1 million. However, very few live to leave the hospital, and half of those who do are debilitated. Some would argue that this is a poor cost-benefit ratio and that both economic and medical resources could be used more productively elsewhere. Similarly, the medical costs for the elderly in the last months of life are exorbitant.

National Data: Costs for the Medicaid program have risen from $51.3 billion in 1988 to $125 billion in 1993.
SOURCE: Hearn 1994
Medicare costs rose from about $88 billion in 1988 to $130 billion in 1992.
SOURCE: Enthoven 1994.

UNEQUAL ACCESS TO MEDICAL CARE

In general, individuals covered by health insurance (who can pass a "wallet biopsy") and with greater financial resources have greater access to better quality medical care than individuals with no health insurance and fewer resources. The increasing numbers of uninsured individuals represent a significant

How will uninsured individuals with medical needs pay for their medical care?

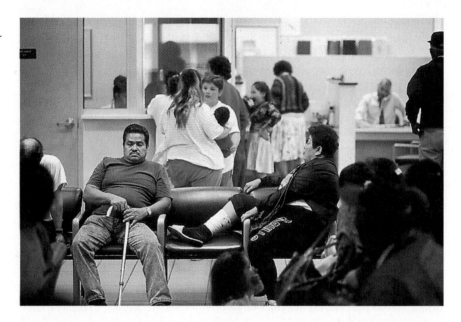

If you like public housing, you'll love public medicine.
—Newt Gingrich
Speaker of the House

problem in the American health care system. Today, more Americans lack health insurance coverage than at any time since the 1960s.

Individuals who are most likely to lack medical insurance include children, young adults, minorities, unmarried individuals, and those with less than a high school education (Weil 1994). The "majority of the uninsured are not poor. [S]even in ten . . . are from families with incomes above the poverty line" (Rowland et al. 1994, 284). Most uninsured individuals work in jobs that do not offer health plans and cannot afford to pay insurance premiums themselves. Still others cannot get insurance because they have a preexisting medical condition such as heart disease or diabetes, which excludes them from health benefits.

Lack of health insurance has negative consequences for the health of the uninsured. The uninsured make fewer visits to a physician each year, delay needed care, are less likely to be admitted to a hospital, receive fewer hospital procedures, and have higher mortality rates. Uninsured women are less likely to seek screening for breast cancer and are 49 percent more likely to die during the four to seven years following diagnosis than insured women (Rowland et al. 1994). The uninsured are also the last to receive organ transplants.

Public insurance programs such as Medicare and Medicaid do not provide an adequate safety net for individuals who do not have private insurance. Because of the soaring costs for Medicaid and Medicare, the government has tightened eligibility requirements, limited benefits, and reduced reimbursements to health care providers. Jecker (1994) reports that more than 25 percent of privately practicing physicians refuse to treat Medicaid patients because reimbursement rates are below costs.

Since the early 1900s, many politicians have advocated establishing a national health insurance program in the United States. The most recent proposal was the Clinton administration's 1994 Health Security Act, which, although supported by many, was opposed by health care industry groups, as well as by citizens who feared its passage would result in a reduction in the quality and choice of health care providers. Though the Clinton plan did not pass, public dissatisfaction with the current state of American health care will continue to pressure policy makers to implement health care reform to control costs and provide universal access to health care.

UNDERSTANDING
ILLNESS AND HEALTH CARE

Several conclusions can be drawn from the material presented in this chapter. Clearly, the physical and mental health of a community's members are essential for the proper functioning of society. As functionalists argue, mental and physical illness are a threat to the social order. However, the cost of health care in the United States is not solely a consequence of a competitive market as functionalists argue. The existence of a medical-industrial complex, as conflict theorists assert, is well documented. Further, if functionalist analysis were correct, the United States, which spends more on health care than any country in the world, would also have the highest quality medical care. Canada, for example, which has universal medical coverage and spends less on health care, has a lower infant mortality rate and a higher life expectancy than the United States.

The problems of American health care are clear: soaring costs and unequal access. Numerous programs and proposals have been devised to deal with both of these problems. One approach has been publicly funded health care programs such as Medicaid and Medicare. These programs provide universal health insurance for the poor and the elderly, leading many to argue for the expansion of such benefits to all citizens in a centralized single-payer model. Nevertheless, various proposals for improving the health care system continue to be debated. The cost of and access to health care may be improved by reform measures, but the health of a society's members is rarely improved by legislative mandate. If the physical and mental health of U.S. citizens are truly to be improved, we must prevent rather than just treat illness and injury. **Health maintenance organizations (HMOs),** which provide complete medical services for a monthly fee, are a significant step toward a preventive model.

Illness is a social phenomenon that is highly correlated with such social variables as race and class. Research indicates, however, that the relationship between race and illness is explained by the fact that racial minorities are over-represented in the lower socioeconomic statuses. That being the case, structural changes in society that eliminate or at least reduce class inequities should significantly decrease illness differentials. As Aday (1994) notes:

> Fundamental investments in enhancing the economic and social well-being of American families and neighborhoods may offer the greatest long-term possibilities for improving their physical, psychological, and social health and well-being. (p. 84)

Further, gender is associated with both physical and mental illness. To a large extent, illness variations between men and women are a consequence of cultural definitions about role performance and the expectations associated with gender roles. Traditional beliefs such as the idea that men must work, succeed, compete, and be responsible for the welfare of their families create much of the stress associated with male morbidity and mortality. Further, stress is

* *

A major cause of children dying is really related to many of the social problems impacting their health.
—Joycelyn Elders
Former Surgeon General

* *

intricately tied to other social status indicators, most notably, race, class, and marital status.

In the early 1900s, infectious diseases such as influenza and pneumonia were the leading causes of death. With the development of antibiotics and other drugs, deaths from these diseases were drastically reduced. Today, the leading causes of death are heart disease and cancer. Each of these, to a large extent, is caused by cultural beliefs that foster self-destructive behaviors—inadequate diets high in salt, fat, and cholesterol, alcohol consumption, smoking, and sedentary lifestyles. Continued educational and media campaigns, employee wellness programs, and community health initiatives that address the dangers of these behaviors must be expanded.

Finally, the continued trend toward medicalization promotes the acceptance of a clinical model whereby a variety of behaviors and conditions are viewed as internally caused, that is, as individual sickness. The collective adoption of such a position often "blames the victim" and undermines social policies that would facilitate needed structural and cultural changes. Stress, for example, is a major risk factor for both physical and mental illness. Yet stress is systemic; it is ". . . tied to social locations and/or social group experiences" and is intricately related to the "social conditions of life" (Turner, Lloyd, and Wheaton 1995, 119). While the clinical model may leave society blameless, it also leaves little hope for meaningful changes in the health status of most Americans.

CRITICAL THINKING

1. Home medical-advice software and computer networks are now available to help consumers manage their own health. Consumers can access a medical library or converse with fellow patients on the Comprehensive Health Enhancement Support System (CHESS) or find answers to routine medical questions with a number of software packages. How do you think this computer technology will affect the U.S. health care system?
2. Explain how corporate concern for profits can both hurt the health of employees and promote health among employees.
3. From a conflict theory perspective, how could one explain the relatively recent designation of premenstrual syndrome as a medical disorder?

KEY TERMS

maternal mortality	life expectancy	single-payer system
infant mortality rate	morbidity	Medicaid
medical-industrial complex	deinstitutionalization	Medicare
medicalization	mental disorder	health maintenance organizations (HMOs)
	defensive medicine	

REFERENCES

Aday, Lu Ann. 1994. "Equity, Accessibility, and Ethical Issues: Is the U.S. Health Care Reform Debate Asking the Right Questions?" In *Health Care Reform in the Nineties,* ed. Pauline Vaillancourt Rosenau, pp. 83–103. Thousand Oaks, Calif.: Sage Publications.

Aitken, Iain, and Laura Reichenbach. 1994. "Reproductive and Sexual Health Services: Expanding Access and Enhancing Quality." In *Population Policies Reconsidered: Health, Empowerment, and Rights,* ed. by Gita Sen, Adrienne Germain, and Lincoln C. Chen, pp. 177–92. Boston: Harvard School of Public Health.

American Psychiatric Association. 1994. *Diagnostic and Statistical Manual of Mental Disorders, 4th Edition (DSM-IV).* Washington, D.C.: American Psychiatric Association.

Angold, Adrian. 1994 (Fall). "Researchers Unite to Help Disruptive Kids: The Leon Lowenstein Center." *Psychiatry at Duke.* Duke University Medical Center. 5(2): 12.

Aral, S. O., and K. K. Holmes. 1991. "Sexually Transmitted Diseases in the AIDS Era." *Scientific American* 264, 62–69.

Avruch, Sheila, and Alicia Puente Cackley. 1995. "Savings Achieved by Giving Benefits to Women Prenatally." *Public Health Reports* 110(1): 27–35.

Baker, Dean B, and Robert A. Karasek. 1995. "Occupational Stress." In *Occupational Health: Recognizing and Preventing Work-Related Disease,* 3d ed., ed. Barry S. Levy and David H. Wegman, pp. 381–406. Boston: Little, Brown.

Bandura, A. 1989. "Perceived Self-Efficacy in the Exercise of Control over AIDS Infection." In *Primary Prevention of AIDS: Psychological Approaches,* ed. V. M. Mays, G. W. Albee, and S. F. Schneider, pp. 128–41. Newbury Park: Calif.: Sage Publications.

Broman, C. L. 1988. "Satisfaction among Blacks: The Significance of Marriage and Parenthood." *Journal of Marriage and the Family* 50: 45–51.

Centers for Disease Control and Prevention. 1994. HIV~AIDS Surveillance Report. 5 (no. 4): 1–33. Available from CDC National AIDS Clearinghouse, P.O. Box 6003, Rockville, MD 20849-6003.

Charlton, Bruce G. 1994 (Jan. 22). "Is Inequality Bad for the National Health?" *The Lancet* 343(8891): 221–22.

Cherner, Linda L. 1995. *The Universal Healthcare Almanac.* Phoenix: Silver & Cherner.

Cockerham, William C. 1989. *Sociology of Mental Disorders,* 2d ed. Englewood Cliffs, N.J.: Prentice-Hall.

Coombs, R. H. 1991. "Marital Status and Person Well-Being: A Literature Review." *Family Relations* 40: 97–102.

Cooper, Mary H. 1995. "Combating Aids: Are Researchers Getting Closer to a Cure?" *Congressional Quarterly Researcher,* April 21.

Cowley, Geoffrey. 1994. "The Ever-Expanding Plague." *Newsweek,* August 22, 37.

Crenshaw, Albert B. 1993. "Diagnosing Medical Fraud." *Society in Crisis,* pp. 232–34. The Washington Post Writers Group. Boston: Allyn & Bacon.

Davis, Morris E., Andrew S. Rowland, Bailus Walker, Jr., and Andrea Kidd Taylor. 1995. "Minority Workers." In *Occupational Health: Recognizing and Preventing Work-Related Disease,* ed. Barry S. Levy and David H. Wegman, pp. 639–49. Boston: Little, Brown.

Enthoven, Alain C. 1994. "Managed Competition Would Improve America's Health Care System." In *Health Care in America: Opposing Viewpoints,* ed. Carol Wekesser, pp. 169–77. San Diego, Calif.: Greenhaven Press.

Fielding, Jonathan, and Neal Halfon. 1994. (Oct. 26). "Where Is the Health in Health System Reform?" *Journal of the American Medical Association* 272(16): 129–34.

Freedman, Lynn P., and Deborah Maine. 1993. "Women's Mortality: A Legacy of Neglect." In *The Health of Women: A Global Perspective,* ed. Marge Koblinsky, Judith Timyan, and Jill Gay, pp. 147–70. Boulder, Colo.: Westview Press.

General Social Survey. 1993. Health Status. Chicago: NORC, A Social Science Research Center.

Glenn, N. D., and C. N. Weaver. 1988. "The Changing Relationship of Marital Status to Reported Happiness." *Journal of Marriage and the Family* 50: 317–24.

Health Is a Right, AIDS Expert Says. 1992 (July 20). *The News and Observer,* Raleigh, N.C., p. 1A.

Hearn, Wayne. 1994. (Dec. 19). "Managing Medicaid." *American Medical News* 37 (47): 15–20.

Hellander, Ida, David U. Himmelstein, Steffie Woolhandler, and Sidney Wolfe. 1994. "Health Care Paper Chase, 1993: The Cost to the Nation, the States, and the District of Columbia." *International Journal of Health Services* 24: 1–9.

Hewlett, Sylvia Ann. 1992. *When the Bough Breaks: The Cost of Neglecting Our Children.* New York: HarperPerennial.

Hoagwood, Kimberly, and Agnes Rupp. 1994. "Mental Health Service Needs, Use, and Costs for Children and Adolescents with Mental Disorders and Their Families: Preliminary Evidence." In *Mental Health, United States,* 1994, ed. R. W. Manderscheid and Mary Anne Sonnenschein, pp. 52–64. Rockville, Md.: U.S. Department of Health and Human Services.

Jecker, Nancy S. 1994. "Employment-Based Insurance Is Unjust." *In Health Care in America: Opposing Viewpoints,* ed. Carol Wekesser, pp. 224–30. San Diego, Calif.: Greenhaven Press.

Johnson, Stanley P. 1994. *World Population—Turning the Tide: Three Decades of Progress.* Boston: Graham & Trotman/Martinus Nijoff.

Kemper, Vicki, and Viveca Novak. 1994. "Powerful Health Care Lobbies Hurt American Health Care." In *Health Care in America: Opposing Viewpoints,* ed. Carol Wekesser, pp. 30–37. San Diego, Calif.: Greenhaven Press.

Kessler, Ronald C., Katherine A. McGonale, Shanyang Zhao, Chritopher B. Nelson, Michael Hughes, Suzann Eshleman, Hans-Ulrich Wittchen, and Kenneth S. Kendler. 1994. "Lifetime and 12-Month Prevalence of DSM-III-R Psychiatric Disorders in the United States." *Archives of General Psychiatry* 51: 8–19.

Klerman, Lorraine V., and Jacob A. Klerman. 1994. "More Evidence for the Public Health Value of Family Planning." *The American Journal of Public Health* 84(9): 1377–78.

Krieger, Nancy, and Elizabeth Fee. 1994. "Man-made Medicine and Women's Health: The Biopolitics of Sex/Gender and Race/Ethnicity." *International Journal of Health Services* 24: 265–83.

Leigh, Wilhelmina A. 1994. "Implications of Health-Care Reform Proposals for Black Americans." *Journal of Health Care for the Poor and Underserved* 5: 17–32.

Levy, Barry S., and David H. Wegman. 1995. "Occupational Health in Global Context: An American Perspective." In *Occupational Health: Recognizing and*

Preventing Work-Related Disease, ed. Barry S. Levy and David H. Wegman, pp. 3–24. Boston: Little, Brown.

Link, Bruce G., Howard Andrews, and Francis T. Cullen. 1992. "The Violent and Illegal Behavior of Mental Patients Reconsidered." *American Sociological Review* 57: 275–92.

McGinnis, Michael J., and Philip R. Lee. 1995. (April 12). "Healthy People 2000 at Mid Decade." *Journal of the American Medical Association* 273: 1123–29.

Mechanic, David. 1990. "Promise Them Everything, Give Them the Streets." *New York Times Book Review,* September 16, 9.

Merchant, Kathleen M., and Kathleen M. Kurz. 1993. "Women's Nutrition through the Life Cycle: Social and Biological Vulnerabilities." In *The Health of Women: A Global Perspective,* ed. Marge Koblinsky, Judith Timyan, and Jill Gay, pp. 63–90. Boulder, Colo.: Westview Press.

National Center for Health Statistics. 1992. *Health, United States, 1991,* pp. 150–51. Hyattsville, Md.: U.S. Public Health Service.

———. 1992. "Serious Mental Illness and Disability in the Adult Household Population: United States." Hyattsville, Md.: U.S. Public Health Service.

———. 1994. Births, Marriages, Divorces, and Deaths for March. *Monthly Vital Statistics Report* 43, no. 3. Hyattsville, Md.: U.S. Public Health Service.

Okie, Susan. 1993. "Health Crisis Confronts 1.3 Billion." *Society in Crisis,* pp. 218–19. The Washington Post Writers Group. Boston: Allyn & Bacon.

Pappas, Gregory. 1994 (June). "Elucidating the Relationship between Race, Socioeconomic Status, and Health." *American Journal of Public Health* 84(6): 892–93.

Parsons, Talcott. 1951. *The Social System.* New York: Free Press.

Pate, Russell R., Michael Pratt, Steven N. Blair, William L. Haskell, Caroline A. Macera, Claude Bouchard, David Buchner, Walter Ettiger, Gregory W. Health, Abby C. King, Andrea Kriska, Arthur L. Leon, Bess H. Marcus, Jeremy Morris, Ralph S. Paffenbarger, Kevin Patrick, Michael L. Pollock, James M. Rippe, James Sallis, and Jack H. Wilmore. 1995 (Feb. 1). "Physical Activity and Public Health: A Recommendation from the Centers for Disease Control and Prevention and the American College of Sports Medicine." *Journal of the American Medical Association* 273(5): 402–6.

Patrick, Susan. 1995. Connecticut Youth Suicide Survey. Governor's Partnership to Protect Connecticut's Workforce. 30 Arbor Street, Hartford, CT 06106.

Pinkney, Deborah Shelton. 1994 (May 2). "Risky Pleasure." *American Medical News* 37(17): 15–16.

Quinn, Margaret M., Susan R. Woskie, and Beth J. Rosenberg. 1995. "Women and Work." In *Occupational Health: Recognizing and Preventing Work-Related Disease,* 3d ed., ed. Barry S. Levy and David H. Wegman, pp. 619–38. Boston: Little, Brown.

Rasell, Edie. 1994. "Overuse of Medical Services Hurts the Health Care System." In *Health Care in America: Opposing Viewpoints,* ed. Carol Wekesser, pp. 38–43. San Diego, Calif.: Greenhaven Press.

Relman, Arnold S. 1980. "The New Medical-Industrial Complex." *New England Journal of Medicine* 303:963–70.

Rosenhan, D. L. 1973. "On Being Sane in Insane Places." *Science* 179: 250–58.

Ross, Catherine E. 1994. "Overweight and Depression." *Journal of Health and Social Behavior* 35: 63–79.

Ross, Catherine E., and Chloe E. Bird. 1994. "Sex Stratification and Health Lifestyle: Consequences for Men's and Women's Perceived Health." *Journal of Health and Social Behavior* 35: 161–78.

Rowland, Diane, Barbara Lyons, Alina Salganicoff, and Peter Long. 1994. "A Profile of the Uninsured in America." *Health Affairs* 13: 283–87.

Scheff, T. J. 1984. *Being Mentally Ill: A Sociological Theory,* 2d ed. New York: Aldine.

Schottenfeld, Richard. 1995. "Disorders of the Nervous System: Psychiatric Disorders." In *Occupational Health: Recognizing and Preventing Work-Related Disease,* 3d ed., ed. Barry S. Levy and David H. Wegman, pp. 533–41. Boston: Little, Brown.

Schwartz, Matthew P. 1995 (Jan. 2). "Nearly 40 Million Americans Uninsured in "93 Study." *National Underwriter Life & Health—Financial Services Edition.* (1): 4.

Schwartz, William B. 1994. "In the Pipeline: A Wave of Valuable Medical Technology." *Health Affairs* 13: 70–79.

Shenkin, Henry A. 1994. *Medical Care Reform: A Guide to Issues and Choices.* Santa Monica, Calif.: Oakvale Press.

Stack, Steven. 1989. "The Impact of Divorce on Suicide in Norway, 1951–1980." *Journal of Marriage and the Family* 51: 229–38.

Statistical Abstract of the United States: 1995, 115th ed. Washington, D.C.: U.S. Bureau of the Census, 1995.

Szasz, Thomas. 1970 (orig. 1961). *The Myth of Mental Illness: Foundations of a Theory of Personal Conduct.* New York: Harper & Row.

Turner, R. Jay, Donald A. Lloyd, and Blair Wheaton. 1995. "The Epidemiology of Social Stress." *American Sociological Review* 60: 104–25.

U.S. Department of Health and Human Services. 1990. *Health Status of the Disadvantaged—Chartbook, 1990.* Washington, D.C.: pp. 23–66.

———. 1991. *Health Status of Minorities and Low-Income Groups,* 3d ed. Washington, D.C.: pp. 37–49.

Weil, Thomas. 1994. "The Clinton Health-Care Reform Plan: Does It Serve the Underserved?" *Journal of Health Care for the Poor and Underserved* 5: 5–16.

Williams, David R., David T. Takeuchi, and Russell K. Adair. 1992. "Socioeconomic Status and Psychiatric Disorder among Blacks and Whites." *Social Forces* 71: 179–94.

World Bank. 1993. *World Development Report 1993: Investing in Health.* New York: Oxford University Press.

World Health Organization. 1946. *Constitution of the World Health Organization.* New York: World Health Organization Interim Commission.

———. 1989. *Coverage of Maternity Care: A Tabulation of Available Information,* 2d ed. Geneva, Switzerland: Division of Family Health.

———. 1994. "AIDS Cases Soar in Past Year." *Global AIDS News* (no. 3). Internet: The Newsletter of the W.H.O. Global Programme on AIDS. Geneva, Switzerland.

3

CHAPTER

Alcohol and Other Drugs

IS IT TRUE?

Cigarettes kill more Americans each year than car accidents, AIDS, murders, suicides, illegal drugs, and fires combined (p. 79).

In 1995, the Supreme Court ruled that random drug testing of student athletes in public school is unconstitutional (p. 80).

In 1994, over half of Americans age 12 and older reported being current users of alcohol (p. 70).

The most commonly used illicit drug in the United States is marijuana (p. 74).

The Dutch have decriminalized small quantities of heroin and have one of the lowest addiction rates in Europe (p. 64).

ANS: 1.T 2.F 3.T 4.T 5.T

> Substance abuse, the nation's number-one preventable health problem, places an enormous burden on American society, harming health, family life, the economy, and public safety, and threatening many other aspects of life.
>
> Robert Wood Johnson Foundation,
> Institute for Health Policy, Brandeis University

One of the more popular television programs is *Beverly Hills 90210*. One reason for its popularity is its willingness to deal with a number of contemporary social problems such as drug addiction. In a series of episodes, viewers were able to observe the individual and social consequences of drug addiction on the part of one of the show's central characters—Kelly Taylor. Her involvement with cocaine jeopardized her health, safety, academic success, and relationships with family and friends.

The use of alcohol and other drugs is a social problem when it interferes with the well-being of individuals and/or the societies in which they live. Managing the drug problem is a difficult undertaking, however. In dealing with drugs, a society must balance individual rights and civil liberties against the personal and social harm that drugs promote—crack babies, suicide, drunk driving, industrial accidents, mental illness, unemployment, and teenage addiction. When to regulate, what to regulate, and who should regulate are complex social issues. Our discussion begins by looking at how drugs are used and regulated in other societies.

The Social Context: Drug Use and Abuse

Pharmacologically, a drug is any substance other than food that alters the structure or functioning of a living organism when it enters the bloodstream. Using this definition, everything from vitamins to aspirin constitutes a drug. Sociologically, the term *drug* refers to any chemical substance that (1) has a direct effect on the user's physical, psychological, and/or intellectual functioning; (2) has the potential to be abused; and (3) has adverse consequences for the individual and/or society.

Societies vary in how they define and respond to drug use. Thus, drug use is influenced by the social context of the particular society in which it occurs.

DRUG USE AND ABUSE IN OTHER SOCIETIES

Since the mid-1970s, the official government policy in the Netherlands has been to treat the use of such drugs as marijuana, hashish, and heroin as a health issue rather than a crime issue. Overall, this "decriminalization" policy has had positive results. Although marijuana and heroin are readily available in Dutch cities, the use of both has declined over the years as have drug overdoses and HIV infections from intravenous drug use. The decline in the number of drug users may have occurred, in part, because addicts are free to seek help without fear of criminal reprisals.

U.S. citizens visiting the Netherlands may be shocked or surprised to find people smoking marijuana and hashish openly in public places.

Great Britain has also adopted a "medical model," particularly in regard to heroin and cocaine. As early as the 1960s, English doctors prescribed opiates and cocaine for their patients who were unlikely to quit using drugs on their own and for the treatment of withdrawal symptoms. By the 1970s, however, British laws had become more restrictive making it difficult for either physicians or users to obtain drugs legally. Today, British government policy provides for limited distribution of drugs to addicts who might otherwise resort to crime to support their habits. Great Britain regulates the use of heroin by allowing physicians to write prescriptions for registered addicts. If addicts commit a crime while receiving heroin, they are treated as other criminals. Further, if unregistered individuals are caught using heroin, they are prosecuted for illegal possession. The result has been to provide medical supervision for registered addicts as well as to reduce the number of crimes associated with heroin use.

In stark contrast to such health-based policies, other countries execute drug users and/or dealers, or subject them to corporal punishment. The latter may include whipping, stoning, beating, and torture. Such policies are found primarily in less developed nations such as Malaysia, where religious and cultural prohibitions condemn any type of drug use including alcohol and tobacco.

DRUG USE IN THE UNITED STATES

American's concern with drugs has varied over the years. Ironically, in the 1970s when drug use was at its highest, concern over drugs was relatively low. Concern about drugs reached its height in 1989 when 64 percent of Americans responding to a *Times/CBS* poll said that drugs were the number one problem in the United States (Goode 1994, 165). Figure 3.1 shows the decline in illicit drug use in the United States from 1979 to 1994.

As Table 3.1 indicates, use of alcohol and cigarettes is much more widespread than use of illicit drugs, such as marijuana and cocaine. In the United States, cultural definitions of drug use are contradictory—condemning it on the one hand (e.g., heroin), yet encouraging and tolerating it on the other (e.g., alcohol).

At various times in U.S. history, many drugs that are illegal today were legal and readily available. In the 1800s and the early 1900s, opium was routinely used

FIGURE 3.1

Illicit Drug Use in the Past Month, All Ages 12 and Older, 1979-1994

SOURCE: Substance Abuse and Mental Health Administration (Office of Applied Statistics) from the 1994 National Household Survey on Drug Abuse. Advance Report #10: Sept. 1995. U.S. Dept. of Health and Human Services.

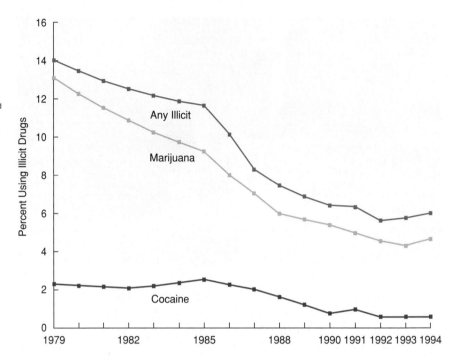

TABLE 3.1

DRUG USE, BY TYPE OF DRUG AND AGE GROUP, 1993

TYPE OF DRUG	EVER USED			CURRENT USER[a]		
	12 to 17 Years Old	18 to 25 Years Old	26+ Years Old	12 to 17 Years Old	18 to 25 Years Old	26+ Years Old
Marijuana	11.7%	47.4%	34.3%	4.9%	11.1%	3.0%
Cocaine	1.1	12.5	12.5	0.4	1.5	0.5
Inhalants	5.9	9.9	4.3	1.4	1.1	0.2
Hallucinogens	2.9	12.5	8.8	0.5	1.3	Unknown
Heroin	0.2	0.7	1.3	0.2	0.4	Unknown
Stimulants[b]	2.1	6.4	6.5	0.5	0.9	0.2
Sedatives[b]	1.4	2.7	3.8	0.2	0.6	0.2
Tranquilizers[b]	1.2	5.4	4.9	0.2	0.6	0.2
Analgesics[b]	3.7	8.7	5.5	0.7	1.4	0.5
Alcohol	41.3	87.1	88.7	18.0	59.3	52.1
Cigarettes	34.5	66.7	76.9	9.6	29.0	25.3

[a]A current user is someone who used the drug at least once within a month prior to the study

[b]Nonmedical use; does not include over-the-counter drugs

SOURCE: *Statistical Abstract of the United States: 1995,* 115th ed., U. S. Bureau of the Census (Washington, D.C.: U.S. Government Printing Office, 1995), Table 217.

in medicines as a pain reliever, and morphine was taken as a treatment for dysentery and fatigue. Amphetamine-based inhalers were legally available until 1949, and cocaine was an active ingredient in Coca-Cola until 1906 when it was replaced with another drug—caffeine (Witters, Venturelli, and Hanson 1992).

Theories of Drug Use and Abuse

Most theories of drug use and abuse concentrate on what are called *psychoactive drugs*; these drugs alter the functioning of the brain affecting the moods, emotions, and perceptions of the user. Such drugs include alcohol, cocaine, heroin, and marijuana. **Drug abuse** occurs when acceptable social standards of drug use are violated resulting in adverse physiological, psychological, and/or social consequences. For example, when an individual's drug use leads to hospitalization, arrest, or divorce, such use is usually considered abusive. Drug abuse, however, does not always entail chemical dependency. **Chemical dependency** refers to a condition in which drug use is compulsive—users are unable to stop because of their dependency. The dependency may be psychological in that the individual needs the drug to achieve a feeling of well-being and/or physical in that withdrawal symptoms occur when the individual stops taking the drug.

Various theories provide explanations for why some people use and abuse drugs. Drug use is not simply a matter of individual choice. Theories of drug use explain how structural and cultural forces, as well as biological factors, influence drug use and society's responses to it.

STRUCTURAL-FUNCTIONALIST PERSPECTIVE

Functionalists argue that drug abuse is a response to the weakening of norms in society. As society becomes more complex and rapid social change occurs, norms and values become unclear and ambiguous, resulting in **anomie**—a state of normlessness. Anomie may exist at the societal level, resulting in social strains and inconsistencies that lead to drug use. For example, research indicates that increased alcohol consumption in the 1830s and the 1960s was a response to rapid social change and the resulting stress (Rorabaugh 1979). Anomie produces inconsistencies in cultural norms regarding drug use. For example, while public health officials and health care professionals warn of the dangers of alcohol and tobacco use, advertisers glorify the use of alcohol and tobacco and the U.S. government subsidizes alcohol and tobacco industries. Further, cultural traditions, such as giving away cigars to celebrate the birth of a child and toasting a bride and groom with champagne, persist.

Anomie may also exist at the individual level as when a person suffers feelings of estrangement, isolation, and turmoil over appropriate and inappropriate behavior. An adolescent whose parents are experiencing a divorce, who is separated from friends and family as a consequence of moving, or who lacks parental supervision and discipline may be more vulnerable to drug use because of such conditions. Such an individual may also be susceptible to peer pressure, particularly by individuals who share his or her feelings of estrangement. Thus, from a structural-functionalist perspective, drug use is a response to the absence of a perceived bond between the individual and society, and to the weakening of a consensus regarding what is considered acceptable.

Structural-functionalists also point out the latent functions of drug policies. For example, the U.S. effort against drugs has focused largely on reducing drug supplies by sealing the nation's borders against drug imports and arresting drug dealers. However, these law enforcement schemes have also increased the price of illicit drugs, contributing to increases in property and violent crime rates since President Richard Nixon created the Drug Enforcement Agency in 1973 (Coombs and Ziedonis 1995).

CONFLICT PERSPECTIVE

Conflict perspectives emphasize the importance of power differentials in influencing drug use behavior and societal values concerning drug use. From a conflict perspective, drug use occurs as a response to the inequality perpetuated by a capitalist system. Societal members, alienated from work, friends, and family, as well as from society and its institutions, turn to drugs as a means of escaping the oppression and frustration caused by the inequality they experience. Further, conflict theorists emphasize that the most powerful members of society influence the definitions of which drugs are illegal and the penalties associated with illegal drug production, sales, and use.

For example, alcohol is legal because it is often consumed by those who have the power and influence to define its acceptability—white males (*Statistical Abstract of the United States: 1995*, Table 218). This group also disproportionately profits from the sale and distribution of alcohol and can afford powerful lobbying groups in Washington to guard the alcohol industry's interests. Since tobacco and caffeine are also commonly used by this group, societal definitions of these substances are also relatively accepting.

Conversely, crack cocaine and heroin are more typically used by minority group members, specifically, blacks and Hispanics. Consequently, the stigma and criminal consequences associated with the use of these drugs are severe. The use of opium by Chinese immigrants in the 1800s provides a good example. The Chinese, who had been brought to the United States to work on the railroads, regularly smoked opium as part of their cultural tradition. As unemployment among white workers increased, however, so did resentment of Chinese laborers. Attacking the use of opium became a convenient means of attacking the Chinese, and in 1877 Nevada became the first of many states to prohibit opium use. As Morgan (1978) observes:

> *The first opium laws in California were not the result of a moral crusade against the drug itself. Instead, it represented a coercive action directed against a vice that was merely an appendage of the real menace—the Chinese—and not the Chinese per se, but the laboring "Chinamen" who threatened the economic security of the white working class. (p. 59)*

The criminalization of other drugs, including cocaine, heroin, and marijuana, follows similar patterns of social control of the powerless, political opponents, and/or minorities. In the 1940s, marijuana was used primarily by minority group members and carried with it severe criminal penalties. But after white middle-class college students began to use marijuana in the 1970s, the government reduced the penalties associated with its use. Though the nature and pharmacological properties of the drug had not changed, the population of users was now connected to power and influence. Thus, conflict theorists regard the regulation of certain drugs, as well as drug use itself, as a reflection of differences in the political, economic, and social power of various interest groups.

SYMBOLIC INTERACTIONIST PERSPECTIVE

Symbolic interactionism, emphasizing the importance of definitions and labeling, concentrates on the social meanings associated with drug use. If the initial drug use experience is defined as pleasurable, it is likely to recur, and over time, the individual may earn the label of "drug user." If this definition is internalized so that the individual assumes an identity of a drug user, the behavior will likely continue and may even escalate.

Drug use is also learned through symbolic interaction in small groups. First-time users learn not only the motivations for drug use and its techniques, but also what to experience. Becker (1966) explains how marijuana users learn to ingest the drug. A novice being coached by a regular user reports the experience:

> *I was smoking like I did an ordinary cigarette. He said, "No, don't do it like that." He said, "Suck it, you know, draw in and hold it in your lungs . . . for a period of time." I said, "Is there any limit of time to hold it?" He said, "No, just till you feel that you want to let it out, let it out," So I did that three or four times. (Becker 1966, 47)*

Marijuana users not only learn how to ingest the smoke, but also learn to label the experience positively. When certain drugs, behaviors, and experiences are defined by peers as not only acceptable but pleasurable, drug use is likely to continue.

> *Because they [first-time users] think they're going to keep going up, up, up till they lose their minds or begin doing weird things or something. You have to like reassure them, explain to them that they're not really flipping or anything, that they're gonna be all right. You have to just talk them out of being afraid. (Becker 1966, 55)*

Interactionists also emphasize that symbols may be manipulated and used for political and economic agendas. The popular DARE (Drug Abuse Resistance Education) program, with its antidrug emphasis fostered by local schools and police, carries a powerful symbolic value that politicians want the public to identify with. "Thus, ameliorative programs which are imbued with these potent symbolic qualities (like DARE's links to schools and police) are virtually assured wide-spread public acceptance (regardless of actual effectiveness) which in turn advances the interests of political leaders who benefit from being associated with highly visible, popular symbolic programs" (Wysong, Aniskiewicz, and Wright, 1994, 461).

BIOLOGICAL THEORIES

Biological research has primarily concentrated on the role of genetics in predisposing an individual to alcohol abuse (Pickens and Svikis 1988). Research indicates that individuals whose parents are alcoholics are as much as four times as likely to abuse alcohol themselves as individuals whose parents did not abuse alcohol (Witters, Venturelli, and Hanson 1992). At the same time,

Drug use by friends is consistently the strongest predictor of a person's involvement in drug use.
—U.S. Department of Justice

many alcoholics do not have parents who abuse alcohol, and many alcoholic parents have offspring who do not abuse alcohol.

Biological theories of drug use hypothesize that some individuals are physiologically predisposed to experience more pleasure from drugs than others and, consequently, are more likely to be drug users. According to these theories, the central nervous system, which is composed primarily of the brain and spinal cord, processes drugs through neurotransmitters in a way that produces an unusually euphoric experience. Individuals not so physiologically inclined report less pleasant experiences and are less likely to continue use (Jarvik 1990).

PSYCHOLOGICAL THEORIES

Psychological explanations focus on the tendency for certain personality types to be more susceptible to drug use. Individuals who are particularly prone to anxiety may be more likely to use drugs as a way to relax, gain self-confidence, and ease tension. Those who have dependent personalities and have a compulsive need for love may be more inclined to use drugs to numb the frustration when other needs are not being met.

Psychological theories of drug abuse also emphasize that drug use is maintained by positive and negative reinforcement. Positive reinforcement occurs when drug use results in desirable experiences, such as excitement, pleasure, and peer approval. Negative reinforcement occurs when drug use results in the temporary alleviation of undesirable experiences, such as pain, anxiety, boredom, and loneliness.

Frequently Used Legal and Illegal Drugs

Drunkenness is the ruin of reason. It is premature old age. It is temporary death.
—St. Basil
Bishop of Caesarea

Social definitions regarding which drugs are legal or illegal have varied over time, circumstance, and societal forces. In the United States, two of the most dangerous and widely abused drugs, alcohol and tobacco, are legal.

ALCOHOL

National Data: In 1994, over half (54%) of Americans age twelve and older reported being current users of alcohol.

SOURCE: 1994 National Household Survey on Drug Abuse. U.S. Dept. of Health and Human Services, 1995.

Americans' attitudes toward alcohol have had a long and varied history. Although alcohol was a common beverage in early America, by 1920 the federal government had prohibited its manufacture, sale, and distribution through the passage of the Eighteenth Amendment to the Constitution. Many have argued that Prohibition, like the opium regulations of the late 1800s, was in fact a "moral crusade" (Gusfield 1963) against immigrant groups who were more likely to use alcohol. The amendment had little popular support and was repealed in 1933. Today, the United States is experiencing a resurgence of concern about alcohol. What has been called a "new temperance" has manifested itself in federally mandated twenty-one-year-old drinking age laws, warning labels on alcohol bottles, increased concern over fetal alcohol syndrome and teenage drinking, and stricter enforcement of drinking and driving regulations. This chapter's *Self and Society* feature on pp. 72–73 assesses attitudes toward alcohol consumption and driving.

Alcohol is the most widely used and abused drug in America. Although most people who drink alcohol do so moderately and experience few negative effects, alcoholics are psychologically and physically addicted to alcohol and suffer various degrees of physical, economic, psychological, and personal harm.

National surveys such as the U.S. Department of Health and Human Services (DHHS) study (1995) indicate that in 1994, about 13 million Americans (6.2 percent of individuals age 12 and older) were heavy drinkers, defined as drinking 5 or more drinks per occassion on 5 or more days in the past month. Individuals 22-25 years old had the highest rate of current drinking (any alcohol use in the past month) and individuals 18-21 years old had the highest rate of heavy drinking. Although whites had the highest rate of past month alcohol use, rates of heavy alcohol use showed no statistically significant differences by race/ethnicity. Sixty percent of men reported using alcohol in the past month, compared to 48 percent of women. Men were much more likely than women to be heavy drinkers (10.3 and 2.5 percent, respectively).

TOBACCO

Although nicotine is an addictive psychoactive drug and tobacco smoke has been classified by the Environmental Protection Agency as a Group A carcinogen, tobacco continues to be among the most widely used drugs in the United States. According to the 1994 National Household Survey on Drug Abuse, the rate of smoking was highest in the 18-25 year old age group (35 percent) and the 26-34 year old age group (32 percent). About 19 percent of Americans 12-17 years old—more than 4 million youths—were smokers in 1994. Smoking rates did not vary by race/ethnicity. However, level of educational attainment was correlated with tobacco usage. Only 16 percent of college graduates smoked while thirty-eight percent of adults who had not completed high school were smokers (U.S. Dept. of Health and Human Services 1995).

Tobacco was first cultivated by Native Americans who introduced it to the European settlers in the 1500s. The Europeans believed it had medicinal properties, and its use spread throughout Europe, assuring the economic success of the colonies in the New World. Tobacco was initially used primarily through chewing and snuffing, but in time smoking became more popular even though scientific evidence that linked tobacco smoking to lung cancer existed as early as 1859 (Feagin and Feagin 1994). Today, the health hazards of tobacco use are well documented and have resulted in the passage of federal laws that require

National Data: In 1994, 29 percent of U.S. citizens age twelve and over reported currently using cigarettes with men reporting slightly higher usage than women (28 percent versus 25 percent). About 6 percent of males and less than 1 percent of females age twelve and older reported consuming smokeless tobacco.

SOURCE: 1994 National Household Survey on Drug Abuse. U.S. Dept. of Health and Human Services, 1995.

Although technology was developed years ago to remove nicotine from cigarettes and to control with precision the amount of nicotine in cigarettes, they are still marketing cigarettes with levels of nicotine that are sufficient to produce and sustain addiction.
—David Kessler
Head of Federal Drug Administration

The passage of the Synar Amendment in January 1996 requires all states to restrict youth access to tobacco. However, tobacco companies continue to target the youth market through such strategies as "give-aways" as depicted in this *Doonesbury* cartoon. The FDA wants to prohibit tobacco companies from using any advertising strategies that target youths.

Alcohol Attitude Test

If you strongly agree with the following statements, write in 1. If you agree, but not strongly write in 2. If you neither agree nor disagree, write in 3. If you disagree, but not strongly, write in 4. If you strongly disagree, write in 5.

Set 1

____ 1. If a person concentrates hard enough, he or she can overcome any effect that drinking may have on driving.

____ 2. If you drive home from a party late at night when most roads are deserted, there is not much danger in driving after drinking.

____ 3. It's all right for a person who has been drinking to drive, as long as he or she shows no signs of being drunk.

____ 4. If you're going to have an accident, you'll have one anyhow, regardless of drinking.

____ 5. A drink or two helps people drive better because it relaxes them.

____ Total score for questions 1 through 5

Set 2

____ 6. If I tried to stop someone from driving after drinking, the person would probably think I was butting in where I shouldn't.

____ 7. Even if I wanted to, I would probably not be able to stop someone from driving after drinking.

____ 8. If people want to kill themselves, that's their business.

____ 9. I wouldn't like someone to try to stop me from driving after drinking.

____ 10. Usually, if you try to help someone else out of a dangerous situation, you risk getting yourself into one.

____ Total score for questions 6 through 10

Set 3

____ 11. My friends would not disapprove of me for driving after drinking.

____ 12. Getting into trouble with my parents would not keep me from driving after drinking.

---

warning labels on cigarette packages and prohibit cigarette advertising on radio and television. Smoking is associated with lung cancer, cardiovascular disease, strokes, emphysema, spontaneous abortion, premature birth, and neonatal death. It is estimated that more than 1,000 Americans die every day from smoking-related causes (DeFronzo and Pawlak 1994).

Despite increased awareness of the dangers of tobacco, the tobacco industry continues to enjoy enormous revenues—$48 billion annually—in part because of its ability to influence public opinion and governmental policy. Tobacco corporations such as Philip Morris and R. J. Reynolds spend millions of dollars annually to influence favorable tobacco legislation such as government price supports.

At the same time, a smoking prohibition movement is gaining momentum. Smokers "have been labeled as drug addicts and neurotics as well as air pol-

Everybody knew it's addictive. Everybody knew it causes cancer. We were all in it for the money.
—Victor Crawford
Former tobacco lobbyist and smoker who developed lung cancer

_____ 13. The thought that I might get into trouble with the police would not keep me from driving after drinking.

_____ 14. I am not scared by the thought that I might seriously injure myself or someone else by driving after drinking.

_____ 15. The fear of damaging the car would not keep me from driving after drinking.

_____ Total score for questions 11 through 15

Set 4

_____ 16. The 55 mph speed limit on the open roads spoils the pleasure of driving for most teenagers.

_____ 17. Many teenagers use driving to let off steam.

_____ 18. Being able to drive a car makes teenagers feel more confident in their relations with others their age.

_____ 19. An evening with friends is not much fun unless one of them has a car.

_____ 20. There is something about being behind the wheel of a car that makes one feel more adult.

_____ Total score for questions 16 through 20

Scoring

Set 1. 13–25 points: realistic in avoiding drinking-driving situations; 5–6 points: tends to make up excuses to combine drinking and driving.

Set 2. 15–25 points: takes responsibility to keep others from driving when drunk; 5–9 points: wouldn't take steps to stop a drunk friend from driving.

Set 3. 12–25 points: hesitates to drive after drinking; 5–7 points: is not deterred by the consequences of drinking and driving.

Set 4. 19–25 points: perceives auto as means of transportation; 5–14 points: uses car to satisfy psychological needs, not just transportation.

SOURCE: Courtesy of National Highway Traffic Safety Administration. National Center for Statistics and Analysis, from _Drug Driving Facts_. Washington, D.C.: NHTSA, 1988.

luters and fire hazards" (Markle and Troyer 1990, 92). Organizations such as the American Cancer Society, the American Heart Association, and the American Lung Association have sought to expose the fatal effects of tobacco and to encourage legislation banning its use. Many states now prohibit smoking in public places such as airports, restaurants, bars, elevators, schools, hospitals, libraries, and retail stores. Although the tobacco companies have organized smoking rights organizations in response, the trend to restrict and/or ban tobacco use continues. An important effect of the anti-smoking campaign is that millions of Americans are giving up the habit annually. Between 1965 and 1992, the percentage of people over eighteen who smoked dropped from nearly 42 percent to 21 percent (Skow 1995). In response, the tobacco companies have begun to redirect their marketing efforts to focus on minority populations and less developed nations.

MARIJUANA

National Data: In 1994, 10 million Americans 12 and older (4.8 percent) were marijuana or hashish users. Marijuana and hashish use among 12-17 year olds has increased since 1992. Current use rates were 4.0% in 1992, 4.9% in 1993 and 7.3% in 1994.

SOURCE: U.S. Dept. of Health and Human Services 1995.

Although drug abuse ranks among the top concerns of many Americans, surveys indicate that illegal drug use of all kinds is far less common than alcohol abuse. According to the 1994 National Household Survey on Drug Abuse (U.S. Dept. of Health and Human Services 1995), marijuana is the most commonly used illegal drug. In 1994, about four-fifths (80 percent) of current illicit drug users were marijuana or hashish users.

Marijuana's active ingredient is THC which, in varying amounts, may act as a sedative or as a hallucinogen. There are an estimated 200 to 250 million marijuana users worldwide, predominantly in Africa and Asia. Marijuana use dates back to 2737 B.C. in China and has a long tradition of use in India, the Middle East, and Europe. In North America, hemp, as it was then called, was used for making rope and as a treatment for various ailments. Nevertheless, in 1937 Congress passed the Marijuana Tax Act, which restricted its use; the law was passed as a result of a media campaign that portrayed marijuana users as "dope fiends" and, as conflict theorists note, was enacted at a time of growing sentiment against Mexican immigrants (Witters, Venturelli, and Hanson 1992, 357–59).

Marijuana use is most common among white males aged eighteen to twenty-five (*Statistical Abstract of the United States: 1995*, Table 218). Its use is higher in urban areas than in rural and varies by region of the country; the West has the highest rates of marijuana use (NIDA 1991). Recent surveys also suggest that after decades of decline, marijuana use is increasing (Bogert 1994); as many as 50 percent of all college students report having used marijuana at least once (Bureau of Justice Statistics 1992).

While the effects of alcohol and tobacco are, in large part, indisputable, there is less agreement about the effects of marijuana. Although the carcinogenic effects of marijuana are as lethal as nicotine's, other long-term physiological effects are unknown. An important concern is that marijuana may be a **gateway drug** that causes progression to other drugs such as cocaine and heroin. More likely, however, is that persons who experiment with one drug are more likely to experiment with another. Indeed, most drug users are polydrug users with the most common combination being alcohol, tobacco, and marijuana.

COCAINE

Cocaine is classified as a stimulant and, as such, produces feelings of excitation, alertness, and euphoria. Although such prescription stimulants as methamphetamine and dextroamphetamine are commonly abused, over the last ten to twenty years societal concern over drug abuse has focused on cocaine. Such concerns have been fueled by its increased use, addictive qualities, physiological effects, and worldwide distribution. More than any other single substance, cocaine has led to the present "war on drugs."

Cocaine, which is made from the coca plant, has been used for thousands of years, but anticocaine sentiment in the United States did not emerge until the early 1900s, when it was primarily a response to cocaine's heavy use among urban blacks (Witters, Venturelli, and Hanson 1992, 260). Cocaine was outlawed in 1914 by the Harrison Narcotics Act, but its use and effects continued to be misunderstood. For example, a 1982 *Scientific American* article suggested that cocaine was no more habit forming than potato chips (Van Dyck and Byck 1982). As demand and then supply increased, prices fell from $100 a dose to $10 a dose, and "from 1978 to 1987 the United States experienced the largest cocaine epidemic in history (Witters, Venturelli, and Hanson 1992, 256, 261).

Since the mid-1980s, cocaine use has declined (U.S. Dept. of Health and Human Services 1995). Whether the decrease is a function of increased government surveillance, anticocaine media messages and celebrity deaths, demographic changes, or a greater awareness of the substance's dangers are unknown.

CRACK COCAINE

Crack is a crystallized product made by boiling a mixture of baking soda, water, and cocaine. The result, also called rock, base, and gravel, is relatively inexpensive and was not popular until the mid-1980s. Its use today is primarily among those between eighteen and thirty-four years old and is higher among minorities in urban areas, those with less education, and the unemployed (NIDA 1991).

Crack is one of the most dangerous drugs to surface in recent years. Its use is associated with high blood pressure, brain hemorrhages, and heart and lung failure (Witters, Venturelli, and Hanson 1992, 268). Crack dealers often give drug users their first few "hits" free, knowing the drug's intense high and addictive qualities are likely to lead to returning customers. Compared to users of other illicit drugs, crack users are characterized by higher rates of consumption and criminal involvement (Johnson, Natarajan, Dunlap, and Elmoghazy 1994). This chapter's *Human Side* graphically describes conditions in a crack house and associated criminal behaviors through the eyes of sociologist-ethnographer Terry Williams.

OTHER DRUGS

Other drugs abused in the United States include hallucinogens (e.g., LSD, MDMA), narcotics (e.g., heroin), amphetamines (e.g., dexedrine) and barbiturates (e.g., Phenobarbitol), and inhalants (e.g. glue or butane). Hallucinogens may be classified as either natural, such as peyote, or synthetic, such as LSD. In either case, however, users report an altering of perceptions and thought patterns. While the use of LSD and heroin, the most potent and addictive of opium-based drugs, has decreased over the last several years, the use of so-called designer amphetamines such as U4Euh and MDMA has increased.

National Data: In 1994 an estimated 1.4 million Americans, or 0.7 percent of the population aged 12 and older, were current cocaine users. Use is highest among 18-34 year olds, men, blacks, the unemployed, and those who had not completed high school.
SOURCE: U.S. Department of Health and Human Services 1995.

National Data: Among high school seniors in 1993, 2.6 percent reported having ever used crack: fewer than 1 percent (0.7) reported having done so in the past month.
SOURCE: U.S. Department of Justice 1994.

Crack is a drug peddler's dream: it is cheap, easily concealed and provides a short-duration high that invariably leaves the user craving more.
—Tom Morganthau
Journalist

AN EXCERPT FROM *THE COCAINE KIDS* (1990)

The door opens a crack before I can knock, a tall African-American man brusquely thrusts his palm toward me and asks, "You got three dollars?" He motions excitedly, "If you ain't got three dollars you can't come in here." The entrance fee. I pay and walk in.

The establishment is desolate, uninviting, dank and smoky. The carpet in the first room is shit-brown and heavily stained, pock-marked by so many smoke burns that it looks like an abstract design. In the dim light, all the people on the scene seem to be in repose, almost inanimate, for a moment.

As my eyes adjust to the smoke, several bodies emerge. I see jaws moving, hear voices barking hoarsely into walkie-talkies—something about money; their talk is jagged, nasal and female. One woman takes out an aluminum foil packet, snorts some of its contents, passes it to her partner then disappears into another room. In a corner near the window, a shadowy figure moans. One woman sits with her skirt over her head, while a bobbing head writhes underneath her. In an adjacent alcove, I see another couple copulating. Somewhere in the corridor a man and woman argue loudly in Spanish. Staccato rap music sneaks over the grunts and hollers.

The smell is a nauseating mix of semen, crack, sweat, other human body odors, funk and filth. Two men dicker about who took the last "hit" (puff); two others are on their hands and knees looking for crack particles they claim they have lost in the carpet.

In the crack houses, the sharing rituals associated with snorting are being supplanted by more individualistic, detached arrangements where people come together for erotic stimulation, sexual activity, and cocaine smoking. They may be total strangers, seeking only brief and superficial physical contact, encounters designed to heighten sensations; the smoking act is a narcissistic fix—there is little thought for the other person. The emotional content is largely due to the momentary excitation of the setting and the cocaine. Much of the sexual behavior is performed to acquire more cocaine.

Nothing better exemplifies the new attitude than the act of *Sancocho* (a word meaning to cut up in little pieces and stew). To sancocho is to steal crack, drugs or money from a friend or other person who is not alert, a regular practice in the crack houses. Another example is the "hit kiss" ritual: after inhaling deeply, basers literally "kiss"—put their lips together and exhale the smoke into each other's mouths. This not only saves all the valuable smoke, but also stimulates the other sexually. Other versions of the kiss extend to other orifices.

SOURCE: Terry Williams. 1990. *The Cocaine Kids: The Inside Story of a Teenage Drug Ring.* © 1990, pp. 106–108. Addison Wesley Publishing Company. Reprinted with Permission.

These drugs, which are synthesized from common chemical forms and marketed illegally under such names as "ecstasy," are dangerously addictive. Designer amphetamines are particularly popular among college students and the affluent (Witters, Venturelli, and Hanson 1992, 255).

Barbiturates, which depress the central nervous system, include sedatives and tranquilizers and are often used in the treatment of psychiatric disorders. Despite most often being obtained through prescription, these drugs continue to be abused, and an illegal market for them persists. Because of their addictive qualities and severe withdrawal symptoms, the American Medical Association has warned physicians about the dangers of prescribing such medication for prolonged use (Witters, Venturelli, and Hanson 1992). Perhaps for this reason, barbiturate use has declined over the last fifteen years (NIDA 1991), and to a large extent, they have been replaced by a class of barbiturate-like drugs called benzodiazepines.

Popular benzodiazepines include Xanax, Valium, and Halcion, which are often prescribed for insomnia and anxiety. They are among the top selling prescription drugs in the United States. Although some evidence suggests that long-term use may have little therapeutic effect, physicians often permit patients to remain on such drugs indefinitely, creating, some argue, "the largest group of prescription drug–dependent people in the United States." Researchers estimate that there are more than one million physically dependent benzodiazepines users in the United States (Witters, Venturelli, and Hanson 1992, 160).

National Data: An estimated 2.1 million Americans have used heroin in their lifetime. More than 18 million Americans (8.7 percent of Americans age 12 and older) have used hallucinogens in their lifetime. The most commonly used hallucinogen is LSD.

SOURCE: U.S. Department of Health and Human Services, 1995.

Societal Consequences of Drug Use and Abuse

Drugs comprise a social problem not only because of their adverse effects on individuals, but also as a result of the negative consequences their use has for society as a whole. Drugs contribute to problems within the family and to the crime rate. The economic costs of drug abuse are enormous, and drug abuse has serious consequences for health on both an individual and a societal level.

FAMILY COSTS

The cost to families of drug use is incalculable. When one or both parents use or abuse drugs, needed family funds may be diverted to purchasing drugs rather than necessities. Children raised in such homes have a higher probability of neglect, behavioral disorders, and absenteeism from school as well as lower self-concepts (Tubman 1993; Easley and Epstein 1991). Drug abuse is also associated with family disintegration. For example, alcoholics are seven times more likely to separate or divorce than nonalcoholics, and as much as 40 percent of family court problems are alcohol related (Sullivan and Thompson 1994, 347).

Family violence is also linked to drug use (Foster, Forsyth, and Herbert 1994). In a study of 320 men who were married or living with someone, twice as many reported hitting their partner only after they had been drinking compared to those who reported the same behavior while sober (Leonard and Blane 1992). Additionally, Straus and Sweet (1992) found that alcohol consumption and drug use were associated with higher levels of verbal abuse among spouses.

National Data: Alcoholics in the United States number between 9 and 10 million, but they affect many more millions of spouses, children, family members, friends, employers, and co-workers.

SOURCE: Witters, Venturelli, and Hanson 1992, 176.

When one or both parents use or abuse drugs, family funds may be diverted to the purchasing of drugs rather than necessities. Children raised in such homes have a higher probability of suffering from neglect.

Consideration Some evidence suggests that the link between alcohol and violence is socially constructed rather than biologically determined. In a cross-cultural study of drinking behavior, MacAndrew and Edgerton (1969) report that behaviors associated with excessive drinking vary significantly from society to society. In some societies, excessive drinking leads to aggressive, hostile behavior; in others, passivity and even complete withdrawal. MacAndrew and Edgerton conclude, consistent with symbolic interactionism, that the "drunk role" is a learned one dependent upon the social context in which it occurs. Such a conclusion is further supported by Levinson (1989) who, in researching ninety small-scale societies, reports that alcohol played little or no role in family violence in most countries around the world.

CRIME COSTS

The only livin' thing that counts is the fix . . . Like I would steal off anybody— anybody, at all, my own mother gladly included.
—Heroin addict

The drug behavior of persons arrested, those incarcerated, and persons in drug treatment programs provides evidence of the link between drugs and crime. About half of those arrested test positive for recent drug use, 40 percent of those in jail report having used drugs in the month prior to arrest, and 60 percent of those in residential treatment programs report that they had committed one or more crimes for money in the year before treatment (Bureau of Justice Statistics 1992; U.S. Department of Justice 1994; Graham and Wish 1994; Lipton 1994).

Consideration The relationship between crime and drug use is a complex one. Researchers disagree as to whether drugs actually "cause" crime or whether, instead, criminal activity leads to drug involvement (Gentry 1995). Further, since both crime and drug use are associated with low socioeconomic status, poverty may actually be the more powerful explanatory variable. Studies on cocaine use among white, middle-class, educated users indicate drugs and crime are not necessarily related (Waldorf, Reinarman, and Murphy 1991). After extensive study of the assumed drug-

crime link, Gentry (1995) concludes that "the assumption that drugs and crime are causally related weakens when more representative or affluent subjects are considered" (p. 491).

Nevertheless, the extent to which heroin- and cocaine-using addicts are involved in property crime is staggering. Violent crime and drugs are also linked. In nearly half the homicides in the United States, either the victim, the offender, or both are drug involved (Conklin 1995). Further, rape, sex crimes, aggravated assault, and other personal crimes are disproportionately committed by drug users (Goldstein et al. 1991; Harrison and Gfroerer 1992).

In addition to the hypothesized crime-drug use link, some criminal offenses are drug defined: possession, cultivation, production, and sale of controlled substances; public intoxication, drunk and disorderly conduct, driving while intoxicated, and miscellaneous liquor law violations. In 1992, arrests for drug offenses numbered more than one million and accounted for about 8 percent (7.6) of all arrests in the United States that year (U.S. Department of Justice 1994).

ECONOMIC COSTS

The economic costs of drug use to society are also high. For example, workers who abuse alcohol have between two and three times the absenteeism rate of nonalcoholics (Laver 1995, 98).

In addition to absenteeism, billions of corporate dollars are lost due to reduced work time and productivity from drug abuse. This cost is passed on to consumers. Concern that on-the-job drug use may impair performance and/or cause fatal accidents has led to drug testing. For many employees, such tests are routine both as a condition for employment and as a requirement for keeping their job. This chapter's *In Focus* reviews some of the issues related to the drug-testing debate.

Other economic costs of drug abuse include the cost of homelessness, the cost to the criminal justice system of processing drug- and alcohol-related crimes, the cost of implementing and maintaining educational and rehabilitation programs, and the cost to government agencies of subsidizing such programs as unemployment benefits, welfare, food stamps, and Medicaid. In 1995, Florida filed a $1.43 billion lawsuit against the tobacco industry in an attempt to recoup public monies spent on Medicaid patients with smoking-related diseases (Farley 1995). The cost to the federal government of fighting the "war on drugs" is also enormous and likely to increase as organized crime develops new patterns of involvement in the illicit drug trade.

HEALTH COSTS

The physical health consequences of drug use for the individual are tremendous: shortened life expectancy; higher morbidity (e.g., cirrhosis of the liver, lung cancer); exposure to HIV infection, hepatitis, and other diseases through shared needles; a weakened immune system; birth defects such as fetal alcohol syndrome; drug addiction in children; and higher death rates. In 1992, nearly 12,000 deaths in the United States were drug-induced and nearly 20,000 deaths were attributed to alcohol-induced causes (*Statistical Abstract of the*

National Data: Heroin and cocaine addicts annually commit forty to sixty robberies and seventy to a hundred burglaries apiece.
SOURCE: Lipton 1994.

National Data: Drug abuse and drug-related crime cost the United States an estimated $67 billion a year. The 1996 federal budget proposes a 1.3 percent increase in drug abuse expenditures over the previous year.
SOURCE: Federal Budget 1996.

National Data: Cigarettes kill more Americans each year than car accidents, AIDS, murders, suicides, illegal drugs, and fires combined.
SOURCE: U.S. Department of Health and Human Services 1995.

Drug Testing

The technology available to detect whether a person has taken drugs was used during the 1970s by crime laboratories, drug treatment centers, and the military. Employers in private industry have turned to chemical laboratories for help in making decisions of employment and retention. An individual's drug use can be assessed through the analysis of that individual's hair, blood, or urine.

In 1986, the President's Commission on Organized Crime recommended that all employees of private companies contracting with the federal government be regularly subjected to urine testing for drugs as a condition of employment. This recommendation was based on the belief that if employees such as air traffic controllers, airline pilots, and railroad operators are using drugs, human lives may be in jeopardy due to impaired job performance.

In 1987, an Amtrack passenger train crashed outside Baltimore, killing sixteen and injuring hundreds. There was evidence of drug use by those responsible for the train's safety. As a result, the Supreme Court ruled in 1989 (by a vote of 7–2), that it is constitutional for the Federal Railroad Administration to administer a drug test to railroad crews if they are involved in an accident. Testing those in "sensitive" jobs for drug use may save lives.

An alternative perspective is that drug testing may be harmful (O'Keefe 1987). First, the tests can be inaccurate in that they may result in either "false positives" (the person who does not use drugs is identified as doing so) or "false negatives" (the person who uses drugs is identified as not doing so). The false-positives problem is serious: an innocent person could lose his or her job because of faulty technology. Second, urinalysis may also reveal that a person is pregnant, is being treated for heart disease, or

has epilepsy. The person may want these aspects of his or her private life to remain private. Third, such drug testing may violate basic constitutional rights. The Fourth Amendment states that "the right of the people to be secure in their persons . . . against unreasonable searches and seizures, shall not be violated." However, where the welfare of the public is at stake, the government has taken the position that it has the right to administer drug tests (e.g., to airline pilots).

Drug testing has enabled employers to detect drug use among employees and applicants. When combined with drug treatment programs, it has contributed to the rehabilitation of drug abusers. However, Ackerman (1995) warns that

to the individual drug user denied a job because of a positive urine test, and to the society on which he or she must remain (unemployed and) dependent, drug testing may compound the problems caused by drug addiction. (p. 487).

As a society, we are moving toward a policy of enforced drug testing for more and more segments of our society. In June, 1995, the Supreme Court ruled that random drug testing of student athletes in public schools is *not* unconstitutional. Public opinion supports drug testing. Seventy-one percent of the nation's college and university freshmen agreed with the statement, "employers should be allowed to require drug testing of employees or job applicants" (American Council on Education and University of California 1994).

SOURCES: Anne Marie O'Keefe. 1987. "The Case against Drug Testing" *Psychology Today,* June, 34–38; American Council on Education and University of California. 1994. *The American Freshman: National Norms for Fall, 1994.* Los Angeles: Higher Education Research Institute. Deborah L. Ackerman. 1995. "Drug Testing," 473–89 in *Handbook on Drug Abuse and Prevention.* Edited by Robert H. Coombs and Douglas Ziedonis. Boston: Allyn and Bacon.

United States 1995, Tables 139 and 140). Death rates for drug-induced and alcohol-induced causes are significantly higher for males and minorities than for females and whites.

Heavy alcohol and drug use are also associated with negative consequences for an individual's mental health. Longitudinal data on both male and female adults have shown that drug users are more likely to suffer from anxiety disorders (e.g., phobias), depression, and antisocial personalities (White and Labouvie 1994). Other data confirm that drug users, particularly in adolescence, have a higher incidence of suicide (Bureau of Justice Statistics 1992). Marijuana, the most commonly used drug by adolescents, is also linked to short-term memory loss, learning disabilities, motivational deficits, and retarded emotional development.

The societal costs of drug-induced health concerns are also extraordinary. Although difficult to estimate, the health costs of illegal drug use are assessed at more than $2 billion annually (U.S. Department of Justice 1993). Societal health costs also include the cost of disability insurance, the effects of second-hand smoke, the spread of AIDS, and the medical costs of accident and crime victims, as well as unhealthy infants and children. For example, infants are five times as likely to die from Sudden Infant Death Syndrome if adults smoke in their rooms (Klonoff-Cohen et al. 1995).

National Data: In 1992, almost half (45 percent) of fatal motor vehicle accidents involved alcohol consumption.

SOURCE: *Statistical Abstract of the United States: 1994*, Table 1016.

Physicians should advise their patients during prenatal care and after delivery not to smoke around an infant.
—Sandra Klonoff-Cohen
Physician/Researcher

Treatment Alternatives

Persons who are interested in overcoming chemical dependency have a number of treatment alternatives from which to choose. Their options include hospitalization, family therapy, drug counseling, private and state treatment facilities, community care programs, drug maintenance programs, and employee assistance programs. Three other commonly used rehabilitative techniques are twelve-step programs, therapeutic communities, and behavioral approaches.

TWELVE-STEP PROGRAMS

Both Alcoholics Anonymous (AA) and Narcotics Anonymous (NA) are voluntary associations whose only membership requirement is the desire to stop drinking or taking drugs. AA and NA are self-help groups in that they are operated by nonprofessionals, offer "sponsors" to each new member, and proceed along a continuum of twelve steps to recovery. These include an acknowledgment of one's helplessness over addiction and a recognition of a higher power as a source of help. In addition to the twelve steps, which require abstinence, humility, penance, and commitment, AA and NA members are immediately immersed in a fellowship of caring individuals with whom they meet daily or weekly to affirm their commitment. Some have argued that AA and NA members trade their addiction to drugs for feelings of interpersonal connectedness by bonding with other group members.

Symbolic interactionists emphasize that AA and NA provide social contexts in which people develop new meanings. Abusers are surrounded by others who convey positive labels, encouragement, and social support for sobriety. Sponsors tell the new members that they can be successful in controlling alcohol and/or drugs "one day at a time" and provide regular interpersonal

AA members essentially trade addiction to the bottle to a network of friends who share a common bond.
—Barry Lubetkin
Psychologist

reinforcement for doing so. Some AA members may also choose to take **antabuse,** a prescribed medication, which when combined with alcohol produces severe nausea. Some alcoholics regard antabuse as a "crutch," but others feel that anything that helps the alcoholic to remain sober should be used.

AA and NA have reputations as two of the most successful drug rehabilitation programs. But because membership is voluntary and anonymous, accurate evaluation of these programs is difficult. Further, since the desire to change is a prerequisite for joining AA or NA, their success rates are artificially elevated, making other programs appear less successful.

THERAPEUTIC COMMUNITIES

In **therapeutic communities,** which house between 35 and 500 people for up to fifteen months, participants abstain from drugs, develop marketable skills, and receive counseling. Synanon, which was established in 1958, was the first therapeutic community for alcoholics and was later expanded to include other drug users. More than four hundred residential treatment centers are now in existence, including Daytop Village and Phoenix House. The longer a person stays at such a facility, the greater the chance of overcoming his or her dependency. Symbolic interactionists argue that behavioral changes appear to be a consequence of revised self-definition and the positive expectations of others.

Stay'N Out, a therapeutic community for the treatment of incarcerated drug offenders, has demonstrated its success in reducing recidivism. When participating in the program for at least nine months, only 23 percent of the inmates, compared to 50 percent of those receiving no treatment, re-offended. The Cornerstone Program has also been successful with drug abusers in prison. Both programs include a holistic treatment approach that focuses on the social and psychological difficulties of returning to acceptable social roles (Lipton 1994, 336).

Treatment for substance abuse often occurs in a group setting where participants may benefit from the support of other substance abusers.

BEHAVIORAL APPROACHES

Behaviorists view drug use as a consequence of positive reinforcement. Treatment involves replacing the rewards of drug use with other positive experiences. For example, some people may be able to substitute the "high" experienced from drugs with the "high" derived from long-distance running or intense aerobic exercise. In addition, drug use is often a very social experience characterized by close friends who are also users, familiar locations where drugs are consumed, and a definition that drug taking is a desirable behavior. Behavioral treatment encourages the person to develop new friends, go to different places, and define drug taking as destructive. Participation of one's family and friends may be necessary to accomplish these changes.

Behaviorists have also used aversive conditioning, whereby a substance abuser begins to associate drugs with negative consequences. For example, an alcoholic may be asked to visualize events leading to consumption: pulling the car off the road to stop at a bar, going inside the bar, sitting at the bar, ordering a drink, picking up the drink, and so on. While the person visualizes each of these scenes, the therapist may administer an electric shock or ask the person to imagine feeling very ill. Previously positive behaviors are thus paired with an aversive stimulus and are, theoretically, less likely to occur. The success of this therapy depends on the substance abuser's ability to transfer contrived experiences from cognitive rehearsal to the real world.

America Responds: Social Policy and Collective Action

Drug use is a complex social issue exacerbated by the structural and cultural forces of society that contribute to its existence. While the structure of society perpetuates a system of inequality creating in some the need to escape, the culture of society, through the media and normative contradictions, sends mixed messages about the acceptability of drug use. Thus, developing programs, laws, or initiatives that are likely to end drug use may be unrealistic. Nevertheless, numerous social policies have been implemented or proposed to help control drug use and its negative consequences.

GOVERNMENT REGULATIONS

The largest social policy attempt to control drug use in the United States was Prohibition. Although this effort was a failure by most indicators, the government continues to impose drug use regulations such as the 1984 Crime Control Act, the 1986 Anti-Drug Abuse Act, the 1988 Drug-Abuse Act, the Crime Control Act of 1990, and the Violent Crime Control and Law Enforcement Act of 1994 (see Table 3.2).

In the 1980s the federal government declared a "war on drugs." Yet, as recently as 1995, the Clinton administration revealed a National Drug Control Strategy that included the largest budget ever for combating drug use. While the manifest function of such "get tough" policies as mandatory prison sentences and capital punishment for drug trafficking is deterrence, the unintended consequences have been quite negative. Yale law professor Steven

> The goal of a drug-free America is an unrealistic one; it is realistic, however, to strive to reduce use to the pre-1960 era when drug use was a small problem in America.
> —Herbert D. Kleber, M.D.
> Former deputy director, White House Office of National Drug Control Policy

TABLE 3.2

FIVE MAJOR FEDERAL ANTIDRUG LAWS FROM THE 1980s AND 1990s

The 1984 Crime Control Act:	• Expanded criminal and civil asset forfeiture laws. • Amended the Bail Reform Act to target pretrial detention of defendants accused of serious drug offenses. • Established a determinate sentencing system. • Increased federal criminal penalties for drug offenses.
The 1986 Anti-Drug Abuse Act:	• Budgeted money for prevention and treatment programs, giving the programs a larger share of federal drug control funds than previous laws. • Restored mandatory prison sentences for large-scale distribution of marijuana. • Imposed new sanctions on money laundering. • Added controlled substances' analogs (designer drugs) to the drug schedule. • Created a drug law enforcement grant program to assist state and local efforts. • Contained various provisions designed to strengthen international drug control efforts.
The 1988 Anti-Drug Abuse Act:	• Increased penalties for offenses related to drug trafficking, created new federal offenses and regulatory requirements, and changed criminal procedures. • Altered the organization and coordination of federal antidrug efforts. • Increased treatment and prevention efforts aimed at reduction of drug demand. • Endorsed the use of sanctions aimed at drug users to reduce the demand for drugs. • Targeted for reduction drug production abroad and international trafficking in drugs.
The Crime Control Act of 1990:	• Doubled the appropriations authorized for drug law enforcement grants to states and localities. • Expanded drug control and education programs aimed at the nations's schools. • Expanded specific drug enforcement assistance to rural states. • Expanded regulation of precursor chemicals used in the manufacture of illegal drugs. • Provided additional measures aimed at seizure and forfeiture of drug trafficker assets. • Sanctioned anabolic steroids under the Controlled Substances Act. • Included provisions on international money laundering, rural drug enforcement, drug-free school zones, drug paraphernalia, and drug enforcement grants.
The Violent Crime Control and Law Enforcement Act of 1994:	• Expanded the federal death penalty to cover large-scale drug trafficking. • Provided new and stiffer penalties for drug trafficking crimes committed by gang members. • Required mandatory life imprisonment without possibility of parole for federal offenders with three or more convictions for serious violent felonies or drug trafficking crimes. • Provided $383 million for prison drug treatment.

SOURCES: U.S. Department of Justice, Office of Justice Programs, Bureau of Justice Statistics. 1992 *Drugs, Crime, and the Justice System*, NCJ–1333652. (Washington, D.C.: U.S. Government Printing Office, December 1992), p. 86, *Violent Crime Control and Law Enforcement Act of 1994*, 1995. World Wide Web.

Duke and co-author Albert C. Gross in a recent book on *America's Longest War* (1994) argue that the war on drugs, much like Prohibition, has only intensified other social problems: drug-related gang violence and turf wars, the creation of syndicate-controlled black markets, unemployment, the spread of AIDS, overcrowded prisons, corrupt law enforcement officials, and the diversion of police from other serious crimes.

Further, U.S. drug policies have implications that extend beyond domestic concerns and affect international relations and the economies of foreign countries. Distributing drugs worldwide requires a complex network of social actors that often parallels the hierarchy of a legitimate business—producers, manufacturers, wholesale and retail distributors, and sales personnel. Many of these roles are occupied by people outside the United States. The largest producers of cocaine, for example, are Peru, Bolivia, and Colombia; opium is predominantly cultivated in Southwest Asia; marijuana comes from Mexico, Jamaica, and Central America (Adler, Mueller, and Laufer 1995).

These countries are often characterized by government corruption and crime, military coups, political instability, and human rights violations. Ironically, the United States provides foreign aid and military assistance to many of these countries. Some argue that trade sanctions should be imposed in addition to crop eradication programs and interdiction efforts. Others, however, noting the relative failure of such programs in reducing the supply of illegal drugs entering the United States, argue that the "war on drugs" should be abandoned and that legalization is preferable to the side effects of regulation.

LEGALIZATION

Proponents for the **legalization** of drugs affirm the right of adults to make an informed choice. They also argue that the tremendous revenues realized from drug taxes could be used to benefit all citizens, that purity and safety controls could be implemented, and that legalization would expand the number of distributors, thereby increasing competition and reducing prices. Drugs would thus be safer, drug-related crimes would be reduced, and production and distribution of previously controlled substances would be taken out of the hands of the underworld.

Those in favor of legalization also suggest that the greater availability of drugs would not increase demand. When a sample of 600 adults was asked, "If cocaine were legalized, would you personally consider purchasing it or not?" less than one percent reported that they would (Dennis 1993). Further, in countries where some drugs have been decriminalized, use has actually declined (Kort 1994). Finally, **decriminalization** of drugs would promote a medical rather than criminal approach to drug use that would encourage users to seek treatment and adopt preventive practices. For example, making it a criminal offense to sell or possess hypodermic needles without a prescription encourages the use of nonsterile needles that spread infections such as HIV and hepatitis.

National Data: Thirty-two percent of U.S. university/college students support legalizing marijuana.

SOURCE: American Council on Education and University of California 1994.

ARGUMENTS AGAINST LEGALIZATION

The official U.S. position has been to impose harsh penalties for the manufacture, sale, and distribution of drugs. Opponents of legalization argue that it would be construed as government approval of drug use and, as a consequence, drug experimentation and abuse would increase. Further, while the legalization of drugs would result in substantial revenues for the government, since all drugs would not be decriminalized (e.g., crack), drug trafficking and black markets would still flourish (Bennett 1993). Legalization would also require an extensive and costly bureaucracy to regulate the manufacture, sale, and distribution of drugs. Finally, the position that drug use is an individual's right cannot guarantee that others will not be harmed. It is illogical to assume that a greater availability of drugs will translate into a safer society.

DEREGULATION

The government has also approached the drug problem through **deregulation** or the reduction of government control of certain drugs. While all states now require that individuals be twenty-one years old to purchase alcohol and eighteen to purchase cigarettes, both substances are legal and purchased freely. Further, in some states, possession of marijuana in small amounts is now a misdemeanor rather than a felony. Deregulation of marijuana permits the criminal justice system to concentrate on fighting more serious drugs such as crack.

U.S. law also allows distribution of methadone in treatment centers for heroin addicts. Methadone, a synthetic opiate, is taken orally and inhibits the euphoric effect of heroin, thus blocking the motivation for its use. The drug produces no "high," and the recovering addict can begin to lead a normal life. Persons in methadone maintenance programs also participate in family counseling and job training programs, both designed to help the addict make a successful return to society. While some research indicates a high recidivism rate and little or no reduction in crime (Kleinman et al. 1977), other research concludes that addicts in methadone maintenance programs are less likely to use heroin again and have lower mortality rates than those not enrolled in similar programs (Yancovitz et al. 1991).

COLLECTIVE ACTION

Social action groups such as Mothers Against Drunk Driving (**MADD**) have lobbied legislators to raise the drinking age to twenty-one and to provide harsher penalties for driving while impaired. MADD, with 3.5 million members, has also put pressure on alcohol establishments to stop "two for one" offers and has pushed for laws that hold the bartender personally liable if a served person is later involved in an alcohol-related accident. Even hosts in private homes can now be held liable if they allow a guest to drive who became impaired while drinking at their house. Perhaps most importantly, MADD seeks to change the meaning of alcohol use by, for example, redefining drunk driving "accidents" as violent crimes.

Sensitized to the danger of driving while impaired, high school principals and school boards have encouraged students to become members of Students Against Drunk Driving (**SADD**). Members often sign a formal pledge and put an emblem on their car to signify a commitment against alcohol. To reduce the number of teenagers driving while drinking, local groups of parents have also organized parties at bowling alleys or school gyms as alternatives to high school graduation parties.

Collective action is also being taken against tobacco companies. One hundred million smokers and ex-smokers have combined to bring the largest class-action lawsuit in U.S. history (Sullivan 1995). They charge that tobacco executives knew over thirty years ago that tobacco was addictive and concealed this fact from both the public and the government. Furthermore, they charge that tobacco companies manipulate nicotine levels in cigarettes with the intention of causing addiction.

In addition to Florida, several other states including Minnesota, Mississippi, and West Virginia have filed health cost–related suits against the tobacco industry (Farley 1995). Since 1954, 808 lawsuits have been filed against the tobacco companies, but they have yet to pay any damages. Thus far, the companies have argued successfully that smokers knew the potential dangers and continued to smoke. What is new in the present wave of lawsuits is the accusation that the tobacco industry concealed knowledge that nicotine is addictive. Attorney Marvin Belli says, "We will prove that the tobacco industry has conspired to catch you, hold you, and kill you" (Sullivan 1995, d3). In addition to these legal pressures, health lobbyists want to force the federal Food and Drug Administration to regulate nicotine as a drug.

UNDERSTANDING
ALCOHOL AND OTHER DRUGS

In summarizing what we know about substance abuse, drugs and their use are socially defined. As the structure of society changes, the acceptability of one drug or another changes as well. As conflict theorists assert, the status of a drug as legal or illegal is intricately linked to those who have the power to define acceptable and unacceptable drug use. There is also little doubt that rapid social change, anomie, alienation, and inequality further drug use and abuse. Symbolic interaction also plays a significant role in the process—if people are labeled as "drug users" and expected to behave accordingly, drug use is likely to continue. If there is positive reinforcement of such behaviors and/or a biological predisposition to use drugs, the probability of drug involvement is even higher. Thus, the theories of drug use complement rather than contradict one another.

Drug use must also be conceptualized within the social context in which it occurs. In a study of high-risk youths who had become drug involved, Dembo et al. (1994) suggest that many youths in their study had been "failed by society":

Many of them were born into economically-strained circumstances, often raised by families who neglected or abused them, or in other ways did not provide for their nurturance and wholesome development . . . few youths in our sample received the mental health and substance abuse treatment services they needed. (p. 25)

However, many treatment alternatives, emanating from a clinical model of drug use, assume that the origin of the problem lies within the individual rather than in the structure and culture of society. While, admittedly, the problem may lie within the individual at the time treatment occurs, policies that address the social causes of drug abuse provide a better means of dealing with the drug problem in the United States.

Prevention is preferable to intervention, and given the social portrait of hard drug users—young, male, minority—prevention must entail dealing with the social conditions that foster drug use. Some data suggest that inner city adolescents are particularly vulnerable to drug involvement due to their lack of legitimate alternatives (Van Kammen and Loeber 1994).

Illegal drug use may be a way to escape the strains of the severe urban conditions and dealing illegal drugs may be one of the few, if not the only, ways to provide for material needs. Intervention and treatment programs, therefore, should include efforts to find alternate ways to deal with the limiting circumstances of inner-city life, as well as create opportunities for youngsters to find more conventional ways of earning a living. (p. 22)

Social policies dealing with drug use have been predominantly punitive rather than preventive. Recently, however, the Clinton administration pledged to concentrate on educating the public on the dangers of alcohol and drug use. DARE is one of the most popular school-based drug education programs in the United States. Uniformed police officers deliver seventeen weekly lessons for forty-five to sixty minutes with the goal of providing students with antidrug views and the social skills to resist using drugs. Short-term effects have been positive (Community Drug Prevention 1990). However, Wysong, Aniskiewicz, and Wright (1994) compared 228 high school seniors exposed to DARE as seventh graders with 355 nonexposed seniors. No significant differences in drug use behaviors or attitudes were found between the two groups. The authors argue that the popularity of the DARE program is part of a "symbolic crusade" against the "drug crisis," as defined by the Bush war on drugs campaign and increased media attention to illicit drugs as a major social problem.

In the United States and throughout the world, millions of people depend on legal drugs for the treatment of a variety of conditions, including pain, anxiety and nervousness, insomnia, overeating, and fatigue. While drugs for these purposes are relatively harmless, the cultural message "better living through chemistry" contributes to alcohol and drug use and its consequences. But these and other drugs are embedded in a political and economic context that determines who defines what drugs, in what amounts, as licit or illicit and what programs are developed in reference to them.

CRITICAL THINKING

1. Which theoretical perspective is most helpful in understanding alcohol and drugs as a social problem? Why?
2. What would be the social, political, and economic consequences of tobacco companies losing the class-action suits against them?
3. Discuss how the manipulation of social definitions might virtually eliminate many "drug" problems.

KEY TERMS

drug abuse	antabuse	decriminalization
chemical dependency	therapeutic communities	deregulation
anomie		MADD
gateway drug	legalization	SADD

REFERENCES

Adler, Freda, Gerhard O. W. Mueller, and William S. Laufer. 1995. *Criminology: The Shorter Version,* 2d ed. New York: McGraw-Hill.

American Council on Education and University of California. 1994. *The American Freshman: National Norms for Fall.* Los Angeles: Higher Education Research Institute.

Becker, H. S. 1966. *Outsiders: Studies in the Sociology of Deviance.* New York: Free Press.

Bennett, William. 1993. "Should Drugs Be Legalized?" In *Social Problems: A Critical Thinking Approach,* 2d ed., ed. Paul J. Baker, Louise E. Anderson, and Dean S. Dorn, pp. 246–48. Belmont, Calif.: Wadsworth.

Bogert, Carroll. 1994. "Good News on Drugs from the Inner City." *Newsweek,* February 14, 28–29.

Bureau of Justice Statistics. 1992. "Drugs, Crime, and the Justice System: A National Report from the Bureau of Justice Statistics." U.S. Department of Justice, Office of Justice Programs. Washington, D.C.: U.S. Government Printing Office, Superintendent of Documents.

Community Drug Prevention Programs Show Progress. 1990. *Public Health Reports* 105: 543.

Conklin, John E. 1995. *Criminology.* Boston: Allyn & Bacon.

Coombs, Robert H., and Douglas M. Ziedonis. 1995. "Preface." In *Handbook on Drug Abuse Prevention,* ed. Robert H. Coombs and Douglas Ziedonis, pp. xiii–xviii. Boston: Allyn & Bacon.

DeFronzo, James, and Rebecca Pawlak. 1994. "Gender Differences in the Determinants of Smoking." *Journal of Drug Issues* 24: 507–16.

Dembo, Richard, Linda Williams, Jeffrey Fagan, and James Schmeidler. 1994. "Development and Assessment of a Classification of High Risk Youths." *Journal of Drug Issues* 24: 25–53.

Dennis, Richard J. 1993. "The Economics of Legalizing Drugs." In *Social Problems: A Critical Thinking Approach,* 2d ed., ed. Paul J. Baker, Louise E. Anderson, and Dean S. Dorn, pp. 249–55. Belmont, Calif.: Wadsworth.

Duke, Steven, and Albert C. Gross. 1994. *America's Longest War: Rethinking Our Tragic Crusade against Drugs.* New York: G. P. Putnam & Sons.

Easley, Margaret, and Norman Epstein. 1991. "Coping with Stress in a Family with an Alcoholic Parent." *Family Relations* 40: 218–24.

Farley, Christopher John. 1995. "Cough Up the Cash." *Time,* March 6, 47.

Feagin, Joe R., and C. B. Feagin. 1994. *Social Problems.* Englewood Cliffs, N.J.: Prentice-Hall.

Federal Budget. 1996. "Controlling Violent Crime and Drug Abuse." Section 4. Washington, D.C.: U.S. Government Printing Office (internet psulias.psu.edu).

Foster, Burk, Craig J. Forsyth, and Stasia Herbert. 1994. "The Cycle of Family Violence among Criminal Offenders: A Study of Inmates in One Louisiana Jail." *Free Inquiry in Creative Sociology* 22: 133–37.

Gentry, Cynthia. 1995. "Crime Control through Drug Control." In *Criminology*, 2d ed., ed. Joseph F. Sheley, pp. 477–93. Belmont, Calif.: Wadsworth.

Goldstein, Paul, Patricia A. Bellucci, Barry J. Spunt, and Thomas Miller. 1991. "Volume of Cocaine Use and Violence." *Journal of Drug Issues* 21: 345–67.

Goode, Erich. 1994. *Deviant Behavior*. Englewood Cliffs, N.J.: Prentice-Hall.

Graham, Nanette, and Eric D. Wish. 1994. "Drug Use among Female Arrestees: Onset, Patterns, and Relationships to Prostitution." *Journal of Drug Issues* 24: 315–29.

Gusfield, Joseph. 1963. *Symbolic Crusade: Status Politics and the American Temperance Movement*. Urbana: University of Illinois Press.

Harrison, Lana, and Joseph Gfroerer. 1992. "The Intersection of Drug Use and Criminal Behavior." *Crime and Delinquency* 38: 422–43.

Jarvik, M. 1990. "The Drug Dilemma: Manipulating the Demand." *Science* 250: 387–92.

Johnson, Bruce D., Mangai Natarajan, Eloise Dunlap, and Elsayed Elmoghazy. 1994. "Crack Abusers and Noncrack Abusers: Profiles of Drug Use, Drug Sales and Nondrug Criminality." *Journal of Drug Issues* 24: 117–41.

Kleinman, Paula Holzman, Irving F. Lukoff, and Barbara Lynn Kail. 1977. "The Magic Fix: A Critical assessment of Methadone Maintenance Treatment." *Social Problems* 25: 208–14.

Klonoff-Cohen, Sandra H., Leightdelstein, Ellen Schneider, Indu Sriwirasan, David Kaegi, Jae Chun Chang, and Karen Wiley. 1995. "The Effect of Passive Smoking and Tobacco Exposure through Breast Milk on Sudden Infant Death Syndrome." *Journal of the American Medical Association* 273: 795–98.

Kort, Marcel de. 1994. "The Dutch Cannabis Debate, 1968–1976." *Journal of Drug Issues* 24: 417–27.

Laver, Robert. 1995. *Social Problems and the Quality of Life*, 6th ed. Madison, Wis.: Brown & Benchmark.

Leonard, K. E., and H. T. Blane. 1992. "Alcohol and Marital Aggression in a National Sample of Young Men." *Journal of Interpersonal Violence* 7: 19–30.

Levinson, D. 1989. *Family Violence in Cross-Cultural Perspective*. Newbury Park, Calif.: Sage Publications.

Lipton, Douglas S. 1994. "The Correctional Opportunity: Pathways to Drug Treatment for Offenders." *Journal of Drug Issues* 24: 331–48.

MacAndrew, C., and R. Edgerton. 1969. *Drunken Comportment: A Social Explanation*. Chicago: Aldine.

Markle, Gerald E., and Ronald J. Troyer. 1990. "Smoke Gets in Your Eyes: Cigarette Smoking as Deviant Behavior." In *Readings on Social Problems*, ed. William Feigelman, pp. 82–94. Fort Worth: Holt, Rinehart & Winston.

Morgan, Patricia A. 1978. "The Legislation of Drug Law: Economic Crisis and Social Control." *Journal of Drug Issues* 8: 53–62.

National Institute on Drug Abuse (NIDA). 1991. "National Household Survey on Drug Abuse: Main Finding 1990." U.S. Department of Health and Human Services Publication No. ADM 91–1788. Washington D.C.: U.S. Government Printing Office.

Pickens, R. W., and D. S. Svikis. 1988. "Biological Vulnerability in Drug Abuse." NIDA *Research Monograph* No. 88. Washington, D.C.: NIDA, 1988.

Robert Wood Johnson Foundation. 1993 (Oct.). "Substance Abuse: The Nation's Number One Health Problem." Report prepared by the Institute for Health Policy, Brandeis University.

Rorabaugh, W. J. 1979. *The Alcoholic Republic: An American Tradition.* New York: Oxford University Press.

Skow, John. 1995. "Our Own Worst Health Enemies." *Time,* January 30, 68–69.

Statistical Abstract of the United States: 1995, 115th ed. U.S. Bureau of the Census. Washington, D.C.: U.S. Government Printing Office, 1995.

Straus, Murry, and S. Sweet. 1992. "Verbal/Symbolic Aggression in Couples: Incidence Rates and Relationships to Personal Characteristics." *Journal of Marriage and the Family* 54: 346–57.

Sullivan, Barbara. 1995. "Tide May Be Turning for Tobacco-Industry Lawsuits." *The Virginia-Pilot and the Ledger-Star,* March 5, D3.

Sullivan, Thomas, and Kenrick S. Thompson. 1994. *Social Problems* New York: MacMillan.

Tubman, J. 1993. "Family Risk Factors, Parental Alcohol Use, and Problem Behaviors among School-Aged Children." *Family Relations* 42: 81–86.

———. 1995. 1994 National Household Survey on Drug Abuse.

U.S. Department of Justice. 1993. "Drugs, Crime and the Justice System." Office of Justice Programs, Bureau of Justice Statistics. Washington, D.C.: U.S. Government Printing Office, 342–471: 80003.

———. 1994. Fact Sheet. Drug Data Summary from 1993 National Household Survey on Drug Abuse. Office of Justice Programs, Bureau of Justice Statistics, July 1994. NCJ-148213.

Van Dyck, C., and R. Byck. 1982. "Cocaine." *Scientific American* 246: 128–41.

Van Kammen, Welmoet B., and Rolf Loeber. 1994. "Are Fluctuations in Delinquent Activities Related to the Onset and Offset in Juvenile Illegal Drug Use and Drug Dealing?" *Journal of Drug Issues* 24: 9–24.

Waldorf, D., C. Reinarman, and S. Murphy. 1991. *Cocaine Changes: The Experience of Using and Quitting.* Philadelphia: Temple University Press.

White, Helene Raskin, and Erich W. Labouvie. 1994. "Generality versus Specificity of Problem Behavior: Psychological and Functional Differences." *Journal of Drug Issues* 24: 55–74.

Witters, Weldon, Peter Venturelli, and Glen Hanson. 1992. *Drugs and Society,* 3d ed. Boston: Jones & Bartlett.

Wysong, Earl, Richard Aniskiewicz, and David Wright. 1994. "Truth and Dare: Tracking Drug Education to Graduation and as Symbolic Politics." *Social Problems* 41: 448–68.

Yancovitz, Stanley R., et al. 1991. "A Randomized Trial of an Interim Methadone Maintenance Clinic." *American Journal of Public Health* 81: 1185–91.

4

Crime and Violence

IS IT TRUE?

Most persons arrested for violent crime are between the ages of thirty-five and forty-five (p. 109).

Although sociologists have different theories about the causes of crime, they agree that crime is always harmful to society (p. 97).

Amnesty International identifies the United States as a country that violates human rights because capital punishment is legal here (p. 118).

The chance of being a victim of a serious crime is fifteen times greater in the United States than in England (p. 94).

The majority of U.S. homicide victims had some type of relationship with their murderer (p. 102).

ANS: 1.F 2.F 3.T 4.T 5.T

> Instead of improving the harsh conditions
>
> that create crime and violence, which
>
> might restore peace and harmony to
>
> our society, we inflict more pain, more
>
> punishment, thus creating more
>
> crime and more violence.
>
> Richard Stratton, Former prison inmate

The murders of Nicole Brown Simpson and Ron Goldman focused national attention on the problems of crime and violence and the complexities of the criminal justice system. For months, television and tabloids focused on the trial of O. J. Simpson complete with sidebars, viewer polls, and daily commentaries. Although the Simpson case was not representative of a typical murder trial, the accusation of intrafamily violence is not unusual. In 1992, 12.2 percent of all homicides were between relatives (FBI 1993).

Crime and violence are among Americans' foremost concerns. In a 1994 poll by the *National Law Journal,* 54 percent of those surveyed responded that crime is the worst problem facing the country today. In the same poll, 62 percent said that they were "truly desperate" about personal safety (Sherman 1994). Such apprehensions are warranted—one or more members of nearly every American family have been or will be the victims of a serious crime (Monk 1993). Heightened awareness of the dangers of victimization have not gone unnoticed. Alamo Rent-a-Car warns its customers, "If you see someone on the road who indicates they need help, call police by dialing 911 when you reach the nearest telephone. Do not stop."

This chapter examines crime rates as well as theories, types, and demographic patterns of criminal behavior. The economic, social, and psychological costs of crime and violence are also examined. The chapter concludes with a discussion of social policies and prevention programs designed to reduce crime and violence in America.

The Social Context: International Crime and Violence

Crime and violence rates vary dramatically by country. United Nations data indicate that the United States has the highest rates of violent crime of all industrialized nations. The chance of being a murder victim or the victim of some other serious criminal injury is four times greater in the United States than in Canada, six times greater than in Sweden, and fifteen times greater than in Japan or England (Beirne and Messerschmidt 1995, 565). Further, the 1992 *International Crime Survey* reveals that regardless of crime type, the United States is consistently one of the top five crime countries in the world (Van Dijk and Mayhew 1993).

The causes and nature of crime and violence vary from society to society. In Brazil, for example, the defense of "honor" has been used successfully in thou-

United Nations data indicate that the U.S. has the highest rate of violent crime of all industrialized nations.

sands of cases where a husband killed his wife because she was unfaithful; in Bosnia-Herzegovina Serbian troops raped, tortured, and murdered thousands of Muslim women as part of the process of ethnic cleansing; and, an Egyptian Islamic group's fundamentalist beliefs led to the bombing of the World Trade Center in New York City in 1993 (Conklin 1995; Adler, Mueller, and Laufer 1995). In each of these examples, as in the United States, the structure and culture of society influences the incidence of crime and violence.

Sources of Crime Statistics

The U.S. government spends millions of dollars annually compiling and analyzing crime statistics. These data help answer such questions as "What is the extent of crime?" and "How do crime rates vary by age, sex, race, and income level of offenders and victims?" A **crime** is a violation of a federal, state, or local law. For a violation to be a crime, however, the offender must have acted voluntarily and with intent and have no legally acceptable excuse (such as insanity) or justification (e.g., self-defense) for the behavior. The three major types of statistics used to measure crime are official statistics, victimization surveys, and self-report offender surveys.

OFFICIAL STATISTICS

Local sheriffs' departments and police departments throughout the United States collect information on the number of reported crimes and arrests. The Federal Bureau of Investigation (FBI) compiles these statistics annually and publishes them, in summary form, in the Uniform Crime Reports (UCR). The UCR lists crime rates or the number of crimes committed per 100,000 population, as well as the actual number of crimes and the percentage of change over time.

These statistics have several shortcomings. Not only do many incidents of crime go unreported, not all crimes reported to the police are recorded. Alternatively, some rates may be exaggerated. Motivation for such distortions

Ultimately, any crime statistic is only as useful as the reader's understanding of the processes that generated it.
—Robert M. O'Brien
Sociologist, University of Oregon

may come from the public (e.g., demanding that something be done) or from political (e.g., election of a sheriff) and/or organizational pressures (e.g., budget requests). For example, a police department may "crack down" on drug-related crimes in an election year. The result is an increase in the recorded number of these offenses. Such an increase reflects a change in the behavior of law enforcement personnel, not a change in the number of drug violations. Thus, official crime statistics may be a better indicator of what police are doing than what criminals are doing.

VICTIMIZATION SURVEYS

Victimization surveys ask people if they have been victims of crime. The Department of Justice's National Crime Victimization Survey (NCVS), conducted annually, interviews nearly 83,000 people about their experiences as victims of crime. Interviewers collect a variety of information including the victim's background (e.g., age, race and ethnicity, sex, marital status, education, and area of residence), relationship to offender (stranger or nonstranger), and the extent to which the victim was harmed. Although victimization surveys provide detailed information about crime victims, they provide less reliable data on offenders.

SELF-REPORT OFFENDER SURVEYS

Self-report surveys ask offenders about their criminal behavior. The sample may consist of a population with known police records, such as a prison population, or it may include respondents from the general population such as college students. Self-report data compensate for many of the problems associated with official statistics but are still subject to exaggerations and concealment. The Criminal Activities Survey (see *Self and Society* on p. 98) asks you to indicate whether you have engaged in a variety of illegal activities.

> **Consideration**   Self-report surveys reveal that virtually every adult has engaged in some type of criminal activity. Why then is only a fraction of the population labeled as criminal? Like a funnel, which is large at one end and small at the other, only a small proportion of the total population of law violators is ever convicted of a crime. For an individual to be officially labeled as a criminal, his or her behavior must first be observed or known to have occurred. Next, the crime must be reported to the police. The police must then respond to the report, find sufficient evidence to substantiate that a crime has taken place, file an official report, and have enough evidence to make an arrest. The arrestee must then go through a preliminary hearing, an arraignment, and a trial and may or may not be convicted. At every stage of the process, an offender may be "funneled" out. In 1990, for example, an estimated 6 million violent crimes occurred; 1.8 million were reported to the police; 580,006 resulted in arrest; 130,226 arrests led to convictions, and 107,302 offenders were incarcerated (Gest 1994).

Sociological Theories of Crime and Violence

Some explanations of crime and violence focus on psychological aspects of the offender such as psychopathic personalities, unhealthy relationships with parents, and mental illness. Other crime theories focus on the role of biological variables such as central nervous system malfunctioning, vitamin or mineral deficiencies, chromosomal abnormalities, and a genetic predisposition toward aggression. Sociological theories of crime and violence emphasize the role of social factors in criminal behavior and societal responses to it.

STRUCTURAL-FUNCTIONALIST PERSPECTIVE

According to Durkheim and other structural-functionalists, crime is functional for society. One of the functions of crime and other deviant behavior is that it strengthens group cohesion:

> The deviant individual violates rules of conduct which the rest of the community holds in high respect; and when these people come together to express their outrage over the offense . . . they develop a tighter bond of solidarity than existed earlier. (Erikson 1966, 4)

Recent research challenges the idea that crime produces social cohesion, however. In a study of twenty-six U.S. cities, Liska and Warner (1991) found that high crime rates in urban areas produced social isolation rather than social cohesion of the citizens.

Crime may also lead to social change. For example, an episode of local violence may "achieve broad improvements in city services . . . [and] be a catalyst for making public agencies more effective and responsive, for strengthening families and social institutions, and for creating public private partnerships" (National Research Council 1994, 9–10). Further, public awareness of illicit drug dealing may call attention to poverty and the lack of employment opportunities.

Poverty is the mother of crime.
—Magnus Aurelius Cassiodorus
Roman historian

While functionalism as a theoretical perspective deals directly with some aspects of crime and violence, it is not a theory of crime per se. Three major theories of crime and violence have developed from functionalism, however. The first, called **strain theory,** was developed by Robert Merton (1957) using Durkheim's concept of anomie, or normlessness. Merton argues that when legitimate means (for example, a job) of acquiring culturally defined goals (for example, money) are limited by the structure of society, the resulting strain may lead to crime.

Individuals, then, must adapt to the inconsistency between means and goals in a society that socializes everyone into wanting the same thing but only provides opportunities for some. When structurally defined means and culturally defined goals are blocked, individuals adapt to the strain by rejecting either the means or the goals. In addition, new goals and means may be substituted for those that are socially approved (see Table 4.1).

Conformity occurs when individuals accept the culturally defined goals and the socially legitimate means of achieving them. Merton suggests that most individuals, even those who do not have easy access to the means and goals, remain conformists. *Innovation* occurs when an individual accepts the goals of society, but rejects or lacks the socially legitimate means of achieving them. Innovation, the mode of adaptation most associated with criminal behavior, explains the high rate of crime committed by uneducated and poor individuals who do not have access to legitimate means of achieving the social goals of wealth and power.

Another adaptation is *ritualism*, in which the individual accepts a lifestyle of hard work, but rejects the cultural goal of monetary rewards. The ritualist goes through the motions of getting an education and working hard, yet is not

Criminal Activities Survey

Read each of the following questions. If, since the age of fifteen, you have ever engaged in the behavior described, place a "+" in the space provided. If you have not engaged in the behavior, put a "0" in the space provided. After completing the survey, read the section on interpretation to see what your answers mean.

Questions	+ (Yes)	0 (No)
1. Have you ever willfully concealed merchandise on your person while in a store without having purchased the merchandise?	___	___
2. Have you ever willfully changed a price tag, marked merchandise at a lower price, or placed a false price tag on merchandise that you wanted to purchase?	___	___
3. Have you ever willfully damaged any land or growing thing or cut, broken, or removed a tree, plant, or flower without the consent of the owner of the land?	___	___
4. Have you ever willfully damaged another person's personal property, causing not more than $200 in damages?	___	___
5. Have you ever, at the age of 16 or 17, gained admission into any theater by claiming to be 18 or older?	___	___
6. Have you ever, in a telephone call, threatened bodily harm to another or threatened to damage another's property?	___	___
7. Have you ever telephoned another repeatedly for the purpose of annoying, threatening, terrifying, harassing, or embarrassing that person?	___	___
8. Have you ever made a telephone call and failed to hang up the phone with the intent of disrupting the other person's phone service?	___	___
9. Have you ever peeped secretly into a room occupied by a female?	___	___
10. Have you ever willfully threatened to physically injure a person or damage another's property and communicated that threat to the other person (orally, in writing, or by any other means)?	___	___
11. Have you ever thrown, dropped, poured, released, discharged, or placed in an area where an athletic or sporting event was taking place any substance or object that was likely to cause injury to persons who were participating in or attending such events or to cause damage to equipment, animals, vehicles, or other things used in the event?	___	___
12. Have you ever intentionally caused a public disturbance by fighting or other violent conduct?	___	___
13. Have you ever intentionally caused a public disturbance by making or using any utterance, gesture, or abusive language that was intended to provoke violent retaliation?	___	___

Questions	+ (Yes)	0 (No)
14. Have you ever been intoxicated in a public place and been disruptive by either (a) blocking traffic; (b) blocking access to a building entrance or passage across a sidewalk; (c) cursing, shouting, or insulting others; or (d) grabbing, pushing, or fighting others or challenging others to a fight?	___	___
15. Have you ever knowingly possessed lottery tickets?	___	___
16. Have you ever driven a vehicle on a public highway or road in a careless manner or at a speed that could endanger other persons or property?	___	___
17. Have you ever played or bet in a game of chance (e.g., card game) at which money, property, or other thing of value was wagered?	___	___

Interpretation: Each of the activities described in these questions represents criminal behavior that was subject to fines, imprisonment, or both under the laws of North Carolina in 1990. For each activity, the following table lists the maximum prison sentence and/or fine for a first-time offender. To calculate your "prison time" and/or fines, sum the numbers corresponding to each activity you have engaged in.

MAXIMUM PRISON SENTENCE FOR FIRST-TIME OFFENDER	MAXIMUM FINE	OFFENSE
1. Six months	Unspecified	Shoplifting
2. Six months	$100	Shoplifting
3. Six months	$500	Criminal mischief
4. Two years	Unspecified	Vandalism
5. None	$50	Criminal fraud
6. Two years	Unspecified	Communicating threats
7. Two years	Unspecified	Annoying communications
8. Two years	Unspecified	Misappropriation of telephone services
9. Two years	Unspecified	Criminal voyeurism
10. Six months	$500	Communicating threats/assault
11. Thirty days	$100	Vandalism/criminal mischief
12. Six months	$500	Disorderly conduct
13. Six months	$500	Disorderly conduct
14. Thirty days	$50	Drunk and disorderly/public intoxication
15. Six months	$2000	Gambling
16. Six months	$500	Reckless driving
17. Two years	Unspecified	Gambling

SOURCE: Adapted from Robert L. Farb and Benjamin B. Sendor. 1990. *1989 Cumulative Supplement to North Carolina Crimes: A Guidebook on the Elements of Crime.* University of North Carolina at Chapel Hill: Institute of Government.

TABLE 4.1

MERTON'S FIVE TYPES OF ADAPTATION

	CULTURALLY DEFINED GOALS	STRUCTURALLY DEFINED MEANS
1. Conformity	+	+
2. Innovation	+	−
3. Ritualism	−	+
4. Retreatism	−	−
5. Rebellion	+/−	+/−

Key: + = acceptance of/access to;
   − = rejection of/lack of access to;
   +/− = rejection of culturally defined goals and structurally defined means and replacement with new goals and means.
SOURCE: Adapted from Robert Merton. 1968. "Social Structure and Anomie." In *Social Theory and Social Structure*, p. 194. Glencoe, Ill.: Free Press.

committed to the goal of accumulating wealth or power. *Retreatism* involves rejecting both the cultural goal of success and the socially legitimate means of achieving it. The retreatist withdraws or retreats from society and may become an alcoholic, drug addict, or vagrant. Finally, *rebellion* occurs when an individual rejects both culturally defined goals and means and substitutes new goals and means. For example, rebels may use social or political activism to replace the goal of personal wealth with the goal of social justice and equality.

While strain theory explains criminal behavior as a result of blocked opportunities, **subcultural theories** argue that certain groups or subcultures in society have values and attitudes that are conducive to crime and violence. Members of these groups and subcultures, as well as other individuals who interact with them, may adopt the crime-promoting attitudes and values of the group. For example, subcultural norms and values contribute to street crime. Sociologist Elijah Anderson (1994) explains that many inner city African-American youths live by a survival code on the streets that emphasizes gaining the respect of others through violence—the tougher you are and the more others fear you, the more respect you have in the community.

But, if blocked opportunities and subcultural values are responsible for crime, why don't all members of the affected groups become criminals? **Control theory** may answer that question. Hirschi (1969), consistent with Durkheim's emphasis on social solidarity, suggests that a strong social bond between individuals and the social order constrains some individuals from violating social norms. Hirschi identified four elements of the social bond: attachment to significant others, commitment to conventional goals, involvement in conventional activities, and belief in the moral standards of society. Several empirical tests of Hirschi's theory support the notion that the higher the attachment, commitment, involvement, and belief, the higher the social bond and the lower the probability of criminal behavior (Krohn and Massey 1980; Sampson and Laub 1993).

CONFLICT PERSPECTIVE

Conflict theories of crime suggest that deviance is inevitable whenever two groups have differing degrees of power; in addition, the more inequality in a society, the greater the crime rate in that society. Social inequality leads individuals to commit crimes such as larceny and burglary as a means of economic survival. Other individuals, who are angry and frustrated by their low position in the socioeconomic hierarchy, express their rage and frustration through crimes such as drug use, assault, and homicide.

According to the conflict perspective, those in power define what is criminal and what is not, and these definitions reflect the interests of the ruling class. Laws against vagrancy, for example, penalize individuals who do not contribute to the capitalist system of work and consumerism. Rather than viewing law as a mechanism that protects all members of society, conflict theorists focus on how laws are created by those in power to protect the ruling class. Wealthy corporations contribute money to campaigns to influence politicians to enact tax laws that serve corporate interests (Jacobs 1988). Despite ample evidence of tobacco's addictive power and devastating health consequences, Congress has failed to pass legislation criminalizing the production and sale of tobacco in part because the tobacco industry makes enormous contributions to legislators.

Furthermore, conflict theorists argue that law enforcement is applied differentially, penalizing those without power and benefiting those with power. For example, female prostitutes are more likely to be arrested than are the men who seek their services. Unlike street criminals, corporate criminals are often punished by fines rather than by lengthy prison terms, and rape laws originated to serve the interests of husbands and fathers who wanted to protect their property—wives and unmarried daughters.

Societal beliefs also reflect power differentials. For example, "rape myths" are perpetuated by the male-dominated culture to foster the belief that women are to blame for their own victimization, thereby, in the minds of many, exonerating the offender. Such myths include the notion that when a woman says "no" she means "yes," that "good girls" don't get raped, that appearance indicates willingness, and that women secretly want to be raped. Not surprisingly, in societies where women and men have greater equality, there is less rape (Sanday 1981).

> *There are two criminal justice systems in this country. There is a whole different system for poor people. It's the same court-house—it's not separate— but it's not equal.*
> —Paul Petterson
> Public defender

> **Consideration** Conflict theorists also point out that by focusing on the problems of street crime and violence, politicians and the media divert public attention away from corporate crime and corporate violence. Powerful corporations, which exert economic influence on politicians and the media, thus benefit from society's preoccupation with street crime. The emphasis on street crime also diverts attention away from other aspects of social life that may be considered crimes against society, such as racism and sexism.

SYMBOLIC INTERACTIONIST PERSPECTIVE

Two important theories of crime and violence emanate from the symbolic interactionist perspective. The first, **labeling theory,** focuses on two questions: How do crime and deviance come to be defined as such, and what are the effects of being labeled as criminal or deviant? According to Howard Becker (1963):

> *Social groups create deviance by making rules whose infractions constitute deviance, and by applying those rules to particular people and labeling them as outsiders. From this point of view, deviance is not a quality of the act a person commits, but rather a consequence of the application by others of rules and sanctions to an "offender." The deviant is one to whom the label has successfully been applied; deviant behavior is behavior that people so label. (p. 238)*

Labeling theorists make a distinction between *primary deviance,* which is deviant behavior committed before a person is caught and labeled as an offender, and *secondary deviance,* which is deviance that results from being caught and labeled. After a person violates the law and is apprehended, that person is stigmatized as a criminal. This deviant label often dominates the social identity of the person to whom it is applied and becomes the person's "master status," that is, the primary basis on which the person is defined by others.

Being labeled as deviant often leads to further deviant behavior because (1) the person who is labeled as deviant is often denied opportunities for engaging in nondeviant behavior, and (2) the labeled person internalizes the deviant label, adopts a deviant self-concept, and acts accordingly. For example, the teenager who is caught selling drugs at school may be expelled and thus denied opportunities to participate in nondeviant school activities (e.g., sports, clubs) and associate with nondeviant peer groups. The labeled and stigmatized teenager may also adopt the self-concept of a "druggie" or "pusher" and continue to pursue drug-related activities and membership in the drug culture.

The assignment of meaning and definitions learned from others are also central to the second symbolic interactionist theory of crime, **differential association.** Edwin Sutherland (1939) proposed that, through interaction with others, individuals learn the values and attitudes associated with crime as well as the techniques and motivations for criminal behavior. Individuals who are exposed to more definitions favorable to law violation (e.g., "crime pays") than unfavorable (e.g., "do the crime, you'll do the time") are more likely to engage in criminal behavior. Thus, children who see their parents benefit from crime, or who live in high crime neighborhoods where success is associated with illegal behavior, are more likely to engage in criminal behavior. In support of differential association, criminologist Charles Tittle (1980) found that respondents who associated with people who had committed criminal acts were themselves significantly more likely to violate the law.

Types of Crime

The FBI identifies eight **index offenses** as the most serious crimes in the United States. The index offenses, which may be against a person (called violent or personal crimes) or against property, are usually considered "street crimes" (see Table 4.2). Other types of crime include vice crime, such as drug use, gambling, and prostitution, as well as organized crime, white-collar crime, computer crime, and juvenile delinquency.

VIOLENT CRIME

In general, violent crime has increased in recent decades. Violent crime includes homicide, assault, rape, and robbery.

Homicide refers to the willful or nonnegligent killing of one human being by another individual or group of individuals. While homicide is the most serious of the violent crimes, it is also the least common, accounting for less than 1 percent of the violent index offenses in 1992 (FBI 1993). The majority of homicide victims had some type of relationship with their murderer (Parker 1995). Most cases of homicide involve friends or acquaintances, neighbors, or co-workers, who kill one another over such issues as jealousy and money. Murders

TABLE 4.2

INDEX CRIMES KNOWN TO THE POLICE

	RATE PER 100,000		
	1984	1993	PERCENTAGE CHANGE IN RATE (1984–1993)
Violent crime			
Murder	7.9	9.5	+20.3%
Forcible rape	35.7	40.6	+13.7
Robbery	205.4	255.8	+24.5
Aggravated assault	290.2	440.1	+51.7
Total	539.2	746.1	+38.4
Property crime*			
Burglary	1,263.7	1,099.2	−13.0
Larceny/theft	2,791.3	3,032.4	+8.6
Motor vehicle theft	437.1	605.3	+38.5
Total	4,492.1	4,736.9	+5.4

*Sufficient data are not available to estimate totals for arson.

SOURCE: Adapted from "Crime in the United States 1993" Pp. 228–236 in *Criminal Justice 95/96*. 1995. John J. Sullivan and Joseph L. Victor (eds.), 1995. Guilford, CT: Dushkin Publishing Group.

by family members or other persons involved in intimate relationships account for nearly one-fifth of all homicides.

In most murders, the victim is the same race as the offender. Ninety-four percent of black victims are killed by other blacks, and 83 percent of white victims are killed by other whites (Press, McCormick, and Wingert 1994). The rate of victimization of young black men is ten times higher than that of young white men. In fact, homicide is the leading cause of death of young black men (Press, McCormick, and Wingert 1994).

Another form of violent crime, *aggravated assault,* involves the attacking of another with the intent to cause serious bodily injury. Like homicide, aggravated assault occurs most often between members of the same race. Unlike homicide, however, aggravated assault is more likely to take place between strangers than between acquaintances and is a fairly common occurrence. In 1993, the assault rate was forty-six times greater than the murder rate: assaults comprised 59 percent of all violent crime.

Rape is also classified as a form of violent crime. The FBI definition of *rape* contains three elements: sexual penetration, force or the threat of force, and nonconsent of the victim. Although men can be victims of rape, the FBI definition recognizes only female rape victims. In 1993, more than 104,000 forcible rapes were reported in the United States, an increase of more than 18 percent from 1988 (FBI 1993; Sullivan and Victor 1995). Given the problems with official statistics, however, this number may be less than 10 percent of the actual number of rapes that occurred that year.

The majority of rapes are **acquaintance rapes**—rapes committed by someone the victim knows (Koss, Gidycz, and Cox 1988). While acquaintance rapes are the most likely to occur, they are the least likely to be reported and the most difficult to prosecute. Unless the rape is what Williams (1984) calls a "classic rape"—that is, the rapist was a stranger who used a weapon, and the attack resulted in serious bodily injury—women hesitate to report the crime out of fear of not being believed.

National Data: Only 15 percent of a national sample of rape victims reported they had been raped by a stranger; 85 percent had been raped by someone they knew.

SOURCE: Koss, Gidycz, and Cox 1988.

Robbery, although involving theft, also includes force or the threat of force, or putting a victim in fear (FBI 1993), and is thus considered a violent crime. Officially, in 1993 more than 659,000 robberies took place in the United States (Sullivan and Victor 1995). However, the National Crime Victimization Survey indicates that less than half of all robberies are reported. Robberies are often committed by strangers (80 percent) with the use of a weapon (70 percent). As with rape, victims who resist a robbery are more likely to stop the crime, but are also more likely to be physically harmed (U.S. Department of Justice 1993).

PROPERTY CRIME

Property crimes are those in which someone's property is damaged, destroyed, or stolen; they include larceny, motor vehicle theft, burglary, and arson. In the United States in 1993, a violent crime occurred, on the average, every sixteen seconds, while a property crime occurred every three seconds; larceny, or simple theft, was the most common, comprising 55 percent of all reported index crimes (Sullivan and Victor 1995).

Larceny involving automobiles and auto accessories is the largest single category of thefts (FBI 1993), but because of the cost involved, theft of a motor vehicle is considered a separate index offense. In 1993, more than 1.5 million auto thefts took place in the United States—over 11 percent of all index crimes (FBI 1993; Sullivan and Victor 1995). Because twice as many cars are stolen to be used temporarily as are sold for economic gain, most stolen vehicles are recovered (Clarke and Harris 1992).

Burglary, which is the second most common index offense, entails entering a structure, usually a house, with the intent to commit a crime while inside. Official statistics indicate that 2,834,800 burglaries were reported to the police in 1993, less than half of all burglaries that took place that year according to the National Crime Victimization Survey (Sullivan and Victor 1995; U.S. Department of Justice 1993).

Arson involves the malicious burning of the property of another. Estimating the frequency and nature of arson is difficult given the legal requirement of "maliciousness." However, 102,009 incidents of arson were reported to the FBI in 1992; two-thirds of the incidents involved residential buildings in large cities (FBI 1993).

VICE CRIMES

Vice crimes are illegal activities that have no complaining party and are therefore often called **victimless crimes.** Vice crimes include using illegal drugs, engaging in or soliciting prostitution (except for legalized prostitution, which exists in Nevada), and illegal gambling.

> *Consideration* Engaging in prostitution and seeking the services of a prostitute are considered high-risk behaviors for the transmission of the HIV infection. Therefore, there is some debate over whether prostitution should be considered a victimless crime.

Most Americans view drug use as socially disruptive. In a 1994 poll, a significant proportion of the population, 66 percent, responded that drugs are the number one cause of crime today (Sherman 1994). There is, however, less consensus that gambling and prostitution should remain criminalized. A number of states have legalized gambling, including casinos in Nevada, New Jersey, Connecticut, and many other states, as well as state lotteries, bingo parlors, horse and dog racing, and jai alai. Further, some have argued that there is little difference, other than societal definitions of acceptable and unacceptable behavior, between gambling and other risky ventures such as investing in the stock market. Conflict theorists are quick to note that the difference is who's making the wager.

International Data: The number of underage prostitutes worldwide is alarming: 400,000 in India, 250,000 in Brazil, and 800,000 in Thailand.

SOURCE: Cited in Adler, Mueller, and Laufer 1995.

ORGANIZED CRIME

Organized crime refers to criminal activity conducted by members of a hierarchically-arranged structure devoted primarily to making money through illegal means. Many of these activities include providing illegal goods and services such as drugs and gambling, as well as the coercion of legitimate businesses for profit. For example, organized crime groups may force legitimate businesses to pay "protection money" by threatening vandalism or violence.

Although most organized crime occurs at the local level (Albanese 1995), it also occurs at the national level. An estimated one in three eighteen-wheelers on the interstate highways is operating on home heating oil, not diesel fuel. The latter is taxed at up to 51 cents a gallon. Truckers avoid this cost by buying home heating oil on the black market through organized crime connections, thereby cheating the government out of billions of tax dollars annually (Brokaw 1994).

Organized crime also occurs at the international level such as smuggling illegal drugs and arms. The traditional notion of organized crime is the Mafia—a national band of interlocked Italian families—but members of many ethnic groups engage in organized crime.

WHITE-COLLAR CRIME

White-collar crime includes both occupational crime, where individuals commit crimes in the course of their employment, and corporate crime, where corporations violate the law in the interest of maximizing profit. Occupational crime is motivated by individual gain; corporate crime benefits the organization.

William Aramony, former president of United Way of America, engaged in occupational crime when he stole $600,000 from the nation's largest charity. He was convicted in 1995 on twenty-five counts of fraud, conspiracy, and money laundering. Physicians who charge Medicaid and Medicare for services never rendered are similarly engaging in criminal activity for their own self-interest. Pilferage (employee theft of merchandise) and embezzlement (employee theft of money) are also examples of occupational crime.

Haagen-Daz's claim that its yogurt was "fat-free," when laboratory analysis revealed that it was not, is an example of corporate crime. Other corporate crimes include price fixing, antitrust violations, and fraud. In 1992, the discount drug-store chain Phar-Mor went bankrupt after a massive fraud scheme in which investors and auditors were given inaccurate information. Phar-Mor's president was indicted on more than a hundred counts of fraud.

Corporate violence, a form of corporate crime, refers to the production of unsafe products and the failure of corporations to provide a safe working environment for their employees. Corporate violence is the result of negligence, the pursuit of profit at any cost, and intentional violations of health, safety, and

The characterization of organized crime as dominated by the Mafia is a gross oversimplification.
—Jay Albanese
Niagara University

Although "street crimes" such as robbery and murder may spark the greatest fear in the public, and gain the most attention from the media, the damage they do is dwarfed by that of "respectable" criminals who wear white collars and work for our most powerful organizations.
—James W. Coleman
Sociologist

Residents of Love Canal were victimized by corporate violence when toxic waste, dumped by the Hooker Chemical Company, began to seep into the basements of homes and schools. Many residents of Love Canal moved out of the area; others complained of high rates of miscarriages, birth defects, and cancer. Although Love Canal was allegedly cleaned up, residents protested against resettling the area.

environmental regulations. Between 1942 and 1953, for instance, Hooker Chemical Company dumped 20,000 tons of toxic waste into an abandoned canal, now called Love Canal, near Niagara Falls. The company then sold the dump site, which was developed as a residential area. Some twenty years later, the toxic sludge, containing twelve known carcinogens, began to appear in basements of schools and homes. One survey found that of sixteen pregnancies in the neighborhood in 1979, one resulted in a healthy baby, four ended in miscarriages, two babies were stillborn, and nine babies were deformed (Thio 1988, 434).

The National Commission on Product Safety estimates that 20 million serious injuries, 100,000 permanently disabling injuries, and 30,000 deaths result each year from unsafe consumer products (reported in Hills 1987). In many cases, corporate executives are aware that the product is unsafe. One example is the Ford Pinto, which had a defective gas tank that exploded in rear-end collisions. Hundreds of burn deaths occurred before the problem was revealed to the public. Yet the Ford Motor Company knew of the dangers of the car and made a profit-motivated decision to do nothing:

> The $11 repairs for all Pintos would cost $137 million but 180 burn deaths and 180 serious burn injuries and 2100 burned vehicles would cost only $49.5 million (each death was figured at $200,000, and each injury at $67,000). Therefore, the company could anticipate a savings or profit [by doing nothing] of $87.5 million. (Hills 1987, 425)

Table 4.3 summarizes some of the major categories of white-collar crime.

COMPUTER CRIME

Computer crime refers to any violation of the law in which a computer is the target or means of criminal activity. Seventy to 90 percent of all cases of com-

TABLE 4.3

TYPES OF WHITE-COLLAR CRIME

Crimes against consumers:
Deceptive advertising
Antitrust violations
Dangerous products
Manufacturer kickbacks
Physician insurance fraud

Crimes against employees:
Health and safety violations
Wage and hour violations
Discriminatory hiring practices
Illegal labor practices
Unlawful surveillance practices

Crimes against the public:
Toxic waste disposal
Pollution violations
Tax fraud
Security violations
Police brutality

Crimes against employers:
Embezzlement
Pilferage
Misappropriation of company funds
Counterfeit production of goods
Business credit fraud

puter crime are committed by employees (Albanese and Pursley 1993). Conklin (1995) has identified several examples of computer crime:

- In 1979, someone purposely tampered with a computerized flight plan that guided a plane's automatic pilot, causing a crash that killed 257 people.
- A programmer made $300 a week by programming a computer to round off each employee's paycheck down to the nearest ten cents and then to deposit the extra few pennies in the offender's account.
- An oil company illegally tapped into another oil company's computer to get information that allowed the offending company to underbid the other company for leasing rights.
- In 1993, thieves placed a phony automatic teller machine (ATM) in a Connecticut mall and recorded the personal identification numbers of the users. After acquiring the numbers, the thieves withdrew thousands of dollars from the unsuspecting depositors.
- In 1995, Kevin Mitnick was arrested for breaking into an Internet provider computer system and stealing 20,000 credit card numbers.

JUVENILE DELINQUENCY

In general, children under the age of eighteen are handled by the juvenile court either as status offenders or as delinquent offenders. A status offense is a violation that can only be committed by a juvenile such as running away from home, truancy, and underage drinking. A delinquent offense is an offense that would be a crime if committed by an adult, such as the eight index offenses. The most common status offenses handled in juvenile court are underage drinking, truancy, and running away. In 1991, 152,000 juveniles were arrested for running away, the only status offense in which arrests of girls exceeded those of boys (*Statistical Abstract of the United States: 1995*, Table 324).

Juveniles commit more property offenses than violent offenses. Of all arrests for serious property crimes in 1991, 32.4 percent of the offenders were under the age of eighteen; of all arrests for the four violent crimes, 17.2 percent were under eighteen (FBI 1992). Murder is the least likely violent crime to be committed by a juvenile and robbery the most likely. The number of juvenile

National Data: Between 1988 and 1992, the number of delinquent and status cases rose 31 and 18 percent, respectively.

SOURCE: U.S. Department of Justice 1995.

gang killings has increased dramatically in recent years, however, rising from around 200 in 1985 to nearly 1,200 in 1993 (Shannon 1995, 66).

Demographic Patterns of Crime

Although virtually everyone violates a law at some time, persons with certain demographic characteristics are disproportionately represented in the crime statistics. Victims, for example, are disproportionately young, lower-class, minority males from urban areas. Similarly, the probability of being an offender varies by gender, age, race, social class, and region.

GENDER AND CRIME

Both official statistics and self-report data indicate that males commit more crime than females. Why are males more likely to commit crime than females? One explanation is that society views female lawbreaking as less acceptable and thus places more constraints on female behavior: "women may need a higher level of provocation before turning to crime—especially serious crime. Females who choose criminality must traverse a greater moral and psychological distance than males making the same choice" (Steffensmeier and Allan 1995, 88).

Further, data suggest that males and females tend to commit different types of crimes. Men, partly because of more aggressive socialization experiences, are more likely than women to commit violent crimes. Men who kill outnumber women by nine to one (Press, McCormick, and Wingert 1994). Females are less likely than males to commit serious offenses, and the monetary value of female involvement in theft, property damage, and illegal drugs is typically less than that for similar offenses committed by males. Nevertheless, a growing number of women have become involved in characteristically male criminal activities such as gang-related crime. This chapter's *In Focus* emphasizes that some female gang members commit crimes traditionally engaged in by males.

National Data: According to the Uniform Crime Reports, the ratio of males to females arrested in 1992 was five male offenders to one female offender.

SOURCE: Adler, Mueller, and Laufer 1995.

International Data: The U.S. homicide rate for 15–24-year-old males is four times higher than Scotland's, and over 21 times higher than Japan's or Austria's.

SOURCE: Fingerhut and Kleinman. 1990.

Females who join gangs often do so to win approval from their boyfriends who are gang members.

Female Gang Members

Witkin (1991) suggests that "gangs are growing like a cancer" (p. 29). In the Los Angeles area, gangs doubled in number from 400 with 45,000 members in 1985 to 800 with 90,000 members in 1990. In Austin, Texas, alone, gang membership climbed from 200 in 1986 to nearly 2,800 in 1991. Although gang members are typically male, some gangs include females. Female gang members tend to come from families characterized by sexual abuse, physical violence, substance abuse, and parental marital problems (Gilligan 1991). Female gang members also seem to be attracted to male gang members who abuse them, both physically and psychologically (Cunningham 1994).

Although female gang members generally engage in such crimes as petty theft, assault, truancy, burglary, and drug sales, some female gang members commit more serious crimes, such as murder and robbery. Male gang members may influence their girlfriends, who are also gang members, to commit violent crimes (Cunningham 1994). One police officer who works with female gang members noted:

Many girls have boyfriends who get into gangs and they join for the love and approval of their mates. This can create a difficult situation for the girls, because they want to be loved by their boyfriends yet, they also know that in order to be loved they may have to commit violent acts within the gang. (Cunningham 1994, 95)

In essence, girls with low self-esteem and frayed family relationships enter gangs in search of greater approval and a sense of belonging. Once they fall in love, they are willing to do what their partners want, including murder. But such behavior may lower their self-esteem at the same time, trapping them in a criminal context with males they have become emotionally dependent on.

Rehabilitation of female gang members includes family therapy to build a positive relationship between parents and their daughters. In addition, rehabilitation involves encouraging gang members to participate in activities that enhance self-worth and teach personal and social responsibility.

SOURCES:

Renee Roreau Cunningham. 1994. "Implications for Treating the Female Gang Member." *Progress: Implications for Treating the Female Gang Member* 3, 91–102;

C. Gilligan. 1991. *Women's Psychological Development: Implications for Psychotherapy.* New York: Haworth Press;

Gordon Witkin. 1991. "Kids Who Kill." *U.S. News and World Report,* April 8, 26–32.

AGE AND CRIME

In general, criminal activity is more prevalent among younger persons than older persons. The highest arrest rate is for individuals under the age of twenty-five. Crimes committed by people in their teens or early twenties tend to involve property crimes like burglary, larceny, arson, vandalism, and liquor/drug violations. The median age of people who commit more serious crimes, such as aggravated assault and homicide, is in the late twenties (Steffensmeier and Allan 1995). These data suggest that the crime rate in the United States is likely to increase in the next decade as the population of young people increases.

National Data: While the total U.S. population will rise about 12 percent by 2005, the number of youths aged 15 to 19 will increase by 21 percent. Young, African-American and Hispanic men—those with the highest violent crime rate—will increase 24 percent and 47 percent, respectively.

SOURCE: Gest and Friedman 1994.

Why is criminal activity more prevalent among individuals in their teens and early twenties? One reason is that juveniles are insulated from many of the legal penalties for criminal behavior. Younger individuals are also more likely to be unemployed or employed in low-wage jobs. Thus, as strain theorists argue, they have less access to legitimate means for acquiring material goods.

Some research suggests, however, that high school students who have jobs become more, rather than less, involved in crime (Felson 1994). In earlier generations, teenagers who worked did so to support themselves and/or their families. Today, teenagers who work typically spend their earnings on recreation and "extras," including car payments and gasoline. The increased mobility associated with having a vehicle also increases opportunities for criminal behavior and reduces parental control. Finally, teenage employment may "bring the worker closer to money and goods suitable for theft" (Felson 1994, 88).

RACE, SOCIAL CLASS, AND CRIME

Race is a factor in who gets arrested. Although whites represented two-thirds of those arrested for all criminal offenses in 1993, (*Statistical Abstract of the United States: 1995*, Table 322), minorities are overrepresented in official crime statistics. For example, although African Americans represent about 13 percent of the population, they account for more than one-fourth of all arrests. While minorities are underrepresented in white-collar crimes, often lacking the opportunity to commit such offenses, blacks are arrested for 44.8 percent of all violent crime, and 31.8 percent of all property crimes (Conklin 1995, 112).

Nevertheless, it is inaccurate to conclude that race and crime are causally related. First, official statistics reflect the behaviors and policies of criminal justice actors. Thus, the high rate of arrests, conviction, and incarceration of minorities may be a consequence of individual and institutional bias (e.g., police prejudice) not only against minorities, but against the lower class in general (Mosher and Hagan 1994). Second, race and social class are closely related in that nonwhites are overrepresented in the lower classes. Since lower-class members lack legitimate means to acquire material goods, they may turn to instrumental, or economically motivated, crimes. Further, while the "haves" typically earn social respect through their socioeconomic status, educational achievement, and occupational role, the "have-nots" more often live in communities where respect is based on physical strength and violence as subcultural theorists argue.

Thus, the apparent relationship between race and crime may, in part, be a consequence of the relationship between these variables and social class. Research indicates, however, that even when social class backgrounds remain the same between blacks and whites, blacks have higher rates of criminality, particularly for violent crime (Wolfgang, Figlio, and Sellin 1972; Elliot and Ageton 1980). Further, to avoid the bias inherent in official statistics, researchers have compared race, class, and criminality by examining self-report data and victim studies. Their findings indicate that while there are racial and class differences in criminal offenses, the differences are not as great as official data would indicate (U.S. Department of Justice 1993).

Consideration Stereotyping particular racial, ethnic, or socioeconomic groups as prone to crime and violence may further contribute to rates of crime and violence among those groups. As one government report describes:

> When groups are negatively stereotyped, they are systematically excluded from the social networks that lead to legitimate economic opportunities. This exclusion further deepens social divisions and weakens commitments to traditional social institutions. Some members of the excluded groups then become involved in high-violence, illegal markets. (National Research Council 1994, 6)

REGION AND CRIME

Crime rates are higher in urban than suburban areas (Winsberg 1994) although suburban crime is growing faster than crime in the cities (Alba, Logan, and Bellair 1994). Higher crime rates in urban areas are due to several factors. First, social control is a function of small intimate groups socializing their members to engage in law-abiding behavior, expressing approval for their doing so and disapproval for their noncompliance. In large urban areas, people are less likely to know each other and thus are not influenced by the approval or disapproval of strangers. Demographic factors also explain why crime rates are higher in urban areas; cities have large concentrations of poor, unemployed, and minority individuals.

Crime also varies by region of the country, the highest percentage of all index crimes in 1993 being in the South (38 percent) followed by the West (25 percent), Midwest (21 percent), and Northeast (17 percent) (Sullivan and Victor 1995). The murder rate in southern states is 32 percent higher than in any other region in the country although rape, assault, and robbery rates are not significantly higher (Conklin 1995). The high rate of southern lethal violence has been linked to high rates of poverty and minority populations in the South, a southern "subculture of violence," higher rates of gun ownership in the South, and a warmer climate that facilitates victimization by increasing the frequency of social interaction.

A lot of people felt that if they could move to the suburbs, it would be a safe place. But all these suburbs have developed tremendous crime problems too.
—Thomas Constantine, Head of Drug Enforcement Administration

National Data: In 1993, the violent crime rate in metropolitan areas was 852 per 100,000 compared to 222 per 100,000 in rural areas. The property crime rate in the same year was 5,193 in metropolitan areas compared to 1,749 in rural areas.

SOURCE: *Statistical Abstract of the United States: 1995,* Table 309.

Costs of Crime and Violence

Crime and violence often result in physical injury and loss of life. In 1993, homicide replaced AIDS as the tenth leading cause of death among Americans and was the second leading killer of those aged fifteen to twenty-four. (Beck et al. 1993). In addition to death, physical injury, and loss of property, crime also has economic, social, and psychological costs.

ECONOMIC COSTS OF CRIME AND VIOLENCE

Conklin (1995, 62–63) suggests that the financial costs of crime can be classified into at least five categories. First are direct losses from crime such as the destruction of buildings through arson, of private property through vandalism, and of the environment by polluters. Second are costs associated with the transferring of property. Bank robbers, car thieves, and embezzlers have all taken property from its rightful owner at tremendous expense to the victim and society. For example, Meyer and Underwood (1994) report that in 1993 computer thieves stole nearly $2 billion worth of copyrighted software programs over the Internet. Additionally, employee theft and shoplifting may add

The financial costs of crime include direct economic losses from crimes such as the destruction of private property through vandalism.

as much as 15 percent to the cost of retail merchandise, victimizing all consumers (Beirne and Messerschmidt 1995).

A third major cost of crime is that associated with criminal violence, such as the loss of productivity of injured workers and the medical expenses of victims. For example, the cost of treating firearm injuries in the United States exceeds $4 billion a year (Thompson and Johnson 1993). Fourth are the costs associated with the production and sale of illegal goods and services, that is, illegal expenditures. The expenditure of money on drugs, gambling, and prostitution diverts funds away from the legitimate economy and enterprises and lowers property values in high crime neighborhoods.

The criminal justice system is also costly. During the 1980s, the state and federal prison population doubled. In 1994, more than a million and a half people were behind bars in the United States (U.S. Dept. of Justice 1995b) at a cost of $15,000 a year per prisoner. The cost of building a new prison is $60,000 per inmate. The cost to U.S. taxpayers of incarcerating offenders is nearly $20 billion a year (reported in Hewlett 1992).

What is the total economic cost of crime? One estimate suggests that the total cost of crime and violence in the United States is more than $450 billion a year (National Research Council 1994). While costs from "street crimes" are staggering, the costs from "crimes in the suites" such as tax evasion, fraud, false advertising, and antitrust violations are estimated to be three times higher (Conklin 1995, 81).

SOCIAL AND PSYCHOLOGICAL COSTS OF CRIME AND VIOLENCE

Crime and violence entail social and psychological, as well as economic, costs. A *Newsweek* poll of children aged ten to seventeen found that over half of white children and two-thirds of minority children were worried about some family member becoming a victim of violent crime (Morganthau 1993). In the same poll, 34 percent of minority children and 16 percent of white children said they did not feel safe from violent crime in their neighborhood after dark. Violence and fear of violence in homes, schools, and communities produce psychological trauma that impedes the social and educational development of children. These social and psychological consequences of crime and violence contribute to an escalating cycle that further increases crime and violence. Fear of crime and violence also affects community life:

> If frightened citizens remain locked in their homes instead of enjoying public spaces, there is a loss of public and community life, as well as a loss of "social capital"—the family and neighborhood channels that transmit positive social values from one generation to the next. (National Research Council 1994, 5–6).

Consideration *The fear of crime sometimes leads to tragedy. In November 1994, fourteen-year-old Matilda Kaye Crabtree, playing a joke on her father, hid in a closet and made noises by pounding on the walls. There had been eight burglaries in the area in the last month, so Matilda's father, thinking a burglar was in the closet, grabbed his .357 caliber pistol. When Matilda jumped out of the closet and said "Boo," her father pulled the trigger and mistakenly killed his own daughter.*

White-collar crimes also take a social and psychological toll at both the individual and the societal level. Moore and Mills (1990, 414) state that the effects of white-collar crime include "(a) diminished faith in a free economy and in business leaders, (b) loss of confidence in political institutions, processes and leaders, and (c) erosion of public morality." Crime also causes personal pain and suffering, the destruction of families, lowered self-esteem, and shortened life expectancy and disease.

Responding to Crime and Violence: Policies and Programs

In 1994, the U.S. Senate passed a $30 billion crime bill. This bill authorized the building of thousands of new prison cells, established new crime-prevention programs, banned assault weapons, increased the number of capital crimes, and provided for the hiring of 100,000 new police officers. In addition to economic policies designed to reduce unemployment and poverty, numerous social policies and programs have already been initiated to alleviate the problem of crime and violence. These policies and programs are directed toward children at risk of being offenders, community crime prevention, media violence, alternative methods of conflict resolution, and criminal justice "get tough" policies.

YOUTH PROGRAMS

Recognizing the link between juvenile delinquency and adult criminality, many anticrime programs are directed toward at-risk youths. For example, Abolish Chronic Truancy (ACT) is a program in Los Angeles in which the prosecutor works closely with school administrators, teachers, parents, and students to deal with the problem of truancy (*Victory Over Violence* 1994). Other

The eight blunders that lead to violence in society: Wealth without Work Pleasure without Conscience Knowledge without Character Commerce without Morality Science without Humanity Worship without Sacrifice Politics without Principle Rights without Responsibilities —Mohandas K. Gandhi Indian nationalist leader and peace activist

I have an open mind on midnight basketball. Certainly, while someone's playing basketball they're not mugging you. At least there's a referee there to blow the whistle if they do. —Henry Hyde U.S. Representative

Youth recreation programs, such as the boys' and girls' clubs, are designed to keep young people "off the streets" and provide a safe and supportive environment offering activities that promote skill development and self-esteem.

Although we seem to go to extraordinarily expensive lengths to punish criminals, we are reluctant to spend money on programs that have proven effective at preventing youngsters from slipping into a life of crime in the first place.
—Sylvia Anne Hewlett
President of National Parenting Association

prevention strategies, including youth recreation programs such as Boys and Girls Clubs, are designed to keep young people "off the streets," provide a safe and supportive environment, and offer activities that promote skill development and self-esteem. According to Gest and Friedman (1994), housing projects with such clubs report 13 percent fewer juvenile crimes and a 25 percent decrease in the use of crack.

Some cities have approved curfews as a means of dealing with juvenile delinquency. In 1993, for example, the mayor of Phoenix enacted a curfew ordinance in an effort to reduce juvenile crime and protect teenage victims. Another trend in youth violence prevention is the establishment of conflict resolution and peer mediation programs in public and private schools. Such programs integrate conflict resolution training into the curriculum for students in grades K through 12. In addition, selected students are trained in mediation and are available to help their peers resolve disputes that erupt in school that might otherwise escalate into violence.

COMMUNITY PROGRAMS

Neighborhood watch programs involve local residents in crime-prevention strategies. For example, MAD DADS in Omaha, Nebraska, patrol the streets in high crime areas of the city on weekend nights, providing positive adult role models for troubled children. Members also report crime and drug sales to police, paint over gang graffiti, organize gun buy-back programs, and counsel incarcerated fathers. Some communities also offer alternative dispute resolution centers. These centers encourage community members who are involved in a conflict to meet with mediators to discuss their conflicts and try to find a mutually agreeable resolution. Most cases that are mediated involve individuals who are referred by the court for relatively minor charges, such as trespassing, harassing phone calls, damage to personal property, and assault. If the individuals resolve their dispute in mediation, the charges are dropped, and they do not have to reappear in court. Mediation may help resolve disputes that would otherwise escalate into violence. Unlike the court process, mediation offers disputants the opportunity to discuss and resolve the issues that led to the violation, thereby preventing further conflicts.

MEDIA VIOLENCE

Violence is portrayed in music lyrics, music videos, video games, cartoons, television series, and movies. A child watching an average amount of television will see nearly 20,000 murders and 80,000 assaults by the age of thirteen (Murray 1993). Such media images may desensitize individuals to violence and serve as models for violent behavior. Exposure to television violence is associated with increased aggressive behavior and decreased sensitivity to the pain and suffering of others (Comstock 1993; Murray 1993).

In response to public concern over television violence, in 1993 television networks voluntarily decided to broadcast parental advisories before violent programming and to send similar advisories to newspapers and magazines that publish TV listings. At the Harvard Center for Health Communications, director Jay Winsten collaborates with entertainment industry executives to promote anti-violence in popular music and television programming. The Center for Health Communications, whose goal is "to mobilize the immense power of mass communication to improve human health," also uses the media to address other social problems such as drug abuse, teen pregnancy, and drunken driving (Rubin 1995, A5). One of the Center's recent campaigns, called "Squash It," aims to teach kids that it is cool to walk away from a confrontation. "Squash it" is an African-American street term for "Back off, let's not fight" (Rubin 1995).

CRIMINAL JUSTICE POLICY

The criminal justice system is based on the principle of **deterrence,** that is, the use of harm or the threat of harm to prevent unwanted behaviors. Thus, the recent emphasis on "get tough" measures holds that maximizing punishment will increase deterrence and cause crime rates to decrease. Research indicates, however, that the effectiveness of deterrence is a function of not only the severity of the punishment, but of the certainty and swiftness of the punishment as well. Further, "get tough" policies create other criminal justice problems including overcrowded prisons and, consequently, the need for plea bargaining and early release programs.

Capital Punishment With capital punishment, the State (the federal government or a state) takes the life of a person as punishment for a crime. Methods of executions include electrocution, lethal injection, the gas chamber, and hanging. States differ in the types of offenses for which capital punishment may be administered and the age at which a person becomes legally eligible for execution. Currently, thirteen states do not have the death penalty (NAACP Legal Defense and Educational Fund 1993). In this chapter's *The Human Side*, Robert Johnson, a professor at American University, describes his reaction as "witness to an execution".

Proponents of capital punishment argue that executions of convicted murderers are necessary to convey the public disapproval and intolerance for such

I feel morally and intellectually obligated to concede that the death penalty experiment has failed.
—Justice Harry Blackmun
U.S. Supreme Court

National Data: Since the 1930s, almost 4,000 people have been executed in the United States.
SOURCE: Smith 1995.
More than 2,800 inmates live on death row in American prisons.
SOURCE: Kaplan 1994.

WITNESS TO AN EXECUTION

At 10:58 the prisoner entered the death chamber. He was, I knew from my research, a man with a checkered, tragic past. He had been grossly abused as a child, and went on to become grossly abusive of others. I was told he could not describe his life, from childhood on, without talking about confrontations in defense of a precarious sense of self—at home, in school, on the streets, in the prison yard. Belittled by life and choking with rage, he was hungry to be noticed. Paradoxically, he had found his moment in the spotlight. . . .

En route to the chair, the prisoner stumbled slightly, as if the momentum of the event had overtaken him. Were he not held securely by two officers, one at each elbow, he might have fallen. . . . Once the prisoner was seated, again with help, the officers strapped him into the chair.

Arms, legs, stomach, chest, and head were secured in a matter of seconds. Electrodes were attached to the cap holding his head and to the strap holding his exposed right leg. A leather mask was placed over his face. The last officer mopped the prisoner's brow, then touched his hand in a gesture of farewell. . . .

The strapped and masked figure sat before us, utterly alone, waiting to be killed . . . waiting for a blast of electricity that would extinguish his life. Endless seconds passed. His last act was to swallow, nervously, pathetically, with his Adam's apple bobbing. I was struck by the

heinous crimes. Those against capital punishment believe that no one, including the State, has the right to take another person's life and that putting convicted murderers behind bars for life is a "social death" that conveys the necessary societal disapproval.

Proponents of capital punishment also argue that it deters individuals from committing murder. Critics of capital punishment hold, however, that since most homicides are situational, and are not planned, offenders do not consider the consequences of their actions before they commit the offense. Critics also point out that the United States has a much higher murder rate than Western European nations that do not practice capital punishment and that death sentences are racially discriminatory. Supreme Court Justice Harry Blackmun argued that the American system of capital punishment is unconstitutional because it is applied unfairly, arbitrarily, and with racial bias (Kaplan 1994).

Capital punishment advocates suggest that executing a convicted murderer relieves the taxpayer of the costs involved in housing, feeding, guarding, and providing medical care for inmates. Opponents of capital punishment

National Data: In 1993, almost half of the inmates on death row were minorities: 39 percent were black and 10 percent represented other racial or ethnic backgrounds; 51 percent were white.

SOURCE: NAACP Legal Defense and Educational Fund 1993.

simple movement then, and can't forget it even now. It told me, as nothing else did, that in the prisoner's restrained body, behind that mask, lurked a fellow human being who, at some level, however primitive, knew or sensed himself to be moments from death.

... Finally, the electricity hit him. His body stiffened spasmodically, though only briefly. A thin swirl of smoke trailed away from his head and then dissipated quickly. The body remained taut, with the right foot raised slightly at the heel, seemingly frozen there. A brief pause, then another minute of shock. When it was over, the body was flaccid and inert.

Three minutes passed while the officials let the body cool. (Immediately after the execution, I'm told, the body would be too hot to touch and would blister anyone who did.)

All eyes were riveted to the chair; I felt trapped in my witness seat, at once transfixed and yet eager for release. I can't recall any clear thoughts from that moment. One of the death watch officers later volunteered that he shared this experience of staring blankly at the execution scene. Had the prisoner's mind been mercifully blank before the end? I hope so.

The physician listened for a heartbeat. Hearing none, he turned to the warden and said, "This man has expired." The warden, speaking to the Director, solemnly intoned: "Mr. Director, the court order has been fulfilled." ...

SOURCE: Robert Johnson, 1989. "'This Man Has Expired': Witness to an Execution." *Commonweal*, January 13, 9–15. Copyright by Commonweal Foundation. Reprinted with permission.

argue that the principles that decide life and death issues should not be determined by financial considerations. In addition, taking care of convicted murderers for life may actually be less costly than sentencing them to death, due to the lengthy and costly appeal process for capital punishment cases (Garey 1985).

Nevertheless, those in favor of capital punishment argue that it protects society by preventing convicted individuals from committing another crime, including the murder of another inmate or prison official. Opponents contend, however, that capital punishment may result in innocent people being sentenced to death. In 1977, Randall Dale Adams was convicted of murdering a Dallas police officer and came within a week of being executed. The Texas Court of Appeals overturned his conviction in 1989 after discovering that the prosecutors in the case had suppressed evidence and knowingly used perjured testimony to convict Adams (Haines 1992). According to Radelet, Bedeau, and Putnam (1992), at least 139 innocent people were sentenced to death in the United States between 1985 and 1990. Twenty-three of these people were executed. Haines (1992, 135) suggests that "these miscarriages or near miscar-

The legal system is greatly overestimated in its ability to sort out innocent from guilty.
—Stephen Bright
Visiting lecturer
Yale Law School

riages of justice will likely prove to be among the more powerful arguments for abolishing capital punishment in coming years."

> **Consideration** *Although the death penalty is common throughout the world, most Western nations have virtually abandoned its use. China, Russia, South Africa and most countries in the Mideast, as well as the United States, continue to practice capital punishment. Zimring and Hawkins (1986) suggest that nations that use capital punishment tend to disregard human rights. Amnesty International lists the United States as a nation with governmental policies that violate human rights, primarily because the United States uses the death penalty.*

Rehabilitation versus Incapacitation Another important debate focuses on the primary purpose of the criminal justice system: Is it to rehabilitate offenders or to incapacitate them through incarceration? Both **rehabilitation** and **incapacitation** are concerned with recidivism rates or the extent to which criminals commit another crime. Advocates of rehabilitation believe recidivism can be reduced by changing the criminal whereas proponents of incapacitation think it can best be reduced by placing the offender in prison so that he or she is unable to commit further crimes against the general public.

Societal fear of crime has lead to a public emphasis on incapacitation and a demand for tougher sentences, a reduction in the use of probation and parole, and support of a "three strikes and you're out" policy. While incapacitation is clearly enhanced by longer prison sentences, rehabilitation may not be. Rehabilitation assumes that criminal behavior is caused by sociological, psychological, and/or biological forces rather than being a product of free will. If such forces can be identified, the necessary change can be instituted. Rehabilitation programs include education and job training, individual and group therapy, substance abuse counseling, and behavior modification. While the evaluation of rehabilitation programs is difficult and results are mixed, incapacitation must of necessity be a temporary measure. Unless all criminals are sentenced to life, at some point they will be returned to society.

Gun Control One of the most passionately debated issues in America is gun control. Those against gun control argue that citizens have the right to own guns and that the nearly 20,000 firearm regulations thus far enacted have not reduced the incidence of violence. After reviewing the research literature, Wright (1995) suggests that "a compelling case for stricter gun controls is difficult to make on empirical grounds and that solutions to the problems of crime and violence in this nation will have to be found elsewhere" (p. 496).

Advocates of gun control insist that the 67 million handguns owned by U.S. citizens contribute to the over 640,000 violent crimes committed with handguns annually (Gibbs 1993). In 1993, 70 percent of murders in the United States were committed with guns (*Statistical Abstract of the United States*, 1995, Table 312). In addition, guns contribute to accidental injury and death, often of friends and family members. Fourteen-year-old Matilda Kaye Crabtree, mentioned earlier, was mistakenly shot by her father, who thought she was a burglar. Matilda's tragic and accidental death would not have occurred if her father had not owned a gun. After a seven-year battle with the National Rifle Association (NRA), gun control advocates achieved a small vic-

The reformative effect of punishment is a belief that dies hard, chiefly, I think, because it is so satisfying to our sadistic impulses.
—Bertrand Russell
Philospher

To do justice, to break the cycle of violence, to make Americans safer, prisons need to offer inmates a chance to heal like a human, not merely heel like a dog.
—Richard Stratton
Former prison inmate

International Data:
Although Switzerland has one of the highest rates of gun ownership in the world, it is virtually "crime-free".
SOURCE: Bierre and Messerschmidt 1995.

tory in 1993 when Congress passed the **Brady Bill.** This law requires a five-day waiting period on handgun purchases so that sellers can screen buyers for criminal records or mental instability. The new regulation has not always been effective. In the fall of 1994, a gunman fired at the White House with a weapon he had recently purchased. He was a convicted felon but lied about his name, and the gun seller did not conduct the required search.

UNDERSTANDING
CRIME AND VIOLENCE

What can we conclude from the information presented in this chapter? Research on crime and violence supports the contentions of both functionalists and conflict theorists. The inequality in society, along with the emphasis on material well-being and corporate profit, produces societal strains and individual frustrations. Poverty, unemployment, urban decay, and substandard schools, the symptoms of social inequality, in turn lead to the development of criminal subcultures and definitions favorable to law violation. Further, the continued weakening of social bonds between members of society and individuals and society as a whole, the labeling of some acts and actors as "deviant," and the differential treatment of minority groups at the hands of the criminal justice system encourage criminal behavior.

While crime and violence constitute major social problems in American society, they are also symptoms of other social problems such as poverty and economic inequality, racial discrimination, drug addiction, an overburdened educational system, and troubled families. The criminal justice system continues to struggle to find effective and just measures to deal with crime and criminal offenders. Many citizens and politicians have embraced the idea that society should "get tough on crime." Get tough measures include building more prisons and imposing lengthier mandatory prison sentences on criminal offenders. Advocates of harsher prison sentences argue that "getting tough on crime" makes society safer by keeping criminals off the streets and deterring potential criminals from committing crime. But skeptics are not convinced. As one argues:

> *Prison . . . has a minimal impact on crime because it is a response after the fact, a mop-up operation. It doesn't work. The idea of punishing the few to deter the many is counterfeit because potential criminals either think they're not going to get caught or they're so emotionally desperate or psychologically distressed that they don't care about the consequences of their actions. (Rideau 1994, 80)*

Prison sentences may not only be ineffective in preventing crime, they may also promote it by creating an environment in which prisoners learn criminal behavior, values, and attitudes from each other.

Rather than get tough on crime after the fact, some advocate getting serious about prevention:

> *The only effective way to curb crime is for society to work to prevent the criminal act in the first place. . . . Our youngsters must be taught to respect the humanity of others and to handle disputes without violence. It is es-*

National Data: A national poll revealed that almost half (43 percent) of the respondents had some type of gun in their home. The same poll revealed that 70 percent of the respondents favored stricter gun control laws and 23 percent favored a law that would make it illegal for any private citizen to own a handgun for any purpose.

SOURCE: Gibbs 1993.

National Data: In 1992, 1,409 U.S. residents lost their lives to accidents involving firearms.

SOURCE: *Statistical Abstract of the United States,* 1995, Table 134.

It is better to prevent crimes than to punish them.
—Cesare Beccaria
Italian economist

sential to educate and equip them with the skills to pursue their life ambitions in a meaningful way. As a community, we must address the adverse life circumstances that spawn criminality. (Rideau 1994, 80).

Reemphasizing the values of honesty, responsibility, and civic virtue is a basic line of prevention with which most agree. In a 1994 poll, 11 percent of Americans, compared to 1 percent in 1989, responded that moral breakdown is the primary cause of crime today (Sherman 1994). Community of Caring is a nationwide program of value socialization in which public school teachers emphasize caring, trust, respect, and responsibility (Henry 1995, D1). As a nation, our focus should be on the moral deficit as well as on the budget deficit. Sociologist Amitai Etzioni observed, "No society can survive moral anarchy" (Potok and Stone 1995, a1).

William DeJong (1994) of the Harvard School of Public Health echoes a similar sentiment concerning violence prevention:

If we are truly committed to preventing violence, we must do more than teach individual children how to survive in the dysfunctional environments in which they are growing up. We must also strive to change those environments by addressing the broader social, cultural, institutional, and physical forces that are at work. (p. 9)

> *We have to do something to try to change or we will be destroyed by violence.*
> —Arun Gandhi
> Peace activist

CRITICAL THINKING

1. Explain why crime rates in the United States began to rise in the 1960s as baby-boom teenagers entered high school.
2. Discuss why the United States has the highest rate of violent crime of all industrialized nations.
3. Identify the most and least useful theoretical frameworks for explaining homicide, burglary, and rape. Explain your choices.

KEY TERMS

crime	index offenses	deterrence
strain theory	acquaintance rape	rehabilitation
subcultural theory	victimless crimes	incapacitation
control theory	organized crime	Brady Bill
labeling theory	white-collar crime	
differential association	computer crime	

REFERENCES

Adler, Freda, Gerhard Mueller, and William Laufer. 1995. *Criminology,* 2d ed. New York: McGraw-Hill. (May).

Alba, Richard, John Logan, and Paul Bellair. 1994. "Living with Crime: The Implications of Racial/Ethnic Differences in Suburban Location." *Social Forces* 73 (2): 395–434.

Albanese, Jay S. 1995. "Organized Crime: The Mafia Mystique." In *Criminology: A Contemporary Handbook,* 2d ed., ed. Joseph F. Sheley, pp. 231–47. Belmont, Calif.: Wadsworth.

Albanese, Jay , and Robert D. Pursley. 1993. *Crime in America: Some Existing and Emerging Problems.* Englewood Cliffs, N.J.: Prentice-Hall.

Anderson, Elijah. 1994(May). "The Code of the Streets: Sociology of Urban Violence." *The Atlantic* 273(5):80–91.

Beck, Melinda, Peter Katel, Vern E. Smith, and Ginny Carroll. 1993. "In a State of Terror." *Newsweek,* September 27, 40–41.

Becker, Howard S. 1963. *Outsiders: Studies in the Sociology of Deviance.* New York: Free Press.

Beirne, Piers, and James Messerschmidt. 1995. *Criminology* 2d ed. Fort Worth: Harcourt Brace.

Brokaw, Tom. 1994. "Diesel Fuel?" NBC Nightly News. November 23.

Clarke, Ronald, and Patricia Harris. 1992. "Auto Theft and Its Prevention," In Michael Tonry, ed., *Crime and Justice: A Review of Research,* vol 16, p. 1–54. Chicago: University of Chicago Press.

Comstock, George. 1993. "The Medium and the Society: The Role of Television in American Life." In *Children and Television: Images in a Changing Sociocultural World,* ed. Gordon L. Berry and Joy Keiko Asamen, pp. 117–31. Newbury Park, Calif.: Sage Publications.

Conklin, John E. 1995. *Criminology,* 5th ed. Boston: Allyn & Bacon.

Corporate Crime Reporter. 1987. "IRS Not Set Up to Monitor Whether Dividend Income to Business Is Being Reported." April 13, 5–6.

DeJong, William. 1994. "School-Based Violence Prevention: From the Peaceable School to the Peaceable Neighborhood."*Forum,* pp. 8–14. Washington, D.C.: National Institute for Dispute Resolution.

Elliot, D., and S. Ageton. 1980. "Reconciling Race and Class Differences in Self-Reported and Official Estimates of Delinquency." *American Sociological Review* 45: 95–110.

Erikson, Kai T. 1966. *Wayward Puritans.* New York: John Wiley & Sons.

Federal Bureau of Investigation (FBI). 1992. *Crime in the United States, 1991: Uniform Crime Reports.* Washington, D.C.: U.S. Government Printing Office.

———. 1993. *Crime in the United States, 1992: Uniform Crime Reports.* Washington, D.C.: U.S. Government Printing Office.

Felson, Marcus. 1994. *Crime and Everyday Life: Insight and Implications for Society.* Thousand Oaks, Calif.: Pine Forge Press.

Filner, Judith. 1994. "Editor's Note." *FORUM,* p. 1. Washington, D.C.: National Institute for Dispute Resolution.

Fingerhut, Lois A. and Joel C. Kleinman. 1990. "International and Interstate Comparisons of Homicide among Young Males." *Journal of the American Medical Association* 263 (June 27): 3292-3295

Garey, M. 1985. "The Cost of Taking a Life: Dollars and Sense of the Death Penalty." *U.C. Davis Law Review* 18: 1221–73.

Gest, Ted, 1994. "Violence in America." *U.S. News and World Report,* January 17, 22–33.

Gest, Ted, and Dorian Friedman. 1994. "The New Crime Wave." *U.S. News and World Report,* August 29, 26–28.

Gibbs, Nancy. 1993. "Up in Arms." *Time,* December 20, 19–26.

Haines, Herb. 1992. "Flawed Executions, the Anti-Death Penalty Movement, and the Politics of Capital Punishment." *Social Problems* 39(2): 125–38.

Henry, Tamara 1995. "Values Enter Classroom Curriculum." *USA Today,* April 5, d1.

Hewlett, Sylvia Anne. 1992. *When the Bough Breaks: The Cost of Neglecting Our Children.* New York: HarperPerennial.

Hills, Stuart. 1987. "Introduction." In *Corporate Violence: Injury and Death for Profit,* ed. Stuart Hills, p. 1–7. Rowman Publishing Co.

Hirschi, Travis. 1969. *Causes of Delinquency.* Berkeley: University of California Press.

Jacobs, David. 1988. "Corporate Economic Power and the State: A Longitudinal Assessment of Two Explanations." *American Journal of Sociology* 93: 852–81.

Kaplan, David A. 1994. "Death Be Not Proud at the Court." *Newsweek,* March 7, 52.

_____. 1994. "Catch-22 at the High Court." *Newsweek,* April 11, 68.

Koss, M. P., C. A. Gidycz, and S. L. Cox. 1988. "Stranger And Acquaintance Rape." *Psychology of Women Quarterly* 12:1–24.

Krohn, Marvin D., and James L. Massey., 1980. "Social Control and Delinquent Behavior: An Examination of the Elements of Social Bond." *Sociological Quarterly* 21: 529–44.

Lesieur, Henry R., and Michael Welch. 1995. "Vice Crimes: Individual Choices and Social Controls." In *Criminology: A Contemporary Handbook,* 2d ed., ed. Joseph F. Sheley, p. 201–29. Belmont, Calif.: Wadsworth.

Liska, A., and B. Warner. 1991. "Functions of Crime: A Paradoxical Process." *American Journal of Sociology* 96: 1441–63.

Merton, Robert. 1957. "Social Structure and Anomie." In *Social Theory and Social Structure.* Glencoe, Ill.: Free Press.

Meyer, Michael, and Anne Underwood. 1994. "Crimes of the 'Net.'" *Newsweek,* November 14, 46–47.

Monk, Richard C. 1993. "Is the Victims' Rights Movement Succeeding?" In *Taking Sides: Clashing Views on Controversial Issues in Crime and Criminology,* 3d ed., ed. Richard C. Monk, p. 286–87. Guilford, Conn.: Dushkin Publishing Group.

Moore, Elizabeth, and Michael Mills. 1990. "The Neglected Victims and Unexamined Costs of White Collar Crime." *Crime and Delinquency* 36: 408–18.

Morganthau, Tom. 1993. "The New Frontier for Civil Rights." *Newsweek,* November 29, 65–66.

Mosher, Clayton, and John Hagan. 1994. "Constituting Class and Crime in Upper Canada: The Sentencing of Narcotics Offenders, circa 1908–1953." *Social Forces* 72(3): 613–41.

Murray, John P. 1993. "The Developing Child in a Multimedia Society." In *Children and Television: Images in a Changing Sociocultural World,* ed. by Gordon L. Berry and Joy Keiko Asamen, pp. 9–22. Newbury Park, Calif.: Sage Publications.

NAACP Legal and Educational Defense Fund. 1993. *Death Row* USA (Spring).

National Research Council. 1994. *Violence in Urban America: Mobilizing a Response.* Washington, D.C.: National Academy Press.

Parker, Robert Nash. 1995. "Violent Crime." In *Criminology: A Contemporary Handbook*, 2d ed., ed. Joseph F. Sheley, pp. 169–85, Belmont, Calif.: Wadsworth.

Potok, Mark, and Andrea Stone. 1995. "Values Get a Chance at Comeback." *USA Today*, February 3–5, 1A, 2A.

Press, Aric, John McCormick, and Pat Wingert. 1994. "A Crime as American as a Colt .45." *Newsweek*, August 15, 22–23.

Radelet, M. L., H. A. Bedeau, and C. E. Putnam. 1992. *In Spite of Innocence: Erroneous Convictions in Capital Cases* Boston: Northeastern University Press.

Rideau, William. 1994. "Why Prisons Don't Work." *Time*, March 21, 80.

Rubin, Amy Magaro. 1995. "Using Pop Culture to Fight Teen Violence." *The Chronicle of Higher Education*, July 21: p. A5.

Sampson, Robert J., and John H. Laub. 1993. *Crime in the Making: Pathways and Turning Points through Life*. Cambridge, Mass.: Harvard University Press.

Sanday, P. R. 1981. "The Socio-cultural Context of Rape: A Cross-cultural Study." *Journal of Social Issues* 37: 5–27.

Shannon, Elaine. 1995. "Crime: Safer Streets yet Greater Fear." *Time*, January 30, 63–67.

Sherman, Rorie. 1994. "Crime's Toll on the U.S.: Fear, Despair and Guns." *National Law Journal*, April 18, A1–A20.

Smith, M. Dwayne. 1995. "The Death Penalty in America." In *Criminology: A Contemporary Handbook*, 2d ed., ed. Joseph F. Sheley, p. 557–72. Belmont, Calif.: Wadsworth.

Statistical Abstract of the United States: 1995, 115th ed. U.S. Bureau of the Census. Washington, D.C.: U.S. Government Printing Office.

Steffensmeier, Darrell, and Emilie Allan. 1995. "Criminal Behavior: Gender and Age." In *Criminology: A Contemporary Handbook*, 2d ed., ed. Joseph F. Sheley, p. 83–113. Belmont, Calif.: Wadsworth.

Sullivan, John J., and Joseph L. Victor. 1995. "Crime in the United States 1993." In *Criminal Justice 95/96*, pp. 228–36. Guilford, Conn.: Dushkin Publishing Group.

Sutherland, Edwin H. 1939. *Criminology*. Philadelphia: Lippincott.

Thio, Alex. 1988. *Deviant Behavior*, 3d ed. New York: Harper & Row.

Thompson, Dick, and Julie Johnson. 1993. "The Exploding Costs of Gunfire." *Time*, October: 11, 59.

Tittle, Charles. 1980. *Sanctions and Social Deviance*. New York: Praeger.

_____. 1993. "Highlights of 20 years of Surveying Crime Victims." Bureau of Justice Statistics. Washington, D. C.: U. S. Government Printing Office (NCJ-144525).

_____. 1995 (May). "Juvenile Court Statistics: 1992." Office of Juvenile Justice and Delinquency Prevention. Washington, D.C.: U.S. Government Printing Office.

_____. 1995b. "Prisoners in 1994." Report NCJ-151614. Washington, D.C.: U.S. Government Printing Office.

Van Dijk, Jan, and Patricia Mayhew. 1993. "Criminal Victimization in the Industrialized World." In *Understanding Crime: Experiences of Crime and Crime Control*, pp. 1–49. Rome: United Nations Publication No. 49.

Victory Over Violence. 1994. New York: Metropolitan Life Insurance Co., Inc., NYC, NY 10010.

Williams, Linda. 1984. "The Classic Rape: When Do Victims Report?" *Social Problems* 31: 459–67.

Winsberg, Morton. 1994. "Crime in the Suburbs: Fact and Fiction." *American Demographics* 16(4): 11–12.

Wolfgang, Marvin, Robert Figlio, and Thorstein Sellin. 1972. *Delinquency in a Birth Cohort*. Chicago: University of Chicago Press.

Wright, James D. 1995. "Guns, Crime, and Violence." In *Criminology: A Contemporary Handbook*, 2d. ed., ed. Joseph F. Sheley, pp. 495–513. Belmont, Calif.: Wadsworth.

Zimring, F. E., and G. Hawkins. 1986. *Capital Punishment and the American Agenda*. Cambridge: Cambridge University Press.

5

Family Problems

IS IT TRUE?

Due to mandatory sex education, the United States has one of the lowest rates of teenage childbirth of any industrialized nation (p. 147).

About half of all U.S. children will experience the breakup of their parents' marriage (p. 145).

The United States has the highest divorce rate in the world (p. 142).

About 30 percent of all U.S. births are to unmarried women (p. 147).

Under U.S. law, a husband forcing his wife to have sex is not considered to be an act of rape (p. 138).

ANS: I. F 2. T 3. T 4. T 5. F

In the fall of 1994, the nation was stunned by the confession of Susan Smith of Union, South Carolina, that she had killed her sons, three-year-old Michael and fourteen-month-old Alex, by strapping them with their seat belts into the family Mazda and pushing the car down a boat ramp into Lake John D. Long. Although the Smith marriage had been troubled by infidelity and divorce, the killing of the boys was the ultimate example of the extent to which family problems can affect individuals, families, and communities. A nation grieved, and, with its collective anger and sorrow, came a heightened concern for family problems and for the health, safety, and happiness of family members.

Politicians often point to the "breakdown" of the family as one of the primary social problems in the world today—a problem of such magnitude that it leads to such secondary social problems as crime, poverty, and substance abuse. Although strengthening family relationships and values is frequently offered as the principal solution of such problems, sociologists argue that family problems and their solutions are rooted in the structure and culture of society. For example, the structure of the economic institution requires many parents to work long hours, often without benefits. Without a national child care system, such as those in France and Sweden, employed parents of young children must often leave their offspring with inadequate or no supervision. Parents and spouses who are stressed by long work hours, poor working conditions, and little pay often bring their stress home, contributing to child abuse, spouse abuse, and divorce.

Families in the United States are also influenced by cultural factors. For example, the American value of **individualism,** which stresses the importance of individual happiness, contributes to divorce as spouses leave marriages to pursue their individual goals. In other countries, such as India, the cultural value of **familism** encourages spouses to put their family's welfare above their individual and personal needs.

In this chapter we look at some of the major social problems facing American families—domestic violence, divorce, unmarried childbirth, and teenage parenthood. Prior and subsequent chapters in this text discuss other problems facing families including poverty, lack of affordable housing, illness and inadequate health care, drug abuse, inequality in education, and prejudice and discrimination.

The United States has long been known as the world's most individualistic society.
—David Popenoe
Sociologist

The Social Context: American Families in Transition

Families are shaped by the society and historical context in which they exist. Next, we look at how the Industrial Revolution influenced the family and some of the variations in the American family today.

Before the Industrial Revolution, large families were common in the United States. In 1994, only 10 percent of U.S. families had three or more children (*Statistical Abstract of the United States: 1995*, Table 74).

EFFECTS OF THE INDUSTRIAL REVOLUTION ON THE FAMILY

The **Industrial Revolution** refers to the social and economic changes that occurred when machines and factories became the primary means for the production of goods. In the United States, industrialization took place during the early and mid-1800s and had profound influences on the family. Before industrialization, a family functioned as an economic unit that produced goods and services for its own consumption. Parents and children worked together in or near the home to meet the survival needs of the family. As the United States became industrialized, men and women increasingly left the home to sell their labor for wages. The family was no longer a self-sufficient unit that determined its own work hours. Rather, employers determined where and when family members would work. Whereas children in preindustrialized America worked on farms and contributed to the economic survival of the family, children in industrialized America became economic liabilities rather than assets. Child labor laws and mandatory education removed children from the labor force and lengthened their dependence on parental support. Soon, both parents had to work away from the home to support their children.

Increased urbanization was another effect of the Industrial Revolution as cities grew up around factories. Living space in the cities was scarce and expensive, which contributed to a decline in the birthrate and smaller families. Unsupervised children roamed the streets increasing the potential for crime and delinquency.

As the cities grew, transportation systems developed within and between cities. These new modes of transport made it possible for family members to travel to work sites far from the home and to move away from extended kin.

With increased mobility, many extended families became separated into smaller nuclear family units consisting of parents and their children. As parents moved away from extended kin and left the home to earn wages, children had less adult supervision and moral guidance.

> **Consideration**   Many Americans attribute social problems to a lack of moral training in the home. A USA Today/CNN/Gallup poll found that 89 percent of the respondents believed that "lack of moral training at home" was the most important factor causing the rapid increase in crime (Meddis and Davis 1993). Children in single-parent or dual-earner families may have limited opportunities to spend time with their parents and thus less time to receive moral guidance from them. Parental moral guidance is also made more difficult by the violence, casual and exploitative sex, and alcohol and drug use that children witness daily on television.

Industrialization also affected the father's role in the family. Employment outside the home prevented men from playing a primary role in child care giving and other domestic activities. The contribution men made to the household became primarily economic. The absence of fathers from the home remains a significant concern today (Blankenhorn 1995).

Finally, the advent of industrialization, urbanization, and mobility is associated with a rise in individualism. When family members functioned together as an economic unit, they were dependent on each other for survival and were concerned about what was good for the family. Some have argued that the focus has since shifted from the needs of the family to self-fulfillment or individualism.

According to Hewlett (1992), the quest for personal fulfillment has contributed to high divorce rates, absent fathers, and parents spending less time with their children. Hewlett suggests that:

> *Like it or not, there are trade-offs between personal fulfillment and family well-being. Creating a home and raising children are supremely time-intensive activities which tend to claim large amounts of adult energy in the prime of life, energy that cannot then be spent on advancing a career, playing golf, or taking aerobics classes. (p. 32)*

VARIATIONS IN U.S. FAMILIES AND HOUSEHOLDS

The U.S. Bureau of the Census defines a **family** as a group of two or more persons related by birth, marriage, or adoption who reside together. As Figure 5.1 illustrates, over the last few decades, two-parent families have declined, while single-parent families have increased.

Another family variation that has increased in recent decades is the blended or stepfamily. A blended family consists of remarried spouses with at least one of the spouses having a child from a previous relationship. Estimates suggest that by the year 2000, blended families will outnumber all other family types in the United States (Darden and Zimmerman 1992).

Other variations include households that are not considered families by the U.S. Census Bureau. A **household** consists of all persons who occupy a housing unit, such as a house or apartment. Although all families form households, not all households are families. Nonfamily households may consist of one person who lives alone, two or more people as roommates, and cohabiting heterosexual or homosexual couples involved in a committed relationship. The percent-

National Data: Women are five times more likely than men to be a single parent; African Americans are almost three times more likely than whites to be single parents.

SOURCE: Ahlburg and De Vita 1992.

National Data: In 1990, about 16 percent of married-couple family households with children were blended families.

SOURCE: *Statistical Abstract of the United States: 1995*, Table 77.

Males are rewarded in our society for emphasizing their careers and making money over spending time with their children. However, many fathers balance their job responsibilities with quality family time.

age of U.S. households that consist of nonfamily members has increased from 19 percent in 1970 to 29 percent in 1994 (U.S. Census Bureau 1995)).

As nonfamily households have become more common, some family scholars have redefined the family to include nonrelated persons who reside together and who are economically, emotionally, and sexually interdependent (Scanzoni and Marsiglio 1993). Segments of U.S. society have begun to regard unmarried heterosexual cohabiting couples and homosexual couples as variations of the American family.

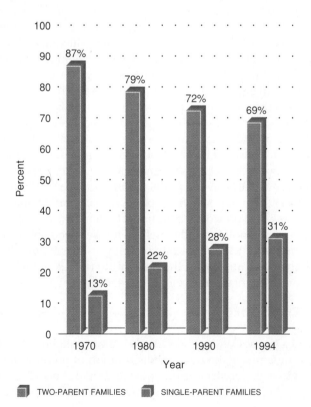

TWO-PARENT FAMILIES   SINGLE-PARENT FAMILIES

FIGURE 5.1
TWO-PARENT AND SINGLE-PARENT FAMILIES SINCE 1970
SOURCE: *Statistical Abstract of the United States: 1995*, 115th ed. Washington, D.C.: U.S. Bureau of the Census, Table 71.

In some U.S. cities and counties, heterosexual cohabiting couples as well as gay couples (with and without children) who apply for a **domestic partnership** designation are granted legal entitlements such as health insurance benefits and inheritance rights that have traditionally been reserved for married couples. In addition, some employers have begun to extend employee benefits to cohabiting partners of employees (Scherreik 1993).

Is the growing popularity of alternatives to the traditional nuclear family evidence that marriage and family have become less important to Americans? Although marriage and family forms have become diversified, marriage and family are still important to most Americans. Over 70 percent of first-year U.S. college students regard rearing a family as "essential" or "very important" (American Council on Education and University of California 1994). Yet even though many Americans share the goal of having a happy and enduring marriage and family, many do not achieve this goal. An examination of the sociological theories of the family will provide a framework for our discussion of various problems related to the family.

Sociological Theories of the Family

Researchers have developed various theories to explain different aspects of the family. Here we will look at three major sociological theories of the family—structural-functionalism, conflict theory, and symbolic interactionism.

STRUCTURAL-FUNCTIONALIST PERSPECTIVE

The structural-functionalist perspective of the family emphasizes that families perform several manifest functions that are important for the survival of society. Families replenish the population through reproduction and contribute to the socialization and education of youth. Well-functioning families also provide emotional and physical care for their members, as well as providing children with a sense of belonging. No other institution focuses so completely on fulfilling the affective needs of its members as does the family.

The structural-functionalist perspective is also concerned with how other institutions affect families. According to structural-functionalism, in order for the family to fulfill its role, it needs the support of other institutions. Families need schools that provide services for children with special needs and that incorporate interpersonal skills and moral training into the curriculum. Families need workplaces that pay sufficient wages to support families, require a shorter workweek, and provide flexible hours for parents, on-site day care, and other family-oriented policies and benefits. Families need politicians to legislate family supports including family planning clinics, affordable housing, health care, and day care. Ideally, these institutions, together with the family, provide for a well-balanced and functioning society.

CONFLICT PERSPECTIVE

Conflict theory focuses on how wealth and power influence marriages and families. Within families, the unequal distribution of power among women, men, and children may contribute to spouse and child abuse. The unequal distribution of wealth between men and women, with men traditionally earning more money than women, contributes to inequities in power and fosters economic dependence of wives on husbands. The term **patriarchy** refers to male-dominated families. Families have traditionally been dominated by men, with the wife taking her husband's name, family residence defined by the husband's place of work, and the standard of living dictated by the male's income.

Conflict theorists emphasize that through the purchase of houses, cars, and appliances, families represent the basic economic unit in society. Reproduction of workers also takes place in the family, as does socialization into the dominant U.S. economic ideology—capitalism. Because of the value of the family to a capitalistic society, the powerful and affluent have a vested interest in promoting the acceptability of the traditional family and the unacceptability of certain family forms. For example, homosexuals have fewer children (future workers), and communal families purchase fewer products and are less likely to extol the virtues of capitalism.

Conflict theorists also emphasize that social programs and policies that affect families are largely shaped by powerful and wealthy segments of society. For example, legislators use the policy of reducing public assistance to single mothers who have additional children as a means of discouraging nontraditional family forms. The interests of corporations and businesses are often in conflict with the needs of families. Corporations and businesses strenuously fought the passage of the 1993 Family Leave Act that guarantees employees of firms with more than fifty workers unpaid time off for parenting leave, illness or death of a family member, and elder care.

SYMBOLIC INTERACTIONIST PERSPECTIVE

As a microsociological approach, symbolic interactionism emphasizes that human behavior is largely dependent upon the meanings and definitions that emerge out of small group interaction. Divorce, for example, was once highly stigmatized and informally sanctioned through the criticism and rejection of divorced friends and relatives. As societal definitions of divorce became less negative, however, the divorce rate increased. The social meanings surrounding single parenthood, cohabitation, and delayed childbearing and marriage have changed in similar ways. As the definitions of each of these family variations became less negative, the behaviors became more common.

Symbolic interactionists also point to the effects of labeling on one's self-concept and the way the self-fulfilling prophecy can affect family members' behavior toward one another. The **self-fulfilling prophecy** implies that we behave according to the expectations of others. When spouses label each other in negative ways through verbal attacks and criticism, they may inadvertently facilitate negative behavior, such as alcohol abuse, infidelity, and abandonment. As a result of being criticized frequently by their partner, spouses may develop negative self-concepts, which in turn contribute to poor job performance, marital discord, and divorce. Mental health problems such as anxiety and depression also result from marital discord.

Children are especially vulnerable to the effects of being negatively labeled by their parents, stepparents, and other family members. When significant adults label children as "bad" or "stupid," the children internalize these labels and view themselves as "bad" or "stupid." For some children, a negative self-concept and the self-fulfilling prophecy contribute to violence, crime and delinquency, school failure, and mental health problems such as depression and anxiety. As the following section explains, painful criticism of spouses, children, and elders may constitute a form of domestic abuse.

Violence and Abuse in the Family

National Data: The National League of Cities estimates that as many as half of all wives will experience violence at some time in their marriage.
SOURCE: Gibbs 1993.

The trial of O. J. Simpson gave national visibility to the issue of domestic violence. Although marriage and family relationships provide many individuals with a sense of intimacy and well-being, for others, these relationships involve violence and abuse causing terror, pain, and, for some, death. Some social scientists believe that family violence is the number one social problem facing America today (Foster, Forsyth, and Herbert 1994, 137).

Domestic abuse can take various forms besides physical violence, including verbal abuse, nonverbal symbolic abuse, sexual abuse, and neglect. Verbal abuse, such as criticism, threats, and name calling, causes mental or psychological distress. *Nonverbal symbolic abuse* includes behaviors such as smashing an object or destroying personal property, tearing up a photograph, and not speaking to or answering a person (Straus and Sweet 1992, 347). **Neglect,** another form of abuse, includes failure to provide adequate attention and supervision, food and nutrition, hygiene, medical care, and a safe and clean living environment. Sexual abuse in the family involves forced or coerced sexual behavior by a family member.

VIOLENCE AND ABUSE IN MARRIAGE AND COHABITING RELATIONSHIPS

Unless we end the cult of silence and complacency toward the violence at the domestic core of our civilizations, we can't hope to end the biased crime and violence against races, religious groups, and nations.
—Daniela Gioseffi
Poet, novelist, activist

Although both men and women may be victims of abuse by intimate partners, domestic violence primarily involves female victims. According to the U.S. Department of Justice (1994), women experience over ten times as many incidents of violence by an intimate as men do. In 1992, 70 percent of the murder victims killed by intimates were female.

The rate and severity of violence are greater among cohabiting couples than between marital partners (Stets and Straus 1989). But both cohabiting and marital couples resort to verbal and nonverbal symbolic abuse more commonly than physical abuse (Straus and Sweet 1992).

Rape is another form of abuse that occurs in marital and cohabiting relationships. One survey found that 14 percent of married women in San Francisco reported that they had been sexually assaulted by their husbands (Russell 1990). Ten percent of married women in a Boston survey reported that they had been raped by their husbands (Finkelhor and Yllo 1988).

Some victims of domestic violence deny that they are being abused. The Abusive Behavior Inventory (see *Self and Society* on pp. 134–135) provides a way to assess the amount of abuse occurring in an adult relationship.

CHILD ABUSE

Child abuse refers to the "physical or mental injury, sexual abuse, negligent treatment, or maltreatment of a child under the age of eighteen by a person who is responsible for the child's welfare . . ." (Willis, Holden, and Rosenberg 1992, 2). The number of children who are physically abused, verbally abused, and/or neglected by their parents or caregivers is staggering. The numbers presented here reflect only the reported cases. Knudsen (1989) estimates that only one in seven cases is reported.

Twice as many cases of child neglect occur than cases of child physical and verbal abuse. In a review of the literature on child abuse, Lloyd and Emery (1993) note that boys are more likely than girls to experience abuse. Other factors associated with an increased risk of child abuse include the following (Krugman, Lenherr, Betz, and Fryer 1986; Oates, Davis, and Ryan 1983; Gelles and Conte 1990; Straus and Sweet 1992; Gelles 1992):

1. The pregnancy is premaritally conceived or unplanned, and the father does not want the child.
2. The child suffers from developmental disabilities or mental retardation.
3. Childrearing techniques are strict and harsh, providing little positive reinforcement for the child.
4. The parents are unemployed or economically disadvantaged.
5. The parents of the child abuse each other.
6. The parents of the child were themselves victims of child abuse.

Sexual abuse of a child by a family member involves sexual contact, or attempted sexual contact, including inappropriate kissing, fondling of the genitals, oral sex, and intercourse. Female children are more likely than male children to be sexually abused. A study of almost 4,000 intrafamilial child sex abuse cases revealed that 85 percent of the victims were female and 15 percent were male (Solomon 1992).

PARENT, SIBLING AND ELDER ABUSE

Spouse and child abuse are widely recognized social problems, in part due to the media coverage of these issues. Other forms of family abuse that are less publicized are parent, sibling, and elder abuse.

Parent Abuse Parents are sometimes the targets of their children's anger, hostility, and frustration. It is not uncommon for teenage and even younger children to physically and verbally lash out at their parents.

Children have pushed their parents down a flight of stairs, set the house on fire while their parents were in it, and used weapons such as guns and knives to cause serious injuries or even death, Reasons children give for killing their parents include collecting insurance money and/or getting back at them for alleged abuse.

Sibling Abuse Seventy-five percent of children with siblings report that they have at least one episode of violent conflict with their siblings during a year's time. Annually, an average of 21 violent acts take place between siblings in a family (Steinmetz 1987).

Some degree of fighting occurs among children in even "well-adjusted" families. Most incidents of sibling violence consist of slaps, pushes, kicks, bites, and punches. However, serious and dangerous violent behavior between siblings occurs as well.

National Data: In 1993, over one million (1,057,255) cases of child maltreatment were substantiated by child protective services agencies.

Source: *Statistical Abstract of the United States: 1995*, Table 346.

National Data: In a national survey of family violence, 10 percent of parents reported that they had been hit, bit, or kicked at least once by their children.

SOURCE: Gelles and Straus 1988.

National Data: About 300 parents are killed by their children each year in the United States.

SOURCE: Heide 1992.

National Data: Each year an estimated 3 percent of children in the United States use a weapon against a brother or sister.

SOURCE: Gelles and Straus 1988.

Abusive Behavior Inventory

This inventory is designed to assess the amount of abuse occurring in a relationship. Circle the number that best represents your closest estimate of how often each of the behaviors happened in your relationship with your partner or former partner during the previous six months.

1 Never   4 Frequently
2 Rarely   5 Very frequently
3 Occasionally

1. Called you a name and/or criticized you.	1	2	3	4	5
2. Tried to keep you from doing something you wanted to do (e.g., going out with friends, going to meetings).	1	2	3	4	5
3. Gave you angry stares or looks.	1	2	3	4	5
4. Prevented you from having money for your own use.	1	2	3	4	5
5. Ended a discussion with you and made the decision himself/herself.	1	2	3	4	5
6. Threatened to hit or throw something at you.	1	2	3	4	5
7. Pushed, grabbed, or shoved you.	1	2	3	4	5
8. Put down your family and friends.	1	2	3	4	5
9. Accused you of paying too much attention to someone or something else.	1	2	3	4	5
10. Put you on an allowance.	1	2	3	4	5
11. Used your children to threaten you (e.g., told you that you would lose custody, said he/she would leave town with the children.)	1	2	3	4	5
12. Became very upset with you because dinner, housework, or laundry was not ready when he/she wanted it done the way he/she thought it should be.	1	2	3	4	5
13. Said things to scare you (e.g., told you something "bad" would happen, threatened to commit suicide).	1	2	3	4	5
14. Slapped, hit, or punched you.	1	2	3	4	5

National Data: Studies on the prevalence of elder abuse in the United States suggest that from 4 to 10 percent of the elderly population are abused.

SOURCE: Johnson 1991.

Elder Abuse Elder abuse includes physical abuse, psychological abuse, financial abuse such as improper use of the elder's financial resources, and neglect. Elder neglect is similar to child neglect and includes failure to provide basic health and hygiene needs such as clean clothes, doctor visits, medication, and adequate nutrition. Neglect also involves unreasonable confinement, isolation of elderly family members, lack of supervision, and abandonment.

In some cases, parent abusers are "getting back" for their parent's maltreatment of them as children. In still other cases, the children are frustrated with the burden of having to care for their elderly parents (White 1988).

15. Made you do something humiliating or degrading (e.g., begging for forgiveness, having to ask his/her permission to use the car or to do something).	1	2	3	4	5
16. Checked up on you (e.g., listened to your phone calls, checked the mileage on your car, called you repeatedly at work).	1	2	3	4	5
17. Drove recklessly when you were in the car.	1	2	3	4	5
18. Pressured you to have sex in a way you didn't like or want.	1	2	3	4	5
19. Refused to do housework or child care.	1	2	3	4	5
20. Threatened you with a knife, gun, or other weapon.	1	2	3	4	5
21. Spanked you.	1	2	3	4	5
22. Told you that you were a bad parent.	1	2	3	4	5
23. Stopped you or tried to stop you from going to work or school.	1	2	3	4	5
24. Threw, hit, kicked, or smashed something.	1	2	3	4	5
25. Kicked you.	1	2	3	4	5
26. Physically forced you to have sex.	1	2	3	4	5
27. Threw you around.	1	2	3	4	5
28. Physically attacked the sexual parts of your body.	1	2	3	4	5
29. Choked or strangled you.	1	2	3	4	5
30. Used a knife, gun, or other weapon against you.	1	2	3	4	5

Scoring: Items of physical abuse are 7, 14, 18, 21, 25–30. Add scores and divide by 10 to obtain physical abuse score. Fifty abusing males scored an average of 1.5 (1 = no physical abuse; 5 = high physical abuse). Psychological abuse items are the remaining 20 items. Add scores and divide by 20. Fifty abusing males scored an average of 2.1 on psychological abuse (1 = no psychological abuse; 5 = high psychological abuse). Thirty-nine abusing females scored 1.8 and 2.8, respectively. Scores from 50 nonabusing males and females were obtained. The respective physical and psychological abuse scores for nonabusing males were 1.1 and 1.5; for nonabusing females, 1.3 and 2.0.

SOURCE: Melanie F. Shepard and James A. Campbell. "The Abusive Behavior Inventory: A Measure of Psychological and Physical Abuse," *Journal of Interpersonal Violence* September 1992: 7, no. 3, 291–305. Inventory on pages 303–304. Used by permission of Sage Publications, 2455 Teller Road, Newbury Park, California 91320

EFFECTS OF DOMESTIC VIOLENCE AND ABUSE

Research indicates that physical, emotional, and sexual abuse have a multitude of negative effects on family members. These effects vary according to the severity, frequency, and type of abuse.

Effects of Abuse in Intimate Relationships Not surprisingly, marital violence is associated with unhappy marital relationships (Bowman 1990). Physical and emotional abuse is, no doubt, a factor in many divorces. In addition to affecting

Verbal abuse is more common than physical abuse and causes mental or psychological distress.

the happiness and stability of relationships, abuse affects the physical and psychological well-being of the victim.

The most obvious effect of physical abuse by an intimate or former partner is physical injury. Indeed, former Surgeon General Antonia Novello notes that battering is the single major cause of injury to women in the United States. As many as 35 percent of women who seek hospital emergency room services are suffering from injuries incurred from domestic violence (Novello 1992).

Violence between intimate partners or ex-partners may also include unintentional death and intentional murder. Each day, four women in the United States are killed by an abusing partner. The FBI reports that 30 percent of female homicide victims were killed by their husbands or boyfriends and 6 percent of male homicide victims were killed by their wives or girlfriends (North Carolina Coalition Against Domestic Violence 1991).

Other effects of abuse by one's intimate partner include fear, feelings of helplessness, confusion, isolation, humiliation, anxiety, depression, stress-induced illness, symptoms of post-traumatic stress disorder, and suicide attempts (Gelles and Conte 1991; Lloyd and Emery 1993). According to Jones (1994), half of the homeless women and children in America are fleeing from violent men.

Effects of Partner Abuse on Children Abuse between adult partners also affects children. About 40 percent of battered women are abused during their pregnancy, resulting in a high rate of miscarriage and birth defects (North Carolina Coalition Against Domestic Violence 1991). Witnessing marital violence is related to emotional and behavioral problems in children and subsequent violence in their own relationships (Busby 1991). Children may also commit violent acts against a parent's abusing partner.

Effects of Physical, Emotional, and Sexual Child Abuse Reviews of research on the effects of child abuse suggest that abused children tend to exhibit aggression, low self-esteem, depression, and low academic achievement (Gelles and Conte 1991; Lloyd and Emery 1993). Children who experience more severe abuse suffer more from intellectual deficits, communication problems, and learning disabilities than children less severely abused. Adults who were physically abused as children may exhibit low self-esteem, depression, unhappiness, anxiety, an increased risk of alcohol abuse, and suicidal tendencies. Physical injuries sustained by child abuse cause pain, disfigurement, scarring, physical disability, and death.

Research on the effects of child sexual abuse indicates that among adolescent females, sexual abuse is associated with lower self-esteem, higher levels of depression, antisocial behavior (e.g., running away from home, illegal drug use), and suicide attempts (Morrow and Sorrell 1989). Sexually abused girls are also more likely to experience teenage pregnancy (Boyer, Fine, and Killpack 1991).

Adult males who were sexually abused as children tend to exhibit depression, substance abuse, and difficulty establishing intimate relationships (Krug 1989). Sexually abused males also have a higher risk of developing negative self-perceptions, anxiety disorders, sleep and eating disorders, and sexual dysfunctions (Elliott and Briere 1992).

FACTORS CONTRIBUTING TO DOMESTIC VIOLENCE AND ABUSE

Research suggests that numerous factors contribute to domestic violence and abuse. These factors occur at various levels from the society and community to the individual and the family (Willis, Holden, and Rosenberg 1992).

Cultural Factors In many ways, American culture tolerates and even promotes violence. Violence in the family stems from our society's acceptance of violence as a legitimate means of enforcing compliance and solving conflicts at personal, national, and international levels (Viano 1992). Violence and abuse in the family may be linked to cultural factors such as violence in the media (see Chapter 4), acceptance of corporal punishment, gender inequality, and the view of women and children as property:

1. *Acceptance of corporal punishment.* Many mental health professionals and child development specialists argue that corporal punishment is ineffective and damaging to children. Yet many parents accept the cultural tradition of spanking as an appropriate form of child discipline. Eighty-three percent of more than 11,000 undergraduate students at the University of Iowa reported that they had experienced some form of physical punishment during their childhood (Knutson and Selner 1994). While not everyone agrees that all instances of corporal punishment constitute abuse, undoubtedly, some episodes of parental "discipline" are abusive.

What some people view as appropriate corporal punishment, others view as abuse.

2. *Gender inequality.* Domestic violence and abuse may also stem from traditional gender roles. Traditional male gender roles have taught men to be aggressive. Traditionally, men have also been taught that they are superior to women and that they may use their aggression toward women because "women need to be put in their place." Traditional female gender roles have also taught women to be submissive to their male partner's control (Straus 1980).

3. *View of women and children as property.* Prior to the late nineteenth century, a married woman was considered to be the property of her husband. A husband had a legal right and marital obligation to discipline and control his wife through the use of physical force. The expression "rule of thumb" can be traced to an old English law that permitted a husband to beat his wife with a rod no thicker than his thumb. This "rule of thumb" was originally intended as a humane measure to limit how harshly men could beat their wives. This traditional view of women as property may contribute to men doing with their "property" as they wish.

According to conflict theorists, the view of women and children as property also explains marital rape and father-daughter incest. Historically, the penalties for rape were based on property right laws designed to protect a man's property—his wife or daughter—from rape by other men; a husband or father "taking" his own property was not considered rape (Russell 1990). In the past, a married woman who was raped by her husband could not have her husband arrested because marital rape was not considered a crime. In 1978, only three states recognized marital rape as a law violation. In 1993, North Carolina became the fiftieth state to recognize marital rape as a crime (National Clearinghouse on Marital and Date Rape 1994).

Community Factors Community factors that contribute to violence and abuse in the family include social isolation, and inaccessible or unaffordable health care, day care, elder care, and respite care facilities:

1. *Social isolation.* Living in social isolation from extended family and community members increases a family's risk for abuse. Isolated families are removed from material benefits, care-giving assistance, and emotional support from extended family and community members. Also, parents who have little contact with others in the community do not have exposure to positive role models for effective parental behavior (Harrington and Dubowitz 1993).

2. *Inaccessible or unaffordable community services.* Failure to provide medical care to children and elderly family members is sometimes due to the lack of accessible or affordable health care services in the community. Failure to provide supervision for children and adults may result from inaccessible day care and elder care services. Without elder care and respite care facilities, socially isolated families may not have any help with the stresses of caring for elderly family members and children with special needs.

Individual and Family Factors Individual and family factors that are associated with domestic violence and abuse include psychopathology, a family history of violence, drug and alcohol abuse, poverty, and fatherless homes:

1. *Psychopathology.* Some abusing spouses and parents have psychiatric conditions that predispose them to abusive behavior. Symptoms of psychiatric conditions that are related to violence and abuse include low frustration tolerance, emotional distress, and inappropriate expressions of anger. Adults who sexually abuse children in their family may have developed a sexual fetish that necessitates the presence of a young child to provide sexual arousal.

2. *Family history of abuse.* Adults who were physically or verbally abused or neglected as children tend to duplicate these patterns in their own families (Gelles and Conte 1991). Still, many adults who were abused as children do not continue the cycle with their own children. Pagelow (1992) emphasizes that a family history of violence is only one factor out of many that may be associated with a greater probability of adult violence.

3. *Drug and alcohol abuse.* Drug and/or alcohol abuse may be related to some instances of abuse in relationships. Indeed, Koss and Gaines (1993) identified regular use of alcohol and nicotine as the most important predictors of sexual aggression severity. A study of crisis calls to the Atlanta Council for Battered Women (Murty and Roebuck 1992) found that 30 percent of abuse victims reported that the perpetrators were intoxicated with alcohol at the time of the abuse. Straus and Sweet (1992) found that drinking alcohol and using drugs were associated with higher levels of verbal and symbolic aggression between spouses.

4. *Poverty.* Abuse in adult relationships occurs among all socioeconomic groups. However, Kaufman and Zigler (1992) point to a relationship between poverty and child abuse:

   > *Although most poor people do not maltreat their children, and poverty, per se, does not cause abuse and neglect, the correlates of poverty, including stress, drug abuse, and inadequate resources for food and medical care, increase the likelihood of maltreatment. (p. 284)*

5. *Fatherless homes.* Living in a home where the father is absent increases a child's risk for being abused. Numerous studies show that children are more likely to be sexually abused by a stepfather or mother's boyfriend than by their biological father (Blankenhorn 1995). This is largely because stepfathers and mothers' boyfriends are not constrained by the cultural incest taboo that prohibits fathers from having sex with their children.

DOMESTIC VIOLENCE AND ABUSE: PREVENTION STRATEGIES

Strategies to prevent family violence and abuse can be applied at three different levels (Gelles 1993; Harrington and Dubowitz 1993). **Primary prevention** strategies target the general population, while **secondary prevention** strategies target groups thought to be at high risk for family violence and abuse. **Tertiary prevention** strategies target families who have experienced abuse; these strategies are designed to reduce the adverse effects of abuse and stop the abuse from happening again.

Primary Prevention Strategies Public education and media campaigns that target the general population may help reduce domestic violence by conveying the criminal nature of domestic assault, offering ways to prevent abuse ("When you are angry at your child, count to ten and call a friend . . ."), and suggesting where abuse victims or perpetrators can get help. Ultimately, though, to prevent or reduce family violence, elements of American culture that contribute to such violence must change. Parents and educators must be taught and encouraged to use methods of child discipline that do not involve physical punishment. Parent training classes are a high school graduation requirement in at least eight states, including California, Delaware, Michigan, New Jersey, New York, Tennessee, Vermont, and Virginia (Shapiro and Schrof 1995). Violence in the media must be curbed or eliminated, and traditional gender roles and views of women and children as property must be replaced with egalitarian gender roles and respect for women and children.

Another strategy involves reducing violence-provoking stress by reducing poverty and unemployment and providing adequate housing, nutrition, medical care, and educational opportunities. While programs such as Aid to Families with Dependent Children (AFDC) and the Special Supplemental Food Program for Women, Infants, and Children (WIC) were not designed to prevent domestic violence and abuse, "they provide crucial assistance to low income families and thus support the functioning of these families" (Harrington and Dubowitz 1993, 264). Integrating families into networks of community and kin would also enhance family well-being and provide support for families under stress.

Secondary Prevention Strategies Families who are at risk of experiencing violence and abuse include low-income families, parents with a history of depression or psychiatric care, single parents, teenage mothers, parents with few social and family contacts, individuals who experienced abuse in their own childhood, and parents or spouses who abuse drugs or alcohol. Secondary prevention strategies, designed to prevent abuse from occurring in high-risk families, include parent education programs, parent support groups, individual counseling, and home visiting programs. Substance abuse treatment may also reduce the risk of violence and abuse in the home. Providing teenagers with access to family planning and contraceptive services may help to prevent teenage and unwanted births and, thus, reduce the child abuse and neglect associated with such births. This chapter's *In Focus* describes a comprehensive program designed to prevent child abuse and neglect in high-risk families.

Tertiary Prevention Strategies What social interventions are available to families that are experiencing abuse or neglect? Abused women and children may seek relief at a shelter or "safe house" for abused women. *Shelters* provide abused women and their children with housing, food, counseling services, and an environment that empowers women by encouraging them to make independent choices about their abusive relationships and about their future. By providing a communal living situation with other abused women, shelters also reduce the

National Data: There are 1,500 shelters for battered women in the United States. There are 3,800 animal shelters.

SOURCE: *General Facts about Domestic Violence* 1995. National Clearinghouse for the Defense of Battered Women. Safety Net Home Page, World Wide Web.

Healthy Families America: A Child Abuse/Neglect Prevention Program

In 1985, a child abuse and neglect prevention project called Healthy Start began in Hawaii. This program was designed to prevent child abuse and neglect by improving family coping skills and functioning, promoting positive parenting skills and parent-child interaction, and encouraging optimal child development. Three years later, not a single case of abuse among the project's 241 high-risk families had been reported (Breakey and Pratt 1991). After Healthy Start expanded into a statewide program, researchers analyzed data from 1,204 at-risk families and found only one case of reported abuse (a 99.99 percent nonabuse rate) and six cases of neglect (a 99.95 percent nonneglect rate).

The National Committee to Prevent Child Abuse, in partnership with Ronald McDonald Children's Charities, initiated a nationwide program modeled after Hawaii's Healthy Start program called Healthy Families America (HFA). The HFA program offers one or two home visits to all new parents. During these visits, service providers share information about baby care and development and parenting skills and explain how parents can utilize other organizations and agencies that provide family support. Families most at risk of child maltreatment are offered intensive home visitation services (at least once a week) for three to five years. All families who participate in the program are linked to a medical provider to assure timely immunizations and well-child care. Depending on the family's needs, they may also be linked to additional services, such as financial aid, food and housing assistance programs, school readiness programs, child care, job training programs, family support centers, substance abuse treatment programs, and domestic violence shelters.

As of spring 1994, more than forty-five communities had HFA programs (Healthy Families America Fact Sheet 1994). Programs such as these cost money, but in the long run, they save money. For every $3 spent on child abuse prevention, we save at least $6 that might otherwise have been spent on child welfare services, special education services, medical care, foster care, counseling, and housing juvenile offenders (Healthy Families America Fact Sheet 1994).

SOURCES: Gail, Breakey, and Betsy Pratt. 1991. "Healthy Growth for Hawaii's 'Healthy Startt': Toward a Systematic Statewide Approach to the Prevention of Child Abuse and Neglect." *Zero to Three* (Bulletin of National Center for Clinical Infant Programs) 11(4):16–22; and Healthy Families America Fact Sheet. 1994 (May). National Committee to Prevent Child Abuse, Healthy Families America. 332 S. Michigan Ave., Suite 1600, Chicago, IL 60604.

women's sense of isolation and help them express their anger and overcome feelings of guilt and inadequacy (Loseke 1992). An alternative to shelters are *safe houses,* which are private homes of individuals who volunteer to provide temporary housing to abused women who decide to leave their violent home. Battered men are not allowed to stay at women's shelters, but many shelters help abused men by providing money for a motel room, counseling, and support services.

Abused or neglected children may be removed from the home. All states have laws that permit abused or neglected children to be placed in out-of-home care, such as foster care (Stein 1993). However, federal law requires that states have programs to prevent family breakup when desirable and possible without jeopardizing the welfare of children in the home. *Family preservation programs* are in-home interventions for families who are at risk of having a child removed from the home due to abuse or neglect.

Alternatively, a court may order an abusing spouse or parent to leave the home. Abused spouses or cohabiting partners may obtain a restraining order prohibiting the perpetrator from going near the abused partner. Another possibility is to have the perpetrator arrested, but many abused spouses refuse. About half of the states and Washington, D.C., now have mandatory arrest policies that require police to arrest abusers, even if the victim does not want to press charges.

Finally, perpetrators and victims of domestic violence and abuse may receive treatment either voluntarily or to comply with a court order. Treatment includes individual and group therapy for abusers and self-help groups such as Parents Anonymous. This chapter's *The Human Side* tells one man's story about how counseling helped him change his abusive behavior.

Divorce

The United States has the highest divorce rate in the world (United Nations 1992). In 1980, the number of divorces per 1,000 population peaked at 5.2 (*Statistical Abstract of the United States: 1995,* Table 142). Since that year, the divorce rate has dropped, reaching 4.6 in 1994 (National Center for Health Statistics 1995). Individuals who get divorced usually explain their divorce on the basis of individual and relationship factors, but a variety of social factors contribute to divorce as well.

INDIVIDUAL AND RELATIONSHIP FACTORS THAT CONTRIBUTE TO DIVORCE

Ask divorced individuals why they divorced and they will probably cite reasons related to themselves, their partner, or their relationship. Individual and relationship factors that contribute to divorce include incompatibility in values or goals, poor communication, lack of conflict resolution skills, sexual incompatibility, extramarital relationships, substance abuse, emotional or physical abuse or neglect, boredom, jealously, and difficulty coping with change or stress related to parenting, employment, finances, in-laws, and illness. Other demographic and life course factors that are predictive of divorce include marriage order (second and subsequent marriages are more prone to divorce than first marriages), cohabitation (couples who live together before marriage are more prone to divorce), teenage marriage, premarital pregnancy, and low socioeconomic status.

SOCIAL FACTORS CONDUCIVE TO DIVORCE

Beyond individual and relationship factors, various social factors contribute to the high rate of divorce in our society. These include the following structural and cultural forces.

Changing Family Functions Prior to the Industrial Revolution, marriage and family relationships served many functions. The family comprised a unit of economic production and consumption, provided care and protection to its members, and was responsible for socializing and educating children. During industrialization, other institutions took over these functions. For example,

The model of the two-parent family, based on a lasting, monogamous marriage, is both possible and desirable. This form of the family, in fact, is by far the most efficacious one for child rearing and for the long-term well-being of individuals and society.
—David Popenoe
Sociologist

ONE MAN'S DETERMINATION TO STOP HIS ABUSIVE BEHAVIOR

I showered and shaved . . . I was excited that I was going out with my partner. Needless to say, I was more than a little disappointed when I found out that she had planned only a short visit all along, and had made plans to go out with her friend . . . I tried to be OK with this, but no matter what I said to her or myself, my disappointment showed on my face . . . and I was really edgy . . . .

I had a couple of hours to cool off, and I did. Unfortunately, not enough. When she returned for her short visit, I became increasingly frustrated . . . I was disappointed that she seemed to choose her friend over me . . . Then it happened. She kissed me goodbye, and turned for the door. I snapped. I picked up a clipboard and threw it across the room. Then I slammed the door hard behind her. It took two seconds for me to realize what I had done, and I ran out the door after her. She was upset. She told me that she didn't think she could continue to see me . . . I stood outside trying to get her to stay and talk to me instead of leaving. Finally she said that we could talk later that evening after she returned home . . . I was afraid I was going to lose someone who was very dear to me.

I went out to get something to eat, and I wrote her a letter. I wrote about how I was sorry, and how I never wanted to let it happen again. I told her that I might explode again sometime, but that I would make sure that she wasn't in the room. We talked that night. She gave me an ultimatum I had already given myself: I would seek counseling, and attend regularly.

Within a week I had enrolled in a batterer's group for men. I returned from the first session, and wrote everything I had learned in a letter to her. I learned that the cycle had begun. I saw something scary in myself. If she had given in instead of standing up to me as she did, I likely would have digressed into a downward spiral of violence and control. As it stands now, we're working through this.

I'm very happy with my group sessions; I'll begin individual counseling later this week. My goal is to learn how to recognize the signs of and stop the violence . . . and to deal with the issues of my past and present that continue to contribute to a need to control . . . I know that this is going to be a long road ahead. I feel lucky that the resources are out there to help me heal myself, and that my partner is willing to be here with me through it all.

SOURCE: World Wide Web. 1995. http://www.marie.az.com

the educational institution has virtually taken over the systematic teaching and socialization of children. Today, the primary function of marriage and the family is the provision of emotional support, intimacy, affection, and love. When marital partners no longer derive these emotional benefits from their marriage, they may consider divorce with the hope of finding a new marriage partner to fulfill these affectional needs.

Increased Economic Autonomy of Women Before 1940, most wives were not employed outside the home and depended on their husband's income. During World War II, the United States needed women in the labor force. Today, the employment rate among married women is higher than in previous decades.

Wives who are unhappy in their marriage are more likely to leave the marriage if they have the economic means to support themselves. Unhappy husbands may also be more likely to leave a marriage if their wives are self-sufficient and can contribute to the support of the children.

Liberalized Divorce Laws Prior to 1970, the law required a couple who wanted a divorce to prove that one of the spouses was at fault and had committed an act defined by the state as grounds for divorce—adultery, cruelty, or desertion. In 1969, California became the first state to initiate **no-fault divorce,** which permitted a divorce based on the claim that there were "irreconcilable differences" in the marriage. Today, all states recognize some form of no-fault divorce. No-fault divorce laws have made divorce easier to obtain.

Cultural Values As noted earlier, individualism in the United States has increased in recent years. In the pursuit of individual happiness, spouses and children may be left behind. Familism is still prevalent among Asian Americans and Mexican Americans, however, which helps to explain why the divorce rate is lower among these groups than among whites and African Americans (Mindel, Habenstein, and Wright 1989). Further, the recent leveling off of the divorce rate may reflect what some researchers regard as a resurgence of familism. Cox (1992) notes that "[T]here are many signs that families and institutions have returned to a more solid foundation of traditional values compared with the departures of the 'me first' 80s" (p. 1).

The value of marriage has also changed in American culture. The increased social acceptance of nonmarital sexuality, nonmarital childbearing, cohabitation, and singlehood reflect the view that marriage is an option, rather than an inevitability. The view of marriage as an option, rather than as an imperative, is mirrored by the view that divorce is also an acceptable option. Divorce today has less social stigma than in previous generations.

CONSEQUENCES OF DIVORCE

Divorce often has numerous negative effects for ex-spouses and their children. Divorce also creates social problems for society as a whole (Blankenhorn 1995; Hewlett 1992; Popenoe 1993; Demo and Acock 1991).

Health Consequences Divorce tends to have deleterious physical and psychological health consequences on ex-spouses. Divorce is associated with personal disorganization, anxiety and psychological distress, unhappiness, loneliness,

National Data: In 1960, only 31.9 percent of married women were employed. By 1994, 60.7 percent of U.S. wives (husbands present) were employed.

SOURCE: *Statistical Abstract of the United States: 1995,* Table 636.

It is now widely accepted that men and women have the right to expect a happy marriage, and that if a marriage does not work out, no one has to stay trapped.
—Sylvia Ann Hewlett
President, National
Parenting Association

depression, illness, and suicide (Kitson and Morgan 1991; Song 1991; Heim and Snyder 1991; Stack 1989; Broman 1988). Furthermore, the more divorces a person has, the greater the negative effects of each subsequent divorce (Kurdek 1991). As discussed in Chapter 2, physical and mental illness are major social problems.

Economic Consequences In general, women and children suffer the economic consequences of divorce more than men. For all racial and ethnic groups, the incomes of women decline significantly after divorce (Smock 1994). In a study in Los Angeles County, the income of divorced men increased 42 percent the first year after divorce while their former wives suffered a 73 percent drop in income (Weitzman 1985). Whether due to divorce or unwed parenthood, single-parent families are more likely to live below the poverty line (Wisensale 1992). Blankenhorn (1995) asserts that "fatherlessness has become the single most powerful determinant of child poverty—more important than race, region, or the educational attainment of the mother" (p. 43). In many cases, the father owes child support, but for one reason or another fails to pay.

> **Consideration** The Family Support Act of 1994 allows child support payments to be automatically withheld from the noncustodial parent's paycheck unless the court finds good cause not to withhold the funds, or parents draw up an alternative written agreement. Increased concern with welfare dependency and, specifically, the cost of such programs as Aid to Families with Dependent Children has led to federal policies aimed at "Deadbeat Dads." Proposed policies include revocation of driver's licenses and professional licenses, property liens across state lines, and expropriation of federal tax refunds. While some programs have been successful in securing child support from absent fathers, more than $34 billion is still owed to 17 million children (Van Biema 1995).

Traditionally, women have curtailed their education and careers in favor of their role as housewives and mothers. Men have not. After a divorce (as well as before divorce), women often do not have the means to earn an income equal to that of their ex-husband. Prior to no-fault divorce laws, divorced women regularly received alimony from their ex-spouses. In 1989, only 16 percent of divorced or separated women were awarded alimony (*Statistical Abstract of the United States: 1993*, Table 612).

Effects on Children A major societal concern is the effect of divorce on children. Although the number of children from divorced families is alarming, researchers disagree on how detrimental divorce may be.

With only one parent in the home, children of divorce, as well as children of never-married mothers, tend to have less adult supervision compared to children in two-parent homes. Lack of adult supervision is related to higher rates of juvenile delinquency, school failure, and teenage pregnancy (Popenoe 1993).

Based on a review of thirty-seven studies involving more than 81,000 adults who experienced the divorce of their parents, researchers concluded that "divorce (or permanent separation) has broad negative consequences for the quality of life in adulthood" (Amato and Keith 1991, 54). These researchers found that adult children of divorced parents experienced lower levels of psychological well-being (depression, low life satisfaction), family

National Data: In 1993, over half (53.7 percent) of children in families headed by single mothers lived below the poverty level.
SOURCE: *Statistical Abstract of the United States 1995*, Table 750.

National Data: Over one million children experience the divorce of their parents every year. About half of all U.S. children—at least one-third of white children and two-thirds of black children—will experience the breakup of their parents' marriage (Ahlburg and De Vita 1992). One-fourth of all freshmen college students in the United States have parents who are divorced or separated.
SOURCE: American Council on Education and University of California 1994.

well-being (low marital quality, divorce), socioeconomic well-being (low educational attainment, income, and occupational prestige), and poorer physical health.

Not all studies reach such pessimistic conclusions. Lauer and Lauer (1991) compared 313 adults (mean age thirty-five) from intact-happy, intact-unhappy, death-disrupted, and divorce-disrupted families and observed "few if any, long-term differences in such things as self-esteem, social competence, dating behavior, and relational attitudes" (p. 289) The researchers conclude:

> *Without minimizing the short-term and long-term trauma of experiencing an unhappy or disrupted family during childhood, it may be that most people are not as handicapped in the long run as some professionals have suggested. In spite of their doubts and various self-deprecating statements, most of those from disrupted and intact-unhappy families were able to form intimate relationships. (p. 289)*

STRENGTHENING POSTDIVORCE FAMILIES

We have to find ways to make marriage work, if for no other reason than marriage is extraordinarily important to children.
—David Popenoe
Sociologist

In general, negative consequences of divorce for children may be minimized if both parents continue to spend time with their children on a regular and consistent basis and communicate to their children that they love them and are interested in their lives. Some research suggests that parental conflict, either in intact families or divorced families, negatively influences the psychological well-being of children (Demo 1992; Demo 1993). By maintaining a civil co-parenting relationship during a separation and after divorce, parents can minimize the negative effects of divorce on their children. However, about 20 percent of separated and divorced spouses have an angry, hostile relationship (Masheter 1991).

What can society do to promote cooperative parenting by ex-spouses? One answer is to encourage, or even mandate, divorcing couples to participate in divorce mediation. In **divorce mediation** divorcing couples meet with a neutral third party, a mediator, who helps them resolve issues of property division, child custody, child support, and spousal support in a way that minimizes conflict and encourages cooperation. Children of mediated divorces adjust better to the divorce than children of litigated divorces (Marlow and Sauber 1990). An increasing number of jurisdictions have mandatory child custody mediation programs, whereby parents in a custody dispute must attempt to resolve their dispute through mediation before a court will hear their case. Some states, including California, Delaware, and Maine, have enacted mandatory child custody and visitation mediation legislation.

Another trend aimed at strengthening postdivorce families is the establishment of parenting programs for divorcing parents (Shapiro and Schrof 1995). Programs such as "Sensible Approach to Divorce" (Wyandotte County, Kansas) and "Parenting After Divorce" (Orange County, North Carolina) emphasize that it is important for both parents to remain involved in their children's lives. Such programs also teach parents skills to help their children adjust to the divorce and advise parents to avoid expressing hostility or criticism toward the ex-spouse in front of the children. Connecticut and Utah require all divorcing parents to attend a parenting program as do more than a hundred courts throughout the United States. Florida goes beyond these programs by offering a course for children of divorcing parents.

Unmarried and Teenage Parenthood

In addition to domestic violence and the high rate of divorce, another pressing social problem related to families is the high rate of unmarried and teenage parenthood. Blankenhorn (1995) notes that "unwed parenthood has . . . become, by far, the nation's fastest-growing family structure trend" (p. 132).

Minority women, who are disproportionately poor, are more likely than white women to give birth without being married. In 1992, 23 percent of white births, 68 percent of black births, and 39 percent of Hispanic births were births to unmarried women (*Statistical Abstract of the United States: 1995*, Table 88). Over the last few decades, however, births to unmarried women have increased more among whites than among blacks (see Table 5.1).

In a society where being married before having children is the traditional norm, why do unmarried women have children? What are the personal and social consequences of unmarried and teenage childbearing? And what kinds of policies might help to alleviate the problems associated with unmarried parenthood?

SOCIAL FACTORS THAT ENCOURAGE UNMARRIED PARENTHOOD

The teenage birthrate in the United States as measured by births per 1,000 teenagers, is significantly higher than in other industrialized countries (see Figure 5.2). Teenagers in other countries are as sexually active as U.S. teenagers, but they grow up in societies that promote responsible contraceptive use. In the Netherlands, for example, individuals are taught to use both the pill and a condom to prevent pregnancy and sexually transmitted diseases (called "Double Dutch").

In the United States, perceived lack of future occupational opportunities also contributes to teenage parenthood (Parnell, Swicegood, and Stevens 1994). Teenage females who do poorly in school may have little hope of success and achievement in pursuing educational and occupational goals. They may think that their only remaining option for a meaningful role in life is to become a parent. In addition, some teenagers feel lonely and unloved and have a baby to create a sense of feeling needed and wanted.

The most rapid rise in single parenthood is among older, educated, professional women, although they still represent only a small fraction of all single mothers (Ingrassia 1993). Most would prefer to be married before having a

> *Marriage has become an almost forgotten institution among black teens. In whole sections of the black community, children are being raised almost exclusively by very young mothers without male role models.*
> —Daniel Patrick Moynihan
> U.S. Senator

National Data: Over one million American teenagers (age 15–19) become pregnant annually, and about half of these give birth to their baby.
SOURCE: Ahlburg and De Vita 1992.

TABLE 5.1			
PERCENTAGE OF BIRTHS TO UNMARRIED WOMEN BY RACE AND YEAR			
	PERCENTAGE OF BIRTHS TO UNMARRIED MOTHERS		
	1970	**1980**	**1992**
Total	11	18	30
White	6	11	23
Black	38	55	68

Source: *Statistical Abstract of the United States:* 1995, 115th ed. Washington, D.C.: U.S. Bureau of the Census, Table 94.

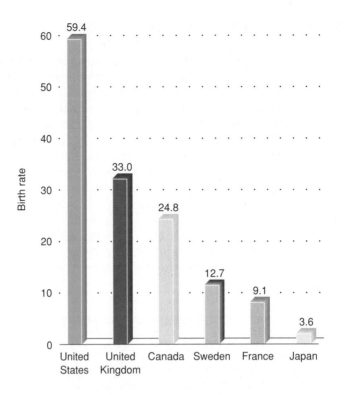

FIGURE 5.2

TEENAGE BIRTHRATE IN SIX INDUSTRIALIZED COUNTRIES

SOURCE: Based on data from *1991 Demographic Yearbook*, 43rd ed. 1992. New York: United Nations, pp 306–11. Used by permission.

. . . .

For many disadvantaged teen-agers, childbearing reflects—rather than causes—the limitations of their lives.
—Ellen W. Freeman
Karl Rickels

. . . .

. . . .

For most women nonmarriage is the consequence, not the cause, of their nonmarital childbearing.
—Neil Bennett
David Bloom
Cynthia Miller

. . . .

child, but feel that their biological clock won't wait (Sapiro 1990). In a pronatalistic society where motherhood is an important avenue to personal fulfillment, women are increasingly seeking this role with or without a husband.

Increased social acceptance of cohabitation also contributes to unmarried parenthood. Births to cohabiting couples are technically considered unwed births, even though the parents are living together.

SOCIAL PROBLEMS RELATED TO UNMARRIED PARENTHOOD

Unmarried childbirth is considered a social problem because of the consequences typically associated with it. Some of these include the following (Blankenhorn 1995; Freeman and Rickels 1993; Musick, 1993; Hewlett 1992; McLanahan and Booth 1991):

1. *Poverty for single mothers and children.* Many unmarried mothers, especially teenagers, have no means of economic support or have limited earning capacity. Single mothers and their children often live in substandard housing and have inadequate nutrition and medical care. The public bears some of the economic burden of supporting unmarried mothers and their children, but even with public assistance, many unwed and teenage parents often struggle to survive economically.

2. *Poor health habits.* Teenage and unmarried women are less likely to seek prenatal care and more likely than older and married women to smoke, drink alcohol, and take drugs. These factors have adverse effects on the health of the baby. Indeed, babies born to unmarried or teenage mothers are more likely to have low birthweights (less than

5 pounds, 5 ounces) and to be born prematurely. Children of teenage and unmarried mothers are also more likely to be developmentally delayed. These outcomes are largely a result of the association between teenage and unmarried childbearing and poverty.

3. *Poor academic achievement.* Poor academic achievement is both a contributing factor and a potential outcome of teenage parenthood. Three-fifths of teenage mothers drop out of school (reported in Hewlett 1992) and, as a consequence, have a much higher probability of remaining poor throughout their lives. Since poverty is linked to unmarried parenthood, a cycle of successive generations of teenage pregnancy may develop.

4. *Children without fathers.* About one-third of U.S. children who live in households without their fathers are the product of unmarried childbirth (U.S. Census Bureau 1989). Blankenhorn (1995) refers to unwed parenthood as "the primary engine of the current growth of father absence in our society" (p. 132). Children without fathers present in the household do not have the opportunity to develop an emotionally supportive relationship with their father. Shapiro and Schrof (1995) report that children who grow up without fathers are more likely to drop out of school, be unemployed, abuse drugs, experience mental illness, and be a target of child sexual abuse. They also note that "a missing father is a better predictor of criminal activity than race or poverty" (p. 39). Family life specialist David Popenoe observed that "[F]atherlessness is a major cause of the degenerating conditions of our young" (Peterson 1995, 6d).

> **Consideration**   *Despite some of the problems associated with single-parent families, many single parents provide a safe and nurturing environment for their children. Conversely, many two-parent families do not provide safe and nurturing environments for their children.*

UNMARRIED PARENTHOOD: SOCIAL STRATEGIES AND INTERVENTIONS

Some interventions regarding unmarried and teenage childbearing aim at prevention, while others attempt to minimize its negative effects. One preventive intervention is to provide sex education and family planning programs before unwanted or unintended pregnancy occurs. Schools, churches, family planning clinics, and public health departments may offer sex education programs. Research on the effectiveness of such programs in preventing pregnancy is disheartening, however. Stout and Rivara (1989) reviewed five studies and concluded that school-based sex education programs have little or no effect on reducing teenage pregnancy. After pregnancy occurs, counseling programs may help unmarried pregnant women decide whether to continue the pregnancy and keep the baby or place it for adoption, or have an abortion. Increasingly, young women are opting to keep their babies.

Other programs aim at both preventing teenage and unmarried childbearing and minimizing its negative effects by increasing the life options of teenagers and unmarried mothers. Such programs include educational programs, job training, and skill-building programs. Other programs designed to

We often fail to recognize that adolescent childbearing is much more than a private tragedy. Teen-age parenthood constitutes a heavy drain on the public purse.
—Sylvia Ann Hewlett
President, National Parenting Association

Fatherlessness is the most destructive trend of our generation.
—David Blankenhorn
President, American Institute for Family Values

Dad is destiny. More than virtually any other factor, a biological father's presence in the family will determine a child's success and happiness.
—Joseph Shapiro
Joannie Schrof

help teenage and unwed mothers and their children include public welfare (such as Aid to Families with Dependent Children), prenatal programs to help ensure the health of the mother and baby, and parenting classes for both teenage fathers and unmarried mothers.

Some programs combine various services. For example, a program at the New Futures School in Albuquerque, New Mexico, offers health care, parenting education, child care services, and vocational training to teenage parents and parents-to-be (reported in Hewlett 1992). The goal of this program is to help teenage parents have healthy babies, complete their high school education, and become self-sufficient.

UNDERSTANDING
FAMILY PROBLEMS

The industrialization of America led to an increase in both the number and the severity of problems in the American family. Societal definitions of the family have also changed with increased acceptance of many previously stigmatized behaviors, such as cohabitation, divorce, and nonmarital parenthood. As these behaviors have become more socially acceptable, they have also become more common.

The impact of family problems, including divorce, abuse, and nonmarital childbearing, is felt not only by family members, but by the larger society as well. Family members experience such life difficulties as poverty, school failure, low self-esteem, and mental and physical health problems. Each of these difficulties contributes to a cycle of family problems in the next generation. The impact on society includes large public expenditures to assist single-parent families and victims of domestic violence and neglect, increased rates of juvenile delinquency, and low academic achievement of children who are struggling to cope with family problems.

Family problems can best be understood within the context of the society and culture in which they occur. Although domestic violence, divorce, and unmarried parenthood may appear to result from individual decisions, these decisions are influenced by a myriad of social forces. Domestic violence, for example, is embedded in a social context. Levinson (1989) found that sixteen of ninety non-Western societies studied were virtually free of family violence. In each of these societies, spouses had equal decision-making power in household and financial matters. In addition, families in these societies did not live in social isolation from extended family and community members. Family members who were victims or were threatened with physical harm by another family member were offered immediate help by neighbors or extended kin who intervened or provided shelter.

In regard to divorce, both the United States and the former Soviet Union have two of the highest divorce rates in the world. Japan and Korea have two of the lowest divorce rates. In the former, liberalized divorce norms and laws prevail; in the latter countries, both the norms and laws are highly restrictive. While restricting access to divorce may simply force unhappy couples to remain married at tremendous emotional costs to all involved, there is a recent trend toward "premarital counseling" as a means of lowering the divorce rate. Such counseling techniques assess a couple's compatibility and, in some cases, boast an 80 to 85 percent success rate in predicting which couples will get a divorce (Gleick 1995). Some have also suggested that a waiting period for marriage licenses would reduce the divorce rate. Advocates argue that rather than making divorce easier, marriage should become more difficult to enter.

Given the social context of family problems, it is important that we look to social intervention for solutions. Cultural changes include a commitment of the media and entertainment industry to stop glamorizing violence, male dominance, and nonmarital sex and instead promote nonviolence, egalitarian relationships, and marital fulfillment. According to Blankenhorn (1995), cultural changes to strengthen the role of the father in American families must begin "from the bottom up, around kitchen tables" (p. 225). Encouraging men to adopt a pro-family attitude requires changing the culturally-defined male gender role so that men "prove" their manhood by being good fathers and husbands instead of too often being violent, patriarchal, and indiscriminately sexually active.

Structural changes in society include creating more workplaces that accommodate family needs (see Chapter 10), expanding school services to include family support programs (see Chapter 13), and prioritizing family well-being in all areas of legislation. Politicians have enormous power in shaping policies that affect families. Recognizing this, Blankenhorn (1995) suggests that:

> *The U.S. Congress should pass, and the President should support, a resolution stating that the first question of policy makers regarding all proposed domestic legislation is whether it will strengthen or weaken the institution of marriage. Not the sole question, of course, but always the first. (p. 231)*

> *It is absolutely necessary that we create that extended family that we grew up with.*
> —Yolanda King
> Daughter, Martin Luther King, Jr.

CRITICAL THINKING

1. Some scholars and politicians argue that "stable families are the bedrock of stable communities." Others argue that "stable communities and economies are the bedrock of stable families." Which of these two positions would you take and why?
2. Is individualism necessarily incompatible with familism? Why or why not?
3. Research has suggested that second-hand smoke from cigarettes represents a health hazard for those who are exposed to it. Consequently, smoking is now banned in many public places and workplaces. Do you think that parents should be banned from smoking in enclosed areas (home or car) to protect their children from second-hand smoke? Do you think that smoking in enclosed areas with one's children present should be considered a form of child abuse? Why or why not?
4. From a structural-functionalist perspective, what latent function does divorce serve for the economic institution?
5. How are cultural definitions of motherhood and fatherhood affected by gender roles?

KEY TERMS

individualism	domestic partnership	primary prevention
familism	patriarchy	secondary prevention
Industrial Revolution	self-fulfilling prophecy	tertiary prevention
family	child abuse	no-fault divorce
household	neglect	divorce mediation

REFERENCES

Ahlburg, Dennis. A., and Carol J. De Vita 1992. "New Realities of the American Family." *Population Bulletin* 47: 2–44.

Amato, Paul. R., and Bruce Keith. 1991. "Parental Divorce and Adult Well-Being: A Metaanalysis." *Journal of Marriage and the Family* 53: 43–58.

American Council on Education and University of California. 1994. "The American Freshman: National Norms for Fall, 1994." Los Angeles, California: Los Angeles Higher Education Research Institute.

Blankenhorn, David. 1995. *Fatherless America: Confronting Our Most Urgent Social Problem*. New York: Basic Books.

Bowman, M. L. 1990. "Measuring Marital Coping and its Correlates." *Journal of Marriage and the Family* 52: 463–74.

Boyer, D., D. Fine, and S. Killpack. 1991. "Sexual Abuse and Teen Pregnancy." *The Network,* Summer, 1–2.

Breakey, Gail, and Betsy Pratt. 1991. "Healthy Growth for Hawaii's 'Healthy Start': Toward a Systematic Statewide Approach to the Prevention of Child Abuse and Neglect." *Zero to Three* (Bulletin of National Center for Clinical Infant Programs), 11(4): 16–22.

Broman, Clifford L. 1988. "Satisfaction among Blacks: The Significance of Marriage and Parenthood." *Journal of Marriage and the Family* 50: 45–51.

Busby, Dean M. 1991. "Violence in the Family." In *Family Research: A Sixty-Year Review,* vol. 1, ed. S. J. Bahr, pp. 335–85. New York: Lexington Books.

Colorado Domestic Violence Coalition. 1991. *Domestic Violence for Health Care Professionals*, 3rd edition.

Cox, E. 1992. "Strengthening Our Values." *California Family* Fall, 1–19.

Darden, E. C., and T. S. Zimmerman. 1992. "Blended Families: A Decade Review, 1970 to 1990." *Family Therapy* 19: 25–31

Demo, David. H. 1992. "Parent-Child Relations: Assessing Recent Changes." *Journal of Marriage and the Family* 54: 104–117.

_____. 1993. "The Relentless Search for Effects of Divorce: Forging New Trails or Tumbling Down the Beaten Path?" *Journal of Marriage and the Family* 55: 42–45.

Demo, David H., and Alan C. Acock. 1991. "The Impact of Divorce on Children." In *Contemporary Families: Looking Forward, Looking Back,* ed. Alan Booth, pp. 162–91. Minneapolis: National Council on Family Relations.

EAP Digest. Nov./Dec. 1991. Troy, Minnesota.

Elliott, D. M., and J. Briere. 1992. "The Sexually Abused Boy: Problems in Manhood." *Medical Aspects of Human Sexuality,* 26: 68–71.

Finkelhor, D., and K. Yllo. 1988. "Rape in Marriage." In *Abuse and Victimization across the Life Span,* ed. M. B. Straus, pp. 140–52. Baltimore: Johns Hopkins University Press.

Foster, Burk, Craig J. Forsyth, and Stasia Herbert. 1994. "The Cycle of Family Violence among Criminal Offenders: A Study of Inmates in One Louisiana Jail." *Free Inquiry in Creative Sociology* 22: 133–37.

Freeman, Ellen W., and Karl Rickels. 1993. *Early Childbearing: Perspectives of Black Adolescents on Pregnancy, Abortion, and Contraception.* Newbury Park, Calif.: Sage Publications.

Gelles, Richard J. 1992. "Poverty and Violence toward Children." *American Behavioral Scientist* 35: 258–74.

_____. 1993. "Family Violence." In *Family Violence: Prevention and Treatment,* ed. Robert L. Hampton, Thomas P. Gullotta, Gerald R. Adams, Earl H. Potter III, and Roger P. Weissberg, pp. 1–24. Newbury Park, Calif.: Sage Publications.

Gelles, Richard J., and Jon R. Conte. 1990. "Domestic Violence and Sexual Abuse of Children: A Review of Research in the Eighties." *Journal of Marriage and the Family* 52: 1045–58.

_____. 1991. "Domestic Violence and Sexual Abuse of Children: A Review of Research in the Eighties." In *Contemporary Families: Looking Forward, Looking Back,* ed. Alan Booth, pp. 327–40. Minneapolis: National Council on Family Relations.

Gelles, Richard J., and Murray Straus. 1988. *Intimate Violence.* New York: Simon & Schuster.

Gibbs, Nancy. 1993. "Till Death Do Us Part." *Time,* January 18: 38–45.

Gleick, Elizabeth. 1995. "Should This Marriage be Saved?" *Time,* February 77: 48–56.

Harrington, Donna, and Howard Dubowitz. 1993. "What Can Be Done to Prevent Child Maltreatment?" In *Family Violence: Prevention and Treatment,* ed. Robert L. Hampton, Thomas P. Gullotta, Gerald R. Adams, Earl H. Potter III, and Roger P. Weissberg, pp. 258–80. Newbury Park, Calif.: Sage Publications.

Healthy Families America Fact Sheet. 1994 (May). National Committee to Prevent Child Abuse, Healthy Families America. 332 S. Michigan Ave., Suite 1600, Chicago, IL 60604.

Heide, K. M. 1992. *Why Kids Kill Parents: Child Abuse and Adolescent Homicide.* Columbus, Ohio: Ohio State University Press.

Heim, Susan C., and Douglas K. Snyder. 1991. "Predicting Depression from Marital Distress and Attributional Processes." *Journal of Marital and Family Therapy* 17: 67–72.

Hewlett, Sylvia A. 1992. *When the Bough Breaks: The Cost of Neglecting Our Children.* New York: Harper Perennial.

Ingrassia, Michelle. 1993. "Daughters of Murphy Brown." *Newsweek,* August 2: 58–59.

Johnson, T. F. 1991. *Elder Mistreatment: Deciding Who is at Risk.* New York: Greenwood Press.

Jones, Ann. 1994. "Crimes against Women: Media Part of Problem for Masking Violence in the Language of Love." *USA Today,* March 10, 9A.

Kaufman, Joan, and Edward Zigler. 1992. "The Prevention of Child Maltreatment: Programming, Research, and Policy." In *Prevention of Child*

Maltreatment: Developmental and Ecological Perspectives, ed. Diane J. Willis, E. Wayne Holden, and Mindy Rosenberg, pp. 269–95. New York: John Wiley & Sons.

Kitson, Gay C., and Leslie A. Morgan. 1991. "The Multiple Consequences of Divorce: A Decade Review." In *Contemporary Families: Looking Forward, Looking Back,* ed. Alan Booth, pp. 150–91. Minneapolis: National Council on Family Relations.

Knudsen, Dean. 1989. "Duplicate Reports of Child Mistreatment: A Research Note." *Child Abuse and Neglect* 13: 41–43.

Knutson, John F., and Mary Beth Selner. 1994. "Punitive Childhood Experiences Reported by Young Adults over a 10-Year Period." *Child Abuse and Neglect* 18: 155–66.

Koss, Mary P. , and John A. Gaines. 1993. "The Prediction of Sexual Aggression by Alcohol Use, Athletic Participation and Fraternity Affiliation." *Journal of Interpersonal Violence* 8: 94–108.

Krug, Ronald S. 1989. "Adult Male Report of Childhood Sexual Abuse by Mothers: Case Description, Motivations, and Long-Term Consequences." *Child Abuse and Neglect* 13: 111–19.

Krugman, R. D., M. Lenherr, B. A. Betz, and G. E. Fryer. 1986. "The Relationship between Unemployment and Physical Abuse of Children." *Child Abuse and Neglect* 13: 111–19.

Kurdek, Lawrence A. 1991. "The Relationship between Reported Well-being and Divorce History, Availability of Proximate Adult, and Gender." *Journal of Marriage and the Family* 53: 71–78.

Lauer, Robert H., and Jeanette C. Lauer. 1991. "The Long-Term Relational Consequences of Problematic Family Backgrounds." *Family Relations* 40: 286–90.

Levinson, D. 1989. *Family Violence in Cross-Cultural Perspective.* Newbury Park, Calif.: Sage Publications.

Lloyd, S. A., and B. C. Emery. 1993. "Abuse in the Family: An Ecological, Life-Cycle Perspective." In *Family Relations: Challenges for the Future,* ed. T. H. Brubaker, pp. 129–52. Newbury Park, CA: Sage Publications.

Loseke, D. R. 1992. *The Battered Woman and Shelters: The Social Construction of Wife Abuse.* Albany, N.Y.: State University of New York Press.

Marlow, L., and S. R. Sauber. 1990. *The Handbook of Divorce Mediation.* New York: Plenum.

Masheter, C. 1991. "Post-Divorce Relationships between Ex-Spouses: The Roles of Attachment and Interpersonal Conflict." *Journal of Marriage and the Family* 53: 103–10.

McLanahan, Sara, and Karen Booth. 1991. "Mother-Only Families." In *Contemporary Families: Looking Forward, Looking Back,* ed. Alan Booth, pp. 405–28. Minneapolis: National Council on Family Relations.

Meddis, Sam Vincent, and Robert Davis. 1993. "Poll: Get Tougher on Crime." *USA Today,* October 28, A1.

Mindel, Charles H., Robert W. Habenstein, and Roosevelt Wright, Jr. 1988. *Ethnic Families in America: Patterns and Variations.* New York: Elsevier, 1988.

Morrow, R. B. and G. T. Sorrell. 1989. "Factors Affecting Self-Esteem, Depression, and Negative Behaviors in Sexually Abused Female Adolescents." *Journal of Marriage and the Family* 51: 677–86.

Murty, K. S., and J. B. Roebuck. 1992. "An Analysis of Crisis Calls by Battered Women in the City of Atlanta." In *Intimate Violence: Interdisciplinary Perspectives,* ed. E. C. Viano, pp. 61–70. Washington, D.C.: Hemisphere Publishing Co.

Musick, Judith S. 1993. *Young, Poor, and Pregnant: The Psychology of Teen-age Motherhood.* New Haven: Yale University Press.

National Center for Health Statistics. 1995. "Births, Marriages, Divorces, and Deaths for September, 1944." *Monthly Vital Statistics Report* 43, no. 9. Hyattsville, Md.: Public Health Service, March 1.

National Clearinghouse on Marital and Date Rape. 1994. Personal communication. Berkeley, Calif.

North Carolina Coalition Against Domestic Violence. 1991 (Spring). *Domestic Violence Fact Sheet.* P.O. Box 51875, Durham, NC 27717-1875.

Novello, A. 1992. "The Domestic Violence Issue: Hear Our Voices." *American Medical News,* March 23, 35(12): 41–42.

Oates, R. K., A. A. Davis, and M. G. Ryan. 1983. "Predictive Factors for Child Abuse." In *International Perspectives on Family Violence,* ed. R. J. Gelles and C. P. Cornell, pp. 97–106. Lexington, Mass.: Lexington Books.

Pagelow, M. D. 1992. "Adult Victims of Domestic Violence: Battered Women." *Journal of Interpersonal Violence* 7: 87–120.

Parnell, Allan M., Gray Swicegood, and Gillian Stevens. 1994. "Nonmarital Pregnancies and Marriage in the United States." *Social Forces* 73 (1): 263–87.

Peterson, Karen S. 1995. "Family Advocates Declare War on Divorce." *USA Today,* March 30, 6d.

Popenoe, David. 1993. "Point of View: Scholars Should Worry about the Disintegration of the American Family." *Chronicle of Higher Education,* April 14, A48

Russell, D. E. 1990. *Rape in Marriage.* Bloomington, Ind.: Indiana University Press.

Sapiro, Virginia. 1990. *Women in American Society,* 2d ed. Mountain View, Calif.: Mayfield.

Scanzoni, John, and W. Marsiglio. 1993. "New Action Theory and Contemporary Families." *Journal of Family Issues* 14: 105–32.

Scherreik, Susan. 1993. "The Practical Part of Living Together." *New York Times,* March 6, 142(L).

Shapiro, Joseph P., and Joannie M. Schrof. 1995 "Honor Thy Children." *U.S. News and World Report,* February 27, 39–49.

Smock, Pamela. 1994. "Gender and the Short-Run Economic Consequences of Marital Disruption." *Social Forces* 73 (1): 243–62.

Solomon, J. C. 1992. "Child Abuse by Family Members: A Radical Feminist Perspective." *Sex Roles* 27: 473–85.

Song, Young I. 1991. "Single Asian American Women as a Result of Divorce: Depressive Affect and Changes in Social Support." *Journal of Divorce and Remarriage* 14: 219–30.

Stack, Steven. 1989. "The Impact of Divorce on Suicide in Norway, 1951–1980." *Journal of Marriage and the Family* 51: 229–38.

Statistical Abstract of the United States: 1993, 113th ed. Washington, D.C.: U. S. Bureau of the Census, 1993.

Statistical Abstract of the United-States: 1995, 115th ed. Washington, D.C.: U.S. Bureau of the Census, 1995.

Stein, Theodore J. 1993. "Legal Perspectives on Family Violence against Children." In *Family Violence: Prevention and Treatment,* ed. by Robert L. Hampton, Thomas P. Gullotta, Gerald R. Adams, Earl H. Potter III, and Roger P. Weissberg, pp. 179–97. Newbury Park, Calif.: Sage Publications.

Steinmetz, Suzanne. 1987. "Family Violence." *In Handbook of Marriage and the Family,* ed. M. B. Sussman and S. K. Steinmetz. New York: Plenum.

Stets, J. E., and M. A. Straus. 1989. "The Marriage as a Hitting License: A Comparison of Assaults in Dating, Cohabiting, and Married Couples." In *Violence in Dating Relationships,* ed. M. A. Pirog-Good and J. E. Stets, p. 33–52. New York: Greenwood Press.

Stout, James W., and Fredrick P. Rivara. 1989. "Schools and Sex Education: Does It Work?" *Pediatrics* 83: 375–79.

Straus, Murray A. 1980 "A Sociological Perspective on the Prevention of Wife-Beating." In *The Social Causes of Husband-Wife Violence,* ed. M. A. Straus and G. T. Hotaling, pp. 211–32. Minneapolis: Minn: University of Minnesota Press.

Straus, M. A. and S. Sweet. 1992. "Verbal/Symbolic Aggression in Married Couples: Incidence Rates and Relationships to Personal Characteristics." *Journal of Marriage and the Family* 54: 346–57.

United Nations. 1992. *1991 Demographic Yearbook,* 43d ed. New York: United Nations.

U.S. Bureau of the Census. 1989. "Studies in Marriage and the Family." *Current Population Reports Series* P-23, no. 162, 5.

U.S. Bureau of the Census. 1995. "Population Profile of the U.S.: 1995." U.S. Government Printing Office. Washington, D.C.

U.S. Department of Justice. Office of Justice Programs. 1994. "Domestic Violence: Violence between Intimates." Washington, D.C.: Bureau of Justice Statistics.

Van Biema, David. 1995. "Dunning Deadbeats." *Time,* April 3, 49–50.

Viano, C. Emilio. 1992. "Violence among Intimates: Major Issues and Approaches." In *Intimate Violence: Interdisciplinary Perspectives,* ed. C. E. Viano, pp. 3–12. Washington, D.C.: Hemisphere.

Weitzman, Lenore J. 1985. *The Divorce Revolution: The Unexpected Social and Economic Consequences for Women and Children in America.* New York: Free Press.

White, Melvin. 1988. "Elder Abuse." In *Aging and the Family,* S. J. Bahr and E. T. Peterson, pp. 261–71. Lexington, Mass.: Lexington Books.

Willis, Diane J., E. Wayne Holden, and Mindy Rosenberg. 1992. "Child Maltreatment Prevention: Introduction and Historical Overview." In *Prevention of Child Maltreatment: Developmental and Ecological Perspectives,* ed. Diane J. Willis, E. Wayne Holden, and Mindy Rosenberg, pp. 1–14. New York: John Wiley & Sons.

Wisensale, Steven. K. 1992. "Toward the 21st Century: Family Change and Public Policy." *Family Relations* 41: 417–22.

Problems of Human Diversity

SECTION 2

People are diverse. They vary on a number of dimensions including age, sexual orientation, gender, and race and ethnicity. In most societies, including the United States, these characteristics are imbued with social significance and are used to make judgments about an individual's worth, intelligence, skills, and personality. Such labeling creates categories of people who are perceived as "different" by others as well as themselves and, as a result, are often treated differently.

A **minority** is defined as a category of people who have unequal access to positions of power, prestige, and wealth in a society. In effect, minorities have unequal opportunities and are disadvantaged in their attempt to gain societal resources. Even though they may be a majority in terms of numbers, they may still be a minority sociologically. Before Nelson Mandela was elected president of South Africa in 1994, South African blacks suffered the disadvantages of a minority, even though they were a numerical majority of the population.

Terms that apply to all minorities include stereotyping, prejudice, and discrimination. A **stereotype** is an exaggerated and overgeneralized truth (e.g., "all Puerto Ricans like spicy food"). **Prejudice** is an attitude, often negative, that prejudges an individual. **Discrimination** is differential treatment by members of the majority group against members of the minority that has a harmful impact on members of the subordinate group. The groups we will discuss in this section are all victims of stereotyping, prejudice, and discrimination.

Minority groups usually have certain characteristics in common. In general, members of a minority group know that they are members of a minority, stay within their own group, have relatively low levels of self-esteem, are disproportionately in the lower socioeconomic strata, and are viewed as having negative traits. Other characteristics of specific minority groups are identified in the accompanying table.

In the following chapters, we discuss categories of minorities based upon age (Chapter 6), sexual orientation (Chapter 7), gender (Chapter 8), and race and ethnicity (Chapter 9). Although other categories of minorities exist (e.g., disabled/handicapped, religious minorities), we have chosen to concentrate on these four because each is surrounded by issues and policies that have far-reaching social, political, and economic implications.

NINE CHARACTERISTICS OF FOUR MINORITIES

	ELDERLY	HOMOSEXUALS	WOMEN	RACIAL AND ETHNIC MINORITIES
1. Status ascribed based on:	Age	Sexual orientation	Sex	Race/ethnicity
2. Visibility:	High	Low	High	High
3. Attribution of minority status (correctly or incorrectly) based on:	Hair Skin elasticity	Mannerisms Style of dress	Anatomy	Skin color Facial features Hair
4. Summary image:	Dependent	Sick or immoral	Weak	Inferior
5. Derogatory and offensive terms:	Old codger Battle-Ax	Faggot Dyke	Bitch Whore	Jap Nigger Spic
6. Control through feigning various characteristics:*	Frailty	Heterosexuality	Weakness	Ignorance
7. Discrimination:	Yes	Yes	Yes	Yes
8. Victims of violence:	Yes	Yes	Yes	Yes
9. Segregation:	Yes	Yes	Yes	Yes

*Being aware of their lack of power, minority group members may try to exert control by feigning certain characteristics. For example, a slave couldn't tell his or her owner, "I'm not going to plow the fields—do it yourself!" But by acting incompetent, the slave may avoid the work. Gays pass as straight by bragging about heterosexual conquests. The elderly in nursing homes whose family members might otherwise not visit act ill in the hope of eliciting a visit. The problem with these acts is that they contribute to and stabilize the summary images.

6

CHAPTER

Youth and Aging

IS IT TRUE?

The more primitive a society, the more likely its members are to practice senilicide—the killing of the elderly (p. 165).

The older a person, the less likely that person is to define a particular age as old (p. 164).

A 1989 federal bill proposed that teenagers be paid less than the minimum wage during training periods (p. 170).

In the United States, individuals age 65 and older are more likely to vote than any other age group (p. 169).

The U.S. poverty rate for children is more than double that of every other major industrialized country (p. 172).

ANS: 1. T 2. T 3. T 4. T 5. T

In many ways, youth and aging are celebrated in our society. A baby's first birthday as well as every birthday of an aging grandparent are significant social events. The first baby born in every new year is often featured on the front page of the local newspaper. And when George Burns turned 99, he was the focus of a national evening news broadcast. When asked if he was glad to be there, he quipped, "[W]hen you're 99 years old, it's nice to be anyplace."

But for every act of celebration that recognizes the specialness of a young or old person, there are countless aspects of social life that oppress children and devalue the elderly. The young and the old represent major population segments of American society. In this chapter, we examine the problems and potential solutions associated with youth and aging. We begin by looking at age as a social variable.

The Social Context: Youth, Aging, and Ageism

In sociology, being a "child" or "senior citizen" is considered an ascribed status. Ascribed statuses are social positions that one is born into or involuntarily assumes later in life. Unlike other ascribed statuses, the status of age changes over time and, thus, represents a continuum.

Age is a social variable that has a dramatic impact on one's life in at least five ways (Matras 1990 identified 1–4):

1. Age determines one's life experiences since the date of birth determines the historical period in which a person lives. Harrigan (1992) notes how fifty years makes a dramatic difference in the world one experiences:

   The America of fifty years ago had a completely different view of society. Americans of that era would not have known what to think of . . . the notion that public schools should distribute condoms to school children. Nor could they have imagined murders in public schools, the placement of metal detectors at school entrances to prevent "students" from entering with pistols or knives.

   Adults in the 1940s and 1950s had come through a terrible depression that made Americans understand the importance of cooperation and concern for one's neighbors. In every way, then, the America of four or five decades ago was a more wholesome society, a better, infinitely more decent place. (p. 4)

2. Different ages are associated with different developmental stages (physiological, psychological, and social) and abilities. Ben Franklin observed, "[A]t 20 years of age the will reigns; at 30 the wit; at 40 judgment."

3. Age defines roles and expectations of behavior. The expression "act your age" implies that some behaviors are not considered appropriate for people of certain ages.
4. Age influences the social groups to which one belongs. Whether one is part of a sixth grade class, a labor union, or a seniors' bridge club depends on one's age.
5. Age defines one's legal status. Sixteen year olds can get a driver's license, 18 year olds can vote and get married without their parents' permission, and 65 year olds are eligible for Social Security benefits.

CHILDHOOD, ADULTHOOD, AND ELDERHOOD

Every society assigns different social roles to different age groups. **Age grading** is the assignment of social roles to given chronological ages (Matras 1990). Although the number of age grades varies by society, most societies make at least three distinctions—childhood, adulthood, and elderhood.

Childhood The period of childhood in our society is from birth through age 17 and is often subdivided into infancy, childhood, and adolescence. Infancy has always been recognized as a stage of life, but the social category of childhood only developed after industrialization, urbanization, and modernization took place. Prior to industrialization, infant mortality was high due to the lack of adequate health care and proper nutrition. Once infants could be expected to survive infancy, the concept of childhood emerged, and society began to develop norms in reference to children. Today, child labor laws prohibit children from being used as cheap labor, educational mandates require that children attend school until the age of 16, and federal child pornography laws impose severe penalties for the sexual exploitation of children.

Adulthood The period from age 18 through 64 is generally subdivided into young adulthood, adulthood, and middle age. Each of these statuses involves dramatic role changes related to entering the workforce, getting married, and

> **National Data:** In 1993, one-quarter (25.6%) of the U.S. population was under the age of 18.
> SOURCE: *Children Now* 1995.

> *That's exactly how it goes. You're young and the whole world is ahead of you, and then one day you're not young anymore, and the whole world is behind you, and it's all over.*
> —David Letterman
> Comedian

Little did members of this age cohort know that they were to become the middle-aged "Sandwich Generation," emotionally and economically responsible for both their young children and their elderly parents.

having children. The concept of "middle age" is a relatively recent one that has developed as life expectancy has been extended. Some people in this phase are known as members of the "**sandwich generation**" since they are often emotionally and economically responsible for both their young children and their aging parents.

Elderhood At age 65 one is likely to be considered elderly, a category that is often subdivided into the young-old, old, and old-old. Membership in one of these categories does not necessarily depend on chronological age. The growing number of healthy, active, independent elderly are often considered to be the young-old, however, while the old-old are the less healthy, less active, and more dependent.

AGE—A MATTER OF DEFINITION

Age is largely socially defined. Cultural definitions of "old" and "young" vary from society to society, from time to time, and from person to person. For example, the older a person, the less likely that person is to define a particular age as old. In a national study of more than 2,503 men and women ages 18 to 75, 30 percent of those under 25 responded that "old" is between 40 and 64 years of age. But only 8 percent of those over the age of 65 reported that 65 was old (Clements 1993). In ancient Greece or Rome where the average life expectancy was 20 years, one was old at 18; similarly, one was old at 30 in medieval Europe and at 40 in the United States in 1850. In the United States today, however, people are usually not considered "old" until they reach age 65.

AGEISM

People in all societies treat each other differently on the basis of age. Although such treatment, the number and definitions of age categories, and the roles provided vary, every society has some form of **ageism**—a belief that age is associated with certain psychological, behavioral, and/or intellectual traits.

Although some elderly people may like to skateboard and some young people may like to play bridge, age tends to influence the range of behavior each group engages in.

Ageism is similar to sexism and racism as discussed in Chapters 8 and 9. Ageism often results in the differential treatment of an individual based on his or her perceived or real chronological age. A person's age is also used to define abilities, opportunities, and appropriateness of social roles and may result in stereotyping, discrimination, and prejudice. Ageism is most often directed toward the young and the elderly; both are often dependent on others for care, discriminated against in housing and employment, and victims of abuse.

THE YOUNG AND THE OLD: A CROSS-CULTURAL LOOK

The young and the old receive different treatment in different societies. Differences in the treatment of the dependent young and old have traditionally been associated with whether the country is developed or less developed. Developed countries are characterized by a higher life expectancy, decreasing fertility, and an aging population, and less developed countries by a shorter life expectancy, higher birthrate, and younger population. Ironically, the elderly are usually most respected in less developed countries where they are viewed as sources of cultural wisdom. In highly developed societies, information is more often obtained through formal education, computer networks, and libraries, making the elderly's knowledge and skills less relevant.

Eastern cultures, such as Japan's, revere their elderly partly because of their presumed proximity to honored ancestors.

Although there are proportionately more elderly in industrial and postindustrial societies than in agricultural ones, these societies have fewer statuses for the elderly to occupy. Their positions as caretakers, homeowners, employees, and producers are often usurped by those aged 18 to 65. Paradoxically, the more primitive the society the more likely that society is to practice senilicide—the killing of the elderly. In some societies the elderly are considered a burden and left to die or, in some cases, actually killed. It could be argued that the treatment of the elderly in the United States is not much better than in countries that practice senilicide. The elderly are often warehoused in state institutions, segregated in nursing homes, abused, and given poor medical attention.

Not all societies treat the elderly as a burden. Scandinavian countries provide government support for in-home care workers for elderly who can no longer perform such tasks as cooking and cleaning. This program allows the elderly to live their final days in their own homes in familiar surroundings (Szulc 1988). Eastern cultures such as Japan revere their elderly, in part, because of their presumed proximity to honored ancestors. This is in stark contradiction to recent evidence that U.S. youth view the elderly as "culturally irrelevant" (Kolland 1994). Japanese elders sit at the head of the table, enter a room and bathe first, and are considered the head of the family. While the United States has Mother's Day and Father's Day, Japan has "Respect for Elders Day" (Palmore 1981).

There were only two periods in the life of a Chinese male when he possessed maximum security and minimal responsibility— infancy and old age. Of the two, old age was the better because one was conscious of the pleasure to be derived from such an almost perfect period.
—Paul T. Welty
Historian

Like the treatment of the elderly, the treatment of the young has changed over time. In the 1800s in Europe, children were ignored and left to fend for themselves. Many were used as inexpensive laborers. Children as young as 4 were used as chimney sweeps in England and as indentured servants in textile mills until the age of 21. In the United States during the same time period, societal concerns for the welfare of children were not much better. Children had to be protected under the Society for the Protection of Cruelty to Animals statutes because no laws protecting children existed (Regoli and Hewitt 1994).

Societies also differ in the way they treat children. In agricultural societies, children work as adults, marry at a young age, and pass from childhood directly to adulthood with no recognized period of adolescence. In contrast, in 1979 the Swedish Parliament passed a law that children could not be subjected to physical punishment, and a 1993 law in Finland banned hair pulling of children. Similarly, in 1992 a bill was introduced into the German Parliament that would prevent parents from "nagging, spanking, boxing ears, or withholding affection from children" (Regoli and Hewitt 1994).

The United States offers countless examples of children being held to a different standard than adults. There is a separate justice system for juveniles and age limits for driving, drinking alcohol, joining the military, entering into a contract, marrying, dropping out of school, and voting. The limitations placed on young adults in the United States would not be tolerated if these same restrictions were placed on individuals on the basis of sex or race. Hence ageism, in reference to children, is significantly more tolerated than sexism or racism in the United States.

Despite the differential treatment of minors, people in the United States are fascinated with youth and being young. This was not always the case. The elderly were once highly valued in the United States—particularly older men who headed families and businesses. Younger men even powdered their hair, wore wigs, and dressed in a way that made them look older (Fischer 1978). It should be remembered, however, that in 1900 only 4 percent of the population was 65; over 40 percent of the population was under 18 (Harris 1990). Being old was rare and respected; to some it was a sign that God looked upon the individual favorably.

One theory argues that the shift from valuing the old to valuing the young took place during the transition from an agriculturally based society to an industrial one. Land, which was often owned by elders, became less important as did their knowledge and skills about land-based economies. With industrialization, technological skills, training, and education became more important than land ownership. Called **modernization theory,** this position argues that as a society becomes more technologically advanced, the position of the elderly declines (Cowgill and Holmes 1972).

Today, being young is portrayed as the quintessence of life; Americans in search for the "fountain of youth" spend billions of dollars on hair coloring, cosmetic surgery, wrinkle creams, and diet pills. Women in particular are targeted by the media as a consequence of society's emphasis on a youthful appearance. Some commentators argue that the preoccupation with youth in the United States has created a "youth culture." Others see the youth culture more as a product of the restrictions placed on youth.

> **Consideration** Using participant observation techniques, Cahill (1993) recorded the treatment of children in public places for nearly 300 hours over a two-year period. He observed that children are restricted in the places they go, for example, often discouraged from eating in some restaurants and excluded from some apartment complexes. Further, public accommodations don't adequately meet the needs of children—pay telephones, sinks, and water fountains are out of children's reach. Cahill concludes that such limitations, as well as the segregation of children in schools, limits communication between children and adults, creating differences in their

respective social worlds. The result is ". ... a distinct [youth] subculture of which adults are only vaguely aware. . ." (p. 400).

Theories of Age Inequality

Three sociological theories help explain age inequality and the continued existence of ageism in the United States. These theories—structural-functionalism, conflict theory, and symbolic interactionism—are discussed in the following sections.

STRUCTURAL-FUNCTIONALIST PERSPECTIVE

Structural-functionalism emphasizes the interdependence of society—how one part of a social system interacts with other parts to benefit the whole. From a functionalist perspective, the elderly must gradually relinquish their roles to younger members of society. This transition is viewed as natural and necessary to maintain the integrity of the social system. The elderly gradually withdraw as they prepare for death, and society withdraws from the elderly by segregating them in housing such as retirement villages and nursing homes. In the interim, the young have learned through the educational institution how to function in the roles surrendered by the elderly. In essence, a balance in society is achieved whereby the various age groups perform their respective functions: the young go to school, adults fill occupational roles, and the elderly, with obsolete skills and knowledge, disengage. As this process continues, each new group moves up and replaces another, benefiting society and all of its members.

The job of parenting is being devalued, and with it the quality of children's lives and society's future.
—"The Progress of Nations" (UNICEF)

This theory is known as **disengagement theory** (Cummings and Henry 1961). Some researchers no longer accept this position as valid, however, given the increased number of elderly who remain active throughout life (Riley 1987). In contrast to disengagement theory, **activity theory** emphasizes that the elderly disengage in part because they are structurally segregated and isolated, not because they have a natural tendency to do so. For those elderly who remain active, role loss may be minimal. The establishment of senior centers and other such facilities is based on the assumption that given opportunities for involvement, the elderly will respond. In studying 1,720 respondents who reported using a senior center in the previous year, Miner, Logan, and Spitze (1993) found that those who attended were less disengaged and more socially active than those who did not.

CONFLICT PERSPECTIVE

The conflict perspective focuses on age grading as another form of inequality as both the young and the old occupy subordinate statuses. Some conflict theorists emphasize that individuals at both ends of the age continuum are superfluous to a capitalist economy. Children are untrained, inexperienced, and neither actively producing nor consuming in an economy that requires both. Similarly, the elderly, although once working, are no longer productive and often lack required skills and levels of education. Both young and old are considered part of what is called the dependent population; that is, they are an economic drain on society. Hence, children are required to go to school in preparation for entry into a capitalist economy, and the elderly are forced to retire.

Other conflict theorists focus on how different age strata represent different interest groups that compete with one another for scarce resources. Debates about funding for public schools, child health programs, Social Security, and Medicare largely represent conflicting interests of the young versus the old.

SYMBOLIC INTERACTIONIST

The symbolic interactionist perspective emphasizes the importance of examining the social meaning and definitions associated with age. The elderly are often defined in a number of stereotypical ways contributing to a host of myths surrounding the inevitability of physical and mental decline. Table 6.1 identifies some of these myths.

Media portrayals of the elderly contribute to the negative image of the elderly. The young are typically portrayed in active, vital roles and are often overrepresented in commercials. In contrast, the elderly are portrayed as difficult, complaining, and burdensome and are often underrepresented in commercials. The elderly are also portrayed as childlike in terms of clothes, facial expressions, temperament, and activities—a phenomenon known as **infantilizing elders** (Arluke and Levin 1990). For example, young and old are often paired together. A promotional advertisement for the movie *Just You and Me, Kid* with Brooke Shields and George Burns described it as "the story of two juvenile delinquents." "Roseanne" Conner comments to her sister Jackie, "You know how cranky Mom gets when she's tired." The media focus on images of Santa visiting nursing homes and local elementary school children teaching residents arts and crafts. Finally, the elderly are often depicted in role reversal, cared for by their adult children as in the situation comedy *Golden Girls.*

Negative stereotypes and media images of the elderly engender **gerontophobia**—a shared fear or dread of the elderly, which may create a self-fulfilling prophecy. For example, an elderly person forgets something and attributes his or her behavior to age. A younger person, however, engaging in the same behavior, is unlikely to attribute forgetfulness to age given cultural definitions surrounding the onset of senility. Thus, the elderly, having learned the social meaning associated with being old, may themselves perpetuate the negative stereotypes.

The negative meanings associated with aging underlie the obsession of many Americans to conceal their age by altering their appearance. With the hope of holding on to youth a little bit longer, aging Americans spend millions of dollars each year on hair products, facial creams, and plastic surgery. In *The Fountain of Age,* Betty Friedan (1993) suggests that the pursuit of eternal youth contributes to the notion that aging is a "problem":

> *What are we doing to ourselves—and to our society—by denying age? . . . the more we seek the perpetual fountain of youth and go on denying age, defining "age" itself as a problem, that "problem" will only get worse. (p. 68)*

It's just a very hard process to watch yourself age. It's sad sometimes.
—Jessica Lange
Actress

TABLE 6.1

MYTHS AND FACTS ABOUT THE ELDERLY

Health	Myth:	The elderly are always sick; most are in nursing homes.
	Fact:	Over 80 percent of the elderly are healthy enough to engage in their normal activities. Only 6 percent are confined to a nursing home.
Automobile Accidents	Myth:	The elderly are dangerous drivers and have a lot of wrecks.
	Fact:	Drivers ages 45 to 74 have only 12 accidents per 100 drivers per year. Drivers under age 20 have 37 accidents per 100 drivers per year. Up to age 75, older drivers tend to drive fewer miles than younger drivers and compensate for their reduced reaction time by driving more carefully. However, drivers 75 and older have 25 accidents per 100 drivers per year. The increased incidence is "rooted in the normal processes of aging: diminishing vision and hearing and decreasing attention spans" (Carney 1989).
Mental Status	Myth:	The elderly are senile.
	Fact:	Although some of the elderly learn more slowly and forget more quickly, most remain oriented and mentally intact. Only 20–25 percent develop Alzheimer's disease or some other incurable form of brain disease. Senility is not inevitable as one ages.
Employment	Myth:	The elderly are inefficient employees.
	Fact:	Although only about 17 percent of men and 9 percent of women 65 years old and over are still employed, those who continue to work are efficient workers. When compared to younger workers, the elderly have lower job turnover, fewer accidents, and less absenteeism. Older workers also report higher satisfaction in their work.
Politics	Myth:	The elderly are not politically active.
	Fact:	In 1986, 1988, 1990, 1992, and 1994, individuals age 65 and older were more likely to vote than any other age group.
Sexuality	Myth:	Sexual satisfaction disappears with age.
	Fact:	Many elderly persons report sexual satisfaction. For example, in a study of 61 elderly men (average age = 71) both with and without sexual partners, sexual satisfaction was rated at an average of 6.3 on a scale where 1 = no satisfaction and 10 = extremely high satisfaction (Mulligan and Paluta 1991).
Adaptability	Myth:	The elderly cannot adapt to new working conditions.
	Fact:	A high proportion of the elderly are flexible in accepting change in their occupations and earnings. Adaptability depends on the individual: many young are set in their ways, and many older people adapt to change readily.

Sources: Binstock, Robert H. 1986. "Public Policy and the Elderly" *Journal of Geriatric Psychiatry* 19: 115–143; Carney, James. 1989. "Can a Driver Be Too Old?" Time, January 16: 28; Harris, Diana K. 1990. *Sociology of Aging*, 2d ed. New York: Harper & Row; Mulligan, T., and R. F. Palguta, Jr. 1991. "Sexual Interest, Activity and Satisfaction among Male Nursing Home Residents." *Archives of Sexual Behavior* 20: 199-204; Palmore, Erdman B. 1984. "The Retired". p. 63-76 In *Handbook on the Aged in the United States* ed. Erdman B. Palmore, Westport, Conn: Greenwood Press; and *Statistical Abstract of the United States: 1995.* 1995. 115th ed. Washington, D.C.: U.S. Bureau of the Census.

Problems of Youth in America

In spite of the presumed benefits of being young, numerous problems are associated with youth. The status of children in the United States is disturbing. In 1993, 43 per 1,000 U.S. children were reported as abused or neglected; almost one in four under 18 were living in poverty; almost one in five had no health insurance. In the same year, one in three U.S. children age two were not appropriately immunized, and a similar percentage of youth did not graduate from high school on time (*Children Now* 1995). Increasingly, what is happening to children is defined as a social problem and has led to a greater concern with children's legal rights in America (see *In Focus*).

CHILDREN AND THE LAW

Children are both discriminated against and granted special protections under the law (see *In Focus*). Although legal mandates require that children go to school until age 16, other laws provide a separate justice system whereby children have limited legal responsibility based upon their age status. As violence by minors increases, many Americans have begun to question the wisdom of a separate legal structure for minors. The laws are changing: most states have lowered the age of accountability, capital punishment of minors is being considered in a number of states, and the number of parent-liability laws has increased. While children's rights may expand in some areas such as self-determination, recent legal changes may cost minors their protected status in the courts.

ECONOMIC DISCRIMINATION

Children are discriminated against in terms of employment, age restrictions, wages, training programs,and health benefits. Traditionally, children worked on farms and in factories but were displaced by the Industrial Revolution. In 1938, Congress passed the Fair Standards Labor Act, which required factory workers to be at least 16. Although the law was designed to protect children, it was also discriminatory in that it prohibited minors from having free access to jobs and economic independence. More recently, a 1989 federal bill proposed that employers pay teenagers less than the minimum wage during their initial training period. No such law exists for any other age group.

> **Consideration** Most of the 3.5 million employees of the fast-food industry are teenagers in their first job, making an average of $5.17 per hour. Not one of the fast-food chains is unionized, which indicates teens' lack of power over their working environment. "Indeed, when Labor Department agents conducted sweeps of work sites around the country in 1990, eighty percent of the 40,000 child labor law violations they uncovered were in the fast food industry" (Clark 1991, 833).

Further, although the federal government gives the American Association of Retired Persons $75 million annually to provide training and placement programs for senior citizens, teenagers, and especially minority adolescents, have the highest rates of unemployment (George 1992). Regarding health benefits, the federal government spends more on health care for the elderly during their last

Children's Rights in America

Recently, the degree to which the courts should empower children with the same legal rights as adults has been the subject of debate (*Congressional Quarterly* 1993). In 1992 a Florida court allowed 12-year-old Gregory Kingsley to "divorce" his biological mother so that he could be adopted by the foster parents who had cared for him during the previous nine months. Aided by his prospective foster parents, Gregory hired an attorney to pursue his case contending that his mother had never given him proper care. In a Vermont case, the court amended a child's birth certificate to include the adoptive mother and biological father as parents.

Leading the cause for children's rights to self-determination is Hillary Rodham Clinton, who has made several recommendations including abolishing minority status for children. In effect, children should be presumed competent to exercise rights and assume responsibilities unless proven otherwise. She also recommends giving children full procedural rights including independent legal counsel in any case where the child's interests are being adjudicated.

In response to these suggestions, conservatives warn that greater legal rights for children will threaten parental authority and the traditional family. They ask, "Where will it stop?" and suggest children would be able to sue their parents over such issues as bedtime, allowances, and household chores.

Historically, children have had little control over their lives. They have been "double dependent" on both their parents and the state. Indeed, colonists in America regarded children as property. Beginning in the 1960s, however, the view that children should have more autonomy became popular and was codified in several legal decisions.

The dominant view of children today, as expressed by the courts as well as the public, involves taking "a protective stance toward children rather than empowering children to care for themselves" (p. 342). Examples of protective legislation include requiring child abuse prevention and treatment programs, ensuring education for disabled children, and setting the constitutional threshold for executions at age 16. Alternatively, empowering children includes such cases as Gregory Kingsley's "divorce" from his mother and more recent court decisions that provide that children aged 15 or older should be permitted to testify as to their custody and visitation preferences.

In spite of these gains, children in the United States have received only limited empowerment. The United States has not ratified the United Nations' Treaty on Children's Rights although 132 countries have, and 25 others have signed the agreement. One reason the United States has not signed the pact may be Article 11, which requires that children be assured "the highest attainable standard of health." Some people are concerned that accepting such a position would result in cases being brought to court that they are simply unwilling, at present, to hear.

SOURCE: *Congressional Quarterly.* 1993. "Children's Legal Rights," April 23, 339–54.

year of life than on all the health care needs of children—eleven times as much money on those 65 and over as on those under the age of 18 (Hewlett 1992).

Worldwide, there is also evidence that when global economic decisions are made, children suffer. Bradshaw et al. (1992) observed that the global debt crisis has led the world's business community to pressure developing countries into financial strategies that directly affect the well-being of children. For example,

Most fast food chain employees are teenagers. None of the fast food chains is unionized, so teens have very little control over their working environment.

funding for immunization programs for children is cut out of economic necessity. "This potential relationship between international debt and children's quality of life is one of the most important sociological issues in poor countries today" (p. 630).

Because of economic discrimination at both the individual and the institutional level, many children live in poverty. The United States does not have a universal government policy to protect children. The Social Security system keeps many elderly out of poverty and, since 1972, has been indexed to keep up with inflation. But Aid to Families with Dependent Children (AFDC) has been cut 42 percent in real dollars since 1970. Social Security keeps eight out of ten elderly from being poor; AFDC keeps less than one in three children out of poverty (Taylor 1993). Nor is there a health care program comparable to Medicare for the elderly for those under 18.

Consideration *Compared to other industrialized nations, the United States has a disturbingly high child poverty rate. Based on a recent worldwide study of children, the U.S. poverty rate for children is more than double that of every other major industrialized country. Twenty percent of U.S. children live below the poverty line, up from 15 percent in 1960 (UNICEF 1994).*

GROWING UP IN THE NINETIES

Childhood is a stage of life that is socially constructed by structural and cultural forces of the past and present. The old roles for children as laborers and farm helpers are disappearing, yet no new roles have emerged. While being bombarded by the media, children must face the challenges of an uncertain economic future, peer culture, music videos, divorce, incidents of abuse, poverty, and crime. Parents and public alike fear children are becoming increasingly involved with sex, drugs, alcohol, and violence. Some even argue that childhood as a stage of life is disappearing (Adler 1994).

In a poll commissioned by *Newsweek* and the Children's Defense Fund, 758 children between the ages of 10 and 17 reported their perspectives on life:

In 1993, about 40 percent of U.S. citizens living below the poverty level were under 18 years old (*Statistical Abstract of the United States: 1995*, Table 747).

What emerges is a portrait of a generation living in fear. The security of their parents' generation, and the optimistic view of the future, is no longer taken for granted by young people today. For them, the poll found, the American Dream may be dying. (Ingrassia 1993, 52)

Many reported that they feared being victims of violent crime (56 percent), not being able to afford a doctor (51 percent), and that their parents would get a divorce (p. 52). A study by the Fordham Institute on the social health of children also found a general decline in the well-being of American youth (Miringoff 1989).

There are some signs of optimism, however, often at the grassroots level where parents, teachers, corporate officials, politicians, and citizens join together in the interest of children. In Kentucky, AmeriCorp volunteers raised the reading competency of underachieving youths 116 percent in just six months; in Dayton, Ohio, behavioral problems of students at an elementary school were significantly reduced once "character education" was introduced; and in Los Angeles's Crenshaw High School, student entrepreneurs established "Food from the Hood," a garden project that is projected to earn $50,000 in profit this year.

Demographics: The "Graying of America"

The population of America is "graying," that is, getting older. Here, the definition of "older" is age 65 or beyond. The origin of this arbitrary age is the Social Security Act of 1935, which established 65 as the age of retirement.

The number of elderly is increasing for three reasons. First, 76 million baby boomers born between 1946 and 1964 are getting older. Additionally, and to a large extent as a consequence of advanced medical technologies, life expectancy has increased and fertility has decreased. Since the proportion of the elderly is influenced by such variables as the fertility rate and life expectancy, different countries have different proportions. Western Europe and the Scandinavian countries have a higher percentage of the elderly than the

National Data: In 1995, about 13 percent of the U.S. population was over age 65. By the year 2050, an estimated 20 percent of the population will be over the age of 65.

SOURCE: *Statistical Abstract of the United States: 1995,* Table 17.

This is the century of old age, or, as it has been called, the "Age of Aging."
—Robert Butler
Gerontologist

United States; Canada, Japan, Israel, and the former Soviet Union have a lower percentage (Matras 1990).

AGE PYRAMIDS

National Data: During the twentieth century, the number of people under 65 in the United States tripled while the number of people 65 and older grew eleven times. In 1900, only one in 25 Americans was elderly; by 1994, one in eight Americans was elderly.

SOURCE: U.S. Census Bureau 1995b.

Age pyramids are a way of showing in graph form the percentage of a population in various age groups. In 1900 the U.S. age pyramid looked very much like a true pyramid: the base of the pyramid was large, indicating that most people were in their younger years, and the top of the pyramid was much smaller, showing that only a small percentage of the population was elderly. By the year 2030, the "pyramid" will look more like a pillar with the exception of the very top, which will reflect the large proportion of elderly people in the population (see Figure 6.1).

The number of people at various ages in a society is important because the demand for housing, education, health care, and jobs varies as different age groups, particularly baby boomers, move through the pyramid. For example, as America "grays," colleges will recruit older students, advertisements will be directed toward older consumers, and elderly housing and medical care needs will increase.

AGE AND RACE/ETHNICITY

In the United States, only 7 percent of racial minorities and Hispanics were 65 and older in 1993, compared with 15 percent of nonhispanic whites (Fowles

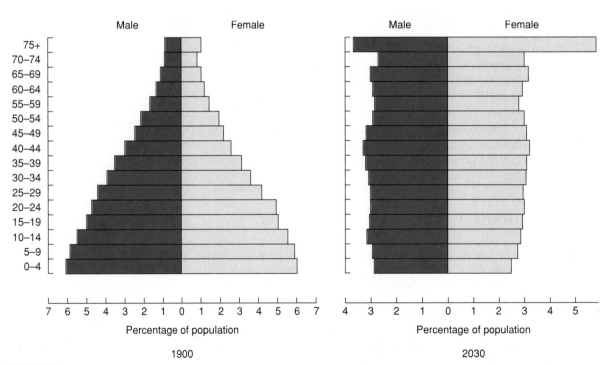

FIGURE 6.1

U.S. POPULATION PYRAMIDS

SOURCE: *Statistical Abstract of the United States: 1993,* 113th ed. Washington, D.C: U.S. Bureau of the Census, Table 17 for 2030 projections.

1995). Racial and ethnic minorities have a lower life expectancy so they have proportionately fewer elderly. Elderly nonwhite individuals suffer from "double jeopardy" in that they are members of two minority groups. In some cases, such as a nonwhite elderly female, they may be in multiple jeopardy categories.

AGE AND GENDER

In the United States, elderly women outnumber elderly men. The 1994 sex ratio for ages 65 and over was 6.6 males for every 10 females. Because differences increase with advanced age, at age 85 and over, there are only 4 males for every 10 females (U.S. Census Bureau 1995b). Men die at an earlier age than women for both biological and sociological reasons—heart disease, stress, and occupational risk (see Chapter 2). The fact that women live longer results in a sizable number of elderly women who are poor. Not only do women, in general, make less money than men, but older women may have spent their savings on their husband's illness, and as homemakers, they are not eligible for Social Security benefits. Further, retirement benefits and other major sources of income may be lost with a husband's death. Half of all older women in 1993 were widows. There were nearly five times as many widows as widowers. (Fowles 1995).

AGE AND SOCIAL CLASS

How long a person lives is influenced by social class (Harris 1990). In general, the higher the social class, the longer the person lives, the fewer the debilitating illnesses, the greater the number of social contacts and friends, the less likely to define oneself as "old," and the greater the likelihood of success in adapting to retirement. Higher social class is also related to fewer residential moves, higher life satisfaction, and more leisure time. In short, the higher one's socioeconomic status, the longer, happier, and healthier one's life.

Problems of the Elderly

Many of the problems of the elderly can be traced to the ideology of ageism, which asserts that one's worth depends on one's age in much the same way that worth is tied to race and gender. In response to this ideology, Betty Friedan (1993) advocates abandoning the cultural emphasis on youth and moving toward "the fountain of age." She suggests looking

> into this new period of life with openness, with change, with vitality . . . It's time to look at age on its own terms, and put names on its values and strengths, breaking through the definition of age solely as deterioration or decline from youth. The problem is how to break through the cocoon of our illusory youth and risk a new stage in life, where there are no prescribed roles, no models, nor rigid rules or visible rewards—how to step out into the true existential unknown of these years of life now open to us and find our own terms for living them. (p. 69)

National Data: Minority populations are projected to represent 25 percent of the elderly population in 2030, up from 13 percent in 1990.

SOURCE: Fowles 1995.

National Data: About 16 percent of elderly women are living in poverty, compared to nine percent of elderly men.

SOURCE: Fowles 1995.

Friedan's book, *The Fountain of Age* (1993), describes how most Americans view the aging process with fear and anxiety over what is believed to be inevitable physical and mental decline. She argues that the problem is not age per se, but the inability to look beyond youth to the possibilities of creative aging. She warns, however, that the elderly cannot reach their full potential if society's barriers, both structural and cultural, remain.

LACK OF EMPLOYMENT

What one does (occupation), for how long (work history), and for how much (wages), are important determinants of retirement income (Hatch 1990). Indeed, employment is important because it provides the foundation for economic resources later in life. Yet, for the elderly who want to work, entering and remaining in the labor force may be difficult because of negative stereotypes, lower levels of education, reduced geographical mobility, fewer employable skills, and discrimination. The likelihood of being employed has decreased for elderly men and women over the last few decades.

In 1967, Congress passed the Age Discrimination in Employment Act (ADEA), which was designed to ensure continued employment for people between the ages of 40 and 65. In 1986, the upper limit was removed making mandatory retirement illegal in most occupations. Nevertheless, thousands of cases of age discrimination occur annually. While employers cannot advertise a position by age, they can state that the position is an "entry level" one or that "2–3 years experience" is required. However, research on job training opportunities at 688 organizations and businesses in the United States found that the elderly, in general, were unlikely to be discriminated against (Knoke and Kalleberg 1994).

If displaced, older workers have difficulty finding a new job. Some research indicates that older workers remain unemployed longer than younger workers and may be more likely to give up looking for work (Moone and Hushbeck 1989).

RETIREMENT

Retirement is a relatively recent phenomenon. Prior to Social Security, individuals continued to work into old age. Today, although the government no longer requires a person to retire at a specific age, it limits Social Security payments to those over 65 years of age—age 67 by the year 2022. Such a policy is certainly an inducement to retire at 65. Many people, however, retire before age 65; 50 percent of all men and an even higher percentage of women retire before they are eligible to receive Social Security benefits.

Retirement is difficult in that in the United States, work is often equated with worth. A job structures one's life and provides an identity; the end of a job culturally signifies the end of one's productivity. Retirement also involves a dramatic decrease in personal income—as much as one-third to one-half (Soldo and Agree 1988). Living on a fixed income is difficult and, unfortunately, few plan for retirement years.

In spite of the potential problems with retirement, only 7 percent retire unwillingly. Most retirees report enjoying retirement and having a greater sense of well-being than younger people who are still working (Russell 1989). Some

National Data: In 1970, about 27 percent of men and 10 percent of women age 65 and over participated in the labor force. By 1994, these rates had decreased to 17 percent and 9 percent, respectively.

SOURCE: *Statistical Abstract of the United States: 1995,* Table 627.

National Data: A USA Today/CNN/Gallup poll of 572 adults ages 30 and older found that less than half (42 percent) were actively saving for retirement.

SOURCE: Willette 1995.

workers benefit from **phased retirement,** which permits them to withdraw gradually. As the number of elderly and, thus, the number of retirees increase, it will become easier to retire—there will be more retirement communities, senior citizen discounts, and products for the elderly. Negative stereotypes of the retired elderly may also change.

POVERTY

A considerable proportion of the elderly report being concerned about money. When a national sample of U.S. citizens was asked what would provide the greatest feeling of security in old age, 40 percent reported that money was at the top of their list compared to spouses (29 percent), children (12 percent), friends (5 percent), career and job (4 percent), or home (4 percent) (Clements 1993). Such concern is justified: the elderly are more likely to be living in poverty than adults of younger ages.

Poverty among the elderly also varies dramatically by such characteristics as gender, race, ethnicity, marital status, and age: women, minorities, those who are single or widowed, and the "old-old" are most likely to be poor (Colburn 1993; *Statistical Abstract of the United States: 1995*). There is also a great deal of diversity among the elderly. The poorest fifth receive only 6 percent of the total resources for the aged while the richest fifth receive 46 percent (Crystal and Shea 1990).

Social Security Actually titled "Old Age, Survivors, Disability, and Health Insurance," Social Security is a major source of income for the elderly. When Social Security was established in 1935, however, it was never intended to be a person's sole economic support in old age; rather, it was to supplement other savings and assets.

Spending on the elderly has increased over time as have Social Security benefits (Hurd 1990). In 1962, programs for the elderly comprised 16 percent of total federal expenditures; by 1994, that number was 38 percent (Samuelson 1995). Although the number of poor elderly has been reduced as a consequence of such spending, the Social Security system has been criticized for being based on number of years worked and preretirement earnings. Hence, women and minorities, who often earn less during their employment years, receive less in retirement benefits. Another concern is whether funding for the Social Security system will be adequate to provide benefits for the increased numbers of elderly in the next decades.

> **Consideration** The term **"new ageism"** refers to viewing the elderly as a burden on the economy and, specifically, on the youth of America. Younger workers are concerned that the size and number of benefits given to the elderly, particularly as the baby boomers move through the ranks, will drain the Social Security system. In 1984, some people, concerned that children and the poor were suffering at the hands of the elderly, formed Americans for Generational Equality (AGE). AGE members argue that as the number of claimants and the size of Social Security benefits grow, present tax levels will be unable to meet future expenditures. If that is the case, the government will have to increase taxes, decrease benefits, or find new sources of revenues.

National Data: Of those 65 and older, 12 percent live below the poverty line in contrast to 9 percent between the ages of 45 and 55.

SOURCE: *Statistical Abstract of the United States: 1995*, Table 747.

One of every nine (11%) elderly whites was poor in 1993, compared to over one-fourth (28%) of elderly blacks and one-fifth (21%) of elderly Hispanics

SOURCE: Fowles 1995.

National Data: The major source of income for elderly couples and individuals in 1992 was Social Security (40%), followed by asset income (21%), public and private pensions (19%), earnings (17%), and all other sources (3%).

SOURCE: Fowles 1995.

HEALTH ISSUES

The biology of aging is called **senescence**. It follows a universal pattern but does not have universal consequences. "Massive research evidence demonstrates that the aging process is neither fixed nor immutable. Biologists are now showing that many symptoms that were formerly attributed to aging—for example, certain disturbances in cardiac function or in glucose metabolism in the brain—are instead produced by disease" (Riley and Riley 1992, 221). Biological functioning is also intricately related to social variables. Altering lifestyles, activities, and social contacts affects mortality and morbidity.

Biological changes are consequences of either **primary aging** due to physiological variables such as cellular and/or molecular variation (e.g., gray hair) or **secondary aging.** Secondary aging entails changes attributable to poor diet, lack of exercise, increased stress, and the like. Secondary aging exacerbates and accelerates primary aging.

Alzheimer's disease received national attention when former President Ronald Reagan announced that he had the disease. Named for German neurologist Alois Alzheimer, the debilitating disease affects both the mental and physical condition of some aging individuals. This chapter's *Self and Society* assesses knowledge about this often misunderstood disease.

Many of the elderly are healthy, but as age increases, health tends to decline. Health is a major quality-of-life issue for the elderly, especially because they face higher medical bills with reduced incomes. Although those over the age of 65 represent only 13 percent of the population, they account for more than a third of all health care spending. The elderly also fill 40 percent of all hospital beds and consume twice as much prescription medication as all other age groups combined (Beck 1993).

Medicare was established in 1966 to provide medical coverage for those over the age of 65; in 1993, the program cost more than $154 billion (*Statistical Abstract of the United States:* 1995, Table 150). Although it is widely assumed that the medical bills of the elderly are paid by the government, the elderly are responsible for as much as 25 to 45 percent of their total health costs. Medicare, for example, pays about half the cost of a visit to the doctor, but does not pay for prescriptions, most nursing home care, dental care, glasses, and hearing aids. The difference between Medicare benefits and the actual cost of medical care is called the **medigap.**

Since health is associated with income, the poorest old are often the most ill: they receive less preventive medicine, have less knowledge about health care issues, and have limited access to health care delivery systems. Medicaid is a federally and state funded program for those who cannot afford to pay for medical care. Thirty-five percent of Medicaid expenditures are for people 65 and over. However, eligibility requirements often disqualify many of the aged poor, often minorities and women.

QUALITY OF LIFE

While some elderly do suffer from declining mental and physical functioning, many others do not. Being old does not mean being depressed, poor, and sick. Roark (1989) found that compared to respondents aged 18 to 49, those over 65 were (1) more satisfied with their standard of living, (2) less lonely, (3) less

---

National Data: When a national sample of U.S. adults was asked to identify their greatest fear about getting old, 35 percent expressed concerns about illness and failing health.

SOURCE: Clements 1993.

We are not a special interest group. We are simply your mothers, fathers, and grandparents. . . . We are simply the generation or two that preceded you. When we are gone you will move up to the vanguard and another generation will wonder what to do with you short of pushing you off a cliff.
—Irene Paull and Bulbul
Authors/Activists

Self & SOCIETY

Alzheimer's Quiz

	True	False	Don't Know
1. Alzheimer's disease can be contagious.	___	___	___
2. A person will almost certainly get Alzheimer's if they just live long enough.	___	___	___
3. Alzheimer's disease is a form of insanity.	___	___	___
4. Alzheimer's disease is a normal part of getting older, like gray hair or wrinkles.	___	___	___
5. There is no cure for Alzheimer's disease at present.	___	___	___
6. A person who has Alzheimer's disease will experience both mental and physical decline.	___	___	___
7. The primary symptom of Alzheimer's disease is memory loss.	___	___	___
8. Among persons older than age 75, forgetfulness most likely indicates the beginning of Alzheimer's disease.	___	___	___
9. When the husband or wife of an older person dies, the surviving spouse may suffer from a kind of depression that looks like Alzheimer's disease.	___	___	___
10. Stuttering is an inevitable part of Alzheimer's disease.	___	___	___
11. An older man is more likely to develop Alzheimer's disease than an older woman.	___	___	___
12. Alzheimer's disease is usually fatal.	___	___	___
13. The vast majority of persons suffering from Alzheimer's disease live in nursing homes.	___	___	___
14. Aluminum has been identified as a significant cause of Alzheimer's disease.	___	___	___
15. Alzheimer's disease can be diagnosed by a blood test.	___	___	___
16. Nursing-home expenses for Alzheimer's disease patients are covered by Medicare.	___	___	___
17. Medicine taken for high blood pressure can cause symptoms that look like Alzheimer's disease.	___	___	___

Answers: 1–4, 8, 10, 11, 13 –16 = False; remaining items = True.

SOURCE: Copyright by Neal E. Cutler, Boettner Institute of Financial Gerontology, University of Pennsylvania. Originally published in *Psychology Today*, 20th Anniversary Issue, "Life Flow: A Special Report—The Alzheimer's Quiz" 1987, "Vol. 21, No. 5, pp. 89, 93. Used by permission of Neal E. Cutler.

likely to think about suicide, and (4) more likely to be happy with their personal lives.

Among the elderly who are depressed, two social factors tend to be in operation. One is society's negative attitude toward the elderly. Words and phrases such as "old," "useless," and "a has-been" reflect cultural connotations of the aged that influence feelings of self-worth. The roles of the elderly also lose their clarity. How is a retiree suppose to feel or act? What does a retiree do? As a result, the elderly become dependent on external validation that may be weak or absent.

The second factor contributing to depression among the elderly is the process of "growing old." This process carries with it a barrage of stressful life events all converging in a relatively short time period. These include health concerns, retirement, economic instability, loss of significant other(s), physical isolation, job displacement, and increased salience of the inevitability of death due to physiological decline. All of these events converge on the elderly and increase the incidence of depression and anxiety.

> **Consideration**   Sherman and Webb (1994) observed that some elderly regard the quality of life as a spiritual journey that includes detachment from things and a renewed value on relationships; as one respondent describes:
>
> I wish I understood then what I know now. I love things, but I don't get attached. I just enjoy that they are there. I love simple things I see and touch everyday—flowers, greenery, a piece of furniture—but I don't own them. Like antiques—I gave them all away to my daughters and friends. The beauty of things is enough for me now. It took my husband's death to see that—that what we had as man and wife was more precious than the "things" we had. (p. 261)

LIVING ARRANGEMENTS

The elderly live in a variety of contexts depending on their health and financial status (see Table 6.2). Most elderly do not want to be institutionalized but prefer to remain in their own homes or in other private households with friends and relatives. Homes of the elderly, however, are usually older, located in inner city neighborhoods, in need of repair, and often too large to be cared for easily.

Although many of the elderly poor live in government housing or apartments with subsidized monthly payments, the wealthier aged often live in retirement communities. These are often planned communities, located in states with warmer climate, and are often very expensive. These communities offer various amenities and activities, have special security, and are restricted by age. One criticism of these communities is that they segregate the elderly from the young and discriminate against younger people by prohibiting them from living in certain areas.

TABLE 6.2		
LIVING ARRANGMENTS OF NONINSTITUTIONALIZED WOMEN AND MEN 65 YEARS OLD AND OVER: 1993		
Men	Living with spouse	75%
	Living with other relatives	7%
	Living alone or with nonrelatives	18%
Women	Living with spouse	41%
	Living with other relatives	17%
	Living alone or with nonrelatives	43%
	SOURCE: Fowles, Donald G. 1995. "A Profile of Older Americans: 1994." Administration on Aging, U.S. Dept. of Health and Human Services.	

Planned retirement communities offer various amenities and activities but are too expensive for most elderly individuals.

Those who cannot afford retirement communities or may not be eligible for subsidized housing often live with relatives in their own home or in the homes of others. It is estimated that more than five million people provide care for aging family members; 90 percent are adult daughters who bear most of the responsibility of caring for their elderly parents as well as for their children (Brody 1990; Dychtwald 1990).

Other living arrangements include shared housing, modified independent living arrangements, and nursing homes. With shared housing, people of different ages live together in the same house or apartment; they have separate bedrooms but share a common kitchen and dining area. They share chores and financial responsibilities. The advantage of this pattern is that it integrates age groups and utilizes skills, talents, and strengths of both the young and the old.

In modified independent living arrangements, the elderly live in their own house, apartment, or condominium within a planned community where special services such as meals, transportation, and home repairs are provided. Skilled or semiskilled health care professionals are available on the premises, and call buttons are installed so help can be summoned in case of an emergency. The advantage of this arrangement is that it provides both autonomy and support for people who are too ill or disabled to live alone. The individual can still maintain some independence even when ill.

Nursing homes are residential facilities that provide full-time nursing care for residents. Nursing homes may be private or public. Private facilities are very expensive and are operated for profit by an individual or a corporation. Public facilities are nonprofit and are operated by a governmental agency, religious organization, or the like. The probability of being in such an extended care facility is associated with race, age, and sex: whites, the old-old, and women are more likely to be in residence. The elderly with chronic health problems are also more likely to be admitted to nursing homes (Garrard et al. 1993). Nursing homes vary dramatically in cost, services provided, and quality of care.

Although abuse may take place in private homes by family members, the elderly, like children, are particularly vulnerable to abuse when they are institutionalized. A 1989 federal report entitled "Board and Care Homes in America: A National Tragedy" details the investigation of facilities for the elderly. Researchers interviewed residents, visited facilities, and collected data on homes in nine states. The result was a list of eighteen categories of victimization including preventable deaths, negligence, overmedication and sedation, poor sanitary conditions, lack of medical care, mail censorship, restriction of movement, inadequate staff, safety violations, inadequate diets, theft of personal funds, and life insurance fraud. The study also cited evidence of sexual and physical abuse and the use of restraining straps.

Media exposure and heightened social awareness of such conditions and practices led to the definition of abused institutionalized elderly as a social problem. The result was the passage of the 1990 Nursing Home Reform Act, which established various rights for nursing care residents: the right to be free of mental and physical abuse, the right not to be restrained unless necessary as a safety precaution, the right to choose one's physician, and the right to receive mail and telephone communication (Harris 1990, 362).

Whether the abuse occurs within the home or in an institution, the victim is most likely to be female, widowed, white, frail, and over 75. The abuser tends to be an adult child or spouse of the victim, who misuses alcohol (Anetzberger, Korbin, and Austin 1994). Some research suggests that the perpetrator of the abuse is more often an adult child who is financially dependent on the elderly victim (Boudreau 1993). Whether the abuser is an adult child or a spouse may simply depend on who the elder victim lives with (Streitfeld 1993).

Many of the problems of the elderly are compounded by their lack of interaction with others, loneliness, and inactivity. This is particularly true for the old-old. The elderly are also segregated in nursing homes and retirement communities, separated from family and friends, and isolated from the flow of work and school. As with most problems of the elderly, the problems of isolation, loneliness, and inactivity are not randomly distributed. They are higher among the elderly poor, women, and minorities. A cycle is perpetuated—being poor and old results in being isolated and engaging in fewer activities. Such withdrawal affects health, which makes the individual less able to establish relationships or participate in activities. This chapter's *The Human Side* provides a glimpse into the life of an elderly woman coping with illness and isolation.

National Data: The National Aging Resource Center on Abuse reports that neglect is the most frequent type of domestic elder abuse (37.2 percent), followed by physical abuse (26.3 percent), financial and material exploitation (20 percent), and emotional abuse (11 percent).

SOURCE: U.S. House of Representatives, Select Committee on Aging 1991.

Studies on the prevalence of elder abuse in the United States suggest that from 4 to 10 percent of the elderly population are abused.

SOURCE: Johnson 1991.

The Elderly Respond

Activism on the part of the elderly has been increasing in recent years and, as their numbers grow, such activism is likely to escalate. It is taking several forms, including collective action through organizations and the exercise of political and economic power.

OLD, ILL, AND ALONE: A GLIMPSE OF AN ELDERLY WOMAN

A hospice volunteer poignantly describes an elderly woman who must cope with illness, pain, and loneliness.

She's eighty-three years old and as frail-looking as a new-born dove. Her spirit is as strong as any young man's. She's worked in sweatshops most of her life. She has two grown children and some grandchildren. Her husband died suddenly thirty years ago from a stroke. She had wanted to die suddenly, like him, but it is cancer that is slowly wearing her down.

She is as frightened of death as anyone. She . . . reminds me of a lotus flower, from the mud of her suffering, her strength is blossoming.

She was in a lot of pain. She lay in bed, her knees bent up. I encouraged her to try . . . to slowly relax her legs. This can help her reduce her muscle tightness and some of her pain. I told her to take deep breaths, and with each breath to gently let her legs stretch out. She tried a little but said she hurt too much.

I stood by her and held her small cold hand. It was as if my mother was there. Or she could have been my lover or either of my grandmothers, who died without me being present . . . Perhaps this was an opportunity to give some of the love I had not given earlier. So it was good to be there. . .

Her pain was getting worse. We gave her some morphine, which helped some.

As her pain diminished, she was able to eat. I fed her oatmeal . . . The afternoon hospice volunteer arrived, and my shift ended. It was time for me to go . . . She seemed distressed that I was leaving . . . I reassured her that . . . the new hospice volunteer could keep her company.

She's in a lot of pain. She's in a strange place, away from the comfortable familiarity of her own home . . . I did my best to make [her] feel comfortable . . . and then left.

SOURCE: Zen Hospice Project Volunteer Newsletter, Issue 1, Oct. 1995.

COLLECTIVE ACTION—GRAY PANTHERS AND THE AARP

More than a thousand organizations are directed toward realizing political power, economic security, and better living conditions for the elderly. These organizations include the National Council of Senior Citizens, the Older Women's League, the National Council on Aging, the National Retired Teachers Association, the National Committee to Preserve Social Security and Medicare, the Gray Panthers, the Senior Action in a Gay Environment, and the American Association of Retired Persons.

One of the earliest and most radical groups is the Gray Panthers, founded in 1970 by Margaret Kuhn. The Gray Panthers were responsible for revealing the unscrupulous practices of the hearing aid industry, persuading the National Association of Broadcasters to add "age" to "sex" and "race" in the Television Code of Ethics statement on media images, and eliminating the mandatory retirement age. In view of these successes, it is interesting to note that the Gray Panthers, with only 50,000 to 70,000 members, is a relatively small organization when compared to the American Association of Retired Persons (AARP).

The AARP has more than 33 million members, age 50 and above, over 90 percent of whom are white. Services of the AARP include discounted mail-order drugs, investment opportunities, travel information, volunteer opportunities, and health insurance. The AARP is the largest volunteer organization in the United States with the exception of the Roman Catholic church.

> **Consideration**   Critics of the AARP argue that the organization is geared more toward making money than toward helping the elderly. "In 1990, for example, the AARP spent about as much on office furniture and equipment as it did on programs to help its 33 million elderly members . . . $43 million was spent on salaries for the 1,110 headquarters employees" (George 1992). Nevertheless, the major stated goal of the AARP is the wielding of political power.

POLITICAL POWER

• • • • • • • • • • • • • • • • • • •

National Data: In the 1992 presidential election, 70 percent of those over 65 voted in contrast to 46 percent of 21 to 24 year olds, 53 percent of 25 to 34 year olds, and 64 percent of 35 to 44 year olds.

SOURCE: *Statistical Abstract of the United States: 1995,* Table 459.

• • • • • • • • • • • • • • • • • • •

Although the elderly represent about 13 percent of the U.S. population, they comprise 16 percent of the voting public. As conflict theorists emphasize, the elderly compete with the young for limited resources. They have more political power than the young and more political power in some states than in others. In Florida, for example, there is concern that the elderly may eventually wield too much political power and act as a voting bloc demanding excessive services at the cost of other needy groups. For example, if the elderly were concentrated in a particular district, they could block tax increases for local schools. To the extent that future political issues are age based and the elderly are able to band together, their political power may increase, as their numbers grow over time (Matras 1990).

ECONOMIC POWER

In constant 1992 dollars, the median annual personal income for the elderly doubled between 1957 and 1992 for both men and women: from $6,537 to $14,548 and from $3,409 to $8,189, respectively (U.S. Census Bureau 1995a). Although these incomes are significantly lower than for men and women between 45 and 54 years of age, income is only once source of economic power:

> Some three quarters of those 65 and over own their own homes (compared to a total U.S. home ownership rate of 65%), and of the total financial assets held by U.S. families, 40% are accounted for by the 12% of the population aged 65 and above. . . . Of even greater significance from the point of view of corporate America is the fact that people 55 and over control about one-third of the discretionary income in the U.S. and spend 30% of it in the

marketplace, roughly twice that of households headed by persons under 35. (Minkler 1989, 18)

Advertisers actively seek the discretionary income of the elderly. Minkler (1989) observed that one favorable outcome of such a marketing focus is a more positive commercial image of the elderly. Better products and more services for older Americans are also benefits.

HEALTH CARE REFORM

Many of the organizations mentioned in the section on collective action have had considerable impact on health care reform in the United States. In 1988, Congress passed the Medicare Catastrophic Coverage Act (MCCA), which was the most significant change in Medicare since its establishment in 1966. The new benefits included unlimited hospitalization, an upper limit on the amount of money recipients would pay for physician's services, home health care and nursing home services, and unlimited hospice care. These changes were particularly significant since many of the illnesses of the elderly are chronic in nature.

The reforms were financed by increasing monthly medical premiums $4 a month and imposing an annual fee based on a person's federal income tax bracket. The maximum premium paid was $800 a person and $1,600 a couple (Harris 1990; Torres-Gil 1990). The AARP initially supported the reforms but later withdrew its support as did many other organizations. The additional monies paid were simply not worth the new benefits, they contended. The AARP also argued that the elderly should not have to bear the burden of reforms necessary for the general public. In 1989, under pressure from the AARP and other organizations of the elderly, Congress repealed the MCCA. As discussed in Chapter 2, Congress is currently in the process of reforming health care policy. The needs of the elderly will be voiced by their lobbyists pressing for change.

UNDERSTANDING
YOUTH AND AGING

What can we conclude about youth and aging in American society? Age is an ascribed status and, as such, is culturally defined by role expectations and implied personality traits. Society regards both the young and the old as dependent and in need of the care and protection of others. Society also defines the young and old as physically, emotionally, and intellectually inferior. As a consequence of these and other attributions, both age groups are sociologically a minority with limited opportunity to obtain some or all of society's resources.

Although both the young and the old are treated as minority groups, different meanings are assigned to each group. In the United States, in general, the young are more highly valued than the old. Functionalists argue that this priority on youth reflects the fact that the young are preparing to take over important statuses while the elderly are relinquishing them. Conflict theorists emphasize that in a capitalist society, both the young and the old are less valued than more productive members of society. Conflict theorists also point out the importance of propagation, that is, the reproduction of workers, which may account for the greater value placed on the young than the old. Finally,

For age is opportunity, no less than youth itself; although in another dress. And as the evening twilight fades away The sky is filled with stars Invisible by day.
—Henry Wadsworth Longfellow
Poet

symbolic interactionists describe the way images of the young and the old intersect and are socially constructed.

The collective concern for the elderly and the significance of defining ageism as a social problem have resulted in improved economic conditions for the elderly. Currently, they are one of society's more powerful minorities. Research indicates, however, that despite their increased economic status, the elderly are still subject to discrimination in such areas as housing, employment, and medical care and are victimized by systematic patterns of stereotyping, abuse, and prejudice.

In contrast, the position of children in the United States has steadily declined as evidenced by a general increase in poverty, homelessness, and unemployment (see Chapters 10 and 11). Wherever there are poor families, there are poor children who are educated in inner city schools, live in dangerous environments, and lack basic nutrition and medical care. Further, age-based restrictions limit their entry into certain roles (e.g., employee) and demand others (e.g., student). While most of society's members would agree that children require special protections, concerns regarding quality-of-life issues and rights of self-determination are only recently being debated.

Age-based decisions are potentially harmful. In 1994, for example, 38 percent of the federal budget was spent on Social Security and Medicare. Yet, not all persons eligible for these entitlements needed the assistance. If budget allocations were based on indigence rather than age, more resources would be available for those truly in need. Further, age-based decisions encourage intergenerational conflict. Government assistance is a zero-sum relationship—the more resources one group gets, the fewer resources another group receives.

Social policies that allocate resources on the basis of need rather than age would shift the attention of policy makers to remedying social problems rather than serving the needs of special interest groups. Age should not be used to impact negatively on an individual's life any more than race, ethnicity, gender, or sexual orientation. While eliminating all age barriers or requirements is unrealistic, a movement toward assessing the needs of individuals and their abilities would be more consistent with the American ideal of equal opportunity for all.

CRITICAL THINKING

1. What stereotypes and problems do the young and elderly share?
2. What cultural and/or structural changes are needed if ageism is to decrease?
3. Regarding children and the elderly, what public policies or programs from other countries might be beneficial to incorporate in the United States?
4. How do different age pyramids influence the treatment of the elderly in the United States?
5. How might the "fountain of age" described by Friedan be accomplished in American society?
6. What structural changes in the United States might benefit the "sandwich generation"?

KEY TERMS

minority

stereotype

prejudice

discrimination

age grading

sandwich generation

ageism

modernization theory

disengagement theory

activity theory

infantilizing elders

gerontophobia

age pyramids

senescence

phased retirement

new ageism

primary aging

secondary aging

medigap

REFERENCES

Adler, Jerry. 1994. "Kids Growing Up Scared." *Newsweek,* January 10: 43–50.

Anetzberger, Georgia J., Jill E. Korbin, and Craig Austin. 1994. "Alcoholism and Elder Abuse." *Journal of Interpersonal Violence* 9: 184–93.

Arluke, Arnold, and Jack Levin. 1990. " 'Second Childhood': Old Age in Popular Culture." In *Readings on Social Problems,* ed. W. Feigelman, pp. 261–65. Fort Worth: Holt, Rinehart & Winston.

Beck, Melinda. 1993. "The Gray Nineties." *Newsweek,* October 4: 65–66.

Boudreau, Francoise A. 1993. "Elder Abuse." In *Family Violence: Prevention and Treatment,* ed. R. L. Hampton, T. P. Gullota, G. R. Adams, E. H. Potter III, and R. P. Weissberg, pp. 142–58. Newbury Park, Calif.: Sage Publications.

Bradshaw, York, Rita Noonan, Laura Gash, and Claudia Buchmann Sershen. 1992. "Borrowing against the Future: Children and Third World Indebtedness." *Social Forces* 71 (3): 629–56.

Brody, Elaine. M. 1990. *Women in the Middle: Their Parent-Care Years.* New York: Springer.

Cahill, Spenser. 1993. "Childhood and Public Life: Reaffirming Biographical Divisions." *Social Problems* 37 (3): 390–400.

Children's Defense Fund. 1989. "A Vision for America's Future." Washington D.C.: Children's Defense Fund, pp. xvi–xvii.

Children Now. 1995. "The Status of America's Children." World Wide Web Children-now.html.

Clark, Charles S. 1991. "Fast-Food Shake-Up." *Congressional Quarterly Researcher* 1, no. 25, November 8: 827–43.

Clements, Mark. 1993. "What We Say about Aging." *Parade Magazine,* December 12: 4–5.

Colburn, Don. 1993. "The Woes of Widows in America." In *Society in Crisis,* ed. The Washington Post Writers Group, pp. 207–11. Needham, Mass.: Allyn & Bacon.

Cowgill, Donald, and Lowell Holmes. 1972. *Aging and Modernization.* New York: Appleton-Century-Crofts.

Crystal, Stephen, and Dennis Shea. 1990. "Cumulative Advantage, Cumulative Disadvantage, and Inequality among Elderly People." *The Gerontologist* 30: 437–43.

Cummings, Elaine, and William Henry. 1961. *Growing Old: The Process of Disengagement.* New York: Basic Books.

Dychtwald, Ken. 1990. *Age Wave.* New York: Bantom Books.

Fischer, David H. 1978. *Growing Old in America.* New York: Oxford University Press.

Fowles, Donald G. 1995. "A Profile of Older Americans: 1994." Administration on Aging, U.S. Dept. of Health and Human Services.

Friedan, Betty. 1993. *The Fountain of Age.* New York: Simon & Schuster.

Garrard, Judith, Joan Buchanan, Edward Ratner, Lukas Makris, Hung-Ching Chan, Carol Skay, and Robert Kane. 1993. "Differences between Nursing Home Admissions and Residents." *Journal of Gerontology* 48 (6): S310–S309.

George, Christopher. 1992. "Old Money." *Washington Monthly,* pp. 16–21.

Harrigan, Anthony. 1992. "A Lost Civilization." *Modern Age: A Quarterly Review* Fall: 3–12.

Harris, Diana K. 1990. *Sociology of Aging.* New York: Harper & Row.

Hatch, Laurie 1990. "Gender and Work at Midlife and Beyond." *Generations* 14 (3): 48–52.

Hewlett, Sylvia. 1992. *When the Bough Breaks: The Cost of Neglecting Our Children.* New York: Basic Books.

Hurd, Michael D. 1990. "The Economic Status of the Elderly." *Science* 244: 659–64.

Ingrassia, Michelle. 1993. "Growing Up Fast and Frightened." *Newsweek,* November 22: 52–53.

Johnson, Thomas F. 1991. *Elder Mistreatment: Deciding Who Is at Risk.* New York: Greenwood Press.

Knoke, David, and Arne L. Kalleberg. 1994. "Job Training in U.S. Organizations." *American Sociological Review* 59: 537–46.

Kolland, Franz. 1994. "Contrasting Cultural Profiles between Generations: Interests and Common Activities in Three Intrafamilial Generations." *Ageing and Society* 14: 319–40.

Matras, Judah. 1990. *Dependency, Obligations, and Entitlements: A New Sociology of Aging, the Life Course, and the Elderly.* Englewood Cliffs, N.J.: Prentice-Hall.

Miner, Sonia, John Logan, and Glenna Spitze. 1993. "Predicting Frequency of Senior Center Attendance." *The Gerontologist* 33: 650–57.

Minkler, Meredith. 1989. "Gold Is Gray: Reflections on Business' Discovery of the Elderly Market." *The Gerontologist* 29 (1): 17–23.

Miringoff, Marc. 1989. *The Index of Social Health, 1989: Measuring the Social Well-Being of a Nation.* Tarrytown, N.Y.: Fordham Institute for Innovation in Social Policy.

Moone, Marilyn, and Judith Hushbeck. 1989. "Employment Policy and Public Policy: Options for Extending Work Life." *Generations* 13 (3): 27–30.

Palmore, E. 1981. "What Can the U.S. Learn from Japan about Aging?" In *Controversial Issues in Gerontology,* ed. H. J. Wershow, pp. 133–39. New York: Springer.

Regoli, Robert, and John Hewitt. 1994. *Delinquency in Society: A Child-Centered Approach.* New York: McGraw-Hill.

Riley, Matilda White. 1987. "On the Significance of Age in Sociology." *American Sociological Review* 52 (February): 1–14.

Riley, Matilda W., and John W. Riley. 1992. "The Lives of Older People and Changing Social Roles." In *Issues in Society,* ed. Hugh Lena, William Helmreich, and William McCord, pp. 220–31. New York: McGraw-Hill.

Roark, Anne C. 1989. "Most Older Persons Say They're Happy with Lives." *Los Angeles Times,* May 4.

Russell, Charles. 1989. *Good News about Aging.* New York: Wiley.

Samuelson, Robert J. 1995. "Social Security: The Facts." *Newsweek,* April 24: 37.

Sherman, Edmund, and Theodore A. Webb. 1994. "The Self as Process in Later-Life Reminiscence: Spiritual Attributes." *Ageing and Society* 14: 255–67.

Soldo, Beth J., and Emily M. Agree. 1988. "America's Elderly." *Population Bulletin* 43 (September): 1–48.

Statistical Abstract of the United States: 1993. 1993. 113th ed. Washington, D.C.: U.S. Bureau of the Census.

Statistical Abstract of the United States: 1995. 1995. 115th ed. Washington, D.C.: U.S. Bureau of the Census.

Streitfeld, David. 1993. "Abuse of the Elderly—Often Its the Spouse." In *Society in Crisis,* ed. The Washington Post Writers Group, pp. 212–13. Needham, Mass.: Allyn & Bacon.

Szulc, Tad. 1988. "How Can We Help Ourselves Age with Dignity?" *Parade,* May 29: 4–7.

Taylor, Paul. 1993. "Revamping Welfare with 'Universalism.' " In *Society in Crisis,* ed. The Washington Post Writers Group, pp. 99–104. Needham, Mass.: Allyn & Bacon.

Torres-Gil, Fernando. 1990. "Seniors React to Medicare Catastrophic Bill: Equity or Selfishness?" *Journal of Aging and Social Policy* 2 (1): 1–8.

UNICEF, United Nations Children's Fund. 1994. "The Progress of Nations." United Nations.

U.S. Census Bureau: Statistical Briefs. 1995a. "Aging of the U.S. Population." May 5: CB95–90.

U.S. Census Bureau. 1995b. "Sixty-five Plus in the United States." May. Economics and Statistics Administration, U.S. Dept. of Commerce.

U.S. House of Representatives, Select Committee on Aging. 1991 (May 15). *Elder Abuse: What Can Be Done?* (hearing) Washington, D.C.: U.S. Government Printing Office.

Willette, Anne. 1995. "Poll: 42% Saving for Retirement." *USA Today,* May 9: A1.

7

CHAPTER

Sexual Orientation

IS IT TRUE?

Anyone who has had sex with both women and men is considered a bisexual (p. 193).

People who believe that gay individuals are "born that way" tend to be more tolerant of gays than people who believe that gay individuals choose their sexual orientation (pp. 199–200).

Most countries throughout the world have laws that protect gay individuals from discrimination on the basis of sexual orientation (p. 205).

The American Psychiatric Association currently classifies homosexuality as a mental disorder (p. 197).

In 1994, the state of Hawaii became the first U.S. state to legally recognize marriages between homosexual partners (p. 209).

ANS: 1.F 2.T 3.F 4.F 5.F

> As long as the anti-gay campaigners continue to spread their message of ignorance and hate, our nation will remain a hostile, dangerous and sometimes deadly place for us, our friends and millions of America's gay and lesbian citizens.
>
> Eric Marcus, Gay activist

To many Americans, sexual orientation is a personal and private matter. Recently, however, homosexuality in American society has become a public issue both for society as a whole and for gay individuals who make up this minority group. Policy makers and citizens are concerned about such questions as "Should homosexuals be allowed to teach elementary school children?" "Should homosexuals be allowed to adopt children?" and "Should homosexual marriages be legally recognized?"

The American public is sharply divided over gay issues, including whether homosexuals should "stay in the closet" or openly reveal their homosexuality, and whether civil rights laws should be extended to homosexuals (Moore 1993). At one end of the continuum are individuals who accept homosexuality, such as Joycelyn Elders, formerly the U.S. surgeon general. She observed that "Sex is . . . a normal part and healthy part of our being, whether it is homosexual or heterosexual" (Bull 1994, 35). On the other end of the continuum are individuals such as David Riley, Jr., who was convicted of first-degree murder for the knifing and drowning of Scott Palmer, a gay man who allegedly propositioned Riley for sex (*Advocate* 1994a, 16).

After discussing the difficulties of defining homosexuality and determining its prevalence in society, we review various theories about the origins of sexual orientation and society's attitudes toward homosexuality. Next, we examine the meaning and origins of homophobia and present cross-cultural data on the topic. The chapter ends with a discussion of social problems associated with homosexuality and the debate over the "gay agenda."

The Social Context: Sexual Orientation

Sexuality involves much more than the biological act of procreation. In all its complexity, "sexuality" encompasses values, emotions, thoughts, lifestyles, identities, behaviors, and relationships. The term **sexual orientation** commonly refers to the aim and object of one's sexual interests—toward members of the same sex, the opposite sex, or both sexes. However, sexual orientation is multifaceted and includes an individual's object of sexual attraction, behavior, and fantasies, as well as issues concerning emotional bonding, lifestyle, and self-identity (Klein 1978, 1985).

DEFINITIONS OF HOMOSEXUALITY, HETEROSEXUALITY, AND BISEXUALITY

Homosexuality refers to the predominance of cognitive, emotional, and sexual attraction to those of the same sex. The term *gay* is synonymous with *homosex-*

ual and may refer to either males or females who have a same-sex orientation. More often *gay* is used to refer to male homosexuals, and **lesbian** is used to refer to homosexual women (Committee on Lesbian and Gay Concerns 1991). **Heterosexuality** refers to the predominance of cognitive, emotional, and sexual attraction to those of the opposite sex.

Bisexuality refers to a sexual orientation that involves cognitive, emotional, and sexual attraction to members of both sexes. Nevertheless, a study of a hundred people who belonged to a bisexual organization found that very few were equally involved with men and women (Weinberg, Williams, and Pryor 1994). Some of the respondents leaned toward homosexuality; others leaned toward heterosexuality. The majority had primary heterosexual relationships and secondary homosexual relationships. Some respondents reported that their sexual behavior leaned one way and their emotional feelings another.

In addition to cognitive, emotional, and sexual attraction, sexual orientation is also defined by sexual self-identity. This complicates the definition of homosexuality, heterosexuality, and bisexuality because attractions and sexual behavior are not always consistent with sexual self-identity. For example, in a study of 52 men who labeled themselves as heterosexual, almost a quarter (23 percent) had had sex with both women and men in the last two years: 6 percent had had sex exclusively with men (Doll et al. 1992). In another study ($n = 6,982$), 69 percent of the men who reported having prior sexual experiences with both men and women described themselves as heterosexual, 29 percent as bisexual, and 2 percent as homosexual (Lever et al. 1992). These data indicate that adult bisexual experiences do not necessarily result in the acquisition of a bisexual self-identity. Also, prior bisexual experience is not required to label oneself as bisexual. In the above study, 18 percent of those who labeled themselves as bisexual reported no adult homosexual experiences.

Although most people view heterosexuality and homosexuality as discrete categories, sex researchers have suggested that sexual orientation exists on a continuum (see Figure 7.1). Using the Heterosexual-Homosexual Rating Scale developed by Kinsey and his colleagues (1949), individuals with ratings of 0 or 1 are entirely or largely heterosexual; those with ratings of 2, 3, or 4 are more bisexual; and those with ratings of 5 or 6 are largely or entirely

> *There is no such thing as "the" homosexual (or "the" heterosexual, for that matter) and statements of any kind which are made about human beings on the basis of their sexual orientation must always be highly qualified.*
> —Alan Bell and
> Martin Weinberg
> Sex researchers

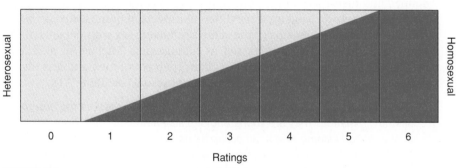

FIGURE 7.1

THE HETEROSEXUAL-HOMOSEXUAL RATING SCALE

SOURCE: A. Kinsey, W. Pomeroy, C. Martin, and P. Gebhard 1953. *Sexual Behavior in the Human Female*, p. 470, Figure 93. Philadelphia: W. B. Saunders. Reprinted by permission of the Kinsey Institute for Research in Sex, Gender, and Reproduction.

homosexual. Kinsey and his colleagues developed the continuum of sexual orientation after finding that many women and men reported having had sexual experiences involving both sexes. Based on this continuum, most people are neither entirely heterosexual nor entirely homosexual, but are somewhere in between.

PREVALENCE OF HOMOSEXUALITY AND HETEROSEXUALITY

Determining the prevalence of homosexuality and heterosexuality is difficult because many gay individuals do not want to reveal their sexual orientation publicly for fear of prejudice and discrimination. Definitional problems add to the difficulty. As noted earlier, the identification of individuals as homosexual or heterosexual is not always clear-cut. Consider the following:

> *Which of the following individuals would you categorize as a homosexual? Is it the young person who fantasizes about someone of their same sex in their class or on their school's swimming team? Is it the young person who has had a few sexual experiences with someone of the same sex? Is it the man who is married to a woman for years who occasionally has sex with men? Is it the woman who is married but unhappy with her sexual relationships with her husband and who has very close but non-sexual attachments to other women? What about the person who struggles against but never acts on desires for members of the same sex? What about those who feel an occasional sexual attraction to people of the same sex? (Blumenfeld and Raymond 1989, 84)*

Establishing the prevalence of homosexuality and heterosexuality is also difficult because "engaging in homosexual sex, or for that matter, heterosexual sex, is not the same as being a homosexual or heterosexual" (Blumenfeld and Raymond 1989, 82). For example, people may engage in heterosexual sex, even though they desire sexual relations with a member of their own sex and view themselves as gay. Conversely, individuals may engage in homosexual sex, even though they view themselves as heterosexuals. Indeed, research supports the conclusion that "more people have homosexual feelings than engage in homosexual behavior, and more engage in homosexual behavior than develop lasting homosexual identification" (Lever et al. 1992, 144).

Thus, the prevalence of homosexuality depends on how homosexuality is defined and measured. In a nationwide study of adults age eighteen to fifty-nine, researchers focused on three different aspects of homosexuality: being sexually attracted to persons of the same sex, having sex with persons of the same sex, and identifying one's self as homosexual (Michael et al. 1994). Results of this study indicate that less than 3 percent of men and less than 2 percent of women identify themselves as homosexual (see Table 7.1).

> *Consideration*   The homosexual population is as diverse as the heterosexual population. They are young and old, single and married, from all educational and income levels, all occupations, races, and religions, and live in both large cities and small towns in all countries (Harry 1990). Because many people believe that homosexuals are easily recognizable—homosexual men being effeminate and homosexual women masculine—assignment to minority status is often, correctly or incorrectly, based on

TABLE 7.1

THREE DIMENSIONS OF SAME-SEX ORIENTATION

	SEXUALLY ATTRACTED TO INDIVIDUALS OF THE SAME SEX	HAD SEXUAL RELATIONS WITH SAME-SEX PARTNER AFTER AGE 18	IDENTIFIES SELF AS HOMOSEXUAL
Women	4%	4%	1.4%
Men	6%	5%	2.8%

Source: Based on Robert T. Michael, John H. Gagnon, Edward O. Laumann, and Gina Kolata. 1994. *Sex in America: A Definitive Survey.* Boston: Little, Brown.

Two, four, six, eight, how do you know your grandma's straight?
Gay slogan

mannerisms and style of dress. In one study, 37 percent of 3,018 respondents believed that they could recognize homosexuals on the basis of their appearance (Klassen, Williams, and Levitt 1989). Research indicates, however, that less than 15 percent of the gay population conform to appearance stereotypes (Tripp 1975).

Theories of Sexual Orientation

Theories of sexual orientation help us understand two separate issues: (1) societal reactions to sexual orientations and (2) the etiology of sexual orientation, that is, what causes a specific sexual orientation. While sociological

Many people believe that homosexuals are recognizable by their appearance. Can you easily identify which one of these men is gay?

theories are more likely to focus on the former, nonsociological theories concentrate on biological and psychological characteristics that are predictive of a specific sexual orientation.

SOCIOLOGICAL THEORIES

Human sexual behaviors and attitudes largely reflect the society in which they occur. Various sociological theories focus on different aspects of society and how they influence human behavior and attitudes. Structural-functionalism, conflict theory, and symbolic interactionism are discussed as they relate to society's response to various sexual orientations.

Structural-Functionalist Perspective Structural-functionalists, consistent with their emphasis on institutions and the functions they fulfill, emphasize the importance of monogamous heterosexual relationships for the reproduction, nurturance, and socialization of children. From a functionalist perspective, homosexual relations, as well as heterosexual nonmarital relations, are defined as "deviant" because they fail to meet societal requisites. Clearly, however, this argument is less salient in a society where other institutions, most notably, schools, have supplemented the traditional functions of the family and where replenishment of the population is no longer a concern.

Some functionalists argue that antagonisms between heterosexuals and homosexuals may disrupt the natural state, or equilibrium, of society. Durkheim, however, recognized that deviation from society's norms may also be functional. Homosexuality, for example, and specifically the recent debate over gay rights, has led to social change. As Durkheim observed, deviation ". . . may be useful as a prelude to reforms which daily become more necessary" (Durkheim [1938] 1993, 66). Additionally, the gay rights movement has motivated many people to reexamine their treatment of sexual minorities and has produced a sense of cohesion and solidarity among members of the gay population.

Conflict Perspective Conflict theorists emphasize that because the nuclear family meets the needs of a capitalist society (see Chapter 5), any threat to the nuclear family is also a threat to the economic system and, therefore, the capitalist class. Homosexuality is one such threat. First, traditionally defined families are the basic units of consumption—they buy homes, invest in their children's education, and purchase a host of specialized consumer goods designed for "family-fun." Since gays are relatively few in number, they represent fewer consumer dollars. Second, reproduction that occurs within the family not only replenishes the labor force, but to some extent provides surplus labor that allows capitalists to keep wages low and profits high. Since gays usually produce few if any offspring, they contribute little to the continuation of the labor force. Third, the family is the primary means by which socialization into the capitalist ideology takes place. Children are instructed to work hard, given an allowance for completing their chores, and taught that a "penny saved is a penny earned." Although other institutions also disseminate capitalistic ideology, the family is the first and the most enduring agent of socialization.

Other conflict theorists, particularly those who do not emphasize a purely economic perspective, note that the antagonisms between heterosexuals and others represent a basic division in society between those with power and those without power. When one group has control of society's institutions and resources, as in the case of heterosexuals, they have the authority to dominate other groups. The recent battle over gay rights is just one example of the political struggle between those with power and those without it.

A classic example of the power struggle between gays and straights took place in 1973 when the American Psychiatric Association (APA) met to revise its classification scheme of mental disorders. Homosexual activists had been appealing to the APA for years to remove homosexuality from its list of mental illnesses but with little success. In 1973, however, the APA's board of directors voted to remove homosexuality from its official list of mental disorders. The board's move encountered a great deal of resistance from conservative APA members and was put to a referendum, which reaffirmed the board's decision (Bayer 1987).

Symbolic Interactionist Perspective Symbolic interactionism focuses on the social meanings of heterosexuality, homosexuality, and bisexuality and how these meanings influence societal reaction to and individual involvement in alternative lifestyles. The meanings we associate with same-sex relations are learned from society—from family, peers, religion, and the media. Freedman and D'Emilio observed that ". . . sexual meanings are subject to the forces of culture. Human beings learn how to express themselves sexually, and the content and outcome of that learning vary widely across cultures and across time" (1990, 485). For example, a person living in Iran is likely to learn that homosexuality is both immoral and illegal (Tielman and Hammelburg 1993). In contrast, a person living in Denmark or the Netherlands is likely to learn that homosexuality is an acceptable lifestyle alternative.

Historical and cross-cultural research on homosexuality reveals the socially constructed nature of homosexuality and its meaning. Although many Americans assume that same-sex romantic relationships have always been taboo in our society, during the nineteenth century, "romantic friendships" between women were encouraged and regarded as preparation for a successful marriage. The nature of these friendships bordered on lesbianism. President Grover Cleveland's sister Rose wrote to her friend Evangeline Whipple in 1890: ". . . It makes me heavy with emotion . . . all my whole being leans out to you . . . I dare not think of your arms" (Goode and Wagner 1993, 49).

The symbolic interactionist perspective may also explain the development of a person's sexual orientation. An individual's sexual self-concept may be influenced by childhood labels such as "sissy" or "tomboy." An early adolescent homosexual experience may also influence an individual to adopt a homosexual identity. Unaware that homosexual contacts in childhood and adolescence are not unusual, children who have same-sex sexual experiences may see these experiences as evidence that they are homosexual. Once individuals label themselves as homosexual, or are labeled by others, they may become locked into a self-fulfilling prophecy whereby their actions and identity conform to the label "homosexual."

Consistent with symbolic interactionism, the development of a gay identity occurs as a process of self-definition and labeling (Troiden 1989). In the first stage, *sensitization*, the person becomes aware of being different in the sense of being relatively uninterested in members of the opposite sex. These feelings

Accepting that one is a homosexual and adopting homosexuality as a lifestyle are important steps in assuming a gay identity. Often associated with this is establishing an emotional and sexual relationship with someone of the same sex.

lead to the second stage, *identity confusion*, in which the person feels attracted to members of the same sex and suspects that he or she might be gay. One individual explained:

> *You feel that you probably are a homosexual, although you're not definitely sure. You feel distant or cut off from other people. You are beginning to think that it might help to meet other homosexuals but you're not sure whether you really want to or not. You prefer to put on a front of being completely heterosexual. (Cass 1984, 156)*

The third stage, *identity assumption*, begins around the age of nineteen to twenty-one for gay men. They report assuming the gay identity as a result of interacting with gay men in social and sexual situations. Lesbians report adopting a gay identity between the ages of twenty-one and twenty-three as a result of involvement in an intense love relationship with a woman (Troiden 1989). Finally, stage four is *commitment*, which involves adopting homosexuality as a lifestyle. This means viewing homosexuality as a legitimate lifestyle that is "right" for oneself, establishing an emotional and sexual relationship with someone of the same sex, and disclosing one's homosexuality to others.

BIOLOGICAL THEORIES

Although symbolic interactionism offers some insight into the process of how someone develops a gay identity, sociological theories, in general, do not address the issue of etiology. Instead, one must turn to psychological and biological theories for attempts to explain what "causes" sexual orientation. In psychology, the Freudian notion that gays suffer from overidentification with their mother and have a hostile or absent father is unsupported by scientific data. The recent movement toward and acceptance of biological explanations of sexual orientation is socially significant. What a society believes is responsible for a social problem, in part, determines the policies adopted to deal with it. Biological explanations usually focus on genetic or hormonal differences between heterosexuals and homosexuals.

Genetics Is sexual orientation an inborn trait that is transmitted genetically like eye color or handedness? Bailey and Pillard (1991) provided support for a genetic basis for sexual orientation with their study of 56 gay men who were twins or had adoptive brothers. In the study, 52 percent of the identical twins, 22 percent of the fraternal twins, and 11 percent of adoptive brothers were homosexual. This finding "provided some support for the view that sexual orientation is influenced by constitutional factors . . . and emphasizes the necessity of considering causal factors arising within the individual, and not just his psychosocial environment" (p. 1095). Research on female twins also concludes that if one twin is gay, there is an increased chance that the other is also gay (Bailey et al. 1993). Since the twins in both studies were reared together, however, it is difficult to "tease apart and quantify the differential contributions of genetic and environmental factors" (Byne and Parsons 1993, 230).

A homosexual orientation among males may be related to the presence of a gene on the X chromosome inherited from the mother. In one study, two-thirds of the gay siblings shared a distinctive pattern along a segment of their X chromosome. "Scientists say the possibility is remote that this genetic pattern would appear by chance" (Park 1995, 95).

Hormones Ellis and Ames (1987) conclude that hormonal and neurological factors operating prior to birth, between the second and fifth month of gestation, are the "main determinants of sexual orientation" (p. 235). Money (1987) suggests that sexual orientation is programmed into the brain during critical periods of prenatal hormonal influence and early childhood experience. In contrast to these observations, Byne and Parsons (1993) reviewed the hormonal studies presented as evidence for a biological basis for homosexuality and concluded that "there is no solid data to suggest that these hormones affect future sexual orientation." (p. 232).

BELIEFS ABOUT THE CAUSES OF HOMOSEXUALITY

Despite the increasing evidence that sexual orientation has a biological basis, many people still believe that gay individuals choose their sexual orientation. Nevertheless, the results of national polls show that the percentage of Americans who believe that homosexuality is inborn increased between 1983 and 1993 (see Table 7.2).

Beliefs about the causes of homosexuality are related to people's attitudes toward gays. In the 1993 poll referred to in Table 7.2, the group that believed that homosexuality is "something that people are born with" displayed a relatively tolerant attitude toward gays (Moore 1993). People who believe that homosexuality is inborn are also more likely to believe that civil rights protection should be extended to gays and to favor ending the ban on gays serving in the military. Parents of gay individuals are likely to believe that homosexuality is inborn. Eighty-seven percent of 402 parents of homosexuals believed that their children were "born that way" (Robinson, Walters, and Skeen 1989; 69).

Consideration Although the terms "sexual preference" and "sexual orientation" are often used interchangeably, the latter term avoids the implication that homosexuality, heterosexuality, and bisexuality are determined

We are maintaining that all the ingredients, biological, individual, and social, codetermine the effects that each has on the other and on the shaping of human sexual preference.
—John P. De CeCecco and John P. Elia
Sex researchers

TABLE 7.2

BELIEFS ABOUT THE CAUSES OF HOMOSEXUALITY, 1983 AND 1993

Survey Question: In your opinion, what causes homosexuality? Is homosexuality something that people are born with, something that develops because of the way people are brought up, or the way that some people prefer to live?

	1983	1993
Inborn	16%	31%
Develops	25	14
Preference	37	35
All/mixed/other	NA	12
No opinion	22	8

SOURCE: David W. Moore. 1993 (April). "Public Polarized on Gay Issue." *Gallup Poll Monthly* 331: 34. Used by permission.

voluntarily. Hence, "orientation" is used more often by those who think there is little choice involved, and "preference" is used more often by those who think choice is important (Weinrich and Williams 1991, 55). Money (1987) suggests that "[p]olitically, sexual preference is a dangerous term, for it implies that if homosexuals choose their preference, then they can be legally forced, under threat of punishment, to choose to be heterosexual" (p. 385).

Heterosexism and Homophobia

The United States, along with many other countries throughout the world, is predominantly heterosexist. **Heterosexism** refers to "an ideological system that denies, denigrates, and stigmatizes any nonheterosexual form of behavior, identity, relationship, or community" (Herek 1990, 316). Heterosexism is based on the belief that heterosexuality is superior to homosexuality and results in prejudice and discrimination against homosexuals and bisexuals. Prejudice refers to negative attitudes, while discrimination refers to behavior that denies individuals or groups equality of treatment. Before reading further, you may wish to assess your attitudes toward homosexuals by completing the "Index of Attitudes toward Homosexuals" in the *Self and Society* feature.

HOMOPHOBIA

National Data: A *Newsweek* poll revealed that 53 percent of respondents do not believe that homosexuality is an acceptable lifestyle; 41 percent of respondents believe that it is an acceptable alternative lifestyle.
SOURCE: Turque 1992.

Negative attitudes toward homosexuality are reflected in a large percentage of the population that disapproves of homosexuality. The term **homophobia** is frequently used to refer to such negative attitudes. Data collected by Bier (1990) suggest that both men and women undergraduate students are "moderately homophobic" with men and first-year students being more homophobic than women and seniors.

Consideration *The term "homophobia" has been criticized because most cases of homophobia do not involve a clinical phobia. According to the Diagnostic and Statistical Manual of Mental Disorders, a phobia involves a compelling desire to avoid the phobic stimuli that arises from a persistent fear or dread. "Invariably the person recognizes that his or her fear is excessive and unreasonable" (American Psychiatric Association 1987, 243). According to these criteria, most individuals who have negative attitudes toward homosexuality are not truly suffering from a phobia because they do not regard their fear as excessive and unreasonable.*

ORIGINS OF HOMOPHOBIA

Why is homosexuality viewed so negatively in the United States? Why does approval or disapproval of homosexuality vary so dramatically between societies and historical time periods? Various reasons, including the following, help to explain American attitudes toward and treatment of homosexuals:

1. *Religion.* Various religions teach that homosexuality is sinful and prohibited by God. The Roman Catholic church rejects all homosexual expression and resists any attempt to validate or sanction the homosexual orientation. Some fundamentalist churches "have been known to endorse the death penalty for homosexual people, and the 'AIDS as God's punishment' argument is a thinly disguised version of the same" (Nugent and Gramick 1989, 31).

   Some religious groups, like the Quakers, accept homosexuality. A controversial book, *Same-Sex Unions in Premodern Europe* by John Boswell (1994), suggests that early Catholic ritual not only tolerated same-sex marriages but blessed them. Boswell further notes that because heterosexual relationships were often based on property or progeny, homosexual relationships in early Christianity were often considered the most pure.

   Some religions are divided on the issue of homosexuality. The Special Committee on Human Sexuality of the Presbyterian Church (USA) reported to the governing body of the church that:

   > *The overwhelming power of God's justice that reaches to all human beings is dawning upon the hearts and consciences of God's people with respect to gays and lesbians. The time has come to embrace more fully the goodness of sexuality, whether it be homosexual or heterosexual. Heterosexuality and homosexuality are both God's good gifts of sexual being. What matters morally and ethically is how we live our lives as faithful people, regardless of our sexual orientation. (Special Committee on Human Sexuality 1991, 103)*

   In spite of the sentiments expressed in the report, the governing body of the Presbyterian church voted not to accept it.

2. *Marital and procreative bias.* Many societies have traditionally condoned sex only when it occurs in a marital context that provides for the possibility of producing and rearing children. Society prohibits homosexuals from marrying. Further, even though new reproductive technologies such as artificial insemination and in vitro fertilization make it possible for gay individuals and couples to have children, many people believe that these advances are best used by heterosexual married couples only (Franklin 1993).

3. *Concern about HIV and AIDS.* Anal intercourse is a sexual behavior that involves high risk of HIV transmission. Thus, many people associate

Self & SOCIETY

Index of Attitudes toward Homosexuals (IAH)

This questionnaire is designed to measure the way you feel about working or associating with homosexuals. It is not a test, so there are no right or wrong answers. Answer each item as carefully and as accurately as you can by placing a number beside each statement as follows:

1 = Strongly agree
2 = Agree
3 = Neither agree nor disagree
4 = Disagree
5 = Strongly disagree

1. _____ I would feel comfortable working closely with a male homosexual.
2. _____ I would enjoy attending social functions at which homosexuals were present.
3. _____ I would feel uncomfortable if I learned that my neighbor was homosexual.
4. _____ If a member of my sex made a sexual advance toward me, I would feel angry.
5. _____ I would feel comfortable knowing that I was attractive to member of my sex.
6. _____ I would feel uncomfortable being seen in a gay bar.
7. _____ I would feel comfortable if a member of my sex made an advance toward me.
8. _____ I would be comfortable if I found myself attracted to a member of my sex.
9. _____ I would feel disappointed if I learned that my child was homosexual.
10. _____ I would feel nervous being in a group of homosexuals.
11. _____ I would feel comfortable knowing that my clergyman was homosexual.
12. _____ I would be upset if I learned that my brother or sister was homosexual.
13. _____ I would feel that I had failed as a parent if I learned that my child was gay.
14. _____ If I saw two men holding hands in public, I would feel disgusted.
15. _____ If a member of my sex made an advance toward me, I would be offended.
16. _____ I would feel comfortable if I learned that my daughter's teacher was a lesbian.
17. _____ I would feel uncomfortable if I learned that my spouse or partner was attracted to members of his or her sex.
18. _____ I would feel at ease talking with a homosexual person at a party.
19. _____ I would feel uncomfortable if I learned that my boss was homosexual.
20. _____ It would not bother me to walk through a predominantly gay section of town.
21. _____ It would disturb me to find out that my doctor was homosexual.
22. _____ I would feel comfortable if I learned that my best friend of my sex was homosexual.
23. _____ If a member of my sex made an advance toward me, I would feel flattered.
24. _____ I would feel uncomfortable knowing that my son's male teacher was homosexual.
25. _____ I would feel comfortable working closely with a female homosexual.

Scoring: To give yourself a score on the IAH, reverse score items 3, 4, 6, 9, 10, 12, 13, 14, 15, 17, 19, 21, 24 in the following way: 1 = 5, 2 = 4, 4 = 2, 5 = 1. For example, if you wrote a 1 for statement number 3 ("I would feel uncomfortable if I learned that my neighbor was homosexual"), change that number to a 5 for scoring purposes. Reverse score the rest of the items in the same way. The remaining questions should be scored as is.

Add up the numbers you assigned to each of the items, then subtract 25 from that sum.

Interpreting your score: Hudson and Ricketts (1980) suggest that the title "Index of Attitudes toward Homosexuals" be placed on the scale when it is administered. Another name for the scale, which might influence a respondent's answers if it were at the top, is the Index of Homophobia. Hudson and Ricketts offer the following classifications of scores, although they caution against putting too much emphasis on the category labels:

0–25	Nonhomophobic
25–50	Moderately nonhomophobic
50–75	Moderately homophobic
75–100	Strongly homophobic

You may be interested in comparing your score or your class' average with those of undergraduate students in psychology classes at a southern state university (Bier 1990).

MEAN SCORES ON THE INDEX OF HOMOPHOBIA

Subgroup	n	Mean Score
Introductory psychology courses		
Men	324	76.79
Women	379	68.66
Senior-level psychology courses		
Men	33	66.94
Women	105	60.29

References:

Bier, M. 1990. "A Comparison of the Degree of Racism, Sexism, and Homophobia between Beginning and Advanced Psychology Students." Unpublished master's thesis, East Carolina University, Greenville, N.C.

Hudson, W. W., and W. A. Ricketts. 1980. "A Strategy for the Measurement of Homophobia." *Journal of Homosexuality* 5: 357–372.

SOURCE: For more information on the IAH, contact Walmyr Publishing Company, P.O. Box 24779, Tempe, AZ 85285-4779. Used by permission.

HIV and AIDS with homosexuality. As noted in Chapter 2, however, worldwide, AIDS is primarily a heterosexual disease. Further, lesbians have a lower risk for sexually transmitted HIV than heterosexual females.

4. *Threat to the power of the majority.* Like other minority groups, the gay minority threatens the power of the majority. Fearing loss of power, the majority group stigmatizes homosexuals as a way of limiting their power. Weinberg (1973) suggests that because they are nonconformists, gay men and lesbians are viewed as a threat to society's values.

5. *Rigid gender roles.* Antigay sentiments also stem from rigid gender roles that dictate that homosexuality violates what is considered to be socially appropriate gender behavior. According to the norms, "real" men don't love men, and "real" women don't love women. Of course, what is defined as appropriate gender role behavior is socially determined and varies over time, place, and person.

Consideration *The homophobic and heterosexist social climate of our society is often viewed in terms of how it victimizes the gay population. However, heterosexuals are also victimized by homophobia and heterosexism. Due to the antigay climate, heterosexuals, especially males, are hindered in their own self-expression and intimacy in same-sex relationships. "The threat of victimization (i.e., antigay violence) probably also causes many heterosexuals to conform to gender roles and to restrict their expressions of (nonsexual) physical affection for members of their own sex" (Garnets, Herek, and Levy 1990, 380).*

6. *Psychiatric witch hunt.* As noted, prior to 1973 the American Psychiatric Association (APA) defined homosexuality as a mental disorder. Treatments for the "illness" of homosexuality included lobotomies, aversive conditioning and, in some cases, castration. The social label of mental illness by such a powerful labeling group as the APA contributed to heterosexuals' negative reactions to gays. Further, it created feelings of guilt, low self-esteem, anger, and depression for many homosexuals. Thus, the psychiatric care system is now busily treating the very conditions it, in part, created.

7. *Myths about homosexuality.* Prejudice and discrimination toward homosexuals may also stem from some of the unsupported beliefs that people have about homosexuality. One negative myth about homosexuals is that they are sexually promiscuous and lack "family values" such as monogamy and commitment to relationships. While some homosexuals do engage in casual sex, as do some heterosexuals, many homosexual couples develop and maintain long-term committed relationships. A study of 560 long-term gay male relationships found that the average length of a relationship was seven years. Ninety-six percent reported that they were committed to be together for "a long time," and 76 percent reported that they were committed for "life" (National Survey Results 1990, 1). In a companion study of lesbian relationships, five years was the average length of time 706 lesbian couples reported that they had been together. Ninety-one percent reported that they were sexually monogamous (National Survey Results 1990).

Another myth that is not supported by data is that homosexuals, as a group, are child molesters. The ratio of heterosexual to homosexual child molesters is approximately eleven to one (Moser 1992). Most often the abuser is a heterosexual relative of the family.

Negative attitudes toward and oppression of lesbians and gay men exist not only in the United States, but throughout the world. The next section provides a global view of social attitudes and laws regarding homosexuality.

GAY OPPRESSION: A GLOBAL VIEW

The International Lesbian and Gay Association (ILGA), along with the International Humanist and Ethical Union and the Department of Gay and Lesbian Studies of the University of Utrecht (Netherlands), sponsored a survey of 202 countries to investigate laws and social attitudes regarding homosexuality. The results of this survey, published in *The Pink Book: A Global View of Lesbian and Gay Liberation and Oppression* (Hendriks, Tielman, and van der Veen 1993), provide a global view of social attitudes regarding homosexuality and the extent to which laws protect, or fail to protect, homosexuals against discrimination.

In 144 of 202 countries (71 percent), "hardly any support for gay and lesbian rights can be found among the population" (p. 250). Oppression of gays is generally worse in Africa than in other regions of the world. Social acceptance of gays is generally higher in Europe than in the rest of the world, although in some less developed countries institutionalized roles exist for gays. In Thai culture, for example, a man who enjoys dressing as a woman and having sex with heterosexual men is known as a *kathoey* and is accepted by society (Weinrich and Williams 1991, 49).

In 7 countries (Denmark, France, Israel, Germany, the Netherlands, Norway, and Sweden) and in some parts of the United States, Canada, Brazil, and Australia, the law protects gay men and women from discrimination. In 98 countries, homosexuality is legal although ages of consent for homosexual and heterosexual behavior vary, and there are no antidiscrimination laws. In 74 countries, homosexual behavior is illegal. Most laws prohibiting homosexual behavior refer to male rather than female homosexuality.

> *There is still no nation in the world that can claim to fully respect the rights and dignity of its homosexual citizens.*
> —John Clark
> Aart Hendriks
> Lisa Power
> Rob Tielman
> Evert van der Veen
> Authors

Social Problems Associated with Homosexuality

Like other minority groups in American society, homosexuals and bisexuals are victims of prejudice and discrimination. Those who are prejudiced against homosexuals regard "them" as a social problem, just as many others define "blacks" or "women" or the "elderly" as the problem. To a large extent, however, the problems of homosexuality in society are created by societal responses to it.

PREJUDICE AGAINST HOMOSEXUALS

In spite of evidence that demonstrates that homosexuals and heterosexuals are similar in personality characteristics, nurturance, and empathy (Whitehead and Nokes 1990), a majority of Americans view gay people negatively. In

National Data When 3,018 adults, representing a national sample of the U.S. population, were interviewed and asked to express their opinion about "homosexuality with affection," 77 percent of the men and 84 percent of the women said it was "always" or "almost always" wrong.

SOURCE: Klassen, Williams, and Levitt 1989, 28.

National Data: Only eight states—California, Connecticut, Hawaii, Massachusetts, Minnesota, New Jersey, Vermont, and Wisconsin—have laws that forbid employment discrimination on the basis of sexual orientation.

SOURCE: Mickens 1994.

general, certain categories of people are more likely to have negative attitudes toward homosexuals than others. Persons who are older, less educated, widowed, living in the South or Midwest, living in lightly populated rural areas, and Protestant are the most likely to have negative attitudes. In contrast, people who are younger, more educated, never married, living in the West, living in heavily populated urban areas, and Jewish are least likely to have antigay attitudes (Klassen, Williams, and Levitt 1989). Public opinion surveys indicate that men are more likely than women to have negative attitudes toward gays. For example, men are more likely than women to oppose extending civil rights protection to homosexuals, gays serving in the military, and gays openly revealing their homosexuality (Moore 1993).

DISCRIMINATION AGAINST HOMOSEXUALS

Weinberg (1973) described homophobia as a prejudice that appears as an antagonism directed toward gay men and women. "Inevitably," he writes, prejudice against a group of people "leads to a disdain of those people, and to mistreatment of them" (pp. 7–8).

Discrimination against homosexuals has occurred for centuries. A statute enacted in England in 1533 during the reign of Henry VIII condemned sodomy, or "buggery" as it was then called, as a crime "against nature" and made it a capital offense. In the first third of the nineteenth century, more than fifty men were hanged for sodomy in England. One year, more men were executed for sodomy than for murder (Weeks 1989). Legal punishments for homosexuality have also included lobotomies, castration, and extermination, the latter occurring in Nazi Germany. In American society, homosexuals are discriminated against in the workplace and in the treatment of their relationships.

Discrimination in the Workplace In recent years, the percentage of Americans who express approval of equal employment rights for homosexuals has increased (see Table 7.3). Nevertheless, most states still do not offer protection against employment discrimination based on sexual orientation.

TABLE 7.3			
ATTITUDES TOWARD EQUAL JOB RIGHTS FOR HOMOSEXUALS, 1977–1993			

Survey Question: In general, do you think homosexuals should or should not have equal rights in terms of job opportunities?

	SHOULD	SHOULD NOT	NO OPINION
1993	80%	14%	6%
1992	74	18	8
1989	71	18	11
1982	59	28	13
1977	56	33	11

SOURCE: David W. Moore. 1993 (April). "Public Polarized on Gay Issue." *Gallup Poll Monthly* 331: 30–34. Used by permission.

Many people who are gay fear being fired, denied salary increases, or not being promoted. The Cracker Barrel restaurant chain fired several openly gay employees in 1991. About 80 percent of the nation's more than 460 Big Brother/Big Sister agencies reject openly gay and lesbian volunteers to work with children (Whitehead and Nokes 1990). The latter discrimination is based, in part, on the belief that "homosexuality is deviant and that children, because they are particularly vulnerable to the influence of role models, should not be exposed to adults who are openly homosexual" (p. 90).

Occupational discrimination is also present in the defense industry where lesbian and gay applicants are routinely denied government security clearances or are subject to unusually lengthy and intensive investigations. One of the most visible and controversial issues concerning job discrimination is the debate over gays in the military. According to a directive issued in 1982 by the Department of Defense, "[h]omosexuality is incompatible with military service" (Tielman and Hammelburg 1993, 337). This directive was implemented in the Army, Air Force, Navy, and Marine Corps and has been applied to enforce dishonorable discharges of gay members of the military.

In 1992, a gay Navy serviceman was fired after revealing his homosexuality, but was reinstated by orders of a federal judge. In 1993, President Clinton moved to lift the ban on homosexuals in the military. The government adopted a "don't ask, don't tell" policy in which recruiting officers are not allowed to ask about sexual orientation, and homosexuals are encouraged not to volunteer such information. Some people feel that the "don't ask, don't tell" policy is oppressive to gays. Eric Marcus (1993) comments:

But my life as a gay man isn't something that takes place only in the privacy of my bedroom. It affects who my friends are, whom I choose to share my life with, the work I do, the organizations I belong to, the magazines I read, where I vacation and what I talk about. I know it's the same for heterosexuals because their sexual orientation affects everything, from choice of senior-prom date and the finger on which they wear their wedding band to the birth announcements they send and every emotion they feel . . . . So the reality of the "don't ask, don't tell" solution for . . . dealing with gays in the military means having to lie about or hide almost every aspect of your life. It's not nearly as simple as just not saying, "I'm gay." (p. 10)

In effect, the "don't ask, don't tell" policy is a subtle message of disapproval. The "not asking" implies that if the answer is gay (and, therefore, the "wrong" answer), negative consequences will follow. Hence, most gays feel the new policy forces them further into the closet. Under the new policy, for example, gays are forbidden to discuss their sexuality at work or to participate in any gay community activities. To do so is to "act on" their homosexuality, which may lead to legal military consequences.

Some changes are occurring, however. In 1995 federal judge Eugene Nickerson ruled that the "don't ask, don't tell" policy is unconstitutional because it discriminates against homosexuals and violates free speech rights. His decision has been appealed by the Department of Justice and is pending before the U.S. Supreme Court.

Discrimination in Relationships No state in the United States grants marriage licenses to gay couples who want to be legally married. Although 1,500

The Constitution does not allow government to subordinate a class of persons simply because others do not like them.
—Chief Judge Abner Mikava

National Data: A *Washington Post* poll revealed that 70 percent of Americans oppose same-sex marriages.

SOURCE: Salholz et al. 1993.

These gay men have been in a committed relationship for over 20 years and consider themselves a "married" couple. They exchanged vows during a "celebration of commitment" ceremony which was attended by family and friends.

homosexual couples participated in a "wedding" replete with ministers and rice during a gay rights march on Washington in 1993, the marriages are not legal. College students are more approving of same-sex marriage than the general public, but a considerable percentage remain disapproving.

As discussed in Chapter 5 (Family Problems), some counties and cities allow unmarried couples, including gay couples, to register as domestic partners. The benefits of domestic partnerships vary from place to place, but may include coverage under a partner's health and pension plans, rights of inheritance and community property, and tax benefits.

In 1993, a male couple and a lesbian couple filed suit against the state of Hawaii for denying them the right to be married. The Hawaii State Supreme Court ruled that Hawaii's marriage law violated the state constitution's equal protection clause, which prohibits discrimination on the basis of gender. In April 1994, however, the Hawaii senate passed a bill outlawing same-sex marriage on the grounds that the purpose of marriage is procreation (Gallagher 1994). The bill did provide for the establishment of a commission to consider recognition of domestic partnerships for gay and lesbian couples.

Discrimination against gays also affects gay women and men who are or want to be parents. Some lesbians artificially inseminate one partner with the sperm of a male relative of the other so that the child will be genetically related to both partners. Other lesbians use sperm from friends. Some homosexual males ask lesbian friends to be surrogate mothers. Still other gay women and men adopt. Phyllis Burke, a lesbian activist from San Francisco, petitioned California for permission to adopt her lover's son and was initially rejected. Later the court granted the adoption (Salholz et al. 1993).

Custody rights for gays are also problematic. Sharon Bottoms of Virginia lost custody of her two-year-old son, Tyler, because she was open about her lesbian relationship with April Wade (Henry 1993). The appeals court overturned the decision and stated that sexual orientation is not a relevant variable in assigning custody rights. Three other states, Arkansas, Missouri, and North Dakota, still take the view that lesbian mothers and homosexual fathers are unfit parents. The basis for such a view rests on the belief that homosexuals are

Some lesbian couples artificially inseminate one partner with the sperm of a male relative of the other so the child will be genetically related to both partners.

unstable and that children reared in such families are likely to be emotionally harmed, sexually molested, impaired in gender role development, or to become homosexuals themselves. Falk (1989) concluded, however, that none of these assumptions is supported by theory or research.

ANTIGAY VIOLENCE

Increasingly, our society is recognizing violence against gays and lesbians as a social problem (Jenness 1995). Surveys indicate that as many as one-fourth of lesbians and gay men report having been victims of physical attacks because of their sexual orientation (Herek 1989). Berrill and Herek (1990, 269) have identified many examples of antigay violence, also known as "gay bashing:"

- In Bangor, Maine, three teenagers yelling "faggot" and "queer" assaulted a gay man and threw him over a bridge into a river, where he drowned.
- In Los Angeles, a man yelling "sick motherfucker" threw a beaker of acid into the face of a lesbian employee of the local Gay and Lesbian Community Services Center.
- In Pensacola, Florida, an arsonist set fire to a Christian church with a ministry in the gay community, causing tens of thousands of dollars in damages. Since the early 1970s, gay community churches have been the targets of arson on more than twenty occasions.

Prejudice and discrimination, including antigay violence, has enraged many gays who are starting to fight back against their attackers. *The Human Side* in this chapter, although not representative of the feelings of all gays, expresses the anger felt by many.

**EXCERPTS FROM A GAY PRIDE PARADE FLIER
AUGUST 15, 1990**

I have friends. Some of them are straight.

Year after year, I see my straight friends. I want to see them, to see how they are doing, to add newness to our long and complicated histories, to experience some continuity.

Year after year I continue to realize that the facts of my life are irrelevant to them and that I am only half listened to, that I am an appendage to the doings of a greater world, a world of power and privilege, of the laws of installation, a world of exclusion. "That's not true," argue my straight friends. There is only one certainty in the politics of power; those left out beg for inclusion, while the insiders claim that they already are. Men do it to women, whites do it to blacks, and everyone does it to queers. . . .

I hate having to convince straight people that lesbians and gays live in a war zone, that we're surrounded by bomb blasts only we seem to hear, that our bodies and souls are heaped high, dead from fright or bashed or raped, dying of grief or disease, stripped of our personhood. . . . .

They've taught us that good queers don't get mad. They've taught us so well that we not only hide our anger from them, we hide it from each other. WE EVEN HIDE IT FROM OURSELVES. We hide it with substance abuse and suicide and overachieving in the hope of proving our worth . . . let yourself be angry that the price of our visibility is the constant threat of violence, anti-queer violence to which practically every segment of this society contributes. Let yourself be angry that THERE IS NO PLACE IN THIS COUNTRY WHERE YOU ARE SAFE, no place where you are not targeted for hatred and attack, the self-hatred, the suicide—of the closet.

The next time some straight person comes down on you for being angry, tell them until things change, you don't need any more evidence that the world turns at your expense . . . . You don't want anymore baby pictures shoved in your face until you can have or keep your own. No more weddings, showers, anniversaries, please, unless they are our own brothers and sisters celebrating . . . tell them to go away until they have spent a month walking hand in hand in public with someone of the same sex. After they survive that, then you'll hear what they have to say. . .

The "Gay Agenda"

The "gay agenda" refers to the concerns of gay individuals and the challenges they face. These concerns and challenges include "coming out" and "outing," developing cohesiveness within the gay community, advocating gay civil rights, and dealing with the conservative backlash against gay initiatives.

COMING OUT AND OUTING

Coming out, an abbreviation for "coming out of the closet," refers to recognizing one's homosexuality and disclosing it to others including parents, siblings, heterosexual partners or spouse, children, friends, employers, and co-workers. Coming out to parents is the most difficult. Rejection is the typical response when parents learn that their son or daughter is gay. Of 37 homosexual and bisexual male high school seniors who came out to their parents, 35 (95 percent) reported that their parents' reaction "varied from extreme family disruption to forcible expulsion from home" (Uribe and Harbeck 1992, 22). One father reacted to his son's disclosure with, "I'd rather have a dead son than a gay son." Over half of the young men in the sample lived with friends or lovers or in residential or foster homes for gay adolescents. Parents may also deny the homosexual orientation of their gay child. Eight out of thirteen lesbian high school seniors in this study told their parents of their sexual orientation. "In each case, their parents told them that it was a passing phase that would go away" (pp. 24–25).

Coming out to strangers is another level in the coming out process. In the last several years, a new level of willingness to go public with one's gayness has emerged. U.S. Representative Barney Frank, Martina Navratilova, and kd Lang are examples of celebrities who have made their homosexuality known to the public.

Coming out is an important aspect of self-affirmation for gay individuals. Coming out also serves to communicate to the heterosexual community the pervasiveness of gay people and the important roles they occupy in society. During World War II, for example, when General Dwight D. Eisenhower learned that there were a number of lesbians in his Women's Army Corps (WAC) command, he asked his assistant, Sgt. Phelps, to draw up a list of all known lesbians in WAC. "We've got to get rid of them," he said (Beck, Glick, and Annin 1993, 60). Sgt. Phelps said that she would do as the general asked, but that her name would be first on the list. Eisenhower's secretary interrupted—Phelps's name would have to be second, her name would be first. Eisenhower told Phelps to "forget that order" (p. 60). Even though the military has no official orders to "get rid of lesbians," Margarethe Cammermeyer, a decorated Army colonel and nurse, jeopardized her military career when she "came out" in 1989.

Sometimes homosexual individuals are involuntarily forced out of the closet. "**Outing**" refers to the practice of publicly identifying the sexual orientation of homosexuals without their consent. The practice of outing is very controversial. Many gays oppose outing, calling it an imposed "demand of gay liberation upon its adherents" (Dankmeijer 1993, 95). They argue that outing robs individuals of their freedom and dignity, violates the right to privacy, and creates mistrust among members of the gay community.

Proponents of outing argue that it is in the best interests of gays to reveal closeted homosexuals to the public. Mohr (1992, 31) suggests that "to accept the closet is to have absorbed society's view of gays, to accept insult so that one avoids harm." Mohr cites the example of Congressman Gerry Studds as evi-

When you find your son is gay, and he brings his lover to your home for a few days, it opens your eyes.
Col. Fred Peck

I've made the choice that my personal liberty and the emancipation that I felt about coming out was definitely more important than my career at that point.
kd Lang
Music artist

dence that outing has positive outcomes. In 1983, Studds was outed by a special counsel to the House Ethics Committee for an affair he had had with a male page a decade earlier.

> *Unlike many outed people, Studds embraced, rather than denied, his sexual orientation. In . . . his self-acceptance, he found for the first time the capacity to love and a sense of freedom and serenity. In his pride, he has taken up a special role in gay projects, heading up congressional opposition to the ban on gays in the military. (pp. 41–42)*

Proponents of outing also recognize that there are "bad reasons" for this practice, such as vindictiveness and self-interest (Mohr 1992, 35). "When the motivation for outing is something other than the perpetuation of self-respect, the reasons for outing are morally dubious."

THE ROLE OF THE GAY SUBCULTURE

Sociologists use the term **subculture** to refer to the distinctive lifestyles, values, and norms of discrete population segments within a society. The gay subculture provides a supportive network within which gay individuals may affirm their sexual identity, develop a positive self-concept, and learn the roles, norms, and values associated with the gay lifestyle. The gay subculture serves to increase the cohesiveness of members of the gay community.

Subcultures provide a similar function for a variety of racial, ethnic, religious, gender, and social class groups. The gay subculture differs from other minority subcultures, however, as Uribe and Harbeck (1992) describe:

> *While most members of minority groups, whether ethnic, national, religious, racial, or gender-related, usually enjoy the support of and enculturation by other family and community members, the homosexual or bisexual young person is usually alone in this process of exploration and identification. (p. 13)*

Some gay and lesbian people live in communities that have a large gay population. In New York, Key West, Los Angeles, and most other large cities, the gay subculture provides gay churches, shops, counseling and health services, bars and other meeting places, and gay newspapers that list social activities for the gay community.

LESBIAN AND GAY RIGHTS MOVEMENT

The Stonewall riots of 1969, in which dozens of gay bar-goers fought back when harassed by police, have come to mark the beginning of the lesbian and gay rights movement in the United States. Various groups such as the National Gay and Lesbian Task Force (NGLTF), Gay and Lesbian Alliance Against Defamation (GLAAD), AIDS Coalition to Unleash Power (ACT-UP), Fund for Human Dignity, Human Rights Campaign Fund, Lambda Legal Defense and Education Fund, National Lesbian and Gay Health Foundation, Lesbian Avengers, and Astraea Lesbian Action Foundation represent the interests of gays and lesbians. These organizations are politically active in their efforts to achieve equal rights for gays and lesbians. The gay rights movement advocates the provision of health insurance benefits, parental leave, and bereavement

To function, every social group must have a culture of its own—its own goals, norms, values, and typical ways of doing things.
—Henry L. Tischler
Sociologist

We don't object to domestic partnerships. We don't agree that it is a substitute for same-sex marriage . . . . Domestic partnership can be a way of helping to eliminate forms of discrimination, but it has nothing to do with marriage. We don't want separate but equal, and domestic partnership is not equal. It doesn't offer the same benefits and recognition.
—Dan Foley
Honolulu attorney

leave for gay couples, the right of gay couples to file joint income tax forms, and the right of gay individuals to inherit assets from their partners without being subject to estate taxes.

The lesbian and gay rights movement has achieved some success in regard to the establishment of domestic partnerships, which are legal relationships that allow unmarried couples to have some of the same benefits as legally married spouses. Some cities including San Francisco, Berkeley, Santa Cruz, and Seattle recognize domestic partnerships. In addition, some states are changing the legal definition of the family to include all relationships in which individuals are emotionally committed and economically interdependent. The New York State Supreme Court has ruled that male and female homosexuals may be considered family in that upon the death of the lease-holding member of a couple, the remaining partner may not be evicted.

The lesbian and gay rights movement has also advocated extending civil rights laws to include homosexuals and has had some success in promoting equal job opportunities for lesbians and gay men. For example, employers are increasingly offering partners of gay employees benefits traditionally granted only to spouses. In 1994, Denver's police department announced that it would begin recruiting openly gay, lesbian, and bisexual officers as part of an effort to diversify its workforce (*Advocate* 1994b). Finally, the gay movement is active in promoting HIV/AIDS research, adequate health care for AIDS victims, and the rights of HIV-infected individuals. Increasingly, openly gay individuals are being elected to political positions. In 1992, two openly gay members of the U.S. Congress and nine gay state legislators were reelected.

The lesbian and gay rights movement is active not only in the United States, but also internationally. The International Lesbian and Gay Association (ILGA) supports lesbian and gay movements in countries throughout the world and represents their interests to international human rights organizations. The ILGA persuaded the World Health Organization (WHO) to declassify homosexuality as a disease (Clark et al. 1993) and has had several successes protesting individual or national injustices against homosexuals. Due to IGLA's efforts, "prisoners have been released, anti-homosexual decisions reversed, and governments embarrassed by exposure of their homophobic actions" (p. 16).

The lesbian and gay rights movement includes heterosexuals as well as homosexuals. Some heterosexuals have joined the gay rights movement because they have friends and/or family members who are gay. For example, P-FLAG (Parents and Friends of Lesbians and Gays) is one of the largest support organizations in the United States. Other heterosexuals have joined the movement because they support human rights and extend that support to lesbians and gays (Kraft 1993).

The lesbian and gay rights movement has also focused on the rights of gay and lesbian college students. This chapter's *In Focus* looks at campus policies regarding homosexuals.

CONSERVATIVE BACKLASH

The growth and successes of the lesbian and gay movement have sparked a conservative backlash spearheaded by political and religious groups that oppose homosexuality. In Aspen, Colorado, for example, voters approved an antigay

God made Adam and Eve, not Adam and Steve.
—Poster at conservative Christian rally

Campus Policies Regarding Homosexuality

Despite the assumption that universities are tolerant of alternative lifestyles, including homosexuality, history professor John D'Emilio reported, ". . . being openly gay on campus still goes against the grain . . . oppression in its many forms is still alive, and the university is not immune to it" (1990, 17).

Student groups have been active in the gay liberation movement since the 1960s. More than 400 gay student groups are organized in community colleges, and public gay student groups have amassed a body of judicial opinion protecting their right to assembly under the First Amendment (D'Emilio 1990). Some campuses, such as the University of Maryland, granted recognition to gay student groups long ago. Maryland's Gay and Lesbian Student Union, recognized in 1970, uses student activity fees to sponsor dances, classes, movies, and counseling services. At other campuses such as Georgetown University and Southern Methodist University, however, disputes over the rights of gay groups have led to litigation (Bartol 1990).

D'Emilio (1990) suggests that colleges and universities have the ability and the responsibility to promote gay rights and social acceptance of homosexual people:

> For reasons that I cannot quite fathom, I still expect the academy to embrace higher standards of civility, decency, and justice than the society around it. Having been granted the extraordinary privilege of thinking critically as a way of life, we should be astute enough to recognize when a group of people is being systematically mistreated. We have the intelligence to devise solutions to problems that appear in our community. I expect us also to have the courage to lead rather than follow. (p. 18)

Among the policies colleges and universities might adopt to meet this challenge are the following:

1. Develop outreach programs to provide support for victims of harassment and violence.
2. Provide training of local law enforcement personnel in lesbian and gay issues.
3. Create institutional policies that clearly affirm the unacceptability of discrimination on the basis of sexual orientation.

Brian McNaught emphasizes that commitment to social policies designed to create an environment free of homophobic behaviors is not an endorsement of any particular lifestyle, but rather an endorsement of tolerance for the diversity of people. He also stresses that homophobia is best addressed with education—providing accurate information about human sexuality, the experience of being gay, and the toll of persecution (McNaught n.d.).

rights measure by a margin of two to one. This measure was similar to Oregon's Measure 9, which would have amended the state constitution to declare homosexuality "abnormal, wrong, unnatural, and perverse." Although the measure did not pass, by March 1994, the number of Oregon jurisdictions that prohibit gay rights bills had increased to twenty. In the same month, Rhode Island's House of Representatives voted 56–43 to reject a gay rights bill.

Conservatives against homosexuals have found support in the Republican-controlled House of Representatives. House Speaker Newt Gingrich promised Rev. Lou Sheldon, head of the Traditional Values Coalition, a hearing on whether the federal government should provide money to school districts that "promote" homosexuality. Commenting on the future, Representative Barney Frank, who is openly gay, stated, "The Republican majority has been consistently and overwhelmingly anti-gay" (Mills 1995, A1–10).

UNDERSTANDING
SEXUAL ORIENTATION

As both functionalists and conflict theorists note, alternatives to a heterosexual lifestyle are threatening, for they challenge traditional definitions of family, childrearing, and gender roles. The result is economic, social, and legal discrimination by the majority. For example, homosexuals are not allowed to marry and thus are denied the tax and insurance benefits available to spouses. Gay men and women are also the most frequent victims of hate crimes. In some countries, homosexuality is formally sanctioned with penalties ranging from fines to imprisonment and even death.

In the past, homosexuality was thought to be a consequence of some psychological disturbance. More recently, some evidence suggests that homosexuality, like handedness, may have a biological component. The debate between biological and social explanations is commonly referred to as the "nature versus nurture" debate. Research indicates that both forces are in operation although debate over which is dominant continues (Byne and Parsons 1993). An interaction effect is the most plausible explanation.

Sexual expression is likely to be a product of complementary biological and social influences (De Cecco and Elia 1993, 1). The way the various elements fuse to create one's sexuality can be viewed as analogous to baking and tasting a cake (Lewontin, Rose, and Kamin 1984). The ingredients, including butter, flour, sugar, and baking soda, are combined in certain amounts and then baked at a particular temperature. The taste of the cake cannot be reduced to the taste of butter, flour, and so on, although each ingredient contributes to the final product. Applied to sexual orientation, this analogy means that genes and hormones may contribute to heterosexual or homosexual orientations, but we cannot reduce sexual orientation to any single ingredient or to various quantities of these ingredients because the ingredients themselves are transformed in the process of social experiences.

The question of etiology, although likely to be a continued area of inquiry, is not of central concern sociologically and may never be answered. What is significant is society's response to the existence of sexual diversity and how that response impacts the quality of life of society's members. Gay rights activists will continue to give gay issues public visibility. Politicians and religious leaders will continue to make decisions that either promote the well-being of the gay minority or hinder it. Ultimately, however, each individual must decide to embrace either an inclusive or an exclusive ideology; collectively, those individual decisions will determine the future treatment of sexual minorities in the United States.

CRITICAL THINKING

1. How do you think the legalization of same-sex marriages in the United States would affect public attitudes toward homosexuals?
2. Why do you think research studies have found that women tend to be more accepting of homosexuality than men, and that men tend to be more homophobic than women?
3. How is the homosexual population similar to and different from other minority groups?
4. Do you think that social acceptance of homosexuality leads to the creation of laws that protect gays? Or does the enactment of laws that protect gays help to create more social acceptance of gays?
5. How is homophobia dysfunctional for the heterosexual population?

KEY TERMS

sexual orientation	bisexuality	outing
homosexuality	heterosexism	subculture
lesbian	homophobia	
heterosexuality	coming out	

REFERENCES

Advocate. 1994a. "Around the Nation." (March 22) 651: 16.

_____. 1994b. "Denver Seeks Gay Cops." (May 3) 654: 18.

American Council on Education and University of California. 1994. "The American Freshman: National Norms for Fall, 1994." Los Angeles: Los Angeles Higher Education Research Institute.

American Psychiatric Association. 1987. *Diagnostic and Statistical Manual of Mental Disorders,* 3d ed., revised. Washington, D.C.: American Psychiatric Association.

Bailey, J. Michael, and R. C. Pillard. 1991. "A Genetic Study of Male Sexual Orientation." *Archives of General Psychiatry* 48: 1089–96.

Bailey, J. Michael, R. C. Pillard, M. C. Neal, and Yvonne Agyei. 1993. "Heritable Factors Influence Sexual Orientation in Women." *Archives of General Psychiatry* 50: 217–23.

Bartol, G. 1990. "The Fight over Gay Rights." *Newsweek on Campus,* 4–10.

Bayer, Ronald. 1987. *Homosexuality and American Psychiatry: The Politics of Diagnosis,* 2d ed. Princeton, N.J.: Princeton University Press.

Beck, Melinda, Daniel Glick, and Peter Annin. 1993. "A (Quiet) Uprising in the Ranks." *Newsweek,* June 21, 60.

Berrill, Kevin T., and Gregory M. Herek. 1990. "Violence against Lesbians and Gay Men: An Introduction." *Journal of Interpersonal Violence* 5: 274–94.

Bier, Mariana. 1990. "A Comparison of the Degree of Racism, Sexism, and Homophobia between Beginning and Advanced Psychology Classes." Unpublished master's thesis, Department of Psychology, East Carolina University, Greenville, N.C.

Blumenfeld, Warren J., and Diane Raymond. 1989. *Looking at Gay and Lesbian Life.* Boston: Beacon Press.

Boswell, John. 1994. *Same-Sex Unions in Premodern Europe.* New York: Villard.

Bull, Chris. 1994 (March 22). "The Condom Queen Reigns." *The Advocate.* 651: 32–38.

Byne, William, and Bruce Parsons. 1993. "Human Sexual Orientation." *Archives of General Psychiatry* 50: 228–39.

Cass, Vienne C. 1984. "Homosexual Identity Formation: Testing a Theoretical Model." *Journal of Sex Research* 20: 143–67.

Clark, John, Aart Hendriks, Lisa Power, Rob Tielman, and Evert van der Veen. 1993. "Introduction." In *The Third Pink Book: A Global View of Lesbian and Gay Liberation and Oppression,* ed. Aart Hendriks, Rob Tielman, and Evert van der Veen, pp. 15–21. Buffalo: Prometheus Books.

Committee on Lesbian and Gay Concerns. 1991. "Avoiding Heterosexual Bias in Language." *American Psychologist* 46: 973–74.

Dankmeijer, Peter. 1993. "The Construction of Identities as a Means of Survival: Case of Gay and Lesbian Teachers." *Journal of Homosexuality* 24: 95–105.

De Cecco, John P., and John P. Elia. 1993. "A Critique and Synthesis of Biological Essentialism and Social Constructionist Views of Sexuality and Gender." *Journal of Homosexuality* 24: 1–26.

D'Emilio, John. 1990. "The Campus Environment for Gay and Lesbian Life." *Academe* 76(1): 16–19.

Doll, Linda S., Lyle R. Peterson, Carol R. White, Eric S. Johnson, John W. Ward, and the Blood Donor Study Group. 1992. "Homosexual and Nonhomosexual Identified Men: A Behavioral Comparison." *Journal of Sex Research* 29: 1–14.

Durkheim, Emile. 1993. "The Normal and the Pathological." Originally published in *The Rules of Sociological Method,* 1938. In *Social Deviance,* ed. Henry N. Pontell, pp. 33–63. Englewood Cliffs, N.J.: Prentice-Hall.

Ellis, Leo, and Ashley M. Ames. 1987. "Neurohormonal Functioning and Sexual Orientation: A Theory of Homsexuality-Heterosexuality." *Psychological Bulletin* 101: 233–58.

Falk, Patricia J. 1989. "Lesbian Mothers: Psychosocial Assumptions in Family Law." *American Psychologist* 44: 941–47.

Finn, Peter, and Taylor McNeil. 1987 (October 7). *The Response of the Criminal Justice System to Bias Crime: An Exploratory Review.* Contract Report submitted to the National Institute of Justice, U.S. Department of Justice.

Franklin, Sarah. 1993. "Essentialism, Which Essentialism? Some Implications of Reproductive and Genetic Techno-Science." *Journal of Homosexuality* 24: 27–39.

Freedman, Estelle B., and John D'Emilio. 1990. "Problems Encountered in Writing the History of Sexuality: Sources, Theory, and Interpretation." *Journal of Sex Research* 27: 481–95.

Gallagher, John. 1994 (May 17). "The Wedding Is Off." *The Advocate* 655: 24–27.

Garnets, L., G. M. Herek, and B. Levy. 1990. "Violence and Victimization of Lesbians and Gay Men: Mental Health Consequences." *Journal of Interpersonal Violence* 5: 366–83.

Gelman, David, and D. Foote. 1992. "Born or Bred." *Newsweek,* February, 46–53.

Goode, Erica E., and Betsy Wagner. 1993. "Intimate Friendships." *U.S. News and Report,* July 5, 49–52.

Harry, Joseph. 1990. "A Probability Sample of Gay Males." *Journal of Homosexuality* 19: 89–104.

Hendriks, Aart, Rob Tielman, and Evert van der Veen, eds. 1993. *The Third Pink Book: A Global View of Lesbian and Gay Liberation and Oppression.* Buffalo: Prometheus Books.

Henry, William A. 1993. "Gay Parents: Under Fire and On the Rise." *Time,* September 20, 66–68.

Herek, Gregory M. 1989. "Hate Crimes against Lesbians and Gay Men." *American Psychologist* 44: 948–55.

_____. 1990. "The Context of Anti-gay Violence: Notes on Cultural and Psychological Heterosexism." *Journal of Interpersonal Violence* 5: 316–33.

Ingrassia, Michele, and Melissa Rossi. 1994. "The Limits of Tolerance?" *Newsweek,* February 14, 47.

Jenness, Valarie. 1995. "Social Movement Growth, Domain Expansion, and Framing Processes: The Gay/Lesbian Movement and Violence against Gays and Lesbians as a Social Problem." *Social Problems* 42: 145–70.

Kinsey, Alfred C., Wardell. B. Pomeroy, and Clyde E. Martin. 1949. *Sexual Behavior in the Human Male.* Philadelphia: W. B. Saunders.

Kinsey, Alfred C., Wardell B. Pomeroy, Clyde E. Martin, and Paul H. Gebhard. 1953. *Sexual Behavior in the Human Female.* Philadelphia: W. B. Saunders

Klassen, Albert D., Colin J. Williams, and Eugene E. Levitt. 1989. *Sex and Morality in the United States.* Middletown, Conn.: Wesleyan University Press.

Klein, Fred. 1978. *The Bisexual Option.* New York: Arbor House.

_____. 1985. "Sexual Orientations: A Multi-variable Dynamic Process." *Journal of Homosexuality* 11: 35–49.

Kraft, Ronald M. 1993. "Hetero Heroes." *The Advocate,* November 16, 64–67.

Lever, Janet, David E. Kanouse, William H. Rogers, Sally Carson, and Rosanna Hertz. 1992. "Behavior Patterns and Sexual Identity of Bisexual Males." *Journal of Sex Research* 29: 141–67.

Lewontin, Richard C., Steven Rose, and Leon J. Kamin. 1984. *Not in Our Genes: Biology, Ideology, and Human Nature.* New York: Pantheon.

McNaught, Brian. (n.d.). "Homophobia on the College Campus: A Discussion Guide." Available from Brian McNaught, 5 St. Louis Avenue, Gloucester, MA 01930.

Marcus, Eric. 1993. "Ignorance Is Not Bliss." *Newsweek,* July 5, 10.

Michael, Robert T., John H. Gagnon, Edward O. Laumann, and Gina Kolata. 1994. *Sex in America: A Definitive Survey.* Boston: Little, Brown.

Mickens, Ed. 1994 (March 22). "WorkLines: Can I Come Out at Work and Be Secure?" *The Advocate* 651: 19–20.

Mills, Kim I. 1995. "Gay Rights Leaders Find Tough Political Climate." *The Daily Reflector,* January 29, A1, A10.

Mohr, Richard D. 1992. *Gay Ideas: Outing and Other Controversies.* Boston: Beacon Press.

Money, John. 1987. "Sin, Sickness, or Status? Homosexual Gender Identity and Psychoneuroendocrinology." *American Psychologist* 42: 384–99.

Moore, David W. 1993 (April). "Public Polarized on Gay Issue." *Gallup Poll Monthly* 331: 30–34.

Moser, Charles. 1992. "Lust, Lack of Desire, and Paraphilias: Some Thoughts and Possible Connections." *Journal of Sex and Marital Therapy* 18: 65–69.

National Survey Results of Gay Couples in Long-Lasting Relationships. 1990 (May/June). *Partners: Newsletter for Gay and Lesbian Couples,* pp. 1–16. Available from Stevie Bryant and Demian, Box 9685, Seattle, WA 98109.

Nugent, Robert, and Jeannine Gramick. 1989. "Homosexuality: Protestant, Catholic, and Jewish Issues: A Fishbone Tale." *Journal of Homosexuality* 18: 7–46.

Park, Alice. 1995. "New Evidence of a 'Gay Gene.'" *Time,* November 13, 95.

Robinson, Bryan E., Lynda H. Walters, and Patsy Skeen. 1989. "Response of Parents to Learning That Their Child Is Homosexual and Concern over AIDS: A National Study." *Journal of Homosexuality* 18: 59–80.

Salholz, Eloise, Lucille Beachy, Dogan Hannah, Vicki Quade, and Melinda Liu. 1993. "For Better or Worse." *Newsweek,* May 24, 69.

Shapiro, Joseph P., Gareth G. Cook, and Andrew Krackov. 1993. "Straight Talk about Gays." *U.S. News and World Report,* July 5, 42–48.

Special Committee on Human Sexuality. 1991. *Part One: Keeping Body and Soul Together: Sexuality, Spirituality, and Social Justice.* General Assembly, Presbyterian Church (USA).

Tielman, Rob, and Hans Hammelburg. 1993. "World Survey on the Social and Legal Position of Gays and Lesbians." In *The Third Pink Book: A Global View of Lesbian and Gay Liberation and Oppression,* ed. Aart Hendriks, Rob Tielman, and Evert van der Veen. Buffalo: Prometheus Books.

Tripp, C. A. 1975. *The Homosexual Matrix.* New York: McGraw-Hill.

Troiden, Richard R. 1989. "The Formation of Homosexual Identities." *Journal of Homosexuality* 17: 43–73.

Turque, Bill. 1992. "Gays under Fire." *Newsweek,* September 14, 35–40.

Uribe, V., and Karen M. Harbeck. 1992. "Addressing the Needs of Lesbian, Gay, and Bisexual Youth: The Origins of PROJECT 10 and School-Based Intervention." In *Coming Out of the Classroom Closet: Gay and Lesbian Students, Teachers, and Curricula,* ed. K. Harbeck, pp. 9–27. New York: Haworth Press.

Weeks, Jeffrey. 1989. *Sex, Politics and Society,* 2nd ed. New York: Longman.

Weinberg, George. 1973. *Society and the Healthy Homosexual.* New York: Anchor Books.

Weinberg, Martin, Colin Williams, and Douglas Pryor. 1994. *Dual Attraction: Understanding Bisexuality.* New York: Oxford University Press.

Weinrich, James D., and W. L. Williams. 1991. "Strange Customs, Familiar Lives: Homosexualities in Other Cultures." In *Homosexuality: Research Implications for Public Policy,* ed. J. C. Gonsiorek and J. D. Weinrich. Newbury Park, Calif.: Sage Publications.

Whitehead, Minnie M., and Kathleen M. Nokes. 1990. "An Examination of Demographic Variables, Nurturance, and Empathy among Homosexual and Heterosexual Big Brother/Big Sister Volunteers." *Journal of Homosexuality* 19: 89–101.

8

CHAPTER

Gender Inequality

IS IT TRUE?

ANS: 1.F 2.T 3.T 4.F 5.F

> Be ready when the hour comes, to show that women are human and have the pride and dignity of human beings. Through such resistance our cause will triumph. But even if it does not, we fight not only for success, but in order that some inward feeling may have satisfaction. We fight that our pride, our self-respect, our dignity may not be sacrificed in the future as they have been in the past.
>
> Christabel Pankhurst, 1911

> *Only a radical transformation of the relationship between women and men to one of full and equal partnership will enable the world to meet the challenges of the 21st century.*
> —Beijing Declaration and Platform for Action, adopted by the 4th World Conference on Women

In 1992, at a convention of Navy personnel at a Las Vegas hotel, male naval officers sexually harassed female naval officers and hotel employees. During the ensuing investigation, women testified that in order to return to their rooms they were forced to pass through a "gauntlet of groping servicemen." Others recalled the use of disparaging names, inappropriate touching, and T-shirts that read "Women are Property." The Tailhook scandal, as the affair was later called, led to the dismissal and forced retirement of several naval officers, the demotion of others, and the sanctioning of many more. Tailhook, along with the Anita Hill–Clarence Thomas controversy, allegations that Senator Bob Packwood of Oregon sexually harassed female employees, and the debates over women in the military and reproductive rights have led to renewed concern over issues of gender equality.

In the previous two chapters, we discussed the social consequences of age and sexual orientation. This chapter looks at **sexism**, which is the belief that there are innate psychological, behavioral, and/or intellectual differences between women and men and that these differences connote the superiority of one group and the inferiority of another. As with age and sexual orientation, such attitudes often result in prejudice and discrimination at both the individual and institutional level. Individual discrimination is reflected by the physician who will not hire a male nurse because he or she believes that women are more nurturing and empathetic and are, therefore, better nurses. Institutional discrimination is exemplified by the difficulty some widows experience in finding employment; they have no work history or job skills as a consequence of living in traditionally defined marriage roles.

Discerning the basis for discrimination is often difficult because gender, age, sexual orientation, and race intersect. The effects of these social variables may interact and reinforce each other. For example, elderly African-American and Hispanic women are more likely to receive lower wages and work in less prestigious jobs than younger white women. They may also experience discrimination if they are "out" as homosexuals. Such **double** or **triple jeopardy** occurs when a person is a member of two or more minority groups. In this chapter, however, we emphasize the impact of gender inequality. **Gender** refers to the social definitions and expectations associated with being female or male.

The Social Context: The Status of Women and Men

Most countries devalue women. "[W]omen's natures, lives, and experiences are not taken as seriously, are not valued as much as those of men" (Walker, Martin, and Thomson 1988, 18). Further, women perceive more gender inequality than men. In a study of attitudes in the United States, England, West Germany, and Austria, Davis and Robinson (1991) found that in each country women perceived less gender equality than men.

INEQUALITY IN THE UNITED STATES

The United States has had a long history of gender inequality. Women have had to fight for equality: the right to vote, equal pay for comparable work, quality education, entrance into male- dominated occupations, and legal equality. Even today most U.S. citizens agree that American society does not treat women and men equally. As discussed later, many national statistics support the belief that men and women are not treated equally: women have lower incomes, hold fewer prestigious jobs, earn fewer academic degrees, and are more likely than men to live in poverty.

Americans' perceptions of the characteristics of men and women also reflect the inequality between the sexes in America. A 1990 Gallup Poll asked whether various characteristics were "generally more true of men or more true of women" (DeStefano and Colasanto 1990). Respondents most frequently described men, in rank order, as aggressive, strong, proud, disorganized, courageous, confident, independent, ambitious, selfish, and logical. In contrast, women were most often described as emotional, talkative, sensitive, affectionate, patient, romantic, moody, cautious, creative, and thrifty. Notice that none of the top ten characteristics were the same. About half of

The history of mankind is a history of repeated injuries and usurpations on the part of man toward woman, having in direct object the establishment of a tyranny over her.
—Manifesto, Seneca Falls, 1848

National Data: When a random sample of American adults were asked if society generally favors one sex over the other, 62 percent reported "men over women," 24 percent reported "equally," and 10 percent reported "women over men;" 4 percent had no opinion.
SOURCE: Newport 1993.

The United States has a long history of gender inequality; women have had to fight for the right to vote, equal pay for comparable work, and other rights.

the respondents thought that biological factors were responsible for the differences, and half thought the differences were due to socio-cultural factors.

A CROSS-CULTURAL VIEW OF INEQUALITY

Societies vary in the degree to which they regard men and women as equals. To assess the views of a hundred university students about the "proper" role relationship between women and men in each of fourteen countries (Canada, England, Finland, Germany, India, Italy, Japan, Malaysia, the Netherlands, Nigeria, Pakistan, Singapore, Venezuela, and the United States), Williams and Best (1990b) developed a series of thirty statements reflecting traditional and modern gender role positions. Agreement with such statements as "[T]he man's job is too important for him to get bogged down with household chores" reflected a traditional orientation. Agreement with such statements as "[M]arriage should not interfere with a woman's career any more than it does with a man's" reflected a modern orientation. Results indicated that the more highly developed the country, the more modern its gender role ideology.

Thus, in many underdeveloped countries, women do much of the physical labor, are forbidden to own land, can be divorced through the mere act of repudiation, and earn as little as half of what a man earns. Even in countries where women have achieved some measure of success, gender inequality is evident. Although more than 69 percent of all physicians in the countries of the former Soviet Union are female, they comprise 90 percent of all pediatricians but only 6 percent of all surgeons (O'Kelly and Carney 1992). The subordinate status of women in many underdeveloped countries is further evidenced by the practice of female genital mutilation (see *In Focus*).

An estimated 110 million women and female children have been mutilated by genital operations throughout the world. The cultural beliefs behind female genital mutilation are economic, social, and religious.

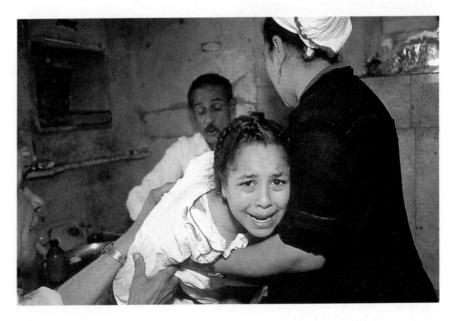

Gender Stratification: Structural Sexism

The social structure underlies and perpetuates much of the sexism in society. **Structural sexism,** also known as "institutional sexism," refers to the ways in which the organization of society, and specifically its institutions, subordinate individuals and groups based on their sex classification. Both structural-functionalism and conflict theory provide explanatory frameworks for understanding structural sexism and the resulting consequences—gender stratification.

SOCIOLOGICAL THEORIES OF GENDER STRATIFICATION

Both structural-functionalism and conflict theory concentrate on how institutions contribute to gender stratification. However, these two theoretical perspectives offer opposing views of the development and maintenance of gender stratification.

Structural-Functionalist Perspective Structural-functionalists argue that preindustrial society required a division of labor based on gender. Women, out of biological necessity, remained in the home performing such functions as bearing, nursing, and caring for children. Men, who were physically stronger and could be away from home for long periods of time, were responsible for providing food, clothing, and shelter for their families. This division of labor was functional for society and, over time, became defined as both normal and natural.

Industrialization rendered the traditional division of labor less functional although remnants of the supporting belief system still persist. Today, because of day care facilities, lower fertility rates, and the less physically demanding and dangerous nature of jobs, the traditional division of labor is no longer as functional. Thus, modern conceptions of the family have, to some extent, replaced traditional ones—families have evolved from extended to nuclear, authority is more egalitarian, more women work outside the home, and there is greater role variation in the division of labor. Functionalists argue, therefore, that as the needs of society change, the associated institutional arrangements also change.

Conflict Perspective Many conflict theorists hold that male dominance and female subordination are shaped by the relationship men and women have to the production process. During the hunting and gathering stage of development, males and females were economic equals, each controlling their own labor and producing needed subsistence. As society evolved to agricultural and industrial modes of production, private property developed and men gained control of the modes of production, while women remained in the home to bear and care for children. Male domination was furthered by inheritance laws that ensured that ownership would remain in their hands. Laws that regarded women as property ensured that women would remain confined to the home.

As industrialization continued and the production of goods and services moved away from the home, the male-female gap continued to grow—women had less education, lower incomes, and fewer occupational skills and were rarely owners. World War II necessitated the entry of large numbers of women into the labor force, but in contrast to previous periods, many did not return

Female Genital Mutilation

An estimated 110 million women suffer serious, even life-threatening, injuries resulting from female genital mutilation (Amnesty International 1995). Clitoridectomy and infibulation are two forms of female genital mutilation. In a clitoridectomy, the entire glans and shaft of the clitoris and the labia minora are removed or excised. With infibulation the two sides of the vulva are stitched together shortly after birth leaving only a small opening for the passage of urine and menstrual blood. After marriage, the sealed opening is reopened to permit intercourse and delivery. After childbirth, the woman is often reinfibulated. About two million girls undergo genital mutilation each year (Amnesty International 1995). The practice is widespread in Africa, where it occurs in twenty countries (Armstrong 1991). An estimated 98 percent of women in Somalia have undergone genital mutilation (Gregory 1994). Although the Kenyan government banned the procedure in 1990, it is still performed on more than 2 million young girls annually (Kaplan and Lewis 1993).

Clitoridectomy and infibulation are usually performed without anesthesia or sterile precautions by illiterate elderly midwives who use such tools as scissors, razor blades, and broken glass (Armstrong 1991). The operation usually occurs in the girl's home with her relatives assisting. Infection, hemorrhage, and chronic pelvic inflammatory disease are not uncommon (Gregory 1994). The practice has been criticized as leaving legions of small girls "in lifelong pain and sexual deprivation" and "vulnerable to disease, infection, and early death" (Kaplan and Lewis 1993, 124).

The societies that practice clitoridectomy and infibulation do so for a variety of economic, social, and religious reasons. A virgin bride can inherit from her father, thus making her an economic asset to her husband. A clitoridectomy increases a woman's worth because a woman whose clitoris is removed is thought to have less sexual desire and therefore to be less likely to be tempted to have sex before marriage. Older women in the community also generate income by performing the surgery so its perpetuation has an economic function (Kopelman 1994, 62). Various cultural beliefs also justify female genital mutilation including the idea that the "female genitalia are unclean and cutting them away purifies a woman; that the sex drive of an uncircumcised woman is uncontrollable; and that unless the labia of a woman are cut they will grow until they hang down between a woman's knees" (Armstrong 1991, 44).

In Muslim cultures, female circumcision is justified on both social and religious grounds. Muslim women are regarded as inferior to men: they cannot divorce their husbands, but their

home at the end of the war. They had established their own place in the workforce and, facilitated by the changing nature of work and technological advances, now competed directly with men for jobs and wages.

Conflict theorists also argue that the continued domination of males requires a belief system that supports gender inequality. Two such beliefs are that (1) women are inferior outside the home (e.g., they are less intelligent, less reliable, and less rational) and (2) women are more valuable in the home (e.g., they have maternal instincts and are naturally nurturing). Thus, unlike functionalists, conflict theorists hold that the subordinate position of women in society is a consequence of social inducement rather than biological differences husbands can divorce them; they are restricted from buying and inheriting property; and they are not allowed to have custody of their children in the event of divorce. Female circumcision is merely an expression of the inequality and low social status women have in Muslim society. Female circumcision also has a religious basis in that Allah is believed to approve of the practice (Hosken 1981, 419).

Interestingly, most women in cultures practicing female genital mutilation maintain that such practices deprive them of nothing. They do not think that women can have orgasms and say their sexual pleasure comes from the knowledge that they contribute to their husbands' enjoyment (Kopelman 1994). When women leave the approving cultural context, they sometimes adopt a different view. After Lydia Oluloro, a Nigerian woman, married an American and came to the United States, she decided she did not want her daughters, ages five and six and both American citizens, to be mutilated. Oluloro and her husband subsequently divorced, and when she learned she would be required to return to Nigeria where her daughters would be subjected to the ritualistic procedure, she sought "cultural asylum" in the United States (her former husband had never completed the papers that would have given her the right to stay). Their case helped make female mutilation an issue of human rights.

There is growing recognition that female genital mutilation occurs in the United States as more and more African immigrants come to this country, bringing their cultural traditions with them. An estimated 7,000 women and girls immigrate to the United States each year from countries where all or most females are circumcised (Burstyn 1995). Many immigrants from these countries either bring their daughters back to their homeland or import someone from their homeland to the United States to perform the circumcision.

As a result of grassroots campaigns, some countries have passed legislation prohibiting genital mutilation (Amnesty International 1995). International organizations, including the UN Commission on Human Rights, UNICEF, and the World Medical Association have also condemned the practice. However, as of 1995, only three states (New York, Minnesota, and North Dakota) have passed laws prohibiting the practice of female circumcision. Aside from laws in these three states, "there is almost no legal protection against FGM [female genital mutilation] for girls in the United States" (Burstyn 1995, 33).

SOURCES: Amnesty International. 1995. *Human Rights are Women's Right.* 322 Eighth Avenue, N.Y.C., N.Y.: Amnesty International USA; S. Armstrong. 1991. "Female Circumcision: Fighting a Cruel Tradition." *New Scientist* 2: 42–46; Linda Burstyn. 1995. "Female Circumcision Comes to America." *The Atlantic Monthly,* October, 28–35; L. P. Cutner. 1985. "Female Genital Mutilation." *Obstetric Gynecology Survey* 40: 437–43; Sophronia Scott Gregory. 1994. "At Risk of Mutilation." *Time* March 21, 45–46; F. P. Hosken. 1981. "Female Genital Mutilation in the World Today: A Global Review." *International Journal of Health Services* 11: 415–30; David A. Kaplan and Shawn D. Lewis. 1993. "Is it Torture or Tradition?" *Newsweek* December 20, 124; Loretta M. Kopelman. 1994. "Female Circumcision/Genital Mutilation and Ethical Relativism." *Second Opinion* 20: 55–71.

that led to the traditional division of labor. In either case, structural sexism has resulted in significant differences between the education and income levels, occupational and political involvement, and civil rights of women and men.

EDUCATION AND STRUCTURAL SEXISM

In 1991, more than half of all bachelor's and master's degrees were awarded to women (*Statistical Abstract of the United States: 1994,* Table 291). However, women still earn fewer doctorates and even fewer degrees in medicine, dentistry, and law (see Table 8.1).

TABLE 8.1

PERCENTAGES OF ADVANCED DEGREES GRANTED TO WOMEN, 1992

TYPE OF DEGREE	PERCENTAGE OF DEGREES EARNED BY WOMEN
Doctorate (Ph. D.)	37%
Medical degree (M. D.)	36
Dentistry degree (D. D. S. or D. M. D.)	32
Law degree (LL. B) or J. D.)	43

SOURCE: *Statistical Abstract of the United States: 1995*, 115th ed., U.S. Bureau of the Census (Washington, D.C.: U.S. Government Printing Office), Tables 301 and 302.

International Data: In 1992, 84 percent of U.S. women ages 25-64 had completed high school, a percentage far higher than that in Japan, Germany, England, France, Canada, or Italy.

SOURCE: U.S. Dept. of Education 1995.

One explanation for why women earn fewer advanced degrees than men is that women are socialized to choose marriage and motherhood over long-term career preparation (Olson, Frieze, and Detlefsen 1990). From an early age, women are exposed to images and models of femininity that stress the importance of domestic family life. When 821 undergraduate women were asked to identify their lifestyle preference, less than 1 percent selected being unmarried and working full-time. In contrast, 53 percent selected "graduation, full-time work, marriage, children, stop working at least until youngest child is in school, then pursue a full-time job" as their preferred lifestyle sequence (Schroeder, Blood, and Maluso 1993, 243). Only 6 percent of 535 undergraduate men selected this same pattern. This lack of career priority on the part of women is reflected in the lack of priority they give to education as preparation for a career.

Structural limitations also discourage women from advancing in the educational profession itself. For example, women seeking academic careers may find that promotion in higher education is more difficult than for men. Long, Allison, and McGinnis (1993) examined the promotions of 556 men and 450 women with Ph.D.'s in biochemistry. They found that women were less likely to be promoted to associate or full professor, were held to a higher standard than men, and were particularly disadvantaged in more prestigious departments. Hente (1993) also observed that in spite of Title IX prohibitions against sex discrimination in colleges, four times as much money is spent on recruiting male athletes as is spent recruiting female athletes.

INCOME AND STRUCTURAL SEXISM

Less education is associated with lower income. Yet even when men and women have the identical level of educational achievement and both work full-time, women still tend to earn only about two-thirds of what men earn (see Table 8.2).

Tomaskovic-Devey (1993) examined the income differences between males and females and found that the percentage of females in an occupation was the best predictor of a gender income gap—the higher the percentage of females, the lower the pay. Supporting this observation, a team of researchers (Kilbourne et al. 1994) analyzed data from the National Longitudinal Survey that included more than 5000 women and 5000 men. They concluded that occupational pay is gendered and that "occupations lose pay if they have a higher

TABLE 8.2

EFFECT OF EDUCATION AND SEX ON INCOME, 1993

| | AVERAGE INCOME FOR FULL-TIME WORKERS | |
LEVEL OF EDUCATIONAL ATTAINMENT	Women	Men
Some high school, no diploma	$18,030	$23,797
High school diploma	20,924	30,384
Some college, no degree	23,655	34,967
Associate degree	26,430	36,002
Bachelor's degree or more	37,109	59,276

SOURCE: *Statistical Abstract of the United States: 1995*, 115th ed., U.S. Bureau of the Census, (Washington, D.C.: U.S. Government Printing Office), Table 742.

percentage of female workers or require nurturant skills" (p. 708). Wellington (1994) also observed that not working full-time, taking time out of the labor force, and having fewer years in a rank accounted for some of the gender gap in earnings. More than half of the wage gap remains unexplained by these variables, however.

WORK AND STRUCTURAL SEXISM

Work is highly gendered. As a group, women tend to work in jobs where there is little prestige and low or no pay, where no product is produced, and where women are the facilitators for others. Women are also more likely to hold positions of little or no authority within the work environment. Investigating the gender gap in organizational authority in seven countries (Australia, Canada, Japan, Norway, Sweden, United Kingdom, and United States), Wright, Baxter, and Birkelund (1995, 419) conclude that in every country, "[W]omen are less likely than men to be in the formal authority hierarchy, to have sanctioning power over subordinates, or to participate in organizational policy decisions."

No matter what the job, if a woman does it, it is less valued than if a man does it. For example, in the early 1800s, 90 percent of all clerks were men, and being a clerk was a very prestigious profession. As the job became more routine, in part because of the advent of the typewriter, the pay and prestige of the job declined and the number of female clerks increased. Today, female clerks predominate, and the position is one of relatively low pay and prestige.

The concentration of women in certain occupations and men in other occupations is referred to as **occupational sex segregation** (see Table 8.3). For example, women are overrepresented in semiskilled and unskilled occupations, and men are disproportionately concentrated in professional and managerial positions (Steiger and Wardell 1995).

In some occupations, sex segregation has decreased in recent years. For example, the percentage of female physicians increased from 16 percent to 22 percent between 1983 and 1994, female dentists increased from 7 to 13 percent, female engineers increased from 6 to 8 percent, and female clergy increased from 6 to 11 percent (*Statistical Abstract of the United States: 1995*, Table 649).

TABLE 8.3

HIGHLY SEX-SEGREGATED OCCUPATIONS, 1994

FEMALE-DOMINATED OCCUPATIONS	PERCENTAGE OF FEMALE WORKERS
Registered nurses	94%
Licensed practical nurses	95
Dietitians	93
Prekindergarten and kindergarten teachers	98
Elementary school teachers	86
Librarians	88
Dental hygienists	100
Secretaries	99
Typists	94
Receptionists	97
Teacher's aides	90
Child care workers	97
Cleaners and servants	94

MALE-DOMINATED OCCUPATIONS	PERCENTAGE OF MALE WORKERS
Engineers	92%
Dentists	87
Physicians	78
Clergy	89
Airplane pilots and navigators	97
Police and detectives	84
Mechanics and repairers	96
Construction	98

SOURCE: *Statistical Abstract of the United States: 1995*, 115th ed., U.S. Bureau of the Census (Washington, D.C.: U.S. Government Printing Office), Table 649.

Nevertheless, despite these and other changes, women are still heavily represented in low-prestige, low-wage **"pink-collar" jobs** that offer few benefits. Even those women in higher- paying jobs are often victimized by a **glass ceiling**—an invisible barrier that prevents women and other minorities from moving into top corporate positions. A 1995 Federal Glass Ceiling Committee found that less than 5 percent of senior managers at the vice-presidential level or higher in Fortune 500 companies are women (Kaufman-Rosen and Kalb 1995, 24).

Sex segregation in occupations continues for several reasons (Martin 1992; Williams 1995). First, cultural beliefs about what is an "appropriate" job for a man or a woman still exist, as do socialization experiences in which males and females learn different skills and acquire different aspirations. Further, opportunity structures for men and women vary. Women have more opportunities in the less prestigious and lower-paying female professions—more than 70 percent of all minimum wage earners are women. Women may also be excluded by male employers and employees who fear the prestige of their profession will be lessened with the entrance of women or who simply believe that "the ideal worker is normatively masculine" (Martin 1992, 220).

Finally, since family responsibilities primarily remain with women, working mothers may feel pressure to choose professions that permit flexible hours and career paths, sometimes known as "mommy tracks." Thus, for example, women dominate the field of elementary education, which permits them to be home when their children are not in school. Nursing, also dominated by women, often offers flexible hours.

Occupational sex segregation perpetuates the limitations imposed by gender stereotypes. Women are stereotyped as nurturing and caring in part because of their service-oriented jobs, while men are believed to be more technically proficient and more competent decision makers because of the kinds of jobs they hold. Williams (1995) notes that "if equal numbers of men and women were employed as mechanics, managers, and airplane pilots, as well as nurses, librarians, and secretaries, these stereotypes would be far more difficult to sustain" (p. 146).

> **Consideration** *Although women entering professions dominated by men are at a disadvantage, the reverse is not true. Williams (1995) interviewed seventy-six men and twenty-three women in four traditionally female professions—elementary school teacher, librarian, nurse, and social worker. She found that men who work in traditional female occupations often receive preferential treatment in hiring and promotion decisions. Williams concludes that men take their "superior" status with them, even into female-dominated professions.*

POLITICS AND STRUCTURAL SEXISM

As a result of the women's suffrage movement led by Susan B. Anthony and Elizabeth Cady Stanton, women received the right to vote in 1920 with the passage of the Nineteenth Amendment. Even though this amendment went into effect more than seventy-five years ago, women today still play a rather minor role in the political arena. In general, the more important the political office, the lower the probability a woman will hold it. The United States has never had a woman president, vice president, or secretary of state. In 1992, often called the "year of the woman," there were only forty-seven female U.S. representatives, six U.S. senators, and three governors; less than 20 percent of the state legislative seats were held by women. Until 1993, when a second woman was appointed, only one woman had been a justice of the U.S. Supreme Court.

The relative absence of women in politics, as in higher education and in high-paying, high-prestige jobs in general, is a consequence of structural limitations. Running for office requires large sums of money, the political backing of powerful individuals and interest groups, and a willingness of the voting public to elect women. Much higher percentages of women hold political office in other industrialized countries.

CIVIL RIGHTS AND STRUCTURAL SEXISM

The 1963 Equal Pay Act and Title VII of the 1964 Civil Rights Act made it illegal for employers to discriminate in wages or employment on the basis of sex. Nevertheless, such discrimination still occurs as evidenced by the thousands of grievances filed each year with the Equal Employment Opportunity Commission (EEOC). One technique used to justify differences in pay is the use of different job titles for the same work. The courts have ruled, however, that jobs that are "substantially equal," regardless of title, must result in equal pay.

Women are also discriminated against in employment. Discrimination, although illegal, takes place at both the institutional and the individual level. Institutional discrimination includes male-dominated recruiting networks,

> *Women are barely tokens in the decision-making bodies of our nation, so the laws that govern us are made by men.*
> —National Organization for Women

International Data: The percentage of legislative positions held by women varies considerably from country to country: Sweden 38 percent, Germany 20 percent, Canada 13.5 percent, Spain 13 percent, Italy 11 percent, England 7 percent, France 6 percent, United States 5 percent, and Greece 3 percent.
SOURCE: Reis and Stone 1992, 440.

employment screening devices designed for men, hiring preferences for veterans, and the practice of promoting from within an organization, based on seniority. One of the most blatant forms of individual discrimination is sexual harassment, an issue that was brought to public attention by the televised confirmation hearings of Supreme Court nominee Clarence Thomas by the Senate Judiciary Committee and also by the resignation of Senator Bob Packwood.

Women are also discriminated against in obtaining credit. For example, having lower incomes, shorter work histories, and less collateral, women often have difficulty obtaining home mortgages or rental property. Further, even though the Equal Credit Opportunity Act of 1974 prohibits discrimination in credit transactions based on sex and/or marital status, a married woman must often request that credit be granted in her name as well as her husband's. If such a request is not made, the lender may issue credit in the husband's name only.

Finally, the rights of women to determine their own reproductive experience are tenuous. Since the U.S. Supreme Court's 1973 *Roe v. Wade* decision, the right of a woman to obtain an abortion has been limited. Today, the debate continues with several recent court decisions weakening the self-determination doctrine (see Chapter 14).

> **Consideration**   *Media attention to women's issues often overshadows the fact that men are victims of discrimination as well. For example, men are discriminated against in custody disputes, pay higher insurance premiums, and may be drafted into the military.*

The Social Construction of Gender Roles: Cultural Sexism

Structural sexism is supported by a system of cultural sexism that perpetuates beliefs about the differences between women and men. **Cultural sexism** refers to the ways in which the culture of society perpetuates the subordination of an individual or group because of the sex classification of that individual or group. Symbolic interactionists emphasize that through the socialization process, both males and females are taught the meanings associated with being masculine and feminine. While women are primarily socialized into expressive or nurturing and emotionally supportive roles, males are more often socialized into instrumental or task-oriented roles. The learning of gender roles begins in the family and continues throughout an individual's socialization experience.

FAMILY RELATIONS AND CULTURAL SEXISM

Is this a photo of a boy's bedroom or a girl's bedroom?

From birth, males and females are treated differently. For example, the toys male and female children receive convey different messages about appropriate gender roles. Research by Rheingold and Cook (1975) revealed how traditional gender role stereotypes are reflected in children's rooms in middle-class homes. Girls' rooms contained dolls, floral prints, and miniature home appliances such as stoves and refrigerators. Boys' rooms were more often decorated with a military or athletic motif and contained such items as building blocks, cars, trucks, planes, and boats. Overall, boys had more toys, more educational toys, and a greater variety in types of toys than girls. This study was replicated more than ten years later with the same results (Stoneman, Brody, and MacKinnon 1986). The significance of these findings lies in the relationship between the toys and the activities they foster: active versus passive play. Traditionally, boys are encouraged to catch the ball and run with it, while girls are encouraged to nurture their dolls.

Household Division of Labor Despite the presumed gender equality in industrialized countries, housework remains primarily women's responsibility (Brines 1994). Calasanti and Bailey (1991) offer three explanations for the continued traditional division of labor in families. The first explanation is the "time-availability approach." Consistent with the structural-functionalist perspective, this position emphasizes that role performance is a function of who has the time to accomplish certain tasks. Because women are more likely to be at home, they are more likely to perform domestic chores.

A second explanation is the "relative resources approach." This explanation, consistent with a conflict perspective, suggests that the spouse with the least power is relegated the most unrewarding tasks. Since men have more education, higher incomes, and more prestigious occupations, they are less responsible for domestic labor. The husband who shouts at his wife, "I pay the bills, the least you can do is keep the house clean!" is expressing the relative resources ideology.

"Gender role ideology," the final explanation, is consistent with a symbolic interactionist perspective. It argues that the division of labor is a consequence of traditional socialization and the accompanying attitudes and beliefs. Females and males have been socialized to perform various roles and to expect their partners to perform other complementary roles. Women typically take care of the house, men the yard. This division of labor is learned in the socialization process through the media, schools, books, and toys. A husband's comment that washing the dishes is "women's work" reflects this perspective.

THE SCHOOL EXPERIENCE AND CULTURAL SEXISM

Sexism is also evident in the schools. It can be found in the books students read, the curricula they are exposed to, and the different ways teachers interact with students.

Textbooks A report entitled "How Schools Shortchange Girls," commissioned by the American Association of University Women (1992), concludes that textbooks still stereotype females. For example, Purcell and Stewart (1990) analyzed 1,883 storybooks used in schools and found that they tended to depict males as clever, brave, adventurous, and income producing and females as passive and as victims. Females were more likely to be in need of rescue and were depicted in fewer occupational roles than males. In a study of twenty-seven introductory psychology and twelve human development textbooks, Peterson and Kroner (1992) determined that the representation of the work, theory, and behavior of males significantly exceeded that of females. Even though 56 percent of psychologists and 78 percent of developmental psychologists receiving Ph.D.'s are women, "the picture presented in textbooks is that the majority of persons working in the various domains of psychology are

National Data: Data from the National Survey of Families and Households on 656 dual-earner marriages revealed that wives performed about 70 percent of household tasks.
SOURCE: Perry-Jenkins and Folk 1994.

Men kinda have to choose between marriage and death. I guess they figure at least with marriage they get meals. Then they get married and find out we don't cook anymore.
—Rita Rudner
Comedian

men" (p. 31). Even textbooks that were designed to promote equality are characterized by "subtle language bias, neglect of scholarship on women, omission of women as developers of history and initiators of events, and an absence of women from accounts of technological developments" (American Association of University Women 1992, 63).

Curricula Encouragement to participate in sports, academic programs, and extracurricular activities is also gender biased despite Title IX of the 1972 Educational Amendments Act, which prohibits "tracking" students by sex. Males are more likely to participate in competitive sports that emphasize traditional male characteristics such as winning, aggression, physical strength, courage, adventurousness, and dominance. Males are also more often encouraged to go into math and science than females.

Teacher-Student Interactions Sexism is also reflected in the way teachers treat their students. Sadker and Sadker (1990) observed that elementary and secondary school teachers pay more attention to boys than to girls. Teachers talk to boys more, ask them more questions, listen to them more, counsel them more, give them more extended directions, and criticize and reward them more frequently. Sadker and Sadker observed that this pattern continues at the postsecondary level.

MEDIA IMAGES AND CULTURAL SEXISM

Media, including television, radio, magazines, and newspapers, reflect the cultural sexism of society. But they also contribute to it in various ways.

Television Although the National Commission on Working Women found that more women on television are strong and intelligent than in earlier years, television roles overall remain stereotypical with many more male than female role models; women continue to be depicted as sex objects and as subordinate to

> **National Data:** In 1992, female high school students scored, on average, four scale points (equivalent to .5 years of schooling) lower than male students on the mathematics portion of a national achievement test; female students scored an average of ten scale points (equivalent to one year of schooling) lower on the science portion of the test.
>
> SOURCE: U.S. Dept. of Education 1995.

Women are often portrayed in ornamental roles that emphasize their appearance rather than their capabilities.

men (Andersen 1993). For example, a study by Sally Steenland of teenage women in eighty prime-time television shows found that adolescent girls are primarily portrayed as being interested in two things—boys and clothes (reported in Barricklow 1992). Television also portrays women as ornaments, who have no purpose or function other than to be attractive (Davis 1990):

> The portrait here is of the young, attractive, and sexy female who is more ornamental in many shows than functional. For example, in one episode of *Miami Vice*, there were 14 speaking characters, all male. There were two female characters with more than three minutes of screen time, but neither spoke. Both were ornamental girlfriends of male episodic characters. (p. 331)

Television programs for children also exhibit gender bias. Almost all of the major characters on *Sesame Street* are male (e.g., Bert, Ernie, Oscar). Where there are female muppets, they disproportionately represent children; male muppets are more often cast as adults (Heiman and Bookspan 1992).

Magazines and Newspapers Magazines carry advertisements that reflect gender stereotypes. For example, one deodorant advertisement boasts "strong enough for a man, gentle enough for a woman." Magazines are also stratified by gender—for example, *Ladies Home Journal* and *Better Homes and Gardens* versus *Field and Stream* and *Gentlemen's Quarterly*. While newer magazines such as *Working Women* are less stereotypical, advertisements continue to encourage excessive concern with appearance in women by suggesting that if a product is not used, a woman will suffer detrimental effects such as wrinkles and dry skin, loss of youthful appearance, gray hair, and weight gain (McCracken 1993). Newspapers are also divided by gender. For example, the "women's section" contains recipes, wedding and engagement announcements, and fashion tips.

LANGUAGE AND CULTURAL SEXISM

In subtle ways, both the words we use and the way we use them can reflect gender inequality. The term *nurse* carries the meaning of "a woman who . . ." and the term *engineer* suggests "a man who . . . ." The embedded meaning of words, as symbolic interactionists note, carry expectations of behavior.

> **Consideration** The terms "broad," "chick," "old maid," and "spinster" convey information about age as well as attaching a stigma to the recipient. There are no comparable terms for men. Further, women have traditionally been designated as either Mrs. or Miss, while Mr. conveys no social meaning about marital status. Language is so gender stereotyped that the placement of female or male before titles is sometimes necessary as in the case of "female police officer" or "male prostitute."
>
> There is a movement away from male-biased language. The American Sociological Association includes suggestions for using nonsexist language in its style manual for preparing articles to be submitted for publication. The recent version of Random House Webster's College Dictionary has adopted terms that reflect the growing trend away from sexist language. Examples include "chairperson" for "chairman," "firefighter" for "fireman," "humankind" for "mankind," and "waitperson" for "waiter" or "waitress."

Virginia Sapiro (1994) has shown how male-female differences in communication style reflect the structure of power and authority relations between men and women. For example, women are more likely to use disclaimers ("I could be wrong but . . . .") and self-qualifying tags ("That was a good movie, wasn't it?"), reflecting less certainty about their opinions. Communication differences between women and men also reflect different socialization experiences. Women are more often passive and polite in conversation; men are less polite, interrupt more often, and talk more (Tannen 1990).

RELIGIOUS BELIEFS AND CULTURAL SEXISM

> *The whole tone of the Church teaching in regard to women is, to the last degree, contemptuous and degrading.*
> —Elizabeth Cady Stanton, 1896
> Feminist

According to Basow (1992), religious beliefs, a major aspect of culture, perpetuate sexism. For example, the Bible emphasizes the **patriarchal** (rule by the father) nature of the family:

> *But I want you to understand that the head of every man is Christ, the head of every woman is her husband, and the head of Christ is God (I Corinthians 11:3).*

> *You shall be eager for your husband, and he shall be your master (Genesis 3:16).*

Sexism is often justified on the basis of such passages and the beliefs they foster.

Furthermore, most of the power and statuses in religious organizations have been accorded to men. Until recently, only men could be priests, ministers, and rabbis. Basow (1992) points out that the Roman Catholic church has no female clergy and that men dominate the nineteen top positions in the U.S. dioceses. Male bias is also reflected in terminology used to refer to God, such as "He," "Father," "King," and "Master."

Social Problems Associated with Traditional Gender Role Socialization

Cultural sexism, transmitted through the family, school, media, language, and religion, perpetuates traditional gender role socialization. Although gender roles are changing, traditional gender roles are still dominant and have consequences for both women and men:

> *There is no denying that the gender system controls men too. Unquestionably, men are limited and restricted through narrow definitions of "masculinity." . . . They, too, face negative sanctions when they violate gender prescriptions. There is little value in debating which sex suffers or loses more through this kind of control; it is apparent that both do. (Schur 1984, 12)*

These traditional socialization experiences lead to several social problems. These include the feminization of poverty, social-psychological costs, health costs, and relationship problems.

POVERTY

Women have only about two-thirds of the income of men, which contributes to the "feminization of poverty" (see also Chapter 11). The U.S. poverty rate is 18.2 percent for women and 12.9 percent for men (Casper, McLanahan, and Garfinkel 1994). As noted earlier, both individual and institutional discrimination contribute to the economic plight of women. Traditional gender role socialization also contributes to poverty among women. Women are often socialized to put family ahead of their education and careers. Women are also expected to take primary responsibility for child care, which contributes to the alarming rate of single-parent poor families in the United States.

SOCIAL-PSYCHOLOGICAL COSTS

Many of the costs of traditional gender socialization are social-psychological in nature. Reid and Comas-Diaz (1990) noted that the cultural subordination of women results in women having low self-esteem and being dissatisfied with their roles as spouses, homemakers/workers, mothers, and friends. In a study of self-esteem among more than three thousand students in grades four through ten, the percentage of girls agreeing with the statement "I'm happy the way I am" dropped from 60 percent during elementary school to 37 percent during middle school and to 29 percent during high school. Negative changes for boys from elementary school through high school were minimal (American Association of University Women 1991).

The negative feelings women have about themselves continue into college where undergraduate women report significantly higher rates of self-dislike, a sense of failure, and self-accusations than undergraduate men (Oliver and Toner 1990). Further, the "ideal person" according to university females at the University of Colorado in Denver is one who is more "masculine than feminine" (Grimmell and Stern 1992).

Not all researchers have found that women have a more negative self-concept than men. Summarizing their research on the self-concepts of women and men in the United States, Williams and Best (1990a) found "no evidence of an appreciable difference" (p. 153). They also found no consistency in the self-concepts of women and men in fourteen countries: "[I]n some of the countries the men's perceived self was noticeably more favorable than the women's, whereas in others the reverse was found" (p. 152). More recent research also documents that women are becoming more assertive and desirous of controlling their own lives rather than merely responding to the wishes of others or the limitations of the social structure (Burger and Solano 1994).

Men also suffer from traditional gender socialization. Men experience enormous cultural pressure to be successful in their work and earn a high income. In a study of 601 adult men, those who reported feeling "more masculine" earned an average of $35,800—those who reported feeling less masculine earned an average of $28,300 (Rubenstein 1990). Further, as a consequence of traditional male socialization, males are more likely than females to value materialism and competition over compassion and self-actualization (Beutel and Marini 1995). Traditional male socialization also discourages males from expressing emotion. In a study of emotional expression among American women and men, Mirowsky and Ross (1995) conclude that "men

> *The poor of America are women: the poor of the world are women.*
> —Marilyn French
> Novelist/author

> *When we are taught that our worth and identity are to be found in loving and being loved, it is indeed devastating to have our attractiveness and womanliness questioned.*
> —Harriet G. Learner

> *I learned from my father how to work. I learned from him that work is life and life is work, and work is hard.*
> —Philip Roth
> Author

keep emotions to themselves more than women, and that women express emotions more freely than men" (p. 449).

HEALTH COSTS

On the average, men in the United States die about seven years earlier than women. Traditional male gender socialization is linked to males' higher rates of heart disease, cirrhosis of the liver, most cancers, AIDS, homicide, suicide, and motor vehicle accidents (*Statistical Abstract of the United States: 1995*, Tables 115 and 126).

Are gender differences in morbidity and mortality a consequence of socialization differentials or physiological differences? Although both nature and nurture are likely to be involved, social rather than biological factors may be dominant. As part of the "masculine mystique," men tend to engage in self-destructive behaviors—heavy drinking and smoking, poor diets, a lack of exercise, stress-related activities, higher drug use, and a refusal to ask for help. Men are also more likely to work in hazardous occupations than women. For example, men are more likely to be miners than women—an occupation with one of the highest mortality rates in the United States. In the following *Human Side*, Cohen (1980) humorously describes the trappings of the "masculine mystique" and how traditional male socialization diminishes physical and emotional well-being among men.

RELATIONSHIP COSTS

Gender inequality also has an impact on relationships. The different ways women and men have been socialized and the unequal opportunities they have been afforded sometimes create resentment. In a study of college students, Reiser (1993) found that women were more likely than men to report feeling resentment toward the opposite sex either "sometimes" or "a lot."

One manifestation of relationship problems is violence that is differentiated by gender (see Chapters 4 and 5). While men are more likely to be victims of violent crime, women are more likely to be victims of rape and domestic violence. Violence against women reflects male socialization that emphasizes aggression and dominance over women.

Toward Gender Equality?

In September 1995, women from across the globe came together at the United Nations' 4th World Conference on Women, in Beijing, to address issues concerning gender inequality and the status of women. Efforts to achieve gender equality have been largely fueled by the feminist movement. Despite a conservative backlash, feminists have made some gains in reducing structural and cultural sexism in the workplace and in the political arena.

FEMINISM AND THE CONSERVATIVE BACKLASH

The modern feminist movement was facilitated by a number of interacting forces: an increase in the number of women in the labor force, an escalating

I was more of a man with you as a woman than I have ever been with a woman as a man. I just need to learn to do it without the dress.
—Dustin Hoffman
to Jessica Lange
in the film *Tootsie*

Men, their rights and nothing more; women, their rights and nothing less.
—Susan B. Anthony
Feminist

IT TAKES A REAL MAN TO ADMIT HE'S UNMANLY

The other day, a bat flew into a house. It was not an ordinary bat, but instead a big, ugly, mean bat that found its way to the bathroom and hung, upside down, over the toilet bowl.

It was not an ordinary house, either. It was, in fact, my house and because it was my house and because I am what is known as the man of the house, it was my job, nay my manly duty, to rid my house of that mean, ugly, reputedly blood-sucking not to mention soul-threatening bat. I did what I had to do.

But I did not do it without hesitation, without saying "Why me?" and without being told the answer—because I'm a man, although being a man does not change the fact that I am afraid of bats. I am also afraid of rats, snakes, sharks and sting rays, but only bats thus far have hung upside down over my toilet bowl. Knock on wood.

I went for the broom. I also went for a cap and a light jacket, knowing full well that the stories about bats clinging to your hair are not true but thinking (logically, you will agree) that a cap could not hurt. Or a jacket. Thus armed and protected, I quickly opened the door and threw a pillow at the thing. It didn't move.

That old feeling came over me. It was the same feeling I experienced when I am dispatched down the stairs in the middle of the night to see what made a noise and it is pretty much the same feeling I had

years ago when I felt obliged to fight to the death some guy who called the girl I was with something like "tootsie." The feeling can be summed up in one word—trapped.

It is about how I would have felt had I been a passenger on the Titanic and someone had yelled "Women and children first." I would have wanted to yell "Why?" but I doubt that I would have had the nerve to do that. Instead, I would have stood stoically on the deck and gone down with the ship like a dumbbell. I'll tell you this: I would have been mad as hell about it.

All men, I think, have had that feeling of being trapped in some male role we want nothing to do with. Sometimes it is as trivial a matter as carving the turkey or arguing with the headwaiter or having to pretend that you know something about cars when dealing with the service manager— "Oh, it's the manifold, is it?"

But sometimes the trap is a vicious one. There are lots of men, after all, who would prefer to be something other than the stereotypical male. Maybe they don't give a hoot about careers or money or, say, competitive sports. Some of them would rather that the women in their lives initiated the dates, or at least some of them, and shared the expense of them and maybe— just maybe—initiated the sex also.

What these men are after is the freedom to be what they want to be

(continued on the next page)

IT TAKES A REAL MAN TO ADMIT HE'S UNMANLY *(continued)*

and still be men. This is something that more and more women are getting to do. All kinds of things that once stigmatized women as either tomboys or weirdos are now routinely done by women with no repercussions at all. Women repair cars and shimmy up telephone poles and jump from airplanes in the Army. Men, though, do not by and large become secretaries or housekeepers or even the male equivalent of housewives—househusbands.

Men, appear to be more hung up, more afraid to abandon the old roles for fear that they will somehow also be abandoning their masculinity. It's as if being a man is not what you are, but what you do and they way you do it.

Anyway, it had only been a couple of days since I talked with a representative of a male liberation group and I thought about him as I stalked the fierce and frightening bat. I wondered what would have happened if I had simply told my

wife that I wasn't going to mess with the thing—that she could, or call someone in the morning—Marlin Perkins for all I care.

But I couldn't do it. I patted my cap and zipped up my jacket and went into the bathroom to do battle with the bat. I slowly opened the window and then closed the toilet bowl cover. I checked the place over and then, slowly, I lifted the broom over my head and sort of swept the thing out the window. Just like that, it was gone.

I closed the windows. I looked around the room and then opened the door. My wife was thrilled. A house guest was awed and in the morning my son was just plain gaga. They asked me how I had gotten rid of the bat. I started to tell them but then stopped.

A man doesn't talk of such things.

SOURCE: Richard Cohen. 1980. "It Takes a Real Man to Admit He's Unmanly." © 1980, Washington Post Writers Group. Reprinted with Permission. May 29. C1, C6.

The growing strength of women's organizations and feminist groups has become a driving force for change.
—Beijing Platform for Action, 1995

divorce rate, the socially and politically liberal climate of the 1960s, student activism, and the establishment of a Commission on the Status of Women by John F. Kennedy. The National Organization for Women (NOW) was established in 1966 and remains the largest feminist organization in the United States with more than 100,000 members. One of NOW's hardest fought battles was the struggle to win ratification of the Equal Rights Amendment (ERA), which states that "[E]quality of rights under the law shall not be denied or abridged by the United States, or by any state, on account of sex." The proposed amendment passed both the House of Representatives and the Senate in 1972, but failed to be ratified by the states by the 1978 deadline, later extended to 1982.

Supporters of the ERA argue that its opponents used scare tactics—saying the ERA would lead to unisex bathrooms, mothers losing custody of their chil-

The beginnings of the modern feminist movement were characterized by public symbolic protests, such as this "bra burning." The socially and politically liberal climate of the 1960s and student activism served as a backdrop for such protests.

dren, and mandatory military service for women—to create a conservative backlash. Susan Faludi in *Backlash: The Undeclared War against American Women* (1991) contends that the arguments against feminism today are the same as those levied against the movement a hundred years ago and that the negative consequences opponents of feminism predict (e.g., women unfulfilled and children suffering) have no empirical support.

CHANGES IN THE WORKPLACE

Changes in the workplace reflect not only an increase in the number of women in the labor force, but a desire by both men and women to balance their lives around work, family, and leisure activities. In one survey, 74 percent of the men and 82 percent of the women declared that they would sacrifice career advancement in order to spend more time with their families (reported in Shor 1991). Corporations have begun to accommodate changing gender roles and the increased emphasis on family life by offering a variety of new programs and benefits such as on-site child care, part-time employment including job sharing, flextime, telecommuting, and assistance with elderly parents.

More women have also begun to enter traditionally male occupations. Williams (1995) suggests that this is an important and essential step on the road to gender equality, because it gives women more economic opportunities and helps to break down limiting stereotypes about women's capabilities. However, Williams warns that:

> Well-meaning efforts directed at getting women to be more "like men" run the risk of reifying the male standard, making men the ultimate measure of success. If the aim is gender equality, then men should be encouraged to become more "like women" by developing, or feeling free to express, interests and skills in traditionally female jobs. (p. 179)

POLITICAL STRATEGIES

A number of statutes have been passed to help reduce gender inequality. They include the 1963 Equal Pay Act, Title IX of the Educational Amendments Act, Title VII of the Civil Rights Act of 1964, the Displaced Homemakers Act, the 1978 Pregnancy Discrimination Act, and the Family Leave Act of 1993. The National Organization for Women (1995) encourages women to be politically active, to run for political office, and to participate in the decision-making processes of the nation. Recently, political activism has focused on the issues of sexual harassment and affirmative action.

Sexual Harassment During the 1980s and 1990s, the courts held that Title VII of the 1964 Civil Rights Act prohibited **sexual harassment** of males or females. Reports of sexual harassment to the EEOC nearly doubled between 1991 and 1992 in response to the publicity surrounding the Anita Hill–Clarence Thomas controversy.

There are two types of sexual harassment: (1) *quid pro quo* in which an employer requires sexual favors in exchange for a promotion, salary increase, or any other employee benefit, and (2) the existence of a hostile environment that unreasonably interferes with job performance as in the case of sexually explicit comments or insults being made to an employee. According to a 1993 Supreme Court decision, a person no longer has to demonstrate "severe psychological damage" in order to win damages. Sexual harassment occurs at all occupational levels, and some research suggests that the incidents of sexual harassment are inversely proportional to the number of women in an occupational category (Fitzgerald and Shullman 1993).

Affirmative Action The 1964 Civil Rights Act provided for **affirmative action** to end employment discrimination based on sex and race (see Chapter 9). Such programs require employers to make a "good faith effort" to provide equal opportunity to women and other minorities. However, in response to the growing sentiment that affirmative action programs constitute "reverse discrimination," recent court decisions have begun to dismantle affirmative action programs (see also Chapter 9).

UNDERSTANDING
GENDER INEQUALITY

Gender roles and the social inequality they create are ingrained in our social and cultural ideologies and institutions and are, therefore, difficult to alter. Nevertheless, as we have seen in this chapter, growing attention to gender issues in social life has spurred some change. For example, women who have traditionally been expected to give domestic life first priority are now finding it acceptable to be more ambitious in seeking a career outside the home. Men who have traditionally been expected to be aggressive and task oriented are now expected to be more caring and nurturing. Women seem to value gender equality more than men, however, perhaps because women have more to gain. For instance, 84 percent of 600 adult women said that the ideal man is caring and nurturing; only 52 percent of 601 adult men said that the ideal woman is ambitious (Rubenstein 1990, 160).

National Data: In a report on sexual harassment in the military, 64 percent of the women and 17 percent of the men reported having experienced some form of harassment.
SOURCE: Martindale 1991.

National Data: In a 1995 survey, 1,003 U.S. adults were asked if affirmative action is needed or not needed to help women overcome discrimination. Forty-one percent responded "needed," 57 percent "not needed," and two percent had no opinion.
SOURCE: Moore 1995.

But men also have much to gain by gender equality. Eliminating gender stereotypes and redefining gender in terms of equality do not mean simply liberating women, but liberating men and our society as well. "What we have been talking about is allowing people to be more fully human and creating a society that will reflect that humanity. Surely that is a goal worth striving for" (Basow 1992, 359). Regardless of whether traditional gender roles emerged out of biological necessity as the functionalists argue or economic oppression as the conflict theorists hold, or both, it is clear today that gender inequality carries a high price: poverty, loss of human capital, feelings of worthlessness, violence, physical and mental illness, and death. Surely, the costs are too high to continue to pay.

> *Give to every other human being every right that you claim for yourself.*
> —Thomas Paine
> Social activist

CRITICAL THINKING

1. Do you think that women and men suffer equally from traditional gender role socialization? Why or why not?
2. What have been the interpersonal costs, if any, between women and men of sensitizing U.S. society to the "political correctness" of interactions between women and men?
3. How has your gender role socialization influenced your educational and career goals?
4. Why are women more likely to work in traditionally male occupations than men are to work in traditionally female occupations?

KEY TERMS

sexism

double or triple (multiple) jeopardy

gender

structural sexism

occupational sex segregation

pink-collar jobs

glass ceiling

cultural sexism

patriarchy

sexual harassment

affirmative action

REFERENCES

American Association of University Women. 1991. *Shortchanging Girls, Shortchanging America.* Washington, D.C.: Greenberg-Lake Analysis Group.

_____. 1992. *How Schools Shortchange Girls.* Washington, D.C.: American Association of University Women.

Andersen, Margaret L. 1993. *Thinking about Women*, 3d ed. New York: Macmillan.

Barricklow, Denise. 1992. "Women in the Media: With Few Exceptions, Sexist Stereotypes Endure." *The Ford Foundation Report* (Summer): 17–19.

Basow, Susan A. 1992. *Gender: Stereotypes and Roles,* 3d ed. Pacific Grove, Calif.: Brooks/Cole.

Beutel, Ann M., and Margaret Mooney Marini. 1995. "Gender and Values." *American Sociological Review* 60: 436–48.

Brines. Julie. 1994. "Economic Dependency, Gender, and the Division of Labor at Home." *American Journal of Sociology* 100: 652–88.

Burger, Jerry M., and Cecilia H. Solano. 1994. "Changes in Desire for Control over Time: Gender Differences in a Ten-Year Longitudinal Study." *Sex Roles* 31: 465–72.

Calasanti, Toni, and Carol A. Bailey. 1991. "Gender Inequality and the Division of Labor in the United States and Sweden: A Socialist-Feminist Approach." *Social Problems* 38(1): 34–53.

Casper, Lynne M., Sara S. McLanahan, and Irwin Garfinkel. 1994. "The Gender-Poverty Gap: What We Can Learn from Other Countries." *American Sociological Review* 59: 594–605.

Cohen, Richard. 1980. "It Takes a Real Man to Admit He's Unmanly." *Washington Post,* May 29, C1, C6.

Davis, Donald M. 1990. "Portrayals of Women in Prime-Time Network Television: Some Demographic Characteristics." *Sex Roles* 23: 325–32.

Davis, Nancy J., and Robert V. Robinson. 1991. "Men's and Women's Consciousness of Gender Inequality." *American Sociological Review* 56: 72–84.

DeStefano, Linda, and Diane Colasanto. 1990. "Unlike 1975, Today Most Americans Think Men Have It Better." *Gallup Poll Monthly* 293: 25–36.

"Economy in Numbers." 1992. *Dollars and Sense* (December): 23.

Faludi, Susan. 1991. *Backlash: The Undeclared War against American Women.* New York: Crown Publishers.

Fitzgerald, Louise F., and Sandra L. Shullman. 1993. "Sexual Harassment: A Research Analysis and Agenda for the '90s." *Journal of Vocational Behavior* 40: 5–27.

Grimmell, Derek, and Gary S. Stern. 1992. "The Relationship between Gender Role Ideals and Psychological Well-Being." *Sex Roles* 27: 487–97.

Heiman, Diane, and Phyllis Bookspan. 1992. "Word on the Street: Bias There, Too." *Rocky Mountain News,* July 28, 30.

Hente, Karl. 1993. "Report Affirms Women Still Playing Catch-Up." In *Society in Crisis,* p. 145–46. Washington Post Writer's Group.

Kaufman-Rosen, Leslie, and Claudia Kalb. 1995. "Holes in the Glass Ceiling." *Newsweek,* March 27, 24–25.

Kilbourne, Barbara S., Georg Farkas, Kurt Beron, Dorothea Weir, and Paula England. 1994. "Returns to Skill, Compensating Differentials, and Gender Bias: Effects of Occupational Characteristics on the Wages of White Women and Men." *American Journal of Sociology* 100: 689–719.

Long, J. Scott, Paul D. Allison, and Robert McGinnis. 1993. "Rank Advancement in Academic Careers: Sex Differences and the Effects of Productivity." *American Sociological Review* 58: 703–22.

Martin, Patricia Yancey. 1992. "Gender, Interaction, and Inequality in Organizations." In *Gender, Interaction, and Inequality,* ed. Cecilia Ridgeway, pp. 208–31. New York: Springer-Verlag.

Martindale, Melanie. 1991. "Sexual Harassment in the Military: 1988." *Sociological Practice Review* 2: 210–16.

McCracken, Ellen. 1993. *Decoding Women's Magazines: From Mademoiselle to Ms.* New York: St. Martin's Press.

Mirowsky, John, and Catherine E. Ross. 1995. "Sex Differences in Distress: Real or Artifact?" *American Sociological Review* 60: 449–68.

Moore, David. 1995. "Americans Today are Dubious about Affirmative Action." *Gallup Poll Newsletter Archive* (March) [internet].

National Organization for Women. 1995. "General Information about NOW." http:1/www.igc.apc.org./homensnet.

Newport, Frank. 1993. "Americans Now More Likely to Say: Women Have It Harder Than Men." *Gallup Poll Monthly* no. 337, October, 11–18.

O'Kelly, Charlotte G., and Larry S. Carney. 1992. "Women in Socialist Societies." In *Issues in Society,* ed. Hugh F. Lena, William B. Helmreich, and William McCord, pp. 195–204. New York: McGraw-Hill.

Oliver, Sarah J., and Brenda B. Toner. 1990. "The Influence of Gender Role Typing on Expression of Depressive Symptoms." *Sex Roles* 22: 775–90.

Olson, Josephine E., Irene H. Frieze, and Ellen G. Detlefsen. 1990. "Having It All? Combining Work and Family in a Male and a Female Profession." *Sex Roles* 23: 515–34.

Perry-Jenkins, Maureen, and Karen Folk. 1994. "Class, Couples, and Conflict: Effects of the Division of Labor on Assessments of Marriage in Dual-Earner Families." *Journal of Marriage and the Family* 56: 165–80.

Peterson, Sharyl B., and Tracie Kroner. 1992. "Gender Biases in Textbooks for Introductory Psychology and Human Development." *Psychology of Women Quarterly* 16: 17–36.

Purcell, Piper, and Lara Stewart. 1990. "Dick and Jane in 1989." *Sex Roles* 22: 177–85.

Reid, Pamela T., and Lillian Comas-Diaz. 1990. "Gender and Ethnicity: Perspectives on Dual Status." *Sex Roles* 22: 397–408.

Reis, Paula, and Anne J. Stone, eds. 1992. *The American Woman, 1992–1993.* New York: W. W. Norton.

Reiser, Christa. 1993. "Gender Hostility: The Continuing Battle between the Sexes." *Free Inquiry in Creative Sociology* 21: 207–12.

Rheingold, Harriet L., and Kaye V. Cook. 1975. "The Content of Boys' and Girls' Rooms as an Index of Parent's Behavior." *Child Development* 46: 459–63.

Rubenstein, Carin. 1990. "A Brave New World." *New Woman* 20(10): 158–64.

Sadker, Myra, and David. Sadker. 1990. "Confronting Sexism in the College Classroom." In *Gender in the Classroom: Power and Pedagogy,* ed. S. L. Gabriel and I. Smithson, pp. 176–87. Chicago: University of Illinois Press.

Sapiro, Virginia. 1994. *Women in American Society.* Mountain View, Calif.: Mayfield.

Schroeder, K. A., L. L. Blood, and D. Maluso. 1993. "Gender Differences and Similarities between Male and Female Undergraduate Students regarding Expectations for Career and Family Roles." *College Student Journal* 27: 237–49.

Schur, Edwin. 1984. *Labeling Women Deviant: Gender, Stigma, and Social Control.* New York: Random House.

Shor, Juliet B. 1991. *The Overworked American: The Unexpected Decline of Leisure.* New York: Basic Books.

Statistical Abstract of the United States: 1995, 115th ed. U.S. Bureau of the Census. Washington, D.C.: U.S. Government Printing Office.

Steiger, Thomas L., and Mark Wardell. 1995. "Gender and Employment in the Service Sector." *Social Problems* 42(1): 91–123.

Stoneman, Z., G. H. Brody, and C. E. MacKinnon. 1986. "Same-Sex and Cross-Sex Siblings: Activity Choices, Behavior and Gender Stereotypes." *Sex Roles* 15: 495–511.

Tannen, Deborah. 1990. *You Just Don't Understand: Women and Men in Conversation*. New York: Ballantine Books.

Tomaskovic-Devey, Donald. 1993. "The Gender and Race Composition of Jobs and the Male/Female, White/Black Pay Gap." *Social Forces* 72(1): 45–76.

U.S. Department of Education. 1995. "The Condition of Education: 1995" (August). http:llwww.ed.gov.801pvbs/conofed95.

Walker, Alexis J., Sally S. Kees Martin, and Linda Thomson. 1988. "Feminist Programs for Families." *Family Relations* 37: 17–22.

Wellington, Alison J. 1994. "Accounting for the Male/Female Wage Gap among Whites: 1976 and 1985." *American Sociological Review* 59: 839–48.

Williams, Christine L. 1995. *Still a Man's World: Men Who Do Women's Work*. Berkeley: University of California Press.

Williams, John E., and Deborah L. Best. 1990a. *Sex and Psyche: Gender and Self Viewed Cross-Culturally*. London: Sage Publications.

_____. 1990b. *Measuring Sex Stereotypes: A Multination Study*. London: Sage Publications.

Wright, Erik Olin, Janeen Baxter, with Gunn Elisabeth Birkelund. 1995. "The Gender-Gap in Workplace Authority: A Cross-National Study." *American Sociological Review* 60: 407–35.

9

CHAPTER

Racial and Ethnic Relations

IS IT TRUE?

The U.S. Census Bureau recognizes only three racial categories: "white," "black," and "other" (p. 250).

In the twenty-first century, the largest racial or ethnic minority group in the United States will be comprised of African Americans (p. 252).

Before 1967, some states in the United States did not permit interracial marriages (p. 252).

According to a 1993 Gallup Poll, 65 percent of Americans believe that the number of immigrants admitted to the United States should be reduced (p. 254).

Due to affirmative action programs, unemployment rates for whites were higher than unemployment rates for blacks in 1994 (p. 261).

ANS: 1.F 2.F 3.T 4.T 5.F

> What treaty that the white man ever made with us have they kept? Not one. When I was a boy the Sioux owned the world; the sun rose and set on their land; they sent ten thousand men to battle. Where are the warriors today? Who slew them? Where are our lands? Who owns them? What law have I broken? Is it wrong for me to love my own? Is it wicked for me because my skin is red? Because I am a Sioux; because I was born where my father lived; because I would die for my people and country?
>
> Sitting Bull, Sioux chief

Movies such as *Dances with Wolves* and *Schindler's List* have given new visibility to the atrocities one group committed against another based on perceived differences. Historical examples are shameful. In 1838, more than 12,000 Cherokee Indians were forced to walk, in the dead of winter, from Georgia to Kansas. More than 4,000 died in what is now known as the "Trail of Tears." For almost two hundred years, Africans and their descendants were sold into slavery, denied their freedom and culture, and separated from their families. During World War II, 120,000 Japanese Americans, 70,000 of whom were U.S. citizens, were declared to be security threats and confined to internment camps. Finally, the horror of the Holocaust, Hitler's obsession with a "superior race," and the systematic extermination of more than 12 million Jews, Ukrainians, Poles, Russians, communists, and homosexuals exemplify the potential consequences of prejudice and discrimination.

In this chapter, we examine the nature, origins, and consequences of racial and ethnic prejudice and discrimination. We also discuss strategies designed to reduce prejudice and discrimination. We begin with an examination of the social meaning of race and ethnicity.

I request you all to keep a three-minute silence, in memory of the countless victims among you who have died in these cruel years.
—Oskar Schindler
Schindler's List

The Social Context: Racial and Ethnic Diversity

The world we live in is filled with diversity. Both living and nonliving things, from rocks and clouds to plants and animals, exist in various forms. Two aspects of human diversity are racial and ethnic variations. In this section, we look at what these variations mean and how they affect social relations.

THE SOCIAL MEANING OF RACE AND ETHNICITY

The terms *race* and *ethnicity* are sometimes used interchangeably. Nevertheless, they are different social constructs.

Race Sociologically, a **race** is a category of people who are believed to share distinct physical characteristics that are deemed socially significant. Racial groups are distinguished on the basis of such physical characteristics as skin color, hair texture, facial features, and body shape and size. Physical variations

The deaths of over 12 million Jews and others considered by Hitler not to be members of his "superior race" exemplify the potential consequences of prejudice and discrimination.

among people are the result of living for thousands of years in different geographical regions (Molnar 1983). For example, humans living in regions with hotter climates developed darker skin from the natural skin pigment, melanin, which protects the skin from the sun's rays. In regions with moderate or colder climates, people had no need for protection from the sun and thus developed lighter skin.

Since the first U.S. Census of 1790, virtually every Census has defined race differently. The first Census divided the population into four groups: free white males, free white females, slaves, and other persons (including free blacks and Indians). In order to increase the size of the slave population, the "one drop of blood" rule appeared, which specified that even one drop of Negroid blood

A Holocaust survivor said, "we are not born with hatred; we learn to hate." Will these children learn to hate others because of differences in physical appearance or cultural backgrounds?

defined a person as black and, therefore, eligible for slavery. In 1960, the Census recognized only two categories: white or nonwhite. In 1970, the Census categories consisted of white, black or "other" (Hodgkinson 1995). Currently, the U.S. Bureau of the Census recognizes four racial classifications: (1) White, (2) Black, (3) American Indian, Aleut, or Eskimo, and (4) Asian or Pacific Islander (*Statistical Abstract of the United States: 1995*).

Classifying people into different races fails to recognize that over the course of human history, migration and intermarriage have resulted in the blending of genetically transmitted traits. Thus, there are no "pure" races; people in virtually all societies have genetically mixed backgrounds. The Census Bureau recognizes that some persons do not identify with a specific racial group and, therefore, includes a racial category called "Other" on its survey forms.

An individual's racial identification is largely socially defined. Because there are no objective criteria for determining a person's race, the Census Bureau relies on self-identification, that is, the individual's perception of his or her racial identity. Since 1970, the number of Native Americans in the United States has increased, not because their birth rates have increased, but because more people who are of mixed descent including Native American have begun to identify themselves as Native American (Harris 1992).

Ethnicity Ethnicity refers to a shared cultural heritage. Each ethnic group has important traditions that give it a unique cultural identity. Ethnic groups may be distinguished on the basis of many cultural characteristics, including language, forms of family structures and roles of family members, religious beliefs and practices, dietary customs, forms of artistic expression such as music and dance, and national origin.

While the classification of race is based on perceived biological or physical characteristics, ethnicity is based on cultural characteristics. Two members of the same race may have different ethnicities. For example, a black American and a black Jamaican have different cultural, or ethnic, backgrounds. Conversely, two individuals with the same ethnic background may belong to different races. Hispanics, for example, may be white or black.

U.S. citizens come from a variety of ethnic backgrounds. More than 20 percent of the U.S. population come from German ancestry, more than 10 percent are of Irish ancestry, and more than 10 percent have English ancestry. In the year 2000, about 11 percent of the U.S. population will be of Hispanic origin, including Cubans, Mexicans, and Puerto Ricans (*Statistical Abstract of the United States: 1995*, Table 19).

Like racial backgrounds, ethnic backgrounds have become increasingly blended due to intermarriage. It is not uncommon for Americans to identify with multiple ethnic backgrounds. Interestingly, a person's identification with a particular ethnic group may change over time and circumstance. For example, people of mixed descent may emphasize their Italian heritage when angry and their Irish ancestry when St. Patrick's Day is near.

Consideration The use of racial and ethnic labels is often misleading. The ethnic classification of "Hispanic," for example, lumps together such disparate groups as Puerto Ricans, Mexicans, Cubans, Venezuelans, Colombians, and others from Latin American countries. The racial term "American Indian" includes more than 300 separate tribal groups that dif-

fer enormously in language, tradition, and social structure. The racial label "Asian American" includes individuals with ancestors from China, Japan, Korea, India, the Philippines, or one of the countries of Southeast Asia.

PATTERNS OF MAJORITY-MINORITY INTERACTION

When two or more racial or ethnic groups come into contact, one of several patterns of interaction may occur, including colonialism, genocide, slavery, segregation, assimilation, pluralism, and amalgamation. These patterns of interaction may occur when two or more groups exist in the same society or when different groups from different societies come into contact.

- **Colonialism** occurs when a racial or ethnic group from one society takes over and dominates the racial or ethnic group(s) of another society. The European invasion of North America, the British occupation of India, and the Dutch presence in South Africa are examples of outsiders taking over a country and controlling the native population.
- **Genocide** refers to the systematic annihilation of one racial or ethnic group by another. The European invasion of the Americas, beginning in the sixteenth century, resulted in the decimation of most of the original inhabitants of North and South America. Some native groups were intentionally killed, while others fell victim to diseases brought by the Europeans. In the twentieth century, Hitler led the Nazi extermination of more than 12 million people, including over 6 million Jews, in what has become known as the Holocaust.
- **Slavery** exists when one group treats another group as property to exploit for financial gain. The dominant group forces the enslaved group to live a life of servitude.
- **Segregation** refers to the physical and social separation of categories of individuals, such as racial or ethnic groups. Segregation may be **de jure** (Latin meaning "by law") or **de facto** ("in fact"). Between 1890 and 1910, a series of U.S. laws were enacted that separated blacks from whites by prohibiting blacks from using "white" buses, hotels, restaurants, and drinking fountains. In 1896, the U.S. Supreme Court (in *Plessy v. Ferguson*) supported de jure segregation of blacks and whites by declaring that "separate but equal" facilities were constitutional. Blacks were forced to live in separate neighborhoods and attend separate schools. Beginning in the 1950s, various rulings overturned these Jim Crow laws, making it illegal to enforce racial segregation. Although de jure segregation is illegal in the United States, de facto segregation still exists in the tendency for racial and ethnic groups to live and go to school in segregated neighborhoods.
- **Assimilation** is the process by which minority groups gradually adopt the cultural patterns of the dominant majority group. Immigrants to the United States may try to become assimilated by adopting the food, dress, customs, and language of the American white majority. Blacks who speak with a "black dialect" may try to abandon their speech patterns and adopt standard white English in an effort to assimilate into the dominant white culture.

National Data: Between 1661, when Virginia enacted a law recognizing slavery, and 1808, when slave trading was outlawed, slave traders forcibly transported about 400,000 Africans to the United States.

SOURCE: Sowell 1981.

- **Pluralism** refers to a state in which racial and ethnic groups maintain their distinctness, but respect each other and have equal access to social resources. In Switzerland, for example, four ethnic groups—French, Italians, Germans, and Swiss Germans—maintain their distinct cultural heritage and group identity in an atmosphere of mutual respect and social equality. In the United States, the political and educational recognition of multiculturalism reflects efforts to promote pluralism. Given the level of prejudice and discrimination toward racial and ethnic minorities (discussed later in this chapter), however, the United States is far from pluralistic.
- **Amalgamation** occurs when different ethnic or racial groups intermingle and produce a new and distinct genetic and cultural population. One way to achieve amalgamation, or a "melting pot" society, is for racial and ethnic groups to intermarry over generations. But in most societies, the norm of **endogamy** influences individuals to marry within their social group. In the United States, marriages between individuals with different ethnic backgrounds is not unusual, but interracial marriages are relatively rare. For many years, some states had antimiscegenation laws that prohibited interracial marriages, but in 1967 , the Supreme Court (in *Loving v. Virginia*) declared these laws unconstitutional and required all states to recognize interracial marriage (Reid 1995).

RACE AND ETHNIC RELATIONS WORLDWIDE

Much of the conflict in the world today is rooted in racial and ethnic hostilities: fighting between Bosnian Serbs and Moslims as the former initiated "ethnic cleansing;" the banning of Koreans from employment in Japan; the slaying of black natives in South Africa despite an official end to apartheid; the continued hostilities between Israelis and Palestinians over the occupied territories; and the rioting by Chinese college students over the increased presence of African schoolmates. Commenting on these racial and ethnic conflicts, Senator Daniel Patrick Moynihan states:

> The defining mode of conflict in the world ahead is ethnic conflict. It promises to be savage. Get ready for 50 new countries in the world in the next 50 years. Most of them will be born in bloodshed. (quoted in Binder and Crossette 1993, 12)

RACE AND ETHNIC RELATIONS: AN AMERICAN DILEMMA

Racial and ethnic minority populations in the United States are growing rapidly. This growth is largely due to immigration and the higher average birth rates among many minority groups. Figure 9.1 shows the estimated racial composition of the United States for selected years.

The 1990 census indicates that the percentage of non-Hispanic whites declined to 76 percent from 80 percent in 1980. Furthermore, the proportion of whites declined in 72 percent of all counties in the United States (Vobejda 1993). Blacks, who represented less than half of all minorities in 1990, will be replaced by Hispanics as the largest minority group in the twenty-first century.

By 2020, while the white population will remain constant, the Hispanic and nonwhite population will double. If present trends continue, by 2056 the "average" U.S. resident will be nonwhite or Hispanic (Henry 1990).

The increased diversity of racial and ethnic groups in the United States assures continued variation in languages, customs, values, beliefs, food, music, and group identity. Ideally, respective groups would revere and appreciate cultural differences. But many Americans have a negative view of racial and ethnic diversity. This chapter's *In Focus* discusses the impact of such views on U.S. immigration policy.

To become a U.S. citizen, immigrants must pass an examination administered by the U.S. Immigration and Naturalization Service. A sample of possible questions included on this examination is presented in this chapter's *Self and Society*.

More than fifty years ago, Myrdal (1944) observed the inherent contradiction between some American values and the treatment of racial and ethnic minorities. Although the Declaration of Independence emphasizes equality and justice for all, racial and ethnic minorities have been persecuted throughout U.S. history. When whites of European descent took charge of America, they began exploiting other racial and ethnic groups. "Justice for all" did not occur when early U.S. settlers stole Indian land and plantation owners enslaved Africans kidnapped from their homeland. "Equality for all" remains an unrealized ideal today as minorities continue to experience prejudice and discrimination in housing, health care, education, politics, and the workplace. The three sociological theories lend insight into the continued subordination of minorities.

Sociological Theories of Race and Ethnic Relations

Numerous theories of race and ethnic relations exist. Some emphasize psychological characteristics arguing, for example, that individuals with certain personality types are more likely to be prejudiced or to direct hostility toward minority group members. Alternatively, biological theories hypothesize that innate differences between racial and ethnic groups may account for behavioral and/or intellectual variations. Sociologists, however, using the sociological imagination, concentrate on the impact of the structure and culture of society on race and ethnic relations.

STRUCTURAL-FUNCTIONALIST PERSPECTIVE

Functionalists emphasize that each component of society contributes to the stability of the whole. In the past, inequality between majority and minority groups was functional for some groups in society. For example, the belief in the superiority of one group over another provided moral justification for slavery, supplying the South with the means to develop an agricultural economy based on cotton. Slaves provided cheap labor and required no training or skills. Further, members of the majority perpetuated the belief that minority members would not benefit from changing structural conditions (Nash 1962). Thus, southern whites felt that emancipation would be detrimental for blacks who were highly dependent upon their "white masters." Indeed, many southerners

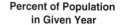

FIGURE 9.1
RACIAL COMPOSITION OF THE UNITED STATES, 1995–2050

Percent of Population in Given Year

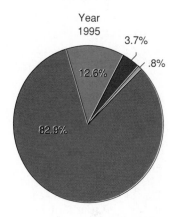

Year 1995

3.7%
.8%
12.6%
82.9%

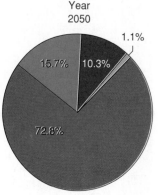

Year 2050

1.1%
15.7%   10.3%
72.8%

■ White
■ Black
■ Asian, Pacific Islander
▨ American Indian, Eskimo, Aleut

SOURCE: *Statistical Abstract of the United States: 1995*, 115th ed., U.S. Bureau of the Census (Washington, D.C.: U.S. Government Printing Office), Table 18.

Immigration Policy in the United States

U.S. immigration policy has had a varied history. Since the early 1800s more than 57 million immigrants have come to the United States (*Statistical Abstract of the United States: 1992*, Table 5). Initially, the immigrants were from England, Ireland, and Germany, but by the early and mid-1900s, they were predominantly from southern and eastern Europe and Mexico. Prejudice and discrimination, particularly against Asians and Hispanics, led to the passage of the Immigration Act of 1921, which for the first time limited the number of immigrants entering the United States.

In 1965, however, the immigration doors were reopened, and the previous bias against non-European immigrants was reversed (Morganthau 1993). The new policy established quotas by hemisphere—120,000 from the Eastern Hemisphere and 120,000 from the Western Hemisphere. Those who had family in the United States, had needed job skills, or were refugees seeking political asylum were given priority. A *refugee* is "any person who is outside his or her country of nationality who is unable or unwilling to return to that country because of persecution or a well-founded fear of persecution" (*Statistical Abstract of the United States: 1995*, p. 3).

Currently, U.S. immigration policy restricts the number of immigrants to 270,000 a year. This limitation has a number of exemptions, however, including refugees. The United States accepted more than 530,000 immigrants in 1980; more than 1,500,000 in 1990 and 1991; and more than 904,000 on 1993 (*Statistical Abstract of the United States: 1995*, Table 6). In addition to legally admitted immigrants, an unknown number of illegal immigrants enter the United States each year. Government estimates of the annual number of illegal immigrants are as high as 500,000 (Morganthau 1993, 20).

The large number of legal and illegal immigrants in the United States has led to increased public concern over immigration policy. According to a 1993 Gallup Poll, 65 percent of Americans feel the number of immigrants admitted to this country should be reduced, twice the percentage who felt that way in 1965 (Moore 1993). Moore suggests that "Americans today . . . are worried about the cultural diversity these newcomers bring with them and their economic impact on local communities" (p. 2). More than half of Americans in the poll believed that "immigrants cost the taxpayers too much by using governmental services like public education and medical services." Less than half of the respondents believed that "immigrants in the long run become productive citizens and pay their fair share of taxes" (Moore 1993, 4).

Anti-immigrant sentiment is based predominantly on the beliefs that immigrants take jobs away from Americans, drive down wages by providing low-cost labor, and consume more than their fair share of tax-subsidized services. For example, immigrants disproportionately settle in certain states—California (40 percent), Texas (12 percent), New York (10 percent), and Florida (8 percent) (Morganthau 1993, 20–21). In California, one out of eight recipients of Aid to Families with Dependent Children is a child of illegal aliens; in 1990, while 7.7 percent of native-born Californians received public assistance, 10.4 percent of new immigrants were on welfare (Thomas and Murr 1993). In 1994, Californians passed Proposition 187, which prevented illegal immigrants from receiving public assistance, but the measure was immediately challenged on constitutional grounds.

The influx of immigrants into certain areas has also aggravated troubled school systems, accelerated the deterioration of cities, escalated crime rates and unemployment, and bankrupted public coffers. In Florida, the number of immigrants has risen so dramatically that the governor estimated the economic cost of immigration, particularly of Haitians, at more than $1 billion in 1994 (Gibbs 1994, 31). Partly as a response to Florida's overburdened economy, in 1994 President Clinton rescinded a decades-old immigration policy that allowed Cuban immigrants automatic asylum (Gibbs 1994).

The United States is, and remains, a nation of immigrants, taking in more aliens each year than all of the other industrialized countries combined. Immigrants bring new skills, ideas, talents, and cultures to the United States, contributing to the same diversity and growth that catapulted America into a position of international leadership a century ago. Immigrants are not always an economic burden. They often take jobs many Americans do not want, and as consumers, they increase the demand for food, clothing, shelter, and other goods and services. Unfortunately, they are also often victimized by the very nation where they seek citizenship: many work as undocumented laborers, paid below the minimum wage, housed in substandard conditions, and denied adequate education and health care.

SOURCES: Nancy R. Gibbs. 1994. "Dire Straights." *Time,* August 29, 27–32; David W. Moore. 1993. "Americans Feel Threatened by New Immigrants." *Gallup Poll Monthly* (July): 2–16; Tom Morganthau. 1993. "America: Still a Melting Pot?" *Newsweek,* August 9, 16–23; *Statistical Abstract of the United States: 1992* and *1995,* 112th and 115th eds. U.S. Bureau of the Census. Washington, D.C.: U.S. Government Printing Office; *Statistical Abstract of the United States: 1992* (112th edition). 1992. U.S. Bureau of the Census. Washington DC: U.S. Government Printing Office, Rich Thomas and Andrew Murr. 1993. "The Economic Cost of Immigration." *Newsweek,* August 9, 18–19.

subscribed to the belief that it was the duty of white landowners to continue their dominance over blacks who would otherwise be unable to survive.

Functionalists recognize, however, that racial and ethnic inequality is also dysfunctional for society (Williams and Morris 1993). First, in a society that values one group over another, the achievements of minorities who might otherwise be productive members of society are obstructed. If the United States is to maintain a competitive edge in the global economy, it must make full use of its human resources. Second, "the expense of coping with vast numbers of human failures in a culture built on achievement" is tremendous (p. 420). This expense includes money spent on law enforcement, social services, health care services, and drug rehabilitation. It also includes lives lost to drugs and homicide, and "occasional destructive outbursts of rage" (p. 420). In addition, cultural beliefs about the superiority of one group over another aggravate existing social problems including crime and violence, drug abuse, poverty, academic underachievement, economic stagnation, urban decay, and health problems. Finally, racial and ethnic inequality contributes to intergroup hostility creating societal tensions that disrupt social equilibrium.

Structural-functionalists are also concerned with how sudden changes in the social system affect society. For example, is immigration functional for society because it brings new consumers and workers who are willing to take

Under Proposition 187, citizens of California voted to deny public schooling, health benefits, and other public health services to illegal aliens.

Becoming a U.S. Citizen: Could You Pass the Test?

Any legal immigrant in the United States for five years may apply for citizenship if he or she has no criminal history and is not a member of the Communist or Nazi parties. The immigrant must also demonstrate knowledge of English and pass a test on U.S. history and government. The following questions are typical of those on the examination given to immigrants seeking U.S. citizenship. Applicants may choose between an oral and a written test. On the oral test, they must answer all the questions correctly. On the written test, they must correctly answer 12 of 20 questions. Based on your answers to these questions, would you be granted U.S. citizenship if you were an immigrant (that is, could you correctly answer 6 out of the following 10 questions)?

1. When was the Constitution written?
2. How can we change the Constitution?
3. Who has the right to vote?
4. What are the three branches of government?
5. Name one qualification to be president.
6. For how many terms can a person be president?
7. Name one duty of the vice president.
8. Name one cabinet department.
9. Which branch of federal government makes the laws?
10. Who is the governor of your state?

SOURCE: Immigration and Naturalization Service, U.S. Department of Justice. 1989. *By the People . . . U.S. Government Structure.* Washington, D.C.: U.S. Government Printing Office.

In the 21st century—and that's not far off—racial and ethnic groups in the U.S. will outnumber whites for the first time. The "browning of America" will alter everything in society, from politics and education to industry, values and culture.
—William Henry

jobs that many Americans are not willing to take? Or is immigration dysfunctional for society because immigrants take jobs away from Americans and enable employers to keep wages low? Immigration has affected not only the economy, but the educational institution as well as it faces the challenge of teaching children from diverse cultural backgrounds.

CONFLICT PERSPECTIVE

Conflict theorists emphasize the role of economic competition in creating and maintaining racial and ethnic group tensions. Majority group subordination of racial and ethnic minorities reflects perceived or actual economic threats by the minority. For example, between 1840 and 1870, large numbers of Chinese immigrants came to the United States to work in mining (California Gold Rush of 1848), railroads (transcontinental railroad completed in 1860), and construction. As Chinese workers displaced whites, anti-Chinese sentiment rose, resulting in increased prejudice and discrimination and the eventual passage of the Chinese Exclusion Act of 1882, which restricted Chinese immigration until 1924.

Further, conflict theorists emphasize the necessity of maintaining a surplus labor force, that is, having more workers than are needed. A surplus labor force assures that wages remain low for someone is always available to take a dis-

As Chinese workers displaced white workers, anti-Chinese sentiment resulted in the eventual passage of the Chinese Exclusion Act of 1882.

gruntled worker's place. Minorities who are disproportionately unemployed serve the interests of the business owners by providing surplus labor, keeping wages low, and, consequently, enabling them to maximize profits.

Conflict theorists also argue that elites foster negative attitudes toward minorities in order to maintain racial and ethnic tensions among workers. As long as workers are divided along racial and ethnic lines, they are less likely to join forces to advance their own interests at the expense of the capitalists. In addition, the "haves" perpetuate racial and ethnic tensions among the "have-nots" to deflect attention away from their own greed. In the 1992 Los Angeles riots instigated by the verdict in the Rodney King case, hardworking small-business owners—predominantly Koreans and Blacks—fought against each other around the same time as public disclosure of the famous S&L scandal and corrupt military overspending. Gioseffi (1993) comments that "it is tragic to realize that poor Los Angeles neighborhoods were burned in race riots . . . while rich majority executives involved in destroying and exploiting the U.S. economy—and costing taxpayers billions—went unprosecuted" (p. xxiv).

Finally, conflict theorists suggest that tensions between majority group and minority group members represent conflict over such fundamental issues as the cause of their subordinate position. While minorities argue that their subordinate position is a consequence of historical circumstances and continued cultural and structural barriers, many majority members argue that minorities are responsible for their own plight. If only minorities worked harder and adhered to the mainstream values of self-reliance and discipline, they too would succeed. Other points of conflict include attitudes toward affirmative action, school busing, bilingual education, and welfare reform.

SYMBOLIC INTERACTIONIST PERSPECTIVE

The symbolic interactionist perspective focuses on how meanings and definitions contribute to the subordinate position of certain racial and ethnic groups. The different connotations of the colors white and black are a case in point. The white knight is good, and the black knight is evil; angel food cake is white, devil's food cake is black. Other negative terms associated with black include black sheep, black plague, black magic, black mass, blackballed and blacklisted. The continued use of such derogatory terms as Jap, Gook, Spic, Frogs, Kraut, Coon, Chink, Wop, and Mick also confirms the power of language in perpetuating negative attitudes toward minority group members.

Negative labeling of minorities leads to a self-fulfilling prophecy. As Schaefer (1993, 18) explains:

> *Self-fulfilling prophecies can be especially devastating for minority groups. Such groups often find that they are allowed to hold only low-paying jobs with little prestige or opportunity for advancement. The rationale of the dominant society is that these minority individuals lack the ability to perform in more important and lucrative positions. Minority-group individuals are then denied the training needed to become scientists, executives, or physicians and are locked into society's inferior jobs. As a result, the false definition becomes real; in terms of employment, the minority has become inferior because he/she was defined at the start as inferior and prevented thereby from achieving equality.*

By being labeled as inferior, racial and ethnic minorities join other minority groups such as women, homosexuals, and the elderly whose achievements are limited by the definitions of others.

Prejudice and Discrimination

Prejudice refers to an attitude or judgment, usually negative, about an entire category of people. Prejudice may be directed toward individuals of a particular religion, sexual orientation, political affiliation, age, social class, sex, race, or ethnicity.

SOURCES OF PREJUDICE

Prejudice is largely a learned attitude that originates in the culture of society. Sources of prejudice include cultural transmission, stereotypes, and the media.

Cultural Transmission Prejudice is taught and learned through the socialization process. One of the first sources of prejudice is the family. Research indicates, for example, that parents who are prejudiced are more likely to have children who are also prejudiced. Other institutions also foster prejudice. Some religious doctrines teach intolerance of racial and ethnic groups. Further, school curricula have traditionally been Eurocentric—that is, biased toward white Europeans—often perpetuating the belief that minority group members are inferior.

Stereotypes Prejudicial attitudes toward racial and ethnic groups are often the result of **stereotypes,** or oversimplified generalizations about a category of individuals. These generalizations, which become deeply embedded in the culture, are either untrue or are gross distortions of reality. For example, ob-

It is never too late to give up your prejudices.
—Henry David Thoreau
Writer/Civil activist

Why are blacks stereotyped as lazy? Wasn't it whites who enslaved blacks to do the hard work on the plantations? If you ask me, whites were too lazy to do the work themselves.
—Student in a sociology class

serving that many professional basketball players are black leads to the stereotype that all blacks have "natural" athletic abilities. Rarely do people who make such observations focus on the other abilities of blacks, the presence of white basketball players, or persons with lesser athletic ability of either race.

Media Stereotypical images presented by the media are particularly harmful in creating and perpetuating prejudice. Although such blatant stereotypes as Amos and Andy, played by two white radio personalities who depicted blacks as temperamental, dishonest and intellectually inferior, no longer exist, more subtle negative images remain. On prime-time television, for example, Hispanics are disproportionately portrayed as criminals (Lichter et al. 1987). Print media are also prone to stereotypes. When blacks are portrayed in magazine advertisements, they are disproportionately pictured as musicians, athletes, and objects of charity (Langone 1993, 30).

RACISM

At the extreme, prejudice takes the form of **racism:** the belief that certain groups of people are innately inferior to other groups. Race then becomes the determining factor in attributing psychological, behavioral, and/or intellectual variations. The perception that certain groups have inferior traits serves to justify discrimination against those groups.

Researchers use surveys to determine the extent to which prejudice and racism exist in an individual, group, or society. According to many survey data on racial attitudes, racism in America has decreased over the last several decades. For example, adjective checklist studies, in which respondents are asked to select traits that are most typical of particular racial and ethnic groups, indicate that negative stereotypes of blacks have faded (Dovidio and Gaertner 1991). A series of Gallup polls revealed that between 1963 and 1978, substantial declines occurred in the percentages of white respondents agreeing with the statements "blacks tend to have less ambition than whites" (from 66 to 49 percent), "blacks have less native intelligence than whites" (from 39 to 25 percent), and "blacks are inferior to whites" (from 31 to 15 percent) (Dovidio and Gaertner 1991).

Dovidio and Gaertner (1991) suggest, however, that "what may have changed across time . . . is what people regard as socially desirable rather than racial attitudes per se" (p. 125). In other words, survey data on racial attitudes may reflect what respondents view as "politically correct" rather than what people really believe or feel. Supporting this hypothesis is a study by Sigall and Page (1981), who found that white subjects who believed that their truthfulness was being monitored through their physiological responses gave more negative evaluations of blacks and more positive evaluations of whites than did control subjects who believed that they were not being monitored. Commentaries surrounding the O.J. Simpson trial certainly suggest that racism still plagues American society.

While prejudice refers to attitudes, **discrimination** refers to behavior that involves treating categories of individuals unequally. The two are not necessarily related—a person may be prejudiced and not discriminate; conversely, a person may discriminate but not be prejudiced.

The great enemy of truth is very often not a lie—deliberate, continued, and dishonest—but the myth, persistent, persuasive and unrealistic.
—John F. Kennedy
Former U.S. President

Racism . . . has been the most persistent and divisive element in this society and one that has limited our growth and happiness as a nation.
—James E. Jones, Jr.
Director, Center for the Study of Affirmative Action

INDIVIDUAL DISCRIMINATION

Sometimes called individual racism, **individual discrimination** refers to the acts by individuals that are based on prejudicial attitudes. There are two types of individual discrimination—overt and adaptive.

Overt Discrimination In *overt discrimination* the individual discriminates because of his or her own prejudicial attitudes. For example, a white landlord may refuse to rent to a Mexican-American family because of her own prejudice against Mexican Americans. Or, a Taiwanese-American college student who shares a dorm room with an African-American student may request a roommate reassignment from the student housing office because he is prejudiced against blacks.

Overt discrimination also takes the form of verbal harassment (McClelland and Hunter 1992). Referring to an adult black male as "boy" or a Native American as "chief" illustrates the demeaning nature of racial and ethnic verbal harassment.

Adaptive Discrimination Suppose a Cuban-American family wants to rent an apartment in a predominantly white neighborhood. If the landlord is prejudiced against Cubans and does not allow the family to rent the apartment, that landlord has engaged in overt discrimination. But what if the landlord is not prejudiced against Cubans but still refuses to rent to a Cuban family? Perhaps that landlord is engaging in *adaptive discrimination,* or discrimination that is based on the prejudice of others. In this example, the landlord may fear that if he rents to a Cuban-American family, other renters who are prejudiced against Cubans may move out of the building or neighborhood and leave the landlord with unrented apartments. Overt and adaptive individual discrimination may coexist. For example, a landlord may not rent an apartment to a Cuban family because of her own prejudices *and* the fear that other tenants may move out.

INSTITUTIONAL DISCRIMINATION

Sometimes called institutional racism, **institutional discrimination** occurs when normal operations and procedures of social institutions result in unequal treatment of minorities. Institutional racism is covert and insidious and maintains the subordinate position of minorities in society. There are two types of institutional discrimination: cultural and structural.

Cultural Discrimination By adhering to their own culture, minorities are systematically excluded from the mainstream of American society. For example, many schools require students to take standardized tests that are culturally biased. Minorities may score lower on these tests not because they are less intelligent, but because they are less familiar with the vocabulary and knowledge tested by these exams (see Chapter 13). Further, cultural discrimination is found in the criminal justice system, which more heavily penalizes crimes that are more likely to be committed by minorities. For example, the penalties for crack cocaine, more often used by minorities, have traditionally been higher than those for other forms of cocaine use even though the same prohibited chemical substance is involved. As conflict theorists emphasize, majority group members make rules that favor their own group.

Structural Discrimination Minorities are also excluded from equal participation in society's institutions because of structural discrimination. For example, many jobs require a college degree. Since minorities are less likely to be college graduates, the probability that the job will be filled by a minority is lowered. Further, infant mortality rates among minorities are disproportionately high because of such structural impediments as a lack of medical care.

As with overt and adaptive discrimination, cultural and structural discrimination are linked. Minorities may not do well in school because of certain language barriers (i.e., cultural discrimination); as a result, they have higher dropout rates and less education. With little education, minorities often find it difficult to secure employment (i.e., structural discrimination).

Social Problems Related to Racial and Ethnic Group Relations

As noted earlier, racial and ethnic hostilities often lead to world conflict, war, and bloodshed (see also Chapter 16). Other social problems related to racial and ethnic group relations include discrimination in employment and income, education, housing, and politics; hate crime victimization, and health and quality of life issues.

EMPLOYMENT AND INCOME DISCRIMINATION

In comparison to U.S. whites, racial and ethnic minorities are more likely to be unemployed. Minorities are also more likely to be fired, work in low-paying and low-status jobs, and earn less income than whites. Differences in educational level do not completely explain differences in unemployment rates. For example, among persons aged 25 to 65 with less than a high school diploma, the black unemployment rate in 1994 was 17.4 percent while the white unemployment rate was 11.7 percent. Among those with a high school diploma but no college experience, the unemployment rate was 12.2 percent for blacks and 5.8 percent for whites (*Statistical Abstract of the United States: 1995*, Table 663).

Minority unemployment is, in part, a function of institutional discrimination. Neckerman and Kirschenman (1991) studied the hiring practices of 185 Chicago area businesses and found that recruitment efforts largely targeted white neighborhoods.

Even when employed, minorities are more likely to be fired than whites. Zwerling and Silver (1993) reached this conclusion after examining job dismissals at a large northeastern city postal office. After taking absenteeism, job tenure, and union membership into consideration, blacks were still twice as likely to be fired as whites.

Minorities are also more likely to be overrepresented at the bottom of an occupational hierarchy and underrepresented at the top. For example, blacks comprise over a quarter of major college athletes. Yet they account for fewer than 8 percent of university and college head coaches and less than 10 percent of university and college athletic directors (Wieberg 1995).

With minorities more likely to be unemployed and to work in low-paying jobs, it is not surprising that minorities are also more likely to live in poverty. Native Americans are the poorest of all minority groups. Native American

National Data: In 1994, unemployment rates for U.S. adults age sixteen and over were 5.2 percent for whites, 9.7 percent for Hispanics, and 10.6 percent for blacks.

SOURCE: *Statistical Abstract of the United States: 1995*, Table 663.

Although over a quarter of major college athletes are black, only 8 percent of head coaches and fewer than 10 percent of athletic directors at the college and university level are black.

household incomes, both on and off the reservation, are only about 70 percent of the household income of whites, and one-third are living in poverty (Feagin and Feagin 1993, 198). Further, the unemployment rate of Native Americans is twice that of the general population.

Hispanics are a diverse ethnic group that includes, among others, Mexicans, Puerto Ricans, and Cubans. Income differentials vary by group with Mexicans and Puerto Ricans, in general, being poorer than Cubans. In 1993, for example, 37 percent of Puerto Ricans lived below the poverty level, compared to 18 percent of Cubans (*Statistical Abstract of the United States: 1995,* Table 53). Possible explanations for such differences include that Cubans have traditionally been concentrated in a limited geographical area that facilitates networking; they came to the United States with many more resources, education, and training; and they are less likely to be involved in agricultural pursuits.

In general, however, Hispanics have lower incomes than whites. The median income of a Hispanic family is two-thirds that of a non-Hispanic family. Only 10 percent of Hispanic men have professional or managerial jobs compared to 27 percent of non-Hispanic men (Langone 1993). As with blacks, occupational and income differences cannot be explained by educational differences alone. Institutional discrimination is responsible for much of the disparity. For example, height and weight regulations for such jobs as police officer and firefighter often exclude Hispanics. Further, there is some evidence that Hispanics who have darker skin, are less Anglo in appearance, and have more Native American features, have lower incomes (Telles and Murguia 1990).

Asian Americans, including Japanese, Chinese, and Koreans, have the highest income and occupational levels of all groups, including whites. They are also targets of the "myth of Asian superiority." Takaki (1990) notes that Asian Americans have come to be viewed as a "model minority" and asks if they are as successful as claimed:

> *For example, figures on the high earnings of Asian-Americans relative to Caucasians are misleading. Most Asian-Americans live in California, Hawaii and New York—states with higher incomes and higher costs of living than the national average.*
>
> *. . . Even Japanese Americans, often touted for their upward mobility, have not reached equality. While Japanese-American men in California earned an average income comparable to Caucasian men in 1980, they did so only by acquiring more education and working more hours. . . . Comparing family incomes is even more deceptive. Some Asian-American groups do have higher family incomes than Caucasians. But they have more workers per family. (p. 15)*

Asian Americans are also underrepresented in professional and managerial positions (Feagin and Feagin 1993) and, as immigrants, may be restricted from employment because of limited English proficiency.

EDUCATIONAL DISCRIMINATION

Minorities, in general, not only have less prestigious jobs and lower incomes, they also have fewer years of education (see Table 9.1). Native Americans have the highest dropout rate of any minority group in the United States—twice the

TABLE 9.1

EDUCATIONAL ATTAINMENT BY RACE AND ETHNICITY FOR U.S. ADULTS AGE 25 AND OLDER, 1994

EDUCATIONAL LEVEL	RACIAL OR ETHNIC GROUP	PERCENTAGE
Completed high school	White	82.0%
	Black	72.9
	Hispanic	53.3
Completed college	White	22.9
	Black	12.9
	Hispanic	9.1

SOURCE: *Statistical Abstract of the United States: 1995*, 115th ed., U. S. Bureau of the Census (Washington, D. C.: U.S. Government Printing Office), Table 238.

dropout rate of whites. The authors of a 1991 report entitled *Indian Nations at Risk* concluded that the Native American dropout rate reflects the lack of teacher attention to Indian concerns, culture, language, and history in public schools (Cooper 1991).

Asian Americans reflect a wider range of educational levels with over half of all Asians over the age of twenty-five having some college. Recent Asian immigrants such as the Vietnamese, however, have higher dropout rates than whites (U.S. Commission on Civil Rights 1992).

Among Hispanics, Cubans are most likely to have a high school degree and Mexicans the least. Like many other minorities, and particularly blacks, Hispanics are often segregated in inner city schools. While de jure segregation ended in 1954 as a result of the Supreme Court's decision in *Brown v. Board of Education of Topeka*, which held that "separate is not equal," schools today remain highly segregated as a result of housing patterns. However, since the passage of the 1964 Civil Rights Act, the federal government has been able to bring suit against a number of school districts that have failed to comply with desegregation regulations. These legal challenges have resulted in "busing" or forced integration. The existence of de facto segregation has taken its toll: blacks are half as likely to attend college as whites and score significantly lower on a variety of standardized tests.

Some reports also suggest that minority students are more than twice as likely to be punished in school as members of the majority group. For example, in the Cincinnati School System, black students are twice as likely as white students to be disciplined. While teachers argue that these statistics are due to differences in behavior between blacks and whites, administrators fear that the teachers' acts may be discriminatory and now require that records be kept on the race of the teacher as well as the student in each discipline case (Hull 1994, 30).

HOUSING DISCRIMINATION

As a consequence of migration patterns in the 1950s and 1960s, minorities are disproportionately trapped in inner city neighborhoods where declining social and economic conditions prevail. They have limited access to safe housing, quality schools, and employment opportunities.

Recent studies indicate that a majority of the nation's black children attend schools that are more than 90 percent black which has caused many to wonder which side actually won in the Brown vs. Board of Education.
—Robert Pratt

National Data: In 1993, 20 percent of children attending inner city public schools were Hispanic, up from ten percent in 1972. Between 1968 and 1992, the percentage of Hispanic students attending schools that are more than 90 percent minority increased from 23 to 34 percent.

SOURCE: U.S. Department of Education 1995.

Blacks have historically been segregated in inner city neighborhoods and in rural counties known as the "black belt." In the 1990 census, there were 400 counties with 25 percent or more black residents (Massey and Denton 1993). Segregation of blacks occurs regardless of income; for example, blacks who earn $50,000 a year are just as segregated as those who make $2,500 a year (Massey and Denton 1993). Further, even when demographic, social class, and family structure variables are taken into consideration, black-owned homes have a lower value than white-owned homes (Horton 1993). Blacks are also half as likely to own their home. This fact is most likely a consequence of the refusal of mortgage companies to make loans available to minority members. As one federal economist noted, it is hard to explain why "white borrowers in the lowest income category were approved for mortgages more often than black borrowers in the highest income group" (Knight 1993, 127).

Many inner city minority neighborhoods are also characterized by high rates of violent crime (see Chapter 4). The emotional cost of living in such neighborhoods is especially high for children (see this chapter's *The Human Side*).

The most fortunate minorities in terms of housing and living conditions are Asian Americans, who are more likely than other minorities to own their own homes. Among Hispanics, Puerto Ricans have the worst living conditions, with over half living in urban inner cities that are deteriorated and overcrowded (Feagin and Feagin 1993). Native Americans have the poorest living conditions of all minorities—poor sanitation, dilapidated housing, inadequate water supplies, and unsafe facilities. While gambling on reservations has generated an estimated $750 million to $1.8 billion (Feagin and Feagin 1993), living conditions generally remain poor. For example, less than 50 percent of all families on reservations have telephones; under half of reservations are connected to public sewers, and one in five American Indian households on reservations lack complete plumbing facilities—hot and cold water, a bath or shower, and a flush toilet (U.S. Census Bureau 1995).

Several discriminatory practices confine minorities to living in certain areas. For example, real estate brokers tell residents that minorities are moving into their neighborhoods and that property values will soon decrease. In an effort to escape quickly, residents sell their property at below-market prices that decrease property values. This practice is called "blockbusting." Other techniques include redlining, racial steering, and restrictive home covenants. Redlining occurs when mortgage companies deny loans for the purchase of houses in minority neighborhoods, arguing that the financial risk is too great. Racial steering occurs when realtors discourage minorities from moving into certain areas by showing them homes only in "their" kind of neighborhood. Restrictive home covenants, illegal since the 1950s, involve a pact between residents that they will not sell their homes to minority group members. Although housing discrimination is illegal, federal regulations are largely unenforced.

> *Consideration* A team of researchers (Farley et al. 1994) studied racial segregation in the Detroit area. They found that stereotypes held by whites fed discriminatory real estate practices. "The stereotypes that emerged ranged from specific beliefs about blacks as bad neighbors (e.g., they let their property run down) to more general beliefs about the behavior of blacks (e.g., they are prone to criminal behavior or they lack the motivation to work)" (p. 775). When asked to explain racial segregation in Detroit, one white responded:

How much do we really value the lives of children? . . . On the basis of what I've seen in the South Bronx, it's hard to believe we love these children. The physical degradation of their neighborhood, the chaotic and dysfunctional medical care we give them, the apartheid school system we proide them, the poisons we pump into their neighborhood by putting every kind of toxic-waste incinerator in their neighborhood, all that together does not give me the impression we value their lives.
—Jonathon Kozol
Author and children's advocate

GROWING UP IN THE OTHER AMERICA

Author Alex Kotlowitz conducted a two-year participant observation research study of children in a Chicago housing project. The following description captures the horrific living conditions endured by Lafeyette, Pharoah, and Dede—three black children living in the "jects."

The children called home "Hornets" or, more frequently, "the projects" or, simply, the "jects" (pronounced *jets*). Pharoah called it "the graveyard." But they never referred to it by its full name: the Governor Henry Horner Homes.

Nothing here, the children would tell you, was as it should be. Lafeyette and Pharoah lived at 1920 West Washington Boulevard, even though their high-rise sat on Lake Street. Their building had no enclosed lobby; a dark tunnel cut through the middle of the building, and the wind and strangers passed freely along it. Those tenants who received public aid had their checks sent to the local currency exchange, since the building's first-floor mailboxes had all been broken into. And since darkness engulfed the building's corridors, even in the daytime, the residents always carried flashlights, some of which had been handed out by a local politician during her campaign.

Summer, too, was never as it should be. It had become a season of duplicity.

On June 13, a couple of weeks after their peaceful afternoon on the railroad tracks, Lafeyette celebrated his twelfth birthday. Under the gentle afternoon sun, yellow daisies poked through the cracks in the sidewalk as children's bright faces peered out from behind their windows. Green leaves clothed the cottonwoods, and pastel cotton shirts and shorts, which had sat for months in layaway, clothed the children. And like the fresh buds on the crabapple trees, the children's spirits blossomed with the onset of summer.

Lafeyette and his nine-year-old cousin Dede danced across the worn lawn outside their building, singing the lyrics of an L. L. Cool J rap, their small hips and spindly legs moving in rhythm. The boy and girl were on their way to a nearby shopping strip, where Lafeyette planned to buy radio headphones with $8.00 he had received as a birthday gift.

Suddenly, gunfire erupted. The frightened children fell to the ground. "Hold your head down!" Lafeyette snapped, as he covered Dede's head with her pink nylon jacket. If he hadn't physically restrained her, she might have sprinted for home, a dangerous action when the gangs started warring. "Stay down," he ordered the trembling girl.

The two lay pressed to the beaten grass for half a minute, until the shooting subsided. Lafeyette held Dede's hand as they cautiously crawled through the dirt toward home. When they finally made it inside, all but fifty cents of Lafeyette's birthday money had trickled from his pockets.

SOURCE: Alex Kotlowitz. 1991. *There Are No Children Here.* New York: Anchor Books, pp. 8–9. Used by permission.

Because they are different. The two races have different ideas as to their responsibilities to a neighbor. . . . A "black neighborhood" is dirtier, less maintained, more inclined to be abused by the residents—throw garbage out the back door and kicking the windows out. (p. 775)

POLITICAL DISCRIMINATION

In general, members of the majority group deprive minorities from participating fully in the political-legal process through discriminatory practices in voter registration, candidate qualifications, and jury selection. Exclusionary techniques include changing elected offices into appointed positions, redrawing the boundaries of voting districts, changing polling places, requiring voters to take literacy tests, and using automobile registration for jury selection. All of these practices make it difficult for minorities to exercise their right to be politically involved.

Blacks have been discouraged from political involvement by segregated primaries, poll taxes, literacy tests, and threats of violence. However, tremendous strides have been made since the passage of the 1965 Voting Rights Act, which prohibited literacy tests and provided for poll observers. Blacks have won mayoral elections in Atlanta, Cleveland, Washington, D.C., and New York City and the governorship in Virginia. In 1993, there were thirty-eight African-American voting members in the U.S. House of Representatives and one non-voting member, one African-American senator, and one African-American Supreme Court Justice. Yet, although Jessie Jackson's multiracial/multiethnic Rainbow Coalition successfully generated support for his presidential candidacy in 1984 and 1988, the two highest political offices in the United States have never been occupied by a black.

Native Americans, Asian Americans, and Hispanics also have low rates of political participation. The Bureau of Indian Affairs (BIA), established in 1824, supervises tribal government, banking, utilities, and highways, as well as millions of dollars in tribal trust funds (Feagin and Feagin 1993). Despite the power of the BIA, in 1988 the Indian Self-Determination Act was amended to permit Native Americans self-governance on the reservation. However, outside of the reservation, Native American involvement in politics is limited. In 1992, there were only thirty-five Native Americans in fourteen state legislatures and even fewer participants in national politics (Feagin and Feagin 1993).

Although one in four Californians is Asian, they comprise only 2 percent of California's top political officials. In addition, in 1991 Asians held only 45 of 8,200 important staff positions in Congress (Bensen 1991).

In 1992, Hispanics represented 28 percent of the population of Houston, but held only one seat on the Houston City Council. In other parts of Texas, however, Hispanics, and specifically Mexicans, have been fairly successful in increasing their representation—they have more than doubled the number of Hispanic officials in the last twenty years. However, voting behavior remains low; fewer than 20 percent of Puerto Ricans voted in the 1992 national election.

HATE CRIME VICTIMIZATION

Perhaps the most brutal form of discrimination takes the form of **hate crimes**—acts of violence motivated by prejudice against racial, ethnic, religious, and sexual orientation groups. Examples of such crimes include the fa-

National Data: In 1991, with less than 20 percent of the FBI agencies reporting, 4,558 hate incidents were identified. The most common offense was intimidation (34 percent), closely followed by vandalism or other property damage (27 percent). Also included were 773 cases of aggravated assault and 12 murders.

SOURCE: Jost 1993, 6.

Mission hate crimes are typically committed by members of white supremacist groups. This scene from the movie *Mississippi Burning* depicts a Ku Klux Klan member brutally attacking a black man.

tal beating of a Vietnamese premed student at the University of Miami, the stabbing of a Jewish scholar by black youths, and the shooting of two blacks by racist soldiers in Fayetteville, North Carolina (Chua-eoan 1995, Jost 1993).

According to an FBI report, in 1991 blacks were the most frequent target of hate crimes—36 percent of the total number; antiwhite offenses accounted for 19 percent of the total (Jost 1993, 6). However, a study of hate crimes reported to the Boston Police Department reveals that Latinos and Asians are the most likely to be attacked followed by gay men and lesbians, and then blacks (Levin and McDevitt 1995).

Levin and McDevitt found that the motivations for hate crimes were of three distinct types: thrill, defensive, and mission. *Thrill hate crimes* are committed by offenders who are looking for excitement and attack victims for the "fun of it." *Defensive hate crimes* involve offenders who view their attacks as necessary to protect their community, workplace, or college campus from "outsiders." Perpetrators of defensive hate crimes are trying to send a message that their victims do not belong in a particular community, workplace, or campus and that anyone in the victim's group who dares "intrude" could be the next victim. *Mission hate crimes* are perpetrated by offenders who have dedicated their lives to bigotry. In Levin and McDevitt's (1995) study of hate crimes in Boston, the most common type of hate crime was thrill hate crime (58%) followed by defensive hate crime (41%). The least common, but most violent type of hate crime is mission hate crime. Levin and McDevitt (1995) describe the 1995 Oklahoma City bombing as "probably the quintessential mission hate crime, perpetrated by individuals whose lives had become consumed with hatred not only for the federal government but possibly for blacks and Jews as well" (9).

Mission hate crimes are often committed by members of white supremacist organizations that endorse racist beliefs and violence against minority group members. In 1987, an African-American schoolteacher was about to step onto a footbridge in a California park when four racist skinheads approached her. They informed the woman that "niggers" had to pay a toll to cross the bridge

Jackie Burden and Michael James died because three soldiers stationed at Fort Bragg . . . decided it was a good night to commit a hate crime.
—Howard Chua-eoan
Jounalist

I'm not against Blacks. I'm against all non-whites.
—Ku Klux Klan member

White supremacy has to die for humanity to live.
—Louis Farrakhan
Nation of Islam leader

and threatened to hang her from a nearby tree if she did not comply. One of the men who was later arrested stated: "We are racist and she was Black. . . . We're into white supremacy" (quoted in Landau 1993, 18).

The Ku Klux Klan, the first major racist, white supremacist group in the United States, began in Tennessee shortly after the Civil War. Klansmen have threatened, beat, mutilated, and lynched blacks as well as whites who dared to oppose them. White Aryan Resistance (WAR), another white supremacist group, fosters hatred that breeds violence. The following message is typical of one received by calling a White Aryan Resistance phone number in one of many states (Kleg 1993, 205):

> *This is WAR hotline. How long, White men, are you going to sit around while these non-White mud races breed you out of existence? They have your jobs, your homes, and your country. Have you stepped outside lately and looked around while these niggers and Mexicans hep and jive to these Africanized rap music? While these Gooks and Flips are buying up the businesses around you? . . . This racial melting pot is more like a garbage pail. Just look at your liquor stores. Most of them are owned by Sand niggers from Iraq, Egypt, or Iran. Most of the apartments are owned by the scum from India, or some other kind of raghead . . . [Jews] are like maggots eating off a dead carcass. When you see what these Jews and their white lackeys have done, the gas chambers don't sound like such a bad idea after all. For more information write us at. . . .*

Other racist groups known to engage in hate crimes are the Identity Church Movement, Neo-Nazis, and the skinheads. While Klan members have traditionally concealed their identities under white hoods and robes, racist skinheads are usually identifiable through their shaved heads, steel-toed boots, jeans, and suspenders. They often have tattoos of Nazi or satanic emblems.

Hate crimes have become a growing threat to the well-being of our society—on college campuses, in the workplace, and in our neighborhoods.
—Jack Levin, Sociologist
Jack McDevitt,
Criminologist

Consideration Not all skinheads are racist. Many youth have adopted the skinhead "look" and lifestyle but do not endorse racism or violence. One nonracist skinhead said: "Being a skinhead does not mean being a Nazi. I happen to have no hair, a black leather jacket, and army boots, and I get stopped all the time by people trying to preach nonviolence to me. I am a pacifist" (quoted in Landau 1993, 43).

In 1990 President Bush signed the Hate Crimes Statistics Act into law. This legislation requires the federal government to collect data on acts of violence motivated by racial, ethnic, and religious hatred. With such data available, the public may become more aware of the scope of hate violence in American society.

HEALTH AND QUALITY OF LIFE

Being a minority in the United States affects every aspect of one's life. While disparities in employment and income, education, housing, and political participation are disturbing, minority members are also characterized by lower life expectancy, higher infant mortality, and increased probabilities of drug involvement, suicide, crime victimization, alcoholism, and mental illness. To a large extent, each of these conditions is a consequence of the relationship they bear to poverty which in turn is related to being a minority group member.

For example, among Native Americans, the infant death rate is seven times the national average, alcoholism rates are the highest in the nation, and life expectancy is less than forty-five for males and forty-seven for females (Feagin and Feagin 1993). Adolescent Native American youth are especially at risk. Research indicates that Native American youths attending reservation schools serviced by the Indian Health Service have a higher suicide rate, are more likely to be victims of sexual abuse, and in general have poorer physical and mental health than white rural youth (Blum et al. 1992).

In a *Newsweek* poll, 51 percent of African Americans believed that the quality of their lives had declined in the last ten years (Morganthau et al. 1992). Compared to whites, blacks have lower life expectancy and higher infant mortality, are more likely to be ill, have higher rates of AIDS and other sexually transmitted diseases, and are less likely to have health insurance (Committee on the Status of Black Americans 1989). Blacks also report lower levels of life satisfaction and happiness than whites (Burton, Armstrong, and Rushing 1993).

Asian Americans, because of their higher levels of income, education, and occupational status, have the highest quality of life among minorities although recent Asian immigrants may be the exception. Hispanics, however, suffer the same lack of life chances as other minorities—lower life expectancy, higher morbidity, inadequate health care, and higher infant mortality. Since infant mortality is, in part, a function of income and education, it is not surprising that the infant mortality rate for Mexicans and Puerto Ricans is higher than for Cubans (Hummer, Eberstein, and Nam 1992).

Strategies Designed to Reduce Prejudice, Discrimination, and Racism

Next we look at strategies designed to reduce prejudice, discrimination, and racism in American society. These include multicultural education, political strategies, affirmative action programs, and diversity training in the workplace.

MULTICULTURAL EDUCATION

Much educational material is biased toward white Europeans. For example, Zinn (1993) observes, "[T]o emphasize the heroism of Columbus and his successors as navigators and discoverers, and to de-emphasize their genocide, is not a technical necessity but an ideological choice. It serves, unwittingly—to justify what was done" (p. 355). **Multicultural education** focuses on the need to represent all racial and ethnic groups in the school curriculum (see also Chapter 13). With multicultural education, the school curriculum reflects the diversity of American society and fosters an awareness and appreciation of the contributions of different racial and ethnic groups to American culture.

One component of multiculturalism is multilingualism. In 1990, one in seven individuals over the age of five (14 percent of the population) grew up speaking a language other than English in the home, the largest proportion speaking Spanish. Further, the number of people in the United States speaking Chinese has almost doubled in recent years. Increasingly, the issue of bilingual education in the public schools will be an issue local school boards will have to address (Barringer 1993). The debate, however, will spill into other arenas as

National Data: In a *Time/CNN* poll, 59 percent of blacks and 37 percent of whites said that race relations in the United States will never get better.
SOURCE: Pooley 1995.

I have a dream that my four little children will one day live in a nation where they will not be judged by the color of their skin, but by the content of their character.
—Martin Luther King, Jr.
Civil rights leader

well. In 1989, a California court held that Japanese and Korean merchants could not be required to have English signs on their stores. As in many other countries throughout the world today, public signs, menus, ballots, newspapers, and television programs are offered in many different languages reflecting the increased diversity of the American population.

POLITICAL STRATEGIES

Various political strategies have been implemented or suggested to reduce prejudice and discrimination. Although some individuals argue that laws cannot change attitudes, there is evidence that changing behaviors can change attitudes. When the military, schools, and housing were integrated, the attitudes of whites toward nonwhites became more positive. Hence, there is a need for laws that prohibit discrimination, for those laws to be strictly enforced, and for sanctions to be imposed when the laws are violated. Denny's restaurant was required to pay $46 million to African-American patrons who were denied service.

One political strategy to decrease discrimination involves increasing minority representation in government. This requires increasing political involvement, action, and participation. For example, the Asian American Voters Coalition has successfully mobilized voters in states with high concentrations of Asian Americans—California, Hawaii, New York, and Texas (Feagin and Feagin 1993). However, the 1995 Supreme Court ruling (in *Miller v. Johnson*) that the creation of congressional districts for the sole purpose of establishing "minority majorities" is unconstitutional will make future minority representation more difficult.

One of the goals of the "Million Man March" in Washington, D.C. in October of 1995 was to emphasize the political clout of the black community. Black leaders who spoke at the march called for black men to pledge themselves to self-reliance, respect for women, and participation in the political process through voting. Glenn C. Loury (1992) suggests implementing more black self-help programs, rather than programs that create and reinforce dependency. He emphasizes the need for an independent, self-guided movement by blacks for blacks—a movement of empowerment that goes beyond "[B]lack elected officials who have done little, other than parrot the lines of white liberals" (p. 167). John E. Jacob, former National Urban League president, disagrees with Loury and argues that the position of minorities today is a consequence of two interrelated forces—a reduction in government programs and changes in the economy that have led to the elimination of jobs. While Loury would reduce or eliminate federal intervention, Jacob (1992) emphasizes the need to reinstate and expand government programs.

AFFIRMATIVE ACTION

Affirmative action refers to programs that provide or seek to provide opportunities or other benefits to persons on the basis of their membership in a specified group (Jones 1993). Affirmative action dates back to 1941 when President Franklin D. Roosevelt issued an executive order concerning fair hiring practices in the defense industry. In 1961, President Kennedy issued an executive order mandating that the government encourage equal opportunity through "positive measures" (McLemore 1993, 174). Avoiding discrimination was not enough—federal contractors had to take "affirmative action" in the hiring of blacks. Women and other minorities were eventually added to the list of "protected" classes (see Chapter 8). Most affirmative action programs have involved one of the following: (1) programs for the enrollment of minorities or women in higher education and professional schools; (2) the setting aside of a percentage of contracts for minority or female subcontractors; or (3) the imposition of quota goals for minority or female employment.

Opponents of affirmative action argue that these programs constitute **reverse discrimination.** Some opponents of affirmative action are white males who feel they have been treated unfairly as a result of efforts to provide minorities with educational and employment opportunities. Bobo and Kluegel (1993) argue that much of the white opposition to race-targeted policies such as affirmative action is due to self-interest and prejudice. But some African Americans are also critical of affirmative action, arguing that it perpetuates feelings of inferiority among minorities and fails to help the "truly disadvantaged" (Steele 1990; Wilson 1987).

Some advocates of affirmative action point to the moral and compensatory justification for such programs. In response to the charge that affirmative action is as discriminatory to whites as prior discrimination was to blacks, Herman Schwartz (1992) argues:

> *No one can honestly equate a remedial preference for a disadvantaged (and qualified) minority member with the brutality inflicted on blacks and other minorities by Jim Crow laws and practices. The preference may take away some benefits from some white men, but none of them is being beaten, lynched, denied the right to use a bathroom, a place to sleep or eat, being forced to take the dirtiest jobs or denied any work at all, forced to attend dilapidated and mind-killing schools, subjected to brutally unequal justice, or stigmatized as an inferior being. (pp. 193–94)*

Other affirmative action advocates suggest that affirmative action is not so much a moral imperative as a matter of the economic health and survival of this nation (Jones 1993). Given the increasing numbers of minorities and the ever-changing job training requirements for high-tech jobs, Jones (1993) says "we cannot afford to have minorities and women excluded from the mainstream education and job activities" (p. 365).

Numerous legal battles have been fought over affirmative action. In 1990, a Hispanic student sued the University of Maryland for denying him a scholarship that was limited to black students. A lower court ruled the black scholarship program was unconstitutional and constituted "reverse discrimination." In 1995, the U.S. Supreme Court refused to hear the appeal, which means that any race-based scholarship in the United States can now be challenged (Stone 1995). In 1995, renewed opposition to affirmative action led to a Supreme Court ruling imposing tough new standards that will effectively eliminate most federal affirmative action programs. Supreme Court Justice Clarence Thomas dismissed affirmative action as "racial paternalism. . . . These programs stamp minorities with a badge of inferiority and may cause them to develop dependencies or to adopt an attitude that they are 'entitled' to preferences" (Mauro 1995, 2A). Civil rights leader Jesse Jackson, who called the

You do not take a person who for years has been hobbled by chains, and liberate him, bring him up to the starting line, and then say, "You are free to compete with all others."
—Lyndon Baines Johnson
Former U.S. President

National Data: In a 1995 Gallup poll, 70 percent of respondents indicated that they believe affirmative action programs have helped racial minorities.
SOURCE: Moore 1995.

While we react to those wearing white sheets, it is those who wear black robes who take away our protection.
—Jesse Jackson
Civil rights leader

ruling a setback, commented: "Clarence Thomas has betrayed the very social justice movement that made his opportunities possible. Without the laws we worked for, he couldn't have gone to Yale . . . he couldn't have gone on the Supreme Court" (Kanamine 1995, 2A).

DIVERSITY TRAINING

Increasingly, corporations have begun to implement efforts to reduce prejudice and discrimination in the workplace through diversity training. Broadly defined, **diversity training** involves "raising personal awareness about individual 'differences' in the workplace and how those differences inhibit or enhance the way people work together and get work done" (Wheeler 1994, 10). Diversity training may address such issues as stereotyping and cross-cultural insensitivity, as well as provide workers with specific information on cultural norms of different groups and how these norms affect work behavior and social interactions.

In a survey of forty-five organizations that provide diversity training, Wheeler (1994) found that for 85 percent of the respondents, the primary motive for offering diversity training was to enhance productivity and profits. In the words of one survey respondent, "The company's philosophy is that a diverse work force that recognizes and respects differing opinions and ideas adds to the creativity, productivity, and profitability of the company" (p. 12). Only 4 percent of respondents said they offered diversity training out of a sense of social responsibility.

UNDERSTANDING
RACIAL AND ETHNIC RELATIONS

After considering the material presented in this chapter, what understanding about racial and ethnic relations are we left with? First, we have seen that racial and ethnic categories are largely arbitrary, imprecise, and misleading. This realization inevitably leads to the question posed by Hodgkinson (1995, 175): "Given that the racial/ethnic categories in the Census are a scientific and anthropological joke, why do we keep the categories at all?" Hodgkinson (1995) suggests that "the answer is a deeply American irony: we need the categories in order to eliminate them. Without knowing who our oppressed minorities are, how can we develop remedies so that they will no longer be oppressed?" (175). For example, by collecting statistics on racial and ethnic categories, the government can monitor and enforce civil rights legislation, and ensure that businesses and public programs comply with equal opportunity provisions in education, housing, and employment (Valentine 1995).

Conflict theorists and functionalists agree that prejudice, discrimination, and racism have benefited certain groups in society. It is also true, however, that racial and ethnic disharmony has created system tensions that disrupt social equilibrium. Further, as symbolic interactionists emphasize, lowered expectations of minority group members, negative labeling, and the use of pejoratives to describe racial and ethnic minority members contribute to their subordinate position.

It is also clear that despite a more educated society, civil rights legislation, and a presumed tolerance for diversity, racism persists in America. Racism varies on a continuum from subtle opposition to race- and ethnic-specific policies to the blatant racism of the Ku Klux Klan and other white supremacy groups. Hostility between minority groups is also increasing: Koreans versus blacks, Hispanics versus Jews, and Native Americans versus Mexicans. From a sociological perspective, such conflicts are understandable in view of the changes in the racial and ethnic composition of the United States and the competition for scarce resources.

Prejudice, discrimination, and racism are debilitating forces in the lives of minorities. In spite of these negative forces, many minority group members succeed in living productive, meaningful, and prosperous lives. But many others cannot overcome the social disadvantages associated with their minority status and become victims of a cycle of poverty (see Chapter 11). Minorities are disproportionately poor, receive inferior education, and, with continued discrimination and prejudice in the workplace, have difficulty improving their standard of living.

Thus, alterations in the structure of society that increase opportunities for minorities—in education, employment and income, and political participation—are crucial to achieving racial and ethnic equality. While government policies or regulations may provide structural opportunities for minorities, policies and regulations often do not change attitudes and beliefs about minority groups embedded in the culture. Changing cultural attitudes begins with the socialization process in the home, school, and place of religious worship. The same socialization process through which children learn prejudice and discrimination may be used to teach children acceptance, compassion, and appreciation for people with varied ethnic and racial backgrounds. In a classic experiment, an elementary school teacher, using only her authority in the classroom and specific examples that reinforced her position (e.g., "Billy's the best reader in the class and he has blue eyes"), convinced students that classmates with blue eyes were superior to those with brown eyes. The results were startling. Children refused to play with their brown-eyed best friends; fights became routine; student successes or failures were attributed to eye color. The next day she reversed the process—blue-eyed children were now inferior. She wanted each group to know what it was like to suffer prejudice and discrimination on the basis of such a superficial quality as eye color (American Broadcasting Company 1970).

Unfortunately, most Americans cannot exchange positions with other racial and ethnic groups in order to learn through experience the injustice of prejudice and discrimination. We can, however, learn through the experiences of others, through contact with different racial and ethnic group members, and through multicultural education and diversity training. Until we as members of a racially and ethnically stratified society fully embrace the American values of equality and justice for all, social inequities are likely to continue.

Ethnic diversity is an opportunity rather than a problem.
—Andrew Greeley
Sociologist/Author

That both black and white in our country can today say we are to one another brother and sister, a united rainbow nation that derives its strength from the bonding of its many races and colours, constitutes a celebration of the oneness of the human race.
—Nelson Mandela
President, Republic of South Africa

CRITICAL THINKING

1. Should race be a factor in adoption placements? Should people be discouraged from adopting a child that is of a different race than the adoptive parents? Why or why not?
2. What compensation would you recommend for Native Americans for past discrimination?
3. Do you think that there will ever be a time in human history when there will be only one "race" due to intermarriage over generations?
4. To what degree are prejudice and discrimination prevalent at the college or university that you attend? Provide evidence or examples to support your answer.
5. How can youths be protected from white supremacy propaganda that is disseminated through computer networks?

KEY TERMS

race

ethnicity

colonialism

genocide

slavery

segregation

de jure segregation

de facto segregation

assimilation

pluralism

amalgamation

prejudice

stereotype

racism

discrimination

individual discrimination

institutional discrimination

hate crime

multicultural education

affirmative action

reverse discrimination

diversity training

REFERENCES

American Broadcasting Company. 1979. "Eye of the Storm." Xerox Films, Human Relations Series. ABC Media Concepts.

Barringer, Felicity. 1993. "For 32 Million Americans, English Is a Second Language." *New York Times*, April 28.

Bensen, Miles. 1991. "Washington's Top Positions Seldom Go to Minorities." *Houston Chronicle*, December 13, 1.

Binder, David (with Barbara Crossette). 1993. "As Ethnic Wars Multiply, U.S. Strives for a Policy." *New York Times (Themes of the Times—Sociology)*, February 7, 12.

Blum, Robert W., Brian Harmon, Linda Harris, Lois Bergeisen, and Michael D. Resnick. 1992. "American Indian–Alaska Native Youth Health." *Journal of the American Medical Association* 267 (March 25): 1637–44.

Bobo, Lawrence, and James R. Kluegel. 1993. "Opposition to Race-Targeting: Self Interest, Stratification Ideology, or Racial Attitudes?" *American Sociological Review* 58(4): 443–64.

Burton, Russell, David Armstrong, and Beth Rushing. 1993. "Social Roles and Subjective Well-Being." *Sociological Spectrum* 13(4): 415–31.

Chua-eoan, Howard. 1995. "Enlisted Killers." *Time*, December 18, 44.

Committee on the Status of Black Americans. 1989. In *A Common Destiny: Blacks and American Society*, ed. G. D. Jaynes, and R. M. Williams. Washington, D.C.: National Academy Press.

Cooper, Kenneth. 1991. "Multicultural Focus Recommended for Education of Native Americans." *Washington Post*, December 27, A19.

Dovidio, John F., and Samuel L. Gaertner. 1991. "Changes in the Expression and Assessment of Racial Prejudice." In *Opening Doors: Perspectives on Race Relations in Contemporary America*, ed. Harry J. Knopke, Robert J. Norrell, and Ronald W. Rogers, pp. 119–48. Tuscaloosa: University of Alabama Press.

Farley, Reynolds, Charlotte Steeh, Maria Krysan, Tara Jackson, and Keith Reeves. 1994. "Stereotypes and Segregation: Neighborhoods in the Detroit Area." *American Journal of Sociology* 100: 750–80.

Feagin, Joe R., and Clairece Booher Feagin. 1993. *Racial and Ethnic Relations*. Englewood Cliffs, N.J.: Prentice-Hall.

Gioseffi, Daniela. 1993. "Introduction." In *On Prejudice: A Global Perspective*, ed. Daniela Gioseffi, pp. xi-1. New York: Anchor Books, Doubleday.

Harris, David. 1992. "An Analysis of the 1990 Census Count of American Indians." Paper presented at the American Sociological Association, Miami, Florida, August 20–24. Used by permission.

Henry III, William A. 1990 "Beyond the Melting Pot." *Time*, April 3, 28–31.

Hodgkinson, Harold L. 1995. "What Should We Call People?: Race, Class, and the Census for 2000." *Phi Delta Kappan*, October, 173-179.

Horton, H. D. 1993. "Race, Class, and Family Structure: Differences in Housing Values for Black and White Homeowners." Paper presented at the Southern Sociological Society, Chattanooga, Tennessee.

Hull, Jon D. 1994. "Do Teachers Punish According to Race?" *Time*, April 4, 30–31.

Hummer, Robert, Isaac Eberstein, and Charles Nam. 1992. "Infant Mortality Differentials among Hispanic Groups in Florida." *Social Forces* 70(4): 1055–75.

Jacob, John E. 1992. "The Future of Black America." In *Taking Sides*, 7th ed., pp. 173–80. Guilford, Conn.: Dushkin Publishing Co.

Jones, James E., Jr. 1993. "The Rise and Fall of Affirmative Action." In *Race in America: The Struggle for Equality*, ed. Herbert Hill and James E. Jones, Jr., pp. 345–69. Madison: University of Wisconsin Press.

Jost, Kenneth. 1993. "Hate Crime: The Issues." *Congressional Quarterly Researchers* 3 (January 8): 1–24.

Kanamine, Linda. 1995. " 'Preference' Programs Oppressive, Thomas Says." *USA Today*, June 13, 2A.

Kleg, Milton. 1993. *Hate Prejudice and Racism*. Albany: State University of New York Press.

Knight, Jerry. 1993. "Race Factor in Mortgage Lending Seen." In *Society in Crisis*, pp. 127–29. Washington Post Writers Group. Boston: Allyn & Bacon.

Landau, Elaine. 1993. *The White Power Movement: America's Racist Hate Groups*. Brookfield, Conn.: Millbrook Press.

Langone, John. 1993. *Spreading Poison*. Boston: Little, Brown.

Levin, Jack and Jack McDevitt. 1995. "Landmark Study Reveals Hate Crimes Vary Significantly by Offender Motivation." *Klanwatch Intelligence Report* (August), 7-9.

Lichter, Robert S., Linda S. Lichter, Stanley Rothman, and Daniel Amundson. 1987. "Prime-Time Prejudice: TV's Images of Blacks and Hispanics." *Public Opinion* (March/April): 12–13.

Loury, Glenn C. 1992. "A Prescription for Black Progress." In *Taking Sides,* 7th ed., pp. 166–72. Guilford, Conn.: Dushkin Publishing Co.

Marble, Manning. 1990. "A New Black Politics." *The Progressive,* August, 18–23.

Massey, Douglas, and Nancy Denton. 1993. *American Apartheid: Segregation and the Making of an American Underclass.* Cambridge, Mass.: Harvard University Press.

Mauro, Tony. 1995. "Court Signals 'End for Era' in Civil Rights." *USA Today,* June 13, 1A.

McClelland, Kent, and Christopher Hunter. 1992. "The Perceived Seriousness of Racial Harassment." *Social Problems* 39(1): 92–107.

McLemore, S. Dale. 1993. *Racial and Ethnic Relations in America.* Needham, Mass.: Allyn & Bacon.

Molnar, Stephen. 1983. *Human Variation: Races, Types, and Ethnic Groups,* 2d ed. Englewood Cliffs, N.J.: Prentice-Hall.

Moore, David W. 1993. "Americans Feel Threatened by New Immigrants." *Gallup Poll Monthly* no. 334, July, 2–16.

_____ 1995. "Americans Today are Dubious about Affirmative Action." *The Gallup Organization Affirmative Action Poll Newsletter Archive* (March) [internet].

Morganthau, Thomas, Marcus Mabry, Frank Washington, Vern Smith, Emily Yoffe, and Lucille Beachy. 1992. "Losing Ground." *Newsweek,* April 6, 20–22.

Myrdal, Gunnar. 1944. *An American Dilemma.* New York: Harper & Row.

Nash, Manning. 1962. "Race and the Ideology of Race." *Current Anthropology* 3: 258–88.

Neckerman, Kathryn, and Joleen Kirschenman, 1991. "Hiring Strategies, Racial Bias, and Inner-City Workers." *Social Problems* 38(4): 433–47.

NORC. 1993. *General Social Surveys, 1972–1993: Cumulative Codebook.* University of Chicago: National Opinion Research Center.

Pooley, Eric. 1995. "To the Beat of His Drum." *Time,* Oct 23, 35-36.

Reid, Evelyn. 1995. "Waiting to Excel: Biraciality in the Classroom." In *Educating for Diversity: An Anthology of Multicultural Voices,* ed. Carl A. Grant, pp. 263–73. Needham Heights, Mass.: Allyn & Bacon.

Schaefer, Richard T. 1993. *Racial and Ethnic Groups.* New York: HarperCollins.

Schwartz, Herman. 1992. "In Defense of Affirmative Action." In *Taking Sides,* 7th ed., pp. 189–94. Guilford, Conn.: Dushkin Publishing Co.

Schwartz, Joe, and Thomas Exter. 1989. "All our Children." *American Demographics* 11 (May): 34–37.

Sigall, H., and Rufus Page. 1981. "Current Stereotypes: A Little Fading, a Little Faking." *Journal of Personality and Social Psychology* 18: 250–54.

Sowell, Thomas. 1981. *Ethnic America.* New York: Basic Books.

Statistical Abstract of the United States: 1995, 115th ed. U.S. Bureau of the Census. Washington, D.C.: U.S. Government Printing Office.

Steel, Melissa. 1995. "New Colors." *Teaching Tolerance* (Spring), 44-49.

Steele, Shelby. 1990. *The Content of Our Character.* New York: St. Martin's Press.

Stone, Andrea. 1995. "Court Kills Blacks-Only Scholarship." *USA Today,* May 23, 1A.

Takaki, Ronald. 1990. "The Harmful Myth of Asian Superiority." *New York Times,* June 16, 15.

Telles, Edward, and Edward Murguia. 1990. "Phenotype Discrimination and Income Differences among Mexican Americans." *Social Science Quarterly* 71(4): 682–96.

United States Commission on Civil Rights. 1992. *Civil Rights Issues Facing Asian Americans in the 1990s.* Washington, D.C.: U.S. Government Printing Office, pp. 68–99.

U.S. Census Bureau. 1995. "Census Bureau Reports on Status of American Indians' Housing on Reservations." Press Release–April 10. CB95-74.

U.S. Department of Education. 1995. "Progress in the Achievement and Attainment of Hispanics" from *The Condition of Education: 1995* [http//www.ed.gov:80/pubs/CondOfEd95].

Valentine, Glenda. 1995. "Shades of Gray: The Conundrum of Color Categories." *Teaching Tolerance* (Spring), 47.

Vobejda, Barbara. 1993. "The Heartland Pulses with New Blood." In *Society in Crisis,* pp. 136–40. Washington Post Writers Group. Boston: Allyn & Bacon.

Wheeler, Michael L. 1994. *Diversity Training: A Research Report.* New York: The Conference Board.

Wieberg, Steve. 1995. "Jackson to Turn up Pressure." *USA Today,* January 11, C1.

Williams, Eddie N., and Milton D. Morris. 1993. "Racism and Our Future." In *Race in America: The Struggle for Equality,* ed. Herbert Hill and James E. Jones, Jr., pp. 417–24. Madison: University of Wisconsin Press.

Wilson, William J. 1987. *The Truly Disadvantaged: The Inner City, the Underclass and Public Policy.* Chicago: University of Chicago Press.

Zinn, Howard. 1993. "Columbus and the Doctrine of Discovery." In *Systemic Crisis: Problems in Society, Politics, and World Order,* ed. William D. Perdue, pp. 351–57. Fort Worth TX: Harcourt Brace Jovanovich.

Zwerling, Craig, and Hilary Silver. 1993. "Race and Job Dismissals in a Federal Bureaucracy." *American Sociological Review* 57(5): 651–60.

Problems of Inequality and Power

SECTION 3

The story of Harrison Bergeron is set in a futuristic society where absolute equality is rigidly enforced (Vonnegut 1968). If people can run faster, they must wear weights in their shoes; if they are brighter, disruptive transistors are implanted in their brains; if they have better vision, blinders are placed over their eyes. The point of the story is that equality, although a cultural ideal, in reality is not always the optimal way to live. The quality of life becomes so unbearable for Harrison Bergeron that he decides that it is better to commit one courageous act of grace and beauty and be killed than to live in a society where everyone is equal.

Differences between people in and of themselves are not what is meant by inequality as a social problem for few would want to live in a society where everyone was the same. Rather, problems of inequality concern inequities in the quality of life. Many of these problems are associated with the nature and structure of work and the economic ideology of capitalism (Chapter 10). Capitalism, as Winston Churchill once said of democracy, may be the worst economic system ever devised—except for all the others. But capitalism's emphasis on the private accumulation of wealth and the profit motive assures that there will be "winners" and "losers" in the competition for resources—the very rich and the very poor (Chapter 11).

Individuals have significantly different "life chances" depending on their position in the resulting stratification system. For those at the bottom of the stratification ladder, life chances are minimal. Recent economic changes have contributed to the deconcentration and deindustrialization of urban areas resulting in high inner city unemployment, displaced workers, deteriorating neighborhoods, and eroding tax bases (Chapter 12). Those who can get out do so, as witnessed by patterns of suburbanization; those who must remain are involuntarily segregated.

As a consequence of these urban processes, city schools, which are heavily dependent upon municipal funds, attract fewer and fewer good teachers, facilities erode, the quality of education declines, and the number of poor minority students increases. Debates begin over the relevance of traditional curricula and the need for multiculturalism. Students graduate without knowing how to read, work simple math problems, or resolve interpersonal conflicts. There is a crisis in education (Chapter 13).

The chapters in Section 3—Work, Wealth and Poverty, Urban Decline and Growth, and Crisis in Education—are highly interrelated and speak to the need for examining both the cultural and the structural underpinnings of the social problems described. Further, all three of the sociological perspectives, structural-functionalism, conflict theory, and symbolic interactionism, are used to understand various aspects of the four problem areas discussed.

10

CHAPTER

Work

IS IT TRUE?

Worldwide, farmers account for half of all workers (p. 282).

The average real wage for workers, or what money actually buys, has steadily increased since 1973 (p. 288).

In 1995, the U.S. unemployment rate was higher than in many other industrialized countries, including Canada, England, and the countries of the European Community (p. 294).

Since 1983, labor union membership has increased steadily (p. 297).

Since 1960, the rate of U.S. workers killed on the job has increased dramatically (p. 299).

ANS: 1. T 2. F 3. F 4. F 5. F

> Throughout the industrialized world, as companies big and small seek higher productivity in the face of cutthroat competition and mind-boggling technological change, jobs have become the economic, political, and social issue of the 1990s.
>
> Marc Levinson, Journalist/Social commentator

" "I owe, I owe . . . It's off to work I go" reads a bumper sticker. Its message reflects the necessity of work and the way many feel about it. Yet nearly eight million people in the United States over the age of sixteen are unemployed and looking for work (*Statistical Abstract of the United States: 1995,* Table 658). Behind this grim statistic are the hopelessness and depression experienced by both individuals and families. Employed individuals may also suffer from work-related problems: alienation, low wages, and hazardous working conditions. These and other social problems associated with work are the focus of this chapter. Indeed, a 1994 *Time/CNN* poll revealed that the economy and jobs closely follow crime as the greatest "problem facing the country today" (*Time* 1994, 25).

The Social Context: The Global Economy

The *economic institution* refers to the structure by which goods and services are produced and distributed. The economic institution is more than statistics about unemployment, interest rates, and the gross domestic product. The economic institution affects every member of society—where we live, where we work, and our quality of life.

INDUSTRIALIZATION AND POSTINDUSTRIALIZATION

The nature of work has been shaped by the **Industrial Revolution,** the period between the mid-eighteenth century and the early nineteenth century when the factory system was introduced in England. The Industrial Revolution dramatically altered society. The nature of work changed: machines replaced hand tools; steam, gasoline, and electric power replaced human or animal power. Industrialization also led to the development of the assembly line and an increased division of labor as goods began to be mass-produced. The development of factories contributed to the emergence of large cities where the earlier informal social interactions dominated by primary relationships were replaced by formal interactions centered around secondary groups. Instead of the family-centered economy characteristic of an agricultural society, people began to work outside the home for wages.

Postindustrialization refers to the shift from an industrial economy dominated by manufacturing jobs to an economy dominated by service-oriented, information-intensive occupations. Postindustrialization is characterized by a highly educated workforce, automated and computerized production meth-

International Data: In the United States, farmers account for less than three percent of all workers. Globally, they account for half.

SOURCE: Reported in Bracey 1995.

ods, increased government involvement in economic issues, and a higher standard of living (Bell 1973). Like industrialization before it, postindustrialization has transformed the nature of work.

THE CHANGING NATURE OF WORK

Industrialization and postindustrialization have changed the nature of work considerably. What we do (grow crops or write business reports), how we do it (use a tractor or a computer), and where we do it (on a farm or in an office complex) have all changed and are likely to continue to do so.

There are three fundamental **work sectors:** primary, secondary, and tertiary. These work sectors reflect the major economic transformations in society—the Industrial Revolution and the Postindustrial Revolution. The *primary work sector,* involving the production of raw materials and food goods, develops when a society changes from a hunting and gathering society to an agricultural one. The *secondary work sector* involves the production of manufactured goods from raw materials (e.g., paper from wood) and emerges as a society becomes industrialized. The third sector is the *tertiary work sector,* which includes professional, managerial, technical-support, and service jobs. Tertiary work sector occupations develop as a response to technological advances that enable fewer workers to maintain the same level of productivity. In a postindustrial society, the highest proportion of jobs are in the tertiary sector. Today, approximately 5 percent, 25 percent, and 70 percent of U.S. workers are in the primary, secondary, and tertiary work sectors, respectively. These percentages are roughly the reverse of those from agricultural days. Between 1981 and 1991, 1.8 million manufacturing jobs were lost (Barlett and Steele 1992). For the first time, white-collar jobs outnumber blue-collar jobs in the American workforce (Adams 1993). Table 10.1 identifies the fastest-growing and fastest-declining occupations as projected from 1992 to the year 2005.

The increased availability of white-collar jobs brings with it two major concerns. First is a "job-to-skill mismatch" leading to millions of unemployed Americans. In a postindustrial society, highly skilled and technological personnel are needed, but many U.S. workers, particularly women and minorities, are not educated and skilled enough for many of these positions (Morris, Bernhardt, and Handcock 1994). It is estimated that one in three youths between the ages of sixteen and twenty-four will not have the skills needed for entry-level, semi-skilled, high-wage occupations (Government Accounting Office 1992). Some disagree with this estimate, however, and argue that service jobs have reached their peak and that manufacturing jobs will increase (Thurow 1993).

Second, even if there are more white-collar jobs, they often pay less than the manufacturing jobs they replace (Cooper 1992). A study by the Congressional Budget Office found that one to three years after losing a job in the 1980s, more than 60 percent of those laid off were not working, or were working at less than 95 percent of their old earnings (Kellam 1994, 56–57).

CAPITALISM, SOCIALISM, AND THE GLOBAL ECONOMY

Societies differ in the way their economic systems are structured. The principal economic systems are capitalism and socialism. Under **capitalism** private individuals or groups invest capital (money, technology, machines) to produce

The job as we know it will not exist in 10 years or less. Job security has disappeared.
—Dennis Waitley
Author, *Empires of the Mind*

The American system of ours, call it Americanism, call it Capitalism, call it what you like, gives each and every one of us a great opportunity if we only seize it with both hands and make the most of it.
—Al Capone
Gangster

TABLE 10.1

OCCUPATIONS OF FASTEST GROWTH AND FASTEST DECLINE, 1992–2005

FASTEST GROWING	FASTEST DECLINING
Home health aides	Frame wirers, central office
Human services workers	Signal or track switch maintainers
Personal and home care aides	Peripheral EDP equipment operators
Computer engineers and scientists	Directory assistance operators
Systems analysts	Central office operators
Physical and corrective therapy assistants and aides	Station installers and repairers, telephone
Physical therapists	Portable machine cutters
Paralegals	Computer operators, except peripheral equipment
Occupational therapy assistants and aides	Shoe sewing machine operators and tenders
Electronic pagination systems workers	Central office and PBX installers and repairers
Teachers, special education	Child care workers, private household
Medical assistants	Job printers
Detectives, except public	Roustabouts
Correction officers	Separating and still machine operators and tenders
Child care workers	Cleaners and servants, private household
Travel agents	Coil winders, tapers, and finishers
Radiologic technologists and technicians	Billing, posting, and calculating machine operators
Nursery (farm) workers	Sewing machine operators, garment
Medical records technicians	Compositors and typesetters, precision
Operations research analysts	Data entry keyers, composing
Occupational therapists	Motion picture projectionists
Subway and streetcar operators	Telephone and cable TV line installers and repairers
Legal secretaries	Cutting and slicing machine setters
Teachers, preschool and kindergarten	Watchmakers
Manicurists	Tire building machine operators
EEG technologists	Packaging and filling machine operators and tenders
Producers, directors, actors, and entertainers	Head sawyers and sawing machine operators and tenders
Speech-language pathologists and audiologists	Switchboard operators
Flight attendants	Farmers
Guards	Machine forming operators and tenders, metal and plastic
Nuclear medicine technologists	Cement and gluing machine operators and tenders
Insurance adjusters, examiners, and investigators	
Respiratory therapists	
Psychologists	

SOURCE: Adapted from *Statistical Abstract of the United States: 1995*, 115th ed. (U. S. Bureau of the Census. Washington, D. C.: U. S. Government Printing Office), Table 651.

goods and services that they then sell for a profit in a competitive market. Capitalism is characterized by economic motivation through profit, the determination of prices and wages primarily through supply and demand, and the absence of governmental intervention in the economy.

Critics of capitalism argue that it creates too many social evils, including alienated workers, poor working conditions, near poverty wages, unemployment, a polluted and depleted environment, and world conflict over resources. **Socialism** emphasizes public rather than private ownership. Theoretically, goods and services are equitably distributed according to the needs of the citizens. Whereas capitalism emphasizes individual freedom, socialism emphasizes social equality. Although all capitalistic and socialistic economies have the general characteristics described here, specific economies vary tremendously.

Both capitalism and socialism claim that they result in economic well-being for society and its members. In reality, capitalist and socialist countries have been unable to fulfill the promises of their respective economic ideologies. Some theorists have suggested that capitalist countries will adopt elements of socialism and socialist countries will adopt elements of capitalism. This idea, known as the **convergence hypothesis,** is reflected in the economies of Germany, France, and Sweden, which are sometimes called "integrated economies" because they have elements of both capitalism and socialism.

> **Consideration** The Great Depression caused the U.S. federal government to reassess its hands-off attitude toward the economy and led to the view that some governmental involvement in the economy is necessary. Today, the U.S. government regulates the stock market, the minimum wage, communications networks, and transportation (air, rail, truck). The government also controls economic programs such as Social Security, unemployment compensation, Medicaid, and Medicare. The government is also actively concerned with the safety and quality of products, services, and the work environment.

In recent decades, advances in communication and information technology have led to the development of a **global economy,** an interconnected network of economic activity that transcends national borders. One result of the global economy is that an increasing number of products pass through the economic systems of several countries. For example, workers in Taiwan may manufacture chairs made from wood that was shipped from Denmark by a French firm. A distributor in Hong Kong then sends the chairs to the United States, where they are sold in a department store that has its headquarters in Germany. Thus, the emergence of a global economy means that more businesses are operating internationally. In fact, a relatively small number of multinational businesses control a large share of the world's economy.

Sociological Perspectives on Work and the Economy

Numerous theories in economics, political science, and history address the nature of work and the economy. In sociology, structural-functionalism and conflict theory, as macrosociological approaches, emphasize the reciprocal effects between society's institutions including the impact of the economy. Symbolic interactionism, as a microsociological perspective, focuses on the meaning of work and work roles for individuals and small groups.

STRUCTURAL-FUNCTIONALIST PERSPECTIVE

According to the structural-functionalists, the economic institution is one of the most important of all social institutions. It provides the basic necessities common to all human societies including food, clothing, and shelter. By providing for the basic survival needs of members of society, the economic institution contributes to social stability.

After the basic survival needs of a society are met, surplus materials and wealth may be allocated to other social uses, such as maintaining military protection from enemies, supporting political and religious leaders, providing formal education, supporting an expanding population, and providing

The real price of everything, what every thing really costs . . . is the toil and trouble of acquiring it.
—Adam Smith
Economist

International Data:
According to one estimate, the six hundred largest multinational companies produce half of the world's total economic output.
SOURCE: Kidron and Segal 1991.

The workers are the saviors of society, the redeemers of the race.
—Eugene V. Debs
American socialist

entertainment and recreational activities. Societal development is dependent on an economic surplus in a society (Lenski and Lenski 1987).

Although the economic institution is functional for society, elements of it may be dysfunctional. For example, prior to industrialization, agrarian societies had a low division of labor in which few work roles were available to members of society. Limited work roles meant that society's members shared similar roles and thus developed similar norms and values (Durkheim [1893] 1966). In contrast, industrial societies are characterized by many work roles, or a high division of labor, and cohesion is based not on the similarity of people and their roles but on their interdependence. People in industrial societies need the skills and services that others provide. The lack of common norms and values in industrialized societies may result in **anomie**—a state of normlessness—which is linked to a variety of social problems including crime, drug addiction, and violence (see Chapters 3 and 4).

CONFLICT PERSPECTIVE

According to Karl Marx, capitalism is responsible for the inequality and conflict within and between societies. The ruling class controls the economic system for its own benefit and exploits and oppresses the working masses. While structural-functionalism views the economic institution as benefiting society as a whole, conflict theory holds that capitalism benefits an elite class that controls not only the economy but other aspects of society as well—the media, politics and law, education, and religion.

As an indication of the ties between business and government, conflict theorists point to the deregulation policies of conservative administrations and the Republican-controlled House of Representatives of 1995. For example, the Democrats had attempted to define tobacco as a drug and restrict its use, a move opposed by the powerful tobacco industry; immediately after gaining control of the House, the Republicans stopped all progress on the measure.

The savings and loan scandal is another example of how government has supported big business. In essence, the federal government increased the federal deposit insurance, which led to more money being deposited in savings and loans; at the same time, the federal government loosened its regulations, which freed savings and loan officers to make risky investments, leading to the collapse of many savings and loan institutions. This scandal cost American taxpayers more than $500 billion (Calavita and Pontell 1990). Both the tobacco and banking examples illustrate how political groups in power provide preferential treatment to lucrative industries that make large campaign contributions.

The conflict perspective provides an explanation for many current work trends, such as worksite health promotion programs and work-family policies and programs. According to conflict theorists, these trends (which are discussed later in this chapter) are not the result of a surge in altruistic or humanitarian concern for workers' well-being. Rather, these policies result in higher job productivity and lower health care costs and thus reflect the "bottom line" profit mentality of corporate leaders.

According to symbolic interactionism, the work role is a central part of a person's identity. When making a new social acquaintance, one of the first questions we usually ask is, "What do you do?" The answer largely defines for us who that person is. As symbolic interactionists note, the label of a job or profession also gives meaning to others about that individual. For example, identifying a person as a truck driver provides a different social meaning than identifying someone as a physician. In addition, the title of one's work status—maintenance supervisor or president of the United States—also gives meaning and self-worth to the individual. An individual's job is one of his or her most important statuses; for many, it comprises a "master status," that is, the most significant status in a person's social identity.

This chapter's *The Human Side*, from the authors' files, articulates the importance of work and employment status as self and other defining attributes. While the husband must deal with feelings of self-doubt and inadequacy, the wife is angry and embarrassed by her husband's unemployment and the meaning assigned to him by friends. In each case, as symbolic interactionists note, definitions and meaning influence behavior.

Problems Experienced by Workers

An increasing number of workers are dissatisfied with their jobs. They feel alienated, fear that their health and safety are jeopardized, and must cope with the frustrations associated with unemployment or underemployment.

JOB DISSATISFACTION

An advertisement for Army recruits claims that joining the Army enables one to "be all that you can be." Indeed, if you read the classified ad section of any newspaper, you are likely to find job advertisements that entice applicants with claims such as "discover a rewarding and challenging career . . ." and "we offer opportunities for advancement and travel . . . ." Unfortunately, most jobs do not allow workers to "be all that they can be." In reality, most employers want you to "be all you can be for them" with limited concern for your career satisfaction. Millions of American workers are dissatisfied with their work.

The degree to which a person is satisfied with a job varies, of course, by type of job. Factors that contribute to job satisfaction include income, prestige, a feeling of accomplishment, autonomy, a sense of being challenged by the job, opportunities to be creative, congenial co- workers, the feeling that one is making a contribution, benefits, promotion opportunities, and job security. These factors often overlap—for example, high-paying jobs tend to have more prestige, be more autonomous, provide more benefits, and permit greater creativity.

When almost two thousand adults ($n = 1,937$) were asked to rate the characteristics most preferred in a job, the most important qualities identified were that the work be important and give the worker a feeling of accomplishment. Other job characteristics respondents identified as important were, in descending order of importance, "income," "chance for advancement," "no

National Data: Less than half (46 percent) of American workers in a Gallup Poll reported that they were "completely satisfied" with their job security. Thirty percent feel that their company does not have a strong sense of loyalty to them.

SOURCE: Moore and McAneny 1993, 19.

ONE COUPLE'S EXPERIENCE WITH UNEMPLOYMENT

The Unemployed Husband's View

Two years ago I was employed in a job in which I earned over $40,000 per year, including health and retirement benefits. I felt I could no longer tolerate the incessant demands being made on me so I quit my job, thinking that I would find another job that was more satisfying. My wife of twenty-one years and three children were aware of my frustrations, but did not want me to stop working until I had another job arranged. Things haven't been the same since I resigned.

Sometimes I feel happier being unemployed in that I no longer have to live with the frustrations that went along with my job. However, I have also experienced depression and suicidal thoughts over being without work. Job op-

portunities for a middle-aged man are limited. The jobs that are available do not pay much. In the past year I have worked in a convenience store, cut grass, and painted houses. I have also sent out over forty-five résumés and interviewed for about ten jobs. Often, the interviewer doesn't even call back or write to say I don't have the job.

The impact on my family has been both good and bad. The good side has been my availability to spend time with my two teenage children. The bad side is that we have plunged deeply into debt and have to watch how every penny is spent. I often feel that my family blames me for the economic hardships we are experiencing. Although I contribute to the family by working odd jobs and doing things around the house, I don't feel that my efforts are recognized or appreciated.

danger of being fired," and "working hours are short, lots of free time." As might be expected, blue-collar workers who do manual and repetitive work experience lower job satisfaction than white-collar workers.

Earning low wages that do not provide an adequate standard of living also contributes to job dissatisfaction. The average real wage for workers in the United States has not risen since 1973.

The twentysomething graduates entering the workplace stand to earn less in inflation-adjusted dollars than their boomer counterparts did a generation ago. Starting pay for new liberal-arts graduates now averages $27,700 a year, according to a Northwestern University annual survey; that falls short of the adjusted entry-level earnings of $28,500 in 1968 (Church 1993, 36).

It isn't easy to be an unemployed male in our society—it's as though I'm nothing if I don't earn money. I resent this view. I've seen plenty of wealthy men who are bankrupt in their interpersonal relationships. They have the "things," those outward signs that show others they are successful, but they are not happy in their marriages and have distant relationships with their children.

The Employed Wife's View

I did not approve of my husband resigning his position. All jobs have their frustrations. I have tried to be supportive, but the longer he has gone without a steady job, the more resentful I have become.

I do not require a lot of money to be happy. I can be thrifty and frugal. But lack of money is intolerable when I don't know where the next meal is coming from and am afraid to answer the phone because it is probably another bill collector.

My husband's anger and quick temper also scare me. There are times I feel he is upset with himself for not having a job and I know he takes it out on me and the children. He expects us to overlook the fact that we are in this mess because of a decision he made.

I have an enjoyable job teaching preschool children but it doesn't pay enough to keep us afloat. I've had friends ask me why I stay married to him and I get embarrassed when people ask me if my husband has found a job yet. It isn't easy being poor compared to the middle-class life to which we were accustomed.

In spite of our economic situation, we continue to have some good times as a couple and as a family. I guess my biggest fear and worry is that I don't know how long my husband will be without stable employment. We won't divorce over this but it has and continues to put a lot of strain on our relationship.

Job satisfaction is also affected by the split labor market. A **split labor market,** also called a dual economy or a segmented labor market, refers to the existence of a primary and a secondary labor market. The primary labor market refers to jobs that are stable, economically rewarding, and come with benefits. These jobs are usually occupied by the most educated and trained individuals (e.g., a corporate attorney, teacher, or accountant), most often white males.

The secondary labor market refers to jobs that involve low pay, no security, few benefits, and little chance for advancement. Domestic servants, clerks, and food servers are examples of these jobs. Women and racial and ethnic minorities are disproportionately represented in the secondary labor market. These workers often have no union to protect them and are more likely to be dissatisfied with their job than workers in the primary labor market.

We must forge a partnership in which the company provides an environment that allows employees to work to their full potential, and where, in exchange, employees agree to perform at their best.
—Sue Osborn
Chevron Corporation

Domestic workers are part of the secondary labor market and typically have no job security, low wages, no benefits and little chance for advancement.

> **Consideration** *Workers who feel that their employer cares about them reciprocate by giving the company a more enthusiastic effort. The reverse is also true. An employee at a U.S. submarine factory observed that disgruntled employees are more likely to do shoddy work, to lose tools, and to take longer to complete a task than satisfied employees (Authors' files 1995).*

ALIENATION

Another aspect of job dissatisfaction is a feeling of alienation. Work in industrialized societies is characterized by a high division of labor and specialization of work roles. As a result, workers' tasks are repetitive and monotonous and often involve little or no creativity (e.g., installing bumpers, typing reports, polishing floors). Limited to specific tasks by their work roles, workers are unable to express and utilize their full potential—intellectual, emotional, and physical. According to Marx, when workers are merely cogs in a machine, they become estranged from their work, the product they create, other human beings, and themselves. Marx called this estrangement "**alienation.**"

Alienation usually has four components: powerlessness, meaninglessness, normlessness, and self-estrangement. Powerlessness results from working in an environment in which one has little or no control over the decisions that affect one's work. Meaninglessness results when workers do no not participate in the total production of a product and thus are unable to see how their role relates to other work roles. Workers may also suffer from normlessness if they see co-workers succeed through questionable tactics. Alienation also involves a feeling of self-estrangement, which stems from the workers' inability to realize their full human potential in their work roles. This chapter's *Self and Society* assesses alienation among college students (see pp.292–293).

The reality of most jobs, according to conflict theorists, is that they are controlled by employers and owners who emphasize efficiency over mean-

National Data: Fifty-three percent of college students say that it is "essential" or "very important" that they obtain recognition from their colleagues for contributions to their occupational field.

SOURCE: American Council on Education and University of California 1994.

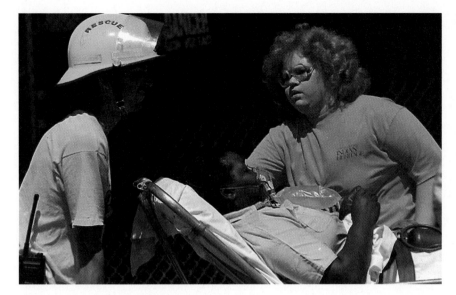

Twenty-five employees died in a fire at a North Carolina poultry processing plant. These deaths could have been avoided if the plant had installed a sprinkler system and provided a safety exit for workers. But such safety measures are costly and, as conflict theorists argue, profit often takes precedence over worker safety.

ing. The owners are indifferent to the workers' alienation unless it affects job performance.

HEALTH AND SAFETY HAZARDS IN THE WORKPLACE

Some people's jobs are literally killing them. Accidents at work and hazardous working conditions contribute to a staggering number of illnesses, injuries, and deaths.

Work-related hazards take many forms. A machine operator can lose a limb or be injured by equipment, a construction worker can fall from a scaffold or from a building, and a bus driver can be injured or killed in a crash. Military personnel and police have dangerous jobs. Gas station attendants and convenience store clerks face the danger of being victims of violent holdups. Employees may also pose a threat to each other. More than 200 assaults by employees occurred in U.S. government post offices in 1993 (Toufexis 1994).

Occupational-related hazards also include inhaling cotton dust in textile mills, coal dust in coal mines, or carcinogens in asbestos factories. Many of these hazards are attributed to company negligence or willful disregard of government and safety laws. For example, the dangers of asbestos were known as early as 1918 when American insurance companies stopped selling life insurance policies to asbestos workers. Nevertheless, the asbestos industry took little action until the 1960s. Of the half million workers exposed to "significant doses of asbestos," 100,000 will die from lung cancer, 35,000 from mesothelioma, and 35,000 from asbestosis (cited in Coleman 1994, 79).

Another example of work-related hazards occurred in 1991 when a North Carolina poultry processing plant caught fire, killing twenty-five workers and injuring fifty-four. The deaths occurred because the plant's doors were locked and there were no evacuation plans or sprinkler system. Conflict theorists argue that the potential loss of revenue from stolen chickens justified, to the owners, not providing a safe exit for workers, and that the cost of a

National Data: An estimated 20 million work-related injuries, 390,000 work-related illnesses, and 100,000 work-related deaths occur each year in the United States.
SOURCE: Levy and Wegman 1995.

In my work I am constantly in danger of injuring myself and others.
—Rigger (moves heavy shipbuilding equipment) Electric Boat Company

Self & SOCIETY

Student Alienation Scale

Indicate your agreement to each statement by selecting one of the responses provided:

1. It is hard to know what is right and wrong because the world is changing so fast.
   _____ Strongly agree   _____ Agree   _____ Disagree   _____ Strongly disagree

2. I am pretty sure my life will work out the way I want it to.
   _____ Strongly agree   _____ Agree   _____ Disagree   _____ Strongly disagree

3. I like the rules of my school because I know what to expect.
   _____ Strongly agree   _____ Agree   _____ Disagree   _____ Strongly disagree

4. School is important in building social relationships.
   _____ Strongly agree   _____ Agree   _____ Disagree   _____ Strongly disagree

5. School will get me a good job.
   _____ Strongly agree   _____ Agree   _____ Disagree   _____ Strongly disagree

6. It is all right to break the law as long as you do not get caught.
   _____ Strongly agree   _____ Agree   _____ Disagree   _____ Strongly disagree

7. I go to ball games and other sports activities at school.
   _____ Always   _____ Most of the time   _____ Some of the time   _____ Never

8. School is teaching me what I want to learn.
   _____ Strongly agree   _____ Agree   _____ Disagree   _____ Strongly disagree

9. I go to school parties, dances, and other school activities.
   _____ Always   _____ Most of the time   _____ Some of the time   _____ Never

10. A student has the right to cheat if it will keep him or her from failing.
    _____ Strongly agree   _____ Agree   _____ Disagree   _____ Strongly disagree

11. I feel like I do not have anyone to reach out to.
    _____ Always   _____ Most of the time   _____ Some of the time   _____ Never

12. I feel that I am wasting my time in school.
    _____ Always   _____ Most of the time   _____ Some of the time   _____ Never

13. I do not know anyone that I can confide in.
    _____ Strongly agree   _____ Agree   _____ Disagree   _____ Strongly disagree

14. It is important to act and dress for the occasion.
    _____ Always   _____ Most of the time   _____ Some of the time   _____ Never

---

National Data:
Approximately 18 percent of the U.S. workforce works nonstandard hours, or shift work.

SOURCE: *Statistical Abstract of the United States: 1995,* Table 647.

sprinkler system would have cut further into profits. Hazardous working conditions exist, according to conflict theorists, because profit takes precedence over safety.

Another work-related health hazard is job stress. Prolonged job stress can cause physical problems, such as high blood pressure, ulcers, and headaches as well as psychological problems. Shift workers are prone to experiencing sleep deprivation and fatigue as well as marital problems due to the lack of time couples have together (Liskowsky 1992; White and Keith 1990).

15. It is no use to vote because one vote does not count very much.
_____ Strongly agree   _____ Agree   _____ Disagree   _____ Strongly disagree

16. When I am unhappy, there are people I can turn to for support.
_____ Always   _____ Most of the time   _____ Some of the time   _____ Never

17. School is helping me get ready for what I want to do after college.
_____ Strongly agree   _____ Agree   _____ Disagree   _____ Strongly disagree

18. When I am troubled, I keep things to myself.
_____ Always   _____ Most of the time   _____ Some of the time   _____ Never

19. I am not interested in adjusting to American society.
_____ Strongly agree   _____ Agree   _____ Disagree   _____ Strongly disagree

20. I feel close to my family.
_____ Always   _____ Most of the time   _____ Some of the time   _____ Never

21. Everything is relative and there just aren't any rules to live by.
_____ Strongly agree   _____ Agree   _____ Disagree   _____ Strongly disagree

22. The problems of life are sometimes too big for me.
_____ Always   _____ Most of the time   _____ Some of the time   _____ Never

23. I have lots of friends.
_____ Strongly agree   _____ Agree   _____ Disagree   _____ Strongly disagree

24. I belong to different social groups.
_____ Strongly agree   _____ Agree   _____ Disagree   _____ Strongly disagree

Interpretation: This scale measures four aspects of alienation: powerlessness, or the sense that high goals (e.g., straight A's) are unattainable; meaninglessness, or lack of connectedness between the present (e.g., school) and the future (e.g., job); normlessness, or the feeling that socially disapproved behavior (e.g., cheating) is necessary to achieve goals (e.g., high grades); and social estrangement, or lack of connectedness to others (e.g., being a "loner"). For items 1, 6, 10, 11, 12, 13, 15, 18, 19, 21, and 22, the response indicating the greatest degree of alienation is "strongly agree" or "always." For all other items, the response indicating the greatest degree of alienation is "strongly disagree" or "never."

SOURCE: Rosalind Y. Mau. 1992. "The Validity and Devolution of a Concept: Student Alienation." *Adolescence* 27: 107, 731–41. Scale items on pp. 739–40. Used by permission of Libra Publishers, Inc. 3089C Clairemont Drive, Suite 383, San Diego, California 92117.

UNEMPLOYMENT AND UNDEREMPLOYMENT

Unemployment is a worldwide problem. In the twenty-five countries belonging to the Organization for Economic Cooperation and Development (OECD), 35 million people, or 8.5 percent of the workforce, are unemployed (OECD 1994). In less developed countries, the problem is extreme and likely to get worse: according to one estimate, in the late 1980s, unemployment and underemployment in the developing world stood at 40–50 percent (Siegel 1994).

Also in the late 1980s, the Overseas Development Council stated that in the developing countries "in the next two decades, at least 600 million new jobs—more than the total number of jobs in all the industrial market economies—will have to be created just to accommodate new entrants into the labor force who are already alive today" (cited in Siegel 1994, 128).

In 1995, the U.S. unemployment rate was 5.6 percent. This percentage represents more than 7.5 million people who were *both* unemployed and actively trying to find a job. The unemployment rate, however, excludes those who are "permanently" unemployed and have given up looking for work such as retired people and full-time housewives/househusbands. An estimated 6.2 million American part-time workers are looking for full-time employment (Congressional Budget Office 1993).

> **Consideration** *There are two types of unemployment: discriminatory and structural. **Discriminatory unemployment** involves high rates of unemployment among particular social groups such as racial and ethnic minorities and women. **Structural unemployment** exists when there are not enough jobs available for those who want them. The sociological imagination suggests that structural unemployment is the result of social factors rather than personal inadequacies of the unemployed. Such social factors include government and business downsizing, job exportation, automation, a reduction in the number of new and existing businesses, an increase in the number of people looking for jobs as the baby boomers move through the workforce, and a recessionary economy where fewer goods are purchased and, therefore, fewer employees are needed. Rather than saying a person is lazy, the sociological imagination suggests that many people are unable to work because of a lack of structural opportunities.*

Unemployment figures also do not include those who are underemployed. **Underemployment** refers to employment in a job that is underpaid; is not commensurate with one's skills, experience, and/or education; and/or involves working fewer hours than desired. A Ph.D. working part-time in a convenience store is an example of underemployment.

The personal consequences of unemployment (and in some cases, underemployment) include lowered self-esteem and confidence, anxiety, depression, and alcohol abuse (Feather 1990; Liem and Liem 1990). Increased suicide rates, increased admissions to state mental hospitals and state prisons, as well as increased rates of cardiovascular-renal disease, have been associated with increased unemployment (Brenner 1978). Unemployment has also been linked to increased family violence (Straus 1980). Unemployment also means losing benefits such as health care.

As devastating as unemployment can be for individuals and families, it is important to keep in mind that unemployment is normal in a dynamic and changing economy. It is also helpful to put U.S. unemployment figures in perspective: the United States has a lower rate of unemployment than many other industrialized countries.

The Congressional Budget Office (1993) projects that the unemployment rate will be 5.7 percent in 1998, or about the same as in 1995. Many economists, however, suggest that the job outlook is grim. A 1992 Department of Labor study found that 30 percent of future college graduates between now and 2005

International Data: The unemployment rate for Canada is 11.1 percent, for England 10.7 percent, and for the countries of the European Community about 11 percent on average.

SOURCE: Church 1993, 35.

will be unemployed or underemployed and will earn less, when inflation is accounted for, than graduates a generation before them (Church 1993, 36).

Threats to Job Security

Just as the unemployed are frustrated at not being able to find a job, some who have a job fear that they may lose it. Automation, foreign competition, job exportation, multinationalism, and declining labor union representation contribute to the vulnerability of American jobs and the associated fear of losing them. Conflict theorists emphasize that, in each case, employers are seeking greater profits at the expense of the workers.

AUTOMATION

Automation, or the replacement of human labor with machinery and equipment, is one of the major changes associated with the Industrial Revolution (see also Chapter 14). Automation is functional for consumers: in the absence of human error, product quality increases and becomes standardized. It is also beneficial for owners because it is efficient and maximizes the production of goods. Automation also minimizes corporate costs since robots do not need health benefits, are not absent because of illness, and never retire.

Automation affects white-collar, as well as blue-collar, job security. In 1991–1992, for example, Sears cut more than 40,000 jobs, mostly clerical and support positions, in the United States and Canada after "installation of computer terminals and telephone kiosks throughout Sears' 868 stores" (Cooper 1992, 178).

FOREIGN COMPETITION

The recent passage of the North American Free Trade Agreement (NAFTA) was due, in part, to concern that the United States was falling behind its foreign competitors. The agreement permits the free movement of goods, services, and investments between the United States, Mexico, and Canada and was created, in part, to help the United States compete with "trade blocs" in Europe and Asia.

Many Americans are concerned about the degree of foreign investment in the United States: foreign investors have purchased American real estate, buildings, baseball teams, and motion picture companies. In 1989, foreign investors spent more than $70 billion in the United States, although this figure has dropped below $20 billion in recent years (Mean 1992).

Another concern is that America has lost its place as the business leader of the world. "American business, with the exception of perhaps space and satellite technology, is no longer leading the world as it did 20 years ago" (Meyer-Larsen 1991, 24). In 1975, for example, eleven of the top fifteen corporations on the *Fortune* 500 list of the world's largest firms were American; by 1991, only seven of the top fifteen were American. Why? According to Meyer-Larsen (1991), it is because the United States responded timidly to the expansion of the global economy. For example, when faced with stiff competition in other countries, U.S. banks simply shut down their branches in those countries.

National Data: When one thousand adult Americans were asked, "Is job security better or worse for Americans compared to two years ago?" 22 percent said "better," 66 percent "worse," 7 percent "no change." Of those who said it was "worse," 53 percent felt it would be worse in the "long term," 37 percent thought it would be worse in the "short term," and 10 percent were "not sure."
SOURCE: Church 1993, 35.

National Data: By 1990, 32 percent of the painters and 17 percent of the welders in the auto industry had been replaced by robotics.
SOURCE: Hodson and Sullivan 1990, 1820.

When some U.S. industries began to falter, they gave up rather than making new investments to increase productivity.

Where does the United States stand in the global economy? Some commentators suggest that the United States is losing its ability to compete:

> More than two hundred years after the Declaration of Independence, the U.S. has lost its position as an independent power. . . . We now conform to the classic model of a failing economic power: with increasingly high levels of foreign dependency, a constantly depreciating currency, and a continuing negative trade balance. (Rohatyn 1988, 8)

In contrast, economist Herbert Stein (1992) argues that whether or not the United States is losing in the world market is a matter of perspective. Pointing out that gross domestic product is steadily increasing, he contends that the U.S. economy is healthy and is simply going through a transitional period that requires adjustments. Workers are left to wonder which view is correct.

JOB EXPORTATION

A more realistic fear for American workers is that their jobs will be exported to other countries where products can be produced more cheaply. In 1990, for example, Levi-Strauss Co. moved its largest Texas plant to Costa Rica and immediately laid off three hundred workers and hundreds more within months (Cockburn 1992). A study conducted by the National Labor Committee found that thirty U.S. apparel manufacturers had plants in El Salvador, Honduras, and Guatemala, and sixty-eight other manufacturers had subcontractors in the three countries. Between 1990 and 1993, these manufacturers closed fifty-eight of their U.S. plants and laid off workers at eleven others; as a result, an estimated 12,000 U.S. workers lost their jobs (Briggs 1993).

> **Consideration** *Some cases of job exportation raise human rights issues. For example, jobs that are exported to developing nations are usually low-paying assembly jobs, 80–90 percent of which are filled by women who legally can be paid less than men in many of these countries. These assembly jobs are tedious and low wage, and workers are forced to live in dirty, crowded "dormitories" provided by multinational corporations.*
>
> *Some exported jobs, such as electronics jobs, are more prestigious but are nevertheless hazardous. A study in South Korea "found that most electronics assembly workers developed severe eye problems after only one year of employment" (Ehrenreich and Fuentes 1992, 168). Further, because pay goes up with seniority, management lays off "older" workers. "We estimate, based on fragmentary data from several sources, that the multinational corporations may already have used up (cast off) as many as six million Third World workers—women who are too ill, too old (30 is over the hill in most industries), or too exhausted to be useful any more" (Ehrenreich and Fuentes 1992, 169).*

CORPORATE MULTINATIONALISM

Automation, foreign competition, and job exportation are all tied to corporate multinationalism. Corporations are becoming multinational, which means that a parent company in one country has branches, known as affiliates, in other countries. International Telephone and Telegraph (ITT) has affiliates in over fifty countries, for example. Exxon has more than a hundred affiliates.

In a process sometimes called "internationalization", corporations build factories in poorer countries where wages are low, while corporate headquarters or research and development offices are located in wealthier countries where an educated workforce is available. Thus, a product is produced not in one country but in many. For example, a Pontiac Le Mans from General Motors, which sells for $20,000, gets its price tag as follows: $6,000 to South Korea for labor and assembly, $3,500 to Japan for the engine, $1,500 to Germany for styling and engineering, $800 to Taiwan, Singapore, and Japan for small components such as computer chips, $500 to England for advertising and marketing services, and $100 to Ireland and Barbados for data processing (Reich 1991, 113). This "global factory" is facilitated by technology, which permits instant communication and the transfer of funds between the various countries; revolutionized transportation systems, which permit raw materials to get from one place to another quickly; and component part production, which allows products to be assembled in different places.

Multinationals are brazen examples of the profit motive. By moving portions of their operation to other countries, corporations are able to find new markets for their products (McDonald's hamburgers to China's millions), lower labor costs (wages for U.S. union members are $30 an hour versus $2 an hour for Korean workers), avoid government regulations (pollution, quality control), and pay lower taxes.

Consideration *Multinationalization provides jobs for U.S. managers, secures profits for U.S. investors, and helps the United States compete in the global economy (Samuelson 1994, 120). It also has "far-reaching and detrimental consequences" (Epstein, Graham, and Nembhard 1993, 206) for American society. First, it contributes to the trade deficit in that more goods are produced and exported from outside the United States than from within. Thus, the United States imports more than it exports. Second, multinationalism contributes to the budget deficit. The United States does not get tax income from U.S. corporations abroad, yet multinationals pressure the government to protect their foreign interests; as a result, military spending increases. Third, multinationalism contributes to U.S. unemployment by letting workers in other countries perform labor that could be completed by U.S. employees. Fourth, multinationals are less committed to solving domestic problems because they are not as directly affected by them. Rather, multinationals are concerned about the problems in the countries where they have affiliates. Finally, corporate multinationalization must take its share of the blame for an array of other social problems such as poverty resulting from fewer jobs, urban decline resulting from factories moving away, and racial and ethnic tensions resulting from competition for jobs.*

International Data: In 1995, the top five countries with which the United States has a trade deficit were Japan, China, Canada, Germany, and Mexico.
SOURCE: U.S. Bureau of Census 1995.

National Data: In the mid-1960s, 35 percent of employed wage and salary workers belonged to a union. In 1995, the percentage had dropped to 15 percent.
SOURCE: Greenwald 1995.

DECLINING LABOR UNION REPRESENTATION

Labor unions originally developed to protect workers and represent them at negotiations between management and labor. But the strength and membership of unions in the United States, as well as in other advanced capitalist countries, has declined (Western 1995). Blue-collar jobs where unions are strong are decreasing in number, and companies have increasingly moved to

"right-to-work" states. These states do not require workers to join a union as a condition of employment and, hence, have weaker unions. In addition, conservative administrations have been probusiness, and public sentiment toward unions has become more hostile. Although the 1935 Wagner Act guarantees the right to strike, this right has been weakened by subsequent amendments and legal interpretations. McCammon (1990) suggests that "the law has diminished the effectiveness of the strike, reduced the likelihood of its occurrence, and limited its legitimate forms, all the while sustaining the right to strike" (p. 206). Although technically most workers can strike, they risk their jobs by doing so. Striking air traffic controllers witnessed their jobs being offered to others.

Greenwald (1995) notes that recent increases in labor union membership may signal a "revival" of labor unions. According to Greenwald, "the very hardships and perceived injustices of the American workplace have begun to stir a new militancy among workers. And that has helped produce signs of a [labor union] comeback" (p. 1).

Responses to Workers' Concerns: Government and Corporate Policies and Programs

Government and private business have implemented a number of programs, policies, and strategies to address concerns of American workers. These responses include displaced workers programs, health and safety regulations and worksite programs, work-family policies and programs, more options in work schedules, and welfare corporatism.

DISPLACED WORKERS PROGRAMS

More than two million workers lose their jobs annually. Among the casualties are "highly trained workers who had ascended the corporate ladder, but not to job security" (Kellam 1994, 51). What happens to these workers?

The U.S. government has implemented various programs for dislocated and displaced workers—the 1962 Manpower Development and Training Act, the 1973 Comprehensive Employment and Training Act, and the 1982 Job Training Partnership Act. Other programs include TAA (Trade Adjustment Assistance), EDWAA (Economic Dislocation and Worker Adjustment Act), CAETA (Clean Air Employment Transition Assistance), DCA (Defense Conversion Adjustment), and DDP (Defense Diversification Program).

Unfortunately, funding for federal job training programs is insufficient to reach more than a small fraction of the workforce (Kenworthy 1995). Even those who complete the retraining do not always find new jobs at comparable wages. As Secretary of Labor Robert B. Reich said, "The truth is that most of the people who lose their jobs now are not going to get their old jobs back. . . . The old concept of unemployment insurance as a bridge to tide you over until you got your old job back, until the recession ended, is simply obsolete" (quoted in Kellam 1994, 53). The rehiring of displaced workers also requires an improved economy that generates new jobs. Without job openings, the value of job retraining is limited.

HEALTH AND SAFETY REGULATIONS

Over the last few decades, health and safety conditions in the workplace have improved as a result of media attention, demands by unions for change, more white-collar jobs, and regulations by the Occupational Safety and Health Administration (OSHA). Through OSHA, the government develops, monitors, and enforces health and safety regulations in the workplace. But OSHA's more than 1,000 inspectors are able to visit only 2 percent of the 6 million workplaces in the United States each year (reported in Kenworthy 1995). Because "the task of monitoring and enforcement simply cannot be effectively carried out by a government administrative agency," Kenworthy (1995) suggests that the United States follow the example of many other industrialized countries: turn over the bulk of responsibility for health and safety monitoring to the workforce (p. 114). Worker health and safety committees are a standard feature of companies in many other industrialized countries and are mandatory in most of Europe. These committees are authorized to inspect workplaces and cite employers for violations of health and safety regulations.

Maximizing the health and safety of workers involves more than implementing, monitoring, and enforcing regulations. Increasingly, businesses and corporations are attempting to maximize worker's health (and corporate profits) by offering worksite health promotion programs as discussed in this chapter's *In Focus*.

National Data: In 1960, the rate of workers killed on the job was 21 per 100,000 workers. This rate decreased steadily through the 1970s and 1980s; in 1993, the rate was 8 per 100,000.

SOURCE: *Statistical Abstract of the United States: 1995*, Table 688.

WORK-FAMILY POLICIES AND PROGRAMS

The influx of women into the workforce (see Figure 10.1) has been accompanied by an increase in government and company policies designed to help

Health Promotion Programs in the Workplace

Along with their briefcases or toolboxes, many American employees now carry a gym bag to work. Before or after work, or perhaps during their lunch hour, employees in many companies may be found in company-provided aerobics classes, weight-training rooms, indoor jogging tracks, basketball courts, or swimming pools. During work hours, many companies provide health-related educational seminars or health screening programs.

Health promotion programs in the workplace have mushroomed in the last decade. In 1995, an estimated half of all large U.S. companies provided worksite health promotion programs. These programs take many forms, including programs in physical fitness (such as weight training, aerobics and cardiovascular training, swimming, and recreational sports), smoking cessation, weight reduction, stress management, yoga, nutrition, prenatal health, and low back care. Some programs also include AIDS education, rape prevention and self-defense, and first aid and CPR certification. Some companies fill their snack dispensers with fruit instead of candy and other "junk food" and hire nutritionists to plan healthy meals that are served in employees' cafeterias. About 10,000 companies have Employee Assistance Programs to help employees and their families with substance abuse, family discord, depression, and other mental health problems. Some companies assume total financial responsibility for health promotion programs; other companies share the expense with employees, who are asked to pay a nominal fee.

Health promotion programs benefit both employees and corporations. Corporations benefit because healthier employees have lower job absenteeism and turnover, file fewer health insurance claims (which results in lower health insurance costs for employers), file fewer worker's compensation claims, and exhibit higher morale and productivity. In addition, health promotion programs can enhance a company's image among workers and the community. Employees enjoy the wide range of physical, mental, and social benefits that are associated with health promotion programs.

Although worksite health promotion programs are often touted as an innovative feature of the American workplace, they existed over a century ago. In 1879, the Pullman Company set up a worksite Physical Fitness Program. In 1894, the president of National Cash Register took employees for prework horseback rides at dawn. He also instituted morning and afternoon exercise breaks and built an employee gym a decade later.

SOURCE: David H. Chenoweth. 1991. *Planning Health Promotion at the Worksite*, 2d ed. Dubuque, Iowa: William C. Brown Publishers. _____ 1995. Personal communication.

women and men balance their work and family roles. In 1993, President Clinton signed into law the Family Leave Act, which requires all companies with 25 or more employees to provide each worker with up to twelve weeks of unpaid leave for reasons of family illness, birth, or adoption of a child. Nevertheless, the United States still lags behind other countries in providing paid time off for new parents. For instance, Germany provides fourteen weeks off with 100 percent salary (Caminiti 1992).

Aside from government-mandated work-family policies, corporations and employers have begun to initiate policies and programs that address the family concerns of their employees. Employer-provided assistance with child

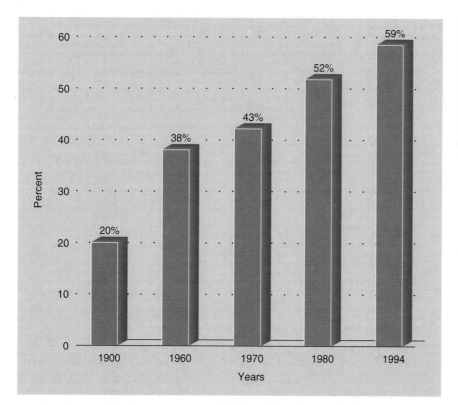

FIGURE 10.1
PERCENTAGE OF WOMEN EMPLOYED IN THE U.S. LABOR FORCE
Figures are rounded.
SOURCES: Phyllis Moen. 1992 *Women's Two Roles: A Contemporary Dilemma*. New York: Auburn House; *Statistical Abstract of the United States: 1995*, 115th ed. U.S. Bureau of the Census (Washington, D.C.: U.S. Government Printing Office), Table 637.

care, assistance with elderly parent care, options in work schedules, and job relocation assistance are becoming more common (Moen 1992). Employees at SAS Institute, a computer software company in Cary, North Carolina, can eat meals with family members and guests at the company cafeteria. The older children from the company preschool can join their parents for lunch (Russo 1993). Pepsi-Co, Inc., in Purchase, New York, has an on-site concierge to do personal chores for its 800 employees (Lopez 1993). In general, though companies that provide help for parents and their children are the exception, rather than the rule.

Work-family policies benefit both employees and their families and the corporations they work for. Hewlett (1992) suggests that:

> *Companies need not be farsighted or altruistic to have [family support] policies; all they need to do is consult their bottom line. Family supports are fast becoming win-win propositions; good for the working parent, good for the child, good for the company. (p. 26)*

For example, Corning Glass Works in upstate New York found that its turnover rate for female employees was twice as high as for male employees. This high turnover rate was costly— replacing each lost worker cost $40,000 (for search costs, on-the-job training costs, and the like). Corning conducted a survey and discovered that "family stress—particularly child-care problems—was the main reason so many women quit their jobs" (Hewlett 1992, 27). Corning decided to implement a family support package that included parenting leave, on-site child care, part-time work options, job sharing, and a parent resource

There is a family and medical leave policy for some of us, some of the time. There are small allowances for childbirth and sickness-unto-death. But the traffic jam of our lives rarely makes way for everyday family problems.
—Ellen Goodman
Columnist

How can you ask your people to unselfishly support the needs of the corporation if the corporation will not support the needs of its people?
—Roger Meade
Scitor Corporation

center. The company's chairman, James P. Houghton, said that Corning's efforts "go way beyond simple justice; it's a matter of good business sense in a changing world . . . it's a matter of survival" (cited in Hewlett 1992, 27).

Fran Rodgers, president of Work/Family Directions explains the need for work-family policies:

> *For over 20 years we at Work/Family Directions have asked employees in all industries what it would take for them to contribute more at work. Every study found the same thing: They need aid with their dependent care, more flexibility and control over the hours and conditions of work, and a corporate culture in which they are not punished because they have families. These are fundamental needs of our society and of every worker.* (Galinsky et al. 1993, 51)

Consideration Corporate adoption of a work-family ethic also benefits the larger community. Corporations that are sensitive to the family responsibilities and needs of employees often make contributions to community agencies that serve families. For example, the Mutual of New York Life Insurance Company funds community day care programs, training programs for day care employees, and child care for teenage mothers so they can continue school or receive job training (Stekas 1993). The Communications Workers of America and the International Brotherhood of Electrical Workers have a Dependent Care Development Fund designed to improve the dependent care programs in the communities where employees live and work (Green 1993).

MORE OPTIONS IN WORK SCHEDULES

Increasingly, workers are gaining greater flexibility in their work schedules. These options, which benefit child-free workers as well as employed parents, include flextime, job sharing, and a reduced workweek. **Flextime** allows the employee to begin and end the workday at different times as long as forty hours per week are maintained. For example, workers may begin at six A.M. and leave at two instead of the traditional nine to five.

With **job sharing,** two people, often husband and wife, share and are paid for one job. U.S. Representative John Conyers has suggested a *reduced workweek* of thirty-two hours instead of forty with the same amount of pay. Conyers argues that a reduced workweek would reduce the unemployment rate and the cost of unemployment benefits. Workers would be healthier, happier, and more productive, and fewer public assistance benefits would have to be paid. Working fewer hours would also allow parents to spend more time at home with their children. Such a trend would likely be associated with increased job satisfaction.

Consideration Although flexible schedules, family leave policies, and employer-funded child care are popular buzzwords that large corporations like to say they offer, these benefits cost money. Rather than provide any of these, corporations can and do save money by hiring part-time workers at lower wages with no benefits. Workers who let their family responsibilities interfere with their job are let go. Corporations also farm out various

National Data: Fifteen percent of U.S. workers with daytime jobs report having flexible schedules.

SOURCE: *Statistical Abstract of the United States: 1995,* Table 647.

National Data: In a 1995 Gallup Poll, women and men were asked if they have enough time or too little time to spend with their spouse and children. Almost half (47 percent) said they had "too little" time to spend with spouse; over half (54 percent) said they had "too little" time to spend with children.

SOURCE: Saad 1995.

tasks, such as desktop publishing, copyediting, and janitorial service, to temporary workers. The result is a corporate structure in which fewer long-term full-time workers receive company benefits and more people are relegated to jobs in the secondary labor market.

WELFARE CORPORATISM

Welfare corporatism is a broad term that refers to varying levels of employee involvement in planning and production. An example is the **quality circle,** which involves meetings of workers and managers who are responsible for production to discuss performance problems and ways to improve morale. Quality circles are similar to "group production," which also involves collaborative work groups. Such circles and groups are used extensively in Japanese organizations. The goal of welfare corporatism is to develop and maintain a common company ideology and to "enhance the commitment and involvement of the employees" (Besser 1994, 873). The company benefits from welfare corporatism through lower absenteeism, fewer turnovers, and higher worker productivity. Employees benefit from a decreased sense of alienation and greater job satisfaction.

EMPLOYEE STOCK OWNERSHIP PLANS

Stock ownership plans allow workers to develop ownership in the company they work for. There are basically three types of plans (Tucker, Nock, and Toscano 1989): (1) In *direct ownership plans*, employees own shares in the company; the more they own, the greater their capacity to profit if the company is successful. (2) In *trust ownership plans*, stocks are transferred to employees as part of a benefit package over a period of time. The longer an employee stays with the company, the more lucrative the benefit package. (3) In *cooperative ownership-employee plans*, the employee not only owns stock in the company but has voting rights based on the proportion of shares he or she holds. Each of these plans may help to increase job satisfaction, decrease worker alienation, and enhance productivity.

UNDERSTANDING WORK

To understand the social problems associated with corporate power and the American worker, it is helpful to examine three aspects of the economy: what we produce, how we produce it, and who does the producing (Dolbeare 1986). In regard to what we produce, the United States is moving away from producing manufactured goods to producing services. In regard to production methods, the labor-intensive blue-collar assembly line is declining in importance, and information-intensive white-collar occupations are increasing. Finally, in regard to who is producing, the workforce is becoming better educated, more technically skilled and trained, and more diverse in terms of racial and ethnic background. Where unskilled labor can be used, production is shifting to developing countries.

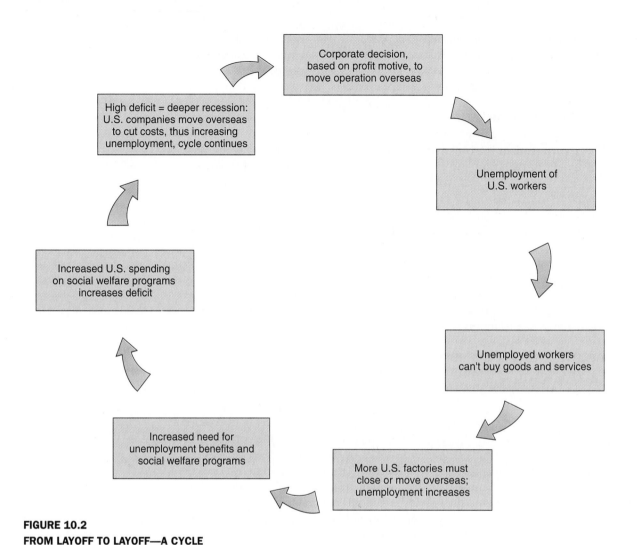

FIGURE 10.2
FROM LAYOFF TO LAYOFF—A CYCLE

Decisions made by U.S. corporations about what and where to invest influence the quantity and quality of jobs available in the United States. As conflict theorists argue, such investment decisions are motivated by profit, which is part of a capitalist system. Profit is also a driving factor in deciding how and when technological devices will be used to replace workers and increase productivity. But if goods and services are produced too efficiently, workers are laid off and high unemployment results. When people have no money to buy products, sales slump, a recession ensues, and social welfare programs are needed to support the unemployed. When the government increases spending to pay for its social programs, it expands the deficit and increases the national debt. Deficit spending and a large national debt make it difficult to recover from the recession, and the cycle continues (see Figure 10.2).

What can be done to break the cycle? Those adhering to the classic view of capitalism argue for limited government intervention on the premise that business will regulate itself via an "invisible hand" or "market forces." For example, if corporations produce a desired product at a low price people will buy it, which means workers will be hired to produce the product, and so on.

Ironically, those who support limited government intervention also sometimes advocate that the government intervene to bail out failed banks and lend money to troubled businesses like Chrysler. Such government help benefits the powerful segments of our society. Yet, when economic policies hurt less powerful groups, such as minorities, there has been a collective hesitance to support or provide social welfare programs. It is also ironic that such bailout programs, which contradict the ideals of capitalism, are needed *because* of capitalism. For example, the profit motive leads to multinationalization, which leads to unemployment, which leads to the need for government programs. The answers are as complex as the problems.

The various forces transforming the American economy are interrelated—technology, globalization, capital flight through multinationalization, and the movement toward a service economy (Eitzen and Zinn 1990). For the individual worker, the concepts of work, job, and career have changed forever:

> *Forget any idea of career-long employment with a big company. Even after downsizing . . . layoffs and early retirements stop, the corporate giants are not going to revert to hiring masses of long-term employees. They have discovered that it is more efficient and profitable to operate as contracting centers, buying goods and services from smaller companies rather than having them produced by their own employees, a process known as "outsourcing." The big corporation of the future will consist of a relatively small core of central employees and a mass of smaller firms working for it under contract. (Church 1993:37)*

As some people have stable jobs and careers and others do not, the gap between the "haves" and the "have-nots" will widen. In the next chapter, we look at the diversity of wealth and power in the United States as another social problem of inequality.

CRITICAL THINKING

1. How can employers minimize worker alienation?
2. Distinguish between discriminatory and structural unemployment and, using the sociological imagination, suggest how unemployment may be unrelated to an individual's qualifications.
3. Specify how solutions to unemployment may involve both less and more governmental involvement.
4. Explain how corporate concern for the "bottom line" may both hurt and help employees.

KEY TERMS

Industrial Revolution

postindustrialization

work sectors (primary, secondary, tertiary)

capitalism

socialism

convergence hypothesis

global economy

split labor market

alienation

discriminatory unemployment

structural unemployment

underemployment

automation

welfare corporatism

quality circle

flextime

job sharing

anomie

REFERENCES

Adams, Bob. 1993. "Class Ceiling." *Congressional Quarterly Researcher* 30(40): 937–60.

American Council on Education and University of California. 1994. *The American College Freshman: National Norms for Fall, 1994.* Los Angeles: Higher Education Research Institute.

Barlett, Donald L., and James B. Steele. 1992. *America: What Went Wrong?* Kansas City: Andrews & McMeel.

Bell, Daniel. 1973. *The Coming of Post-Industrial Society.* New York: Basic Books.

Besser, Terry. 1994. "The Commitment of Japanese Workers and U.S. Workers: A Reassessment of the Literature." *American Sociological Review* 58: 873–81.

Bracey, Gerald W. 1995. "The Fifth Bracey Report on the Condition of Public Education." *Phi Delta Kappan* (October), 149–162.

Brenner, Meyer H. 1978. "The Social Costs of Economic Distress." In *Consultation on the Social Impact of Economic Distress.* New York: American Jewish Committee, Institute of Human Relations.

Briggs, Barbara. 1993. "Aiding and Abetting Corporate Flight." *Multinational Monitor*, January/February.

Calavita, Kitty, and Henry N. Pontell. 1990. "Heads I Win, Tails You Lose": Deregulation, Crime, and Crisis in the Savings and Loan Industry." *Crime and Delinquency* 36: 309–41.

Caminiti, S. 1992. "Who's Minding America's Kids?" *Fortune,* August 10: 50–53.

Church, George. 1993. "Jobs in an Age of Insecurity." *Time,* November 22, 31–39.

Cockburn, Alexander. 1992. "Clinton, Labor, and Free Trade." *Nations,* November 2, 508–9.

Coleman, James. 1994. *The Criminal Elite: The Sociology of White Collar Crime,* 3d. ed. New York: St. Martin Press.

Congressional Budget Office. 1993. "The Economic and Budget Outlook: Fiscal Years 1994–1998." Report to the Senate and House Committees. January. Internet.

Cooper, Mary H. 1992. "Jobs in the '90s." *Congressional Quarterly Researcher* 2: 169–92.

Dolbeare, Kenneth M. 1986. *Democracy at Risk: The Politics of Economic Renewal,* rev. ed. Chatham, N.J.: Chatham House.

Durkheim, Emile. [1893] 1966. *On the Division of Labor in Society,* trans. G. Simpson. New York: Free Press.

Ehrenreich, Barbara, and Annette Fuentes. 1992. "Life on the Global Assembly Line." In *Sociology: Windows on Society,* 2d. ed., ed. John W. Heersen and Marylee Mason, pp. 166–71. Los Angeles: Roxbury Publishing Co.

Eitzen, Stanley, and Maxine Baca Zinn, eds. 1990. *The Reshaping of America: Social Consequences of the Changing Economy.* Englewood Cliffs, N.J.: Prentice-Hall.

Epstein, Gerald, Julie Graham, and Jessica Nembhard, eds. 1993. "Third World Socialism and the Demise of COMECON." In *Creating a New World Economy: Forces of Change and Plans of Action,* pp. 405–20. Philadelphia: Temple University Press.

Feather, Norman T. 1990. *The Psychological Impact of Unemployment.* New York: Springer-Verlag.

Galinsky, Ellen, James E. Riesbeck, Fran S. Rodgers, and Faith A. Wohl. 1993. "Business Economics and the Work-Family Response." In *Work-Family Needs: Leading Corporations Respond,* pp. 51–54. New York: The Conference Board.

Government Accounting Office. 1992. "Labor Issues." Transitions Series No. OCG-93-19TR. December. Internet.

Green, Michelle. 1993. "NYNEX's Dependent Care Development Fund." In *Work-Family Needs: Leading Corporations Respond,* pp. 45–46. New York: The Conference Board.

Greenwald, John. 1995. "The Battle to Revive U.S. Unions." *Time* 146(18) (Oct. 30). [http://www.pathfinder.com].

Hewlett, Sylvia Ann. 1992. *When the Bough Breaks: The Cost of Neglecting Our Children.* New York: HarperCollins.

Hodson, Randy, and Teresa A. Sullivan. 1990. *The Social Organization of Work.* Belmont, Calif.: Wadsworth.

Kellam, Susan. 1994. "Worker Retraining." *Congressional Quarterly Researcher* 4: 51–71.

Kenworthy, Lane. 1995. *In Search of National Economic Success.* Thousand Oaks, Calif.: Sage Publications.

Kidron, Michael, and Ronald Segal. 1991. *The New State of the World Atlas.* New York: Simon & Schuster.

Lenski, Gerard, and J. Lenski. 1987. *Human Societies: An Introduction to Macrosociology,* 5th ed. New York: McGraw-Hill.

Levinson, Marc. 1994. "Help Wanted Reluctantly." *Newsweek,* March 14, 36–37.

Levy, Barry S., and David H. Wegman. 1995. "Occupational Health in Global Context: An American Perspective." In *Occupational Health: Recognizing and Preventing Work-Related Disease,* ed. Barry S. Levy and David H. Wegman, pp. 3–24. Boston: Little, Brown.

Liem, Joan H., and G. Ramsey Liem. 1990. "Understanding the Individual and Family Effects of Unemployment." In *Stress Between Work and Family,* ed. J. Eckenrode and S. Gore, pp. 175–204. New York: Plenum Press.

Liskowsky, David R. 1992. "Biological Rhythms and Shift Work." *Journal of the American Medical Association* 268 (December 2): 3047.

Lopez, J. A. 1993. "Undivided Attention: How PepsiCo Gets Work Out of People." *Wall Street Journal,* April 1, 1.

McCammon, Holly. 1990. "Legal Limits on Labor Militancy: U.S. Labor Law and the Right to Strike since the New Deal." *Social Problems* 37(2): 206–29.

Mean, Walter R. 1992. "Outer Limits to America's Turn Inward." *New Progressive Quarterly* 9(3): 28–30.

Meyer-Larsen, Werner. 1991. "America's Century Will End with a Whimper." *World Press Review* (January): 24–29.

Moen, Phyllis. 1992. *Women's Two Roles: A Contemporary Dilemma.* New York: Auburn House.

Moore, David W., and Leslie McAneny. 1993. "Workers Concerned They Can't Afford to Retire." *Gallup Poll Monthly* May, 16–20.

Morris, Martina, Annette D. Bernhardt, and Mark S. Handcock. 1994. "Economic Inequality: New Methods for New Trends." *American Sociological Review* 59 (April): 205–19.

OECD. 1994. *OECD Societies in Transition: The Future of Work and Leisure.* Paris, France: Organisation for Economic Cooperation and Development.

Reich, Robert. 1991. *The Work of Nations: Preparing Ourselves for 21st Century Capitalism.* New York: Knopf.

Rohatyn, Felix. 1988. "Restoring American Independence." *New York Review of Books* 18 (February): 8–10.

Russo, David F. 1993. "Do You Employ Women? How about Common Sense?" In *Work-Family Needs: Redefining the Business Case,* pp. 23–24. New York: The Conference Board.

Saad, Lydia. 1995. "Children, Hard Work Taking Their Toll on Baby Boomers." *The Gallup Organization Newsletter Archive* (April): Vol. 59, No. 47.

Samuelson, Robert J. 1994. "It Could Last until 2000." *Newsweek,* December 26, 120.

Shanker, Albert. 1992. "How Far Have We Come?" *New York Times,* August 16, E9.

Siegel, Richard Lewis. 1994. *Employment and Human Rights: The International Dimension.* Philadelphia: University of Pennsylvania Press.

Statistical Abstract of the United States: 1995, 115th ed. U.S. Bureau of the Census. Washington, D.C.: U.S. Government Printing Office.

Stein, Herbert. 1992. "America's Economy Is Strong." In *Taking Sides,* pp. 17–23. San Diego, Calif.: Greenhaven Press.

Stekas, Lynn. 1993. "Corporate Contributions." In *Work-Family Needs: Leading Corporations Respond,* pp. 43–44. New York: The Conference Board.

Straus, Murray A. 1980. "A Sociological Perspective on the Prevention of Wife-beating." *The Social Causes of Husband-Wife Violence,* ed. M. A. Straus and G. T. Hotaling, pp. 211–32. Minneapolis: University of Minnesota Press.

Thurow, Lester. 1993. "American Mirage: A Post-Industrial Economy?" In *Systemic Crisis,* ed. William D. Perdue, pp. 97–101. Fort Worth: Harcourt.

Time. 1994. "Gripe, Gripe, Gripe." April 25, 25.

Toufexis, Anastasia. 1994. "Workers Who Fight Fire with Fire." *Time,* April 25, 35–37.

Tucker, James, Steven L. Nock, and David J. Toscano. 1989. "Employee Ownership and Perceptions of Work." *Work and Occupations* 16: 26–42.

U.S. Bureau of Census. 1995. "Top Ten Countries with which the United States has a Trade Deficit." (August). [http://www.census.gov./ftp/pub/foreign-trade].

Vonnegut, Kurt, Jr. 1968. *Welcome to the Monkey House: A Collection of Short Works.* New York: Delacorte Press/S. Lawrence, pp. 7–14.

Western, Bruce. 1995. "A Comparative Study of Working Class Disorganization: Union Decline in Eighteen Advanced Capitalist Countries." *American Sociological Review* 60: 179–201.

White, Lynn, and Bruce Keith. 1990. "The Effect of Shift Work on the Quality and Stability of Marital Relations." *Journal of Marriage and the Family* 52: 453–62.

CHAPTER

11

Wealth and Poverty

IS IT TRUE?

The United States has the lowest poverty rate of all industrialized nations (p. 313).

In a 1993 survey of U.S. adults, most said that the government spent too much on public assistance (p. 325).

More than 20 percent of the world's population live in poverty (p. 313).

The United States contributes more per capita economic aid to developing countries than does any other industrialized country (p. 334).

In 1995, a full-time minimum wage job fell 30 percent short of keeping a family of three above the poverty line (p. 338).

ANS: 1. F 2. F 3. T 4. F 5. T

U nemployment, homelessness, and poverty are themes that permeate the media. As companies downsize, individuals lose their jobs, their homes, and their ability to pay for adequate medical care. A feeling of despair blankets American society. But news reports also focus on affluent politicians at black-tie dinners and corporate executives with multimillion dollar salaries. The inequities are obvious and have led to heightened public resentment. As F. Scott Fitzgerald (1926) wrote in *All the Sad Young Men:*

Poverty blights whole cities; spreads horrible pestilence; strikes at the soul of all those who come within sight, sound or smell of it.
—George Bernard Shaw
Irish dramatist

Let me tell you about the rich. They are different than you and me. They possess and enjoy early, and it does something to them, makes them soft where we are hard, and cynical where we are trustful, in a way that, unless you were born rich, it is difficult to understand. They think, deep down in their hearts, that they are better than we are because we had to discover the compensations and refuges of life for ourselves. Even when they enter into our world or sink below us, they still think they are better than we are. They are different. (pp. 1–2)

This chapter examines the social problems associated with economic inequities. After discussing the extent of inequality and the stratification system associated with it, various theories, individual and societal costs, and possible solutions for the problems created are explored. We begin by focusing on the social context of inequality.

The Social Context: The Haves and the Have-Nots

There are great disparities in the way people live. This is true not only in the United States but around the world.

INEQUALITY IN THE UNITED STATES AND AROUND THE WORLD

News reports often focus on affluent politicians at black tie dinners and corporate executives with multi-million dollar salaries; all this as companies downsize and individuals lose their jobs. The inequities have led to heightened public resentment.

The United States is a nation of tremendous economic variation ranging from the very rich to the very poor. Signs of this disparity are visible everywhere, from opulent mansions perched high above the ocean in California to shantytowns in the rural South where people live with no running water or electricity. We are a society that speaks of "the homeless and the hungry, the truly disadvantaged, the underclass, [and] the permanently poor . . ." (Devine and Wright, 1993, xv), yet we have the highest production of goods and services per man, woman, and child in the world. Despite political slogans about easing "the economic burdens of American citizens," inequality in the United States began to escalate during the 1980s after decades of little change or decline (Morris, Bernhardt, and Handcock 1994) and continues to escalate today.

Of the wealthier industrialized nations, the United States has one of the largest income differentials. For example, the highest paid 10 percent of workers in the United States earn 5.6 times as much as the lowest 10 percent of the workers. In contrast, in England, the highest 10 percent make only 3.4 times as much as the lowest 10 percent. Sweden and the Netherlands have the lowest wage differences (*The Economist* 1993).

Compared to other industrialized countries, the United States also has one of the highest rates of poverty. One reason is the U.S. unemployment rate, which, though lower than the rate in most industrialized countries, is still higher than in some nations. In 1960–1990, the average U.S. unemployment rate was 6.0. In the same time period, the unemployment rates for Germany, Austria, Sweden, Norway, New Zealand, and Japan were 3.4, 2.3, 2, 2, 1.9, and 1.8, respectively (Kenworthy 1995). Additionally, when compared to other industrialized nations, the United States has very few government-provided benefits such as nationalized health care and child care.

> **International Data:**
> According to a 1990 United Nations' Human Development Report, more than 1 billion people worldwide, over 20 percent of the world's population, live in poverty.
> SOURCE: Perdue 1993.

SOCIAL STRATIFICATION

Every society ranks its members in a system of **social stratification,** a system which divides people into categories based on their access to resources, opportunities, power, and prestige. Sociologists describe social stratification systems that allow little change in social position as "closed" systems. In a closed system, individuals are born into a social position and remain in that position over a lifetime. In India, for instance, individuals are confined to the social position into which they are born with little opportunity for social mobility based on individual achievements. Closed systems also discourage individuals from marrying outside their position. Sociologists describe stratification systems that permit considerable **social mobility,** or change in people's position, as "open" systems. Open stratification systems allow individuals to move from one social position to another. In the United States, for example, individuals may change their social position through achievement, marriage, or inheritance. The United States purports to be an open system where anyone can achieve the "American dream." In reality, many Americans are restricted by limited opportunity and discrimination.

THE COMPONENTS OF INEQUALITY

Inequality has three major components: wealth, prestige, and power. Wealth is the sum of an individual's material resources including but not limited to income, land, real estate, trusts, stocks, and bonds—the total assets of an individual or family. Prestige is the social esteem or respect an individual commands because of specific attributes, personal qualities, or achievements. In the United States, prestige tends to be associated primarily with one's occupation. This chapter's *Self and Society* allows you to rank various occupations on the basis of prestige and compare your responses with a national sample of U.S. adults.

Power is the ability of an individual to achieve desired goals despite resistance from others. Although Marx argued that power is based in economics, Weber believed that there are many other sources of power, particularly the

Occupational Prestige Rankings

Directions: Rank order the following twenty occupations based on how much prestige you associate with each occupation. Assign the number "1" to the occupation that you think has the highest prestige; assign "2" to the occupation with the next highest prestige, and so on. The least prestigious occupation will be ranked number "20." Then compare your rankings with the results of a national survey of U.S. adults.

Occupation	Rank Order	Occupation	Rank Order
1. Librarian	___	11. Janitor	___
2. Bulldozer Operator	___	12. Carpenter	___
3. Secretary	___	13. Garbage collector	___
4. College/university professor	___	14. Bank teller	___
5. Farmer	___	15. Physician	___
6. Registered nurse	___	16. Computer programmer	___
7. Social worker	___	17. Hairdresser	___
8. Bartender	___	18. Elementary school teacher	___
9. Mail carrier	___	19. Clergy	___
10. Lawyer	___	20. Police officer	___

U.S. Sample Results (Occupation Followed by Rank): 1 = 9, 2 = 17, 3 = 12, 4 = 3, 5 = 14, 6 = 5, 7 = 10, 8 = 19, 9 = 11, 10 = 2, 11 = 20, 12 = 15, 13 = 18, 14 = 13, 15 = 1, 16 = 7, 17 = 16, 18 = 6, 19 = 4, and 20 = 8.

SOURCE: Adapted from *General Social Surveys 1972–1993: Cumulative Codebook.* 1993. Chicago: National Opinion Research Center, pp. 937–45. Used by permission.

> *Wealth . . . means power, it means leisure, it means liberty.*
> —James Russell Lowell
> American poet

power of those who run bureaucracies. To Max Weber, power, like prestige, is an independent dimension of stratification. He believed that one can be powerful independent of one's economic position and that Marx's analysis with its emphasis on wealth was too limited.

Social status is a combination of the three elements of wealth, prestige, and power. Indeed, all three are frequently correlated as in the case of a physician who is wealthy, enjoys high prestige, and, because of his or her position, also wields a great deal of power. Most would agree that physicians have higher social status than janitors who are low on the dimensions of wealth, prestige, and power. However, it is a mistake to assume that the three characteristics always occur together. University professors, for example, have high prestige, but relatively low power and wealth.

> **Consideration** In the United States, it is assumed that one's social status is achieved rather than ascribed. Therefore, if someone scores low on any of the three stratification dimensions, there is a tendency to regard the individual, rather than the system, as a failure. For example, a person who is a janitor and hence has low income, prestige, and power is assumed to lack motivation. Alternative explanations such as the failure of the schools to teach fundamental skills are less often considered.

The term **social class** refers to groups of people who share a similar position or social status within the stratification system. The most important objective dimension of social class is wealth since it is closely tied to power and prestige. We commonly speak of the lower class, the middle class (which most Americans define themselves as), and the upper class. In this chapter, the primary concern is economic polarization: the division of society into the two most extreme classes—the very rich and the very poor.

LIFE CHANCES AND LIFESTYLES

Individual position in the stratification system determines what Weber calls **life chances,** or the opportunity to obtain all that is valued in society including happiness, health, income, and education (Weber in Gerth and Mills 1958). For example, the higher one's position in the stratification system, the lower one's chances of becoming divorced, being arrested, or dying in a war, and the higher one's chances of going to college and securing employment.

The term **lifestyle** refers to a distinct subculture associated with a particular social class. Each subculture has its own beliefs, aspirations, and preferences. For example, the upper-middle-class car, alcoholic beverage and leisure pursuit of the 1990s are, respectively, the Range Rover, Cristal, and playing with computers; for the lower middle class, a Geo, domestic lite beer, and sports (Labich 1994). The affluent also vary by such characteristics as race and ethnicity, gender, age, and region of the country. This chapter's *In Focus* answers the question, "Who are the affluent?"

> *The accumulation of material goods is at an all-time high, but so is the number of people who feel an emptiness in their lives.*
> —Al Gore
> U.S. Vice President

Theories of Stratification

Stratification is a cultural universal. The two macro-level sociological theories, structural-functionalism and conflict theory, help to explain why all societies are stratified.

STRUCTURAL-FUNCTIONALISM

Structural-functionalists argue, as put forth decades ago by Davis and Moore (1945), that the distribution of resources in society is a consequence of different individual abilities. For society to function, certain tasks must be accomplished. For example, someone must care for children, others must build roads, and still others must be trained to heal the sick. Each task requires different levels of expertise and knowledge, and a differential reward system helps to assure that the person who performs a particular role is the most qualified. As people acquire certain levels of expertise (e.g., B.A., M.A., Ph.D., M.D.), they are progressively rewarded. Such a system, argued Davis and Moore, motivates people to achieve by offering higher rewards for higher achievements. If physicians were not offered high salaries, for example, who would want to endure the arduous years of medical training and long, stressful hours at a hospital? Functionalists suggest that offering differential rewards for different occupational roles is both functional and necessary for society's survival.

Who Are the Affluent?

The term *affluence* typically refers to those with considerably higher than average incomes. The affluent might begin with those having household incomes of $50,000 or more, while the moderately affluent would include those with household incomes between $75,000 and $100,000. Many Americans, though, regard only those with household incomes over $100,000 as the truly affluent. In general, affluence varies by race and ethnicity, gender, age, and region.

1. *Race and ethnicity.* As a group, non-Hispanic whites are more affluent than nonwhites. The percentage of white, black, and Hispanic households with incomes of $75,000 and over in 1993 were 13.4, 5.2, and 5.4 percent respectively (*Statistical Abstract of the United States: 1995*, Table 729). In the same year, however, 19.5 percent of Asian-American households had incomes of $75,000 and over. Almost forty percent of Asian-headed households had incomes of $50,000 or more, compared to only 30 percent of white households (Table 729). As noted in Chapter 9, the higher incomes of Asian-American households are the result of several factors: Asian-Americans are concentrated in California, Hawaii, and New York—states with higher incomes and higher costs of living than the national average. As a group, Asian-Americans tend to be highly educated and work more hours than whites. They also have more workers per family.

2. *Gender.* Men have higher incomes than women. The 1993 median incomes of civilian men and women employed full-time were $31,077 and $22,469, respectively (*Statistical Abstract of the United States: 1995*, Table 739). When incomes of $75,000 a year or more are examined, 5.2 percent of men but only 0.9 percent of women can be considered "affluent" (*Statistical Abstract of the United States: 1995*, Table 740). As discussed in Chapter 8, income differences between women and men result from occupational segregation, discrimination, a lower percentage of women in full-time jobs, and fewer advanced educational and professional degrees among women.

3. *Age.* Persons between the ages of forty-five and fifty-four earn the highest median annual incomes (*Statistical Abstract of the United States: 1995*, Table 740). The age group with the lowest median income includes individuals between the ages of fifteen and twenty-four. The age group with the next lowest income consists of the elderly—individuals aged sixty-five and older. Although older people have lower annual incomes, they generally have higher net worth (U.S. Census Bureau 1994a).

4. *Region.* Waldrop and Jacobsen (1992) observed that the affluent tend to cluster in certain geographic regions, including the northeast from Portland, Maine, down to Alexandria, Virginia. "Of the 20 counties with the highest concentration of households earning $50,000 or more, 15 are in the northeastern megalopolis" (p. 29). One of the most affluent counties is Westchester County, New York, where 18 percent of the households have annual incomes of $100,000 or more. Nationwide, only 4 percent of households earn $100,000 or more annually.

SOURCES: *Statistical Abstract of the United States: 1995*, 115th ed. U.S. Bureau of the Census. (Washington, D.C.: U.S. Government Printing Office); Judith Waldrop and Linda Jacobsen. 1992. "American Affluence" *American Demographics* (December): 29–42.

The functionalist perspective seems to accept poverty as a necessary evil. Do you agree?

Functionalists also hold that society is characterized by social mobility. Vertical mobility occurs when one's position changes in the stratification system, as when a laborer becomes a supervisor. Horizontal mobility entails movement within a given stratum, as when a cab driver becomes a bus driver. An open stratification system with considerable mobility is the most functional for society, but it also leads to tremendous inequities.

Although such inequities are dysfunctional in many ways, the stratification system in general and poverty in particular serve a number of positive functions. People are motivated to work harder to achieve success, and those who are unable to succeed are limited to undesirable jobs that no one would otherwise want to perform. Other functions include creating a "poverty infrastructure" by providing employment for such people as welfare workers and supplying a market for inferior goods such as older homes and automobiles (Gans 1972).

Critics of structural-functionalism argue that a successful society can be achieved without limiting the success of individuals. Lack of individual achievement may reflect the scarcity of top positions in society rather than a lack of individual ability. Further, many people who provide important tasks, such as child care workers, are not adequately rewarded, while others, such as sports figures and rock stars, are overcompensated. Functionalism also appears to accept poverty as a necessary evil and ignores the role of inheritance in the distribution of rewards.

We talk about the American Dream, and want to tell the world about the American Dream, but what is that dream, in most cases, but the dream of material things? I sometimes think that the United States for this reason, is the greatest failure the world has ever seen.
—Eugene O'Neill
Playwright

CONFLICT THEORY

Conflict theorists regard inequality in society as a consequence of the continuous struggle between the bourgeoisie (owners of the means of production) and the proletariat (workers). Inequality is dependent upon an individual's relation to the means of production, that is, whether he or she is an owner or a worker. As a result of this relationship, over time, the bourgeoisie become dominant over the proletariat through the private accumulation of wealth. As wealth is transferred from one generation to the next, opportunity for others is limited, as is upward social mobility in the stratification system. Thus, from a conflict perspective, social status is ascribed rather than achieved.

Conflict theorists also note that in the political arena, laws and policies are adopted that favor the wealthy. Sometimes this is called the **wealthfare system.** Such laws include the U.S. tax structure, which permits deductions for such things as charitable contributions, stock market losses, and income earned abroad. Similarly, low-interest government loans to failing businesses, import taxes that increase the price of foreign-made goods thereby making American-made products competitive, and government spending policies are all part of the wealthfare system.

In addition, the educational institution furthers the ideals of capitalism by perpetuating the belief in equal opportunity, the "American Dream," and the value of the work ethic. The proletariat, dependent on the capitalistic system, continue to be exploited by the wealthy and accept the belief that poverty is a consequence of personal failure rather than a flawed economic structure.

Poverty in America

Many Americans associate the word *poverty* with media images of starving children in less developed countries. But impoverished women, men, children, and elderly individuals can be found across America—in our inner cities, schools, homeless shelters, and isolated pockets in rural areas. Although poverty is not as widespread or severe in America as it is in many less developed countries, it nevertheless represents a significant social problem.

DEFINITIONS AND MEASUREMENT OF POVERTY

Sociologists distinguish between two types of poverty: absolute and relative. **Absolute poverty** refers to the chronic absence of the basic necessities of life including food, clothing, and shelter. **Relative poverty** refers to not being able to live up to the standard of living considered normal to members of society. Both definitions are problematic, however. For example, how much food is enough food? Can a cardboard box under an overpass be considered a shelter? Alternatively, since most people feel poor when compared to someone else, how relatively deprived does one need to be to be considered "poor"?

In an effort to measure poverty objectively, the Social Security Administration establishes a federal **poverty line,** an annual dollar amount below which individuals or families are considered officially poor. The specific amount is calculated by estimating how much money is needed to provide a nutritionally adequate diet, and then multiplying that number by three based on the assumption that Americans spend one-third of their income on food. The number of persons in the household also affects the level of poverty identified for that family (see Table 11.1).

The use of an official poverty line has been criticized on several grounds. First, the poverty index is based solely on money income and does not take into consideration noncash benefits received by many low-income persons, such as food stamps, Medicaid, and public housing. The poverty index also

TABLE 11.1

POVERTY LINE BY SIZE OF FAMILY, 1993

SIZE OF UNIT	OFFICIAL POVERTY LEVEL
1 person	$ 7,363
Under 65 years	7,518
65 years and over	6,930
2 persons	9,414
Householder under 65	9,728
Householder 65 years and older	8,740
3 persons	11,522
4 persons	14,763
5 persons	17,499
6 persons	19,718
7 persons	22,383
8 persons	24,838
9 or more persons	29,529

SOURCE: *Statistical Abstract of the United States: 1995*, 115th ed. U. S. Bureau of the Census (Washington, D. C.: U. S. Government Printing Office), Table 739.

disregards regional differences in the cost of living and uses inadequate baseline figures on nutritional data (Devine and Wright 1993, 13).

DEMOGRAPHIC VARIATIONS

The poor are a diverse group. Table 11.2 provides a demographic profile of individuals living below the poverty line in terms of race, age, education, and family structure and size.

As Table 11.2 indicates, women and minorities are disproportionately poor. In 1994, nearly 35 percent of all female-headed households were below the poverty level (U.S. Census Bureau 1995b). Minority women are three times as likely as white women to be poor. The growing trend for women to be poorer than men is called the **feminization of poverty.** Explanations for the feminization of poverty include lower paying jobs and educational levels of women, care of dependent children, longer life expectancy (and thus the higher number of elderly women who are poor compared to elderly men), the increase in divorce and the number of unmarried births and teenage pregnancy, and a reduction in welfare payments (Gimenez 1990). Several factors contribute to the lower incomes of minority households: high unemployment, low levels of educational achievement, and limited career options due to individual and institutional discrimination.

Children are also overrepresented among the poor. More than 20 percent of the poor in the United States are under age sixteen. Although the number of poor children is growing, the assistance they are receiving is not. Cutbacks under the Reagan administration reduced the amount of support for poor children. Today only about 50 percent of poor children receive any welfare bene-

Poverty is the open mouthed relentless hell which yawns beneath civilized society. And it is hell enough.
—Henry George
Economist

TABLE 11.2

DEMOGRAPHICS OF INDIVIDUALS AND FAMILIES BELOW THE POVERTY LINE, 1994

INDIVIDUALS	PERCENTAGE OF INDIVIDUALS BELOW POVERTY LINE
	Total: 14.5%
Race/ethnicity:	
Black	30.6%
Hispanic	30.7
White (not of Hispanic origin)	9.4
Age in years:	
Under 18	21.8
18–24	18.0
25–44	11.9
45–54	7.8
55–59	10.4
60–64	11.4
65 and older	11.7

FAMILIES	PERCENTAGE OF FAMILIES BELOW POVERTY LINE
	Total: 11.6%
Family structure:	
Female householder (no husband present)	34.6%
Married couples	6.1

SOURCE: U.S. Census Bureau 1995b.

fits compared to nearly 80 percent in 1970 (DeParle 1992). Ironically, not only has the number of poor children grown, but the number of rich children has also grown as well, increasing the economic polarization between the classes (Lichter and Eggebeen 1993).

The U.S. poverty rate also varies according to geographic region. The poverty rate is higher in small towns and rural areas than in urban areas, 16 and 13 percent, respectively (Devine and Wright 1993, 71). The South has a higher rate of poverty than the West, Midwest, and Northeast. High unemployment, fewer job opportunities, and lower wages account for some of the differences. Because the rural poor live in remote places and are less visible than other poor individuals, they are often called the "forgotten poor." Who are the rural poor? Smith (1991) describes them as follows:

[They are] farmhands, who never had any land to mortgage. They are also coal miners, sawmill cutters, foundry men, and Jacks of whatever trades

FIGURE 11.1

PERCENTAGE BELOW THE POVERTY LINE BY STATE, 1993

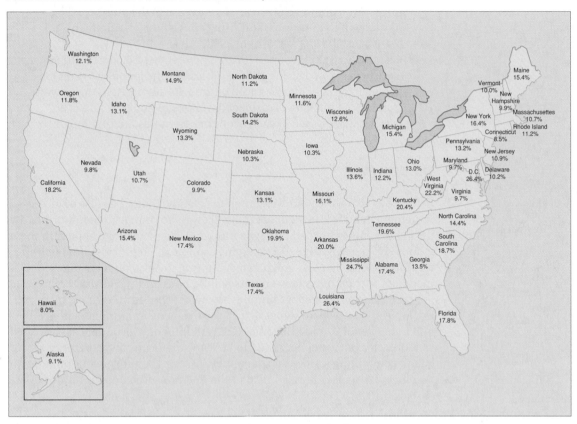

SOURCE: *Statistical Abstract of the United States: 1995*, 115th ed. U. S. Bureau of the Census (Washington, D. C.: U. S. Government Printing Office), Table 749.

are hiring. Or Janes. Women make up 45% of the rural work force. A "go-getter" in many places refers not to a striver but to a fellow who picks up his wife after her shift. (p. 210).

Figure 11.1 shows where the poor live in the United States. As this map indicates, Mississippi, Louisiana, West Virginia, and the District of Columbia have the highest percentages of persons below the poverty line.

VARIATIONS BY EMPLOYMENT STATUS

The typical image of a poor person is someone who is unemployed. But many employed people also live under the poverty line.

1. *Working poor.* In 1990, about 60 percent of the poor were employed or living with someone who was employed at least part of the year.

Hence, a majority of the poor are not poor because they do not work or do not want to work, but because of such structural economic forces as declining relative pay, an increase in the number of low-paying or part-time jobs, and rising educational requirements for many jobs (Devine and Wright 1993).

2. *Unemployed.* Of the poor who are unemployed, 50 percent do not work because of age, disabilities, illness, or the inability to find employment after being displaced or fired. As discussed in the previous chapter, the inability of displaced workers to find new jobs is, in part, a consequence of such economic trends as multinationalization (see Chapter 10).

THE NEW POOR

In previous years, the poor were often the elderly. Today, because of increased retirement benefits, the poor are more likely to be young, often minorities living in households headed by single mothers. The percentage of poor in these groups has increased due to a changing economy that provides little opportunity for the unskilled and uneducated. Many of the new poor are referred to as members of the **underclass**—a persistantly poor and socially disadvantaged group. The term "underclass" implies several attributes and behaviors, including joblessness, welfare dependency, involvement in criminal activity, dysfunctional families, and low educational attainment. The underclass are often stereotyped as being constrained to African-Americans living in inner city or ghetto communities. However, the underclass are a heterogeneous population that includes poor whites living in urban and non-urban communities (Alex-Assensoh 1995).

Theories of Poverty

Two theoretical frameworks dominate explanations of poverty: structural explanations of poverty and cultural explanations of poverty.

STRUCTURAL EXPLANATIONS OF POVERTY

Structuralists emphasize that the source of poverty is in the structure of society rather than in individual failure. First, due to changes in the labor market and, specifically, the development of a split labor market, fewer and fewer high-paying jobs are being created for the uneducated and/or unskilled.

Second, such macro-level economic trends as multinationalization, automation, and a relative loss of manufacturing jobs have increased unemployment. Further, the jobs that are available pay proportionately less due to inflation and offer less job security than in previous years (see Chapter 10).

Third, structural changes in the family contribute to poverty. Single-headed households and households headed by females are increasing. Since single-headed households have only one wage earner, and women make less money than men, poverty is increasing. Finally, from a conflict perspective, those who have wealth and power want to maintain their advantage. Hence, structural changes, or the lack thereof, are designed to maintain the status quo. For example, the relatively low benefits paid to those on welfare help to keep production costs down and corporate profits high by assuring that a surplus labor force willing to work for minimum wages is always available.

CULTURAL EXPLANATIONS OF POVERTY

Lewis (1966) argues that, over time, the poor develop norms, values, and beliefs that contribute to their own plight. According to Lewis, the *culture of poverty* is characterized by female-centered households, the belief in instant rather than deferred gratification, and a relative lack of participation in society's major institutions. Early sexual experimentation, early marriage, and unmarried parenthood are also normative. Certain groups, according to this view, remain poor over time as the culture of poverty is transmitted from one generation to the next.

In support of the cultural explanation of poverty, Banfield (1992) states that "[T]he lower-class forms of all problems are, at bottom, a single problem: the existence of an outlook and style of life which is radically present-oriented and which therefore attaches no value to work, sacrifice, self-improvement, or service to family, friends, or community" (p. 150). Critics of the culture of poverty approach argue that it blames the victim rather than the structure of society for poverty, justifies the status quo, and perpetuates inequality (Ryan 1992).

Furthermore, researchers disagree as to why the poor believe and act as they do. In contrast to the view that the norms and values of the poor cause their poverty, Valentine (1968) suggests that living in poverty itself creates a set of norms and values. The cultural differences that exist between the poor and the nonpoor are a means of coping with the deprivations suffered by the poor. Thus, dropping out of school may be a rational response to school failure and the belief that success in school is unrelated to success in life. Another view suggests that the poor do have mainstream traditional values but, finding them unattainable, "stretch" them to include additional values in order to minimize the frustrations of failure (Rodman 1963).

Consequences of Poverty

Poverty has enormous negative consequences. They may be divided into those experienced by the individual and those experienced by society.

INDIVIDUAL CONSEQUENCES OF POVERTY

Poverty has a tremendous impact upon the individual. It affects health, hunger, education, housing, and crime and justice and also entails several social-psychological costs.

Health   The poor are less healthy in almost every way. They are less likely to see a doctor despite higher morbidity rates, have a shorter life expectancy, and, because of hazardous working conditions, are more likely to be the victim of an accident at work. The poor also have higher infant mortality rates. Although the United States spends more money on health care than any other industrialized nation in the world (see Chapter 2), a black baby born in an inner city

Poverty is a great enemy of human happiness; it certainly destroys liberty and it makes some virtues impracticable, and others extremely difficult.
—Samuel Johnson
English essayist and poet

The poor spend a higher proportion of their income on food than those above the poverty line. They often lack transportation, which means that they may pay more because they have to shop in ghetto grocery stores where prices are often higher.

neighborhood in Boston has less chance of surviving the first year of life than an infant born in Uruguay or Panama (Phillips 1991).

Hunger Millions of poor children go hungry each day. Yet the elderly are even more likely to be malnourished. A 1993 report by the Urban Institute estimates that as many as 50 percent of the elderly living in inner city neighborhoods go hungry and/or must choose between food and paying rent (Lee 1993).

The poor spend a higher proportion of their income on food than those above the poverty line. In 1990, those with the lowest 20 percent of household incomes before taxes spent about 43 percent of their income on food while the highest 20 percent spent about 9 percent of their income on food (*Statistical Abstract of the United States: 1993*, Table 692). Furthermore, the poor pay more per food item because they often lack transportation and thus must shop in small local grocery stores where prices are usually higher.

Crime and Justice The poor are more likely to be arrested, convicted, and imprisoned for criminal offenses. Sociologists debate whether the poor are actually more likely to commit a crime or simply more likely to be processed by the criminal justice system. Nevertheless, research suggests that severe poverty is positively associated with lethal-violence rates among both blacks and whites (Huff-Corzine, Corzine, and Moore 1991). Other research, however, suggests that income inequality is a better predictor of white violent crime than black violent crime (Harer and Steffensmeier 1992). The poor are also more likely to be the target of violent crime, particularly young, African-American males who are disproportionately homicide victims (see Chapter 4).

Housing The poor are more likely to live in inner city neighborhoods where the houses are old, crowded, dangerous, and owned by an absentee landlord. According to estimates, more than 25 percent of Americans live in substandard housing, many without heat or proper plumbing facilities (Sivard 1991, 48).

International Data:
Worldwide, 55 million children under the age of twelve suffer from hunger.
SOURCE: Sivard 1991, 448.

National Data: In 1990, those with the lowest 20 percent household income spent about 43 percent of their income on shelter; the highest 20 percent spent only about 13 percent of their income on shelter.
SOURCE: *Statistical Abstract of the United States: 1992*, 560.

The poor also pay a higher percentage of their income for shelter compared to the rich.

Education Because school districts are determined by residential patterns, the poor often attend inner city schools. These schools are characterized by lower-quality facilities, overcrowded classrooms, and a higher teacher turnover rate. Further, poor students are less likely to graduate from high school or go to college, creating a vicious cycle whereby subsequent generations remain poor over time (see Chapter 13).

Social-Psychological Consequences In a society that values success, the poor are defined as failures. Such definitions, as symbolic interactionists note, result in lower self-concepts and higher rates of depression, frustration, and despair. Many of these characteristics are a result of the poverty infrastructure, which requires the poor to verify their daily activities in order to receive public assistance. Regulations that require signatures for everything from school attendance to job interviews reinforce the notion that the poor cannot be trusted and, like children, need constant monitoring. As a result, many of the poor are docile and dependent, a psychological condition known as learned helplessness (Seligman 1967). Associated with this sense of helplessness are feelings of alienation because the poor have little control over their lives. One study of welfare recipients found that the longer individuals were on welfare, the more their sense of efficacy and optimism about the future declined (Popkin 1990). Not surprisingly, the poor also have higher rates of suicide, alcoholism, and mental illness.

Poverty demoralizes.
—Ralph Waldo Emerson
American poet and essayist

SOCIETAL CONSEQUENCES OF POVERTY

Poverty also has negative consequences for society. One of the most notable costs is the tremendous loss of human resources and potential contributions as generations of poor are denied access to society's institutions. Increasingly, however, public attention has focused on the economic cost of supporting the poor. **Public assistance** is a general term that refers to some form of economic support by the government to citizens who meet certain criteria.

No society can surely be flourishing and happy, of which the far greater part of the members are poor and miserable.
—Upton Sinclair
Author

> **Consideration** Despite recent antiwelfare sentiment, in a 1993 General Social Survey, 64.6 percent of adults said the government spent too little on public assistance while only 12.4 percent responded that it spent too much. These percentages have not changed significantly over the last ten years (NORC 1993).

HOMELESSNESS—PERSONAL DISASTER AND SOCIETAL EMBARRASSMENT

There have always been homeless people in the United States, but they were particularly numerous during the Industrial Revolution and the Great Depression of the 1930s. Other countries also experience homelessness; large cities in Japan, for example, have reported as many as 10,000 homeless. In the United States, homelessness has risen dramatically since the 1980s. The following *Human Side* conveys the hopelessness and despair of the more than 600,000 homeless in the United States (Mead 1993).

DIARY OF A HOMELESS MAN

John Coleman is a middle-class white male in New York City who wanted to know what it was like to be homeless. In the excerpt that follows, he describes his experiences.

Having changed out of my normal clothes in the Penn Station's men's room and stowed them in the locker, I was ready for the street. Or thought so.

Was I imagining it, or were people looking at me in a completely different way? I felt that men, especially the successful-looking ones in their forties and over, saw me and wondered. For the rest, I wasn't there. . . . .

At Seventh Avenue and 35th Street, I went into a coffee shop. The counterman looked me over carefully. When I ordered the breakfast special—99 cents—he told me I'd have to pay in advance. . . I did . . . but I noticed that the other customers were given checks, and paid only when they left.

. . . My wanderings were all aimless. There was no plan, no goal, no reason to be anywhere at any time. Only hours into this role, I felt a useless part of the city streets. . . . A weathered drifter told me about a hideaway down in the bowels of the station, where it was warm and quiet. I found my way there and lay down on some old newspapers to sleep.

How long did I sleep? It didn't seem long at all. I was awakened by a flashlight shining in my eyes, and a voice, not an unkind one, saying, "You can't sleep here. Sorry, but you have to go outside."

. . . I left and walked up to 47th Street, between Fifth and Madison Avenues, where I knew there was a warm grate in the sidewalk (I've been passing it every morning for over five years on my way to work). One man was asleep there already. But there was room for two, and he moved over.

. . . In Manhattan's earliest hours, you get the feeling that the manufacture and removal of garbage is the city's main industry. So far, I haven't been lucky or observant enough to rescue much of use from the mounds of trash waiting for the trucks and crews. The best find was a canvas bag that will fit nicely over my feet at night.

I'm slipping into a routine: Washing up at the station. Coffee on the street. Breakfast at Blimpie. A search for the *Times* in the trash baskets. And then a leisurely stretch of reading in the park.

. . . A man I squatted next to in a doorway on 29th Street said it all: "The onliest thing is to have a warm place to sleep. That having somebody care about you. That'd be even onlier."

. . . Watching people come and go at the Volvo tennis tournament at Madison Square Garden, I sensed how uncomfortable they were at the presence of the homeless. Easy to love in the abstract, not so easy to face the face.

It's no wonder the railway police are under orders to chase us out of sight.

Perhaps a saving factor is that we're not individuals. We're not people anybody knows. . . .

There was an ageless, shaggy woman in Bryant Park this morning who delivered one of the more interesting monologues I've heard. For a full ten minutes, with no interruption from me beyond an occasional, "Uh-huh," she analyzed society's ills without missing a beat.

. . . At 3:30 P.M., with more cold ahead, I sought out the Men's Shelter at 8 East 3rd Street. This is the principal entry point for men seeking the city's help. It provides meals for 1,300 or so people every day and beds for some few of those. . . .

I've seen plenty of drawings of London's workhouses and asylums in the times of Charles Dickens. Now I've seen the real thing, in the last years of the twentieth century in the world's greatest city.

The lobby and the adjacent "sitting room" were jammed with men standing, sitting, or stretched out in various positions on the floor. It was as lost a collection of souls as I could have imagined. Old and young, scarred and smooth, stinking and clean, crippled and hale, drunk and sober, ranting and still, parts of another world and parts of this one. The city promises to take in anyone who asks. Those rejected everywhere else find their way to East 3rd Street.

The air was heavy with the odors of Thunderbird wine, urine, sweat, and above all, nicotine and marijuana. Three or four Human Resources Administration police officers seemed to be keeping the violence down to tolerable levels, but barely so.

After a long delay, I got a meal ticket for dinner and was told to come back later for a lodging ticket. . . .

The shouting and the obscenities didn't stop once we had our food. Again and again we were told to finish and get out. Eating took perhaps six minutes, but those minutes removed any shred of dignity a man might have brought in with him from the street. . . .

I decided to ask a question anyway, about whether there would be a chance for me to go to Brooklyn once I got my lodging ticket. He turned on me and let me have the full force of his bullhorn: "Don't ask questions, I said. You're not nobody."

Long after the scheduled departure, the lines moved. We sped by school buses to the armory at Ft. Washington Avenue . . . . They marched us into showers (very welcome), gave us clean underwear, and sent us upstairs to comfortable cots arranged in long rows in a room as big as a football field.

There were 530 of us there for the night, and we were soon quiet. . . .

SOURCE: Excerpted from John R. Coleman. 1990. "Diary of a Homeless Man." In *Social Problems Today: Coping with the Challenges of a Changing Society*, ed. James M. Henslin. Englewood Cliffs, N.J.: Prentice-Hall, pp. 160–69. Used by permission.

Although sympathy for the homeless was high in the '80's, with the '90's it has faded into an attitude of blaming the homeless for their own situation.

National Data: In the 1960s and 1970s, a full-time minimum wage job kept a family of three above the poverty line. In 1995, a full-time minimum wage job fell 30 percent short of keeping a family of three above the poverty line. In 1995, the minimum wage would have needed to be $6.05 in order to keep a family of three (with one full-time employee) above the poverty line.

SOURCE: Quigley 1995.

Some argue that homelessness is caused by problems within the individual. The homeless are characterized by high rates of mental and physical illness; one-third are estimated to have psychiatric disorders and one-half substance abuse problems (Devine and Wright 1993). But, social forces are also responsible for homelessness: increased poverty, a shortage of affordable housing, the deindustrialization of urban areas (see Chapter 12) leaving unskilled workers with fewer job options, the erosion of public welfare benefits, increased unemployment, deinstitutionalization of the mentally ill, and recessionary periods. Homeless individuals also tend to have few family ties (Sosin 1992). Although the typical homeless person is an unmarried, middle-aged male of minority status (Rossi and Wright 1993), many women, children, and elderly individuals are also homeless.

Americans' sympathy for the homeless in the 1980s turned to hostility in the 1990s—a backlash reflecting changing opinions. While many Americans thought homelessness was caused by a housing shortage, more recently there has been a tendency to blame the victims for their own homelessness. These beliefs have become institutionalized as cities institute "get-tough" measures against the homeless: sleep-proof benches in San Francisco, citations to loiterers in Santa Monica, laws against panhandling in Madison, making it illegal to sleep on park benches in Atlanta, and ejecting the homeless from New York City shelters after ninety days. Donations to community shelters and soup kitchens have also declined in recent years.

Rectifying Inequality

In the United States, federal, state, and local governments, have devoted considerable attention and resources to antipoverty programs for the last fifty years. Here we describe some of these programs and proposals. Finally, we look at international responses to poverty.

MINIMUM WAGE INCREASE?

One strategy for improving the standard of living for low-income American families is to increase the minimum wage. In early 1995, President Clinton proposed an hourly minimum wage increase of 45 cents per year for two years. Under Clinton's proposal, the minimum wage would increase from $4.25 to $4.70 in 1995 and to $5.15 in 1996. However, Republicans strongly opposed Clinton's proposal because they believe that small businesses would suffer from increased wage costs and jobs would be eliminated. Some economists agree that increasing the minimum wage would mean higher unemployment for minorities, teenagers, and other workers at low-paying jobs; businesses would reduce wage costs by hiring fewer employees. Other economists suggest that wage increases could create new jobs. Card and Krueger (1995) collected data on the impact of wage increase on employment in various states and found that employment opportunities increased after a pay rise.

Many of todays antipoverty programs have their roots in Franklin D. Roosevelt's New Deal of the 1930s, which included Aid to Dependent Children (now AFDC), the Public Works Administration, the 1935 Social Security Act, and the Works Progress Administration. The central goal of the Roosevelt administration was to help the 25 percent of the population who were unemployed, many of whom were starving and homeless. Roosevelt's programs were largely successful in creating enough jobs and economic activity to bring the country out of the Great Depression.

In 1964 President Lyndon B. Johnson launched his "war on poverty," which created ten antipoverty programs for which Congress appropriated $800 million in 1965. Although the success of these programs is debated, Devine and Wright (1993) argue that they were very effective in reducing poverty. Ten years after the programs were implemented, the poverty rate was down by 50 percent. In the 1970s, however, recession and high unemployment took their toll; the poverty rate stopped dropping and stayed relatively unchanged until the early 1980s. With the election of conservative Ronald Reagan, federal poverty programs were cut and the poverty rate began to rise, reaching a fifteen-year high in 1983—as high as in the early 1960s (Devine and Wright 1993).

Today, numerous government programs exist to help the poor. Many public assistance programs stipulate that households are not eligible for benefits unless their income and/or assets fall below a specified guideline. Forms of public assistance include food benefits, cash aid, medical care, housing benefits, education aid, services (such as child care), employment and job training programs, and low-income energy assistance to help with heating bills.

Food Benefits Food benefits include food stamps, school lunch and breakfast programs, the special supplemental food program for women, infants, and children (WIC), and nutrition programs for the elderly. Food stamp recipients use vouchers to purchase edible goods. The largest group receiving food stamps are women with dependent children. It is estimated that less than half of those who could receive food stamps actually do (Cloward and Piven 1993). Women eligible for WIC also receive vouchers to purchase food items such as milk, cheese, fruit juice, and cereal, which are deemed important for pregnant and nursing mothers and their young children.

Cash Aid Cash aid includes Aid to Families with Dependent Children (AFDC) and Federal Supplemental Security Income (SSI). Administered by the Social Security Administration, SSI provides a minimum income for the aged, blind, and disabled.

Aid to Families with Dependent Children, which targets single mothers, is administered by the state and funded by both federal and state dollars. In 1992, only 22 percent of families receiving AFDC reported having any other source of income (U.S. Department of Health and Human Services 1994).

Social Security (SS), which was established in 1935 by the Social Security Act, is arranged so that individuals pay into the program during their working years and draw from their earlier investments during retirement. Social

The inevitable consequence of poverty is dependence.
—Samuel Johnson
English essayist and poet

National Data: AFDC benefit levels range from $120 per month for a family of three in Mississippi to $923 per month in Alaska, with the median state paying $367 in AFDC benefits (January 1993 figures). In all 50 states, AFDC benefits are below the Census Bureau's poverty threshold, varying from 13 percent of the poverty threshold in Mississippi to 79 percent in Alaska (median of 39 percent).

SOURCE: U.S. Department of Health and Human Services 1994.

Security provides income for retired or disabled workers, payments for those disabled on the job, and survivor benefits for spouses and children. Some people regard Social Security as a form of public assistance or welfare, while others view it as a form of insurance.

Medical Care Various programs provide medical aid to economically disadvantaged persons. Medical care assistance programs include Indian Health Services, maternal and child health services, and Medicaid, which provides medical services and hospital care for the poor through reimbursing physicians and hospitals.

Housing and Energy Assistance Housing assistance includes lower-income housing, low-rent public housing, and rural housing loans to the economically disadvantaged. Low-income energy assistance is also available to help the poor pay for home heating costs.

Education Public education aid for the economically disadvantaged includes educational loans and Pell grants for qualifying college students. Head Start programs, paid for by federal, state, and local money, provide educational services for disadvantaged preschool-age children. The first Head Start programs, which were established in 1964 by the Economic Opportunity Act, were based on the philosophy that if a child can succeed in school, he or she has an excellent chance at succeeding in life. Most research suggests that Head Start programs have been enormously successful. Today, these programs provide services for parents as well as health and educational training to more than 750,000 preschool children. Poor children enrolled in Head Start programs have higher levels of school achievement, higher self-concepts, and better health than poor children who do not participate in the programs (Besharov 1992). In 1994, President Clinton signed legislation expanding Head Start programs to include toddlers and infants and increasing full-day and year-round services.

Employment and Job Training Programs Various employment and job training programs are available to help individuals out of poverty. These include summer youth employment programs, Job Corps, and training for disadvantaged adults and youth. These programs fall under the Job Training and Partnership Act (JTPA), a federally funded program passed in 1982 and amended in 1992.

WELFARE REFORM

Numerous welfare reforms have been proposed including the 1995 Welfare Reform Act, which returns funding of many welfare programs to the states. Previously, Congress passed the 1988 Family Support Act authorizing states to require welfare recipients without dependent children to either be employed or in school—sometimes called workfare. Another provision required the states to be more aggressive in collecting child support payments from delinquent parents. Results of the legislation have been mixed, in part, because states did not take a proactive stance.

President Clinton "wants to end welfare as we know it" and is "prepared to support cutting off benefits if people are able to work without hurting their

National Data: Of a national sample of adults, 81 percent reported that the welfare system is in need of fundamental reform; 95 percent favored taking money out of the paychecks of fathers who refuse to make child support payments, and 92 percent favored requiring all able-bodied people on welfare to work or learn a job or skill.

SOURCE: Gibbs 1994.

children, and if there is a job available." He has proposed limiting welfare to two years, requiring AFDC recipients to work, and eliminating payment increases for women who have additional children while on welfare, called a family cap. Women with infant children, learning disabilities, emotional disorders, and/or substance abuse problems would be exempt. Given these proposed restrictions, the number of families who would actually lose benefits would be around 300,000.

> **Consideration** As conflict theorists are quick to point out, much of the money intended for welfare recipients actually ends up in the hands of the bureaucracy:
>
> This system fails us all, not by spending too much money on poor people, but by spending too much on their surrogates: the social welfare middlemen who claim to represent the interests of impoverished families. They consume at least 10 times the nation's actual cash payments to welfare families. (Funciello 1995, 11a)

THE FAILURE OF U.S. POVERTY PROGRAMS

The persistence of poverty may, in part, be due to the faulty assumptions on which federal and state programs are based, inherent problems within the implemented "solutions," and public opinion. Some of these assumptions, problems and opinions are examined in the next paragraphs.

The Charity Ethic The *charity ethic* holds that charity is bad and that people who receive charity are somehow fundamentally flawed. Public assistance, particularly in hard economic times, is defined as a handout rather than an entitlement. The public often becomes hostile to the poor, defining "them" as part of the problem, and myths emerge that justify such beliefs. Table 11.3 identifies the myths and realities of welfare in America.

When welfare is more attractive than work, the solution is not to make welfare less attractive but rather to make work more attractive.
—Joel A. Devine and James D. Wright
Sociologists

The Work Ethic The *work ethic* holds that only those who work are worthy of positive social recognition; in other words, work = wealth = worth. Because of this ethic, welfare recipients internalize the negative definitions of others and, through a self-fulfilling prophecy, may be less likely to finish school, find a job, and become economically self-sufficient.

Assistance Should Be Temporary The 1935 Social Security Act argued that assistance should be minimal and temporary. The Clinton administration echoes this position. Yet, as discussed in Chapter 10, in an age of multinationalization, postindustrialization, automation, and the like, some people may be permanently unemployed. Is it then realistic to base welfare programs on the assumption that payments should be minimal and temporary since not all recipients will eventually find work?

Blaming the Victim The "government needs to abandon its hostile attitude and punitive approach to recipients of social welfare" (Caputo 1993, 523). Blaming the poor creates a scapegoat, incites fear in the larger population, and divides the population along class lines. Further, blaming the victim contributes to

TABLE 11.3

THE MYTHS AND REALITIES OF WELFARE

- *Myth:* Welfare benefits are more than adequate to live on.
- *Fact:* Welfare benefits are actually quite small. In 1993, the median AFDC payment was $367 a month; in 1992, the average SSI payment was $358 a month. In all 50 states, welfare payments are below the federally established poverty line.

- *Myth:* Women on welfare have more children in order to receive more welfare benefits.
- *Fact:* Numerous studies report that women on AFDC are no more likely to have additional children than poor women who are not on AFDC (Devine and Wright 1993, 141).

- *Myth:* Many people on welfare don't deserve to be—they are cheating the taxpayers.
- *Fact:* In fact, more people who are deserving of welfare do not receive it than the reverse. This is particularly true in rural areas where "spatial and geographic factors" make enrollment difficult (Hirschl and Rank 1991).

- *Myth:* Once people are on welfare, they remain on welfare.
- *Fact:* On the average, people receive welfare for two years; more than half of all women on welfare receive it for less than four years (Sklar 1992).

- *Myth:* People on welfare either do not work or do not want to work.
- *Fact:* Harris (1993), studying women on welfare, found that at any given time one-third of welfare mothers are employed, and that two-thirds of those who escape welfare do so by becoming employed.

- *Myth:* Families on welfare have many more children than nonwelfare families.
- *Fact:* The average number of children in an AFDC family is 2.6 compared to 2.1 for non-AFDC families (U. S. Census Bureau 1995a).

- *Myth:* Reducing welfare benefits motivates people to work.
- *Fact:* Studies indicate that reducing welfare payments does not motivate people out of poverty but rather increases the number of people who are poor (Caputo 1993).

stereotyping of the poor, which interferes with the development of sound economic policy and also reinforces a self-fulfilling prophecy.

Bureaucratic Inadequacies The bureaucratic structures that administer public welfare programs are fragmented, underfinanced, and often lead to an unnecessary duplication of services. Because of a lack of resources, high caseloads lead to overworked and frustrated caseworkers. Welfare workers also deal with only one aspect of the client's needs and rarely deal with the client's problems holistically. For example, a family might need assistance with housing, food stamps, job training, child care, and medical care, each of which is delivered by a different social welfare agency. As a result, "disadvantaged recipients of agencies' services are typically shunted from agency to agency. . . . This shunting creates even more difficulties in the lives of people whose lives are already enormously burdened and who may have few coping mechanisms" (Waddock 1995, 60–61).

Race-Specific Policies Wilson (1987) argues that many antipoverty programs have failed because they are race-specific; that is, they are directed toward specific minority groups rather than the poor as a whole. He argues that:

the shift from preferential treatment for those with certain racial or ethnic characteristics to those who are truly disadvantaged in terms of their life chances would not only help the white poor, but would also direct more ef-

fectively the problems of the minority . . . in the last few years of the twen-
tieth century, the problems of the truly disadvantaged in the United States
will have to be attacked through universal programs that enjoy the sup-
port and commitment of a broad constituency. (Wilson 1987, 117 and 120)

Societal Ambivalence There is an all-too-obvious contradiction between the ideal of "equality and opportunity for all" and the reality of "inequality and limited opportunity" for so many. While most Americans subscribe to the former, they are unwilling to pay for changing the latter. Although some simply may not care, it is more likely that the majority of Americans are just preoccupied with their own lives and economic well-being. The result, however, is that officials supporting welfare reform and a reduction in funding for antipoverty programs were elected in record numbers in the 1994 Congressional elections. Apparently, politicians have learned that "running for office promising better service to those most in need is an exercise in political self-destruction" (Galbraith 1992, 31). The poor have low rates of voting and thus have minimal influence on elected government officials and the policies they advocate.

INTERNATIONAL RESPONSES TO POVERTY

The World Bank estimates that over one billion people worldwide are living in poverty. The number of people living in poverty is expected to *increase*, not decrease (Jolly, Rosenthal, and Tokman 1994). Alleviating worldwide poverty continues to be a major concern of both developing and developed countries.

One strategy for alleviating poverty on a worldwide basis involves "increasing the demand for the poor's most abundant asset—their labour power" through economic development and the creation of jobs (Kanbur 1995:90). As emphasized in Chapter 15, economic development necessitates controlling population growth and protecting the environment and natural resources which are often destroyed and depleted in the name of economic growth.

Alleviating poverty on a global level also requires social expenditures to provide the poor with better health care and education. Poor health is both a consequence and a cause of poverty; improving the health status of a population is a significant step toward breaking the cycle of poverty. Increasing the educational levels of a population better prepares individuals for paid employment and for participation in political affairs that affect poverty and other economic and political issues. Improving the educational level of women in developing countries is also associated with lower birth rates, which in turn fosters overall economic development (see also Chapter 15).

Achieving improvements in health and education require economic and material resources that impoverished countries do not have. Kanbur (1994) argues that "the international community must also do its share, by supporting these efforts through greatly increased capital flows to developing countries" (93). With so many cutbacks in public spending and an increasing national debt, many U.S. citizens are reluctant to support the economic needs of other countries. Indeed, several countries contribute significantly more to developing countries than does the United States (see Figure 11.2).

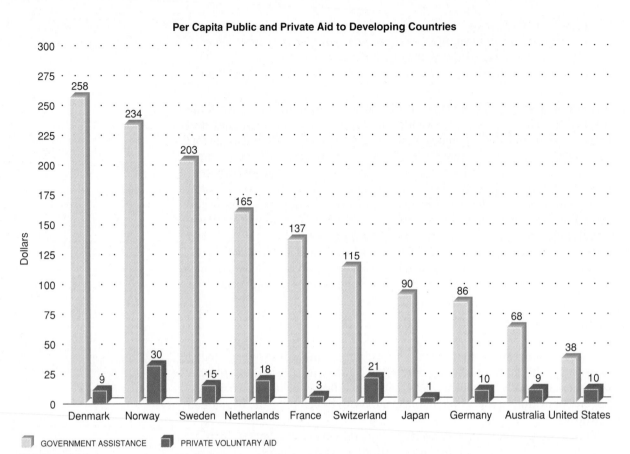

Per Capita Public and Private Aid to Developing Countries

FIGURE 11.2

PER CAPITA PUBLIC AND PRIVATE AID TO DEVELOPING COUNTRIES: 1993 (IN DOLLARS)

SOURCE: *Statistical Abstract of the United States; 1995,* 115th ed. U.S. Bureau of the Census (Washington, D.C.: U.S. Government Printing Office), Table 1414.

UNDERSTANDING
WEALTH AND POVERTY

As we close this chapter, we emphasize that several structural factors in the economic institution contribute to poverty: multinationalization, the transition to a service economy and the corresponding loss of jobs in the manufacturing sector, a split labor market, increased technology that displaces workers, and fewer jobs for unskilled laborers. Gans (1992) suggests that "the war on the poor is best ended by job-centered economic growth that creates decent public and private jobs" (p. 462).

Education is also important in breaking the cycle of poverty. Overcrowded and inadequate schools contribute to poverty by failing to provide students with the skills, motivation, and confidence to pursue a meaningful job or career. Women and minorities, who are disproportionately poor, tend to live in impoverished areas with inferior schools. As a result, many drop out of school or have low academic achievement. Unskilled, jobless, and uneducated, the poor are unable to escape deteriorated neighborhoods characterized by a lack

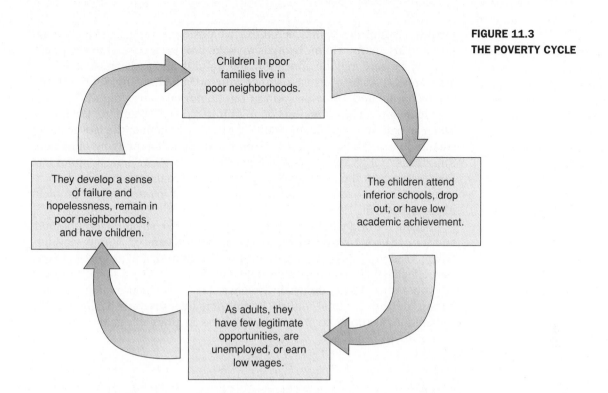

FIGURE 11.3
THE POVERTY CYCLE

Children in poor families live in poor neighborhoods.

The children attend inferior schools, drop out, or have low academic achievement.

As adults, they have few legitimate opportunities, are unemployed, or earn low wages.

They develop a sense of failure and hopelessness, remain in poor neighborhoods, and have children.

of legitimate opportunities and positive adult role models. Hence, they remain poor over time and pass this legacy on to their children (see Figure 11.3).

While structural changes in the economic institution and improvements in the educational institution may reduce poverty, such changes take time. A **guaranteed annual income** would eliminate poverty immediately. In many European countries, the government guarantees that the poor will not fall below 60 to 70 percent of the country's median income. In the United States, welfare payments bring an individual to only 20 percent of the median income. By spending $60 billion a year, we could eliminate poverty in the United States by guaranteeing a minimum standard of living to all citizens (Devine and Wright 1993).

Poverty is often justified by the **equity principle,** which, as functionalists assert, holds that those who have more resources deserve them because of their greater contributions to society. In the United States, even many economically disadvantaged people believe this principle which, according to conflict theorists, attests to the strength of the "false consciousness." (Ritzman and Tomaskovic-Devey 1992). The problem with the equity principle is that it justifies inequality by perpetuating the belief that the rich are deserving and the poor are failures. Blaming poverty on individual rather than structural and cultural factors implies not only that poor individuals are responsible for their plight, but also that they are responsible for improving their condition. If we hold individuals accountable for their poverty, we fail to make society accountable for providing expanded educational and job opportunities for disadvantaged populations (Caputo 1993). There is a middle ground between the idea that the poor are helpless victims and the idea that only the strongest and most deserving survive. This middle ground involves a compromise between these two positions: provide help and support and also empower individuals to make productive use of this support. Support services include education, job training and assistance, child care assistance, and short-term assistance with food and housing. Such services, when coordinated, "provide support but do not take away dignity or make recipients into helpless victims of an unjust society" (Waddock 1995, 187). When a national sample of adults was asked whether the government should do everything possible to improve the standard of living of all poor Americans or if each person should take care of him- or herself, about half (48.7 percent) of the respondents, indicated they believed that the government and the individual should be equally involved in resolving the problem of poverty (NORC 1993).

Imagine a world where everyone had comfortable shelter, plentiful food, and enough economic resources to pay for medical care, education, clothing, and recreation. If this imaginary world were achieved, and absolute poverty were effectively eliminated, what would the effects be on such social problems as crime, drug abuse, domestic violence, health problems, prejudice and racism, and international conflict? Ending or reducing poverty begins with the recognition that doing so is a worthy ideal and an attainable goal.

CRITICAL THINKING

1. If absolute poverty did not exist in the United States, would relative poverty still exist? How would relative poverty change, if at all?
2. Why does poverty exist in America if this is the land of "equality and opportunity for all"?
3. What are the benefits and drawbacks of using an absolute versus a relative measurement of poverty?
4. Why are women more likely to live below the poverty line than men?
5. Explain what the poverty cycle is and how it can be broken.

KEY TERMS

social stratification	wealthfare system	underclass
social mobility	absolute poverty	public assistance
social class	relative poverty	guaranteed annual income
life chances	poverty line	
lifestyle	feminization of poverty	equity principle

REFERENCES

Alex-Assensoh, Yvette. 1995. "Myths about Race and the Underclass." *Urban Affairs Review* 31:3–19.

Banfield, Edward. 1992. "The Future of the Lower Class." In *Taking Sides,* 7th ed., ed. Kurt Finsterbusch and George McKenna, pp. 150–54. Guilford, Conn.: Dushkin Publishing Group.

Besharov, Douglas J. 1992. "A New Start for Head Start." *American Enterprise* 3 (March/April): 52–57.

Caputo, Richard K. 1993. "Family Poverty, Unemployment Rates, and AFDC Payments: Trends among Blacks and Whites." *Families in Society: The Journal of Contemporary Human Services* (November): 515–26.

Card, David and Alan Krueger. 1995. *Myth and Measurement: The New Economics of the Minimum Wage.* Princeton, NJ: Princeton University Press.

Cloward, Richard A., and Frances Fox Piven. 1993. "A Class Analysis of Welfare." *Monthly Review* 44 (February): 25–31.

Davis, Kingsley, and Wilbert Moore. 1945. "Some Principles of Stratification." *American Sociological Review* 10: 242–49.

DeParle, Jason. 1992. "Why Marginal Changes Don't Rescue the Welfare System." *New York Times,* March 1, Section 4, p. 3.

Devine, Joel A., and James D. Wright. 1993. *The Greatest of Evils: Urban Poverty and the American Underclass.* New York: Aldine de Gruyter.

Fitzgerald, F. Scott. 1926. *All the Sad Young Men.* New York: Charles Scribner's Sons.

Funciello, Theresa. 1995. "The Soup-Kitchen Elite." *USA Today,* February 2, 11A.

Galbraith, John Kenneth. 1992. "The Tyranny of the Contended." *Washington Monthly* (June): 29–31.

Gans, Herbert J. 1972. "The Positive Functions of Poverty." *American Journal of Sociology* 78 (September): 275–388.

_____. 1992. "The War against the Poor." *Dissent* 39 (Fall): 461–65.

Gerth, H. H., and C. Wright Mills. 1958. *From Max Weber: Essays in Sociology.* New York: Galaxy.

Gibbs, Nancy. 1994. "The Vicious Cycle." *Time,* June 20, 25–30.

Gimenez, Martha E. 1990. "The Feminization of Poverty: Myth or Reality?" *Social Justice* 17(3): 43–69.

Harer. Miles D., and Darrell Steffensmeier. 1992. " The Differing Effects of Economic Inequality on Black and White Rates of Violence." *Social Forces* 70(4): 1035–54.

Harris, Kathleen Mullan. 1993. "Work and Welfare among Single Mothers in Poverty." *American Journal of Sociology* 99(2): 317–52.

Hirschl, Thomas A., and Mark R. Rank. 1991. "The Effect of Population Density on Welfare Participation." *Social Forces* 70(1): 225–35.

Huff-Corzine, Lin, Jay Corzine, and David C. Moore. 1991. "Deadly Connections: Culture, Poverty, and the Direction of Lethal Violence." *Social Forces* 69(3): 715–32.

Jolly, Richard, Gert Rosenthal and Victor Tokman. 1994. "Foreword: The Challenge of Poverty." In *Poverty Monitoring: An International Concern,* ed. Rolph van der Hoeven and Richard Anker, pp. xvii–xix. New York, N.Y.: St. Martin's Press.

Kenworthy, Lane. 1995. *In Search of National Economic Success.* Thousand Oaks, CA: Sage Publications.

Labich, Kenneth. 1994. "Class in America." *Fortune,* February 7, 114–26.

Lee, F. R. 1993. "Fear of Hunger Stalks Many Elderly." *New York Times,* November 16, B4.

Lewis, Oscar. 1966. "The Culture of Poverty." *Scientific American* 2(5): 19–25.

Lichter, Daniel T., and David J. Eggebeen. 1993. "Rich Kids, Poor Kids: Changing Income Inequality among American Children." *Social Forces* 71(3): 761–80.

Mead, Lawrence. 1993. "The Politics of Poverty: Toward a New Debate." *Current* (December): 21–25.

Morris, Martina, Annette D. Bernhardt, and Mark S. Handcock. 1994. "Economic Inequality: New Methods for New Trends." *American Sociological Review* 59 (April): 205–19.

NORC. 1993. General Social Survey. Roper Organization. Storrs, Conn.: Roper Organization, Inc. Internet.

Perdue, William Dan. 1993. "To Have and Have Not." In *Systemic Crisis,* pp. 270–73. Fort Worth: Harcourt.

Phillips, Kevin. 1991. *The Politics of Rich and Poor.* New York: Simon & Schuster.

Popkin, Susan. 1990. "Welfare: Views from the Bottom." *Social Problems* 37(1):64–79.

Quigley, William. 1995 (June 3). "The Minimum Wage and the Working Poor." *America,* 172(20):6–7.

Ritzman, Rosemary L., and Donald Tomaskovic-Devey. 1992. "Life Chances and Support for Equality and Equity as Normative and Counternormative Distribution Rules." *Social Forces* 70(3): 745–63.

Rodman, Hyman. 1963. "The Lower-Class Value Stretch." *Social Forces* 42: 205–15.

Rossi, Peter H., and James D. Wright. 1993. "The Urban Homeless: A Portrait of Urban Dislocation." In *The Ghetto Underclass,* ed. William Julius Wilson, pp. 149–59. Newbury Park, Calif.: Sage Publications.

Ryan, William. 1992 ."Blaming the Victim." In *Taking Sides,* 7th ed., ed. Kurt Finsterbusch and George McKenna, pp. 155–62. Guilford, Conn.: Dushkin Publishing Group.

Seligman, Martin E. P. 1967. "Failure to Escape Traumatic Shock." *Journal of Experimental Psychology* 74: 1–9.

Sivard, Ruth Leger. 1991. *World Military and Social Expenditures.* Washington, D.C.: World Priorities.

Sklar, Holly. 1992. "Reaffirmative Action." *Zeta Magazine* 5: 9–15.

Smith, Lee. 1991. "Rural Poverty: The Forgotten Poor." *Current* (May): 16–19.

Sosin, Michael R. 1992. "Homeless and Vulnerable Meal Program Users: A Comparison Study." *Social Problems* 39(2): 170–88.

Statistical Abstract of the United States: 1992, 112th ed. U.S. Bureau of the Census. Washington, D.C.: U.S. Government Printing Office.

Statistical Abstract of the United States: 1993, 113th ed. U.S. Bureau of the Census. Washington, D.C.: U.S. Government Printing Office.

Statistical Abstract of the United States: 1995, 115th ed. U.S. Bureau of the Census. Washington, D.C.: U.S. Government Printing Office.

The Economist. 1993. " Rich Man, Poor Man." July 24, p. 71.

U.S. Census Bureau. 1994a. "Median Net Worth of Households Dropped 12 Percent." (January 26): Internet.

_____. 1994b. "Number of Americans in Poverty up for 4th Year." (October 6): CB94-159. Internet.

_____. 1995a. "Fertility and Economic Characteristics of AFDC Mothers." (March 3): CB95-42. Internet.

_____. 1995b. "Income and Poverty: 1994 Summary." [http://www.census.gov/ftp/pub].

U.S. Department of Health and Human Services. 1994. "Facts Related to Welfare Reform: Aid to Families with Dependent Children (AFD)." Press Release (June). [http://www.fedworld.com].

Valentine, Charles A. 1968. *Culture and Poverty: Critiques and Counter-Proposals.* Chicago: University of Chicago Press.

Waddock, Sandra A. 1995. *Not by Schools Alone: Sharing Responsibility for America's Education Reform.* Westport, Conn.: Praeger Publishers.

Waldrop, Judith, and Linda Jacobsen. 1992. "American Affluence." *American Demographics* (December): 29–42.

Wilson, W. J. 1987. *The Truly Disadvantaged: The Inner City, the Underclass, and Public Policy.* Chicago: University of Chicago Press.

12

CHAPTER

Urban Decline and Growth

IS IT TRUE?

"Urban psychosis" has been used successfully as a defense for murder (p. 348).

Between 1995 and 2000, the growth rates of the three most populated U.S. Cities (New York, Los Angeles, and Chicago) are estimated to be less than one percent (p. 342).

Most of the world's largest cities are in industrialized countries (p. 342).

Violent crime rates are much higher in metropolitan areas than in rural areas (p. 350).

Between 1980 and 1990, federal funding to U.S. cities had been cut by over one-half (p. 352).

ANS: 1. F 2. T 3. F 4. T 5. T

America and its cities are at a crossroads.

If they choose to make their separate ways

into the future, decline and decay almost

surely lie ahead for both. But if they stride

together as partners into the twenty-first

century, the nation and its great urban areas

will compete and brilliantly succeed in

the new global economy.

1993 Final Report of the 82nd American Assembly

Waiting in snarled traffic amid the beeping horns and bumping fenders on a hot summer day is enough to make one question the benefits of urban living. Yet, as a population, Americans have always been intrigued by the idea of building and living in large cities and have been drawn by the lure of culture, entertainment, and fine dining. Many argue, however, that the problems of urban living outweigh its advantages. In this chapter, we look at the historical social forces that have created our cities, the modern social forces that are shaping our cities today, and the social problems that affect and are affected by cities in America and throughout the world.

The Social Context: The Urban Environment

Urbanization has profound implications for the livelihood, way of life and values of individuals.
—United Nations International Conference on Population and Development
Cairo 1994

Cities, and their accompanying metropolitan areas, are at the core of the nation. Cities are where most people reside, work, go to school, and shop. They are the center of our financial establishments (e.g., Wall Street), communication infrastructures (e.g., phone companies), medical institutions (e.g., hospitals), transportation networks (e.g., airports), and governmental agencies (e.g., state capitols). In spite of the majesty of some cities, many are deteriorating and must cope with physical decline, high crime, poverty, homelessness, racial inequality, and failing educational systems. These urban problems are not unique to the United States—they are worldwide.

A WORLD VIEW OF URBANIZATION

National Data: Seventeen of the twenty largest cities in the world are in developing countries.
SOURCE: Sassen 1994.

As early as 5000 B.C., cities of 7,000 to 20,000 people existed along the Nile, Tigris-Euphrates, and Indus river valleys. But it was not until the Industrial Revolution in the nineteenth century that cities grew rapidly and began to house most of the world's population. **Urbanization,** the transformation of a society from a rural to an urban one, has also transformed social life throughout the world.

U.S. citizens tend to think of New York, Los Angeles, and Chicago when they think of large cities, yet most of the world's large cities are not in industrialized countries. Table 12.1 lists the ten most populated cities in the world and their projected populations for the year 2000.

The growth rate of urban populations in developing countries is phenomenal. Between 1995 and 2000, the growth rates of the three most populated U.S. cities (New York, Los Angeles, and Chicago) are estimated to be less than

TABLE 12.1

THE WORLD'S TEN LARGEST CITIES

	PROJECTED POPULATION IN 2000
1. Tokyo-Yokohama, Japan	29,971,000
2. Mexico City, Mexico	27,872,000
3. São Paulo, Brazil	25,354,000
4. Seoul, South Korea	21,976,000
5. Bombay, India	15,357,000
6. New York City, USA	14,648,000
7. Osaka-Kobe-Kyoto, Japan	14,287,000
8. Tehran, Iran	14,251,000
9. Rio de Janeiro, Brazil	14,169,000
10. Calcutta, India	14,088,000

SOURCE: *Statistical Abstract of the United States : 1994*, 114th ed. U.S. Bureau of the Census (Washington, D. C.: U.S. Government Printing Office), Table 1355.

one percent. Meanwhile, cities such as Tehran, Iran; Lagos, Nigeria; Dhaka, Bangladesh; and Kinshasa, Zaire, are estimated to be growing between 4 and 5 percent a year—10 to 100 times the growth rate in the most populated U.S. cities! Both developed and developing countries are going through the process of shifting from predominantly rural to predominantly urban societies. By the year 2005, urban areas are expected to house more than half of the world population (United Nations 1994). Urban growth in less developed countries is largely due to high birthrates (see Chapter 15).

Cities across the globe contend with a number of problems, but many problems are most severe in cities in less developed countries. These cities are especially vulnerable to health risks caused by inadequate housing, water, food, and medical care. For example, in Calcutta, more than half of the city's ten million residents have no toilets. Human waste—urine and feces—contaminates the city streets causing disease.

HISTORY OF URBANIZATION IN THE UNITED STATES

About two hundred years ago, most U.S. citizens—more than 90 percent of the population—lived in rural areas. Nevertheless, urbanization began as early as the 1700s, when most major industries were located in the largest metropolitan areas including New York City, Philadelphia, and Boston. Unskilled laborers, seeking manufacturing jobs, moved into urban areas as the associated processes of urbanization and industrialization accelerated in the nineteenth century (Feagin 1983). People were also lured to the cities by the higher incomes they offered and such urban amenities as museums, libraries, and entertainment.

The "pull" of the city was not the only reason for urbanization, however. Technological advances were making it possible for fewer farmers to work the same amount of land. Thus, "push" factors were also involved—making a living as a farmer became more and more difficult as technology, even then, replaced workers.

The rate of growth of a city in an underdeveloped country can be phenomenal, and when city services don't keep pace, the risk of disease escalates.

According to the 1990 census definition, an **urban population** consists of persons living in cities or towns of 2,500 or more inhabitants. An **urbanized area** refers to one or more places and the adjacent surrounding territory that together have a minimum population of 50,000. Figure 12.1 depicts the tremendous growth of the U.S. urban population over the last two hundred years.

SUBURBANIZATION

In the late nineteenth century, railroad and trolley lines enabled people to live outside the city and still commute into the city to work. As more and more people moved to the **suburbs**—urban areas surrounding central cities—America underwent **suburbanization.** Following World War II, many U.S. city dwellers moved to the suburbs out of concern for the declining quality of city life and the desire to own a home on a spacious lot. Suburbanization was also spurred by racial and ethnic prejudice, as the white majority moved away from cities that, due to immigration, were becoming increasingly diverse. The greater accessibility of automobiles and the availability of mass transit systems also contributed to suburbanization. In the 1950s, VA and FHA loans made housing more affordable, enabling many city dwellers to move to the suburbs. As increasing numbers of people moved to the suburbs, so did businesses and jobs.

Those who did not have jobs in the suburbs could commute to work or work in a satellite branch in suburbia that was connected to the main downtown office. The new technologies of fax machines, home computers, cellular phones, pagers, and E-mail have also facilitated the movement to the suburbs.

**FIGURE 12.1
PERCENTAGE OF U.S. POPULATION THAT IS URBAN, 1790–1990***

*An urban population consists of persons living in cities or towns of 2,500 or more inhabitants.
SOURCES: *Statistical Abstract of the United States: 1991,* 111th ed. U.S. Bureau of the Census (Washington, D.C.: U.S. Government Printing Office), pp. 17, 27; *Statistical Abstract of the United States: 1993,* 113th ed., p. 34.

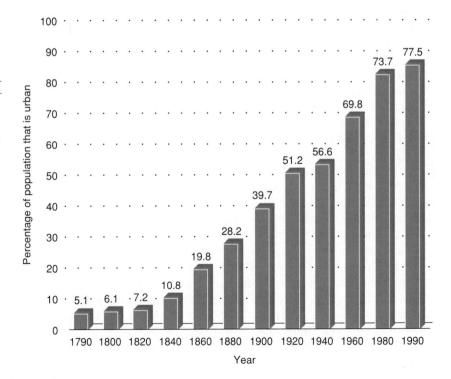

Consideration *Some suburban residents are becoming dissatisfied with living conditions in the suburbs. Many suburbs have become overdeveloped and are now characterized by strip malls, office buildings, and large apartment complexes. Many suburban residents would prefer to live in a community based on the village model where a cluster of homes surrounds a central location that is the focus of social life. They want "communities with parks and outdoor public spaces in which people can gather and interact" (Adler 1995, 43).*

METROPOLITAN GROWTH IN THE UNITED STATES

A **metropolitan area** consists of a central core area containing a large population, together with adjacent communities that have a high degree of social and economic integration with the core. Simply defined, metropolitan areas are large cities and their surrounding suburbs. Another term for "metropolitan area" is **metropolis,** from the Greek meaning "mother city." Metropolises have grown rapidly in the United States. Table 12.2 shows how metropolitan areas have grown as a percentage of both U.S. population and land area since 1960.

Metropolitan populations are likely to continue to grow. From 1980 to 1992, the total U.S. metropolitan population increased by almost 15 percent. In contrast, the nonmetropolitan population grew by only 4.5 percent (*Statistical Abstract of the United States: 1995,* Table 42).

URBANIZATION AND SOCIOLOGICAL THEORIES

Structural-functionalists view the development of urban areas within the context of other societal changes. As technology provided freedom from the farm, and industrialization provided new job opportunities in factories in the city, people flocked to urban areas. An expanding population also made urbanization inevitable. Thus, the development of cities is a natural and functional one. Although cities initially functioned as centers of production and distribution, today they are centers of finance, administration, and information.

Conflict theorists emphasize that the development of cities involves power struggles as people and corporations make decisions about urban growth that are economically based. The decision to build a mall or not and where to locate that mall are economic decisions based on the desire to maximize profits.

> *The ratio of workers to residents has narrowed, and suburban jobs are growing faster than city jobs.*
> —Richard L. Forstall
> Demographer

> *You can't keep spreading out. The cost to make roads and sewers gets to the point where it doesn't work.*
> —Mike Burton
> Executive director
> Portland's metro government

TABLE 12.2

PERCENTAGE OF U.S. POPULATION AND U.S. LAND AREA WITHIN METROPOLITAN AREAS

YEAR	PERCENTAGE OF U.S. POPULATION	PERCENTAGE OF U.S. LAND AREA
1960	63.0%	8.7%
1970	66.7	10.9
1980	73.2	16.0
1990	74.3	16.4
1993	79.7	19.0

SOURCE: *Statistical Abstract of the United States: 1994,* 114th ed. U.S. Bureau of the Census (Washington, D. C.: U.S. Government Printing Office), Table C, Appendix 2.

The decision to tear down inner city homes to make room for office complexes or parking decks is also profit motivated. The decision maker rarely considers that residents in low-income housing will be displaced or that 200-year-old oak trees will be cut down.

Conflict theorists also point out that the movement of many businesses and corporations out of northern and northeastern cities to Sun Belt cities is a consequence of cheaper labor, an anti-union climate, and tax incentives. In this regard, cities compete to encourage industries to locate within their boundaries.

Symbolic interactionists emphasize the effects of urbanization on interaction patterns and social relationships. These effects are discussed in detail later in the chapter.

Urbanism as a Way of Life

The term **urbanism** refers to the culture and lifestyle of city dwellers. This culture and lifestyle is characterized by individualistic and cosmopolitan norms, values, and styles of behavior. In contrast to the slow paced and traditional nature of rural life, life in the city is fast-paced and always on the "cutting edge" in terms of the latest technology, entertainment, fashions, food trends, and other manifestations of cultural change. Urban dwellers develop an "urban consciousness"—an awareness of the consequences of city living. Although some urban dwellers long to "get out of the city," many view city life as dynamic and exciting. Some city dwellers are ambivalent about city living— they both enjoy the urban environment and yet also long for the country (see this chapter's *The Human Side* for one city dweller's account of city life). Outsiders, however, often view cities as places to avoid.

ANTI-URBAN BIAS

In general, cities have a reputation for being crowded, dirty, and crime-ridden. Los Angeles is the most crowded U.S. city with a population of 11.4 million and a density of over 5,000 people per square mile (Larson 1993). Cities generally have higher concentrations of air pollutants than non-urban areas, with Los Angeles having the worst air quality of all U.S. cities. Big cities, such as Miami, Chicago, Atlanta, Tampa and Fort Worth also have high crime rates and are thus viewed as dangerous places to live, work, or visit.

Cities are also tainted by the reputation of being cold and impersonal. As early as 1902, George Simmel (see Wolff 1978) observed that urban living involved an overemphasis on punctuality, individuality, and a detached attitude toward interpersonal relationships. It is not difficult to find evidence to support Simmel's observations: witness New Yorkers pushing each other to get onto the subway during rush hour, hear motorists curse each other in Los Angeles traffic jams, watch Chicago residents ignore the homeless man asleep on the sidewalk. Simmel's observations of city life provided the basis for the classical view of urbanism.

THE IDIOCY OF URBAN LIFE

. . . These rats are social creatures, as you can tell if you look out on the city street during an insomniac night. But after 6 A.M., the two-legged, daytime creatures of the city begin to stir; and it is they, not the rats, who bring the rat race. You might think that human beings congregate in large cities because they are gregarious. The opposite is true. Urban life today is aggressively individualistic and atomized. Cities are not social places.

The lunacy of modern city life lies first in the fact that most city dwellers who can do so try to live outside the city boundaries. So the two-legged creatures have created suburbs, exurbs, and finally rururbs (rubs to some). Disdaining rural life, they try to create simulations of it. No effort is spared to let city dwellers imagine they are living anywhere but in a city: patches of grass in the more modest suburbs, broader spreads in the richer ones further out; prim new trees planted along the streets. . . .

. . . The professional people buy second homes in the country as soon as they can afford them, and as early as possible on Friday head out of the city they have created.

. . . As the farmer walks down to his farm in the morning, the city dweller is dressing for the first idiocy of his day, which he not only accepts but even seeks—the journey to work. . . . This takes two forms: solitary confinement in one's own car, or the discomfort of extreme overcrowding on public transport. Both produce angst. There are no more grim faces than those of the single drivers we pedestrians can glimpse at the stoplights during the rush hour. It is hard to know why they are so impatient in the morning to get to their useless and wearisome employments; but then in the evening, when one would have thought they would be relaxed, they are even more frenetic. Prisoners in boxes on wheels, they do not dare wonder why they do it. . . . Life in the suburbs and exurbs has become a bondage to the hours of journeying.

. . . On the bus or subway each morning and evening other urban dwellers endure the indignity of being crushed into unwelcome proximity with strangers whom they have no wish to communicate with except in terms of abuse, rancor, and sometimes violent hostility. . . even eye contact on public transport is treated as an act of aggression or at least harassment.

. . . The primary urban activity of getting to and from work has other curious features. As every Englishman visiting America for the first time remarks, the smell of deodorants on a crowded bus or subway in the morning is overpowering. Even the stale smell of the human body would be preferable. It must account for the glazed looks—perhaps all deodorants contain a gas introduced by the employers to numb the urban office workers to the fatuity of their labors.

SOURCE: Henry Fairlie. 1987. "The Idiocy of Urban Life." *New Republic,* January 5 and 12. Used by permission.

Various theories of urbanism focus on how living in a city affects interaction patterns and social relationships. Here we examine both the classical and the modern theoretical views, as well as attempts to synthesize the two perspectives.

> *Our cities are more pestilential than yellow fever to the morals, the health and the liberties of man.*
> — Thomas Jefferson
> Former U.S. President

> *"The city," an alien place where by definition middle class Americans refuse to live.*
> — Jerry Adler
> Journalist

Classical Theoretical View Lewis Wirth (1938), a second-generation student of Simmel, argued that urban life is disruptive for both families and friendships. He believed that because of the heterogeneity, density, and size of urban populations, interactions become segmented and transitory, resulting in weakened social bonds. Those bonds that do develop are superficial and detract from the closeness of primary relationships. Wirth held that as social solidarity weakens, people develop certain social-psychological conditions including loneliness, depression, stress, and antisocial behavior.

> *Consideration* The presumed effect of the urban environment on antisocial behavior has been used in court. In 1991, a seventeen-year-old youth with a history of victimization and neighborhood violence unsuccessfully used "urban psychosis" as a defense after shooting another teenager for a leather jacket (Shoop 1993). In a subsequent legal case, Daimion Osby contended that he shot two unarmed men to death because of "urban survival syndrome" (Davis 1994).

Wilson (1993) empirically assessed the validity of Wirth's classical view of cities by examining the effects of city size on a number of variables. He used General Social Survey data, which are representative of noninstitutionalized adults in the United States. Wilson hypothesized that urbanism inhibits family completeness in that people are less likely to marry; that it disrupts family relationships in terms of the number and frequency of contacts between relatives; and that it changes the functions served by kin—as community size increases, relatives are less likely to rely on one another for help.

Although Wilson has been criticized for the way he operationalized urbanism, he found little support for Wirth's theory. Urbanism did not inhibit family completeness, and contact with and reliance on relatives were unaffected. He did find, however, that the larger the urban area, the greater the likelihood that individuals were separated or divorced. The fact that there are fewer informal social controls and that attitudes are generally more liberal in an urban environment may contribute to the higher divorce rate. Further, in opposition to Wirth's theory, the prevalence of psychiatric disorders does not differ significantly between urban and rural areas (Kessler et al. 1994).

Modern Theoretical View In stark contrast to Wirth's pessimistic view of urban areas, Herbert Gans ([1962] 1984) argued that cities do not interfere with the development and maintenance of functional and positive interpersonal relationships. Among other communities, he studied an Italian urban neighborhood in Boston called the West End and found such neighborhoods to be community oriented and marked by close interpersonal ties. Rather than finding the social disorganization described by Wirth, Gans observed that kinship and ethnicity helped bind people together. These enclaves were characterized by intimate small groups with strong social bonds. Thus, Gans saw the city as

The diversity of urban populations facilitates the development of subcultures in which there is a sense of community ties. An example is this Jewish community in Brooklyn, New York.

a patchwork quilt of different neighborhoods or **urban villages**, each of which helped individuals deal with the pressures of urban living.

A Theoretical Synthesis To what degree are these theoretical views supported by empirical research? Fisher (1982) interviewed more than 1,000 respondents in various urban areas and found evidence for both the classical and the modern theoretical perspectives of urbanism. From the classical perspective, he found that heterogeneity does make community integration and consensus difficult—there is less community cohesion. Ties that do exist are less often kin-related than in nonurban areas and are more often based on work relationships, memberships in voluntary and professional organizations, and proximity to neighbors.

Fisher also found, however, that the diversity of urban populations facilitates the development of subcultures that have a sense of community ties. For example, large urban areas include such diverse groups as gays, ethnic and racial minorities, and artists. These individuals "find each other" and develop their own unique subcultures.

Another researcher (Tittle 1989) empirically examined each of the three theories of the effects of urbanism—classical, modern, and Fisher's theoretical synthesis. Holding such demographic variables as race, education, age, length of residence, and marital status constant, Tittle examined the effects of community size on a respondent's social bonds, anonymity, tolerance, alienation, and deviant behavior. His sample consisted of 1,993 respondents from Iowa, New Jersey, and Oregon.

Tittle (1989) found some support for both the classical and modern view and, thus, for Fisher's synthesis. As predicted by the classical view, the larger the size of the community, the weaker a respondent's social bonds and the higher his or her anonymity, tolerance, alienation, and reported incidence of deviant behavior. He also found that racial and ethnic groups created their own sense of community, lending support to the modern theory of urbanism.

Cities and Social Problems

Urban areas in the United States are the context for a number of social problems. These include crime and violence, drug trafficking, joblessness, inadequate schools, overburdened transportation systems, segregation, inadequate housing, poverty, and problems associated with immigration.

CRIME AND VIOLENCE

National Data: In 1993, there were 852 violent crimes (murder, robbery, rape, assault) reported to the police per 100,000 population in metropolitan areas compared to 222 violent crimes per 100,000 population in rural areas.

SOURCE: *Statistical Abstract of the United States: 1995*, Table 309.

Evening television news stories, newspaper headlines, and magazine articles emphasize the frightening state of crime and violence in our cities. Drive-by shootings, crack houses, gang activity, and random violence all contribute to the negative images of urban life. In 1994, the number of murders in New Orleans climbed to nearly 400, leading some to call the city known as the "Big Easy," the "Big Queasy" (Woodbury 1994). In general, the incidence of violence is higher in urban areas than in rural areas. This observation is based on data that compare rates of violence in large cities (250,000+) to those in small cities (10,000 or less).

Youth gangs, although often the focus of public concerns about urban violence, often develop as a response to the social disorganization of many urban neighborhoods. While ideally one's community provides a source of social support, identity, and status, many inner city youths resort to gang membership as a means of achieving these ends.

> **Consideration**   Gangs in New York City in the nineteenth and early twentieth centuries were so brazen and violent they roamed the streets passing out flyers advertising their services—$10 for breaking a person's nose and jaw, $15 for chewing a person's ear off, $50 for poisoning a team of horses, and $100 or more for the "big job" (Messinger and Breslau 1993, 34).

Community policing involves uniformed police officers patrolling and being responsible for certain areas of the city, as opposed to simply responding to crimes as they occur. Frequent police-community resident contacts are an important feature of community policing.

Two tactics have been helpful in reducing urban crime. One method is **community policing** in which uniformed police officers patrol and are responsible for certain areas of the city as opposed to simply responding to crimes as they occur. New York City implemented this tactic in 1991 under the "Safe Streets, Safe City" program. Other features of the program included frequent police–community resident contacts, the creation of precinct management teams with neighborhood representatives, and an ideology of working together with residents to deal with local crime problems (Brown 1993).

A second method of dealing with urban neighborhood crime is the creation of **defensible space.** For example, Five Oaks, a district in Dayton, Ohio, had an inordinate amount of crime—much of it caused by drive-by shootings. Architects and urban planners added speed bumps, closed selected streets, and made other streets one way. The goal was to structurally rearrange the neighborhood so that "cruising" became virtually impossible. Also, large neighborhoods were divided into smaller ones providing a heightened sense of community on the part of residents. Results revealed that traffic in Five Oaks was reduced 67 percent, violent crime 50 percent, and property crime 26 percent (Cose 1994).

DEINDUSTRIALIZATION AND BLUE-COLLAR UNEMPLOYMENT

Unemployment in urban areas is related to **deindustrialization,** or the loss and/or relocation of manufacturing industries (McNulty 1993). Since the 1970s, many urban factories have closed or relocated, forcing blue-collar workers into unemployment. General Motors, for example, is the only one of the big three U.S. automobile makers left in Detroit—the "Motor City." When such companies close their plants, many blue-collar inner city residents not only are jobless, but also lack the education and training needed to obtain white-collar jobs.

As cities experience deindustrialization, they also experience **deconcentration,** or the redistribution of the population from cities to suburbs and surrounding areas. One of the primary causes of deconcentration is the introduction of new technologies (e.g., robotics), which facilitate the relocation of production to less developed nations and to nonmetropolitan areas in the United States. Entire manufacturing outfits can be moved out of the country and, with current telecommunication technology, remain in contact with corporate offices located anywhere in the United States. Multinationalization also contributes to deconcentration (see also Chapter 10).

Deindustrialization and deconcentration have a dramatic impact on urban residents. Flint, Michigan, was once the site of a large General Motors plant boasting 70,000 manufacturing employees in 1980. When the plant closed, Flint's manufacturing workforce dropped by almost half, to 40,000, and by 1987 the city was ranked last out of 300 U.S. cities in a quality of life survey (Lord and Price 1992). In 1939, Camden, New Jersey, had almost 300 factories. More than 37,000 people worked in the shipyards alone. When RCA, Campbell Soup, and other large companies moved out of the area or dramatically reduced their workforce, local unemployment and poverty rates soared. Today, a third of the 88,000 residents and nearly two in three children in Camden live below the federally established poverty line.

National Data: In 1994, almost half (42.3 percent) of all workers who lost their jobs did so because the plant or company for which they worked either closed down or moved.

SOURCE: *Statistical Abstract of the United States: 1995,* Table 657.

INADEQUATE CITY SERVICES

Loss of the manufacturing sector in central cities has resulted in a lower tax base and, hence, inadequate city services. Inadequate city services are particularly evident in the poorer sections of cities. One researcher lived in East Harlem, a 200-square-block area in New York City, to assess what inner city life was like. He observed:

> The telephone company took six weeks to install my phone; the garbage trucks don't make their rounds at least once a month; about as often, the letter carrier fails to appear; and careless oil truck operators frequently spill heating oil all over the sidewalk. . . for the second summer [the pool] has been closed down while a corrupt construction company "renovates" it. . . . For the third year in a row, the basketball courts . . . are marred by deep potholes; only every other hoop on the courts is still in place. Broken beer bottles, human feces, crack vials, and an occasional hypodermic needle litter the jungle gym where I take my two-year-old son to play on weekends. (Bourgois 1993, 30)

In the 1970s, when deindustrialization was taking place, the federal government provided loans and grants to cities to compensate for the loss of revenues from fleeing employers and residents. Between 1980 and 1990, however, federal aid was reduced 64 percent, and cities had to rely primarily on property taxes as a source of revenue. At the same time, these tax receipts were decreasing as more people moved out of the city. The problem was further complicated by the fear that raising taxes might result in an even greater flight to the suburbs (Sclar and Hook 1993).

A lack of city revenues may also mean the city cannot pay its employees—sanitation workers, police and fire personnel, and schoolteachers. City services can literally come to a halt as employees refuse to work without pay. While all city services may be disrupted as a consequence of what amounts to municipal bankruptcy, the effects on schools may be the most devastating.

<aside>
National Data: A 1992 annual report by the National League of Cities revealed that expenditures exceeded revenues in 54 percent of all cities.

SOURCE: Cozic 1993.
</aside>

DETERIORATING SCHOOLS

As local revenues decrease, the quality of city schools, particularly in inner city neighborhoods, declines, leading many city residents to move to the suburbs. Although public schools in other countries are often supported at the national level, U.S. schools depend primarily on local funding. The result is dramatic differences between inner city and suburban schools. The former are highly segregated with an estimated 90 percent of the school population being nonwhite (Kozol 1991). Teachers, often from middle-class backgrounds, are unprepared to deal with the diverse student population and, out of frustration, may move to suburban school districts. Further, as discussed in Chapter 13, inner city schools are often the oldest and most deteriorated. Consequently, they lack adequate facilities, such as computer laboratories, and have higher teacher turnover because of the often dangerous working conditions. As educational quality continues to deteriorate, those who can afford to move out do so, leaving the poorest residents behind. As a result, property values continue to decline, the tax base decreases, schools further erode, and the cycle repeats itself.

OVERBURDENED TRANSPORTATION SYSTEMS

People who live and work in cities depend either on public transportation, such as buses and subways, or on roads and highways. The vast numbers of people relying on city transportation systems have placed an enormous burden on these systems.

The heaviest commuter flow is into New York City where every day 554,000 more people enter the city to go to work than leave it; next are Washington with 426,000 and Boston with 215,000 (Forstall 1993). Heavy use of city streets by commuters has resulted in numerous potholes, and many streets are impassable; those that are adequate support cars that contribute to air pollution in inner cities. Forty percent of U.S. bridges are estimated to be unsafe. For many municipalities, however, the cost of repairs is simply prohibitive.

Many mass transit systems are outdated and are not properly maintained—they are not federally funded as highways, expressways, and interstates are. Some cities have contracted privately for mass transit systems. In 1989, Denver became the first large city to do so; many others have followed, and some report savings of as much as 30 to 40 percent (Pool 1990).

SEGREGATION

Although more minorities are moving to the suburbs than ever before, minorities are still largely concentrated in central cities. Table 12.3 presents the percentages of racial minorities and Hispanics living in the four major U.S. metropolitan areas and the central city within each of these metropolitan areas. As the table indicates, the percentage of minority populations in central

TABLE 12.3

PERCENTAGE OF MINORITY POPULATIONS WITHIN FOUR MAJOR U. S. METROPOLITAN AREAS AND THEIR CENTRAL CITIES, 1990

	RACIAL MINORITY POPULATION*	HISPANIC POPULATION†
New York		
City	36.1%	24.4%
Metropolitan area	22.5	14.6
Los Angeles		
City	24.3	39.9
Metropolitan area	18.3	32.9
Chicago		
City	43.1	19.6
Metropolitan area	22.2	10.9
Washington, D.C.		
City	67.8	5.4
Metropolitan area	29.2	3.9

*Includes blacks, American Indians, Eskimos, Aleuts, Asians, and Pacific Islanders.
†Persons of Hispanic origin may be of any race.
SOURCE: *Statistical Abstract of the United States: 1994*, 114th ed. U. S. Bureau of the Census (Washington, D. C.: U. S. Government Printing Office), Tables 43, 46.

cities is significantly higher than in the total metropolitan area. This suggests that minorities are largely segregated in central cities, while non-Hispanic whites disproportionately comprise the suburban population.

Early government policies contributed to the concentration of minorities in large urban areas. In the 1930s and 1940s, the Federal Housing Authority and the Veterans Administration made it difficult for minorities to secure loans. Minorities were required to move into nonwhite-only neighborhoods. Since neighborhoods were segregated by race, and nonwhites lived in the center cities, the only available housing for minorities was in downtown areas. Additionally, most lending institutions often considered loans to minorities in central city neighborhoods to be too risky (Judd 1991).

The fact that many minorities do not have the resources to move out of inner city neighborhoods results in involuntary segregation—whites move out leaving nonwhites behind. Segregation is particularly evident in public housing. Bickford and Massey (1991) examined data from the U.S. Department of Housing and Urban Development (HUD) on segregation in public housing projects and found that blacks were invariably concentrated in high-density projects. The researchers concluded that "for blacks in the nation's largest cities, public housing segregation appears to be almost universal" (p. 1034).

> **Consideration** *African-Americans who leave inner city areas do not always prefer integrated settings. Some choose to live in suburbs or neighborhoods that are predominantly black. This pattern of residential separation is called voluntary segregation (Shannon, Kleniewski, and Cross 1991).*

INADEQUATE HOUSING

In an attempt to solve some of the housing needs of urban residents, the federal government has provided public housing for those who might otherwise not afford it. In New York City alone, the Housing Authority has a waiting list of 250,000 families, and it is one of the country's more successful programs. In addition, failure to screen residents has led to highly undesirable tenants—drug pushers who sell controlled substances to residents, making it dangerous for families and other law-abiding persons (Wagner and Vitullo-Martin 1993).

Available housing in urban areas is often inadequate, characterized by outdated plumbing and wiring, overcrowding, and fire hazards. The city does not repair these buildings because of a lack of funds. More often the money goes to suburban housing and urban renewal projects. The latter displace the poor with subsidized nonresidential projects such as office complexes. New, clean, inexpensive public housing units are almost nonexistent. This chapter's *Self and Society* demonstrates one of the most urgent problems faced by urban dwellers—the cost of housing (see pp. 356–357).

For some, there is no housing at all (see Chapter 11). New York City has more than 70,000 homeless. As Specter (1993) notes:

> *. . . in a city of houses such as Washington, the homeless can become almost invisible. Not here. Here we all live on top of each other so that no matter who you are, the problem never goes away. They are mentally ill, they use drugs, they have no hope. They are the dark reflection of a sick society. They symbolize the housing crisis and the jobs crisis and the uncomfortable Darwinian reality that the strong rarely do help the weak. (p. 86).*

National Data: About three out of four houses built before 1978 have some lead-based paint; children under six and women of childbearing ages are at the greatest risk for lead poisoning.

SOURCE: Housing and Urban Development 1995.

The homeless often live in abandoned buildings, including factories, houses, apartments, and businesses. These abandoned buildings, or TOADS (an acronym for "temporarily obsolete abandoned derelict sites"), are common in cities with insufficient industry and many poor and minority residents. Using TOADS for shelter is dangerous because they may expose people to toxic waste and diseased rodents. The homeless also build fires inside these structures for warmth, which sometimes results in the property catching fire and endangering thousands of nearby residents (Greenberg, Popper, and West 1990).

Sometimes owners intentionally set deteriorated properties on fire in order to collect insurance payments and to make land available for upscale development. Tenements that house people are often replaced by large commercial buildings with no housing units. To conflict theorists, profit over people is the reality of inner city development.

IMMIGRATION AND MIGRATION

The thousands of Cuban boats that landed on Florida shores in August of 1994 resensitized U.S. citizens to the potential problems of immigration. Immigrants typically settle in urban areas. Historically, a large influx of European immigrants in the late 1800s and early 1900s settled in U.S. urban areas. This was followed by a major migration of southern rural blacks to northern urban areas. Today, a large percentage of immigrants into inner cities are Asian or Hispanic. Minority immigrants, along with many inner city African Americans, are often economically disadvantaged, live in substandard housing, and receive inferior education (see also Chapter 9).

Recent immigrants settle disproportionately in certain cities, namely, Miami, San Francisco, Los Angeles, and Chicago. Unchecked immigration creates three major problems. First, as diversity increases, the possibility of violence may also increase as a response to hostile intergroup relations (e.g., the riots in Los Angeles). Second, recent immigrants may fail to assimilate socioeconomically. Such assimilation has been slowed by the development of the

Recent immigrants may fail to assimilate socioeconomically, and the tendency to settle in enclaves means that intra-group solidarity increases, which further lowers the probability of assimilation.

Housing Costs in U.S. Cities

The following U.S. cities each had a population of 200,000 or more in 1990. For each column, rank the cities from 1 to 15 in terms of median housing value and monthly rental payment. For example, if you think Mobile, AL, had the second highest median housing value, assign a number 2, and so forth. Use the same process for ranking monthly rental payments. When finished, compare your answers with the correct rankings.

1990 Median Value of Owner-Occupied Housing Units*		1990 Median Gross Rent of Renter-Occupied Housing Units†	
New York, NY	_____	San Jose, CA	_____
Chicago, IL	_____	Birmingham, AL	_____
Detroit, MI	_____	Buffalo, NY	_____
Indianapolis, IN	_____	Minneapolis, MN	_____
San Antonio, TX	_____	Jersey City, NJ	_____
Washington, DC	_____	Atlanta, GA	_____
Louisville, KY	_____	Richmond, VA	_____
Albuquerque, NM	_____	Boston, MA	_____
Honolulu, HI	_____	Portland, OR	_____
Wichita, KS	_____	New York, NY	_____
Anchorage, AK	_____	St. Louis, MO	_____
Mobile, AL	_____	Anchorage, AK	_____
Akron, OH	_____	Phoenix, AZ	_____
Baton Rouge, LA	_____	New Orleans, LA	_____
Pittsburgh, PA	_____	Ft. Worth, TX	_____

split labor market, the loss of blue-collar jobs in urban areas, and increased intragroup solidarity that lowers the probability of assimilation (Espiritu and Light 1991). Finally, an influx of immigrants places an even greater burden on the already struggling urban infrastructures as new residents require increased city services.

In some developing countries, the influx of migrants into the cities from surrounding rural areas is also creating problems. In China, for example, as many as 100 million people flocked into Chinese cities in 1992 looking for employment. Unable to find work, they crowded into ghetto areas and drained city services. To combat such an influx, China required all city residents to have a *hukou,* a police-issued residence permit that was required for such routine requests as having a telephone installed or enrolling a child in school. With so many people flooding urban areas, however, police resources were inadequate to regulate the masses. As a result, there has been an increase in crime and corruption associated with the black-market sale of permits (Kuhn and Kaye 1994).

URBAN POVERTY AND THE CYCLE OF DECAY

While the official poverty rate is higher in small towns and rural areas, the actual number of people who are poor is highest in urban areas, and the per-

Interpretation: The following table shows the correct ranking of the cities and their associated median housing values and monthly rental costs in 1990.

	RANK	VALUE		RANK	RENT
New York, NY	2	($189,600)	San Jose, CA	1	($755)
Chicago, IL	6	($78,700)	Birmingham, AL	15	($322)
Detroit, MI	15	($25,600)	Buffalo, NY	12	($352)
Indianapolis, IN	9	($60,800)	Minneapolis, MN	14	($329)
San Antonio, TX	12	($49,700)	Jersey City, NJ	4	($527)
Washington, DC	3	($123,900)	Atlanta, GA	7	($422)
Louisville, KY	7	($70,900)	Richmond, VA	8	($413)
Albuquerque, NM	5	($85,900)	Boston, MA	2	($625)
Honolulu, HI	1	($353,900)	Portland, OR	10	($392)
Wichita, KS	10	($56,700)	New York, NY	5	($496)
Anchorage, AK	4	($109,700)	St. Louis, MO	13	($342)
Mobile, AL	11	($55,400)	Anchorage, AK	3	($564)
Akron, OH	13	($43,800)	Phoenix, AZ	6	($442)
Baton Rouge, LA	8	($67,900)	New Orleans, LA	11	($379)
Pittsburgh, PA	14	($41,200)	Ft. Worth, TX	9	($403)

*A housing unit, as defined by the U.S. Census Bureau, is any unit intended for occupancy as the separate living quarters.

†Units for which the occupant pays rent in cash.

SOURCE: U.S. Census Bureau. 1995. "City and County Data Book." U.S. Census Government Gopher, Main Data Bank [Internet].

centage is increasing. The concentration of poor people in urban areas has many ramifications.

As a consequence of declining tax revenues, city services to the poor are severely cut; inadequate police protection leads to high crime, which frightens away prospective employees, employers, and/or residents; inferior schools result in high rates of truants, dropouts, and students with weak academic skills; blue-collar jobs are lost due to deindustrialization; and residents who remain segregated in these areas are ill prepared to meet the needs of an increasing technological and service-oriented society. Inner city landlords try to make a profit by raising rents or selling property for office complexes, parking decks, or public buildings. Doing so leads to an even greater housing shortage, reduced city revenues, and continued urban decay.

New Orleans, for example, is experiencing extensive urban decay. In 1993, the crime rate was up 36 percent from 1992, and it continued to climb in 1994. Violence in the city hurts the tourist industry and deters new businesses from locating there. New Orleans' problems began in the 1980s with the drop in oil prices, which led to a shortage of jobs and a loss of revenues. The city government went bankrupt, and those who could escape the deteriorating conditions did so—most often affluent whites moving to the suburbs. The urban population is now 65 percent black, and 10 percent of the city residents live in ten public housing projects. It is also estimated that there are 37,000 vacant

We will neglect our cities to our peril, for in neglecting them we neglect the nation.
— John F. Kennedy
Former U.S. President

National Data: In 1959, only 27 percent of the poor lived in metropolitan central cities; by 1991, the percentage had increased to 43 percent.

SOURCE: Kasarda 1993.

houses in New Orleans (Woodbury 1994). Moore, Livermore, and Galland (1991, 353) observe that New Orleans is a haven of

> . . . *joblessness, misguided welfare policies, and ineffectual corrections and educational programs. In the final stage, the kids and younger adults of this underclass cannibalize their own neighborhoods, stripping vacant apartments of anything of value, doing $30,000 worth of damage to a house to get a few pounds of brass fittings and copper wiring to sell to junk dealers for a few pennies.*

Saving Our Cities

Numerous federal, state and private policies and programs have been implemented to attempt to revitalize the cities. A number of these programs are reviewed here; some have worked while others have had questionable success.

FEDERAL PROGRAMS

The federal government has assisted cities through public housing and urban renewal programs.

In the film Field of Dreams Kevin Costner was told by unseen voices to "build it and they will come"; the Republican approach to cities seems to be "ignore them and they will go away."
— Ruth Messinger and Andrew Breslau
Social scientists

National Data: In 1977, the federal government gave cities $9.3 billion. By 1990, the funding had dropped to $4.6 billion.
SOURCE: Wagner and Vitullo-Martin 1993.
During the Reagan-Bush Republican years, federal funds as a percentage of city budgets were cut by over 64 percent.
SOURCE: Messinger and Breslau 1993.

Public Housing The oldest of the federal programs, public housing was intended to provide inexpensive housing for working poor families in inner cities. Under the program's policies, however, if residents' incomes increased above a certain level, they were evicted. As a result of these policies, public housing came to have a high concentration of people on welfare. Additionally, since the program was administered federally, it was not responsive to local needs (Wagner and Vitullo-Martin 1993).

Urban Renewal The urban renewal program was designed to rebuild blighted areas of the inner city and to provide low-cost housing for the poor. Unlike public housing programs, local authorities played a significant role in the design and location of the housing units and in the implementation of the program. Problems still existed, however. In some cases, houses in inner cities were torn down and replaced with office complexes or, alternatively, with middle- and upper-income housing, which displaced lower-income residents.

Other Federal Programs In the 1970s, the federal government began to assist cities through community development block grants "to benefit low and moderate income families, eliminate slums and blight, or meet urgent needs" (Brophy , 1993, 216). These grants also allowed cities more control over revitalization efforts.

Between 1977 and 1985, urban development action grants, which required commitments from local investors before being awarded, were implemented. The federal monies, which were unlimited in amount, were intended to create jobs and stimulate local economies. This program was highly successful. In 1990, HUD spent $4.6 billion on urban development action grants. Coupled with the $31.8 billion spent by private investors, these grants resulted in nearly 3,000 urban renewal projects in 1,209 locales. Additionally, the program created 592,000 new jobs and rehabilitated 113,000 houses. Due to budget cuts during the Reagan years, this program was discontinued in 1988 (Brophy 1993).

The Reagan-Bush administrations de-emphasized housing needs in cities and instead advocated broad-based economic development. Arguing that a healthy economy, both locally and nationally, would resolve the housing problem, "Reaganomics" assumed that if the economy fared well, prosperity would "trickle down" to the poor by providing jobs and, therefore, money for housing.

Reduced support, continued unfunded federal mandates, and bureaucratic breakdowns make it difficult for cities to recoup and prosper. In addition, it is estimated that "65% of every dollar of federal aid for the urban poor is absorbed by the urban bureaucracy that is supposed to deliver it" (*The Economist* 1993, 13).

PRIVATE INVESTORS

With the loss of federal support, cities have had to develop creative ways to fund projects. One successful tactic has been the development of partnerships between corporate leaders and local government entities. Cleveland Tomorrow, Portland Progress Associates, and the Greater Baltimore Committee have all been successful in revitalizing downtown areas. This chapter's *In Focus* describes in detail the efforts of the Greater Baltimore Committee. In 1991, the Atlanta city government and the Chamber of Commerce formed the Atlanta Neighborhood Development Partnership with financial support from the Ford Foundation. It raised more than $10.5 million for private investment in urban neighborhoods (Brophy 1993).

> *There are no quick fixes or dazzling new policy options for the problems that beleaguer America's cities.*
> — Ruth Messinger and Andrew Breslau
> Social scientists

COMMUNITY-BASED DEVELOPMENT PROGRAMS

Some residents of deteriorating urban areas have begun grassroots programs to improve living conditions in their neighborhoods. Community-based development programs involve small-scale developers and volunteers working with a small professional staff who are concerned with improving the community. In 1991, there were 2,000 community-based programs nationally, financed in part by the 1990 federal HOME program. A major advantage of community-based development programs is their holistic approach that focuses on formulating a comprehensive response to neighborhood concerns and empowering residents (Brophy 1993).

REPOPULATING THE CITIES

In an effort to stop the flight of urban residents to suburban areas and bring suburbanites back as city residents, tactics such as gentrification, urban homesteading, and the creation of enterprise zones have been used.

Gentrification Sometimes called neighborhood revitalization, **gentrification** is the process by which housing in older neighborhoods is purchased and renovated by private individuals and/or developers. In reality, old housing is

Baltimore: A Case Study in Central-City Renewal through Human Investment Programs

Human investment programs are aimed at making people more productive members of society. Such programs include education and job training, as well as programs that promote health and well-being. Baltimore provides a case study demonstrating how important human investment programs can be in the revitalization of cities plagued with poverty, unemployment, public health problems, and hopelessness.

In one innovative program, all students in the Baltimore public schools who maintain 95 percent attendance records during their junior and senior years are offered a "guarantee of opportunity." Each high school student with a good attendance record is guaranteed three job interviews with companies belonging to the Greater Baltimore Committee; if the interviews do not produce a job, the city Office of Employment Development evaluates the individual and provides additional training.

The Greater Baltimore Committee has also formed a CollegeBound Foundation to provide students with financial assistance to attend college. CollegeBound advisers go into the high schools to help students learn about scholarship opportunities, college options, and required courses and to assist them with SAT registration and financial aid applications.

The CollegeBound program has achieved impressive results. During the 1990–91 school year, the percentage of students taking the SAT increased 24 percent over the previous year.

During the same period, the proportion of seniors completing financial aid forms for assistance with college expenses rose 46 percent. The percentage of seniors who completed college applications increased from 26 percent in 1990 to 46 percent in 1991.

The long-term effects of Baltimore's "guarantee of opportunity" and CollegeBound programs have yet to be documented. But documenting the results is not the biggest obstacle to implementing and continuing human investment programs. The biggest obstacle is funding. Imbroscio, Orr, Ross, and Stone (1995) point to the importance of recognizing the long-term gains of human investment programs rather than the short-term costs:

A popular myth holds that urban human investment programs—education and job training specifically—have been amply funded and that continuing social ills are evidence that more money is not a solution to the problems cities face. . . . The reality is different. Many human investment programs do work, but they are poorly funded. . . . Consequently, many needs go unmet, in some cases even when money spent in the short run would save expenses over the long run. (p. 51)

SOURCE: Adapted from David Imbroscio, Marion Orr, Timothy Ross, and Clarence Stone. 1995. "Baltimore and the Human Investment Challenge." In *Urban Revitalization: Policies and Programs*, ed. Fritz W. Wagner, Timothy E. Joder, and Anthony J. Mumphrey, Jr., pp. 38–68. Thousand Oaks, Calif.: Sage Publications.

often bought by cosmopolitans, single individuals, and child-free couples who want the advantages of living in an urban setting (Gans 1991). The city provides tax incentives for investing in old housing with the goal of attracting wealthier residents back into these neighborhoods and increasing the tax base. However, low-income residents are often forced into substandard housing as fewer and fewer rentals or affordable units are available. In effect, gentrification often displaces the poor and the elderly.

Urban Homesteading While gentrification encourages residents to buy and renovate older houses, **urban homesteading** encourages individuals and investors to buy abandoned houses at reduced prices. Restrictions may require the buyer to live in the house for a specified time period or dictate the type of renovations that must be made. Urban homesteading brings people back into the neighborhoods, reduces the number of vacant houses, increases the property tax base, and encourages people to take pride in their homes and in their neighborhoods.

Enterprise Zones In addition to attracting residents, local governments may provide tax incentives to businesses that locate in low-income areas with the stipulation that they must hire a certain proportion of local employees. Thus, **enterprise zones** stimulate the local economy, provide jobs for the unemployed, and increase city revenues.

REGIONALIZATION

Revitalizing cities is difficult because the city and suburban areas are constantly in conflict over the distribution of government-funded resources. Residents of suburbs "use" city services (e.g., roads, water supplies, sewer systems, mass transit systems) and cultural offerings (e.g., museums, theater) without paying taxes for them. One solution is to merge city and suburban governments—a technique known as **regionalization.** A metropolitan-wide government must be formed to handle the inequities and concerns of both suburban and urban areas. As might be expected, suburban officials resist regionalization because they believe it will hurt their neighborhoods economically by draining off money for the cities.

STRATEGIES FOR ALLEVIATING URBAN GROWTH IN LESS DEVELOPED COUNTRIES: POPULATION CONTROL AND REDISTRIBUTION

In less developed countries, limiting population growth is essential for alleviating social problems associated with rapidly growing urban populations. Strategies for lowering the birth rate and reducing population growth are discussed in detail in Chapter 15.

Another strategy for minimizing urban growth in less developed countries involves redistributing the population from urban to rural areas. The document resulting from the 1994 United Nations International Conference on Population and Development suggests how governments can lure industry and people away from overcrowded cities (United Nations 1994): (1) promote agricultural development in rural areas, (2) provide incentives to industries and businesses to relocate from urban to rural areas, (3) provide incentives to encourage new businesses and industries to develop in rural areas, (4) develop the infrastructure of rural areas, including transportation and communication systems, clean water supplies, sanitary waste disposal systems, and social services. Of course, these strategies require economic and material resources, which are in short supply in less developed countries.

What can we conclude from our analysis of urban life? Clearly, deindustrialization, deconcentration, and suburbanization have seriously and, for the most part, negatively affected urban life. U.S. cities are suffering from fewer jobs, higher crime rates, inadequate schools, failing services, and deteriorating housing. Many residents who could afford to leave have done so; those who remain are often the poor, the elderly, and/or minorities. Without jobs or an adequate education, their chances of getting out are limited.

Urban problems are multifaceted and interrelated. It is difficult to know what causes what. For example, did suburbanization contribute to the deterioration of the inner cities or vice versa? Is poverty a cause of urban ills or the result? It is difficult to determine the ordering of the variables and, therefore, what to do to resolve the problems.

We do know that as cities deteriorate, the surrounding suburbs tend to do so as well. Although the suburbs would like to remain detached from the responsibility of protecting the inner cities from decline, their efforts are misguided. The interconnectedness of city and suburbs is like a malignancy that affects us all either directly if we live in the cities or indirectly as museums close and we fear for our lives when walking city streets.

Addressing the problems of America's cities requires a societal commitment to a "pro-growth urban policy." The goals of such a policy would include the following (Sclar and Hook 1993; Wagner and Vitullo-Martin 1993; Wagner, Joder, and Mumphrey 1995):

1. *Reduce conflict between the suburbs and inner cities.* Regionalization or some other structural changes are needed to assure that those who benefit from a service contribute to its cost. While conflict theorists emphasize that competition and exploitation between groups are inevitable, cooperation would better serve the needs of the two areas as evidenced by municipalities where regional governments have been implemented.

2. *Improve city services.* Inadequate city services lead to unsafe and undesirable living conditions in urban areas. If we want our cities to flourish, we must be willing to commit the financial funds that are necessary to improve and maintain top-quality city services.

3. *Maximize human capital.* Residents in inner city neighborhoods must receive quality education and job training to prepare them for an increasingly competitive marketplace. Employment programs such as the depression era's Works Progress Administration (WPA), which successfully built libraries, roads, and the like and created jobs, could also be implemented. Workers, for example, could be used to make capital improvements in distressed areas.

4. *Revitalize urban neighborhoods.* This includes revitalizing abandoned houses and industrial real estate complexes so that residents have clean affordable places to live and work. Community block grants in the mid-1970s, provide an excellent model—money was directed specifically for deteriorating communities and not siphoned off for other causes.

Public space must also be reclaimed to eliminate physical and social disorder:

Physical disorder is sometimes characterized as "broken windows," but it includes vacant unkempt lots, abandoned buildings, and informal graveyards for junked cars. Social disorder includes not only illegal behavior, such as open-air drug markets, but also nonviolent disorderly behavior, such as groups of young men insulting or threatening passers-by, public drinking, and other behaviors that make people feel uncomfortable or unsafe. (Violence in Urban America 1994, 21)

5. *Reinstitute public housing.* Not only should applicants be screened but residents should be provided the opportunity to purchase the house. Such housing should be single-family units, not high-rise projects, and those cities where revitalization is needed the most should have highest priority.
6. *Take responsibility.* The federal government needs to take responsibility for the problems it creates and to rethink and/or alter unsuccessful policies. For example, some immigration policies encourage an influx of immigrants into cities that simply cannot absorb the population increase. The federal government also imposes mandates without providing funding for them.

It is not clear which of these social actions can realistically be enacted or what the priority should be. What is clear is that to not act affirmatively is to abandon our cities and watch them deteriorate into armed camps. No other country in the industrial world neglects its cities as does the United States. Japan is in the midst of an $8 trillion investment in its urban infrastructure; Paris, London, Bonn, and Rome all enjoy levels of national support that, if they were offered here, would make the nation's mayors cry with joy. By ignoring our cities' needs, we are jeopardizing our future competitiveness in the world economy (Messinger and Breslau 1993, 35–36).

Progress is being made. "Pittsburgh resuscitated itself from dependence on one dominant and dying industry—steel—into a diverse and thriving economy. Chicago is thriving both downtown and in its neighborhoods. Atlanta, Dallas, and Houston have made themselves models of economic efficiency in the new global markets" (Wagner and Vitullo-Martin 1993). There is hope for our cities.

CRITICAL THINKING

1. Why does the federal government pass legislation to reduce urban decline without providing the funds for its mandates?
2. What common interests of urbanites and suburbanites might encourage them to cooperate in resolving problems of urbanization?
3. Which theories of urbanization might become more in vogue as cities change in the next thirty years?

KEY TERMS

urbanization

urban population

urbanized area

suburbs

suburbanization

metropolitan area

metropolis

urbanism

community policing

defensible space

deindustrialization

deconcentration

gentrification

urban homesteading

enterprise zones

regionalization

urban villages

REFERENCES

Adler, Jerry. 1995. "Bye-Bye, Suburban Dream." *Newsweek,* May 15, 40–45.

Bickford, Adam, and Douglas S. Massey. 1991. "Segregation in the Second Ghetto: Racial and Ethnic Segregation in American Public Housing, 1977." *Social Forces* 69(4): 1011–36.

Bourgois, Philippe. 1993. "Growing Up." In *Social Problems,* ed. Leroy W. Barnes, pp. 28–31. Guilford, Conn.: Dushkin Publishing Group.

Brophy, Paul C. 1993. "Emerging Approaches to Community Development." In *Interwoven Destinies: Cities and the Nation,* ed. Henry Cisneros, pp. 213–30. New York: W. W. Norton.

Brown, Lee P. 1993. "Police-Community Partnerships Reduce Urban Crime." In *American Cities: Opposing Viewpoints,* ed. Charles P. Cozic, pp. 128–34. San Diego, Calif.: Greenhaven Press.

Cose, Ellis. 1994. "Drawing Up Safer Streets." *Newsweek,* July 11, 57.

Cozic, Charles P., ed. 1993. *American Cities: Opposing Viewpoints.* San Diego, Calif.: Greenwood Press.

Davis, Robert. 1994. "We Live in Age of Exotic Defenses." *USA Today,* November 22, 1A.

The Economist. 1993. "Hell Is a Dying City." November 6, 13–14.

Espiritu, Yen, and Ivan Light. 1991. "The Changing Ethnic Shape of Contemporary Urban America." In *Urban Life in Transition,* ed. M. Gottdiener and Chris G. Pickvance, pp. 35–54. Newberry Park, Calif.: Sage Publications.

Fisher, Claude. 1982. *To Dwell among Friends: Personal Networks in Town and City.* Chicago: University of Chicago Press.

Feagin, Joe R. 1983. *The Urban Real Estate Game.* Englewood Cliffs, N.J.: Prentice-Hall, pp. 20–37.

Forstall, Richard L. 1993. "Going to Town." *American Demographics* (May): 42–47.

Gans, Herbert. [1962] 1984. *The Urban Villagers,* 2d ed. New York: Free Press (first edition published in 1962).

_____. 1991. *People, Plans, and Policies: Essays.* New York: Columbia University Press and the Russell Sage Foundation.

Greenberg, Michael R., Frank J. Popper, and Bernadette M. West. 1990. "The TOADS Go to New Jersey: Implications for Land Use and Public Health in Mid-Sized and Large U.S. Cities." *Urban Studies* 29: 117–25.

Housing and Urban Development. 1995. "Lead-based Paint: A Threat to your Children." Gopher.hud.gov [internet].

Judd, Dennis R. 1991. "Segregation Forever?" *The Nation*, December 9, 740–43.

Kasarda, John. 1993. "Cities as Places Where People Live and Work: Urban Change and Neighborhood Distress." In *Interwoven Destinies: Cities and the Nation,* ed. Henry Cisneros, pp. 81–124. New York: W. W. Norton.

Kessler, Ronald C., Katherine A. McGonale, Shanyang Zhao, Christopher B. Nelson, Michael Hughes, Suzann Eschleman, Hans-Ulrich Wittchen, and Kenneth S. Kendler. 1994. "Lifetime and 12-Month Prevalence of DSM-III-R Psychiatric Disorders in the United States." *Archives of General Psychiatry* 51: 18–19.

Kozol, John. 1991. *Savage Inequalities: Children in American Schools.* New York: Crown Publishing.

Kuhn, Anthony, and Lincoln Kaye. 1994. "Bursting at the Seams." *Far Eastern Economic Review* (March 10): 27–28.

Larson, Jan. 1993. "Density Is Destiny." *American Demographics* (February): 38–42.

Lord, George F., and Albert C. Price. 1992. "Growth Ideology in a Period of Decline: Deindustrialization and Restructuring, Flint Style." *Social Problems* 39(2): 155–69.

McNulty, Robert. 1993. "Quality of Life and Amenities as Urban Investment." In *Interwoven Destinies: Cities and the Nation,* ed. Henry Cisneros, pp. 231–49. New York: W. W. Norton.

Messinger, Ruth, and Andrew Breslau. 1993. "I Am City, Hear Me Roar." *Social Policy* (Spring): 26–37.

Moore, Winston, Charles Livermore, and George F. Galland, Jr. 1991. "Woodlawn: The Zone of Destruction." In *Social Problems: Contemporary Readings,* 2d ed. John Stinson, Ardyth Stinson, and Vincent N. Parrillo, pp. 351–64. Itasca, Ill.: F. E. Peacock Publishers.

Pool, Robert. 1990. "Urban Transit Savings." Speech delivered to The Heritage Foundation, March 13.

Sassen, Saskia. 1994. "The Urban Complex in a World Economy." *International Social Science Journal* 46: 43–62.

Sclar, Elliot, and Walter Hook. 1993. "The Importance of Cities to the National Economy." In *Interwoven Destinies: Cities and the Nation,* ed. Henry Cisneros, pp. 48–80. New York: W. W. Norton.

Shannon, Thomas R., Nancy Kleniewski, and William M. Cross. 1991. *Urban Problems in Sociological Perspective,* 2d ed. Prospect Heights, Ill.: Waveland Press.

Shoop, Julie Gannon. 1993. "Criminal Lawyers Develop 'Urban Psychosis' Defense." *Trial* (August): 12–13.

Specter, Michael. 1993. "Calcutta on the Hudson: We New Yorkers Are Learning How to Escape from the Giant Army of Homeless People." *Society in Crisis,* ed. The Washington Post Writer's Group, pp. 85–87. Boston: Allyn & Bacon.

Statistical Abstract of the United States: 1993, 113th ed., U.S. Bureau of the Census. Washington , D.C.: U.S. Government Printing Office.

Statistical Abstract of the United States: 1994, 114th ed., U.S. Bureau of the Census. Washington, D.C.: U.S. Government Printing Office.

Statistical Abstract of the United States: 1995, 115th ed., U.S. Bureau of the Census. Washington, D.C.: U.S. Government Printing Office.

Tittle, Charles. 1989. "Influences on Urbanism: A Test of Predictions from Three Perspectives." *Social Problems* 36(3): 270–88.

United Nations. 1994. *Programme of Action.* The United Nations International Conference on Population and Development (ICPD). Cairo, Egypt. September 5–13, 1994.

Violence in Urban America. 1994. Summary of a Conference Held by Committee on Law and Justice, Commission on Behavioral and Social Sciences and Education, National Research Council, and John F. Kennedy School of Government. Washington, D.C.: National Academy Press.

Wagner, Fritz W., Timothy E. Joder, and Anthony J. Mumphrey Jr., eds. 1995. "Conclusion." In *Urban Revitalization: Policies and Programs,* pp. 203–11. Thousand Oaks, Calif.: Sage Publications.

Wagner, Robert F., and Julia Vitullo-Martin. 1993. "Can Clinton Save Our Cities?" *Journal of the American Planning Association* (Summer): 267–70.

Wilson, Thomas C. 1993. "Urbanism and Kinship Bonds." *Social Forces* 71(3): 703–12.

Wirth, Louis. 1938. "Urbanism as a Way of Life." *American Journal of Sociology* 44: 8–20.

Wolff, Kurt H. 1978. *The Sociology of George Simmel.* Toronto: Free Press.

Woodbury, Richard. 1994. "Down in the Big Queasy." *Time,* February 28, 43.

13

CHAPTER

Crisis in Education

IS IT TRUE?

Due to court-ordered busing and a national emphasis on the equality of education, segregation in the public schools has been largely eliminated (p. 384).

When researchers asked a national sample of U.S. public school parents to give a grade to the nation's public schools, most respondents (over 50 percent) gave either an "A" or a "B" to the schools (p. 376).

In 1993, almost one-third of Hispanic Americans ages eighteen to twenty-one were high school dropouts (p. 377).

More than half of people in developing nations are illiterate (p. 368).

IQ is the best predictor of school success (p. 381).

ANS: 1. F 2. F 3. T 4. T 5. F

> . . . we are dealing, it would seem, not so much with culturally deprived children as with culturally depriving schools. And the task to be accomplished is not to revise, and amend, and repair deficient children but to alter and transform the atmosphere and operations of the schools to which we commit these children. Only by changing the nature of the educational experience can we change its product.
>
> William Ryan, Sociologist

American education is experiencing a crisis. Former Secretary of Education William Bennett, who supported ending the Department of Education as a cabinet position, said that the agency "has come to contain bad ideas, harmful practices, needless expenditures, obsolete programs and dysfunctional regulations" (Henry 1995, 1D). Other problems associated with public education include teenagers who drop out of school, high school graduates who are unable to read or solve simple math problems, and teachers who are not adequately trained or are leaving the profession because of uncontrollable discipline problems. In this chapter, we focus on many of these social problems as part of the crisis in education. We begin with a cross-cultural look at education.

The Social Context: Cross-Cultural Variation in Education

Education is an indispensable tool for the improvement of the quality of life.
—United Nations Conference on Population and Development Cairo 1994

Looking only at the American educational system might lead one to conclude that most societies have developed some method of formal instruction for their members. After all, in the United States there are more than 80,000 schools, 2.5 million teachers, and 50 million students. In reality, many societies have no formal mechanism for educating the masses. As a result, more than half of the people in the developing nations are illiterate. In India alone, more than 250 million people cannot read or write—a number approximately equal to the entire population of the United States.

On the other end of the continuum are societies that emphasize the importance of formal education. In Japan, students attend school on Saturday, and the school calendar is forty days longer than in the United States. Germany, Israel, Scotland, England, and France also have more mandatory school days than the United States (Barrett 1990).

Some countries also empower professionals to organize and operate their school systems. Japan, for example, hires professionals to develop and implement a national curriculum and to administer nationwide financing for its schools. In contrast, school systems in the United States are often run at the local level by school boards and local PTAs composed of lay people. In effect, local communities raise their own funds and develop their own policies for operating the school system in their area; the result is a lack of uniformity from district to district. Thus, parents who move from one state to another often find the quality of education available to their children differs radically. In so-

Because teaching is a highly respected vocation in Japan, students treat their teachers with respect and obedience. Teaching is less well-regarded in the U.S. and the consequences are felt by our teachers every day.

cieties with professionally operated and institutionally coordinated schools such as Japan, teaching is a prestigious and respected profession. Consequently, Japanese students are attentive and obedient to their teachers. In the United States, the phrase "Those that can, do; those that can't, teach" reflects the lack of esteem for the teaching profession. The insolence and defiance among students in American classrooms are evidence of the disrespect that many American students have for their teachers.

Sociological Theories of Education

The three major sociological perspectives—structural-functionalism, conflict theory, and symbolic interactionism—are important in explaining different aspects of American education.

STRUCTURAL-FUNCTIONALIST PERSPECTIVE

According to structural-functionalism, the educational institution serves important tasks for society including instruction, socialization, the provision of custodial care, and the sorting of individuals into various statuses. Many social problems, such as unemployment, crime and delinquency, and poverty, may be linked to the failure of the educational institution to fulfill these basic functions (see Chapters 4, 10, and 11). Structural-functionalists also examine the reciprocal influences of the educational institution and other social institutions, including the family, political institution, and economic institution.

Instruction A major function of education is to teach students the knowledge and skills that are necessary for future occupational roles, self-development, and social functioning. Although some parents teach their children basic knowledge and skills at home, most parents rely on schools to teach their chil-

Education is the key to prosperity and the wisest investment we can make in our children's and our nation's future.
—Richard Riley
U.S. Secretary
of Education

dren to read, spell, write, tell time, count money, type, and use computers. As we will discuss later, many U.S. students display a low level of literacy skills and academic achievement. The failure of schools to instruct students in basic knowledge and skills both causes and results from many other social problems including unemployment, poverty, drug abuse, family problems, and crime and delinquency.

Socialization The socialization function of education involves teaching students to respect rules and authority—behavior that is essential for social organization (Merton 1968). Students learn to respond to rules and authority by asking permission to leave the classroom, sitting quietly at their desks, and raising their hands before asking a question. Students who do not learn to respect and obey teachers may later disrespect and disobey employers, police officers, and judges.

The educational institution also socializes youth into the dominant culture. Schools attempt to instill and maintain the norms, values, traditions, and symbols of the culture in a variety of ways, such as celebrating holidays (Martin Luther King, Jr. Day, Thanksgiving); requiring students to speak and write in standard English; displaying the American flag; and discouraging violence, drug use, and cheating.

As the number and size of racial and ethnic minority groups increase, American schools are faced with a dilemma: Should public schools promote only one common culture or should they emphasize the cultural diversity reflected in the American population? We examine this dilemma in this chapter's *In Focus*.

Sorting Individuals into Statuses Schools sort students into different educational statuses through a mechanism called **tracking**—grouping students together on the basis of similar levels of academic achievement and abilities. In elementary grades, students may be tracked into groups such as the Blue Birds, Yellow Birds, and Red Birds. In high school, students may be tracked into honors programs, college preparatory programs, and vocational programs.

Tracking attempts to facilitate instruction and promote learning by enabling teachers to gear instruction to the ability levels of their students. Critics of tracking argue that it creates inequities in the educational system because high-track pupils enjoy several advantages (Hallinan 1995). Students in high tracks are exposed to a wider and more interesting curriculum than lower-track students; they receive higher-quality instruction and experience fewer classroom disruptions from disciplinary problems. Higher-track students are also more highly regarded by their peers and have stronger self-images; teachers have high expectations for high-track students, but low expectations for students in low tracks. In a study on math and science tracking, Oakes (1990) found that students in the lower tracks had poorer teachers, inferior materials (e.g., books), and more difficulty getting the classes they needed for entry into college. Sernau (1993) argues that school tracking improves the performance of higher-track students, but depresses the performance of lower-track students and increases the social isolation of each from the other.

Some evidence suggests that students may actually learn better in heterogeneous groups where students of varying abilities help one another in what Oakes (1985) calls **cooperative learning.** In cooperative work groups, small groups of students work together, helping each other with either individual or

Monoculturalism or Multiculturalism in the Public Schools?

Throughout the United States, minority students comprise an increasing percentage of the school-age population. By the year 2000 over half of California's school-age population will be minority members. It is not surprising then that most Americans (75 percent) in a recent national poll believe that schools should promote both one common culture *and* diverse cultural traditions (Elam, Rose, and Gallup 1994). About half of those surveyed (53 percent) said that a common cultural tradition and diverse traditions should receive equal emphasis in the schools. Banks and Banks (1993) suggest that multicultural education is necessary to "help students to develop the knowledge, attitudes, and skills needed to function within their own micro cultures, the U.S. macro culture, other micro cultures, and within the global community" (p. 25). But in many schools across the nation, **multiculturalism** is either an unrealized or a nonexistent ideal. In Lake County, Florida, for example, the school board voted in May 1994 to teach students that American culture and institutions are "superior to other foreign or historic cultures" (Elam, Rose, and Gallup 1994, 52).

Neglecting or devaluing the norms, values, traditions, and languages of American minority students damages their self-esteem. A Mexican-American student recalled his feelings about being required to speak English (Rodriquez 1990:203):

When I became a student , I was literally "remade"; neither I nor my teachers considered anything I had known before as relevant. I had to forget most of what my culture had provided, because to remember it was a disadvantage. The past and its cultural values became detachable, like a piece of clothing grown heavy on a warm day and finally put away.

In addition to its negative effect on minority students' self-esteem, the failure to recognize and validate the cultural traditions of minority students contributes to the continuing cycle of prejudice and discrimination against them. Finally, misunderstanding or intolerance of differences between groups of people often leads to conflict and violence.

What can schools do to promote multiculturalism? Some schools regularly serve foods associated with different cultures such as tacos or fried rice, recognize religious and secular holidays celebrated by different cultures such as Kwanzaa (an African-American cultural celebration), and sponsor multicultural events such as Native American craft shows, and Mexican-American folk dances. Teachers may require students to read literature and poetry as well as nonfiction work written by members of cultural minorities. Some schools use achievement tests developed specifically for certain minority students. Schools may also emphasize the importance of languages other than American English and encourage students to be bilingual. Finally, some schools have incorporated multicultural or "diversity" issues into the curriculum.

In 1991, the Southern Poverty Law Center in Montgomery, Alabama launched a project called "Teaching Tolerance" to provide teachers with ideas and materials to teach young people how to accept those who are different from them. For example, in March 1995, the Center began free distribution of a teaching package called *The Shadow of Hate: A History of Intolerance in America*. More than 38,000 schools have requested a copy of this teaching package, which includes a 40-minute video, textbook, and complete lesson plans.

group assignments. Cooperative learning methods produce greater social engagement and learning for all students (Hallinan 1995; Sautter 1995).

> **Consideration**   Perhaps a meaningful and productive learning experience for students can be achieved in both tracked and detracked classrooms. Hallinan (1995) argues:
>
> Regardless of how students are grouped, if the educational processes provide quality instruction, increase student motivation, and foster positive social experiences, students will learn. . . . Quality instruction and a high level of student involvement will produce learning regardless of grouping. (p. 38)

Schools also sort individuals by providing credentials for individuals who achieve various levels of education within the system. These credentials sort people into various statuses such as "high school graduate," "college graduate," and "English major." Finally, schools sort individuals into professional statuses by awarding degrees for such professions as medicine, nursing, and law.

Custodial Care   The educational system also serves the function of providing custodial care (Merton 1968), which is particularly valuable to single-parent and dual-earner families. The school system provides supervision and care for children and adolescents for twelve years of school totaling almost 13,000 hours. Some states also offer full-day kindergarten in the public schools, and some school districts are experimenting with offering classes on a twelve-month basis, Saturday classes, and/or longer school days. Providing more hours of supervision for children and adolescents may reduce juvenile delinquency and teenage pregnancy. Indeed, "lack of parental supervision is one of the strongest predictors of the development of conduct problems and delinquency" (cited in Sautter 1995, K8). In most districts, adolescents are required to attend school until they reach age sixteen.

CONFLICT PERSPECTIVE

Conflict theorists emphasize that the educational institution solidifies the class positions of groups and allows the elite to control the masses. Although the official goal of education in society is to provide a mechanism for everyone to achieve, in reality educational opportunities and the quality of education are not equally distributed.

Conflict theorists point out that the socialization function of education is really indoctrination into a capitalist ideology. In essence, students are socialized to value the interests of the state and function to sustain it. Such indoctrination begins in kindergarten. Rosabeth Moss Kanter (1972) coined the term "the organization child" to refer to the child in nursery school who is most comfortable with supervision, guidance, and adult control. Teachers cultivate the organization child by providing daily routines and rewarding those who conform. In essence, teachers train future bureaucrats to be obedient to authority.

Finally, the conflict perspective focuses on what Kozol (1991) calls the "savage inequalities" in education that perpetuate racial inequality. Kozol documents gross inequities in the quality of education in poorer districts, largely

Kozol contends that schools in poorer, mostly minority districts tend to have less funding, and therefore, less adequate facilities, books, materials, and personnel.

comprised of minorities, compared to districts that serve predominantly white middle-class and upper-middle-class families. Kozol reveals that schools in poor districts tend to receive less funding and have inadequate facilities, books, materials, equipment, and personnel. This problem is discussed further later in the chapter.

SYMBOLIC INTERACTIONIST PERSPECTIVE

Whereas structural-functionalism and conflict theory focus on macro-level issues such as institutional influences and power relations, symbolic interactionism examines education from a micro perspective. This perspective is concerned with individual and small group issues, such as teacher-student interactions, the student's self-esteem, and the self-fulfilling prophecy.

Teacher-Student Interactions Symbolic interactionists have examined the ways in which students and teachers view and relate to each other. For example, children from economically advantaged homes bring social and verbal skills into the classroom that elicit approval from teachers. From the teachers' point of view, middle-class children are easy and fun to teach: they grasp the material quickly, do their homework, and are more likely to "value" the educational process. Children from economically disadvantaged homes often bring fewer social and verbal skills to those same middle-class teachers who may, inadvertently, hold up social mirrors of disapproval. Teacher disapproval contributes to the lower self-esteem among disadvantaged youth.

Students also influence the self-concepts of each other. Kinney (1993) observes that the most popular students sometimes label outsiders as "nerds" or "geeks" and that these labels have negative influences on how the students feel about themselves. Some students try to change such definitions by becoming involved in school clubs and activities, which provide a different reference for their self-concepts.

Self-Fulfilling Prophecy The **self-fulfilling prophecy** occurs when people act in a manner consistent with the expectations of others. For example, a teacher who defines a student as a slow learner may be less likely to call on that student or to encourage the student to pursue difficult subjects. As a consequence of the teacher's behavior, the student is more likely to perform at a lower level. Thus, students who are labeled as underachievers and placed in slower-paced classes are often less likely to succeed. Further, students who are labeled as "behavioral problems" or "class bullies" may also internalize these labels and act accordingly.

A study by Rosenthal and Jacobson (1968) provides empirical evidence of the self-fulfilling prophecy in the public school system. Five elementary school students in a San Francisco school were selected at random and identified for their teachers as "spurters." Such a label implied that they had superior intelligence and academic ability. In reality, they were no different from the other students in their classes. At the end of the school year, however, these five students scored higher on their IQ tests and made higher grades than their classmates who were not labeled as "spurters." In addition, the teachers rated the spurters as more curious, interesting, and happy and more

"THEY THINK I'M DUMB"

The following excerpt poignantly recounts a conversation between author-ethnographer Thomas Cottle (1976) and Ollie, an eleven-year-old boy, labeled as "dumb."

"You know what, Tom?" he said, looking down at his ice cream as though it suddenly had lost its flavor, "nobody, not even you or my Dad, can fix things now. The only thing that matters in my life is school, and there they think I'm dumb and always will be. I'm starting to think they're right. . . .

"Even if I look around and know that I'm the smartest in my group, all that means is that I'm the smartest of the dumbest, so I haven't gotten anywhere at all, have I? I'm right where I always was. Every word those teachers tell me, even the ones I like most, I can hear in their voice that what they're really saying is, 'alright you dumb kids, I'll make it easy as I can, and if you don't get it then, then you'll never get it.' That's what I hear every day, man. From every one of them. Even the other kids talk to me that way too. . . ."

"I'll tell you something else," he was saying, unaware of the ice cream that was melting on his hand. "I used to think, man, that even if I wasn't so smart, that I could talk in any class in that school, if I did my studying, I mean, and have everybody in that class, all the kids and the teacher too, think I was alright. Maybe better than alright too. You know what I mean?"

"That you were intelligent," I said softly.

"Right. That I was intelligent like they were. I used to think that all the time, man. Had myself convinced that whenever I had to stand up and give a little speech, you know, about something, that I'd just be able to go do it." He tilted his head back and forth. "Just like that," he added excitedly.

"I'm sure you could too."

"I could have once, but not anymore."

"How do you know, Ollie?"

"I know."

"But how?" I persisted.

"Because last year just before they tested us and talked to us, you know, to see what we were like, I was in this one class and doing real good. As good as anybody else. Did everything they told me to do. Read what they said, wrote what they said, listened when they talked. . . ."

"Then they told me, like on a Friday, that today would be my last day in that class. That I should go to it today, you know, but that on Monday I had to switch to this other one. They just gave me a different room number, but I knew what they were doing. Like they were giving me one more day with the brains, and then I had to go to be with the dummies, where I was suppose to be. . . . So I went with the brains one more day, on that Friday like I said, in the afternoon. But the teacher didn't know I was moving, so she acted like I belonged there. Wasn't her fault. All the time I was just sitting there thinking this is the last day for me. This is the last time I'm ever going to learn anything, you know what I mean? Real learning."

He had not looked up at me even once since leaving the ice cream store. . . . "From now on," he was saying, "I knew I had to go back where they made me believe I belonged . . . then the teacher called on me, and this is how I know just how not smart I am. She called on me, like she always did, like she'd call on anybody, and she asked me a question. I knew the answer, 'cause I'd read it the night before in my book. . . . So I began to speak, and suddenly I couldn't say nothing. Nothing, man. Not a word. Like my mind died in there. And everybody was looking at me, you know, like I was crazy or something. My heart was beating real fast, I knew the answer, man. And she was just waiting, and I couldn't say nothing. And you know what I did? I cried. I sat there and cried, man, 'cause I couldn't say nothing. That's how I know how smart I am. That's when I really learned at that school, how smart I was. I mean, how smart I thought I was. I had no business being there. Nobody smart's sitting in no class crying. That's the day I found out for real. That's the day that made me know for sure."

Ollie's voice had become so quiet and hoarse that I had to lean down to hear him. We were walking in silence, I was almost afraid to look at him. At last he turned toward me, and for the first time I saw the tears pouring from his eyes. His cheeks were bathed in them. Then he reached over and handed me his ice cream cone.

"I can't eat it now, man," he whispered. "I'll pay you back for it when I get some money."

SOURCE: Excerpted from Thomas J. Cottle. 1976. *Barred from School.* Washington, D.C.: The New Republic Book Company, Inc., pp 138–40. Used by permission.

likely to succeed than the "nonspurters." Because the teachers expected the "spurters" to do well, they treated the students in a way that encouraged better school performance. This chapter's *The Human Side* illustrates how negative labeling affects a student's self-concept and performance.

Problems in the American Educational System

Half of public school parents in a national poll rated the quality of the education their children receive as average or below-average (Elam and Rose 1995). The concerns Americans have about the schools their children attend are not misplaced. In 1983, the National Commission on Excellence in Education claimed that "for the first time in history, the education skills of one generation will not surpass, will not equal, will not even approach, those

> *The quality of education our children attain is central to our survival as a society.*
> —Sandra A. Waddock
> Boston College

We need to give up the notion of a single ideal of the educated person and replace it with a multiplicity of models designed to accommodate the multiple capacities and interests of students.
—Nel Noddings
Educational reformer

of their parents" (p. 11). Student alienation, illiteracy and low academic achievement, high dropout and truancy rates, inadequate school facilities and personnel, and student violence and discipline problems contribute to the widespread concern over the quality of American education.

STUDENT ALIENATION

In the typical U.S. public school, students have little or no input into school rules, regulations, and curricula. Students have few choices regarding the courses they take, the books they read, the school projects they do, and the methods by which they are evaluated. Consequently, many students experience **alienation,** or a sense of powerlessness and meaninglessness in the role of student (see Self and Society in Chapter 10). This state of powerlessness and meaninglessness generalizes to relationships with others and ultimately leads to a sense of estrangement from one's self. Alienation among students manifests itself in such problems as absenteeism and dropping out of school, failure to complete assignments, careless work and poor test performance, low motivation, vandalism, and discipline problems on school grounds (Newmann 1980).

Increasingly, educational reformers are arguing against "an ideology of control that forces all students to study a particular, narrowly prescribed curriculum devoid of content they might truly care about" and arguing for "greater respect for a wonderful range of human capacities now largely ignored by schools" (Noddings 1995, 366). Some alternative and innovative schools, described later in this chapter, have found ways to empower students and involve them in meaningful educational experiences without loss of academic rigor.

ILLITERACY AND LOW ACADEMIC ACHIEVEMENT

In 1992, the Educational Testing Service for the Department of Education conducted the National Adult Literacy Survey, which involved interviewing and testing 26,000 adults age sixteen and older. This survey required respondents to demonstrate that they could understand basic written information, complete a job application form, and balance a checkbook. The results were embarrassing (see National Data).

Although literacy levels tend to be lowest among students who attend the poorest schools in the nation (Kozol 1991), apathy and ignorance may be found among students at more affluent schools as well. For example, a 1988 ABC News Special entitled "Burning Questions: America's Kids: Why They Flunk" began with the following interview with students from middle-class high schools:

Interviewer: Do you know who's running for president?

First Student: Who, run? Ooh. I don't watch the news.

Interviewer: Do you know when the Vietnam War was?

Second Student: Don't even ask me that. I don't know.

Interviewer: Which side won the Civil War?

Third Student: I have no idea.

Interviewer: Do you know when the American Civil War was?

Fourth Student: 1970.

Hewlett (1992) reports evidence that paints a disturbing picture of the academic achievement levels of U.S. students. Average SAT scores of high school seniors in 1989 were 70 points below those in the early to mid-1960s. In 1989, only 5 percent of seventeen-year-old high school students could calculate the unit cost of electricity on a utility bill; in the early 1970s, 12 percent of seventeen-year-olds could solve this problem. In 1987, almost half of seventeen-year-olds in the United States could not determine whether 87 percent of 10 is greater than, less than, or equal to 10. About 35 percent of American eleventh-graders write at or below the following level:

"I have been experience at cleaning house Ive also work at a pool for I love keeping thing neat organized and clean. Im very social Ill get to know people really fast." (reported in Hewlett 1992, 83)

In most international comparisons of educational achievement, U.S. students rank at or near the bottom. Survey results reported by Hewlett (1992) show that U.S. students placed seventh out of ten countries in physics; ninth out of ten countries in chemistry; and tenth, or last place, in mathematics proficiency.

Consideration *Adults who do not graduate from high school or who do poorly in school tend to work in low-income jobs. Thus, society attributes poverty largely to the academic failure that characterizes impoverished people. Noddings (1995) offers a different perspective:*

No person who does honest, useful work—regardless of his or her educational attainments—should live in poverty. A society that allows this to happen is not an educational failure; it is a moral failure. (p. 366)

HIGH TRUANCY AND DROPOUT RATES

More than one out of every ten Americans ages eighteen to twenty-four has not completed high school. The highest dropout rate is among Hispanic Americans. Truancy and dropout rates are also highest among poor students living in school districts that are inadequately funded. Kozol (1991) examined some of the poorest schools in the nation and found dropout rates of up to 86 percent in some Chicago schools, 60 percent in some Cincinnati schools, and over 60 percent in Jersey City schools.

Why do students drop out of high school? In the National Educational Longitudinal Survey (McMillen et al. 1992), students who dropped out of school between the eighth and tenth grades reported several reasons for dropping out (see Table 13.1).

The economic and social consequences of dropping out of school are significant. Dropouts are more likely than those who complete high school to be unemployed and to earn less when they are employed. Individuals who do not complete high school are also more likely to engage in criminal activity, have poorer health and lower rates of political participation, and require more government services such as welfare and health care assistance (Natriello 1995; Rumberger 1987).

National Data: In 1993, 12.6 percent of Americans ages eighteen to twenty-one were high school dropouts. In that age group, 12.3 percent of whites, 15.9 percent of blacks, and almost one-third of Hispanics (28.6 percent) were high school dropouts.

SOURCE: *Statistical Abstract of the United States: 1995*, Table 269.

National Data: In 1992, high school dropouts were three times more likely to receive AFDC or other public assistance payments than high school graduates with no college.

SOURCE: National Center for Education Statistics 1995.

TABLE 13.1

WHY STUDENTS DROP OUT OF HIGH SCHOOL*

REASON	PERCENT
1. Did not like school	51%
2. Failing in school	40
3. Could not keep up with schoolwork	31
4. Did not feel they belonged	23
5. Could not work and go to school at the same time	14
6. Became a parent	14
7. Had to support a family	9

*Reasons reported by students who dropped out of school between the eighth and tenth grades.
SOURCE: Marilyn M. McMillen, Phillip Kaufman, Elvie Hausken, and Denise Bradby. 1992. *Dropout Rates in the United States, 1991*. Washington, D. C.: National Center for Education Statistics, U. S. Department of Education.

There is a growing realization that completion of high school is the absolute minimal educational level necessary to prepare youngsters for the vast majority of jobs in the modern economy.
—Gary Natriello
Teachers College
Columbia University

National Data: In a national survey of students between the ages of twelve and nineteen, 16 percent reported the presence of street gangs in school; 16 percent reported that their teachers had been attacked or threatened with attack.

SOURCE: U.S. Department of Education 1992, p. 116.

In 1994, gunfire resulted in 35 deaths and 92 injuries in U.S. schools.

SOURCE: Sautter 1995.

Consideration *The consequences of dropping out of school have become more serious. In the early 1950s, only 60 percent of U.S. students graduated from high school. But those with little education could find manual labor jobs that did not require technical skills. Today, the uneducated have fewer job opportunities. "Gone are the days when society could absorb the uneducated in industrial jobs" (Lays 1991, 20). According to Tom Shannon, president of the National School Board Association:*

There are very few jobs left for those with strong backs but undeveloped minds. For example, the army is no longer looking for potato peelers. It's looking for people who can repair the machines that do the potato peeling. (Cited in Lays 1991, 20)

Dropout prevention programs and strategies are designed around various goals, including the following: (1) enhance the prospects for academic success; (2) strengthen the positive social relationships and climate of support and concern students experience in school; (3) make the school curriculum more relevant to the current and future lives of students; (4) involve parents in their children's educational experience; and (5) integrate educational and human services to address the social and economic problems that impede student progress (Natriello 1995).

STUDENT VIOLENCE

As we discussed in Chapter 4, the high rate of violence in U.S. society has infiltrated the nation's schools. A University of Michigan study estimates that each day 270,000 guns are brought to school, and that 160,000 students stay home from school because of fear of violence in or on the way to school (reported by Sautter 1995).

Many schools have responded to the problem of violence by taking drastic measures, such as installing metal detectors at entrances.

School violence affects more than individual victims. Sautter (1995) reminds us that "all students are victimized by the fear, the anger, the guilt, the anguish, and the sense of helplessness that follow an act of school violence" (p. K6).

In response to violence, many schools throughout the country have police officers patrolling the halls, require students to pass through metal detectors before entering school, and conduct random locker searches. Video cameras set up in classrooms, cafeterias, halls, and buses purportedly deter some student violence. More than 2,000 schools nationwide conduct peer mediation and conflict resolution programs to help youth resolve conflict in nonviolent ways (see also Chapter 4).

INADEQUATE SCHOOL FACILITIES AND PERSONNEL

In *Savage Inequalities,* Jonathan Kozol (1991) provides vivid and shocking descriptions of some of our nation's poorer schools. His descriptions reveal the gross inadequacies in school facilities and personnel that plague our school system. For example, in Crown Heights, Brooklyn, school officials have used bathrooms, gymnasiums, hallways, and closets as classrooms. At P.S. 94 in District 10, where 1,300 children study in a building suitable for 700, the gym has been transformed into four noisy, makeshift classrooms. The gym teacher improvises with no gym. In a reading classroom, huge pieces of the ceiling have collapsed onto the floor, desks, and books. The rain spills in through the roof.

Inadequate school facilities not only impede learning, but also contribute to behavioral problems and low self-esteem among students. Consider the following description:

These are not just cosmetic concerns. We are referring to conditions that are unsafe or even harmful.
—Carol Moseley-Braun
U.S. Senator

It's not enough to reform schools. We've also got to rebuild them.
—Tom Harkin
U.S. Senator

At Irvington High School . . . . the gym is used by up to seven classes at a time. To shoot one basketball, according to the coach, a student waits for 20 minutes. There are no working lockers. Children lack opportunities to bathe. They fight over items left in lockers they can't lock. They fight for their eight minutes on the floor. Again, the scarcity of things that other children take for granted in America—showers, lockers, space and time to exercise—creates the overheated mood that also causes trouble in the streets. The students perspire. They grow dirty and impatient. They dislike who they are and what they have become. (Kozol 1991, 159)

In addition to inadequacies in school facilities, there are inadequacies in school personnel. In the New York City school system, one school counselor must serve 700 students. In Paterson, New Jersey, one counselor serves 3,600 elementary school children. At P.S. 94 one truant officer is responsible for finding and retrieving no less than 400 children at a given time (Kozol 1991).

School districts with inadequate funding often have difficulty attracting qualified school personnel. Unfortunately, these poorer districts are in dire need for talented teachers who can meet the needs of children from diverse backgrounds and of varying abilities. Many schools have a shortage of minority teachers who can provide professional role models, have had similar life experiences, and have similar language and cultural backgrounds as minority students. Black and Hispanic male ghetto children may perceive that white middle-class female teachers are less understanding of what they experience than minority male teachers.

Undisciplined and violent students and inadequate teaching materials and school facilities contribute to low teacher morale. Low morale interferes with teaching effectiveness and drives some teachers out of the profession. The relatively low pay of teachers also contributes to morale problems and the questionable quality of instruction.

Individuals who enter and remain in the teaching profession are not necessarily competent and effective teachers. More than half of the states have implemented mandatory competency testing, which requires prospective teachers to pass the National Teacher's Examination or some other test of knowledge on the subject they intend to teach. Knowledge-based competency tests do not accurately predict a teacher's effectiveness in the classroom, however. A teacher may know how to solve algebra problems but may not have the skills to communicate this knowledge to a student.

In an effort to recruit teachers, more than half of the states have adopted **alternative certification programs,** whereby college graduates with degrees in fields other than education may become certified if they have "life experience" in industry, the military, or other jobs. *Teach for America,* originally conceived by a Princeton University student in an honor's thesis, is an alternative teacher education program aimed at recruiting liberal arts graduates into teaching positions in economically deprived and socially disadvantaged schools. After completing an eight-week training program, recruits are placed as full-time teachers in rural and inner city schools. Critics argue that these programs may place unprepared personnel in schools.

Later we will discuss some of the educational trends and strategies designed to improve the quality of American education. Next, we focus on another problem of education: inequality in the school system.

Who Succeeds? The Inequality of Educational Attainment

As noted earlier, conflict theory focuses on inequalities in the educational system. Educational inequality is based on social class and family background, race and ethnicity, and gender. Each of these factors influences who succeeds in school.

SOCIAL CLASS AND FAMILY BACKGROUND

Assume you want to predict a student's future educational success (as measured by grades and performance on standardized tests) and future educational attainment (number of years completed). What information will best help you make these predictions? IQ? No. The best predictor of educational success and attainment is socioeconomic status (Flanagan 1993). Children whose families are in middle and upper socioeconomic brackets are more likely to perform better in school and to complete more years of education than children from lower socioeconomic families. For example, students in the lowest quarter of family income levels are about a tenth as likely to finish four years of college by the age of twenty-four as those in the top quarter (Mortenson 1991).

Families with low incomes have fewer resources to commit to educational purposes. Low-income families have less money to buy books, computers, tutors, and lessons in activities such as dance and music and are less likely to take their children to museums and zoos. Parents in low income brackets are also less likely to expect their children to go to college, and their behavior may lead to a self-fulfilling prophecy. Disproportionately, children from low-income families do not go to college.

Low-income parents are also less involved in their children's education. Yet parental involvement is crucial to the academic success of the child. According to Barton (1992), the most powerful measure of school quality is a high parent-teacher ratio. Although working-class parents may value the education of their children, in contrast to middle- and upper-class parents, they are intimidated by their child's schools and teachers, don't attend teacher conferences, and have less access to educated people to consult with about their child's education (Lareau 1989). In addition, middle- and upper-class parents bring work home from the office; children in lower-class families do not see their parent(s) bring paperwork home. In the absence of a family norm or model for "homework," very little homework may be accomplished in lower socioeconomic families.

Because low-income parents are often themselves low academic achievers, their children are exposed to parents who have limited language and academic skills. Children learn the limited language skills of their parents, which restricts their ability to do well academically. Low-income parents are unable to help their children with their math, science, and English homework because they often do not have the academic skills to do the assignments.

Lower socioeconomic families tend to have more children and smaller homes than middle- and upper-class families. Low-income parents often spend less "quality time" with their children (because there are more of them),

Educational reform measures alone can have only modest success in raising the educational achievements of children from low-income families. The problems of poverty must be attacked directly.
—Richard J. Murnane
Graduate School
of Education
Harvard University

The family plays a key role in their children's success in school.
—Albert Bandura
Social scientist

Give me children from a two-parent Asian-American family. They will outscore almost everybody because they are taught at home that school is special, that teachers must be respected.
—William Bennett
Former Secretary
of Education

and the home environment and neighborhood are often noisy and not conducive to studying and learning.

Children from poor families also have more health problems and nutritional deficiencies. Children cannot learn when they are hungry, malnourished, sick, or in pain. Kozol (1991) interviewed children in the South Bronx and observed:

> Bleeding gums, impacted teeth and rotting teeth are routine matter for the children I have interviewed. . . . Children get used to feeling constant pain. They go to sleep with it. . . . Children live for months with pain that grown-ups would find unendurable. The gradual attrition of accepted pain erodes their energy and aspiration. I have seen children in New York with teeth that look like brownish, broken sticks. I have also seen teen-agers who were missing half their teeth. . . . Many teachers in urban schools have seen this. It is almost commonplace. (pp. 20–21).

Consideration In 1965, Project Head Start began to help preschool children from disadvantaged families. It provided an integrated program of care emphasizing four primary areas: (1) education, (2) health care (medical, dental, nutritional, and mental health), (3) parental involvement, and (4) social services. According to the Select Committee on Children, Youth and Families, every dollar spent on such programs as Head Start saves taxpayers six dollars in reduced costs for special education, truant officers, welfare benefits, and crime (cited in Hewlett 1992, 67). Hewlett notes, however, that due to underfunding, Head Start serves only 25 percent of those eligible.

Lack of adequate funding for Head Start is part of a larger problem: children who live in lower socioeconomic conditions receive fewer public educational resources (Kozol 1991). Schools that serve low socioeconomic districts are largely overcrowded and understaffed; they lack adequate building space and learning materials.

The U.S. tradition of decentralized funding means that local schools depend upon local taxes, usually property taxes; about 45 percent of school funding comes from local sources. The amount of money available in each district varies by the socioeconomic status, or SES, of the district. This system of depending on local communities for financing has several consequences:

- Low SES school districts are poorer because less valuable housing means lower property values; in the inner city, houses are older and more dilapidated; less desirable neighborhoods are hurt by "white flight" with the result that there is a low tax base for local schools in deprived areas.
- Low SES school districts are less likely to have businesses or retail outlets where revenues are generated; such businesses have closed or moved away.
- Because of their proximity to the downtown area, low SES school districts are more likely to include hospitals, museums, and art galleries, all of which are tax-free facilities. These properties do not generate revenues.
- Low SES neighborhoods are often in need of the greatest share of city services; fire and police protection, sanitation, and public housing consume the bulk of the available revenues. Precious little is left for education in these districts.

- In low SES districts, a disproportionate amount of the money has to be spent on maintaining the school facilities, which are old and in need of repair, so less is available for the children themselves.

While the state provides additional funding to supplement local taxes, it is not enough to lift schools in poorer districts to a level that even approximates the funding available to schools in wealthier districts.

RACE AND ETHNICITY

Socioeconomic status interacts with race and ethnicity. Because race and ethnicity are so closely tied to socioeconomic status, it appears that race or ethnicity alone can determine school success. While race and ethnicity also have independent effects on educational achievement (Pollard 1993), their relationship is largely due to the association between race and ethnicity and socioeconomic status. As Table 13.2 shows, educational attainment varies by race and ethnicity.

As the percentage of minority students in the classroom increases, so does concern for the negative correlation between minority status and educational achievement. One reason why some minority students have academic difficulty is that they did not learn English as their native language. Indeed, English is a second language for more than 32 million Americans. To help American children who do not speak English as their native language, some educators advocate **bilingual education**—teaching children in both English and their non-English native language. Advocates claim that bilingual education results in better academic performance of minority students, enriches all students by exposing them to different languages and cultures, and enhances the self-esteem of minority students. Critics argue that bilingual education limits minority students and places them at a disadvantage when they compete outside the classroom, reduces the English skills of minorities, costs money, and leads to hostility with other minorities who are also competing for scarce resources.

Another factor that hurts minority students academically is the fact that many tests used to assess academic achievement and ability are biased against minorities. Questions on standardized tests often require students to have knowledge that is specific to the white middle-class majority culture. Non-Hispanic students who take the Chicano Intelligence Scale of Cultural

In no school that I saw anywhere in the United States were nonwhite children in large numbers truly intermingled with white children.
—Jonathan Kozol
Author and
education specialist

TABLE 13.2

EDUCATIONAL ATTAINMENT BY RACE AND ETHNICITY (ADULTS 25 OR OLDER)

EDUCATIONAL ATTAINMENT	RACE/ETHNIC BACKGROUND	PERCENT
Four years of high school or more	Whites	82.1%
	Blacks	72.9
	Hispanics	53.3
Four years of college or more	Whites	23.0
	Blacks	12.9
	Hispanics	9.1

SOURCE: *Statistical Abstract of the United States: 1995*, 115th ed. U. S. Bureau of the Census (Washington, D. C.: U. S. Government Printing Office), Table 240.

Orientation (Ramirez 1988) generally do poorly because they do not have knowledge or language skills specific to the Hispanic culture (see this chapter's *Self and Society* on pp. 386–387). Similarly, minority students do poorly on tests that are biased toward the white middle class.

In addition to being hindered by speaking a different language and being from a different cultural background, minority students in white school systems are also disadvantaged by overt racism and discrimination. Much of the educational inequality experienced by poor children is due to the fact that a high percentage of them are also nonwhite or Hispanic. Discrimination against minority students takes the form of unequal funding, as discussed earlier, and school segregation.

In 1954, the U.S. Supreme Court ruled in *Brown v. Board of Education* that segregated education was unconstitutional because it was inherently unequal. Despite this ruling, many schools today are racially segregated. In 1966, a landmark study entitled *Equality of Educational Opportunity* (Coleman et al. 1966) revealed the extent of segregation in U.S. schools. In this study of 570,000 students and 60,000 teachers in 4,000 schools, the researchers found that almost 80 percent of all schools attended by whites contained 10 percent or fewer blacks, and that whites outperformed minorities (excluding Asian Americans) on academic tests. Coleman and his colleagues emphasized that the only way of achieving quality education for all racial groups was to desegregate the schools. This recommendation, known as the **integration hypothesis,** advocated busing to achieve racial balance.

In spite of the Coleman report, court-ordered busing, and an emphasis on the equality of education, public schools in the 1990s remain largely segregated. Racial segregation is particularly evident in poorer urban schools. Kozol (1991) found that most of the urban schools he visited in various U.S. cities were 95 to 99 percent nonwhite. Central-city schools have become more, not less, segregated since the Coleman report. In 1971, minority students comprised 43.5 percent of the student population of nineteen large U.S. central-city schools. By 1986, this percentage had increased to 78.1 percent (Wong 1995).

GENDER

Worldwide, women receive less education than men. Three-fourths of illiterate persons in the world are women (United Nations 1994).

Historically, U.S. schools have discriminated against women. Prior to the 1830s, U.S. colleges accepted only male students. In 1833, Oberlin College in Ohio became the first college to admit women. Even so, in 1833, female students at Oberlin were required to wash male students' clothes, clean their rooms, and serve their meals and were forbidden to speak at public assemblies (Fletcher 1943; Flexner 1972).

In the 1960s, the women's movement sought to end sexism in education. Title IX of the Education Amendments of 1972 states that no person shall be discriminated against on the basis of sex in any educational program receiving federal funds. These guidelines were designed to end sexism in the hiring and promoting of teachers and administrators. Title IX also sought to end sex discrimination in granting admission to college and awarding financial aid. Finally, the guidelines called for an increase in opportunities for female athletes by making more funds available to their programs. The push toward equality in education for women has had a positive effect on the aspirations of women.

Traditional gender roles account for many of the differences in educational achievement and attainment between women and men. As noted in Chapter 8, schools, teachers, and educational materials reinforce traditional gender roles in several ways. Some evidence suggests, for example, that teachers provide less attention and encouragement to girls than to boys and that textbooks tend to stereotype females and males in traditional roles (Bailey 1993).

Studies of academic performance suggest that females tend to lag behind males in math and science. One explanation is that women experience workplace discrimination in these areas, which restricts their occupational and salary opportunities. The perception of restricted opportunities, in turn, negatively impacts academic motivation and performance among girls and women (Baker and Jones 1993).

Bushweller (1995) notes, however, that while boys tend to excel in math and science, girls tend to excel in English. To help girls achieve in math and science, some schools have implemented all-girls classes in these subjects. Bushweller suggests that "if girls-only classes are being considered for science and math—subjects in which girls tend not to do as well as boys—then boys-only classes should be considered for subjects like English, where boys don't do as well as girls" (p. 12).

> **Consideration** Noddings (1995) also suggests that the concern over women lagging behind in traditionally male subjects should be accompanied by concern over men lagging behind in traditionally female subjects. She states:
>
> Women's lack of success or low rate of participation in fields long dominated by men is seen as a problem to be treated by educational means. But researchers do not seem to see a problem in men's low rate of participation in nursing, elementary school teaching, or full-time parenting. (p. 366)
>
> Noddings suggests that a high value should be placed on traditional female occupations. In her view, "care for children, the aged, and the ill must be shared by all capable adults, not just women, and everyone should understand that these activities bring special rewards as well as burdens" (p. 366).

Most of the research on gender inequality in the schools focuses on how female students are shortchanged in the educational system. But what about male students? For example, schools fail to provide boys with adequate numbers of male teachers to serve as positive role models. To remedy this, some school systems actively recruit male teachers, especially in the elementary grades where female teachers dominate.

The problems that boys bring to school may indeed require schools to devote more resources and attention to them. More than 70 percent of students with learning disabilities, such as dyslexia, are male, as are about 75 percent of students identified as having serious emotional problems. Boys are also more likely than girls to have speech impairments and to be labeled as mentally retarded. Lastly, boys are more likely than girls to exhibit discipline problems (Bushweller 1995).

Chicano Intelligence Scale of Cultural Orientation (CISCO)

Circle the letter of the correct answer.

1. Which one of the following is not associated with el movimiento?
    a. Miguel Aleman   b. Rodolfo Gonzales   c. César Chávez   d. Reis Tijerina

2. Which of the following organizations is not a Chicano organization?
    a. LULAC   b. PASO   c. American G.I. Forum   d. RUCA

3. One important ingredient of tortillas de harina:
    a. corn flour   b. vegetable oil   c. white flour   d. corn starch

4. My parents and the Silvas are "compadres" because I am the Silva's _____.
    a. godson   b. first cousin   c. orphan   d. grandson

5. The treaty signed by the United States and Mexico in 1848 is known as the Treaty of:
    a. Guadalupe Hidalgo   b. Chapultepec   c. San Joaquin   d. Chamizal

6. Which of the following are you least likely to find in a "barrio"?
    a. a church   b. a bakery   c. a dancehall   d. a Chamber of Commerce

7. A light-complected Mexican-American boy is likely to be nicknamed _____.
    a. blanco   b. gringo   c. prieto   d. güero

8. Rosita Alvirez:
    a. died from the three gunshots   b. married Hipolito
    c. had two sons and one daughter   d. did not like to go dancing.

9. That part of the southwestern United States from which it is believed the Aztecs migrated before they settled in Mexico City is:
    a. San Diego   b. Aztlan   c. Colorado   d. Santa Barbara

10. Chicken is to "mole" as intestine is to:
    a. chorizo   b. rice   c. menudo   d. gaspacho

11. The Chicano writer who was killed by a policeman in East Los Angeles in 1970:
    a. Francisco Madero, Jr.   b. Ruben Salazar
    c. José Espinosa   d. Juan Gallo

12. "Ranchera" music has a special quality when sung by:
    a. Trini Lopez   b. Libertad Gomez   c. Roberto Medina   d. Jorge Negrete

13. The poem "I am Joaquin" was written by:
    a. Joaquin Castillo   b. César Chávez   c. Miguel Aleman   d. Rodolfo Gonzales

14. The flag of the soldier:
    a. blue, white, red   b. green, white, red   c. yellow, white, red   d. green, white, yellow

15. Chante and canton:
    a. champion   b. home   c. shirt   d. song

16. As an act of faith and sacrifice many Chicanos stop having their favorite foods or drinks during:
    a. lent   b. police time   c. "las posadas"   d. hangover

17. A person who is my madrina is my:
    a. stepmother   b. legal guardian   c. mother-in-law   d. godmother

18. "These are 'las mananitas' that were sung by":
    a. the old woman Inez   b. the King David   c. the chicanito   d. the Queen Mary

19. Carnalismo:
    a. a purely physical attraction   b. a relationship through kinship
    c. sins of the flesh   d. a feeling of brotherhood

20. The Mexican composer famous throughout the world:
    a. Lee Treviño   b. Agustin Lara   c. José-Torres   d. Pedro Armindariz

21. El grito de Dorlores is most associated with:
    a. Benito Juarez   b. Emiliano Zapata   c. Pancho Villa   d. Padre Hidalgo

22. Which of the following terms does not appear in the Chicano movement?
    a. strike   b. overcome   c. assimilate   d. teatro campesino

23. Elected in El Paso, 1972, as chairman of La Raza Unida Party was:
    a. Alberto Casso   b. Corky Gonzales   c. José Angel Gutiérrez   d. César Chávez

24. Rice with _____.
    a. tongue   b. chicken   c. tamales   d. oranges

25. Chicano term for the police:
    a. la migra   b. la chota   c. el gabacho   d. el pachuco

26. The "barrio" is the home of:
    a. la migra   b. la chota   c. el gabacho   d. el pachuco

27. *Pocho* was written by:
    a. Angel Gutiérrez   b. Rodolfo Gonzales   c. Jose Villareal   d. Pedro Infante

28. The Virgin of Guadalupe appeared before:
    a. Christopher Columbus   b. Juan Diego   c. Jesus Villa   d. Pedro Pistolas

Answer Key:

1. a	8. a	15. b	22. c
2. d	9. b	16. a	23. c
3. c	10. c	17. d	24. b
4. a	11. b	18. b	25. b
5. a	12. d	19. d	26. d
6. d	13. d	20. b	27. c
7. d	14. b	21. d	28. b

SOURCE:Albert Ramirez. 1988. "Racism toward Hispanics: The Culturally Monolithic Society." In *Eliminating Racism: Profiles in Controversy*, ed. by Phyllis A. Katz and Dalmas A. Taylor, pp. 137–58. New York: Plenum Press. The scale is on pages 142 and 143. Used by permission of Dr. Albert Ramirez.

Scoring: Out of a possible score of 140 (28 items, 5 points for each correct answer), the average score for 133 Anglo-American students was 36.4 with a standard deviation of 14.42; the average score for 81 Chicanos was 93.3 with a standard deviation of 24.03. If the results of the test were interpreted in the same manner as traditional IQ test results, the conclusion would be that 16 percent of Anglo-American university students are severely defective and 52 percent are moderately defective (Ramirez 1988, 141).

Trends and Innovations in American Education

National Data: Between 1980 and 1993, the proportion of U.S. high school graduates going directly to college increased from 49 to 62 percent.

SOURCE: U.S. Department of Education 1995.

Since the 1983 publication of *A Nation at Risk,* which documented the dismal state of public education, American public schools have made attempts to improve. For example, 84 percent of the states have raised their graduation requirements, 70 percent of schools no longer permit students to participate in extracurricular activities if they are failing academic subjects, and 40 percent of schools have lengthened their school year (Celis 1993). However, educational reformers are calling for changes that go beyond get-tough policies that maintain the status quo.

MORAL AND INTERPERSONAL EDUCATION

Violence, divorce, teen pregnancy, and drug abuse suggest that more attention needs to be placed on moral education. Most school curricula neglect the human side of education—the moral and interpersonal aspects of developing as an individual and as a member of society. Some educational reformers oppose the current emphasis on increasing academic standards and recommend that the main goal of education should be "to encourage the growth of competent, caring, loving and lovable people" (Noddings 1995, 366). To achieve this, Noddings suggests that students work together on school projects, help younger students, contribute to the care of buildings and grounds, and do supervised volunteer work in the community. She recommends that:

> *All students should be engaged in a general education that guides them in caring for self, intimate others, global others, plants, animals, the environment, objects and instruments, and ideas. Moral life so defined should be frankly embraced as the main goal of education. (p. 368)*

Some educational reformers oppose the current emphasis on increasing academic standards and believe that education should encourage students to be "competent, caring, loving people."

A moral and interpersonal emphasis in education implies that schools should prepare students not only for the world of work, but also for parenting and for civic responsibility. Noddings (1995) notes that:

> Almost all of us enter into intimate relationships, but schools largely ignore the centrality of such interests in our lives. And although most of us become parents, evidence suggest that we are not very good at parenting—and again the schools largely ignore this huge human task. (p. 367)

How does the public feel about moral education? In a national poll, the majority of public school parents approved of teaching courses on values and ethical behavior in the public schools. Although public schools are constitutionally prohibited from teaching any particular religion, about two-thirds of public school parents favor nondevotional instruction about various religions (Elam, Rose, and Gallup 1994).

Moral and interpersonal education occurs to some extent in schools that have peer mediation and conflict resolution programs (discussed earlier and in Chapter 4). Such programs teach the value of nonviolence, collaboration, and helping others as well as skills in interpersonal communication and conflict resolution. Moral and interpersonal education also occurs in micro-society schools as discussed in the following section.

> *Our society does not need to make its children first in the world in mathematics and science. It needs to care for its children—to reduce violence, to respect honest work of every kind, to reward excellence at every level, to ensure a place for every child and emerging adult in the economic and social world, to produce people who can care competently for their own families and contribute effectively to their communities.*
> —Nel Noddings
> Educational reformer

MICRO-SOCIETY SCHOOLS

A **micro-society school** is a simulation of the "real" or nonschool world. In a micro-society school, the students—with the help and guidance of their teachers—design and run their own democratic, free-market society within the school (Clinchy 1995b). At the first micro-society school, the City Magnet School in Lowell, Massachusetts, developed in the early 1980s, students set up their own government, complete with legislative, executive, and judicial branches. They write their own school constitution and elect a legislature to make their own school laws. The school has its own courts and system of justice, as well as its own police force, called the City School Crime Stoppers. Students also devised and implemented a tax system operated by their own internal revenue service.

The school has an economic system with its own currency and banks in which every student has an account. Students have started numerous retail businesses that sell such things as pencils and stationery. They also set up their own publishing business within the language arts program.

All these micro-society activities are real jobs for which students get paid. "Everyone has to have and hold at least one job in the micro-society in order to earn wages or her keep, just as people do in real life" (Clinchy 1995b, 403). To learn all the basic skills necessary to hold a job and participate in the micro-society, students go to the school within the school—the City School Academy. Students pay tuition to "go to school" from the money they earn by holding jobs in the rest of the micro-society.

Through participation in the micro-society school, both students and their teachers "constantly face moral dilemmas that they must solve as they strive to build a 'good' society" (Richmond 1989, 232):

Do you want a society with the extremes of poverty and wealth? Do you want a state of fear and violence? Should the microsociety's government assist or ignore children who may not be succeeding? Do you want a democracy or a totalitarian state? What liberties should children have? And what responsibilities should they shoulder? What kinds of activities should be taxed? When does one put the community's welfare ahead of the rights of the individual? What civil rights should children enjoy in their microsociety?

NATIONAL EDUCATIONAL STANDARDS

When the fiscal crisis in most of our urban areas is so severe that classes are being held in gymnasiums and hallways, when many schools do not have enough funds to stay open for the full 180 days a year, when buildings are disintegrating before our very eyes, when in some cities three classrooms must share one set of textbooks . . . it is simply a flight of fantasy to assume that more standardized testing and national curriculum guidelines are the answer.
—Michael W. Apple
University of
Wisconsin—Madison

During the Clinton administration, Congress passed Goals 2000: The Educate America Act. This national agenda identified eight national goals for education to be achieved by the year 2000. These goals include increasing the high school graduation rate to at least 90 percent, eliminating drugs and violence in the schools, eliminating illiteracy among U.S. adults, and enabling U.S. students to rank first in the world in math and science. Parental involvement and teacher training are also important goals. To achieve the academic objectives in Goals 2000, the United States is moving toward a system of national standards that will define what students should know and be able to do at each grade level. To achieve national standards, "experts" are working on developing a national curriculum; to assess whether students are mastering the national curriculum objectives, educators are developing national tests. The national standards, curriculum, and tests are, officially, voluntary, but, Clinchy (1995a) points out that "the legislation passed by Congress contains language making it clear that states and local districts hoping to qualify for future federal funding will be expected to use national standards and tests—or roughly similar goals, standards, and tests—as their own" (p. 354).

Michael Apple (1995), an opponent of a national curriculum, suggests that "the national curriculum is a mechanism for the political control of knowledge" (p. 360). Critics argue that the power to make decisions about what will be taught and how it will be taught should be in the hands of parents, teachers, and students in local schools. In addition, schools that rely on national standards for what an educated person should know may fail to recognize and nurture the multiple capacities, interests, and cultural backgrounds of their students. The emphasis on testing may also be detrimental to learning. Toch (1992) notes that:

Many educators believe that the tests themselves are contributing to the poor performance of the nation's students, in part because test preparation consumes tremendous amounts of classroom time. . . . There is also less student participation in classrooms where tests drive teaching, less debate and fewer opportunities for students to develop original solutions to problems. (pp. 68–69)

Consideration *Imposing standards of test performance sometimes leads to cheating—not by students, but by teachers. Teachers cheat by giving students advance copies of tests, helping students during tests, teaching what is on the test, and altering students' responses. Toch (1992) reports that in a national survey of educators in 1990, one in eleven teach-*

ers reported pressure from administrators to cheat on standardized tests. Why are teachers and administrators motivated to cheat? School superintendents with high scores in their district may gain a national reputation and contract for larger salaries. Increasingly, states give funding bonuses to schools with the highest test scores. Teachers whose students perform well on standardized tests are also sometimes eligible to receive bonuses.

COMPUTER TECHNOLOGY IN EDUCATION

Computers in the classroom allow students to access large amounts of information. The proliferation of computers both in school and at home may mean that teachers will become facilitators and coaches rather than sole providers of information. Not only do computers enable students to access enormous information including that from the World Wide Web independently, but they also allow students to progress at their own pace. Unfortunately, computer technology is not equally accessible by all students. Students in poor school districts are less likely to have access to computers either in school or at home.

At the college level, many traditional and nontraditional programs rely on computer technology. New York Institute of Technology offers the American Open University, which provides 130 courses and three B.S. degrees by means of computer technology. The computer emulates traditional classrooms in that students enrolled in courses can ask questions of other students or of teachers. The "at-home" student also has a syllabus, a text, and library privileges. Graduate students at the New School of Social Research in New York can connect via computer modem with a specialist in a particular field (Meeks 1989).

ALTERNATIVE SCHOOL CHOICES

Traditionally, children have gone to school in the district where they live. School vouchers, home schooling, and private schools provide parents with alternative school choices for their children. **School vouchers** are tax credits that are transferred to the public or private school the parents select for their child. More than a quarter of the states now offer such vouchers. Proponents of the voucher system argue that it reduces segregation and increases the quality of schools since they must compete for students to survive. Opponents argue that vouchers increase segregation because white parents use the vouchers to send their children to a private school with few minorities. Vouchers, opponents argue, are also unfair to economically disadvantaged students who are not able to attend private schools because of the high tuition. Sernau (1993) argues that only "troubled students who are unable to escape will remain in the public school system" (p. 90).

Some parents are choosing not to send their children to school at all but to teach them at home. For some parents, **home schooling** is part of a fundamentalist movement to protect children from perceived non-Christian values in the public schools. Other parents are concerned about the quality of their children's education as well as their safety. How does being schooled at home instead of attending public school affect children? Webb (1989) found that children educated at home, either partly or completely, were equally successful in going to college and securing employment as those educated in the public school system.

Every adult American has the right to vote, the right to decide where to work, where to live. It's time parents were free to choose the schools that their children attend. This approach will create the competitive climate that stimulates excellence. . . .
—George Bush
Former U.S. President

One form of school choice involves parents teaching their children at home. Some research has found that children taught at home were equally as successful in college and employment as those educated in the public schools.

National Data: In 1994, an estimated 11 percent of U.S. students at the elementary and secondary levels attended private schools.

SOURCE: *Statistical Abstract of the United States: 1995,* Table 233.

Another choice parents may make is to send their children to a private school. The primary reason parents send their children to private schools is for religious instruction. The second most frequent reason is that private schools are superior to public schools in terms of academic achievement, percentage of graduates attending college, and other factors such as discipline, order, and environment (Coleman 1987). Parents also choose private schools for their children in order to have greater control over school policy, to avoid busing, or to obtain a specific course of instruction such as dance or music.

PRIVATIZATION

Privatization, or the use of private services in the public educational system, is a growing trend in education. Examples of privatization range from private practice teachers hired to teach selected courses to private management corporations that run entire public school systems. For example, nine Baltimore schools are now run by Education Alternatives, Inc., of Minneapolis. Elam, Rose, and Gallup (1994) explain that:

> *Superintendents have said that they sought contracts with private firms because they were frustrated by bureaucracies so complex and cumbersome that they could not get leaking roofs repaired or teachers transferred from under- to over-enrolled schools in a timely way. (p. 50)*

National Data: In 1992, almost half of all public schools participated in some partnership. In the same year, corporations and corporate foundations donated about $2 billion— or one-third of their total donations—for education-related projects.

SOURCE: Cited in Goldring and Sullivan 1995.

One form of privatization is the development of partnerships with businesses and private foundations, which provide schools with equipment, personnel, expertise, and money. Partnerships benefit schools by providing needed resources and help corporations by creating a better educated workforce for the future. Corporations can contribute in other ways as well. In 1987, for example, Procter & Gamble adopted a Cincinnati school and established Project ASPIRE, enlisting ninety-five Procter & Gamble employees to work one-to-one with students at risk for dropping out.

Eugene Lang, a wealthy businessman, promised 62 sixth graders in one of the poorest school districts in New York City that he would personally finance their college education if they graduated from high school. Eight years later, all but a few had graduated, and over half were in college. Lang had given students with little academic future a vision of hope—and the certainty of a paid college education. Subsequently, Lang started the "I Have a Dream Foundation" in which 140 classes in forty cities now participate. Lang recruits sponsors who, during the class's sixth grade, commit to paying college tuition for all who attain specified academic levels (Evans 1992).

UNDERSTANDING
THE EDUCATIONAL CRISIS

What can we conclude about the educational crisis in the United States? Any criticism of education must take into account that over a century ago the United States had no systematic public education system at all. Many American children did not receive even a primary school education. Instead, they worked in factories and on farms to help support their families. Whatever education they received came from the family or the religious institution. In the mid-1800s, educational reformer Horace Mann advocated at least five years of mandatory education for all U.S. children. Mann believed that mass education would function as a "balanced wheel of social machinery" to equalize social differences among members of an immigrant nation. His efforts resulted in the first compulsory education law in 1852, which required twelve weeks of attendance each year. By World War I, every state mandated primary school education, and by World War II, secondary education was compulsory as well.

Public schools are supposed to provide all U.S. children with the academic and social foundations necessary to participate in society in a productive and meaningful way. But, as conflict theorists note, for many children the educational institution perpetuates an endless downward cycle of failure, alienation, and hopelessness.

Breaking the cycle requires providing adequate funding for teachers, school buildings, equipment, and educational materials. In spite of the political rhetoric about the importance of education, the $30.4 billion budget for 1996 represents a 4.4 percent decrease from the 1995 budget (Kelly 1995). Commenting on this reduction, Secretary of Education Richard Riley said, "This is not the time to slam the door on educational progress" (p. 3d). Even with adequate funding, as functionalists argue, education alone cannot bear the burden of improving our schools. The education institution needs support from the political and economic institutions as well.

The political and economic institutions must also provide jobs. Students with little hope of school success will continue to experience low motivation as long as job prospects are bleak and earnings in available jobs are low. Ray and Mickelson (1993) explain:

. . . School reforms of any kind are unlikely to succeed if non-college bound students cannot anticipate opportunity structures that reward diligent efforts in school. Employers are not apt to find highly disciplined and motivated young employees for jobs that are unstable and low paying. (pp. 14–15)

We need a system where there are consequences for students and reasons to learn. You should not get into college just because you are 18 and breathing. Today, in many schools, you can.
—Albert Shanker
President, American
Federation of Teachers

I'd like parents to go into the school and be involved with the teacher, the principal, the PTA. . . .
—Richard Riley
U.S. Secretary
of Education

National Data: In a 1995 NBC/Wall Street Journal survey, two out of three Americans favored increased spending for education; 89% believed a U.S. Department of Education is necessary.

SOURCE: Cited in U.S. Department of Education 1995.

Finally, "if we are to improve the skills and attitudes of future generations of workers, we must also focus attention and resources on the quality of the lives children lead outside the school" (Murnane 1994: 290). We must provide support to families so children grow up in healthy, safe, and nurturing environments. Children are the future of our nation and of the world. Whatever resources we provide to improve the lives and education of children are sure to be wise investments in our collective future.

CRITICAL THINKING

1. Would you want your child to go to a micro-society school? Why or why not?
2. How may a teenager's dropping out of high school be explained as a failure of the educational institution rather than as a "motivation" problem on the part of the teenager?
3. How have changes in the family affected the educational institution?
4. As the U.S. population ages, a greater percentage of the population will be elderly and will not have children in public school. How will this demographic trend affect the allocation of critical or necessary resources to public schools?

KEY TERMS

multiculturalism

tracking

cooperative learning

self-fulfilling prophecy

alienation

alternative certification programs

bilingual education

integration hypothesis

micro-society school

school vouchers

home schooling

privatization

REFERENCES

American Council on Education and University of California. 1994. "The American Freshman: National Norms for Fall, 1994." Los Angeles: Los Angeles Higher Education Research Institute.

Apple, Michael W. 1995. "The Politics of a National Curriculum." In *Transforming Schools*, ed. Peter W. Cookson, Jr., and Barbara Schneider, pp. 345–70. New York: Garland Publishing Co.

Bailey, Susan M. 1993. "The Current Status of Gender Equity Research in American Schools." *Educational Psychologist* 28: 321–40.

Baker, David P., and Deborah P. Jones. 1993. "Creating Gender Equality: Cross-National Gender Stratification and Mathematical Performance." *Sociology of Education* 66: 91–103.

Banks, James A., and Cherry A. Banks, eds. 1993. *Multicultural Education*, 2d ed. Boston: Allyn & Bacon.

Barrett, Michael. 1990. "The Case for More School Days." *Atlantic Monthly* 266 (November): 78–106.

Barton, Paul. 1992. *America's Smallest School: The Family.* Princeton, N.J.: Educational Testing Service.

Bushweller, Kevin. 1995. "Turning Our Backs on Boys." *Education Digest* (January): 9–12.

Celis, William. 1993. "10 Years after a Scathing Report, Schools Show Uneven Progress." *New York Times,* April 28.

Clinchy, Evans. 1995a. "Sustaining and Expanding the Educational Conversation." *Phi Delta Kappan* (January): 352–54.

_____. 1995b. "Learning in and about the Real World: Recontextualizing Public Schooling." *Phi Delta Kappan* (January): 400–404.

Coleman, James. 1987. *Public and Private High School: The Impact of Communities.* New York: Basic Books.

Coleman, James S., J. E. Campbell, L. Hobson, J. McPartland, A. Mood, F. Weinfield, and R. York. 1966. *Equality of Educational Opportunity.* Washington, D.C.: U.S. Government Printing Office.

Elam, Stanley M. and Lowell C. Rose. 1995. "The 27th Annual Phi Delta Kappa/ Gallup Poll of the Public's Attitudes Toward the Public Schools." *Phi Delta Kappan* (September): 41–56.

Elam, Stanley M., Lowell C. Rose, and Alec M. Gallup. 1994. "The 26th Annual Phi Delta Kappa/Gallup Poll of the Public's Attitudes toward the Public Schools." *Phi Delta Kappan* (September): 41–56.

Evans, Thomas W. 1992. *Mentors: Making a Difference in Our Public Schools.* Princeton, N.J.: Peterson's Guides.

Flanagan, Constance. 1993. "Gender and Social Class: Intersecting Issues in Women's Achievement." *Educational Achievement* 28: 357–78.

Fletcher, Robert S. 1943. *History of Oberlin College to the Civil War.* Oberlin, Ohio: Oberlin College Press.

Flexner, Eleanor. 1972. *Century of Struggle: The Women's Rights Movement in the United States.* New York: Atheneum.

Goldring, Ellen B., and Anna V. Shaw Sullivan. 1995. "Privatization: Integrating Private Services in Public Schools." In *Transforming Schools,* ed. Peter W. Cookson, Jr., and Barbara Schneider, pp. 537–59. New York: Garland Publishing Co.

Hallinan, Maureen T. 1995. "Tracking and Detracking Practices: Relevance for Learning." In *Transforming Schools,* ed. Peter W. Cookson, Jr., and Barbara Schneider, pp. 35–55. New York: Garland Publishing Co.

Henry, Tamara. 1993. "Public Schools Becoming as Segregated as in the 1960s." *USA Today,* December 14, 1.

_____. 1995. "Cuomo Talks on Education Department." *USA Today,* January 27, D1.

Hewlett, Sylvia Ann. 1992. *When the Bough Breaks: The Cost of Neglecting Our Children.* New York: HarperPerennial.

Kanter, Rosabeth Moss. 1972. "The Organization Child: Experience Management in a Nursery School." *Sociology of Education* 45: 186–211.

Kelly, Dennis. 1995. "Education Budget Shows Priority Shift." *USA Today*, February 7, 3d.

Kinney, David A. 1993. "From Nerds to Normals: The Recovery of Identity among Adolescents from Middle School to High School." *Sociology of Education* 63: 21–40.

Kozol, Jonathan. 1991. *Savage Inequalities: Children in America's Schools.* New York: Crown Publishers.

Lareau, Annette. 1989. *Home Advantage: Social Class and Parental Intervention in Elementary Education.* Philadelphia: Falmer Press.

Lays, Julie. 1991. "Educating Eddie." *State Legislatures* 17(4): 20–22.

McMillen, Marilyn M., Phillip Kaufman, Elvie Hausken, and Denise Bradby. 1992. *Dropout Rates in the United States, 1991.* Washington, D.C.: National Center for Education Statistics, U.S. Department of Education.

Meeks, Brooks. 1989. "Changing Schools." In *The Reshaping of America,* ed. S. Eitzen and M. B. Zinn, pp. 278–84. Englewood Cliffs, N.J.: Prentice-Hall.

Merton, Robert K. 1968. *Social Theory and Social Structure.* New York: Free Press.

Mortenson, Thomas G. 1991. "Equity of Higher Education Opportunity for Women, Black, Hispanic, and Low Income Students." *ACT Student Financial Aid Research Report Series,* January.

Murnane, Richard J. 1994. "Education and the Well-Being of the Next Generation." In *Confronting Poverty: Prescriptions for Change,* ed. Sheldon H. Danziger, Gary D. Sandefur and Daniel H. Weinberg, pp. 289–307. New York: Russell Sage Foundation.

National Center for Education Statistics. 1995. *The Condition of Education.* Pittsburgh, PA: U.S. Government Printing Office.

National Commission on Excellence in Education. 1983. *A Nation at Risk.* Washington, D.C.

Natriello, Gary. 1995. "Dropouts: Definitions, Causes, Consequences, and Remedies." In *Transforming Schools,* ed. Peter W. Cookson, Jr., and Barbara Schneider, pp. 107–28. New York: Garland Publishing Co.

Newmann, Fred M. 1980. "Organizational Factors and Student Alienation in High Schools: Implications of Theory for School Improvement." Washington, D.C.: National Institute of Education.

Noddings, Nel. 1995. "A Morally Defensible Mission for Schools in the 21st Century." *Phi Delta Kappan* (January): 365–68.

Oakes, Ann. 1985. *Keeping Track: How Schools Structure Inequality.* New Haven: Yale University Press.

_____. 1990. *Multiplying Inequalities: The Effects of Race, Social Class, and Tracking on Opportunities to Learn Mathematics and Science.* Santa Monica, Calif.: Rand Corporation.

Pollard, Diane S. 1993. "Gender, Achievement, and African-American Students' Perceptions of their School Experience." *Educational Psychologist* 28: 341–56.

Ramirez, Albert. 1988. "Racism toward Hispanics: The Culturally Monolithic Society." In *Eliminating Racism: Profiles in Controversy,* ed. Phyllis A. Katz and Dalmas A. Taylor, pp. 137–58. New York: Plenum Press.

Ray, Carol A., and Roslyn A. Mickelson. 1993. "Restructuring Students for Restructured Work: The Economy, School Reform, and Non-College-Bound Youths." *Sociology of Education* 66: 1–20.

Richmond, George. 1989. "The Future School: Is Lowell Pointing Us toward a Revolution in Education?" *Phi Delta Kappan* (November): 232–36.

Rodriquez, Richard. 1990. "Searching for Roots in a Changing World." In *Social Problems Today,* ed. James M. Henslin, pp. 202–13. Englewood Cliffs, N.J.: Prentice-Hall.

Rosenthal, Robert, and Lenore Jacobson. 1968. *Pygmalion in the Classroom: Teacher Expectations and Pupils' Intellectual Development.* New York: Holt, Rinehart & Winston.

Rumberger, Russell W. 1987. "High School Dropouts: A Review of Issues and Evidence." *Review of Educational Research* 57: 101–21.

Sautter, R. Craig. 1995. "Standing Up to Violence: Kappan Special Report." *Phi Delta Kappan* (January): K1–K12.

Schlosstein, Steven. 1989. *The End of the American Century.* New York: Congdon & Weed.

Schultz, Tom and M. Elena Lopez. 1995. "Early Childhood Reform: Local Innovations in a Flawed Policy System." *Phi Delta Kappan* (September): 60–63.

Sernau, Scott. 1993. "School Choices, Rational and Otherwise: A Comment on Coleman." *Sociology of Education* 66: 88–90.

Simpson, Janice. 1993. "Adding Up the Under Skilled." *Time,* September 20, 75.

Statistical Abstract of the United States: 1995, 115th ed. U.S. Bureau of the Census. Washington, D.C.: U.S. Government Printing Office.

Toch, Thomas. 1992. "Schools for Scandal." *U.S. News and World Report,* April 27, 66–70.

United Nations. 1994. *Programme of Action.* The United Nations Conference on Population and Development (ICPD). Cairo, Egypt. September 5–13, 1994.

U.S. Department of Education, National Center for Education Statistics. 1992. *The Condition of Education 1992.* Washington, D.C.: U.S. Government Printing Office.

U.S. Department of Education. 1995. Press release. [http://www.ed.gov/press release].

Webb, Julie. 1989. "The Outcomes of Home-Based Education: Employment and Other Issues." *Educational Review* 41: 121–33.

Wong, Kenneth K. 1995. "Can the Big-City School System be Governed?" In *Transforming Schools,* ed. Peter W. Cookson, Jr., and Barbara Schneider, pp. 457–88. New York: Garland Publishing Co.

Problems of Modernization

SECTION 4

Section 4 focuses on problems of modernization—the cultural and structural changes that occur as a consequence of society changing from traditional to modern. Both Durkheim and Marx were concerned with the impact of modernization. Each theorized that as societies moved from "mechanical" to "organic solidarity" (in Durkheimian terms) or from "production for use" to "production for exchange" (in Marxian terms), fundamental changes in social organization would lead to increased social problems.

Although modernization has contributed to many of the social problems we have already discussed, it is more directly related to the three problems we examine in this section—technology, population and the environment, and global conflict.

One of the difficulties in understanding social problems involves sorting out the numerous social forces that contribute to social problems. Every social problem is related, in some way, to many other social problems. Nowhere is this more apparent than in the final three chapters. For example, even though scientific and technological advances are designed and implemented to enhance the quality and conditions of social life, they contribute to other social problems. Science and technology (Chapter 14) have extended life through various medical advances and have successfully lowered the infant mortality rate in many developing nations. However, these two "successes" (fewer babies dying and an increased life expectancy), when coupled with a relatively high fertility rate, lead to expanding populations. Many nations struggle to feed, clothe, house, or provide safe drinking water and medical care for their increased numbers.

Further, in responding to problems created by overpopulation, science and technology have contributed to the growing environmental crisis. For example, many developing countries use hazardous pesticides to increase food production for their growing populations, overuse land which leads to desertification and, out of economic necessity, agree to deforestation by foreign investors.

Developed countries also contribute to the environmental crisis. Indeed modernization itself, independent of population problems, exacerbates environmental concerns as the fragile ecosystem is overburdened with the by-products of affluent societies and scientific and technological triumphs: air pollution from the burning of fossil fuels, groundwater contamination from chemical runoff, nuclear waste disposal, and destruction of the ozone layer by chlorofluorocarbons. Thus, science and technology, as well as population and the environment (Chapter 15), are inextricably related.

While population patterns and the resultant increased scarcity of resources provide a motivation for global conflict (Chapter 16), science and technology provide more efficient means of worldwide destruction. Conversely, global conflict has devastating effects on the environment (e.g., nuclear winter) and has inspired much scientific and technological research and development such as laser-based and nuclear technologies. Thus, each of the chapter topics to follow is both an independent and a dependent variable in a complex web of cause and effect.

14

CHAPTER

Science and Technology

IS IT TRUE?

In 1995, most U.S. federal research and development funds were spent on health, space research and technology, and energy (p. 405).

In 1994, a defective Pentium chip was discovered to exist in over two million computers in aerospace, medical, scientific, and financial institutions as well as schools and government agencies (p. 409).

Over 30 million people in 160 countries use the Internet (p. 412).

The clock was invented by capitalistic industrialists as a means of controlling the time workers spent on the job (p. 410).

About one-third of American homes have a personal computer (p. 411).

ANS: 1. F 2. T 3. T 4. F 5. T

> Most of the consequences of technology that are causing concern at the present time—pollution of the environment, potential damage to the ecology of the planet, occupational and social dislocations, threats to the privacy and political significance of the individual, social and psychological malaise . . . are with us in large measure because it has not been anybody's explicit business to foresee and anticipate them.
>
> Emmanuel Mesthene, Former Director of the Harvard Program on Technology and Society

If religion was formerly the opiate of the masses, then surely technology is the opiate of the educated public today.
—John McDermott
State University
of New York

Virtual reality, CD-ROMS, and cloning are examples of cutting edge technologies. Virtual reality is now used to train workers in occupations as diverse as medicine, engineering, and professional sports. CD-ROM has brought the sights, sounds, images, and characters of history into our homes. The ability to genetically replicate embryos has sparked worldwide debate over the ethics of reproduction. Just as the telephone, the automobile, the television, and countless other technological innovations have forever altered social life, so will more recent technology.

Science and technology go hand in hand. **Science** is the process of discovering, explaining, and predicting natural or social phenomena. A scientific approach to understanding AIDS, for example, might include investigating the molecular structure of the virus, the means by which it is transmitted, and public attitudes about AIDS. **Technology,** as "a form of human cultural activity that applies the principles of science and mechanics to the solution of problems," is intended to accomplish a specific task—in this case, the development of an AIDS vaccine.

Some sociologists argue that science and technology should be considered one of the basic social institutions, along with family, education, government, economics, and religion. Indeed, some academicians suggest that science and technology have replaced religion as the source of ultimate truth and knowledge. Belief in *scientism*—the idea that science holds the answer to all important questions—has displaced religion in much of the modern world. As Postman (1992) describes:

> [Scientism involves] the desperate hope, and wish, and ultimately the illusory belief that some standardized set of procedures called "science" can provide us with an unimpeachable source of moral authority, a suprahuman basis for answers to questions like "What is life . . . ?" "Why is death and suffering?" "What is right and wrong to do?" "What are good and evil ends?" "How ought we to think and feel and behave?" (p. 162)

What are the effects of science and technology on humans and their social world? How do science and technology help to remedy social problems and how do they contribute to social problems? Is technology, as Postman (1992) suggests, both a friend and a foe to humankind? This chapter addresses each of these questions.

The world was made a smaller place in the mid to late 1800's by the Pony Express. And it gets smaller all the time, particularly now that much of the world is connected to the Internet.

The Social Context: The Technological Revolution

Less than fifty years ago, traveling across state lines was an arduous task, a long-distance phone call was a memorable event, and mail carriers brought belated news of friends and relatives from far away. Today, travelers journey between continents in a matter of hours, and for many, E-mail, faxes, and electronic fund transfers have replaced conventional means of communication.

The world is a much smaller place than it used to be and will become even smaller as the technological revolution spreads. While America is the most "wired" of all countries having, for example, 32 personal computers per 100 citizens, other countries are gaining ground (Jackson 1995). Japan hopes to have all homes interconnected by the year 2000. In England, one can go to the Cyberia Cafe and pay $2.85 for coffee and half an hour on the Internet.

LEVELS OF TECHNOLOGICAL DEVELOPMENT

Societies differ in their level of technological sophistication and development. In agricultural societies, which emphasize the production of raw materials, **mechanization,** or the use of tools to accomplish tasks previously done by hand, dominates. As societies move toward industrialization and become more concerned with the mass production of goods, **automation** prevails. Automation involves the use of self-operating machines, as in an automated factory where autonomous robots assemble automobiles. Finally, as a society moves toward postindustrialization, it emphasizes service and information professions (Bell 1973). At this stage, technology shifts toward **cybernation** whereby machines control machines—making production decisions, programming robots, and monitoring assembly performance.

To achieve technological development, societies need material and economic resources. Technological development also requires the support of society's members and political leaders. For example, although abortion has been technically possible for years, 24 percent of the world's population live in countries where abortion is either prohibited or permitted only when the life

Science is committed to the universal. A sign of this is that the more successful a science becomes, the broader the agreement about its basic concepts; there is not a separate Chinese or American or Soviet thermodynamics, for example, there is simply thermodynamics.
—O. B. Hardison, Jr.
Humanities professor

One of the major differences between modern and traditional societies is that in modern societies we expect change. The future will be different from the past. Technology is the key to change in modern society.
—Albert H. Teich
American Association for the Advancement of Science

FIGURE 14.1
SOURCES OF FUNDS FOR
RESEARCH AND
DEVELOPMENT, 1994

SOURCE: *Statistical Abstract of the United States: 1995,* 115th ed. U. S. Bureau of the Census (Washington, D. C.: U. S. Government Printing Office), Table 980.

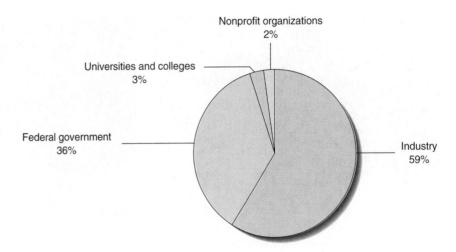

Printing, gunpowder, and the magnet . . . have changed the whole face and state of things throughout the world; the first in literature, the second in warfare, the third in navigation; whence have followed innumerable changes; insomuch that no empire, no sect, no star seems to have exerted greater power and influence in human affairs than these changes.
—Francis Bacon
Sixteenth-century scientist

National Data: In 1994, more than $172 billion were spent on research and development in the United States.

SOURCE: *Statistical Abstract of the United States: 1995,* Table 980.

of the mother is in danger (United Nations Population Fund 1991). As we see in the next section, the United States has both the material and economic resources and the public support necessary for technological development.

RESEARCH AND DEVELOPMENT IN THE UNITED STATES

Scientific investigation and technological innovation are also called "research and development." Research entails the pursuit of knowledge; development refers to the production of needed materials, systems, processes, or devises directed toward the solution of a practical problem.

Research and development are funded by four sectors: private industry, the federal government, colleges and universities, and other nonprofit organizations such as research institutes (see Figure 14.1). Most research and development funds from the federal government are spent on national defense (see Figure 14.2). Other research and development funds are spent on technological innovations that are sold in the private sector. This chapter's *In Focus* feature describes some recent technological innovations—"winners" at the 1994 Discover Awards.

SCIENCE AND TECHNOLOGY: FRIEND OR FOE?

The vast investment in research and development reflects, in part, the tremendous faith Americans have in science and technology. Many Americans believe that technological innovations are a sign of progress and a means of exerting control over their lives and the environment. In addition, many believe that science and technology will solve many of today's social problems related to food and energy, global security, and economic revitalization (Glendinning 1990).

Weinberg (1966) suggests that many Americans believe that social problems can be resolved through a "**technological fix**" rather than through social engineering. For example, a social engineer might approach the problem of water shortages by persuading people to change their lifestyle: use less water, take shorter showers, and wear clothes more than once before washing. A technologist would avoid the challenge of changing people's habits and moti-

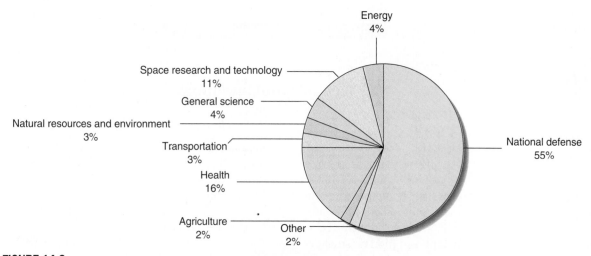

FIGURE 14.2

ESTIMATED FEDERAL FUNDING FOR RESEARCH AND DEVELOPMENT IN VARIOUS AREAS, 1995*

SOURCE: *Statistical Abstract of the United States: 1995,* 115th ed. U. S. Bureau of the Census (Washington, D. C.: U. S. Government Printing Office), Table 984.

vations and instead concentrate on the development of new technologies that would increase the water supply. Social problems may be tackled through both social engineering *and* a "technological fix." In recent years, for example, social engineering efforts to reduce drunk driving have included imposing stiffer penalties for drunk driving and disseminating public service announcements such as "Friends Don't Let Friends Drive Drunk." An example of a "technological fix" for the same problem is the development of car air bags, which reduce injuries and deaths due to car accidents. Similarly, religious leaders who promote nonviolence are using a social engineering approach to the problem of war, while technologists who develop new and better weapons that deter aggressors are attempting a "technological fix" for the problem of global conflict.

Not all individuals agree that science and technology are good for society. Skeptics point out that science and technology have sometimes resulted in unforeseen and often unwanted consequences. For example, automobiles began to be mass-produced in the 1930s in response to consumer demands. But the proliferation of automobiles also led to increased air pollution and the deterioration of cities as suburbs developed, and today, traffic fatalities are the number one cause of death from all accidents. Despite such results, most Americans believe that science and technology have been good for society.

> **Consideration** Postman (1992) suggests that technology is both a friend and an enemy:
>
> Technology . . . makes life easier, cleaner, and longer. Can anyone ask more of a friend? . . . It is the kind of friend that asks for trust and obedience, which most people are inclined to give because its gifts are truly bountiful. But of course, there is a dark side to this friend. Its gifts are not without a heavy cost. . . . The uncontrolled growth of technology destroys the vital sources of our humanity. It creates a culture without a moral foundation. It

National Data: In a 1993 General Social Survey of U.S. adults, only 17 percent agreed or strongly agreed with the statement, "Overall, modern science does more harm than good"; 62 percent disagreed or strongly disagreed; and 21 percent neither agreed nor disagreed.

SOURCE: General Social Survey 1993.

New Technological Inventions

- **Whole Plane Parachute**
  Are you afraid of flying? You may avoid some airplane crashes by flying in planes equipped with a large parachute that deploys when the aircraft begins to plummet. Such chutes are now available and have been approved by the Federal Aviation Administration for smaller aircraft. The development of chutes for larger commercial airplanes is underway.

- **Cars That Fly**
  The Aircar is no wider than a mobile home and combines the technology of a car and a plane. A single engine powers both the propeller for flying and the wheels for driving. The Aircar's flying capacity is similar to a helicopter or a small plane, although further testing and funding are needed.

- **The DataGlove**
  This lightweight glove enables victims of neurological diseases who cannot talk to speak through the use of hand signs. Users simply store gestures and what they represent into the glove's memory. When the user re-creates these signs, a voice synthesizer speaks the correct words or phrases for the person.

- **Robot Rescue Ranger**
  When a tanker truck hauling dangerous gases overturns, a robot can motor into the area, shut off a valve, open a door, or pick up and return objects. It can also climb steps and has onboard cameras that can relay important information about the accident and victims to on-site workers. Formerly, individuals in heavy protective hot suits were put in jeopardy by walking into the dangerous rubble.

- **Lead Paint Detector**
  Have you moved into an old apartment or house and want to know if the paint on the windowsills has lead in it? The XL Spectrum Analyzer is a pocket-size instrument that can quickly and accurately measure the lead present in paint on exposed surfaces, where it is most likely to be inhaled or ingested. The device, which costs around $12,000, will be used mainly by building inspectors to detect lead that might otherwise cause brain injury, blindness, and even death.

- **Environmentally Friendly Car**
  When a car is stalled in traffic, its running engine continues to waste fuel and emit carbon monoxide into the air. With the help of Volkswagen's ecomatic system, the diesel engine in a standard VW Golf turns itself off after 1.5 seconds of inactivity. Pressure on the gas pedal instantly and smoothly restarts the car. Tests indicate a 22 percent fuel saving and a 36 percent reduction in carbon monoxide emissions. Ecomatically equipped cars are already available in Europe and cost about $1,000 more than a standard VW Golf.

undermines certain mental processes and social relations that make human life worth living. Technology, in sum, is both friend and enemy. (p. xii)

Sociological Theories of Science and Technology

Each of the three major sociological frameworks helps us to better understand the nature of science and technology in society.

STRUCTURAL-FUNCTIONALIST PERSPECTIVE

Functionalists view science and technology as emerging in response to societal needs—that "[science] was born indicates that society needed it" (Durkheim [1973] 1925). As societies become more complex and heterogeneous, finding a common and agreed-upon knowledge base becomes more difficult. Science fulfills the need for an assumed objective measure of "truth" and provides a basis for making intelligent and rational decisions. In this regard, science and the resulting technologies are functional for society.

If society changes too rapidly as a result of science and technology, however, problems may emerge. When the material part of culture (i.e., its physical elements) changes at a faster rate than the nonmaterial (i.e., its beliefs and values) a **cultural lag** may develop (Ogburn 1957). For example, the typewriter, the conveyor belt, and the computer expanded opportunities for women to work outside the home. With the potential for economic independence, women were able to remain single or to leave unsatisfactory relationships and/or establish careers. But while new technologies have created new opportunities for women, beliefs about women's roles, expectations of female behavior, and values concerning equality, marriage, and divorce have "lagged" behind.

Robert Merton (1973), a functionalist and founder of the subdiscipline sociology of science, also argued that scientific discoveries or technological innovations may be dysfunctional for society and create instability in the social system. For example, the development of time-saving machines increases production, but also displaces workers and contributes to higher rates of employee alienation. Defective technology can have disastrous effects on society. In 1994, a defective Pentium chip was discovered to exist in over two million computers in aerospace, medical, scientific, and financial institutions as well as schools and government agencies. Replacing the defective chip was a massive undertaking, but was necessary to avoid thousands of inaccurate computations and organizational catastrophe.

CONFLICT PERSPECTIVE

Conflict theorists, in general, emphasize that science and technology benefit a select few. For some conflict theorists, technological advances occur primarily as a response to capitalist needs for increased efficiency and productivity and thus are motivated by profit. As McDermott (1993) notes, most decisions to increase technology are made by "the immediate practitioners of technology, their managerial cronies, and for the profits accruing to their corporations" (p. 93). As Figure 14.1 illustrated, in the United States, private industry spends more money on research and development than the federal government does. The Dalkon Shield and silicone breast implants are examples of technological advances that promised millions of dollars in profits for their developers. However, the rush to market took precedence over thorough testing of the products' safety. Subsequent lawsuits filed by consumers who argued that both products had compromised the physical well-being of women resulted in large damage awards for the plaintiffs.

Science and technology also further the interests of dominant groups to the detriment of others. The need for scientific research on AIDS was evident in the early 1980s, but the required large-scale funding was not made available as long

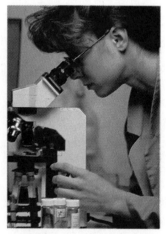

Motivated by profit, private industry spends more money on research and development than the federal government does.

Science and technology are . . . essential for strengthening the economy, creating high quality jobs, protecting the environment, improving our health care and education systems, and maintaining our national security. This country must sustain world leadership in science, mathematics, and engineering if we are to meet the challenges of today . . . and tomorrow.
—Bill Clinton
U.S. President

Many of the things that we like to think of as mere tools or instruments now function as virtual members of society.
—Langdon Winner
Social scientist

as the virus was thought to be specific to homosexuals and intravenous drug users. Only when the virus became a threat to mainstream Americans were millions of dollars made available for AIDS research. Hence, conflict theorists argue that granting agencies act as gatekeepers to scientific discoveries and technological innovations. These agencies are influenced by powerful interest groups and the marketability of the product rather than by the needs of society.

> **Consideration**   Some feminists argue that technology is an extension of the patriarchal nature of society that promotes the interest of men and ignores the needs and interests of women. For example, washing machines, although time saving devices, disrupted the communal telling of stories and the resulting friendships among women who gathered together to do their chores. Bush (1993) observes:
>
> Technology always enters into the present culture, accepting and exacerbating the existing norms and values. In a society characterized by a sex-role division of labor, any tool or technique . . . will have dramatically different effects on men than on women. (p. 204)
>
> Other feminists acknowledge that technological innovations have improved the lives of women by balancing employment opportunities, especially in new, skilled, blue-collar and technical jobs such as computer repair specialist and telecommunication operator. Walshok (1993) studied women in these occupations and found that they reported high levels of job satisfaction and a strong sense of job security.

SYMBOLIC INTERACTIONIST PERSPECTIVE

This new regimen is simpler and potentially allows greater privacy than any other abortion method.
—Dr. Etienne-Emile Raulieu
Inventor of RU486

New technologies alter the structure of our interests: the things we think about. They alter the character of our symbols: the things we think with. And they alter the nature of community: the arena in which thoughts develop.
—Neil Postman
New York University

Knowledge is relative. It changes over time, over circumstances, and between societies. We no longer believe that the world is flat nor that the earth is the center of the universe, but such beliefs once determined behavior as individuals responded to what they thought to be true. The scientific process is a social process in that "truths" result from the interactions between scientists and researchers and the lay public.

Kuhn (1973) argues that the process of scientific discovery begins with assumptions about a particular phenomenon (e.g., the world is flat). Since there are always unanswered questions about a topic (e.g., why don't the oceans drain?), science works to fill these gaps. When new information suggests that the initial assumptions were incorrect (e.g., the world is not flat), a new set of assumptions or framework emerges to replace the old one (e.g., the world is round). It then becomes the dominant belief or paradigm.

Symbolic interactionists emphasize the importance of this process and the impact social forces can have on it. Technological innovations are also affected by social forces, and their success is, in part, dependent upon the social meaning assigned to any particular product. If a product is defined as impractical, cumbersome, inefficient, or immoral, it is unlikely to gain public acceptance. Such is the case with RU486, an oral contraceptive, which is widely used in France, Great Britain, and China, but is rarely prescribed in the United States.

Not only are technological innovations subject to social meaning, but who becomes involved in what aspects of science and technology is also socially defined. Men, for example, outnumber women three to one in earning computer science degrees. They also score higher on measures of computer aptitude and report higher computer use than women (Williams et al. 1993). Societal definitions of men as being rational, mathematical, and scientifically minded and having greater mechanical aptitude than women are, in part, responsible for these differences.

Technology and the Transformation of Society

A number of modern technologies are considerably more sophisticated than technological innovations of the past. Nevertheless, older technologies have influenced the social world as profoundly as the most mind-boggling modern inventions. Indeed, without older technological innovations, such as the clock and printing press, most modern technology would not have been possible.

Technology has far-reaching effects on every aspect of social life. As noted earlier, technology has altered the very concept of society. New transportation and communication systems have created interconnections between previously separated societies and thus led to the development of a global society. The following sections discuss other societal transformations due to various modern technologies, including workplace technology, computers, the information highway, and science and biotechnology.

TECHNOLOGY IN THE WORKPLACE

All workplaces, from doctor's offices to factories and from supermarkets to real estate corporations, have felt the impact of technology. The Office of Technology Assessment of the U.S. Congress estimates that seven million U.S. workers are under some type of computer surveillance (Winner 1993), which lessens the need for supervisors and makes control by employers easier. Further, technology can make workers more accountable by gathering information about their performance. Through such time-saving devices as personal digital assistants and battery-powered store shelf labels, technology can enhance workers' efficiency. Technology is also changing the location of work. Already three million employees *telecommute* that is, complete all or part of their work away from the workplace. The number of telecommuters is rising by 20 percent every year (Jaroff 1995, 38).

Robotic technology, sometimes called computer-aided manufacturing (CAM), has also revolutionized work, particularly in heavy industry such as automobile manufacturing (see Chapter 10). An employer's decision to use robotics is dependent upon direct (e.g., initial investment) and indirect (e.g., unemployment compensation) costs, the feasibility and availability of robots performing the desired tasks, and the increased rate of productivity. Use of robotics may also depend on whether there is union resistance to the replacement of workers by machines. Although it is often assumed, as some conflict theorists would argue, that technology in the workplace is only advantageous to the employer, Shaiken (1984) notes that "[C]omputers and microelectronics present a dazzling array of alternatives in the workplace; more worker autonomy or greater managerial authority; more skills or fewer skills, increased hierarchy or more democratic decision making" (p. 4).

The information super-highway is going to change the way we work, creating jobs that don't exist today . . . eliminating some others.
—Stone Phillips
Journalist

We will witness the loss of many jobs to wholly automated systems, which will soon change the white-collar workplace to the same degree that it has already transformed the factory floor.
—Nicholas Negroponte
Professor of Media Technology
M.I.T.

Early computers were very large and were thought to have use only in the scientific community. But when IBM began producing them for commercial use, they greatly underestimated their sales potential; and today about 30% of homes in the United States have a personal computer.

Consideration *Postman (1992) describes how the clock—a relatively simple innovation that is taken for granted in today's world—profoundly influenced not only the workplace but the larger economic institution:*

The clock had its origin in the Benedictine monasteries of the twelfth and thirteenth centuries. The impetus behind the invention was to provide a more or less precise regularity to the routines of the monasteries, which required, among other things, seven periods of devotion during the course of the day. The bells of the monastery were to be rung to signal the canonical hours; the mechanical clock was the technology that could provide precision to these rituals of devotion. . . . What the monks did not foresee was that the clock is a means not merely of keeping track of the hours but also of synchronizing and controlling the actions of men. And thus, by the middle of the fourteenth century, the clock had moved outside the walls of the monastery, and brought a new and precise regularity to the life of the workman and the merchant. . . . In short, without the clock, capitalism would have been quite impossible. The paradox . . . [is] that the clock was invented by men who wanted to devote themselves more rigorously to God; it ended as the technology of greatest use to men who wished to devote themselves to the accumulation of money. (pp. 14–15)

THE COMPUTER REVOLUTION

Early computers were much larger than the small machines we have today and were thought to have only esoteric uses among members of the scientific and military communities. In 1951, only about half a dozen computers existed (Ceruzzi 1993). The development of the silicon chip and sophisticated microelectronic technology allowed tens of thousands of components

to be imprinted on a single chip smaller than a dime. The silicon chip led to the development of laptop computers, mini-television sets, cellular phones, electronic keyboards, and singing birthday cards. The silicon chip also made computers affordable. Although the first personal computer was developed only twenty years ago (Levy 1995), today about one-third of American homes have one (Kantrowitz and Rosenberg 1994).

Today, computers form the backbone of universities, government agencies, corporations, and businesses. Between 1984 and 1993, the percentage of U.S. public schools using computers for student instruction increased from 85 percent to 99 percent (*Statistical Abstract of the United States: 1995*, Table 258).

Computers are big business, and the United States is one of the most successful producers of computer technology. The top four selling computers in Europe—Apple, Compaq, IBM, and Hewlett-Packard—are all American made (Powell and Deane 1994). The computer industry has mushroomed in the last two decades. In 1971, 2,388 U.S. college students earned a bachelor's degree in computer and information sciences; by 1992 that number had increased to 24,557 (*Statistical Abstract of the United States: 1995*, Table 300).

Aside from their word processing, data analysis, spreadsheet, and graphics capabilities, computers today are "smarter" than ever before. Through computer technology known as **virtual reality,** individuals use headphones, goggles, gloves, and body suits to move through a three-dimensional world that changes in response to movements of the head or hand. With virtual reality, one can have a simulated experience of people, places, sounds, and sights without leaving home. Though used mainly as a means of entertainment today, virtual reality also has practical uses, such as in training medical students and airline pilots. Virtual reality's potential is unlimited and its implications are startling. As Rheingold (1993, 360) observes, "[V]irtual reality vividly demonstrates that our social contract with our own tools has brought us to a point where we have to decide fairly soon what it is we as humans ought to become because we are on the brink of having the power of creating any experience we desire."

> **National Data:** In 1993, almost one-half (46 percent) of U.S. workers used a computer on the job.
>
> SOURCE: *Statistical Abstract of the United States: 1995*, Table 671.

THE INFORMATION SUPERHIGHWAY

Information technology, or **infotech** for short, refers to any technology that carries information. Most information technologies were developed within a hundred-year span: photography and telegraphy (1830s), rotary power printing (1840s), the typewriter (1860s), transatlantic cable (1866), telephone (1876), motion pictures (1894), wireless telegraphy (1895), magnetic tape recording (1899), radio (1906), and television (1923) (Beniger 1993). The concept of an "information society" dates back to the 1950s when an economist identified a work sector he called "the production and distribution of knowledge." In 1958, 31 percent of the labor force were employed in this sector—today more than 50 percent are. When this figure is combined with those in service occupations, more than 75 percent of the labor force are involved in the information society (Beniger 1993).

The Clinton administration embraces the development of a national information infrastructure as outlined in the Communications Act of 1994. An information infrastructure performs three functions (Kahin 1993). First, it carries information, just as a transportation system carries passengers. Second, it collects data in digital form that can be understood and used by people. Finally, it

> *The information superhighway may be mostly hype today, but it is an understatement about tomorrow. It will exist beyond people's wildest predictions.*
> —Nicholas Negroponte
> Professor of Media
> Technology
> M.I.T.

National Data: In a national poll, 58 percent of
adults reported that if they
or their spouse were pregnant, they would want their
unborn child to be tested
for genetic defects.

SOURCE: Elmer-Dewitt 1994b.

permits people to communicate with one another by sharing, monitoring, and exchanging information based on common standards and networks. In short, an information infrastructure facilitates telecommunications, knowledge, and community integration.

The **Internet** is an international information infrastructure available through many universities, research institutes, government agencies, and businesses. Today 30 to 40 million people in 160 countries use the Internet, which was developed in the 1970s as a Defense Department experiment (Elmer-Dewitt 1995). With a personal computer, a modem, and a telephone line, users can log into locations around the world to access information, transfer files, and send and receive E-mail. The Internet also provides access to thousands of discussion groups, shopping networks, databases, bulletin boards, videos, and reservation systems from around the global village. Commercial access to the Internet is available through such services as *Prodigy, America On-line,* and *Compuserve.*

SCIENCE AND BIOTECHNOLOGY

While recent computer innovations and the establishment of an information superhighway have led to significant cultural and structural changes, science and its resulting biotechnologies have led to not only dramatic changes, but also hotly debated issues. Here we will look at some of the issues raised by developments in genetics and reproductive technology.

Genetics Molecular biology has led to a greater understanding of the genetic material found in all cells—DNA (deoxyribonucleic acid)—and with it the ability for **genetic screening.** Currently, researchers are trying to complete genetic maps that will link DNA to particular traits. Already, specific strands of DNA have been identified as carrying such physical traits as eye color and height, as well as such diseases as breast cancer, cystic fibrosis, prostate cancer, and Alzheimer's. "By the end of the 1990s, routine tests will detect predispositions to dozens of diseases as well as indicate a wide range of normal human traits" (Weinberg 1993, 319).

> *Consideration* While technology may be neutral, its uses are not. In some countries, for example, most notably developing nations, female fetuses are disproportionately aborted. Further, in the 1980s, urban blacks were genetically screened for sickle-cell anemia. Once individuals with the sickle-cell trait were identified, health care providers counseled them either not to have children or not to marry someone who also had the trait. Yet, even though detection of Tay-Sachs, a genetic disease in Jews, was more accurate and less expensive, health care providers did not routinely test and counsel Jews to remain child-free.

The Human Genome Project, a fifteen-year effort to map human DNA, has, on the average, located a gene at the rate of one a day with the goal of identifying 100,000 genes by the year 2005. The hope is that if a defective or missing gene can be identified, it may be possible to get a healthy duplicate and transplant it to the affected cell. This is known as **gene therapy.** Alternatively, viruses have their own genes that can be targeted for removal. Experiments are now under way to accomplish these biotechnological feats.

Genetic engineering is the ability to manipulate the genes of an organism in such a way that the natural outcome is altered. Genetic engineering is accomplished by splicing the DNA from one organism into the genes of another. For example, a herbicide-resistant gene from a petunia was recently placed in a soybean plant making it less susceptible to disease (Springer 1995). Theoretically, genetic engineering could enable parents to choose the genetically determined traits of their offspring.

> **Consideration** Gregory Carey, a geneticist at the University of Colorado, poses an interesting question. Suppose scientists discovered a genetic marker that would permit accurate prediction of violent behavior before a child's birth. If we knew that this child was, say, nine times more likely to be arrested and convicted of a violent act, should that child be aborted? What if the child had Down's syndrome or was physically handicapped, an alcoholic, or gay? What if the child had a known life expectancy of thirty-five? Which, if any, of these fetuses should be aborted? Carey reminds us that we have already identified the gene that predicts violent behavior—males are nine time more likely to be arrested and convicted of a violent crime than females (Elmer-Dewitt 1994a).

Reproductive Technologies The evolution of "reproductive science" has been furthered by scientific developments in biology, medicine, and agriculture. At the same time, however, its development has been hindered by the stigma associated with sexuality and reproduction, its link with unpopular social movements (e.g., contraception), and the feeling that such innovations challenge the natural order (Clarke 1990). Nevertheless, new reproductive technologies have been and continue to be developed.

In **in-vitro fertilization (IVF),** an egg and a sperm are united in an artificial setting such as a laboratory dish or test tube. Although the first successful attempt at IVF occurred in 1944, it was not until 1978 that the first test tube baby, Louise Brown, was born. Today, more than three hundred fertility clinics in the United States provide this procedure. Criticisms of IVF are often based on traditional definitions of the family and the legal complications created when a child can have as many as five potential parental ties—egg donor, sperm donor, surrogate mother, and the two people who raise the child (depending on the situation, IVF may not involve donors and/or a surrogate). Litigation over who are the "real" parents has already occurred.

Parenthetically, we should note that even without IVF, surrogacy raises many legal and social issues. The most publicized case thus far concerned Mary Beth Whitehead of New Jersey, a paid surrogate mother, who was artificially inseminated with the sperm of William Stern and agreed to bear the child for him and his wife. When the baby was born, Whitehead refused to relinquish her. A judge upheld the surrogacy contract, severed Whitehead's parental rights, and gave Baby M to the Sterns. One year later, the Supreme Court of New Jersey ruled surrogacy for hire was illegal and awarded Whitehead visitation rights.

The availability of test tube fertilization also has significant policy implications. A fifty-nine-year-old British woman gave birth to twins as a result of donated eggs implanted in her uterus. Since postmenopausal women can now have children, should retirement benefits also include child care? Some countries,

> *It is now a matter of a handful of years before biologists will be able to irreversibly change the evolutionary wisdom of billions of years with the creation of new plants, new animals, and new forms of human and post human beings.*
> —Ted Howard
> Jeremy Rifkin
> Biotechnology critics

National Data: In a 1990 General Social Survey, 744 adults were asked whether they would have an abortion if tests indicated the fetus had a serious genetic defect. Of the respondents, 50.7 percent said yes, 46.6 percent no, and 2.7 percent refused to answer.
SOURCE: General Social Survey 1990.

> *I don't want the people who are bringing us a more packageable, storable, cost-efficient tomato turning their attention to my grandchildren.*
> —Barbara Katz Rothman
> Former President, Society for the Study of Social Problems

Although the first successful attempt at in-vitro fertilization occurred in 1944, it was 1978 before the first test tube baby was born. Today over 300 fertility clinics in the United States provide this procedure. This photo depicts a reunion of children born by this method, and their families.

such as Germany, have outlawed IVF. Should its use be restricted—perhaps to persons under thirty years of age, to married couples, to individuals with no previous children? As of 1995, the federal government does not require fertility clinics to consider the marital status of IVF recipients, but clinics are required to inform consumers of the success rates of various fertility procedures. Less than 15 percent of couples who use IVF give birth to a baby.

> **Consideration**   In vitro fertilization is a good example of cultural and structural inequality. Since donor eggs cost between $10,000 and $20,000 each, IVF is usually not an option for the poor—a consequence of the structure of society. The culture, however, defines women as primary caregivers. When a woman in her fifties wants to have a child, she's often asked, Who will care for the child later in life? However, when a man in his fifties fathers a child, he's seldom asked, Who will care for the child later in life?

Ironically, science and technology have assisted contraception as well as fertility. In 1990, the Federal Drug Administration (FDA) approved the use of Norplant, a long-acting reversible hormonal contraceptive consisting of six thin flexible silicone capsules that are implanted under the skin of the upper arm. Tested by more than 55,000 women in forty-six countries, Norplant provides a continuous low dosage of levonorgestrel, which protects against pregnancy for up to five years. Norplant-2 consists of two capsules and is effective for about three years.

Like fertility technologies, contraception raises numerous social issues. Should adolescents have unrestricted access to contraceptive devices? Should contraception be used as a means of social control and, if so, for who? In California, a judge granted probation to a convicted child abuser on condition that she have a Norplant implant for three years. "Distressed by her fear of a longer prison sentence, the woman agreed to submit to state control over her body" (Planned Parenthood Federation of America 1991, 8). While Norplant may be viewed as a new contraceptive choice for all women, it has "come to be promoted as a new kind of control over the poorest and most vulnerable" (p. 8). As Robert Blank (1990) explains:

> Given the current negative attitude of the public toward those on welfare, the increased emphasis on the population problem, the scarcity of public funds for welfare programs, and the emerging focus on the competency of parents, it would not be surprising if the availability of reversible sterilization (such as Norplant) gave impetus to pressures for widespread use of incentives (or coercion) to encourage (or force) sterilization of the poor, retarded, and those otherwise deemed "unfit." (p. 130)

Perhaps more than any other biotechnology, abortion epitomizes the potentially explosive consequences of new technologies. **Abortion** is the removal of an embryo or fetus from a woman's uterus before it can survive on its own. Since the U.S. Supreme Court's ruling in *Roe v. Wade* in 1973, abortion has been legal in the United States. However, recent Supreme Court decisions have limited the *Roe v. Wade* decision. In *Planned Parenthood of Southeastern Pennsylvania v. Casey*, the Court ruled that a state may restrict the conditions under which an abortion is granted, such as by requiring a twenty-four-hour waiting period or parental consent for minors.

Abortion is a complex issue for everyone, but especially for women, whose lives are most affected by pregnancy and childbearing. Women who have abortions are more often poor, unmarried, minorities who say they intend to have children in the future (Facts in Brief 1992). Abortion is also a complex issue for societies, which must respond to the pressures of conflicting attitudes toward abortion and the reality of high rates of unintended and unwanted pregnancy. Table 14.1 shows the results of three national surveys on the conditions under which abortion is acceptable.

Attitudes toward abortion tend to be polarized between two opposing groups of abortion activists—prochoice and prolife. Advocates of the prochoice movement hold that freedom of choice is a central human value, that

What most Americans want to do with abortion is to permit it but also to discourage its use.
—Roger Rosenblatt
Author/Social
commentator

TABLE 14.1

ABORTION UNDER WHAT CONDITIONS?

In 1973, 1983, and 1993, the General Social Survey included a question on abortion. Respondents were asked "whether it should be possible for a pregnant woman to obtain a legal abortion if. . . ." The percentages responding "yes" follow.

	1993	1983	1973
1. SERIOUS DEFECT IN BABY	81.3%	78.9%	84.5%
2. MARRIED, WANTS NO MORE CHILDREN	47.1	38.9	47.7
3. HEALTH SERIOUSLY ENDANGERED BY PREGNANCY	89.8	89.7	92.3
4. FAMILY HAS LOW INCOME, CAN'T AFFORD CHILD	49.9	43.7	53.4
5. PREGNANCY BECAUSE OF RAPE	82.9	82.8	83.5
6. NOT MARRIED, DOESN'T WANT TO MARRY FATHER	48.1	39.4	49.1
7. ANY OTHER REASON	45.3	34.3	86.3

SOURCE: General Social Survey. 1973, 1983, 1993. Storrs, Conn.: Roper Organization. [Internet].

Abortion Attitude Scale

This is not a test. There are no wrong or right answers to any of the statements, so just answer as honestly as you can. The statements ask you to tell how you feel about legal abortion (the voluntary removal of a human fetus from the mother during the first three months of pregnancy by a qualified medical person). Tell how you feel about each statement by circling one of the choices beside each sentence. Respond to each statement and circle only one response.

	Strongly Agree	Agree	Slightly Agree	Slightly Disagree	Disagree	Strongly Disagree
1. The Supreme Court should strike down legal abortions in the United States.	5	4	3	2	1	0
2. Abortion is a good way of solving an unwanted pregnancy.	5	4	3	2	1	0
3. A mother should feel obligated to bear a child she has conceived.	5	4	3	2	1	0
4. Abortion is wrong no matter what the circumstances are.	5	4	3	2	1	0
5. A fetus is not a person until it can live outside its mother's body.	5	4	3	2	1	0
6. The decision to have an abortion should be the pregnant mother's.	5	4	3	2	1	0
7. Every conceived child has the right to be born.	5	4	3	2	1	0
8. A pregnant female not wanting to have a child should be encouraged to have an abortion.	5	4	3	2	1	0
9. Abortion should be considered killing a person.	5	4	3	2	1	0
10. People should not look down on those who choose to have abortions.	5	4	3	2	1	0
11. Abortion should be an available alternative for unmarried, pregnant teenagers.	5	4	3	2	1	0

procreation choices must be free of government interference, and that since the woman must bear the burden of moral choices, she should have the right to make such decisions. Alternatively, prolifers hold that the unborn fetus has a right to live and be protected, that abortion is immoral, and that alternative means of resolving an unwanted pregnancy should be found (Callahan and Callahan 1984). This chapter's *Self and Society* assesses attitudes toward abortion and documents the differences between the two positions.

Despite what appears to be a universal race to the future and the indisputable benefits of such scientific discoveries as the workings of DNA and the technology of IVF, some people are concerned about the duality of science and technology. Science and the resulting technological innovations are often life assisting and life giving; they are also potentially destructive and life threatening. The same scientific knowledge that led to the discovery of nuclear fission, for example, led to the development of both nuclear power plants and the po-

	Strongly Agree	Agree	Slightly Agree	Slightly Disagree	Disagree	Strongly Disagree
12. Persons should not have the power over the life or death of a fetus.	5	4	3	2	1	0
13. Unwanted children should not be brought into the world.	5	4	3	2	1	0
14. A fetus should be considered a person at the moment of conception.	5	4	3	2	1	0

Scoring and Interpretation As its name indicates, this scale was developed to measure attitudes toward abortion. It was developed by Sloan (1983) for use with high school and college students. To compute your score, first reverse the point scale for Items 1, 3, 4, 7, 9, 12, and 14. Total the point responses for all items. Sloan provided the following categories for interpreting the results:

70–56 Strong proabortion
55–44 Moderate proabortion
43–27 Unsure
26–16 Moderate prolife
15–0 Strong prolife

Reliability and Validity The Abortion Attitude Scale was administered to high school and college students, Right to Life group members, and abortion service personnel. Sloan (1983) reported a high total test estimate of reliability (0.92). Construct validity was supported in that Right to Life members' mean scores were 16.2; abortion service personnel mean scores were 55.6, and other groups' scores fell between these values.

SOURCE: L. A. Sloan, 1983. "Abortion attitude scale." *Health Education* 14(3): 41–42. Used by permission.

tential for nuclear destruction. Thus, we now turn our attention to the problems associated with science and technology.

Societal Consequences of Science and Technology

Scientific discoveries and technological innovations have implications for all social actors and social groups. As such, they also have consequences for society as a whole.

ALIENATION AND DESKILLING

As technology continues to play an increasingly important role in the workplace, workers tend to feel there is no creativity in what they do—they feel

Men [and women] have become the tools of their tools.
—Henry David Thoreau
Author/Social activist

alienated. The movement from mechanization, to automation, to cybernation increasingly removes individuals from the production process, often relegating them to flipping a switch, staring at a computer monitor, or entering data at a keyboard. Not only are these activities experienced as routine, boring, and meaningless, but they also promote **deskilling;** that is, "labor requires less thought than before and gives them [workers] fewer decisions to make" (Perrolle 1990, 338). Deskilling stifles development of alternative skills and limits opportunities for advancement and creativity.

To conflict theorists, deskilling also provides the basis for increased inequality for "[T]hroughout the world, those who control the means of producing information products are also able to determine the social organization of the 'mental labor' which produces them" (Perrolle 1990, 337). Such control includes control of the social context of work; yet "the conditions of computerized work do not facilitate the formation of class consciousness in the same way that the early industrial revolution . . . did" (p. 339). Deskilling has existed for years, but it has been heightened by the increasing use of technology and is likely to continue as employers, in search of efficiency and productivity, introduce more technological changes.

The electronic sweatshops that are becoming more and more numerous are especially conducive to worker alienation and deskilling (Garson 1992). Here, low-paid employees, many of them women, sit at computer terminals for hours entering data and keeping records for thousands of businesses, corporations, and agencies. The work is monotonous and solitary and provides little autonomy. Nevertheless, these sweatshops are efficient and cost-effective. Women who work on computers at home are called "cottage keyers." They are especially exploited in that they have no sick leave, no company benefits, no insurance, and no paid vacation (Mattera 1983).

SOCIAL RELATIONSHIPS AND SOCIAL INTERACTION

National Data: In a Gallup survey, 38 percent feared that computer technology would result in their losing face-to-face contact with other people.

SOURCE: Wiseman and Enrico 1994.

Technology affects social relationships and the nature of social interaction. The development of telephones has led to fewer visits with friends and relatives; with the coming of VCRs and cable television, the number of places where social life occurs (e.g., movie theaters) has declined. As technology increases, social relationships and human interaction are transformed—and often disrupted.

Technology also makes it easier for individuals to live in a cocoon—to be self-sufficient in terms of finances (e.g., Quicken), entertainment (e.g., pay-per-view movies), work (e.g., telecommuting), recreation (e.g., virtual reality), shopping (e.g., QVC), communication (e.g., Internet), and many other aspects of social life. Ironically, although the information highway can bring people together, it can also isolate them from each other.

Some technological innovations replace social roles. For example, an answering machine may replace a secretary, a computer-operated vending machine may replace a waitperson, an automatic teller machine may replace a banker, and closed circuit television, a teacher (Johnson 1988; Winner 1993). These technologies may improve efficiency, but they also reduce human contact.

LOSS OF PRIVACY AND SECURITY

When M.I.T. professor of media technology Nicholas Negroponte was asked "what do you fear most in thinking about the digital future?," his response was "privacy and security."

> When I send you a message in the future, I want you to be sure it is from me; that when that message goes from me to you, nobody is listening in; and when it lives on your desk, nobody is snooping later. (Negroponte 1995: 88)

Schools, employers, and the government are increasingly using technology to monitor individuals' performance and behavior. Today, through cybernation, machines monitor behavior by counting a key punch operator's keystrokes, a checkout clerk's scanned food items, or a telephone operator's minutes on line.

Employers and schools may subject individuals to drug testing technology (see Chapter 3). Through computers, individuals can obtain access to phone bills, tax returns, medical reports, credit histories, bank account balances, and driving records. Some companies sell such personal information. Unauthorized disclosure is potentially devastating. If a person's medical records indicate that he or she is HIV positive, for example, that person could be in danger of losing his or her job or health benefits. DNA testing of hair, blood, or skin samples can be used to deny individuals insurance, employment, or medical care. A report by the National Academy of Sciences indicates that some citizens have already lost their jobs and health insurance based on genetic tests (Elmer-Dewitt 1994a).

People aren't aware that mouse clicks can be traced, packaged, and sold.
—Larry Irving
Commerce Department

Technology has created threats not only to the privacy of individuals, but also to the security of entire nations. Computers and modems can be used (or misused) in terrorism and warfare to cripple the infrastructure of a society and tamper with military information and communication operations (see *In Focus* "Information Warfare" in Chapter 16).

National Data: In a Gallup survey, more than half (56 percent) of white-collar workers reported being afraid that the proliferation of computers would threaten their privacy.
SOURCE: Wiseman and Enrico 1994.

To protect unauthorized access to information stored in or transmitted through computers and communication technologies, groups, organizations, and corporations may code information using a technique called "encryption." Information that is encrypted is unintelligible without the code to unscramble it. The U.S. government, however, wants to expand its power to have access to encrypted, or coded, information. The U.S. National Security Agency (NSA) has devised a computer microchip called the Clipper Chip that is designed to make it easier for federal agencies like the Central Intelligence Agency (CIA) to unscramble encrypted information. The NSA, CIA, and other agencies want the Clipper Chip installed in every fax, modem, and telephone produced in the United States. To tap a line, law enforcement agencies would need to obtain a warrant that would allow them to get the code for the specific chip. The Clipper Chip is already in use at government agencies for all unclassified communications. At this time, commercial use of the chip is voluntary (Elmer-Dewitt 1994b).

National Data: A national survey of Americans revealed that 80 percent were opposed to the use of the "Clipper Chip." Two-thirds said that privacy was more important than allowing police to conduct wiretaps.
SOURCE: Elmer-Dewitt 1994b.

UNEMPLOYMENT

Some technologies replace human workers—robots replace factory workers, word processors displace secretaries and typists, and computer-assisted

Technology changes the nature of work and the types of jobs available. Fewer semi-skilled workers are needed, since many of these jobs have been replaced by machines.

diagnostics reduce the need for automobile mechanics (see Chapter 10). It is estimated, for example, that 52,000 branch banks will be replaced by automatic teller machines in the next decade. The cost of a teller transaction is $1.07; an electronic transaction, seven cents (Fix 1994).

Technology also changes the nature of work and the types of jobs available. For example, fewer semiskilled workers are needed since many of these jobs have been replaced by machines. The jobs that remain, often white-collar jobs, require more education and technological skills. Technology thus contributes to the split labor market (see also Chapter 10).

THE HAVES AND THE HAVE-NOTS

One of the most significant social problems associated with science and technology is the increased division between the classes. As Mitch Kapor, founder of Lotus Development Corporations, observes, those who are disfranchised from the new technologies "will be highly correlated with the general have-nots" (Ratan 1995, 25). The wealthier the family, the more likely the family is to have a computer. Of American families with an income of $75,000 a year or more, 74 percent have at least one PC. However, only about one-third of all U.S. homes have a computer. Further, white families are three times more likely to have a computer than black or Hispanic families (Hancock, 1995, 50–51).

One source of technological inequality is the school system. Richer school districts have more technological equipment than poorer ones, and "schools in the more affluent suburbs have twice as many computers per student as their less-well-funded urban counterparts" (Ratan 1995). Infrastructures in poor rural and urban areas are often unable to support many of the more sophisticated technological innovations. For example, inner city neighborhoods are less likely to be "wired," that is, to have the telecommunications hardware necessary for schools to access on-line services. The tendency for cable and telephone companies to lay fiber optics in the more affluent neighborhoods

National Data: In a 1995 poll of Americans, 23 percent reported that computers intensified the division between rich and poor; 58 percent responded that computers made little difference because the rich and poor are already so far apart.

SOURCE: Hancock 1995.

has been called "information apartheid" or "electronic redlining." Further, any direct access is impossible for the seven million homes in the United States, predominantly of the poor, that are without telephones (Ratan 1995).

The cost of equalizing such differences is enormous, but the cost of not equalizing them may be even greater. Employees who are technologically skilled earn up to 15 percent higher pay than those who are not, according to Labor Department economists (Hancock 1995, 51). Further, technological disparities exacerbate the structural inequities perpetuated by the split labor force and the existence of primary and secondary labor markets (see Chapter 10).

> **Consideration** *Inner city areas, which are often financially strained, find it difficult to finance the information highway. Five years ago, an inner city school in Union City, New Jersey, was put "on-line," and Bell Atlantic donated a computer for every seventh grader. Parents began E-mailing the principal, student test scores increased dramatically, and attendance is now the best in the school district (Hancock 1995).*

HEALTH RISKS OF TECHNOLOGY

Some new technologies have unknown risks. Biotechnology, for example, has promised and, to some extent, has delivered everything from life-saving drugs to heartier pest-free tomatoes. The risks of releasing the genetically altered organisms into the atmosphere are unknown, however. "These genetically engineered microbes are alive and are inherently unpredictable," says leading biotechnology critic Jeremy Rifkin. "Unlike chemicals, they reproduce, migrate, grow. If something goes wrong, you can't recall them, seal them up, clean them up or do anything about them" (Trafford and Gabor, 1991, 404).

Other technologies pose clear risks to large numbers of people. Examples include nuclear power plants, DDT, automobiles, X rays, food coloring, and breast implants. Another problem is **technology-induced diseases** such as those experienced by Chellis Glendinning (1990) when she used the "pill" and the Dalkon Shield (see *The Human Side*).

The production of new technologies may also place manufacturing employees in jeopardy. For example, the electronics industry uses thousands of hazardous chemicals including freon, acetone, and sulfuric and nitric acids:

> *[Semiconductor] workers are expected to dip wafer-thin silicon that has been painted with photoresist into acid baths. The wafers are then heated in gas-filled ovens, where the gas chemically reacts with the photosensitive chemicals. After drying, the chips are then bonded to ceramic frames, wires are attached to contacts and the chip is encapsulated with epoxy. These integrated circuits are then soldered onto boards, and the whole device is cleaned with solvents. Gases and silicon lead to respiratory and lung diseases; acids to burning and blood vessel damage and, solvents to liver damage. (Hosmer 1986, 2)*

THE CHALLENGE TO TRADITIONAL VALUES AND BELIEFS

Technological innovations and scientific discoveries often challenge traditionally held values and beliefs, in part because they enable people to achieve goals that were previously unobtainable. Before recent advances in reproductive

The history of the "rocky road of progress" is made up of apparent technological wonders that turned out to be techno-threats or outright disasters.
—Abigail Trafford
Andrea Gabor
Journalists

In the case of the Dalkon Shield IUD, the rush to market of this supposed technological advance took precedence over thorough testing of the product's safety. The toll in human suffering cannot be calculated.

SURVIVING TECHNOLOGY-INDUCED DISEASE: ONE WOMAN'S EXPERIENCE

I am a technology survivor. I became sick from an encounter with a health-threatening technology, and I survived.... when I was twenty years old, I went to a women's health clinic looking for advice about birth control.... the attitude at the clinic unequivocally transmitted the message that women should use... the Pill.

I took them for two years. During that time I developed chronic vaginal infections, hives, food allergies, and paralyzing depression. Although no doctor was able to diagnose my condition at the time, I had contracted a disease called systemic candidiasis.

... after public hearings had revealed some of the Pill's more blatant medical effects, a gynecologist told me that "God's gift to woman" had arrived. It was the Dalkon Shield intrauterine device (IUD). He inserted one... I began to experience pain, fevers, and fatigue: pelvic inflammatory disease (PID) caused by the Shield. The antibiotics used to treat it worsened the candida problem until I suffered a total collapse.

Despite my efforts to get help, medical professionals did not seem to know the root of my condition lay in immune dysfunction caused by ingesting artificial hormones and worsened by chronic inflammation. In all, my life was disrupted by illness for twenty years, including six years spent in bed....

For most of the years of illness, I lived in isolation with my problem. Doctors and manufacturers of birth control technologies never acknowledged it or its source. Neither did my family, friends, or colleagues. I continually met with such incomplete and uncompassionate responses as: "What's your problem? You look fine to me!" "But your blood test is normal," and "What are you trying to teach yourself by giving yourself this illness?" There are many sources for the ignorance and denial that surround technology-induced disease, but the ultimate results of such frames of mind is that they alienate sick people from the support and caring they deserve and they alienate all of us from addressing the collective problems of technology's dangers.

SOURCE: Chellis Glendinning. 1990. *When Technology Wounds*, pp. 15–16. New York: Wiliam Morrow and Company, Inc. Used with permission.

technology, for example, women could not conceive and give birth after menopause. Technology that allows postmenopausal women to give birth challenges societal beliefs about childbearing and the role of older women. Macklin (1991) notes that the techniques of egg retrieval, in vitro fertilization, and gamete intrafallopian transfer (GIFT) make it possible for two different women to each make a biological contribution to the creation of a new life. Such technology requires society to reexamine its beliefs about what a family is and what a mother is. Should family be defined by custom, law, or the intentions of the parties involved?

Medical technologies that sustain life lead us to rethink the issue of when life should end. The increasing use of computers in the classroom challenges the traditional value of human interaction in the learning process. New weapons systems challenge the traditional idea of war as something that can be survived and even won. Toffler (1970) coined the term **future shock** to describe the confusion resulting from rapid scientific and technological changes that unravel our traditional values and beliefs.

The Public Debate: Controlling Science and Technology

As technology increases, so does the need for social responsibility. Nuclear power, genetic engineering, cloning, and computer surveillance techniques all increase the need for social responsibility: ". . . technological change has the effect of enhancing the importance of public decision making in society, because technology is continually creating new possibilities for social action as well as new problems that have to be dealt with" (Mesthene 1993, 85). Schumacher (1993) argues that science and technology have simply gone too far and that what is needed is "appropriate technology"—appropriate in the sense that it respects human values and needs and returns control to the people.

Science and technology raise many public policy issues. Policy decisions, for example, address concerns about the safety of nuclear power plants, the privacy of electronic mail, the hazards of chemical warfare, and the legality of surrogacy. In formulating policy about the direction of scientific research and the implementation of technologies, decision makers must consider the costs versus the benefits of a specific technology.

COSTS VERSUS BENEFITS OF SCIENCE AND TECHNOLOGY

Each new technology introduced into society involves both costs and benefits. Often, the corporate class benefits at the expense of employees. For example, robotics improve corporate efficiency and maximize profits, but displace workers. Biotechnology has the capacity to both benefit and harm all of society's members. Genetic screening can be used to assess the health risks of a fetus, for example, but can also prevent someone from finding a job because of "genetic inferiority."

Costs and benefits are also economic. Health costs have escalated, in part, because of the cost of increasingly advanced medical technology. But this technology is also leading to increased life expectancy. By the year 2000, U.S. life expectancy is estimated to be 76.7, up from 70.8 in 1970 (*Statistical Abstract of the United States: 1995*, Table 114). Further, as a society, members must ask whether the billions of dollars spent on scientific research and technological development would be better devoted to repairing deteriorating schools, reducing crime, or improving life among the poor.

> *Science has liberated the ideas of those who read and reflect, and the American example had kindled feelings of right in the people. An insurrection has consequently begun, of science, talents and courage, against rank and birth, which have fallen into contempt. . . . Science is progressive.*
> —Thomas Jefferson
> Former U.S. President

In creating science and technology, have we created a monster that has begun to control us rather than the reverse? What controls, if any, should be placed on science and technology? The government, often through such regulatory agencies and departments as the Food and Drug Administration, the Federal Communications Commission, and the Department of Transportation, prohibits the use of some technologies (e.g., assisted suicide devices) and requires others (e.g., seatbelts). Further, all proposed research and development projects seeking federal funds must be accompanied by an environmental impact statement. The Office of Technology Assessment, established in 1973, also provides information to Congress about the environmental impact of proposed projects. Additionally, the National Institute of Standards and Technology, a part of the Commerce Department's Technology Administration, promotes economic growth through working with industry in developing new technologies.

In 1993, President Clinton, by executive order, established the National Science and Technology Council (NSTC), which includes the vice president and the secretaries of defense, energy, and commerce, among others. The major function of the NSTC is to coordinate the interagency science and technology policy-making process and to implement and integrate the president's science and technology agenda (NSTC 1994). President Clinton also created the President's Committee of Advisers on Science and Technology (PCAST), which advises him on issues of science and technology and assists the NSTC in securing private sector cooperation.

UNDERSTANDING
SCIENCE AND TECHNOLOGY

What are we to understand about science and technology from this chapter? As functionalists argue, science and technology evolve as a social process and are a natural part of the evolution of society. As society's needs change, scientific discoveries and technological innovations emerge to meet these needs, thereby serving the functions of the whole. Consistent with conflict theory, however, science and technology also meet the needs of select groups and are characterized by political components. As Winner (1993) notes, the structure of science and technology conveys political messages including "[P]ower is centralized," "[T]here are barriers between social classes," "[T]he world is hierarchically structured," and "[T]he good things are distributed unequally" (Winner 1993, 288).

The scientific discoveries and technological innovations that are embraced by society as truth itself are socially determined. Research indicates that science and the resulting technologies have both negative and positive consequences—a technological dualism. Technology saves lives and time and money; it also leads to death, unemployment, alienation, and estrangement. Weighing the costs and benefits of technology poses ethical dilemmas as does science itself. Ethics, however, "is not only concerned with individual choices and acts. It is also and, perhaps, above all concerned with the cultural shifts and trends of which acts are but the symptoms" (McCormick 1994, 16).

Thus, society makes a choice by the very direction it follows. Such choices should be made on the basis of guiding principles that are both fair and just (Winner 1993; Goodman 1993):

1. Science and technology should be prudent. Adequate testing, safeguards, and impact studies are essential. Impact assessment should include an evaluation of the social, political, environmental, and economic factors.

2. No technology should be developed unless all groups, and particularly those who will be most affected by the technology, have at least some representation "at a very early stage in defining what that technology will be" (Winner 1993, 291). Traditionally, the structure of the scientific process and the development of technologies has been centralized (that is, decisions have been in the hands of a few scientists and engineers); decentralization of the process would increase representation.

3. There should be no means without ends. Each new innovation should be directed toward fulfilling a societal need rather than the more typical pattern in which a technology is developed first (e.g., high-definition televisions) and then a market is created (e.g., "you'll never watch a regular TV again!"). Indeed, from the space program to research on artificial intelligence, the vested interests of scientists and engineers, whose discoveries and innovations build careers, should be tempered by the demands of society.

It would be nice if the scientist and the engineer were cognizant of, and deeply concerned about, the potential risks, secondary consequences, and other costs of their creations.
—Allan Mazur
Sociologist

What the twenty-first century will hold, as the technological transformation continues, may be beyond the imagination of most of society's members. Technology empowers; it increases efficiency and productivity, extends life, controls the environment, and expands individual capabilities. But, as Steven Levy (1995) notes, there is a question as to whether society can accommodate such empowerment (p. 26).

As this century closes and we enter the first computational millennium, one of the great concerns of civilization will be the attempt to reorder society, culture, and government in a manner that exploits the digital bonanza, yet prevents it from running roughshod over the checks and balances so delicately constructed in those simpler precomputer years.

CRITICAL THINKING

1. Should white supremacist groups have the right to disseminate information about their organizations and recruit members through the Internet?

2. In 1996, President Clinton signed a bill that requires TV manufacturers to equip future sets with the "V-chip"—a technological device designed to prevent children from watching programs their parents find objectional. Hollywood executives opposed the "V-chip" on the grounds that it is an intrusion into freedom of expression. How might a conflict theorist explain opposition to the "V-chip"?

3. What currently existing technologies have had more negative than positive consequences for individuals and for society?

KEY TERMS

REFERENCES

Bell, Daniel. 1973. *The Coming of Post-Industrial Society: A Venture in Social Forecasting.* New York: Basic Books.

Beniger, James R. 1993. "The Control Revolution." In *Technology and the Future,* ed. Albert H. Teich, pp. 40–65. New York: St. Martin's Press.

Blank, R. H. 1990. *Regulating Reproduction.* New York: Columbia University Press.

Bush, Corlann G. 1993. "Women and the Assessment of Technology." In *Technology and the Future,* ed. Albert H. Teich, pp. 192–214. New York: St. Martin's Press.

Callahan, S., and D. Callahan. 1984. "Abortion; Understanding Differences." *Family Planning Perspectives* 16: 219–21.

Ceruzzi, Paul. 1993. "An Unforeseen Revolution: Computers and Expectations, 1935–1985." In *Technology and the Future,* ed. Albert H. Teich, pp. 160–74. New York: St. Martin's Press.

Clarke, Adele E. 1990. "Controversy and the Development of Reproductive Sciences." *Social Problems* 37(1): 18–37.

Discovery Magazine. 1994. "5th Annual Discover Awards for Technological Innovation." October.

Durkheim, Emile. [1925] 1973. *Moral Education.* New York: Free Press.

Elmer-Dewitt, Philip. 1994a. "The Genetic Revolution." *Time,* January 17, 46–53.

_____. 1994b. "Who Should Keep the Keys." *Time,* March 14.

_____. 1995. "Welcome to Cyberspace." *Time,* Spring, 4–11.

Facts in Brief: Abortion in the United States. 1992. New York: Alan Guttmacher Institute.

Fix, Janet L. 1994. "Automation Makes Bank Branches a Liability." *USA Today,* November 28, 1B.

Garson, Barbara. 1992. "Computers and the Electronic Sweatshops of the Future." In *Sociology: Windows on Society,* ed. John Heeren and Marylee Mason, pp. 263–74. Los Angeles: Roxbury Publishing Co.

General Social Survey, 1973, 1983, 1990, 1993. Storrs, Conn.: Roper Organization, Inc. [Internet].

Glendinning, Chellis. 1990. *When Technology Wounds: The Human Consequences of Progress.* New York: William Morrow.

Goodman, Paul. 1993. "Can Technology Be Humane?" In *Technology and the Future,* ed. Albert H. Teich, pp. 239–55. New York: St. Martin's Press.

Hancock, LynNell. 1995. "The Haves and the Have-Nots." *Newsweek,* February 27, 50–53.

Hosmer,. Ellen. 1986. "High Tech Hazards: Chipping Away at Workers Health." *Multinational Monitor* 7 (January 31): 1–5.

Jackson, James O. 1995. "Its a Wired, Wired World." *Time,* Spring, 80–82.

Jaroff, Leon. 1995. "Age of the Road Warrior." *Time,* Spring, 38–41.

Johnson, Jim. 1988. "Mixing Humans and Nonhumans Together: The Sociology of a Door-Closer." *Social Problems* 35: 298–310.

Johnson, Robert C. 1993. "Science, Technology and the Black Community." In *Technology and the Future,* ed. Albert H. Teich pp. 265–82. New York: St. Martin's Press.

Kahin, Brian. 1993. "Information Technology and Information Infrastructure." In *Empowering Technology: Implementing a U.S. Strategy,* ed. Lewis M. Branscomb, pp. 135–66. Cambridge, Mass: MIT Press.

Kantrowitz, Barbara, and Deborah Rosenberg. 1994. "Ready, Teddy? You're Online." *Newsweek,* October 12, 60–61.

Kuhn, Thomas. 1973. *The Structure of Scientific Revolutions.* Chicago: Chicago University Press.

Levy, Steven. 1995. "TechnoMania." *Newsweek,* February 27, 25–29.

Macklin, Ruth. 1991. "Artificial Means of Reproduction and Our Understanding of the Family." *Hastings Center Report* (January/February): 5–11.

Mattera, Philip. 1983. "Home Computer Sweatshops." *The Nation,* April 2, 390–92.

McCormick, S. J. Richard A. 1994. "Blastomere Separation." *Hastings Center Report* (March/April): 14–16.

McDermott, John. 1993. "Technology: The Opiate of the Intellectuals." In *Technology and the Future,* ed. Albert H. Teich, pp. 89–107. New York: St. Martin's Press.

Merton, Robert K. 1973. "The Normative Structure of Science." In *The Sociology of Science,* ed. Robert K. Merton. Chicago: University of Chicago Press.

Mesthene, Emmanuel G. 1993. "The Role of Technology in Society." In *Technology and the Future,* ed. Albert H. Teich, pp. 73–88. New York: St. Martin's Press.

National Science and Technology Council Executive Secretariat Office. 1994. "PCAST Fact Sheet." August 3, 1994. Washington, D.C.: U.S. Government Printing Office.

"Nicholas Negroponte: The *Multimedia Today* Interview." 1995. *Multimedia Today,* July-September: 86–88.

Ogburn, William F. 1957. "Cultural Lag as Theory." *Sociology and Social Research* 41: 167–74.

Perrolle, Judith A. 1990. "Computers and Capitalism." In *Social Problems Today,* ed. James M. Henslin, pp. 336–42. Englewood Cliffs, N.J.: Prentice-Hall.

Planned Parenthood Federation of America. 1991. *Norplant: The Promise of New Choices or the Threat of New Control.* Annual Report. New York: Planned Parenthood.

Postman, Neil. 1992. *Technopoly: The Surrender of Culture to Technology.* New York: Alfred A. Knopf.

Powell, Bill, and Daniella Deane. 1994. "Road Kill on the Infoban." *Newsweek,* October 24, 42–44.

Ratan, Suneel. 1995. "A New Divide between the Haves and the Have-Nots." *Time,* Spring, 25–26.

Rheingold, Howard. 1993. "Virtual Reality and Teledildonics." In *Technology and the Future*, ed. Albert H. Teich, pp. 350–65. New York: St. Martin's Press.

Schumacher, E. F. 1993. "Buddhist Economics." In *Technology and the Future*, ed. Albert H. Teich, pp. 231–38. New York: St. Martin's Press.

Shaiken, Harlen. 1984. *Work Transformed: Automation and Labor in the Corporate Age*. New York: Holt.

Springer, Laura. 1995. "Chow of the Future." *Newsweek*, January 2, 114.

Statistical Abstract of the United States: 1995, 115th ed. U.S. Bureau of the Census. Washington, D.C.: U.S. Government Printing Office.

Toffler, Alvin. 1970. *Future Shock*. New York: Random House.

Trafford, Abigail, and Andrea Gabor. 1991. "Living Dangerously." In *Social Problems: Contemporary Readings,* ed. John Stimson, Ardyth Stimson, and Vincent N. Parrillo, pp. 399–405. Itasca, Ill.: F. E. Peacock Publishers.

United Nations Population Fund. 1991. *Population Policies and Programmes: Lessons Learned from Two Decades of Experience,* ed. Nafis Sadik. New York: New York University Press.

Walshok, Mary Lindenstein. 1993. "Blue Collar Women." In *Technology and the Future*, ed. Albert H. Teich, pp. 256–264. New York: St. Martin's Press.

Weinberg, Alvin. 1966. "Can Technology Replace Social Engineering?" *University of Chicago Magazine* 59 (October): 6–10.

Weinberg, Robert A. 1993. "The Dark Side of Genome." In *Technology and the Future,* ed. Albert H. Teich, pp. 318–28. New York: St. Martin's Press.

Williams, Sue Winkle, Shirley M. Ogletree, William Woodburn, and Paul Raffeld. 1993. "Gender Roles, Computer Attitudes, and Dyadic Computer Interaction Performance in College Students." *Sex Roles* 29: 515–25.

Winner, Langdon. 1993. "Artifact/Ideas as Political Culture." In *Technology and the Future*, ed. Albert H. Teich, pp. 283–94. New York: St. Martin's Press.

Wiseman, Paul, and Dottie Enrico. 1994. "Techno Terror Slows Info Highway Traffic." *USA Today,* November 14, 1B.

15

CHAPTER

Population and the Environment

IS IT TRUE?

The United States, with 4.8 percent of the world's population, uses 25 percent of the world's commercial energy (p. 450).

Ninety-five percent of the one billion people who will be added to the world's population between 1992 and 2002 will be in less developed countries (p. 431).

According to the National Center for Environmental Health Strategies, perfume and cologne are air pollutants that have harmful health effects on some individuals (p. 445).

Nuclear waste from power plants remains dangerously radioactive for 10,000 years (p. 448).

The World Bank estimates that the earth's rainforests will disappear within sixty years (p. 450).

ANS: 1. T 2. T 3. T 4. T 5. T

> Population may be the key to all the issues that will shape the future: economic growth; environmental security; and the health and well-being of countries, communities, and families.
>
> Nafis Sadik, Executive Director,
> UN Population Fund

In early 1992, the U.S. National Academy of Sciences and the Royal Society of London issued a report that warned:

> *If current predictions of population growth prove accurate and patterns of human activity on the planet remain unchanged, science and technology may not be able to prevent either irreversible degradation of the environment or continued poverty for much of the world. (cited in Brown 1995, 411)*

In the previous chapter, we noted that science and technology are both friend and foe. The same can be said for population growth. In one sense, population growth reflects the ability of humans to overcome disease, famine, and harsh environmental conditions. Uncontrolled, it results in a variety of social problems such as disease and death, food shortages, and depletion of natural resources.

In this chapter, we discuss population growth and the concomitant environmental implications. These concerns reflect two branches of social science: demography and human ecology. **Demography** is the study of the size, distribution, movement, and composition of human populations. **Human ecology** is the study of the relationship between human populations and their natural environment. After discussing population growth in the world and in the United States, we examine theories of population growth and the social factors that contribute to rapidly expanding populations. We also explore how population growth contributes to a variety of social problems and examine strategies for limiting population growth. We end the chapter by looking at the extent, social causes, and solutions to environmental problems.

The Social Context: Population Growth

For thousands of years, the world's population grew at a relatively slow rate. During 99 percent of human history, the size of hunting and gathering societies was restricted by disease and limited food supplies. Around 8000 B.C., the development of agriculture and the domestication of animals led to increased food supplies and population growth, but even then harsh living conditions and disease still put limits on the rate of growth.

This pattern continued until the mid-eighteenth century when the Industrial Revolution improved the standard of living for much of the world's population. The improvements included better food, cleaner drinking water, and improved housing, as well as advances in medical technology such as vaccinations against infectious diseases; all contributed to rapid increases in population. Today, population growth continues worldwide.

WORLD POPULATION

In the year A.D. 1, the world's population was about 250 million. The **doubling time**—or time it takes for a population to double in size from any base year—decreases as the population grows. Although the population in A.D. 1 took 1,650 years to double, the second doubling took only 200 years, the third 80 years, and the fourth 45 years. In 1994, the doubling time for the world's population was 41 years; for the U.S. population, doubling time was 89 years (Waldrop 1994).

Population growth is generally highest in less developed countries. Compared to the developed countries, these nations are characterized by greater illiteracy, higher infant mortality rates, more people per square mile, less industrialization, shorter life expectancies, more poverty, lower-quality health care, and poorer nutrition. Ninety-five percent of the one billion people who will be added to the world's population between 1992 and 2002 will be in less developed countries ("Population Growth Threatens Natural Resources Renewal" 1992).

As the populations of the developed countries grow at slower rates, these countries will come to represent less and less of the world's total population. In 1950, for example, North American countries comprised 6.6 percent of the world's population. This percentage had dropped to 5.2 percent by 1990 and is projected to decrease to 3.3 percent by 2050. Similarly, Europe, which is comprised mostly of developed countries, accounted for 15.6 percent of the world's population in 1950, but only 9.4 percent in 1990; this percentage is projected to drop to 4.9 percent by the year 2050 (United Nations 1992).

UNITED STATES POPULATION

During the colonial era (c. 1650), the U.S. population included about 50,000 colonists and 750,000 Native Americans. By 1859, disease and warfare had reduced the Indian population to 250,000, but the European population had increased to 23 million. The U.S. population continued to increase into the 1900s. From the mid-1940s to the late 1960s the U.S. birth rate had increased significantly. This period of high birth rates, commonly referred to as the *baby boom*, peaked in 1957 when the crude birth rate (number of live births per 1,000 people) reached 25.3. Although the birth rate dropped to 15.3 in 1986, the U.S. population continues to increase. As Table 15.1 shows, the U.S. population is expected to be over 276 million by the year 2000 (*Statistical Abstract of the United States: 1995,* Table 1361).

THEORIES OF POPULATION GROWTH

There have been two dominant theories of population growth—the Malthusian theory and the demographic transition theory.

Malthusian Theory In 1798, Thomas Malthus observed that the population was growing faster than the food supply and predicted that masses of people were destined to be poor and hungry. According to Malthus, food shortages would lead to war, disease, and starvation that would eventually slow population growth.

International Data: The world's population is projected to be 6.1 billion by the year 2000.

SOURCE: *Statistical Abstract of the United States: 1995,* Table 1361.

By the year 2025, it is estimated that the planet will be inhabited by 8.5 billion people.

SOURCE: Urzua 1992.

Population growth is generally highest in developing countries, which are characterized by high illiteracy, higher infant mortality rates, larger per square mile population, less industrialization, lower life expectancy, higher poverty, inadequate health care, and poor nutrition.

National Data: From 1990 to 1995, the U.S. population grew by 13 million people, an increase of 5.2%.

SOURCE: Deardorff and Montgomery 1995.

TABLE 15.1

U. S. POPULATION IN SELECTED YEARS

YEAR	POPULATION
1650	50,000 colonists 750,000 Native Americans
1859	23 million persons of European heritage 250,000 Native Americans
1990	250 million
1995	263 million
2000 (projected)	276 million
2050 (projected)	392 million

SOURCES: Dennis Ahlburg. 1993. "The Census Bureau's New Projections of the U. S. Population." *Population and Development Review* 19: 159–74; National Center for Health Statistics. 1994. Births, Marriages, Divorces, and Deaths for April. Monthly Vital Statistics Report, Vol. 43 No. 4. Hyattsville, Md.: Public Health Service. *Statistical Abstract of the United States: 1995*, 115th ed. U. S. Bureau of the Census. (Washington, D. C.: U. S. Government Printing Office).

The greatest single obstacle to the economic and social advancement of the majority of the peoples of the underdeveloped world is rapid population growth.
—Robert McNamara
Former Secretary of Defense

Eighteenth-century England provides an example of how **Malthusian theory** may have actually operated. When wheat became scarce, it became very expensive, and people delayed marriage because they could not afford to feed a family. Once the marriage rate slowed and the birth rate declined, fewer people competed for wheat, the price of bread dropped, and marriage and birth rates began to increase again.

Critics of Malthusian theory argue that it is possible to provide enough food for the world's population. Conflict theorists argue that food producers artificially limit the supply of food in order to command a high price for their products. According to these theorists, present agricultural technology could produce enough food for an expanding population, yet food shortages exist due to capitalism and the inequitable distribution of resources. For example, farmers concentrate on cash crops, such as sugarcane, tobacco, and coffee beans, rather than growing less lucrative crops such as grains, which would help feed the world's population. Malthusian theory also assumes that population growth is inevitable, but the availability of contraceptive technology negates this assumption. Today, access to contraception enables people to control family size and slow or reverse population growth.

Demographic Transition Theory The **demographic transition theory** explains how industrialization affects population growth. Consistent with structural-functionalism, this theory suggests that as one component of the social system changes, other elements also change. The population changes in three stages as a society makes the transition from preindustrial to industrial (see Figure 15.1):

- *Stage I.* In preindustrial society, both the birth rate and the death rate are high. The result is a fairly stable population that either does not grow or grows very slowly.

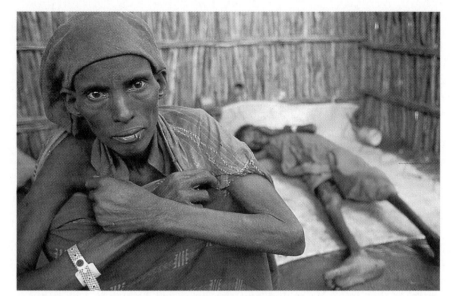

Critics of Malthus' theory argue that it is possible to provide enough food for the world's population. According to conflict theorists, food producers artificially limit the food supply to command a high price. The human result is the same, however.

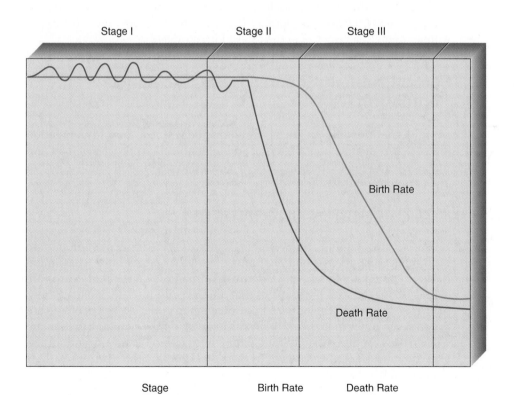

Stage		Birth Rate	Death Rate
I	(preindustrial)	High	High
II	(industrial)	High	Low
III	(advanced industrial)	Low	Low

FIGURE 15.1
DEMOGRAPHIC TRANSITION STAGES

- *Stage II.* As a society makes the transition from agricultural to industrial, the death rate decreases due to improvements in sanitation, health care, and the supply and distribution of food. The continuing high birth rate, in conjunction with the declining death rate, leads to a rapid increase in population. In some cases, the population may grow so rapidly that it cripples a country's chance of industrial growth.
- *Stage III.* As a society reaches an advanced stage of industrialization, the birth rate declines due to the availability of inexpensive forms of contraception, the economic liability of children, and social pressures to have smaller families. The declining birth rate compensates for the low death rate, and population growth slows or may even decline.

The demographic transition theory describes how population growth has changed in countries that are already industrialized. Functionalists emphasize that industrialization results in the employment of women outside the home, thus decreasing the birth rate. It is unknown, however, whether countries that are not yet industrialized will follow a similar pattern. Some evidence suggests that industrialization and the increased economic well-being it brings do not always lead to decreased fertility. Anthropologist Virginia Abernethy noted that as a sense of economic well-being increases, people may want to have more children, not fewer. In Kenya, for example, even though income increased between decades, the fertility rate rose from 7.5 live births per woman in the 1950s to 8.12 in the 1960s (Linden 1994b).

Social Problems Related to Unrestrained Population Growth

Some of the most urgent social problems today are related to population growth. They include poor maternal and infant health, shortages of food and water, environmental degradation, overcrowded cities, and conflict within and between countries.

INADEQUATE MATERNAL AND INFANT HEALTH

Having several children at short intervals increases the chances of premature birth, infectious disease, and death for the mother or the baby. The United Nations Population Fund (1991) warns that "maternal and infant deaths are closely correlated with pregnancies that are too early, too late, too many, and too close" (p. 57). In developing countries, women under the age of fifteen are five to seven times more likely to die during pregnancy or childbirth than are women ages twenty to twenty-four. Babies born to mothers younger than sixteen are much more likely to die in their first month of life (United Nations Population Fund 1991).

FOOD SHORTAGES, MALNOURISHMENT, AND DISEASE

Countries with large populations, few resources, and limited land are particularly vulnerable to food shortages. Food shortages lead to malnourishment

The United Nations' Food and Agriculture Organization now lists virtually every major commercial species of fish as depleted, fully exploited or overexploited.
—Melissa Healy
Journalist

and a variety of diseases and health concerns. A quarter of a million children go blind every year from vitamin A deficiency. In addition, many suffer from iodine deficiency disorder (IDD), which is the greatest cause of brain damage in children and infants (World Health Organization 1994). McNamara (1992) summarizes the health consequences of malnutrition:

> Surveys have shown that millions of children in low-income families receive insufficient protein and calories to permit optimal development of their brains, thereby limiting their capacity to learn and to lead fully productive lives. Additional millions die each year before the age of five, from debilitating disease caused by nutritional deficiencies. (p. 12).

According to Dyson (1994), most people who are undernourished are so because they are poor and do not have the resources to purchase food. Dyson suggests that world hunger may best be overcome through increasing employment and income, rather than increasing food production.

WATER SHORTAGES AND DEPLETION OF OTHER NATURAL RESOURCES

The surface of planet Earth is approximately 70 percent water. Water is essential to plant, animal, and human life; the human body is composed of approximately 70 percent water. According to Population Action International, however, by the year 2025, one in three people will be living in a country with a shortage of water. During the early 1990s, the ratio was one in fifteen (Associated Press 1993).

> **Consideration** In rural China, for example, over 82 million people are threatened by a water shortage. The problem is worse in urban areas; over 300 Chinese cities have water shortages or have water that is polluted or contaminated with pesticides. In the 1950s, Beijing wells drew water from 16 feet below the earth's surface. In the early 1990s, the city's 40,000 wells had to reach down 160 feet on average for water. The water shortage has prompted official debate over the viability of Beijing as China's capital (Associated Press 1993).

Uncontrolled population growth also contributes to the depletion of other natural resources such as forests, oil, gas, coal, and certain minerals. Whether our planet will be able to sustain the world's population depends not only on how many people there are to sustain, but also on how these people make use of the resources that sustain them.

URBAN CROWDING AND HIGH POPULATION DENSITY

Population growth contributes to urban crowding and high population density. In 1950 Shanghai was the only city in a developing country with a population of more than 5 million. By the year 2000, the United Nations projects that more than forty cities in developing countries will have over 5 million inhabitants (McFalls 1991). Without economic and material resources to provide for basic living needs, urban populations in developing countries often live in severe poverty. Urban poverty in turn produces environmental problems such as unsanitary disposal of waste. In Nigerian urban ghettos, for example, "mounds

International Data: Thirty-eight percent (192 million) of the world's children under the age of five are underweight and malnourished.

SOURCE: World Health Organization 1994.

The greatest challenge of the coming century is the maintenance of growth in global food production to match or exceed the projected doubling (at least) of the human population.
—Paul Ehrlich
Anne H. Ehrlich
Gretchen C. Daily
Demographers/Biologist

of refuse (including human wastes) that litter everywhere—gutters, schools, roads, market places and town squares—have been accepted as part of the way of life" (Nzeako, quoted in Agbese 1995).

Population growth also affects the density of a country's population. Singapore has nearly 12,000 people per square mile of land. In contrast, the United States has an average density of 75 people per square mile (*Statistical Abstract of the United States: 1995*, Table 1361). India has one-third the land area of the United States, but more than three times the population. Imagine tripling the U.S. population. Then imagine that this tripled population all lived in the eastern third of the United States. That will give you an idea of how crowded countries like India are.

MIGRATION AND CONFLICT

If we don't control the population with justice, humanity and mercy, it will be done for us by nature—brutally.
—Henry Kendall
Nobel Laureate in Physics

Conflict theorists emphasize that as populations grow, competition for scarce resources increases the probability of conflict within and between countries. In the 1980s, food riots and demonstrations in the Sudan led to a military takeover of the government (Brown and Wolf 1986). Conflict may also occur between countries as people migrate to neighboring nations in search of food and other needed resources. As large numbers of immigrants seek improved life conditions, they compete with native-born populations for limited resources. Gioseffi (1993) warns that, "If nothing is done to check the population growth now threatening the quality of life everywhere, we are bound to see issues of prejudice constantly on the rise—because of the shrinking resources and land areas available . . ." (xlix). Immigration into the United States has led to increased conflict between racial and ethnic groups (see Chapter 9).

Structural and Cultural Influences on Population Growth

Various structural and cultural factors contribute to population growth. These factors include lack of access to birth control methods, pronatalistic cultural values, roles of women, and economic underdevelopment.

LACK OF ACCESS TO BIRTH CONTROL METHODS

National Data: Seven in ten first-year college students report that "raising a family" is an important life goal.

SOURCE: American Council on Education and University of California 1994.

Although researchers have developed a wide range of contraceptives, many of these methods are not widely available or are prohibitively expensive. One report suggests that less than half the population in many developing countries has access to affordable contraception ("Birth control" 1991). In Chad, an IUD would cost nearly three-fourths of a year's income for an average woman, and in Kenya, female sterilization could cost as much as 90 percent of a person's average annual income.

In some countries, methods of birth control are provided only to married women. Family planning personnel often refuse, or are forbidden by law or policy, to make referrals for contraceptive and abortion services for unmarried women. In addition, "lack of confidentiality and long waiting times discourage unmarried young people from attending clinics, where they may be spotted by family, friends, or teachers " (Hawkins and Meshesha 1994, 16).

Finally, many women throughout the world do not have access to legal abortion. As of 1986, only 76 percent of the world's population lived in countries where abortion was legally permitted. Of that number, 39 percent had access to abortion on request; 24 percent could obtain abortions for socioeconomic reasons such as inadequate income, housing, or unwed status; and 13 percent could obtain them on broader health grounds. The remaining 24 percent of the world's population lived in countries where abortion was either prohibited or permitted only to save the life of the mother (United Nations Population Fund 1991).

PRONATALISTIC CULTURAL VALUES

Making contraceptives available does not reduce fertility unless women and men want to use birth control methods to prevent childbearing. In many societies, pronatalistic cultural values promote having children. In America, national observances such as Mother's Day and Father's Day, parents who ask "When will I be a grandparent?" and friends who have children may influence couples toward parenthood.

Pronatalist cultural values also proliferate throughout the world. In traditional Chinese culture, having many children was considered a blessing and a way of honoring one's ancestors. Confucius, the ancient Chinese philosopher, said that the greatest sin is to die without an heir. Throughout history, many religions have worshiped fertility and recognized it as being necessary for the continuation of the human race. In many countries, religions prohibit or discourage birth control, contraceptives, and abortion.

Sometimes, governmental regulations and policies enforce or encourage pronatalism. In pre-1989 Romania, for example, the pronatalist regime of Nicolae Ceausescu prohibited sterilization and abortion, as well as the sale of contraceptives (Bok 1994). In pronatalist America, couples are allowed dependency deductions on their income tax for each child. In effect, child-free couples pay higher taxes.

STATUS OF WOMEN

Throughout the developing world, the status of women is primarily restricted to that of wife and mother. Women in developing countries are not encouraged to seek education or employment, but to marry early, have children, and stay home. In parts of South Africa, for example, girls are expected to leave school and get married when they reach age fourteen. A community health worker in South Africa describes women's roles:

> Generally, married women are not allowed to make any decisions or say anything which contradicts their husbands. They cannot use contraception of any kind because they should "give birth until the babies are finished inside the stomach." It does not matter whether you give birth ten or fourteen times. (Klugman, cited in Mahmud and Johnston 1994, 155)

ECONOMIC UNDERDEVELOPMENT

Economic underdevelopment is associated with high birth rates for a number of reasons. First, economically underdeveloped countries tend to highly restrict the roles of women. In these societies, women are expected to marry young and have children—lots of children. In contrast, women in industrialized societies are more likely to have educational and occupational goals. Pursuing such goals encourages women to delay marriage and limit family size.

Economically underdeveloped societies also have high birth rates because children in these societies are regarded as an economic asset to the family. Although a large family means more mouths to feed, it also means more hands to work in the fields to help support the family. In industrialized societies, children generally are not an economic asset, but a liability. Child labor laws and mandatory education in developed countries restrict children from contributing economically to the family.

In underdeveloped countries, large families also provide income and security to the aged, as surviving children support their elderly parents. In developed countries, social security or other government programs are available to help take care of the elderly.

Finally, underdeveloped countries may impose pronatalistic policies in order to increase their population size and stimulate economic development. In the 1970s, Romania implemented a campaign to raise the rate of population growth and boost economic development. Among other things, the campaign prohibited abortion and contraception (Boland, Rao, and Zeidenstein 1994).

Strategies for Limiting Population Growth

Should governments attempt to reduce the world's rapid rate of population growth? Most social scientists and government leaders would answer "yes." The question, "What population control strategies should be implemented?" is not so easily answered. Nevertheless, various strategies on the local, national, and international levels have been tried, with some degree of success.

PROVIDE ACCESS TO BIRTH CONTROL METHODS

> *The question that society must answer is this: Shall family limitation be achieved through birth control or abortion? Shall normal, safe, effective contraceptives be employed, or shall we continue to force women to the abnormal, often dangerous surgical operation? Contraceptives or Abortion—which shall it be?*
> —Margaret Sanger
> Birth control advocate

Family planning specialists emphasize that access to birth control methods is important to population control. One way to limit population growth is to provide women and men with safe and effective means of birth control. Sterilization, the most effective method of birth control other than abstinence, has become the most widely used method of family planning in both developing and developed countries (United Nations Population Fund 1991). Worldwide the next most common methods of contraception are IUDs (intrauterine devices), oral contraceptives, and condoms.

As noted earlier, however, many individuals, especially in poor countries, do not have access to affordable contraceptives. The United Nations Population Fund (1991) estimates that only 48 percent of couples in developing countries use contraceptives; in developed countries, the corresponding figure is 71 percent.

Increasing contraceptive usage requires providing access to affordable contraceptive methods along with appropriate instruction and education concerning their use. Unless contraceptive and family planning services are available to all sexually active individuals, including young and unmarried individuals, many women will continue to experience high pregnancy rates. While contraceptive availability is necessary for limiting population growth, it

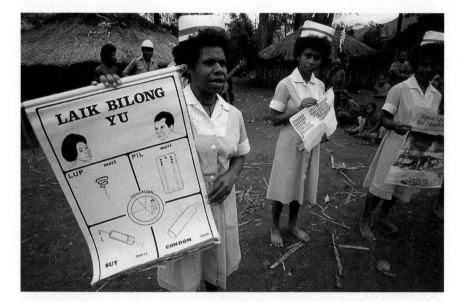

Information about birth control and contraceptives are provided more freely in some countries than in others. Here nurses provide contraceptive information to local people at a family planning clinic in Papua, New Guinea.

is not sufficient by itself. In many pronatalistic societies, women have high fertility rates because they either want large families or are forced by their husbands to have many children. One answer to these problems is to improve the status of women.

IMPROVE THE STATUS OF WOMEN

Improving the status of women is vital to curbing population growth. Nafis Sadik, executive director of the United Nations Population Fund, argues that population control cannot be achieved without gender equality and the social empowerment of women to control their lives, especially their reproductive lives. Toward this end, the 1994 Cairo Conference on Population passed a proposal allocating, by the year 2000, $17 billion annually for programs supportive of women. Such programs would include education, family planning, and health care.

Education plays a key role in improving the status of women and reducing fertility rates. In a study of sixty-two low-income countries, Schultz (1993) found that the higher the educational level of women, the lower the fertility rate and the slower the population growth. World Fertility Survey data reveal a strong association between women's education and age of marriage, desired family size, and contraceptive use in developing countries. Based on data for thirty countries, the United Nations reports that women with no education had an average of 6.9 children, three more than women with seven or more years of education (reported in Mahmud and Johnston 1994). Researchers hypothesize that more education results in reduced fertility in developing countries because it delays marriage and reduces desired family size by stimulating aspirations for a higher standard of living. Education empowers women by preparing them for employment in the economic sector and offers them a meaningful role other than that of wife and mother. Lastly, education exposes women to nontraditional values and to knowledge and positive attitudes about contraceptive use (Mahmud and Johnston 1994).

In my opinion, if we are to make genuine progress in economic and social development, if we are to make progress in achieving population goals, women increasingly must have greater freedom of choice in determining their roles in society.
—Jay Rockefeller
U.S. Senator

The increase in education of women and girls contributes to greater empowerment of women, to a postponement of the age of marriage and to a reduction in the size of families.
—Program of Action of the 1994 International Conference on Population and Development (Chapter XI)

Researchers hypothesize that more education for women results in reduced fertility in developing countries, because it delays marriage and reduces desired family size by stimulating aspirations for a higher standard of living.

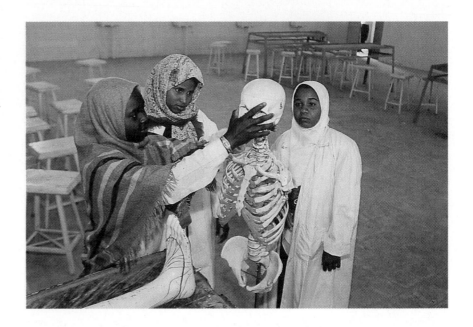

INCREASE ECONOMIC DEVELOPMENT

Another strategy for slowing population growth involves stimulating a society's economic development by building more factories, increasing industrial output, and increasing employment and income levels. Women in economically developed countries are more likely to have more education and gender equality than women in less developed countries. As previously noted, women's education and status are related to fertility levels.

Economic development also changes the economic value of children. Whereas children in agricultural societies contribute economically to the family, they are economic liabilities in industrialized countries.

Although economic development can result in reduced fertility, it can also contribute to environmental problems such as pollution and depletion of natural resources. These concerns are addressed later in this chapter. Next, we consider a form of population control that some criticize as being coercive and in violation of basic human rights—the imposition of government regulations and policies on reproductive behavior.

IMPOSE GOVERNMENT REGULATIONS AND POLICIES

To ensure a healthier and more abundant world, we simply must slow the world's explosive growth in population.
—Bill Clinton
U.S. President

The government can socially engineer population control. Some countries have imposed strict governmental regulations on reproduction. In the 1970s, India established mass sterilization camps and made the salaries of public servants contingent on their recruiting a quota of citizens who would accept sterilization. The Indian state of Maharashtra enacted compulsory sterilization legislation and in a six-month period sterilized millions of people, many of them against their will (Boland, Rao, and Zeidenstein 1994). This policy has since been rescinded.

Governmental population regulations in China are less extreme, but still controversial. In 1979, China developed a one-child family policy whereby parents get special privileges for limiting their family size. Specifically, parents who pledge to have only one child receive an allowance for health care for five years that effectively increases their annual income by 10 percent. Parents who have only one child also have priority access to hospitals and receive a pension when they reach old age. In addition, their only child is given priority enrollment in nursery school and exempted from school tuition. Chinese couples who have three or more children lose these privileges and must pay a special tax that effectively lowers their income for the first fourteen years of the child's life. Couples with higher educations and incomes are more likely to sign the one-child certificate, which states that they agree to restrict their family to one child (Zhang and Strum 1994).

China also implemented mandatory gynecological exams. Twice each year health care workers visit each village and, theoretically, check every woman of reproductive age. Under the guise of reproductive health care, each woman is checked for gynecological problems, inserted with an IUD if she has already had a child, and subjected to an abortion if she already has a child and her new pregnancy has not been approved by her village. The Chinese government also promotes sterilization (Greenhalgh, Zhu Chujuzhu, and Li Nan 1994).

Critics of China's population policy argue that government policies that are intended to directly influence fertility are coercive and abusive of women's right to choose the number and timing of their children (McIntosh and Finkle 1995). The 1994 International Conference on Population Development advanced the agenda to replace coercive population programs with those that empower women, improve their health, and raise their status in the family and community.

Advocates of government-imposed fertility control policies point to the success of China's one-child policy in reducing fertility. Many Chinese couples, however, still view the ideal family size as containing two children—one boy and one girl. Based on interviews with Chinese couples, researchers conclude that "if and when administrative pressure is relaxed, many of today's single-child families will move to a second" (Greenhalgh, Zhu Chujuzhu, and Li Nan 1994, 390). In addition, the base population is so large (1.2 billion people), that even with the reduction in the fertility rate, China's population is still growing by 17 million people a year (Linden 1994a).

One by-product of China's one-child policy has been an increase in female infanticide and the abortion of female fetuses. When couples are limited to one child, many would prefer to have a son. By 1992, the sex ratio of newborn children was 118.5 boys for every 100 girls, leading to estimates that 1.7 million girls are "missing" each year (Boland, Rao, and Zeidenstein 1994).

Consideration *According to Tannahill, throughout history, the "simplest and most obvious method of keeping the population down was infanticide" (1982, 31). Commonly, infants are simply abandoned and left to die from lack of nourishment and shelter from the elements. In most cases of infanticide, the victim is female. Tannahill (1982) suggests that the female infant is usually the target of infanticide because she was herself a child-producer of the future, a threat not only in her person but in her progeny to the food*

International Data: The fertility rate in China has fallen almost 25 percent since the one-child policy was implemented—down from 2.6 in 1987 to about 1.90 births per woman today.

SOURCE: Greenhalgh, Zhu Chujuzhu, and Li Nan 1994.

In China, parents who have only one child have priority access to hospitals and receive a pension when they reach old age. Additionally, their only child is given priority enrollment in nursery school and exempted from school tuition.

supply. Alternatively, it can be argued that it would be more effective to kill males since they can impregnate many females in the same nine months it takes a female to gestate one fetus. Sons may be spared because it is they, not daughters, who support parents in their old age.

Environmental Problems

An expanding population is one of many factors that contributes to environmental problems such as land, water, and air pollution and depletion of natural resources. Each of these environmental problems poses a growing threat to the physical, economic, and social well-being of all people throughout the world. In this chapter's *The Human Side*, children from around the world address the issue of environmental degradation.

AIR POLLUTION

Transportation vehicles, fuel combustion, industrial processes (such as the burning of coal and wood), and solid waste disposal have contributed to the growing levels of air pollutants, including carbon monoxide, sulfur dioxide, nitrogen dioxides, and lead. Air pollution levels are highest in areas with both heavy industry and traffic congestion, such as Los Angeles and Mexico City.

National Data: Over sixty percent of carbon monoxide pollution results from emissions from transportation vehicles.

SOURCE: *Statistical Abstract of the United States: 1995*, Table 375.

Depletion of the Ozone Layer The use of human-made chlorofluorocarbons (CFCs), which are used in refrigerators, cleaning computer chips, hospital sterilization, solvents, dry cleaning, and aerosols, has damaged the ozone layer of the earth's atmosphere. Industrial countries account for 84 percent of CFC production; Americans use six times more CFCs than the global average (Vajpeyi 1995).

The depletion of the ozone layer allows hazardous levels of ultraviolet rays to reach the earth's surface. Ultraviolet light causes drying of human skin and increases the incidence of skin cancers, including melanoma, which kills about a third of its victims. Depletion of the ozone layer has also been linked to cataracts of the eye, suppression of the human immune system, declining food crops, rising sea levels, and global warming (Brown 1995; Vajpeyi 1995).

The rising atmospheric concentration of greenhouse gases is potentially the most economically disruptive and costly change that has been set in motion by our modern industrial society.
—Lester R. Brown
Worldwatch Institute

Greenhouse Effect and Global Warming As increasing amounts of CFCs, carbon dioxide, methane, and other gases collect in the atmosphere, they act like the glass in a greenhouse holding heat from the sun close to the earth and preventing it from rising back into space. This **greenhouse effect** threatens to raise the average temperature of the globe by as much as 9.9 degrees Fahrenheit by the year 2040, if greenhouse gases continue to rise at the current rate (Chandler 1989). The resulting heat and drought would cause crop failures, accelerate the extinction of numerous species, and lead to the death of various plants and trees that require a narrow temperature band to survive.

The greenhouse effect would also cause the polar ice caps and other glaciers to melt, resulting in a rise in sea level. Some island countries would become uninhabitable. Low-lying deltas, such as in Egypt and Bangladesh, would be flooded, displacing millions of people. Brown (1995) warns that "rising seas in a warming world would be not only economically costly, but politically disruptive as well" (p. 415).

VOICES OF YOUTH

In March of 1995, global leaders met in Copenhagen, Denmark, at a World Summit for Social Development sponsored by the United Nations. One of the many issues they addressed was the environment. Children from around the world were invited to contribute suggestions for dealing with environmental concerns. The following are some of the more than 3,000 responses received and distributed over the Internet.

Dear World Summit Leaders:

I wish that the people would stop polluting so that we don't end up swimming in garbage. Would you want to swim in garbage?

—Martin Torrey, 8 years old,
Germany

We can take better care of the environment by passing a law to stop cutting off trees. Severe penalties should be imposed on the offender. There should be a rule to plant four trees for every one cut . . . . Our world is becoming polluted and cruel. This should be stopped. I have voiced my opinion and would be grateful if some notice is taken.

—Debanti Sengupta, 10 years old,
India

Some bad things I've observed in overcrowded cities are pollution, crime, unemployment, traffic, and noise. To fix it I suggest making the city bigger to make more space.

—Alex W., 9 years old, United States

I asked myself what we could do to help save the environment . . . stop buying wooden furniture. If people don't buy wooden furniture they would not sell it anymore.

—Pablo Gomez, 11 years old, Spain

. . . I think that economic sanctions should be taken against countries that destroy rain forests (or any type of forest) more than is absolutely required to. I think that paper could be recycled 100%, without any need for further tree-killing. Reduce, Reuse, Recycle.

—Alex Krasavin, 16 years old, Russia

We attempted to think of a sensible solution, but short of sending people to the moon, we couldn't come up with one . . . . We believe the world should put more money into solar powered vehicles and appliances.

—Tim, Richard, and Rob,
14 years old, Australia

Lack of fare [sic] use of world resources, and extreme consumption of unnecessary products are the main cause of poverty and under development.

—Alisa Varasteh, 12 years old, Iran

I don't think people should spend money on things . . . and just throw away when they are bored of using it.

—Nhu Nguyen, 10 years old,
Vietnam

Pollution is a major part of the environment. Australia is not a major polluted country like Russia. Rivers and lakes are polluted all the time by rubbish pouring into the rivers. Oil

(continued on the next page)

tipped down the sink or drain eventually flows into the rivers through to the oceans. Fish, plants and other living things are dying from this happening in our environment.

—Annabel McKay, 13 years old, Australia

Here in Denmark we got a very good water cleaning system, so we don't pollute the seas around us. But in other countries they don't have any water cleaning system, so they pollute the seas. So it doesn't matter that we don't pollute when the other countries any way pollute the seas. What could the top leaders do, from those countries that have got a water cleaning system? They could send some money, building material, and some experts that could help build some cleaning systems, in those countries that don't get one.

—Martin Hahn, Magnus Bentsen, and Peter Nielsen, 13 years old, Denmark

I wish that there was no more polluting in the world and that every body would stop treating the world as a junk yard.

—Sophia Campana, 8 years old, France

Hello, my name is Natasha. I think we can take better care of the environment by . . . not polluting the air, water, forests, and cities . . . throwing rubbish in the bin . . . not leaving food lying around . . . using spray cans that are kind to the environment . . . only taking as much as you need or can use of water, wood, power, and food. I'm going to a school dance tonight and I am looking forward to it. I hope it will not be too hard on the environment—but then again, it's only one night. Will you write back to me?

—Natasha Cook, 13 years old, New Zealand

Overall consequences of greenhouse, global warming, and depletion of ozone caused by excessive and reckless energy emissions on the earth's environment could be, in the long run, rivaled only by a devastating total war.
—Dhirendra K. Vajpeyi
University of Northern
Iowa

Air pollution is not just a problem outdoors. As this chapter's *In Focus* explains, air pollution is found indoors in our homes, schools, workplaces, and public buildings.

LAND POLLUTION

About 30 percent of the world's surface is land, which provides soil to grow the food we eat. Increasingly, humans are polluting the land with toxic and nuclear waste, solid waste, and pesticides.

Toxic and Nuclear Waste The global community generates more than a million tons of hazardous waste each day (Brown 1995). The highly publicized incident at Love Canal near Niagara Falls, New York, is an example of the problems toxic waste can create. In 1953, the Hooker Chemical Company filled in a dump site with toxic waste and subsequently gave the land to the local

Indoor Air Pollution

When we hear the phrase "air pollution," we typically think of smoke stacks and vehicle exhausts pouring gray streams of chemical matter into the air. But much air pollution is invisible to the eye and exists where we least expect it—in our homes, schools, workplaces, and public buildings. Fumes from common household, personal, and commercial products contribute to indoor pollution. For some individuals, exposure to these products can result in a variety of temporary acute symptoms such as drowsiness, disorientation, headache, dizziness, nausea, fatigue, shortness of breath, cramps, diarrhea, and irritation of the eyes, nose, throat, and lungs. Long-term exposure can affect the nervous system, reproductive system, liver, kidneys, heart, and blood. Mary Lamielle, director of the National Center for Environmental Health Strategies, suggests that "it's very possible that maybe about one-third of the population is variously sensitive to chemicals" (Edwards 1995, 16E). Some solvents found in household, commercial, and workplace products cause cancer; others birth defects (*The Delicate Balance* 1994). The following are some of the most common indoor pollutants:

1. *Carpeting.* New carpeting emits nearly one hundred different chemical gases that have caused illness in many people. The Carpet and Rug Institute has adopted a new labeling system to alert consumers of adverse health effects that may occur when carpet is installed.
2. *Mattresses.* Mattresses may emit a number of volatile organic chemicals as well as formaldehyde and aldehydes from the sizing or ticking on the box spring.
3. *Household and commercial products.* Numerous products used in public buildings, workplaces, and homes emit potentially harmful chemicals. Such products include drain cleaners, oven cleaners, spot removers, shoe polish, dry-cleaned clothes, paints, varnishes, furniture polish, potpourri, mothballs, fabric softener, and caulking compounds. Air fresheners, deodorizers, and disinfectants emit the pesticide paradichlorobenzene.
4. *Office supplies.* Potentially harmful organic solvents are present in numerous office supplies, including glue, white-out, printing ink, carbonless paper, and felt-tip markers.
5. *Perfumes and colognes.* There are about 800 fragrances on the market today. According to the National Center for Environmental Health Strategies, these products contain neurotoxic and allergenic substances that cause adverse health effects in some individuals (*The Delicate Balance* 1994). According to a survey of 750 people done for Bristol-Myers Squibb Company's Excedrin, sitting next to heavily perfumed individuals is the biggest cause of headaches for airline passengers. In 1992, a New Jersey woman died after a perfume salesperson held a perfume sample near her nose, causing a severe allergic reaction (reported in *The Delicate Balance* 1994). The Cosmetic, Toiletry and Fragrance Association denies that fragrances adversely affect public health. Nevertheless, the state of California proposed a bill to ban perfume in the workplace (Twombly 1994). More and more businesses are voluntarily limiting fragrances in the workplace or banning them altogether to accommodate employees who experience ill effects from them. After an employee and a student at the University of Minnesota's School of Social Work reported that they could not tolerate fragrances, the school instituted an informal policy banning fragrances, hand lotions, and strong deodorants (Fry 1995).

(continued on the next page)

Indoor Air Pollution *(continued)*

Nancy Johnson, an associate director at the school, commented:

At first, students and employees took the problem lightly, but when a student had an asthma-like attack and had to receive oxygen for half an hour, people realized it was serious (Sixel 1995, 4B).

6. *Chemicals in heating, ventilation, and air conditioning (HVAC) systems.* The air in public and commercial buildings often contains deodorizers, disinfectants, perfumes, and scents that are emitted through the building's HVAC system. Many people have reported illness resulting from various chemicals present in these products. In testimony before the Occupational Safety and Health Administration (OSHA), Mary Lamielle, director of the National Center for Environmental Health Strategies, proposed that the use of deodorizers, disinfectants, perfumes, and scents be discouraged or prohibited in HVAC systems in the workplace and in public buildings (Lamielle 1995).

Indoor air pollution is particularly problematic for sufferers of a controversial condition known as "multiple chemical sensitivity" (MCS). People suffering from MCS say that after one or more acute or traumatic exposures to a chemical or group of chemicals, they began to experience adverse effects from low levels of chemical exposure that do not produce symptoms in the general public. But even individuals who are not diagnosed as having MCS may experience adverse health effects from indoor air pollution. Further, Lamielle says that "If you improve the indoor air then everyone benefits whether or not they have chemical sensitivities" (Melson 1994, 2).

SOURCES: John G. Edwards. 1995 (March 19). Chemical Illnesses Growing." *Las Vegas Review Journal*, pp. 14E, 16E; Jason Fry. 1995. "School's Fragrance Ban Raises Volume of Disagreement over Multiple Chemical Sensitivity." *Indoor Air Review* 4(12): 3, 23; Mary Lamielle. 1995 (January 9). "Testimony of Mary Lamielle, President, National Center for Environmental Health Strategies: OSHA Indoor Air Quality Proposed Rule 29 CFR Parts 1910, 1915, 1926, and 1928." National Center for Environmental Health Strategies, 1100 Rural Avenue, Voorhees, NJ 08043; Gail Melson. 1994. "Multiple Chemical Sensitivities: See You in Court?" *INvironment* (The Newsletter of Building Management and Indoor Air Quality) 4(1): 2–10; L. M. Sixel. 1995 (February 20). "Businesses Try to Limit Fragrances." *Houston Chronicle*, 1B, 4B; *The Delicate Balance*. 1994. National Center for Environmental Health Strategies. Vol. 5, Nos . 3–4. 1100 Rural Avenue, Voorhees, NJ 08043. Renee Twombly. 1994. "MCS: A Sensitive Issue." *Environmental Health Perspectives* 102(9): 746–50.

school district. Homes were also built in the area, and by the 1970s toxic waste was seeping into basements. Residents complained of high rates of miscarriages, cancer, and chromosomal abnormalities (Shribman 1990). Some moved away, others stayed. The area has allegedly been cleaned up, and homes are being sold there once again (see Chapter 4).

In 1992, 1,700 plaintiffs from Southbend, Texas, were awarded $207 million in damages related to toxic waste. The plaintiffs lived in a suburb of Houston, Texas, where two waste disposal plants released chemicals responsible for birth defects and heart and organ problems (Voorst 1993b). Figure 15.2 shows the location of hazardous waste sites in the United States. Victims of environmental poisoning experience not only adverse physical health effects, but also social and psychological stresses, including the feeling of loss of control over the environment (Picou and Rosebrook 1993; Dyer 1993).

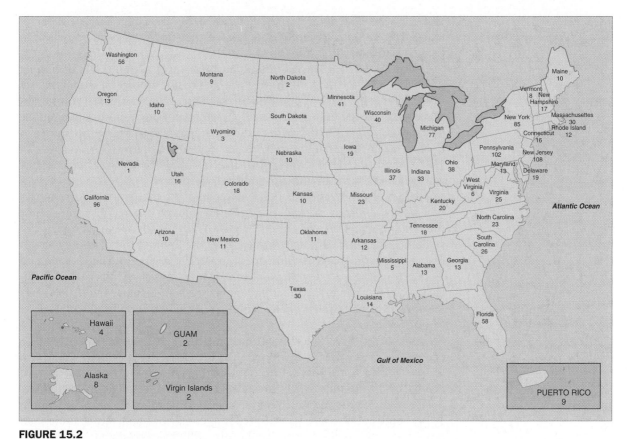

FIGURE 15.2
HAZARDOUS WASTE SITES BY STATE, 1994
SOURCE: *Statistical Abstract of the United States: 1995*, 115th ed. U.S. Bureau of the Census (Washington, D.C.: U.S. Government Printing Office), Table 382.

The disposal of nuclear waste, which comes from the manufacture of nuclear weapons and radioactive by-products from nuclear power plants, is particularly problematic. The U.S. Nuclear Regulatory Commission licenses nuclear reactors for forty years. When nuclear reactors reach the end of their forty-year licenses, the radioactive waste must be stored somewhere. For economic reasons, many nuclear plants close down before their licenses have expired. As reactors age and deteriorate, repairing and maintaining them is so expensive that fixing them often is not worthwhile. But closing a nuclear power plant is also costly. Of the 109 nuclear power plants in the United States, 32 have waste storage facilities that will exceed their capacity before 1998 (Stover 1995). About 28,000 metric tons of nuclear waste are already stored around the United States. This figure is expected to grow to 48,000 metric tons by 2003 and 87,000 metric tons by 2030 (not including waste from military nuclear operations) (Stover 1995). The United States has also promised to accept nuclear waste from about forty nations with nuclear research reactors.

The cost of storing nuclear waste and cleaning other hazardous waste sites is immense. Cleaning up hazardous waste sites in the United States would require an estimated $750 billion, roughly three-fourths of the U.S. federal budget in

National Data: In 1994, 1,283 U.S. hazardous waste sites were on the national priority list.

SOURCE: *Statistical Abstract of the United States: 1995*, Table 382.

In the United States, 41 million people live within a four-mile radius of a hazardous waste site, and about 3,325 people live within a one-mile radius of a hazardous waste site.

SOURCE: Reported in *The Delicate Balance* 1994, 20.

1990 (Brown 1995). But not cleaning these sites is also costly. Brown (1995) remarks that "one way or another, society will pay—either in clean up bills or in rising health care costs" (p. 416).

Under the Nuclear Waste Policy Act, which was passed in 1982, beginning in 1998, the Department of Energy will handle the storage of nuclear waste from commercial nuclear power plants. Scientists have proposed several options for disposing of nuclear waste, including burying it in rock formations deep below the earth's surface or under Antarctic ice, injecting it into the ocean floor, or hurling it into outer space. Each of these options is risky and costly. In 1987, Congress decided to investigate the feasibility of building a nuclear storage facility at Yucca Mountain in southern Nevada.

The act also provides for utility companies to charge their customers a penny for every kilowatt-hour generated by nuclear power. This money, now more than $10 billion, goes into a Nuclear Waste Fund to be used for the development of a nuclear waste disposal site. The Department of Energy has already spent more than $6 billion from the Nuclear Waste Fund and is spending about $1 million a day to assess if Yucca Mountain is a safe place to store nuclear waste—waste that will remain dangerously radioactive for 10,000 years (Stover 1995). Assessment of Yucca Mountain could take a decade or more.

Solid Waste In 1960, each U.S. citizen generated 2.7 pounds of garbage on average every day. By 1993, this figure had increased to 4.4 pounds (*Statistical Abstract of the United States: 1995,* Table 380). In the United States, we discard nearly 160 million tons of solid waste each year, enough to bury 2,700 football fields in a layer ten stories high (National Solid Wastes Management Association 1991). Some of this waste is converted into energy by incinerators; more than half is taken to landfills. The availability of landfill space is limited, however. For example, Seattle has a landfill capacity sufficient for only 100 years (Voorst 1993a). Some states have passed laws that limit the amount of solid waste that can be disposed of; instead, they require that bottles and cans be returned for a deposit or that lawn clippings be used in a community composting program.

Pesticides The Northwest Coalition for Alternatives to Pesticides (1993) reports that U.S. agriculture uses more than 800 million pounds of pesticides every year. In 1992, the U.S. Food and Drug Administration analyzed a dozen commonly eaten foods, including flour, apples, oranges, and strawberries, and found pesticides in over half the samples. The Environmental Protection Agency (EPA) estimates that 40 percent of lawns in the United States are treated with pesticides, which amounts to 70 million pounds of pesticides used annually (*The Delicate Balance* 1994). Many of the chemicals used on crops are hazardous not only to pests but to humans who consume them through contaminated food and water and to those who work in the fields. Pesticides contaminate food, water, and air and can be absorbed through the skin, swallowed, or inhaled. Many common pesticides are considered potential carcinogens and neurotoxins.

Furthermore, pesticides that are used routinely have not been adequately tested. Only about 20 percent of the nearly 750 active pesticide ingredients have been tested for chronic health effects (Weiss 1991). Even when a pesticide is found to be hazardous and is banned in the United States, other countries may continue to use it. Although DDT is banned in the United States, the pesticide is used in many other countries from which we import food.

> **Consideration** *A 1990 EPA study found that minority communities have a higher than average exposure to environmental contaminants such as air and water pollution (Weisskopf 1993). EPA officials argued that the overexposure was a result of housing and employment patterns, not environmental racism. In response, Benjamin Chavis, director of the National Association for the Advancement of Colored People (NAACP), said that "the disproportionate exposure to minorities has been the result of systematic policymaking, not a function of historical coincidence" (p. 130). A study of toxic waste site locations in five cities conducted by sociologist Robert Bullard supports an institutional discrimination position. Bullard concluded that "race was a big factor in determining where these facilities go" (quoted in Weisskopf 1993, p. 131).*

WATER POLLUTION

Our water is being polluted by a number of harmful substances, including pesticides, industrial waste, acid rain, and oil spills. The *Exxon Valdez* oil spill in Alaska is one of the more memorable accidents, yet many more incidents have occurred. Although 80 percent of the spills are attributed to "human error," doubling the amount of steel in the hulls of tankers would keep oil from spilling in 27 out of 30 cases (Begley 1994). Conflict theorists argue that owners' resistance to reinforcing tanker hulls is based on cost considerations.

Acid Rain Air pollutants, such as sulfur and nitrous oxide, mix with precipitation to form acid rain. Polluted rain, snow, and fog contaminate crops, lakes, and rivers.

> **Consideration** *Environmental problems often lead to conflict between nations. International relations between the United States and Canada are strained because the sulfur dioxide from U.S. industries continues to kill marine life in the lakes and streams around the Adirondack Mountains, as well as in other parts of the Northeast and Canada.*

Industrial and Human Waste About half of all the drinking water in the United States comes from wells, which tap water trapped underground. In many areas, however, toxic industrial waste and human waste have seeped into groundwater and have poisoned lakes, rivers, and oceans. Since 1986, 10 million tons of waste from sewage plants have been dumped in the ocean just beyond the continental shelf off the northeast coast (Toufexis 1993).

One of the most dangerous contaminants is the chemical PCB, used in manufacturing everything from baby bottles to pesticides. When ingested, PCB affects the reproductive system of both men and women, which may explain why men's sperm counts have dropped by 50 percent since 1938 and testicular cancer has tripled. PCB may also be related to breast cancer and endometriosis, a condition suffered by only 21 women in the world seventy years ago and, today, by 5 million women in the United States alone (Begley and Glick 1994).

The very survival of the human species depends upon the maintenance of an ocean clean and alive, spreading all around the world. The ocean is our planet's life belt.
—Jacques Cousteau
Oceanographer

National Data: 1993, 9,672 oil-polluting incidents in and around U.S. waters were reported. A total of 1,543,578 gallons of oil were spilled in these incidents.

SOURCE: *Statistical Abstract of the United States: 1995,* Table 372.

DEPLETION OF NATURAL RESOURCES

Overpopulation contributes to the depletion of natural resources, such as coal, oil, and forests. The demand for new land, fuel, and raw materials has resulted in **deforestation**—the destruction of the earth's rain forests. In Africa, Southeast Asia, and Central and South America, an area of tropical rain forest the size of Ireland vanishes every year. The World Bank estimates that the earth's rain forests will disappear within the next sixty years (Vajpeyi 1995). The major cause of deforestation is commercial logging.

Deforestation represents a serious threat to global ecological well-being because forests absorb carbon dioxide from the air and thus regulate the supply of fresh air. Deforestation also displaces native peoples from their lands.

A related concern is **desertification,** which occurs when semiarid land on the margins of deserts is overused. Overgrazing by cattle and other herd animals and the cutting of brush and trees for firewood leave the land denuded of vegetation and allow the desert to expand. By the year 2000 the world will have lost 25 million acres of cultivated land. An estimated 35 percent of the earth's land surface is now at some stage of desertification (Jacobson 1990). Once the process of desertification has begun, it is very difficult to reverse.

> ***Consideration*** *Air, water, and land pollution as well as deforestation threaten biodiversity and the delicate balance of nature. **Biodiversity** refers to the great variety of plant and animal species that are dependent on each other for survival. But due most to pollution and deforestation, over 27,000 species a year become extinct. Biologist E. O. Wilson estimates that deforestation leads to the extinction of at least 50,000 invertebrate species every year—about 140 every day (Vajpeyi 1995). According to the World Watch Institute (1988), if plant and animal extinctions continue at their present rate, one-fifth of all species will disappear by the year 2000. Reduced biodiversity threatens the ecological balance by affecting the food chain (Wilson 1992).*

Social Causes of Environmental Problems

In addition to population growth, various other structural and cultural factors have also played a role in environmental problems.

INDUSTRIALIZATION AND ECONOMIC DEVELOPMENT

Many of the environmental problems confronting the world have been caused by industrialization and economic development. Industrialized countries, for example, consume more energy and natural resources than developing countries.

Environmental problems of developed countries are due to industrialization, overconsumption of natural resources, and the demand for increasing quantities of goods and services. Industrialization and economic development have been the primary cause of global environmental problems such as the ozone hole and global warming (Koenig 1995). Conflict theorists argue that governments pursue economic development and industrialization at the expense of environmental conditions.

In less developed countries, environmental problems are largely due to poverty and the priority of economic survival over environmental concerns. Vajpeyi (1995) explains:

> Policymakers in the Third World are often in conflict with the ever-increasing demands to satisfy basic human needs—clean air, water, adequate food, shelter, education—and to safeguard the environmental quality. Given the scarce economic and technical resources at their disposal, most of these policymakers have ignored long-range environmental concerns and opted for short-range economic and political gains. (p. 24)

CULTURAL VALUES AND ATTITUDES

Cultural values and attitudes that contribute to environmental problems include individualism, capitalism, and materialism. Individualism, which is a characteristic of American culture, puts individual interests over collective welfare. Even though recycling is good for our collective environment, many individuals do not recycle because of the personal inconvenience involved in washing and sorting recyclable items. Similarly, individuals often indulge in countless behaviors that provide enjoyment and convenience at the expense of the environment: long showers, use of dishwashing machines, recreational boating, meat eating, and use of air conditioning, to name just a few.

Capitalistic values also contribute to environmental degradation. While the environmentalist makes preservation of the environment the first priority, the capitalist emphasizes making profits from industry regardless of the damage done to the environment. Further, to maximize sales, manufacturers design products intended to become obsolete. As a result of this **planned obsolescence** (Turner 1977), consumers continually throw away used products and purchase replacements. Industry profits at the expense of the environment, which must sustain the constant production and absorb ever-increasing amounts of waste.

Finally, the influence of materialism, or the emphasis on worldly possessions, also encourages individuals to continually purchase new items and throw away old ones. The media bombard us daily with advertisements that tell us life will be better if we purchase a particular product. Materialism contributes to pollution and environmental degradation by supporting industry and contributing to garbage and waste. The cultural value of militarism also contributes to environmental degradation. This issue is discussed in detail in Chapter 16.

Limited Solutions and Limited Gains

Solving environmental problems is difficult and costly. Lowering fertility, as discussed earlier, helps reduce population pressure on the environment. Environmentalist groups, government regulations, recycling programs, and the use of alternative sources of energy can also contribute to solutions.

Modern industrial civilization, as presently organized, is colliding violently with our planet's ecological system . . . . We must make the rescue of the environment the central organizing principle for civilization.
—Al Gore
U.S. Vice President

The earth has enough for everyone's need but not enough for everyone's greed.
—Mahatma Gandhi
Peace activist

Trash-Reducing Activities

Every year, Americans generate millions of tons of trash. In less than thirty years, the amount of durable goods (appliances, furniture) and nondurable goods (paper, clothing, disposable products) in the solid waste stream has nearly tripled (Environmental Protection Agency 1992). Individuals can reduce the amount of trash produced by engaging in a variety of practices and behaviors. The following questionnaire will help you assess the degree to which you minimize solid waste production. For each of the following items, indicate whether you engage in the behavior described on a scale of one to four. Also, consider the social values (e.g., consumerism, materialism, comfort and ease, individualism, and the like) underlying your behavior.

Item	1 (Never)	2 (Sometimes)	3 (Often)	4 (Always)
1. At the grocery store, do you purchase items in bulk rather than in prepackaged containers whenever possible (e.g., tomatoes, garlic, mushrooms)?	____	____	____	____
2. Whenever possible, do you buy large or economy-size items for household products that are used frequently (e.g., laundry soap, shampoo)?	____	____	____	____
3. Do you use cloth napkins, sponges, and dishcloths around the house rather than paper napkins and paper towels?	____	____	____	____
4. When possible, do you use rechargeable batteries instead of disposable batteries?	____	____	____	____
5. Do you buy second-hand clothing?	____	____	____	____
6. Do you mend or repair clothes, shoes, boots, handbags, and briefcases instead of throwing them away?	____	____	____	____
7. Do you resell or give away unwanted furniture and appliances rather than throwing them away?	____	____	____	____

ENVIRONMENTALIST GROUPS

Environmentalist groups exert pressure on the government to initiate or intensify actions related to environmental protection. Environmentalist groups also design and implement their own projects, and disseminate information to the public about environmental issues. In the United States, environmentalist groups date back to 1892 with the establishment of the Sierra Club followed by the Audubon Society in 1905. More recent groups include Greenpeace and Friends of the Earth.

Environmentalist groups also attempt to educate the public about environmental issues and promote attitudes and behaviors that protect and restore the environment. Such behaviors include using car pools or public transportation, recycling, building energy-efficient homes, and minimizing use of electric lights, home heat, and air conditioning. This chapter's *Self and Society* allows you to assess the degree to which you participate in reducing solid waste in our society.

Item	1 (Never)	2 (Sometimes)	3 (Often)	4 (Always)
8. Do you resell or give away unwanted clothes rather than throwing them away?	___	___	___	___
9. Do you use low-energy fluorescent lightbulbs rather than incandescent ones?	___	___	___	___
10. Do you reuse plastic bags and containers?	___	___	___	___
11. Do you reuse scrap paper and use both sides of paper for writing notes?	___	___	___	___
12. Do you save and reuse gift boxes, ribbons, and larger pieces of wrapping and tissue paper?	___	___	___	___
13. Do you save and reuse packaging "peanuts" and "bubble wrap"?	___	___	___	___
14. Do you take plastic grocery bags back to the grocery store for recycling?	___	___	___	___
15. Do you share newspapers and magazines with others to reduce the generation of waste paper?	___	___	___	___
16. Do you choose recyclable products and containers and recycle them?	___	___	___	___
17. Do you select products made from recycled materials?	___	___	___	___

Total score ___

Scoring Add your responses to compute your total score. The higher the score, the more you are helping to minimize solid waste.

SOURCE: Adapted from the Environmental Protection Agency. 1992. *Consumer's Handbook for Reducing Solid Waste*. Washington, D.C.: U.S. Government Printing Office (Document EPA/530-K-92-003).

Despite the efforts of environmental groups, public concern about environmental issues has declined in recent years. In 1995, a Gallup poll revealed that about a third (35 percent) of Americans agreed that life on earth would be able to continue without major environmental disruptions only if "immediate and drastic actions" were taken to preserve the environment (Moore 1995, 17). Four years earlier, over half (57 percent) of Americans agreed with that view. Further, 63 percent of Americans in 1995 said they consider themselves environmentalists compared to 78 percent in 1991 (Moore 1995). According to Stisser (1994), less than 15 percent of the U.S. population are "true blue greens" who are committed to environmental issues and work to bring about positive change.

National Data: A quarter of university/college first-year students in the United States report that "helping to clean up the environment" is an important life goal.

SOURCE: American Council on Education and University of California 1994.

RECYCLING

Recycling, or reusing useful materials found in waste, has become more common in recent years. More than forty states have comprehensive recycling programs.

In recent years, recycling has become more common in public places as well as in households.

· ·

In their gas-guzzling lives full of electric gadgetry and plastic and chemical waste dumping, [many citizens] can't imagine that the freedom of all to breathe air everywhere is threatened by their pollutants. . . . Can they come to realize that so-called primitive tribal ways are more intelligently in tune with Earth, in terms of saving Earth's resources, than those of obscenely exploitative nation-states which call themselves 'civilized'?
—Daniela Gioseffi
Poet, novelist, editor, journalist, performer, and activist

· ·
· ·

International Data:
Worldwide, thirty-three countries produce some of their electricity from nuclear power plants.
SOURCE: Stover 1995.

· ·

At the local level, recycling programs grew from 50 to 4,000 communities between 1990 and 1993 (Voorst 1993a). The National Recycling Coalition has persuaded twenty-five large U.S. companies, including Walmart, Coca-Cola, and Johnson and Johnson, to participate in buying recycled products. McDonald's is also known for using recycled materials in its packaging.

ALTERNATIVE SOURCES OF ENERGY

Generating energy from coal and oil contributes to the world's growing level of pollution. In addition, our supplies of coal and oil are finite and are being depleted. One solution to the problems associated with the use of coal and oil for energy is to use alternative sources of energy, such as solar power, geothermal power, wind power, ocean thermal power, nuclear power, tidal power, and power from converting corn, wood, or garbage. Even though solar-powered home heating is costly to install, over 100,000 homes in the United States have solar power (Greenwald 1993). More efficient and less expensive solar panels are being developed and "the forecast for the industry in the 21st century is bright and sunny" (p. 85).

Nuclear power is controversial due to the potential dangers it presents. The explosion at the Chernobyl nuclear reactor in the Soviet Ukraine in 1986 resulted in environmental disaster and the evacuation of 100,000 people from their homes (Brown, Flavin, and Postel 1990). As discussed earlier, disposal of radioactive waste from nuclear plants is also costly and problematic. Nevertheless, about 21 percent of the electricity used in the United States comes from nuclear power plants (Stover 1995).

GOVERNMENT REGULATIONS AND FUNDING

Through regulations and the provision of funds, governments play a vital role in protecting and restoring the environment. Governments have responded to concerns related to air and water pollution, ozone depletion, and global warming by imposing regulations affecting the production of pollutants. Governments have also been involved in the preservation of deserts, forests, reefs, wetlands, and endangered plant and animal species.

For example, to reduce air pollution caused by automobiles, the U.S. government requires cars to have catalytic converters. In 1990, Congress amended the Clean Air Act to provide marketable pollution rights for sulfur dioxide emissions by electric companies. The Environmental Protection Agency issued more than 5 million marketable permits, each allowing the emission of one ton of sulfur dioxide annually, to 110 companies, which must have permits for all of their sulfur dioxide emissions or face large fines. Companies that want to emit more sulfur dioxide can buy permits from other companies, while those that reduce their own pollution can profit from selling their permits (Holcombe 1995).

Government regulations are only effective if they are enforced. However,

. . . largely because of political pressure from industry, the EPA has been slow to implement and enforce congressionally required regulations, allowing massive pollution to continue. Polluting industries have poured millions of dollars into congressional campaigns and lobbying efforts to

help assure that congressional action to halt pollution was minimal. (Feagin and Feagin 1994, 385)

Conflict theorists emphasize that the competing interests of capitalists and environmentalists collide in Congress as politicians weigh their political futures against the fate of the environment. Punishing industries in violation of environmental regulations would mean risking large campaign contributions and, potentially, one's job.

INTERNATIONAL COOPERATION

No single government working alone can restore and protect the environment. International cooperation among governments is vital. The 1972 Stockholm Conference on the Human Environment, the United Nations Environment Program (UNEP) since the 1970s, and the 1983 World Commission on Environment and Development represent efforts to address environmental concerns at the international level. More recently, the 1992 Earth Summit in Rio de Janeiro—a twelve-day event—brought together heads of states, delegates from more than 170 nations, nongovernmental organizations, representatives of indigenous people, and the media to discuss an international agenda for both economic development and the environment. Maurice Strong (1991) suggested that "no conference has ever faced the need to make such an important range of decisions . . . that will virtually determine the face of the earth" (pp. v–vi). International cooperative efforts have resulted in, for example, the Global Environmental Facility (GEF), located at the World Bank in Washington, and the United Nations' International Environmental Technology Center in Osaska and Shiga, Japan. The United Nations Development Program supports countries in environmental management. The 1992 Earth Summit in Rio resulted in the Rio Declaration—"a nonbinding statement of broad principles to guide environmental policy, vaguely committing its signatories not to damage the environment of other nations by activities within their borders and to acknowledge environmental protection as an integral part of development" (Koenig 1995, 15).

Because industrialized countries have more economic and technological resources, they bear primary responsibility for leading the nations of the world toward environmental cooperation. Jan (1995) emphasizes the importance of international environmental cooperation and the role of developed countries in this endeavor:

Advanced countries must be willing to sacrifice their own economic well-being to help improve the environment of the poor, developing countries. Failing to do this will lead to irreparable damage to our global environment. Environmental protection is no longer the affair of any one country. It has become an urgent global issue. Environmental pollution recognizes no national boundaries. No country, especially a poor country, can solve this problem alone. (pp. 82–83)

An example of international cooperation on environmental issues is the effort to curb the production of chlorofluorocarbons (CFCs), which contribute to ozone depletion and global warming. So far 70 nations—accounting for more than 90 percent of global CFC production and consumption—have signed an agreement to pursue alternatives to CFCs. The largest consumers of

. . . as long as 70 million Americans live in communities where the air is dangerous to breath; as long as half our rivers, our lakes and our streams are too polluted for fishing and swimming; as long as people in our poorest communities face terrible hazards from lead paint to toxic waste dumps . . . our journey is far from finished.
—Bill Clinton
U.S. President

Protection of the environment is a goal that virtually everyone believes is worthwhile and would enhance the quality of life. The disagreement comes in deciding how to implement policies to achieve the goal.
—Randall G. Holcombe
Florida State University

CFCs have established a fund to help developing countries acquire alternatives to CFCs (Koenig 1995).

SUSTAINABLE ECONOMIC DEVELOPMENT: AN INTERNATIONAL AGENDA

Achieving global cooperation on environmental issues is difficult, in part, because developed countries (primarily in the northern hemisphere) have different economic agendas from developing countries (primarily in the southern hemisphere). The northern agenda emphasizes preserving wealth, affluent lifestyles, and the welfare state while the southern agenda focuses on overcoming mass poverty and achieving a higher quality of life (Koenig 1995). Southern countries are concerned that northern industrialized countries—having already achieved economic wealth—will impose international environmental policies that restrict the economic growth of developing countries just as they are beginning to industrialize. Global strategies to preserve the environment must address both wasteful lifestyles in some nations and the need to overcome overpopulation and widespread poverty in others.

The authors of *Beyond the Limits* suggest that rather than strive toward economic growth, nations should strive toward development, defined as "expanding or realizing potentialities and bringing to a fuller, better state" (Meadows, Meadows, and Randers 1992, xix). Development involves more than economic growth, it involves sustainability. The World Commission on Environment and Development (1987) defines **sustainable development** as "development that meets the needs of the present without compromising the ability of future generations to meet their own needs" (p. 43). Achieving sustainable development has become a primary goal of governments throughout the world.

UNDERSTANDING
POPULATION AND THE ENVIRONMENT

Because population increases exponentially, the size of the world's population has grown and will continue to grow at a staggering rate. Given research that indicates the problems associated with population growth—deteriorating socioeconomic conditions, depletion of natural resources, and urban crowding—most governments recognize the value of controlling population size. Efforts to control population must go beyond providing safe, effective, and affordable methods of birth control. Slowing population growth necessitates interventions that change the cultural and structural bases for high fertility rates. These interventions include increasing economic development and improving the status of women, which includes raising their levels of education, their economic position, and their (and their children's) health (Pritchett 1994).

Rapid and dramatic population growth has contributed to environmental problems because the greater numbers of people make increased demands on natural resources and generate excessive levels of pollutants. Environmental problems are due not only to large populations, but also to the ways in which these populations live and work. As conflict theorists argue, individuals, private enterprises, and governments have tended to choose economic and political interests over environmental concerns.

Many Americans believe in a "technological fix" for the environment—that science and technology will solve environmental problems. Paradoxically, the same environmental problems that have been caused by technological progress may be solved by technological innovations designed to clean up pollution and preserve natural resources. Koenig (1995) points out, however, that while technological innovation is important in resolving environmental concerns, "it is not sufficient in providing adequate responses to deep-rooted social causes of the environmental catastrophe" (p. 9). Addressing the values that guide choices, the economic contexts in which the choices are made, and the governmental policies that encourage various choices is critical to resolving environmental and population problems.

Global cooperation is also vital to resolving environmental concerns, but is difficult to achieve because rich and poor countries have different economic development agendas: developing poor countries struggle to survive and provide for the basic needs of its citizens; developed wealthy countries struggle to maintain their wealth and relatively high standard of living. Can both agendas be achieved without further pollution and destruction of the environment? Is sustainable economic development an attainable goal? The answer must be yes.

Man is here for only a limited time, and he borrows the natural resources of water, land and air from his children who carry on his cultural heritage to the end of time. . . . One must hand over the stewardship of his natural resources to the future generations in the same condition, if not as close to the one that existed when his generation was entrusted to be the caretaker.
—Delano Saluskin
Yakima Indian Nation

CRITICAL THINKING

1. What macro and micro policies would you recommend in socializing a new generation to engage in reasonable consumption behavior that is respectful of the environment?
2. Discuss how a country can become more industrialized and reduce its population and consumption of resources at the same time.
3. Do you think governments should regulate reproductive behavior in order to control population growth? If so, how?

KEY TERMS

demography

human ecology

doubling time

Malthusian theory

demographic transition theory

greenhouse effect

deforestation

biodiversity

desertification

planned obsolescence

sustainable development

REFERENCES

Agbese, Pita Ogaba. 1995. "Nigeria's Environment: Crises, Consequences, and Responses." *Environmental Policies in the Third World: A Comparative Analysis*, ed. O. P. Dwivedi and Dhirendra K. Vajpeyi, pp. 125–44. Westport, Conn.: Greenwood Press.

Ahlburg, Dennis A. 1993. "The Census Bureau's New Projections of the US Population." *Population and Development Review* 19: 159–74.

American Council on Education and University of California. 1994. *The American Freshman: National Norms for Fall, 1994.* Los Angeles: Higher Education Research Institute.

Associated Press. 1993. "Water Becoming Scarce Worldwide, Group Says." *Cleveland Plain Dealer,* November 8, C6.

Begley, Sharon. 1994. "Oil and Water Don't Mix." *Newsweek,* March 28, 54.

Begley, Sharon, and Daniel Glick. 1994. "The Estrogen Complex." *Newsweek,* March 21, 76–77.

Birth Control a Luxury in Much of the World. 1991 (July 1). *Asheville* [North Carolina] *Citizen-Times,* 4B.

Bok, Sissela. 1994. "Population and Ethics: Expanding the Moral Space." In *Population Policies Reconsidered: Health, Empowerment, and Rights,* ed. Gita Sen, Adrienne Germain, and Lincoln C. Chen, pp. 15–26. Boston: Harvard School of Public Health.

Boland, Reed, Sudhakar Rao, and George Zeidenstein. 1994. "Honoring Human Rights in Population Policies: From Declaration to Action." In *Population Policies Reconsidered: Health, Empowerment, and Rights,* ed. by Gita Sen, Adrienne Germain, and Lincoln C. Chen, pp. 89–105. Boston: Harvard School of Public Health.

Brown, Lester R. 1995. "The State of the World's Natural Environment." In *Seeing Ourselves: Classic, Contemporary, and Cross-Cultural Readings in Sociology,* 3d ed., ed. John J. Macionis and Nijole V. Benokraitis, pp. 411–16. Englewood Cliffs, N.J.: Prentice-Hall.

Brown, Lester R., Christopher Flavin, and Sandra Postel. 1990. "A World at Risk." In *Social Problems Today,* ed. James M. Henslin, pp. 348–57. Englewood Cliffs, N.J.: Prentice-Hall.

Brown, Lester, and Edward Wolf. 1986. "Assessing Ecological Decline." In *State of The World, 1986: A Worldwatch Institute Report on Progress toward a Sustainable Society,* ed. Lester Brown et al. New York: W. W. Norton.

Chandler, William. 1989. "Development and Global Environmental Change." *Cooperation for International Development: The United States and the Third World in the 1990s,* ed. Robert J. Berg and David F. Gordon, p. 51. Boulder, Colo.: Lynne Reinner.

Deardoff, Kevin E. and Patricia Montgomery. 1995. "National Population Trends" in *Population Profile of the United States: 1995.* U.S. Census Bureau. http://www.census.gov.

Dwivedi, O. P., and Renu Khator. 1995. "India's Environmental Policy, Programs, and Politics." In *Environmental Policies in the Third World: A Comparative Analysis,* ed. O. P. Dwivedi and Dhirendra K. Vajpeyi, pp. 47–69. Westport, Conn.: Greenwood Press.

Dyer, Christopher. 1993. "Tradition Loss as Secondary Disaster: Long-Term Cultural Impacts of the Exxon Valdez Oil Spill." *Sociological Spectrum* 13: 65–88.

Dyson, Tim. 1994. "Population Growth and Food Production: Recent Global and Regional Trends." *Population and Development Review* 20: 397–411.

Feagin, Joe R., and Clairece Booher Feagin. 1994. *Social Problems,* 4th ed. Englewood Cliffs, N.J.: Prentice-Hall.

Gibbs, Nancy R. 1994. "Dire Straits." *Time,* August 29, 27–32.

Gioseffi, Daniela. 1993. "Introduction." In *On Prejudice: A Global Perspective,* ed. Daniela Gioseffi, pp. xi–1. New York: Anchor Books, Doubleday.

Greenhalgh, Susan, Zhu Chujuzhu, and Li Nan. 1994. "Restraining Population Growth in Three Chinese Villages, 1988–93." *Population and Development Review* 20: 365–95.

Greenwald, John. 1993. "Here Comes the Sun." *Time,* October 18, 84–85.

Hawkins, Kirstan, and Bayeligne Meshesha. 1994. "Reaching Young People: Ingredients of Effective Programs." In *Population Policies Reconsidered: Health, Empowerment, and Rights,* ed. Gita Sen, Adrienne Germain, and Lincoln C. Chen, pp. 211–22. Boston: Harvard School of Public Health.

Holcombe, Randall G. 1995. *Public Policy and the Quality of Life: Market Incentives versus Government Planning.* Westport, Conn.: Greenwood Press.

Jacobson, Jodi L. 1990. "Environmental Refugees: Nature's Warning System." *Populi* 16(1): 29–32.

Jan, George P. 1995. "Environmental Protection in China." *Environmental Policies in the Third World: A Comparative Analysis,* ed. O. P. Dwivedi and Dhirendra K. Vajpeyi, pp. 71–84. Westport, Conn.: Greenwood Press.

Koenig, Dieter. 1995. "Sustainable Development: Linking Global Environmental Change to Technology Cooperation." *Environmental Policies in the Third World: A Comparative Analysis,* ed. O. P. Dwivedi and Dhirendra K. Vajpeyi, pp. 1–21. Westport, Conn.: Greenwood Press.

Linden, Eugene. 1994a. "Population: The Awkward Truth." *Time,* June 20, 74.

_____ .1994b. "Showdown in Cairo." *Time,* September 5, 52–53.

Mahmud, Simeen, and Anne M. Johnston. 1994. "Women's Status, Empowerment, and Reproductive Outcomes." In *Population Policies Reconsidered: Health, Empowerment, and Rights,* ed. Gita Sen, Adrienne Germain, and Lincoln C. Chen, pp. 151–60. Boston: Harvard School of Public Health.

McFalls, Joseph A., Jr. 1991. "Population: A Lively Introduction." *Population Bulletin* 46 (October).

McIntosh, C. Alison and Finkle, Jason L. 1995. "The Cairo Conference on Population and Development: A New Paradigm?" *Population and Development Review* 21: 223–60.

McNamara, Robert S. 1992. "The Population Explosion." *The Futurist* 26 (November/December): 9–13.

Meadows, Donella H., Dennis L. Meadows, and Jorgen Randers. 1992. *Beyond the Limits.* Post Mills, Vt.: Chelsea Green.

Moore, David W. 1995. "Public Sense of Urgency about Environment Wanes." *The Gallup Poll Monthly* (April): 17–20.

National Center for Health Statistics. 1994. Annual Summary of Births, Marriages, Divorces, and Deaths: United States, 1993. Monthly Vital Statistics Report, Vol. 42 No. 13. Hyattsville, Md.: Public Health Service, 1994.

National Solid Wastes Management Association. 1991. "New Landfills Can Solve the Garbage Crisis." In *The Environmental Crisis,* ed. David L. Bender and Bruno Leone, pp. 122–27. San Diego, Calif.: Greenhaven Press.

Northwest Coalition for Alternatives to Pesticides. 1993. "Healthy Food and Health Farms." Northwest Coalition for Alternatives to Pesticides. P.O. Box 1393, Eugene OR 97440.

Perdue, William, ed. 1993. *Systemic Crisis.* Forth Worth, Tex.: Harcourt, Brace Jovanovich.

Picou, Steven J., and Donald D. Rosebrook. 1993. "Technological Accident, Community Class-Action Litigation, and Scientific Damage Assessment: A Case Study of Court Ordered Research." *Sociological Spectrum* 13: 117–38.

"Population Growth Threatens Natural Resources Renewal." 1992. *Public Health Reports* 107 (September/October): 608.

Pritchett, L. H. 1994. "Desired Fertility and the Impact of Population Policies." *Population and Development Review* 20: 1–55.

Schultz, Paul T. 1993. *Sources of Fertility Decline in Modern Economic Growth: Is Aggregate Evidence on the Demographic Transition Credible?* Working Paper Series, Institute for Policy Reform, No. 58.

Shribman, David. 1990. "Love Canal 10 Years Later." In *Social Problems Today,* ed. James Henslin, pp. 343–45. Englewood Cliffs, N.J.: Prentice-Hall.

Statistical Abstract of the United States: 1992, 112th ed. U.S. Bureau of the Census. Washington, D.C.: U.S. Government Printing Office.

Statistical Abstract of the United States: 1995, 115th ed. U.S. Bureau of the Census. Washington, D.C.: U.S. Government Printing Office.

Stisser, Peter. 1994. "A Deeper Shade of Green." *American Demographics* (March).

Stover, Dawn. 1995 (August). "The Nuclear Legacy." *Popular Science,* 52–83.

Strong, Maurice. 1991. "Introduction." In *Beyond Interdependence,* ed. Jim MacNeil, Pieter Winsemius, and Taizo Yakushiji. New York: Oxford University Press.

Tannahill, R. 1982. *Sex in History.* New York: Stein & Day.

The Delicate Balance. 1994. The National Center for Environmental Health Strategies, Vol. 5 Nos. 3–4. 1100 Rural Avenue, Voorhees, NJ 08043.

Toufexis, Anastasia. 1993. "The Dirty Seas." In *Readings in Social Problems,* ed. William Feigelman, pp. 360–66. Fort Worth: Holt, Rinehart & Winston.

Turner, Jonathan H. 1977. *Social Problems in America.* New York: Harper & Row.

United Nations. 1992. *Long Range World Population Projections: Two Centuries of Population Growth, 1950–2150,* p. 24. Sales No. E.92. 13 2. New York.

United Nations Population Fund. 1991. *Population Policies and Programmes: Lessons Learned from Two Decades of Experience.* New York: New York University Press.

Urzua, R. 1992. (January). "The Demographic Dimension." *UNESCO Courier,* 14.

Vajpeyi, Dhirendra K. 1995. "External Factors Influencing Environmental Policymaking: Role of Multilateral Development Aid Agencies." *Environmental Policies in the Third World: A Comparative Analysis,* ed. O. P. Dwivedi and Dhirendra K. Vajpeyi, pp. 24–45. Westport, Conn.: Greenwood Press.

Voorst, Bruce V. 1993a. "Recycling: Stalled at Curbside." *Time,* October 18, 78–80.
_____ .1993b. "Toxic Dumps: The Lawyer's Money Pit." *Time,* September 13, 63–64.

Waldrop, Judith. 1994. "This Is Not a Doomsday Scenario." *American Demographics* 16 (March): 22–23.

Weiss, Laura. 1991. "Pesticides Must be More Closely Regulated." In *The Environmental Crisis,* ed. David L. Bender and Bruno Leone, pp. 66–72. San Diego, Calif.: Greenhaven Press.

Weisskopf, Michael. 1993. "Minorities' Pollution Risk Is Debated." In *Societies in Crisis,* pp. 130–32. Washington Writers Group.

Wilson, Edward O. 1992. *The Diversity of Life.* Cambridge, Mass.: Harvard Universtiy Press.

World Commission on Environment and Development. 1987. *Our Common Future.* New York: Oxford University Press.

World Health Organization .1994. "Report on Infants and Young Child Nutrition: Global Problems and Promising Developments." Press Release, January 18, 1994. [Internet].

World Watch Institute. 1988. *State of the World.* New York: W. W. Norton.

Zhang, Junsen, and Roland Strum. 1994. "When Do Couples Sign the One-Child Certificate in Urban China?" *Population Research and Policy Review* 13: 69–81.

Global Conflict

IS IT TRUE?

1 Most of the casualties of war today are civilians (p. 475).

2 The resolution of conflict between nations also tends to result in the resolution of conflict within nations (p. 483).

3 Although the military causes a great deal of environmental damage during wartime, during times of peace military forces are geared to help clean up the environment and remediate environmental damage done during wartime (p. 482).

4 Military spending in the world as a whole has far exceeded spending for health care and education, especially in poor countries (p. 466).

5 In 1995, there were more than 36,000 nuclear weapons on the planet with a combined explosive power of 650,000 Hiroshima-sized bombs (p. 488).

ANS: 1.T 2.F 3.F 4.T 5.T

> Every gun that is made, every warship launched, every rocket fired, signifies in the final sense a theft from those who hunger and are not fed, those who are cold and not clothed. The world in arms is not spending money alone. It is spending the sweat of its laborers, the genius of its scientists, and the hopes of its children.
>
> Dwight D. Eisenhower, Former U.S. President/Military Leader

The history of the world is a history of conflict. Never in recorded history has there been a time when conflict did not exist between and within groups. The most violent form of conflict—**war**—refers to organized armed violence aimed at a social group in pursuit of an objective. Wars have existed throughout human history and continue in the contemporary world.

War is one of the great paradoxes of human history. It both protects and annihilates. It creates and defends nations, but also destroys them. Whether war is just or unjust, defensive or offensive, it involves the most horrendous atrocities known to humankind. The victims of these atrocities include both military personnel and civilians:

International Data: In the 1980s, twenty-two wars were fought; in the early 1990s, thirty-five different countries were involved in armed conflict.

SOURCE: Renner 1993a.

A man with no arm came into my shop, the blood gushing from his stump. Then he ran away. I saw the torso of a woman. She was still moving, but her legs were gone. The other day I saw something similar in a film. A beast cut a young man in two, torso and legs. One was a movie, the other is our reality here in Bosnia. We are like a flock of little chickens squeezed into this cage of a town, chirping for help. (Ferid Durakovic, after a Serb mortar shell landed near his food store in Sarejevo, killing 43 people and wounding more than 80; quoted in Fedarko 1995, 50)

This chapter focuses on the causes and consequences of global conflict and war. Along with population and environmental problems, war and global conflict are among the most serious of all social problems in their threat to the human race and life on earth.

The Social Context: Global Conflict in a Changing World

As societies have evolved and changed throughout history, the nature of war has also changed. Before industrialization and the sophisticated technology that resulted, war occurred primarily between neighboring groups on a relatively small scale. In the modern world, war can be waged between nations that are separated by thousands of miles, as well as between neighboring nations. In the following sections, we examine how war has changed our social world and how our changing social world has affected the nature of war in the industrial and postindustrial information age.

WAR AND THE DEVELOPMENT OF CIVILIZATION

The very act that now threatens modern civilization—war—is largely responsible for creating the advanced civilization in which we live. Before large political states existed, people lived in small groups and villages. War broke the barriers of autonomy between local groups and permitted small villages to be incorporated into larger political units known as "chiefdoms." Centuries of warfare between chiefdoms culminated in the development of the state. The **state** is "an apparatus of power, a set of institutions—the central government, the armed forces, the regulatory and police agencies—whose most important functions involve the use of force, the control of territory and the maintenance of internal order" (Porter 1994, 5–6). The creation of the state in turn led to other profound social and cultural changes:

> And once the state emerged, the gates were flung open to enormous cultural advances, advances undreamed of during—and impossible under—a regimen of small autonomous villages. . . . Only in large political units, far removed in structure from the small autonomous communities from which they sprang, was it possible for great advances to be made in the arts and sciences, in economics and technology, and indeed in every field of culture central to the great industrial civilizations of the world. (Carneiro 1994, 14–15)

Thus, war, in a sense, gave rise to the state. As Porter (1994) notes, "there are few states in the world today whose existence, boundaries, and political structure did not emerge from some past cauldron of international or civil war" (p. 1).

THE INFLUENCE OF INDUSTRIALIZATION AND TECHNOLOGY ON WAR

Industrialization and technology could not have developed in the small social groups that existed before military action consolidated them into larger states.

The significance of wars is not just that they lead to major changes during the period of hostilities and immediately after. They produced transformations which have turned out to be of enduring significance.
—Anthony Giddens
Sociologist

Industrialization may decrease a society's propensity to war, but, at the same time, it increases the potential destructiveness of war because with industrialization, warfare technology becomes more sophisticated and more lethal.

Thus, war contributed indirectly to the industrialization and technological sophistication that characterize the modern world.

Industrialization, in turn, has had two major influences on war. Cohen (1986) calculated the number of wars fought per decade in industrial and preindustrial nations and concluded that "as societies become more industrialized, their proneness to warfare decreases" (p. 265). Cohen summarized the evidence for this conclusion: the preindustrial nations had an overall mean of 10.6 wars per decade, while the industrial nations averaged 2.7 wars per decade. Perhaps industrialized nations have more to lose, so they avoid war and the risk of defeat. Or, perhaps, industrialized nations are more preoccupied with manufacturing and commerce than with militarism.

Although industrialization may decrease a society's propensity to war, it also increases the potential destruction of war. With industrialization, military technology became more sophisticated and more lethal. Rifles and cannons, replaced the clubs, arrows, and swords used in more primitive warfare and in turn, were replaced by tanks, bombers, and nuclear warheads. This chapter's *In Focus* looks at how modern computer and information technology is transforming warfare capabilities.

THE ECONOMICS OF MILITARY SPENDING

National Data: In the United States, over $270 billion was spent on national defense in 1995.

SOURCE: *Statistical Abstract of the United States: 1995,* Table 548.

The increasing sophistication of military technology has commanded a large share of resources in countries throughout the world. Military spending in the world as a whole far exceeds spending for health care and education, especially in poor countries (Galbraith 1994). Klein (1994) notes that military expenditures for all developing countries amounted to 1.7 times the combined expenditures for education and health. Military spending includes expenditures for salaries of military personnel, research and development, weapons, veterans' benefits, and other defense-related expenses.

The U.S. government not only spends money on its own military, but it also sells military equipment to other countries either directly or by helping U.S. companies sell weapons abroad (see Figure 16.1). Although the purchasing countries may use these weapons to defend themselves from hostile attack, foreign military sales may pose a threat to the United States by arming potential antagonists. For example, the United States, which provides more than half of the world's arms exports, supplied weapons to Iraq to use against Iran. These same weapons were then used against Americans in the Gulf War. In addition, export competition between the United States and Russia poses a threat to their newly improved relations (O'Prey 1995).

National Data: U.S. defense spending decreased each year between 1992 and 1995.

SOURCE: *Statistical Abstract of the United States: 1995,* Table 548.

The **Cold War,** the state of political tension and military rivalry that existed between the United States and the former Soviet Union, provided justification for large expenditures on military preparedness. The end of the Cold War, along with the rising national debt, have resulted in cutbacks in the U.S. military budget.

The economic impact of these defense cutbacks has been mixed. On the negative side, defense cutbacks result in job losses and the closure of military bases, facilities, factories and plants in defense industries. Nationally, a 1 percent cutback in defense purchases would reduce employment in the United States by less than 0.03 percent (Taylor 1993). However, certain industries and the regions and states where they are located suffer disproportionately as a re-

Information Warfare

In the postindustrial information age, computer technology has revolutionized the nature of warfare and future warfare capabilities. O'Prey (1995) notes that "the growing availability of high-performance sensors, information processing capabilities, and precision-guided munitions . . . is fundamentally changing combat operations" (pp. 17–18). With the increasing proliferation and power of computer technology, military strategists and political leaders are exploring the horizons of "information warfare," or **infowar.** Essentially, infowar utilizes technology to attack or manipulate the military and civilian infrastructure and information systems of an enemy. For example, infowar capabilities include the following (Waller 1995):

- Breaking into the communications equipment of the enemy army and disseminating incorrect information to enemy military leaders.
- Inserting computer viruses into the computer systems that control the phone system, electrical power, banking and stock exchanges, and air-traffic control of an enemy country.
- Jamming signals on the enemy's government television station and inserting a contrived TV program that depicts enemy leaders making unpopular statements that will alienate their people.
- Incapacitating the enemy's military computer systems, such as the one that operates the weapons system.

By 2010, the U.S. Army hopes to "digitize the battlefield" by linking every soldier and weapons systems electronically. Further, a prototype of the equipment to be used by the infantry in the twenty-first century is currently being developed:

His helmet will be fitted with microphones and earphones for communications, night-vision goggles and thermal-imaging sensors to see in the dark, along with a heads-up display in front of his eyes to show him where he is on the ground and give him constant intelligence reports. (Waller 1995, 41)

The U.S. Army, Navy, and Air Force are setting up infowar offices. In 1995, the first sixteen infowar officers graduated from the National Defense University in Washington after being specially trained in everything from defending against computer attacks to using virtual reality computer technology to plan battle maneuvers.

A major problem of infowar technology is that much of it is inexpensive and readily available. With a computer, a modem, and some rudimentary knowledge of computers, anyone could be an "infowarrior." The U.S. government's Joint Security Commission described U.S. vulnerability to infowar as "the major security challenge of this decade and possibly the next century" (quoted in Waller 1995, 40).

SOURCES: Kevin P. O'Prey. 1995. *The Arms Export Challenge: Cooperative Approaches to Export Management and Defense Conversion.* Washington, D.C.: The Brookings Institute; Douglas Waller. 1995. "Onward Cyber Soldiers." *Time,* August 21, 38–44.

sult of defense cutbacks. In 1992, over 150,000 U.S. defense industry workers were laid off, and over one million more are expected to be laid off by the end of the decade (Bischak 1993).

On the positive side, defense cutbacks provide a **peace dividend,** in that resources previously spent on military purposes can be used for private or

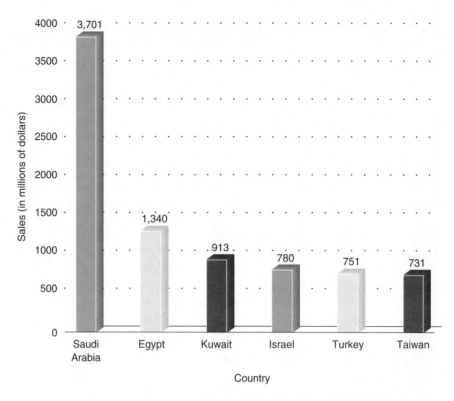

International Data: In 1990, the industrialized countries had more than 10 million military personnel while the developing countries had more than 18 million. An additional 22 million people worldwide were employed directly or indirectly in defense industries, and between 750,000 and 1.5 million scientists and engineers were doing military research and development.

SOURCE: Reported in Sandler and Hartley 1995, 8.

public investment or consumption. For example, the peace dividend could be used for new manufacturing plants and machinery (private investment) or for public education, transportation, housing, health, and the environment. The peace dividend could also be used to lower the national debt and/or lower taxes.

Achieving a peace dividend requires the reallocation of resources from military forces and defense industries to other sectors of the economy—a process referred to as **economic conversion** (Sandler and Hartley 1995). Military bases could be converted to civil airports, prisons, housing developments, or shopping centers. Defense research facilities could shift their emphasis to environmental or health problems, food production, or alternative sources of energy. Workers in the defense industry could be employed in the civil sector. In 1993, President Clinton committed nearly $20 billion over a five-year period for the "Defense Reinvestment and Conversion Initiative" to help workers and communities adjust to defense cutbacks (Bischak 1993). This initiative includes money for retraining and education programs for displaced defense industry workers and military personnel. On an international scale, this represents an enormous task.

Do the benefits of the peace dividend justify the costs associated with economic conversion? According to defense economists Sandler and Hartley (1995), the dividends of peace are likely to be small in the short run due to the costs associated with economic conversion. In the long term, however, the benefits of having more goods and services for public consumption could very well outweigh the short-term costs.

Sociological Perspectives on Conflict and War

Sociological perspectives can help us understand various aspects of war. In this section, we describe how structural-functionalism, conflict theory, and symbolic interactionism may be applied to the study of conflict and war.

STRUCTURAL-FUNCTIONALIST PERSPECTIVE

Structural-functionalism focuses on the functions war serves and suggests that war would not exist unless it had positive outcomes for society. It has already been noted that war has served to consolidate small autonomous social groups into larger political states. An estimated 600,000 autonomous political units existed in the world around the year 1000 B.C. Today, that number has dwindled to less than 200 (Carneiro 1994).

Another major function of war is that it produces social cohesion and unity among societal members by giving them a "common cause" and a common enemy. Unless a war is extremely unpopular, military conflict promotes economic and political cooperation. Internal domestic conflicts between political parties, minority groups, and special interest groups dissolve as they unite to fight the common enemy. During World War II, U.S. citizens worked together as a nation to defeat Germany and Japan.

In the short term, war also increases employment and stimulates the economy. The increased production needed to fight World War II helped pull the United States out of the Great Depression. The investments in the manufacturing sector during World War II also had a long-term impact on the U.S. economy. Hooks and Bloomquist (1992) studied the effect of the war on the U.S. economy between 1947 and 1972 and concluded that the U.S. government

A major function of war is that it produces unity among society members. They have a common cause, and a common enemy. They feel a sense of cohesion and work together to defeat the enemy.

Intersocietal conflicts have furthered the development of social structures.
—Herbert Spencer
Sociologist

"directed, and in large measure, paid for a 65% expansion of the total investment in plant and equipment" (p. 304). Specific cities also benefited from government investments; the petroleum industry in Houston and airframe production in Los Angeles, Dallas, and Atlanta are examples.

Another function of war is the inspiration of scientific and technological developments that are useful to civilians. Research on laser-based defense systems led to laser surgery, for example, and research in nuclear fission and fusion facilitated the development of nuclear power. The airline industry owes much of its technology to the development of air power by the Department of Defense (Schafer and Hyland 1994). The Internet was created by the Pentagon for military purposes (Waller 1995).

Finally, war serves to encourage social reform. After a major war, members of society have a sense of shared sacrifice and a desire to heal wounds and rebuild normal patterns of life. They put political pressure on the state to care for war victims, improve social and political conditions, and reward those who have sacrificed lives, family members, and property in battle. As Porter (1994) explains:

> Only the promise of a better world can give meaning to a terrible conflict. Since . . . the lower economic strata usually contribute more of their blood in battle than the wealthier classes, war often gives impetus to social welfare reforms. (p. 19)

CONFLICT PERSPECTIVE

Conflict theorists emphasize that the roots of war often stem from antagonisms that emerge whenever two or more ethnic groups (e.g. Bosnians and Serbs), countries (United States and Vietnam), or regions within countries (the U.S. North and South) struggle for control of resources or have different political, economic, or religious ideologies. Further, conflict theory suggests that war benefits the corporate, military, and political elites. Corporate elites benefit because war often results in the victor taking control of the raw materials of the losing nations, thereby creating a bigger supply of raw materials for its own industries. Indeed, many corporations profit from defense spending. Under the Pentagon's Bid and Proposal program, for example, corporations can charge the cost of preparing proposals for new weapons as overhead on their Defense Department contracts. Also, Pentagon contracts often guarantee a profit to the developing corporations. Even if the project's cost exceeds initial estimates, called a cost overrun, the corporation still receives the agreed-upon profit. In the late 1950s, President Dwight D. Eisenhower referred to this close association between the military and the defense industry as the **military-industrial complex.**

The military elite benefit because war and the preparations for it provide prestige and employment for military officials. War benefits the political elite by giving government officials more power. Porter (1994) observed that "throughout modern history, war has been the lever by which . . . governments have imposed increasingly larger tax burdens on increasingly broader segments of society, thus enabling ever-higher levels of spending to be sustained, even in peacetime" (p. 14). Political leaders who lead their country to a military victory also benefit from the prestige and hero status conferred on them.

As war becomes more sophisticated, it continuously increases governmental authority and decreases the power of the people.
—J. C. L. Simonde de Sismondi
Swiss economist

War . . . has but one thing certain, and that is to increase taxes.
—Thomas Paine
American revolutionary writer

SYMBOLIC INTERACTIONIST PERSPECTIVE

The symbolic interactionist perspective focuses on how meanings and definitions influence attitudes and behaviors regarding conflict and war. The development of attitudes and behaviors that support war begins in childhood. American children learn to glorify and celebrate the Revolutionary War, which created our nation. Movies romanticize war, children play war games with toy weapons, and various video and computer games glorify heroes conquering villains.

> **Consideration** *Monuments to wars and war heroes are scattered throughout our nation's capital, but none are dedicated to peace. The first national monument to honor peace, the National Peace Garden, is scheduled to be built on the Potomac River in 1997. Within this 10-acre public garden, peace messages will be displayed against a backdrop of pools, waterfalls, and flower beds (Peace Garden 1995).*

Symbolic interactionism helps to explain how military recruits and civilians develop a mindset for war by defining war and its consequences as acceptable and necessary. The word "war" has achieved a positive connotation through its use in various phrases—the "war on drugs," the "war on poverty," and the "war on crime." Positive labels and favorable definitions of military personnel facilitate military recruitment and public support of armed forces. Military personnel wear uniforms that command public respect and earn badges and medals that convey their status as "heroes."

Many government and military officials convince the masses that the way to ensure world peace is to be prepared for war. Most world governments preach peace through strength rather than strength through peace. Governments may use propaganda and appeals to patriotism to generate support for war efforts and motivate individuals to join armed forces.

To legitimize war, the act of killing in war is not regarded as "murder." Deaths that result from war are referred to as "casualties." Bombing military and civilian targets appears more acceptable when nuclear missiles are "peacekeepers" that are equipped with multiple "peaceheads." Killing the enemy is more acceptable when derogatory and dehumanizing labels such as Gook, Jap, Chink, and Kraut convey the attitude that the enemy is less than human.

In addition, international law defines and enforces ethics and rules of war. For example, chemical, toxic, and biological warfare generally are considered unjust, as are poisoning streams, firing on a flag of truce, mistreatment of corpses, and purposeless destruction (Von Glahn 1970).

Pilgrim settlers had to imagine Native Americans as subhuman savages in order to kill and rob them of their very sustenance and rightful use of their own lands and hunting grounds.
—Daniela Gioseffi
Poet, novelist, editor, journalist, performer, and activist

Causes of War

The causes of war are numerous and complex. Most wars involve more than one cause. The immediate cause of a war may be a border dispute, for example, but religious tensions that have existed between the two countries for decades may also contribute to the war (Van Evera 1994). The following section reviews various causes of war.

> **Consideration** *The reasons why a society goes to war may be different from the reasons why a given individual of that society engages in war. In*

The issue of war is always uncertain.
—Cicero
Roman orator/statesman

some cases, societal causes may translate into individual motives. But in other cases, "an individual may have his [or her] own private reasons for fighting which may be entirely distinct from those driving the society as a whole to go to war" (Carneiro 1994, 13).

CONFLICT OVER LAND AND OTHER NATURAL RESOURCES

Nations often go to war in an attempt to acquire or maintain control over nat-ural resources, such as land, water, and oil (Ramsey 1993). Disputed borders are one of the most common motives for war. Conflicts are most likely to arise when borders are physically easy to cross and are not clearly delineated by nat-ural boundaries, such as major rivers, oceans, or mountain ranges.

Water is another valuable resource that has led to wars. At various times the empires of Egypt, Mesopotamia, India, and China all went to war over irriga-tion rights. Recently, Serbia's desire for access to the Adriatic Sea has con-tributed to the conflict between the Bosnian Serbs and the Muslims of Bosnia and Herzegovina.

Not only do the oil-rich countries in the Middle East present a tempting tar-get in themselves, but war in the region can threaten other nations that are de-pendent on Middle Eastern oil. Thus, when Iraq seized Kuwait and threatened the supply of oil from the Persian Gulf, the United States and many other nations reacted militarily in the Gulf War. However, in a document prepared for the Center for Strategic and International Studies, Starr and Stoll (1989) warn that:

> *By the year 2000, water, not oil will be the dominant resource issue of the Middle East. According to World Watch Institute, "despite modern technology and feats of engineering, a secure water future for much of the world remains illusive." The prognosis for Egypt, Jordon, Israel, the West Bank, the Gaza Strip, Syria, and Iraq is especially alarming. If present consumption patterns continue, emerging water shortages, combined with a deterioration in water quality, will lead to more competition and conflict. (p. 1)*

CONFLICT OVER VALUES AND IDEOLOGIES

Many countries initiate war not over resources, but over beliefs. World War II was largely a war over differing political ideologies: democracy versus fascism. The Cold War involved the clashing of opposing economic ideologies: capital-ism versus communism. Wars over differing religious beliefs have led to some of the worst episodes of bloodshed in history, in part, because some religions are partial to *martyrdom*—the idea that dying for one's beliefs leads to eternal salvation. The Shiites (one of the two main sects within Islam) in the Middle East represent a classic example of holy warriors who feel divine inspiration to kill the enemy.

Conflict between religious groups may stem from conflicting values, ethnic hostilities, and/or territorial disputes. The ongoing conflict between Irish Catholics and Irish Protestants stems largely from a territorial dispute over Northern Ireland. Many Muslims hate the West and regard Westerners as the "enemy of God;" they also see the world as divided into two camps, those who belong to the House of Islam and those who are members of the House of Unbelief. In their view, Muslims have a duty to bring Islam to all unbelieving countries. Conflicts over values or ideologies are not easily resolved. The conflict between secularism and Islam has lasted for fourteen centuries (Lewis 1990). According to Brown (1994), wars fought over values and ideologies are less likely to end in compromise or negotiation because they are fueled by people's convictions and their desire to spread their way of life.

If ideological differences can contribute to war, do ideological similarities discourage war? The answer seems to be "yes;" in general, countries with similar ideologies are less likely to engage in war with each other than countries with differing ideological values (Dixon 1994). Democratic nations are particularly disinclined to wage war against one another (Doyle 1986).

RACIAL AND ETHNIC HOSTILITIES

Ethnic groups vary in their cultural and religious beliefs, values, and traditions. Thus, conflicts between ethnic groups often stem from conflicting values and ideologies. Racial and ethnic hostilities are also fueled by competition over land and other natural and economic resources. Gioseffi (1993) notes that "experts agree that the depleted world economy, wasted on war efforts, is in great measure the reason for renewed ethnic and religious strife. 'Haves' fight with 'have-nots' for the smaller piece of the pie that must go around" (xviii). As noted in Chapter 9, racial and ethnic hostilities are also perpetuated by the wealthy majority to divert attention away from their exploitations and to maintain their own position of power.

Gioseffi (1993) conveys the idiocy and irony of racial and ethnic hostilities:

> At this dangerous juncture, as we near the year 2000, after more than eighty centuries of art and human creativity, philosophy, music, poetry, social and biological science—we humans, considered the paragon of animals in our ability to think, named Homo sapiens, meaning wise or knowing animal, persist, brutishly, in hating and killing each other for the colors of our skin, the shapes of our features, our places of origin on our common terra firma, our styles of culture or language, and most ironically of all our "religious" beliefs—despite the fact that all the great religions of the Earth teach the same basic golden rule: "Do unto others as you would have them do unto you" (xlix).

The most important divide in this hard world is not over bloodlines or ways of worship. It's between those who pursue reason and those who dismiss it. It's between those who build and those who bomb.
—Ellen Goodman
Columnist

DEFENSE AGAINST HOSTILE ATTACKS

The threat or fear of being attacked may cause the leaders of a country to declare war on the nation that poses the threat. The threat may come from a foreign country or from a group within the country. After Germany invaded Poland in 1939, Britain and France declared war on Germany out of fear that they would be Germany's next victims. In Bosnia-Herzegovina, when Bosnian Serbs engaged in "ethnic cleansing," Muslims feared for their survival. Germany attacked Russia in World War I, in part out of fear that Russia had entered the arms race and would use its weapons against Germany. Japan bombed Pearl Harbor hoping to avoid a later confrontation with the U.S. Pacific fleet, which posed a threat to the Japanese military. In 1981, the Israelis conducted an air raid against Iraq's nuclear facilities in an attempt to disarm Iraq and remove its threat to Israel (Brown 1994).

REVOLUTION

Revolutions involve citizens warring against their own government. A revolution may occur when a government is not responsive to the concerns and demands of its citizens and when there are strong leaders willing to mount opposition to the government (Brown 1994).

The birth of the United States resulted from colonists revolting against British control. More recently, civil war broke out in Rwanda when the dissatisfied Tutsis in the Rwanda Patriotic Front (RPF) rebelled against the Hutus who were content with the government. In August of 1994, the RPF took over the government, but the 2.2 million citizens who fled the country when the war began were afraid to return. With no stable government, conflict in Rwanda persists. Similar situations have existed in Guatemala, Chile, and Uganda.

NATIONALISM

Some countries engage in war in an effort to maintain or restore their national pride. For example, Scheff (1994) argues that "Hitler's rise to power was laid by the treatment Germany received at the end of World War I at the hands of the victors" (p. 121). Excluded from the League of Nations, punished by the Treaty of Versailles, and ostracized by the world community, Germany turned to nationalism as a reaction to material and symbolic exclusion.

In the late 1970s, Iranian fundamentalist groups took hostages from the American Embassy in Iran. President Carter's attempt to use military forces to free the hostages was not successful. That failure intensified doubts about America's ability to effectively use military power to achieve its goals. The hostages in Iran were eventually released after President Reagan took office. But doubts about the strength and effectiveness of America's military still called into question America's status as a world power. Subsequently, U.S. military forces invaded the small island of Grenada because the government of Grenada

Civil war in Rwanda reflects revolutionary efforts by dissatisfied citizens against those content with the government.

was building an airfield large enough to accommodate major military armaments. U.S. officials feared that this airfield would be used by countries in hostile attacks on the United States. From one point of view, the large scale and "successful" attack on Grenada functioned to restore faith in the power and effectiveness of the American military.

Social Problems Associated with War and Militarism

Social problems associated with war and militarism include death and disability; rape, forced prostitution, and displacement of women and children; disruption of social-psychological comfort; diversion of economic resources; and destruction of the environment.

DEATH AND DISABILITY

Thus far in the twentieth century, war has taken the lives of more than 100 million persons—more than the total number of deaths in all previous wars or massacres in human history combined (Porter 1994). Many American lives have been lost in wars, including over 53,000 in World War I, 292,000 in World War II, 34,000 in Korea, and 58,000 in Vietnam. In our modern world, sophisticated weapons technology combined with increased population density has made it easier to kill large numbers of people in a short amount of time. When the atomic bomb was dropped on the Japanese cities of Hiroshima and Nagasaki during World War II, 250,000 civilians were killed. More recently, in the war in Rwanda, over half a million people died within three months (Gibbs 1994). Most of the casualties in war today are civilians (see Figure 16.2).

War's impact extends far beyond those who are killed. Many of those who survive war incur disabling injuries. War also harms the larger society. War-related deaths and disabilities deplete the labor force, create orphans and

We owe it to future generations to explain why.
—Robert McNamara on Vietnam
Former U.S. Secretary of Defense

There never was a good war or a bad peace.
—Benjamin Franklin
American scientist/writer

The object of war is not to die for your country but to make the other bastard die for his.
—Gen. George Patten

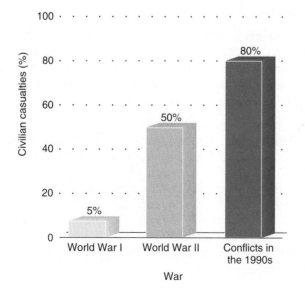

FIGURE 16.2
CIVILIAN CASUALTIES OF WAR
SOURCE: Amnesty International. 1995. *Human Rights Are Women's Right.* New York: Amnesty International Publications.

single-parent families, and burden taxpayers who must pay for the care of orphans and disabled war veterans.

Persons who participate in experiments for military research may also suffer physical harm. Representative Edward Markey of Massachusetts identified thirty-one experiments dating back to 1945 in which U.S. citizens were subjected to harm from participation in military experiments. Markey charged that many of the experiments used human subjects who were captive audiences or populations considered 'expendable' such as the elderly, prisoners, and hospital patients. In 1963, for example, 131 inmates at two prisons in Oregon and Washington were paid $200 each if they agreed to have as much as 600 roentgens of radiation applied to their scrotum. Today, the largest recommended dose is 6 roentgens for an entire year.

For military research purposes, Eda Charlton of New York was injected with plutonium in 1945. She and seventeen other patients did not learn of their poisoning until thirty years later. Her son, Fred Shultz, said of his deceased mother:

> *I was over there fighting the Germans who were conducting these horrific medical experiments . . . at the same time my own country was conducting them on my own mother. (Miller 1993, 17)*

RAPE, FORCED PROSTITUTION, AND DISPLACEMENT OF WOMEN AND CHILDREN

Half a century ago, the Geneva Conventions prohibited rape and forced prostitution in war. Nevertheless, both continue to occur in modern conflicts.

Before and during World War II, the Japanese military forced an estimated 100,000 to 200,000 women and teenage girls into prostitution as military "comfort women" (Amnesty International 1995). These women were forced to have sex with dozens of soldiers every day in "comfort stations." Many of the women died as a result of untreated sexually transmitted disease, harsh punishment, or indiscriminate acts of torture.

More recently, armed forces in Bosnia-Herzegovina have raped women civilians and prisoners. Most of the victims have been Muslim women raped by Bosnian Serbian soldiers:

> *In one such case, a 17-year-old Muslim girl was taken by Serbs from her village to huts in woods near by. . . . She was held there for three months. . . . She was among 12 women who were raped repeatedly in the hut in front of the other women—when they tried to defend her they were beaten off by the soldiers. (Amnesty International 1995, 19)*

In 1994, militia forces roamed through the town of Kibuye, Rwanda, burning houses and killing civilians. "Women found sheltering in the parish church were raped, then pieces of wood were thrust into their vaginas, and they were left to die slowly" (Amnesty International 1995, 17).

War also displaces women and children from their homes, forcing them to flee to other countries or other regions of their homeland. Refugee women and female children are particularly vulnerable to sexual abuse and exploitation by locals, members of security forces, border guards, or other refugees. In refugee camps, women and children may also be subjected to sexual violence from officials and male refugees.

DISRUPTION OF SOCIAL-PSYCHOLOGICAL COMFORT

War and living under the threat of war interfere with social-psychological well-being. In a study of 269 Israeli adolescents, Klingman and Goldstein (1994) found a significant level of anxiety and fear, particularly among younger females, in regard to the possibility of nuclear and chemical warfare. Even during peacetime, the threat of war creates concern and insecurity.

This disruption of social-psychological comfort ranges from vague concern to unspeakable psychological horror. Imagine being in a concentration camp, such as Dachau or Auschwitz, and witnessing your friends and loved ones being tortured and killed. Or, imagine dropping a bomb on a village and experiencing the horror of knowing that innocent children were victimized by the blast. The accompanying *The Human Side* conveys the psychological horror of war as experienced by two children.

Civilians who are victimized by war and military personnel who engage in combat may experience a form of psychological distress known as **post-traumatic stress disorder,** a clinical term referring to a set of symptoms that may result from any traumatic experience including crime victimization, rape, or war. Symptoms of post-traumatic stress disorder include sleep disturbances, recurring nightmares, flashbacks, and poor concentration. Post-traumatic stress disorder is also associated with other personal problems such as alcoholism, family violence, divorce, and suicide.

One study estimates that about 30 percent of male veterans of the Vietnam War have experienced post-traumatic stress disorder, and about 15 percent continue to experience it (Hayman and Scaturo 1993). In another study of 215 Army National Guard and Army Reserve troops who served in the Gulf War and who did not seek mental health services upon return to the states, 16 to 24 percent exhibited symptoms of post-traumatic stress disorder (Sutker et al. 1993).

DIVERSION OF ECONOMIC RESOURCES

As discussed earlier, maintaining the military and engaging in warfare require enormous financial capital and human support. An estimated $100 billion annually is spent worldwide on military research and development. This amount exceeds the combined government research expenditures on developing new energy technologies, improving human health, raising agricultural productivity, and controlling pollution (Renner 1993c).

Money that is spent for military purposes could be allocated for social programs. The decision to spend $1.4 billion for one Trident submarine, equal in cost to a five-year immunization program that would prevent nearly one million childhood deaths annually (Renner 1993a), is a political choice. Similarly, world leaders could choose to allocate the $774 billion needed to reverse environmental damage in four priority areas: reforesting the earth, raising energy efficiency, protecting croplands from erosion of topsoil, and developing renewable sources of energy (Renner 1993c). Although the end of the Cold War has resulted in a relative decrease in defense spending, in 1995 the U.S. government spent more on national defense than on education, social services, the justice system, the environment, and health combined (see Figure 16.3 on p. 480).

> *Some countries have seen the use of systematic sexual violence against women as a weapon of war to degrade and humiliate entire populations. Rape is the most despicable crime against women; mass rape is an abomination*
> —Boutros Boutros-Ghali
> UN Secretary-General on International Women's Day, 1993

> *I have seen enough of one war never to wish to see another.*
> —Thomas Jefferson
> Former U.S. President

National Data: In a national poll, four in ten U.S. adults reported that they believe that the United States is vulnerable to surprise attack. Fifty percent of those over age fifty have this belief.
SOURCE: Laird 1993.

National Data: Between 1940 and 1995, the United States spent an estimated $3.5 trillion to prepare for nuclear war. In 1995, the United States spent $27 billion to prepare for nuclear war.
SOURCE: Center for Defense Information 1995.

THE EXPERIENCE OF WAR THROUGH THE EYES OF TWO CHILDREN

Zlata Filipovic (1995), age ten, is a Bosnian girl who kept a diary of her life in Sarajevo. The following entries reflect her private thoughts and experiences of war:

March 30, 1992:

It's almost half-term. We're all studying for our tests. Tomorrow we're suppose to go to a classical music concert at the Skenderija Hall. Our teacher says we shouldn't go because there will be 10,000 people, pardon me, children, there and somebody might take us as hostages or plant a bomb in the concert hall. Mommy says I shouldn't go. So I won't. (pp. 27–28)

May 2, 1992:

. . . The gunfire was getting worse . . . so we ran down to our own cellar. The cellar is ugly, dark, smelly. . . . We listened to the pounding shells, the shooting, the thundering noise overhead. We even heard planes. . . . We heard glass shattering in our street. Horrible, I put my fingers in my ears to block out the terrible sounds. (p. 39)

June 1, 1993:

. . . Breakfast, lunch and dinner were all uncooked because the gas went off yesterday. As you know, there is no electricity either, so we're on the verge of suicide. . . . I can't take it anymore. . . . There is a growing possibility of my killing myself, if all these morons up there and down here don't kill me first. I'm losing it. (p. 53)

October 17, 1993:

We went down into the cellar. Into the cold dark, stupid cellar which I hate. We were there for hours and hours. They kept pounding away. All the neighbors were with us. . . . Sometimes I think it would be better if they kept shooting so that we wouldn't find it so hard when it starts up AGAIN. I am convinced now that it will never end. Because some people don't want it to, some evil people who hate children and ordinary folk. We haven't done anything. We're innocent. But helpless! (p. 187)

Consideration Using examples such as France under Napoleon and Turkey under the Ottoman Empire, Paul Kennedy (1987) argues that countries with the highest military expenditures eventually become among the least powerful nations. He hypothesizes that "the United States now runs the risk, so familiar to historians of the rise and fall of previous Great Powers, of what may roughly be called imperial overstretch"—the inability to defend and maintain all of American interests and obligations (p. 514).

Anne Frank was thirteen in 1942 when the Nazis occupied Amsterdam and she began to write in her diary. She wrote the following words while hiding in a secret part of a house with eight others over a two-year period. She and the others were discovered in 1944; Anne was sent to the concentration camp of Bergen-Belsen and died two months before Holland was liberated by the Allies.

January 13, 1943

It is terrible outside. Day and night more of those poor miserable people are being dragged off, with nothing but a rucksack and a little money. On the way they are deprived even of these possessions. Families are torn apart, the men, women, and children all being separated. Children coming home from school find that their parents have disappeared. Women return from shopping to find their homes shut up and their families gone. (p. 57)

July 23, 1943:

Just for fun I'm going to tell you each person's first wish, when we are allowed to go outside again. Margot and Mr. Van Daan long more than anything for a hot bath filled to overflowing and want to stay in it for half an hour. Mrs. Van Daan wants most to go and eat cream cakes immediately. Dussel thinks of nothing but seeing Lotju, his wife; Mummy of her cup of coffee; Daddy is going to visit Mr. Vossen first; Peter the town and a cinema, while I should find it so blissful, I shouldn't know where to start! But most of all, I long for a home of my own, to be able to move freely. . . . (p. 81)

June 15, 1944.

I wonder if it's because I haven't been able to poke my nose outdoors for so long that I've grown so crazy about everything to do with nature? I can perfectly well remember that there was a time when a deep blue sky, the song of the birds, moonlight and flowers could never have kept me spellbound. That's what changed since I've been here. (p. 225)

SOURCES: Zlata Filipovic. 1995. *Zlata's Diary: A Child's Life in Sarejevo* New York: Penguin Books; Anne Frank. 1952. *The Diary of a Young Girl.* New York: Pocket Books.

DESTRUCTION OF THE ENVIRONMENT

Traditional definitions of and approaches to national security have assumed that political states or groups comprise the principal threat to national security and welfare. This assumption implies that national defense and security are best served by being prepared for war against other states. The environmental costs of military security are often overlooked or minimized in such

My God . . . what have we done?
—Robert Lewis
Co-pilot of the Enola Gay after dropping the atomic bomb on Hiroshima

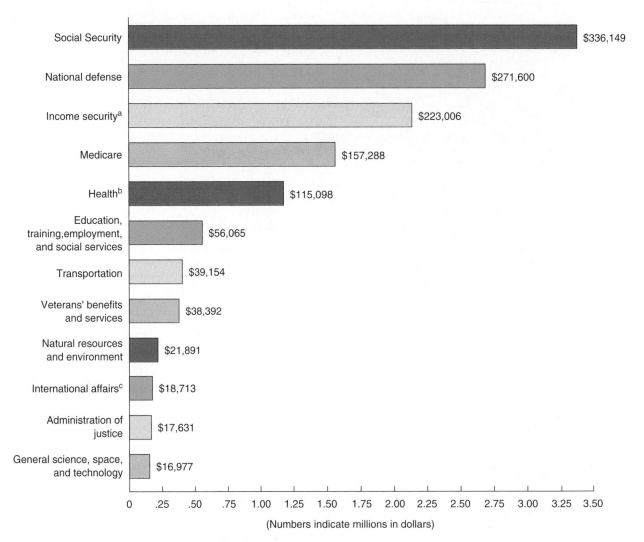

a Includes retirement and disability insurance, unemployment compensation, housing assistance, and food assistance
b Includes health research and health care services
c Includes international development and humanitarian assistance

FIGURE 16.3

SELECTED U.S. FEDERAL OUTLAYS, 1995 (estimated)

SOURCE: *Statistical Abstract of the United States: 1995* 115th ed. U.S. Bureau of the Census. (Washington, D.C.: U.S. Government Printing Office), Table 522.

discussions. But environmental security is also vital to national and global security, and achieving one at the expense of the other is like taking one step forward and two steps back.

We have already noted that military spending diverts economic resources available for other social issues, including environmental issues. In addition, militarism and war directly contribute to environmental problems, even during times of peace.

Oil smoke from the 650 burning oil wells left in the wake of the Gulf War contains soot, sulphur dioxide, and nitrogen oxides, the major components of acid rain, and a variety of toxic and potentially carcinogenic chemicals and heavy metals.

Destruction of the Environment during War The environmental damage that occurs during war continues to devastate human populations long after war ceases. In Vietnam, 13 million tons of bombs left 25 million bomb craters. Nineteen million gallons of herbicides, including Agent Orange, were spread over the countryside. An estimated 80 percent of Vietnam's forests and swamp lands were destroyed by bulldozing or bombing (Funke 1994).

The Gulf War also illustrates how war destroys the environment (Funke 1994; Renner 1993c). In six weeks, one thousand air missions were flown, dropping 6,000 bombs. In 1991, Iraqi troops set 650 oil wells on fire, releasing oil, which still covers the surface of the Kuwaiti desert and seeps into the ground, threatening to poison underground water supplies. The estimated 6–8 million barrels of oil that spilled into the Gulf waters are threatening marine life. This spill is by far the largest in history—25–30 times the size of the 1989 *Exxon Valdez* oil spill in Alaska.

The clouds of smoke that hung over the Gulf region for eight months contained soot, sulfur dioxide, and nitrogen oxides—the major components of acid rain—and a variety of toxic and potentially carcinogenic chemicals and heavy metals. The U.S. Environmental Protection Agency estimates that in March 1991 about ten times as much air pollution was being emitted in Kuwait as by all U.S. industrial and power-generating plants combined. Acid rain destroys forests and harms crops. It also activates several dangerous metals normally found in soil, including aluminum, cadmium, and mercury. Acid rain makes these metals more soluble and, therefore, more of a threat to water supplies and fish. The environmental effects of the Kuwait oil fires have affected regions as far away as Chad and the South Pacific. Kuwaiti soot has also been found in Japan, Hawaii, and parts of the continental United States.

Bullets with a core of radioactive nuclear waste were used during the Gulf War, and a thousand of them were left on the ground. Children who played with them risked uranium poisoning. Uranium from these bullets also contaminated water and soil, resulting in the uranium poisoning of thousands of people (Hoskins 1993). After the cease-fire in Iraq, about 80 percent of those who died were children (Burleigh 1991).

The ultimate environmental catastrophe facing the planet is a massive exchange thermonuclear war (Funke 1994). Aside from the immediate human casualties, poisoned air, poisoned crops, and radioactive rain, many scientists agree that the dust storms and concentrations of particles would block vital sunlight and lower temperatures in the northern hemisphere, creating a **nuclear winter.** In the event of large-scale nuclear war, most living things on earth would die. The fear of nuclear war has greatly contributed to the military and arms buildup, which, ironically, also causes environmental destruction even in times of peace.

Destruction of the Environment in Peacetime Even when military forces are not engaged in active warfare, military activities assault the environment. Ecological damage occurs from training troops and from building, testing, and practicing with weapons.

Modern military maneuvers require large amounts of land. The Department of Defense owns 100,000 square kilometers, an area equivalent in size to the state of Virginia. In addition, the armed services lease another 80,000 square kilometers from other federal agencies (Renner 1993c). The use of land for military purposes prevents other uses, such as agriculture, habitat protection, recreation, and housing. More importantly, military use of land often harms the land. In practicing military maneuvers, the armed forces demolish natural vegetation, disturb wildlife habitats, erode soil, silt up streams, and cause flooding. Military bombing and shooting ranges leave the land pockmarked with craters and contaminate the soil and groundwater with lead and other toxic residues.

The armed forces also consume large amounts of energy and thus contribute to air pollution and global warming. Worldwide, nearly one-quarter of all jet fuel is used for military purposes (Renner 1993c). The use of petroleum products in military operations contributes to air pollution. Carbon emissions and the use of ozone-depleting substances contribute to the depletion of the ozone layer and global warming.

The production, maintenance, and storage of weapons and military equipment also poison the environment and its human, plant, and animal inhabitants. According to Renner (1993c), "the U.S. military is the largest generator of hazardous wastes in the country and quite likely in the world" (p. 104).

Bombs exploded during peacetime leak radiation into the atmosphere and groundwater. From 1945 to 1990, 1,908 bombs were tested—that is, exploded—at more than thirty-five sites around the world. Although underground testing has reduced radiation, some still escapes into the atmosphere and is suspected of seeping into groundwater (Renner 1993c).

Arms-control and disarmament treaties of the last decade call for the disposal of huge stockpiles of weapons. Yet, there are no completely safe means of disposing of weapons and ammunition. Greenpeace has called for placing weapons in storage until safe disposal methods are found (Renner 1993c). But the longer weapons are stored, the more they deteriorate, increasing the likelihood of dangerous leakage.

National Data: Nine nuclear weapons facilities have qualified for inclusion on the U.S. Environmental Protection Agency's "Superfund" National Priorities List of the worst contaminated sites in America. Cleaning up the contamination from nuclear weapons will cost an estimated $230 billion over the next 75 years.

SOURCE: Center for Defense Information 1995.

National Data: In recent years, U.S. military activities generated between 400,000 and 500,000 tons of toxins each year, more than the top five U.S. chemical companies combined.

SOURCE: Renner 1993c.

In the United States, the volume of high-level toxic wastes generated during weapons production is seven times greater than that produced by power plants.

SOURCE: Funke 1994.

Conflict and Politics in the Post–Cold War Era

One of the most significant recent events affecting global conflict has been the end of the Cold War due to the collapse of the communist regime of the former Soviet Union. Prospects for world peace in the post–Cold War era are examined next.

INTERNAL CONFLICT IN THE POST–COLD WAR ERA

In the discussion of the structural-functionalist view of global conflict and war, we noted that war functions as a catalyst for social cohesion. The corollary to the cohesive effect of war is that without a common enemy to fight, internal strife is likely to occur. Porter (1994) identifies a historical pattern in which "the end of an era of international rivalry and conflict has marked the beginning of internal conflict and disarray almost everywhere" (p. 300). According to Porter, the post–Cold War era is likely to be an era of political turmoil and divisiveness among social, racial, religious, and class groups:

> *Given the growing diversity of American culture and values today, our society, no longer united by foreign threats, might find that its own internal cleavages are greater than anyone realized. . . . We can expect growing public disdain for the political process, rising unrest in the inner cities, proposals for radical constitutional change, third-party movements, one-term presidents, and a serious national identity crisis over what it means to be an American. (Porter 1994, 295)*

TERRORISM AND GUERRILLA WARFARE: A GROWING THREAT

Terrorism is the premeditated use, or threatened use, of violence by an individual or group to gain a political objective. Terrorism may be used to publicize a cause, promote an ideology, achieve religious freedom, attain the release of a political prisoner, or rebel against a government. Terrorists use a variety of tactics, including assassinations, skyjackings, armed attacks, kidnapping and hostage taking, threats, and various forms of bombing. Terrorist activities capture worldwide media attention, which publicizes the terrorists' cause.

Terrorism can be either domestic or transnational. Transnational terrorism occurs when a terrorist act in one country involves victims, targets, institutions, governments, or citizens of another country. The 1993 bombing of the World Trade Center in New York exemplifies transnational terrorism. Four Muslim extremists were convicted of the bombing, which killed six people and injured a thousand. Domestic terrorism is exemplified by the 1995 truck bombing of a nine-story federal office building in Oklahoma City, resulting in 168 deaths and more than 200 injured. Gulf War veteran Timothy McVeigh, who, along with Terry Nichols, was charged with the bombing, is reported to have been a member of a paramilitary group that opposes the U.S. government.

Another example of terrorism occurred in 1995, when the Prime Minister of Israel, Yitzhak Rabin, was assassinated by Yigal Amir, a fellow Jew. Amir was part of an extremist Jewish group that insisted that lands seized by Israel during the Six-Day War in 1967 (the Sinai, West Bank and Gaza Strip) must remain as part

Perhaps for the first time, world leaders can move from responding to the Cold War to shaping environmentally healthy societies. The environment can then move to the center of the economic decision making, where it belongs.
—Worldwatch Institute

National Data: According to the Southern Poverty Law Center's Militia Task Force (1995), 171 paramilitary groups are operating in thirty-eight states.

SOURCE: Militia Task Force 1995.

If you ask me what is the obstacle to the implementation [of the peace plan], it is terror. We face a unique kind of terrorism— the suicidal terror mission. There is no deterrent to a person who goes with high explosives in his car in his bag and explodes himself.
—Yitzhak Rabin
Former Prime Minister
of Israel

of Israel's biblical birthright. Amir and other extremists opposed Rabin's plan to trade land for peace with the Palestinians. Amir assassinated Rabin in an attempt to thwart the peace process.

A government can use both defensive and offensive strategies to fight terrorism. Defensive strategies include using metal detectors at airports and strengthening security at potential targets, such as embassies and military command posts. Offensive strategies include retaliatory raids, group infiltration, and preemptive strikes. Unfortunately, efforts to stop one kind of terrorism may result in an increase in other types of terrorist acts. For example, after the use of metal detectors in airports increased, the incidence of skyjackings decreased, but the incidence of assassinations increased (Enders and Sandler 1993).

Following the bombing in Oklahoma City, President Clinton called for new powers against domestic terrorists, including the following measures: (1) laws to establish an FBI-run counterterrorism center, (2) creation of a fund for infiltrating suspected domestic terrorist organizations, and (3) legislation to give the FBI more authority to search hotel registers, phone logs, and credit cards.

Since the early 1980s, the Southern Poverty Law Center's Militia Task Force has been instrumental in fighting antigovernment militia groups. For example, in 1986, the Militia Task Force brought a court action that exposed the North Carolina White Patriot Party's thousand- member militia unit's plans to blow up federal facilities with stolen military explosives (Militia Task Force 1995). Over a fifteen-year period, the Militia Task Force has built extensive computerized files on militias and hate groups. The files include more than 11,000 photographs, records of over 61,000 hate activities, reports on 14,000 individuals who have committed hate acts or are affiliated with hate groups, and intelligence on more than 3,200 hate group and militia organizations. Six times a year the Militia Task Force reports its findings to more than 6,000 law enforcement agencies. This chapter's *Self and Society* deals with American attitudes and beliefs about terrorism.

Unlike terrorist activity, which targets civilians and may be committed by lone individuals, **guerrilla warfare** is committed by organized groups opposing a domestic or foreign government and its military forces. Guerrilla warfare often involves small groups who use elaborate camouflage and underground tunnels to hide until they are ready to execute a surprise attack. Since 1945, more than 120 armed guerrilla conflicts have occurred, resulting in the death of over 20 million people (Perdue 1993). Most of these conflicts occurred in developing countries. Fidel Castro's guerrillas in Cuba and the Vietcong guerrillas in Vietnam are examples.

Two theories have been advanced to explain why guerrilla warfare occurs most often in less developed countries (Moaddel 1994). First, as societies change from a traditional to a modern industrialized society, they experience institutional instability, which leads to conflict as various groups compete for control and resources. A second theory holds that the conflicts arise from external international relations. Less developed countries are dependent on more developed countries, which exploit their labor forces and resources. The growing inequality between less developed and more developed countries creates conflict.

POLITICS IN THE POST–COLD WAR ERA: THREE POSSIBLE SCENARIOS

Porter (1994) outlines three possible scenarios for the future of global security. In the first scenario, civil strife grows out of the extreme dissatisfaction

International Data: By the early 2000s, there will be about 200 nation-states. Their authority and sovereignty will be challenged by 4,000 ethnic minorities.

SOURCE: Ramsey 1993.

American Attitudes and Beliefs about Terrorism

Answer the following questions about terrorism by checking one of the answer choices for each question. Answers obtained in a 1995 Gallup survey of American adults are presented following the questions.

Question	Answer Choices
1. How likely do you think it is that bombings or similar acts of violence will occur in the United States in the near future?	Very likely ___ Somewhat likely ___ Somewhat unlikely ___ Very unlikely ___
2. How worried are you that you or someone in your family will become a victim of a terrorist attack similar to the bombing in Oklahoma City?	Very Worried ___ Somewhat worried ___ Not too worried ___ Not worried at all ___
3. Do you personally feel any sense of danger from terrorist acts where you live and work, or not?	Yes ___ No ___
4. Do you think there are any actions that the United States government could take to prevent future terrorist attacks in this country, or is it not possible to prevent future attacks?	Yes, actions possible ___ No, can't prevent ___

Answers obtained in a 1995 Gallup survey of American adults:

1. Very likely—50%
   Somewhat likely—36%
   Somewhat unlikely—9%
   Very unlikely—3%

2. Very worried—14%
   Somewhat worried—28%
   Not too worried—33%
   Not worried at all—24%

3. Yes—17%
   No—82%

4. Yes, actions possible—45%
   No, can't prevent—46%

SOURCE: David W. Moore. 1995. "Americans Brace Themselves Against More Terrorism." *Gallup Poll Monthly* (April): 1–5, 45. Used by permission.

of ethnic communities living in a state dominated by other ethnic groups. Conflict between ethnic groups may ultimately result in each group forming its own independent political community. In Europe, which currently consists of 1,000 or more possible political communities, this scenario would result in the devolution of state structures. Small independent polities would replace centralized states, and Europe would essentially be remedievalized. "Post-modernity," suggests Porter, "would loom as a return to the past" (p. 301).

In the second scenario, terrorism, low-intensity conflict, and street-level violence replace state-centered, large-scale warfare. As the tools of war slip out of the control of central states and fall into the hands of guerrilla militia forces and terrorist groups, the state will become increasingly powerless.

The third scenario Porter (1994) envisions is entirely different. In this view, independent states are threatened by a return of empire. "In a complex world of economic interdependence and mass communications, large-scale organizations that transcend national borders are growing in importance. . . . By the year 2000 or 2010, it is conceivable that Western Europe will again be a unified empire" (p. 301).

In Search of Global Peace: Strategies and Policies

Various strategies and policies are aimed at creating and maintaining global peace. These include the redistribution of economic resources, the creation of a world government, peacekeeping activities of the United Nations, arms control, and mediation and arbitration.

REDISTRIBUTION OF ECONOMIC RESOURCES

National Data: In 1991, the U.S. federal government spent over $273 million on national defense. In the same year, U.S. foreign economic aid totaled less than $12 million.

SOURCE: *Statistical Abstract of the United States: 1994*, Tables 504 and 1319.

Inequality in economic resources contributes to conflict and war as the increasing disparity in wealth and resources between rich and poor nations fuels hostilities and resentment. Therefore, any measures that result in a more equal distribution of economic resources are likely to prevent conflict. John J. Shanahan (1995), retired U.S. Navy Vice Admiral and director of the Center for Defense Information, suggests that wealthy nations can help reduce social and economic roots of conflict by providing economic assistance to poorer countries. Nevertheless, U.S. military expenditures for national defense far outweigh U.S. economic assistance to foreign countries.

As we discussed in Chapter 15, strategies that reduce population growth are likely to result in higher levels of economic well-being. Conversely, unrestrained population growth contributes to economic hardship of impoverished countries. Funke (1994) explains that "rapidly increasing populations in poorer countries will lead to environmental overload and resource depletion in the next century, which will most likely result in political upheaval and violence as well as mass starvation" (p. 326). Although achieving worldwide economic well-being is important for minimizing global conflict, it is important that economic development does not occur at the expense of the environment. Otherwise, we are simply trading one form of human destruction (war) for another (environmental degradation). As we emphasized in Chapter 15, economic development that is not sustainable is not, in the long run, development, but disaster.

WORLD GOVERNMENT

Some analysts have suggested that world peace might be attained through the establishment of a world government. The idea of a single world government is not new. In 1693, William Penn advocated a political union of all European monarchs and in 1712, Jacques-Henri Bernardin de Saint-Pierre of France suggested an all-European Union with a "Senate of Peace." Proposals such as these have been made throughout history. President Bush spoke of a new world order that became possible after the fall of communism in Eastern Europe. Jervis (1994) claims that "we cannot eliminate the possibility of war without creating world government" (p. 239).

If a world government is to be formed, poorer countries struggling for recognition and an end to suppression must have a voice. Otherwise, their struggle will produce wars of succession or wars against other nations (Van Evera 1994). The prospects for creating world governance are dim, however. Rich and powerful countries are reluctant to give up their power to a larger controlling political force. And, as Terhal (1994) argues, "poor countries feel themselves so vulnerable that they also refuse to accept any supra-national rule, clinging desperately to their national sovereignty, as the only . . . security system left" (p. 115).

THE UNITED NATIONS

The United Nations (UN), whose charter begins, "We the people of the United Nations—Determined to save succeeding generations from the scourge of war. . . ," has engaged in at least twenty-six peacekeeping operations since 1948. The UN Security Council can use force, when necessary, to restore international peace and security. Recently, the UN has been involved in overseeing multinational peacekeeping forces in Somalia, Haiti, Kuwait, and Bosnia-Herzagovina.

A major problem with the concept of the UN is that its members represent individual nations, not a region or the world. And because nations tend to act in their own best economic and security interests, UN actions performed in the name of world peace may be motivated by nations acting in their own interests. Nevertheless, the UN is regarded as an international agency dedicated to keeping, making, and enforcing peace.

MEDIATION AND ARBITRATION

Mediation and arbitration are nonviolent strategies used to resolve conflicts and stop or prevent war. In mediation, a neutral third party intervenes and facilitates negotiation between representatives or leaders of conflicting groups. Mediators do not impose solutions, but rather help disputing parties generate options for resolving the conflict. Ideally, a mediated resolution to a conflict meets at least some of the concerns and interests of each party to the conflict. In other words, mediation attempts to find "win-win" solutions in which each side is satisfied with the solution. Although mediation is used to resolve conflict between individuals, it is also a valuable tool for resolving international conflicts. For example, former President Jimmy Carter successfully mediated between Israeli Prime Minister Menachem Begin and Egypt's President Anwar Sadat to negotiate the Egypt-Israel Peace Treaty of 1979 (Brown 1994).

Arbitration also involves a neutral third party who listens to evidence and arguments presented by conflicting groups. Unlike mediation, however, in arbitration, the neutral third party arrives at a decision or outcome that the two conflicting parties agree to accept.

If you want peace, work for justice.
—Pope Paul VI

Peace must first be developed within an individual. And I believe that love, compassion, and altruism are the fundamental basis for peace. Once these qualities are developed within an individual, he or she is then able to create an atmosphere of peace and harmony. This atmosphere can be expanded and extended from the individual to his family, from the family to the community and eventually to the whole world.
—H. H. Dalai Lama
Peace activist and
Buddhist teacher

In his role as a mediator, former President Jimmy Carter successfully negotiated a treaty between Egypt and Israel in 1979.

The real danger is that we will be tempted more and more to resort to the use of military forces as we diminish our capacity to respond by other means. As the saying goes, if all you have is a hammer then every problem starts to look like a nail.
—Vice Admiral John J. Shanahan
U.S. Navy (retired)
Director of the Center for Defense Information

ARMS CONTROL

In the 1960s, the United States and the Soviet Union led the world in an arms race, each competing to build a more powerful military arsenal than its adversary. The Pentagon justified the arms race on the assumption that large stockpiles of weapons were necessary to defend against possible Soviet attack and, more importantly, to act as a deterrent of war. If either superpower—the United States or the Soviet Union—were to initiate a full-scale war, the retaliatory powers of the other nation would result in the destruction of both nations. Thus, the principle of **mutually assured destruction (MAD)** that developed from nuclear weapons capabilities transformed war from a win-lose proposition to a lose-lose scenario. If both sides would lose in a war, the theory goes, neither side would initiate war.

Due to the end of the Cold War and the growing realization that current levels of weapons literally represented "overkill," governments have moved in the direction of arms control, which involves reducing or limiting defense spending, weapons production, and armed forces. There have been many arms limitation initiatives since 1945, when the United Nations established the International Atomic Energy Commission to develop a plan to eliminate all nuclear weapons. More recent arms-control initiatives have included SALT (Strategic Arms Limitation Treaty), START (Strategic Arms Reduction Treaty), and NPT (Nuclear Nonproliferation Treaty).

Strategic Arms Limitation Treaty Under the 1972 SALT agreement (SALT I), the United States and the Soviet Union agreed to limit both their defensive weapons and their land-based and submarine-based offensive weapons. Also in 1972, Henry Kissinger drafted the Declaration of Principles, known as **detente,** which means "negotiation rather than confrontation." A further arms limitation agreement (SALT II) was negotiated in 1979, but was never ratified by Congress due to the Soviet invasion of Afghanistan. Subsequently, the arms race continued with the development of new technologies and an increase in the number of nuclear warheads.

Strategic Arms Reduction Treaty Strategic arms talks resumed in 1982, but made relatively little progress for several years. During this period, President Reagan proposed the Strategic Defense Initiative (SDI), more commonly known as "Star Wars," which purportedly would be able to block missiles launched by another country against the United States (Brown 1994). Star Wars was controversial for several reasons. Some critics questioned whether it would be effective, while others argued that it would undermine the principle of mutually assured destruction by enabling one side to survive a nuclear war. Although some research was conducted on the system, Star Wars was never actually built.

By 1991, the international situation had changed. The communist regime in the Soviet Union had fallen, the Berlin Wall had been dismantled, and many Eastern European and Baltic countries were under self-rule. SALT was renamed START (Strategic Arms Reduction Treaty) and was signed in 1991. A second START agreement signed in 1993 signaled the end of the Cold War. START II called for the reduction of nuclear warheads to 3,500 by the year 2003, about one-third the level present in the early 1990s (Brown, 1994). Nevertheless, only 500 to 2,000 nuclear warheads are needed to induce a nuclear winter and the destruction of most life on earth (Sagan 1990).

Nuclear Nonproliferation Treaty The Nuclear Nonproliferation Treaty (NPT) was signed by 156 countries in 1970. The agreement held that countries without nuclear weapons would not to try to get them; in exchange, the nuclear-capable countries (the United States, United Kingdom, France, China, and Russia are known to have nuclear weapons; Israel, India, Pakistan, and South Africa are suspected of having them) agreed they would not provide nuclear weapons to countries that did not have them (Brown 1994).

Even if military superpowers honor agreements to limit arms, the availability of black market nuclear weapons information and materials presents a threat to global security. More than 100,000 workers in Russian labs, research institutes, and military facilities have access to hundreds of tons of plutonium and can easily steal samples. Since most of the workers earn less than $1,200 annually, they might be tempted to sell nuclear materials.

> *In my opinion, in the nuclear world the true enemy is war itself.*
> —Denzel Washington acting as Hunter in *Crimson Tide*

Consideration If all nuclear, chemical, and biological weapons were disposed of, conventional weapons could still result in massive human and environmental destruction. For example, an attack by conventional weapons on any of the approximately 466 civil nuclear power plants in twenty-six countries would release radioactive gases over a wide area (Westing 1990). Destroying industrial chemical facilities with conventional weapons could release toxic gases. Conventional weapons can also destroy dams and cause massive and life-threatening floods. In 1938, the Chinese dynamited a dike on the Yellow River to stop the advancing Japanese. In the process, eleven Chinese cities and more than 4,000 villages were flooded; several hundred thousand Chinese drowned and several million were left homeless (Westing 1990). Matousek (1990) *suggests that the damage from a major conventional war could approach the damage that would result from a war in which chemical or nuclear weapons were employed:*

It thus becomes clear that the prevention of nuclear or chemical war no longer suffices for the avoidance of human and environmental catastrophes. Such prevention must now be extended to include all war, in both industrialized and industrializing countries. (Matousek 1990, 36)

UNDERSTANDING
GLOBAL CONFLICT

> *The first victim of war is not truth—it is conscience. Otherwise human beings could not bear the guilt of participating in a savage conflict in which armed force is not a last resort, but a hair trigger.*
> —William Perdue
> Sociologist

As we come to the close of this chapter, how might we have an informed understanding of global conflict? Each of the three theoretical positions discussed in this chapter reflects the realities of war. As functionalists argue, war offers societal benefits—social cohesion, economic prosperity, scientific and technological developments, and social change. Further, as conflict theorists contend, wars often occur for economic reasons as corporate elites and political leaders benefit from the spoils of war—land and water resources and raw materials. The symbolic interactionist perspective emphasizes the role that meanings, labels, and definitions play in creating conflict and contributing to acts of war.

Ultimately, we are all members of one community—earth—and have a vested interest in staying alive and protecting the resources of our environment for our own and future generations. But conflict between groups is a feature of social life and human existence that is not likely to disappear. What is at stake—human lives and the ability of our planet to sustain life—merits serious attention. Traditionally, nations have sought to protect themselves by maintaining large military forces and massive weapons systems. These strategies are associated with serious costs. In diverting resources away from other social concerns, militarism undermines a society's ability to improve the overall security and well-being of its citizens. Conversely, defense spending cutbacks can potentially free up resources for other social agendas, including lowering taxes, reducing the national debt, addressing environmental concerns, eradicating hunger and poverty, improving health care, upgrading educational services, and improving housing and transportation. Therein lies the promise of a "peace dividend."

Hopefully, future dialogue on the problem of global conflict and war will redefine national and international security to encompass social, economic, and environmental concerns. These other concerns play a vital role in the security of nations and the world. The World Commission on Environment and Development (1990) concluded that:

> *The deepening and widening environmental crisis presents a threat to national security—and even survival—that may be greater than well-armed, ill-disposed neighbors and unfriendly alliances. . . . The arms race in all parts of the world—pre-empts resources that might be used more productively to diminish the security threats created by environmental conflict and the resentments that are fueled by widespread poverty. . . . There are no military solutions to environmental insecurity.*

National and global policies aimed at reducing poverty and ensuring the health of our planet and its present and future inhabitants are important aspects of world peace. But as long as we define national and global security in military terms, we will likely ignore the importance of nonmilitary social policies in achieving world peace. According to Funke (1994), changing the definition of national security "is the first step to changing policy" (p. 342).

CRITICAL THINKING

1. Under what conditions, if any, do you believe war is justified?
2. What economic, social, and psychological contexts are conducive to the development of war?
3. What role can the educational institution play in attaining global security?
4. What role do the media play in shaping public opinion and views on military spending and warfare?

KEY TERMS

war	economic conversion	terrorism
state	military-industrial complex	guerrilla warfare
infowar		mutually assured destruction (MAD)
Cold War	post-traumatic stress disorder	detente
peace dividend	nuclear winter	

REFERENCES

Amnesty International. 1995. *Human Rights Are Women's Right.* New York: Amnesty International USA.

Bischak, Gregory A. 1993. "President Clinton's 1993 Conversion Program." In *Real Security: Converting the Defense Economy and Building Peace,* ed. Kevin J. Cassidy and Gregory A. Bischak, pp. 294–98. Albany: State University of New York Press.

Brown, Seyom. 1994. *The Causes and Prevention of War.* New York: St. Martin's Press.

Burleigh, Nina. 1991. "Watching Children Starve to Death." *Time,* June 10, 56–58.

Carneiro, Robert L. 1994. "War and Peace: Alternating Realities in Human History." In *Studying War: Anthropological Perspectives,* ed. S. P. Reyna and R. E. Downs, pp. 3–27. Langhorne, Pa.: Gordon & Breach Science Publishers.

Center for Defense Information. 1995. *The Defense Monitor* (September/October). Washington, D.C.

Cohen, Ronald. 1986. "War and Peace Proness in Pre- and Postindustrial States." In *Peace and War: Cross-Cultural Perspectives,* ed. M. L. Foster and R. A. Rubinstein, pp. 253–67. New Brunswick, N.J.: Transaction Books.

Dixon, William J. 1994. "Democracy and the Peaceful Settlement of International Conflict." *American Political Science Review* 88(1): 14–32.

Doyle, Michael. 1986. "Liberalism and World Politics." *American Political Science Review* 80 (December): 1151–69.

Enders, Walter, and Todd Sandler. 1993. "The Effectiveness of Anti-Terrorism Policies: A Vector-Autoregression-Intervention Analysis." *American Political Science Review* 87(4): 829–44.

Fedarko, Kevin. 1995. "Louder than Words." *Time,* September 11, 50–59.

Filipovic, Zlata. 1994. *Zlata's Diary: A Child's Life in Sarejevo.* New York: Viking Penguin Books.

Funke, Odelia. 1994. "National Security and the Environment." In *Environmental Policy in the 1990s: Toward a New Agenda,* 2d ed., ed. Norman J. Vig and Michael E. Kraft, pp. 323–45. Washington, D.C.: Congressional Quarterly, Inc.

Galbraith, John Kenneth. 1994. "Autonomous Military Power: An Economic View." In *The Economics of International Security,* ed. Manas Chatterji, Henk Jager, and Annemarie Rima, pp. 9–13. New York: St. Martin's Press.

Gibbs, Nancy. 1994. "Cry the Forsaken Country." *Time,* August 1, 27–37.

Gioseffi, Daniela. 1993. "Introduction." In *On Prejudice: A Global Perspective,* ed. Daniela Gioseffi, pp. xi–1. New York: Anchor Books, Doubleday.

Hayman, Peter, and Douglas Scaturo. 1993. "Psychological Debriefing of Returning Military Personnel: A Protocol for Post-Combat Intervention." *Journal of Social Behavior and Personality* 8(5): 117–30.

Hooks, Gregory, and Leonard E. Bloomquist. 1992. "The Legacy of World War II for Regional Growth and Decline: The Effects of Wartime Investments on U.S. Manufacturing, 1947–72." *Social Forces* 71(2): 303–37.

Hoskins, Eric. 1993. "The First Casualties of War." *New Statesman and Society* (January 29): 16–17.

Jervis, Robert. 1994. "Arms Control, Stability, and Causes of War." *Political Science Quarterly* 108: 239–53.

Kennedy, Paul. 1987. *The Rise and Fall of the Great Powers.* New York: Vintage Books.

Klein, Lawrence R. 1994. "Development and Disarmament: The Meaning." In *The Economics of International Security,* ed. Manas Chatterji, Henk Jager, and Annemarie Rima, pp. 14–19. New York: St. Martin's Press.

Klingman, Avigdor, and Zehava Goldstein. 1994. "Adolescents' Response to Unconventional War Threat Prior to the Gulf War." *Death Studies* 18: 75–82.

Laird, Bob. 1994. "Another Pearl Harbor?" *USA Today,* December 7, 1.

Lewis, Bernard. 1990. "The Roots of Islamic Rage." *The Atlantic* (September): 47–60.

Matousek, Jiri. 1990. "The Release in War of Dangerous Forces from Chemical Facilities." In *Environmental Hazards of War,* ed. Arthur H. Westing, pp. 30–37. Newbury Park, Calif.: Sage Publications.

Militia Task Force. 1995. "Emergency Update of Militia Terrorists." The Southern Poverty Law Center, 400 Washington Avenue, Montgomery, AL 36104.

Miller, Susan. 1993. "A Human Horror Story." *Newsweek,* December 27, 17.

Moaddel, Mansoor. 1994. "Political Conflict in the World Economy: A Cross-National Analysis of Modernization and World-System Theories." *American Sociological Review* 59: (April): 276–303.

Nelan, Bruce. 1994. "Formula for Terror." *Time*, August 29, 46–51.

O'Prey, Kevin P. 1995. *The Arms Export Challenge: Cooperative Approaches to Export Management and Defense Conversion.* Washington, D.C.: The Brookings Institute.

Peace Garden. 1995. "Hear & Now: News and Musings of Interest." *Teaching Tolerance*, Spring: 6.

Perdue, William Dan. 1993. *Systemic Crisis: Problems in Society, Politics and World Order.* Fort Worth, Tex.: Harcourt Brace Jovanovich.

Porter, Bruce D. 1994. *War and the Rise of the State: The Military Foundations of Modern Politics.* New York: Free Press.

Ramsey, Russell W. 1993. "World Systems, Challenges: 1993–2025." *The Officer* (April). Washington, D.C.: Reserve Officers Association of the United States.

Renner, Michael. 1993a. "National Insecurity." In *Systematic Crisis: Problems in Society, Politics and World Order,* ed. William D. Perdue, pp. 136–41. Fort Worth, Tex.: Harcourt Brace Jovanovich.

Renner, Michael. 1993b. *Critical Juncture: The Future of Peacekeeping.* Washington D.C.: Worldwatch Institute.

_____ . 1993c. "Environmental Dimensions of Disarmament and Conversion." In *Real Security: Converting the Defense Economy and Building Peace,* ed. Kevin J. Cassidy and Gregory A. Bischak, pp. 88–132. Albany: State University of New York Press.

Sagan, Carl. 1990. "Nuclear War and Climatic Catastrophe: Some Policy Implications." In *Readings on Social Problems,* ed. William Feigelman, pp. 374–88. Fort Worth, Tex.: Holt, Rinehart & Winston.

Sandler, Todd, and Keith Hartley. 1995. *The Economics of Defense.* New York: Cambridge University Press.

Schafer, Todd, and Paul Hyland. 1994. "Technology Policy in the Post–Cold War World." *Journal of Economic Issues* 28(2): 597–608.

Scheff, Thomas. 1994. *Bloody Revenge.* Boulder, Colo.: Westview Press.

Shanahan, John J. 1995. "Director's Letter." *The Defense Monitor.* Center for Defense Information, Washington, D.C. Volume XXIV, Number 6:8.

Starr, J. R., and D. C. Stoll. 1989. "U.S. Foreign Policy on Water Resources in the Middle East." Washington, D.C.: The Center for Strategic and International Studies.

Statistical Abstract of the United States: 1993, 113th ed. U.S. Bureau of the Census. Washington, D.C.: U.S. Government Printing Office.

Statistical Abstract of the United States: 1995, 115th ed. U.S. Bureau of the Census. Washington, D.C.: U.S. Government Printing Office.

Sutker, Patricia B., Madeline Uddo, Kevin Brailey, and Albert N. Allain, Jr. 1993. "War- zone Trauma and Stress-related Symptoms in Operation Desert Shield/Storm (ODS) Returnees." *Journal of Social Issues* 49(4): 33–50.

Taylor, Lori L. 1993. "Estimating Regional Sensitivities to Defense Purchases." In *Defense Spending and Economic Growth,* ed. James E. Payne and Anandi P. Sahu, pp. 203–20. Boulder, Colo.: Westview Press.

Terhal, Piet H. J. J. 1994. "Comprehensive Global Security: A Copernican Reversal." In *The Economics of International Security,* ed. by Manas Chatterji, Henk Jager and Annemarie Rima, pp. 106–17. New York: St. Martin's Press.

Van Evera, Stephen. 1994. "Hypotheses on Nationalism and War." *International Security* 18(4): 5–39.

Von Glahn, Gerhard. 1970. *Law among Nations.* New York: Macmillian.

Waller, Douglas. 1995. "Onward Cyber Soldiers." *Time,* August 21, 38–44.

Westing, Arthur H. 1990. "Environmental Hazards of War in an Industrializing World." In *Environmental Hazards of War,* ed. Arthur H. Westing, pp. 1–9. Newbury Park, Calif.: Sage Publications.

World Commission on Environment and Development (Brundtland Commission). 1990. *Our Common Future.* New York: Oxford University Press.

Epilogue

Today, there is a crisis—a crisis of faith: faith in the ideals of equality and freedom, faith in political leadership, faith in the American dream, and, ultimately, faith in the inherent goodness of humankind and the power of one individual to make a difference. To some extent, faith is shaken by texts such as this one. Crimes are up; marriages are down; political corruption is everywhere; bigotry's on the rise; the environment is killing us—if we don't kill it first. Social problems are everywhere, and what's worse, many solutions only seem to create more problems.

The transformation of American society in recent years has been dramatic. With the exception of the Industrial Revolution, no other period in human history has seen such rapid social change. The structure of society, forever altered by such macrosociological processes as multinationalization, deindustrialization, and globalization, continues to be characterized by social inequities—in our schools, in our homes, in our cities, and in our salaries.

The culture of society has also undergone rapid change, leading many politicians and lay persons alike to call for a return to traditional values and beliefs and to emphasize the need for moral education. The implication is that somehow things were better in the "good old days," and if we could somehow return to those times, things would be better again. Some things were better—for some people.

Fifty years ago, there were fewer divorces and less crime. AIDS and crack cocaine were unheard of, and violence in schools was almost nonexistent. At the same time, however, in 1950, the infant mortality rate was over three times what it is today; racial and ethnic discrimination flourished in an atmosphere of bigotry and hate, and millions of Americans were routinely denied the right to vote because of the color of their skin; more than half of all Americans smoked cigarettes; and persons over the age of twenty-five had completed a median of 6.8 years of school.

The social problems of today are the cumulative result of structural and cultural alterations over time. Today's problems are not necessarily better or worse than those of generations ago—they are different and, perhaps, more diverse as a result of the increased complexity of social life. But, as surely as we brought the infant mortality rate down, prohibited racial discrimination in education, housing, and employment, increased educational levels, and reduced the number of smokers, we can continue to meet the challenges of today's social problems. But how does positive social change occur? How does one alter something as amorphous as society? The answer is really quite simple. All social change takes place because of the acts of individuals. Every law, every regulation and policy, every social movement and media exposé, and every court decision began with one person.

A human being is part of the whole . . . He experiences himself, his thoughts and feelings, as something separate from the rest, a kind of optical delusion of his consciousness. This delusion is a kind of prison for us, restricting us to our personal desires and to affection for a few persons nearest to us. Our task must be to free ourselves from this prison by widening our circle of compassion to embrace all living creatures.
—Albert Einstein
Scientist

Never doubt that a small group of thoughtful, committed citizens can change the world. Indeed, it's the only thing that ever has.
—Margaret Mead
Anthropologist

Sociologist Earl Babbie (1994) recounts how the behavior of one person—Rosa Parks—made a difference. Rosa Parks was a seamstress in Montgomery, Alabama, in the 1950s. Like almost everything else in the South in the 1950s, public transportation was racially segregated. On December 1, 1955, Rosa Parks was on her way home from work when the "white section" of the bus she was riding became full. The bus driver told black passengers in the first row of the black section to relinquish their seats to the standing white passengers. Rosa Parks refused.

She was arrested and put in jail, but her treatment so outraged the black community that a boycott of the bus system was organized by a new minister in town—Martin Luther King, Jr. The Montgomery bus boycott was a success. Just eleven months later, in November of 1956, the U.S. Supreme Court ruled that racial segregation of public facilities was unconstitutional. Rosa Parks had begun a process that in time would echo her actions—the civil rights movement, the March on Washington, the 1963 Equal Pay Act, the 1964 Civil Rights Act, the 1965 Voting Rights Act, regulations against discrimination in housing, and affirmative action.

Was social change accomplished? In 1960, the median school years completed by black and white Americans differed by nearly three years; by 1991, that difference was less than one. While many would point out that such changes and thousands like them have created other problems that need to be addressed, who among us would want to return to the "good old days" of the 1950s in Montgomery, Alabama?

Millions of individuals make a difference daily. Chuck Beattie and Bret Byfield, two social workers in Minneapolis, began Phoenix Group in 1991. Purchasing houses with a few grants and some private donations, they hired "street people" to renovate the homes and then let them move in. Today, Phoenix Group has more than thirty-nine properties, 300 residents, and eleven businesses. Susan Brotchie, deserted by her husband and unable to get child support, began Advocates for Better Child Support, which has helped more than 9,000 people establish and collect child support payments. Pedro José Greer was an intern in Miami when he treated his first homeless patient. Appalled by the fatal incidence of tuberculosis, a curable disease, Dr. Greer opened a medical clinic in a homeless shelter. Today, he heads the largest provider of medical care for the poor in Florida—Camillus Health Concern—annually serving over 4,500 patients (Chinni et al. 1995, 34). After suffering chronic illness from exposure to air pollutants from a sewage plant and home renovation materials, Mary Lamielle founded the National Center for Environmental Health Strategies (NCEHS), a national nonprofit organization dedicated to the development of creative solutions to environmental health problems (Lamielle 1995). Through her work as director of the NCEHS, Lamielle has influenced policy development and research and has provided support and advocacy to sufferers of environmental pollution.

College students have also worked to bring about social change. According to Paul Loeb (1995), college students have prompted the adoption of multicultural curriculums, helped the homeless, and made their schools more environmentally accountable. College students also influenced universities to rid themselves of South African investments and played an important role in building the international movement that helped end apartheid.

While only a fraction of the readers of this text will occupy social roles that directly influence social policy, one need not be a politician or member of a social reform group to make a difference. We, the authors of this text, challenge you, the reader, to make individual decisions and take individual actions to make the world a more humane, just, and peaceful place for all. Where should we begin? Where Rosa Parks and others like her began—with a simple individual act of courage, commitment, and faith.

REFERENCES

Babbie, Earl. 1994. *The Sociological Spirit: Critical Essays in a Critical Science.* Belmont, Calif.: Wadsworth.

Chinni, Dante, Marc Peyser, John Leland, Annetta Miller, Tom Morganthau, Peter Annin, and Pat Wingert. 1995. "Everyday Heroes." *Newsweek,* May 29, 26–39.

Lamielle, Mary. 1995. Personal communication. National Center for Environmental Health Strategies. 1100 Rural Avenue, Voorhees, NJ 08043.

Loeb, Paul Rogat. 1995. "The Choice to Care." *Teaching Tolerance,* Spring, 38–43.

Appendix A:
Methods of Data Analysis

There are three levels of data analysis: description, correlation, and causation. Data analysis also involves assessing reliability and validity.

Description

Qualitative research involves verbal descriptions of social phenomena. Having a homeless and single pregnant teenager describe her situation is an example of qualitative research.

Quantitative research often involves numerical descriptions of social phenomena. Quantitative descriptive analysis may involve computing the following: (1) means (averages), (2) frequencies, (3) mode (the most frequently occurring observation in the data), (4) median (the middle point in the data; half of the data points are above, and half are below the median), and (5) range (the highest and lowest values in a set of data).

Correlation

Researchers are often interested in the relationship between variables. *Correlation* refers to a relationship among two or more variables. The following are examples of correlational research questions: What is the relationship between poverty and educational achievement? What is the relationship between race and crime victimization? What is the relationship between religious affiliation and divorce?

If there is a correlation or relationship between two variables, then a change in one variable is associated with a change in the other variable. When both variables change in the same direction, the correlation is positive. For example, in general, the more sexual partners a person has, the greater the risk of contracting a sexually transmissible disease. As variable A (number of sexual partners) increases, variable B (chance of contracting an STD) also increases. Similarly, as the number of sexual partners decreases, the chance of contracting an STD decreases. Notice that in both cases, the variables change in the same direction, suggesting a positive correlation (see Figure A.1).

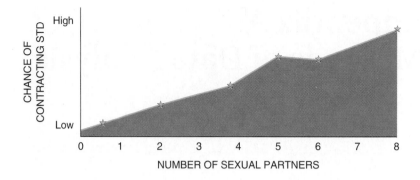

When two variables change in opposite directions, the correlation is negative. For example, there is a negative correlation between condom use and contracting STDs. In other words, as condom use increases, the chance of contracting an STD decreases (see Figure A.2).

The relationship between two variables may also be curvilinear, which means that they vary in both the same and opposite directions. For example, suppose a researcher finds that after drinking one alcoholic beverage, research participants are more prone to violent behavior. After two drinks, violent behavior is even more likely, and this trend continues for three and four drinks. So far, the correlation between alcohol consumption and violent behavior is positive. After the research participants have five alcoholic drinks, however, they become less prone to violent behavior. After six and seven drinks, the likelihood of engaging in violent behavior decreases further. Now the correlation between alcohol consumption and violent behavior is negative. Because the correlation changed from positive to negative, we say that the correlation is curvilinear (the correlation may also change from negative to positive) (see Figure A.3)

A fourth type of correlation is called a spurious correlation. Such a correlation exists when two variables appear to be related, but the apparent relationship occurs only because they are both related to a third variable. When the third variable is controlled through a statistical method in which the variable is held constant, the apparent relationship between the variables disappears. For example, blacks have a lower average life expectancy than whites do. Thus, race and life expectancy appear to be related. However, this apparent correlation exists because both race and life expectancy are related to socioeconomic

FIGURE A.2
NEGATIVE CORRELATION

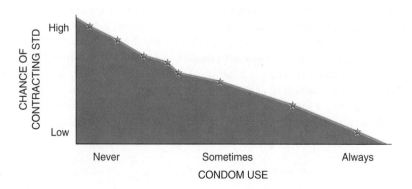

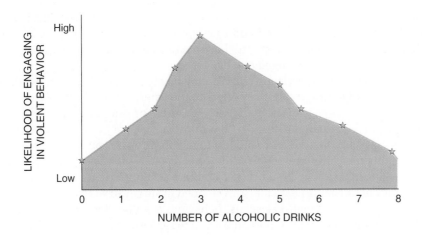

FIGURE A.3
CURVILINEAR CORRELATION

status. Since blacks are more likely than whites to be impoverished, they are less likely to have adequate nutrition and medical care.

Causation

If the data analysis reveals that two variables are correlated, we know only that a change in one variable is associated with a change in another variable. We cannot assume, however, that a change in one variable *causes* a change in the other variable unless our data collection and analysis are specifically designed to assess causation. The research method that best assesses causality is the experimental method (discussed in Chapter 1).

To demonstrate causality, three conditions must be met. First, the data analysis must demonstrate that variable A is correlated with variable B. Second, the data analysis must demonstrate that the observed correlation is not spurious. Third, the analysis must demonstrate that the presumed cause (variable A) occurs or changes prior to the presumed effect (variable B). In other words, the cause must precede the effect.

It is extremely difficult to establish causality in social science research. Therefore, much social science research is descriptive or correlative, rather than causative. Nevertheless, many people make the mistake of interpreting a correlation as a statement of causation. As you read correlative research findings, remember the following adage: "Correlation *does not* equal causation."

Reliability and Validity

Assessing reliability and validity is an important aspect of data analysis. *Reliability* refers to the consistency of the measuring instrument or technique; that is, the degree to which the way information is obtained produces the same results if repeated. Measures of reliability are made on scales and indexes (such as those in the *Self-Assessments* in this text) and on information-gathering techniques, such as the survey methods described in Chapter 1.

Various statistical methods are used to determine reliability. A frequently used method is called the "test-retest method." The researcher gathers data on the same sample of people twice (usually one or two weeks apart) using a particular instrument or method and then correlates the results. To the degree that the results of the two tests are the same (or highly correlated), the instrument or method is considered reliable.

Measures that are perfectly reliable may be absolutely useless unless they also have a high validity. *Validity* refers to the extent to which an instrument or device measures what it intends to measure. For example, police officers administer "breathalyzer" tests to determine the level of alcohol in a person's system. The breathalyzer is a valid test for alcohol consumption.

Validity measures are important in research that uses scales or indices as measuring instruments. Validity measures are also important in assessing the accuracy of self-report data that are obtained in survey research. For example, survey research on high-risk sexual behaviors associated with the spread of HIV relies heavily on self-report data on such topics as number of sexual partners, types of sexual activities, and condom use. Yet, how valid are these data? Do survey respondents underreport the number of their sexual partners? Do people who say they use a condom every time they engage in intercourse really use a condom every time? Because of the difficulties in validating self-reports of number of sexual partners and condom use, we may not be able to answer these questions.

Ethical Guidelines in Social Problems Research

Social scientists are responsible for following ethical standards designed to protect the dignity and welfare of people who participate in research. These ethical guidelines include the following (Nachmias and Nachmias 1987; American Sociological Association 1984; Committee for the Protection of Human Participants in Research 1982):

1. *Freedom from coercion to participate.* Research participants have the right to decline to participate in a research study or to discontinue participation at any time during the study. For example, professors who are conducting research using college students should not require their students to participate in their research.

2. *Informed consent.* Researchers are required to inform participants "of all aspects of the research that might reasonably be expected to influence willingness to participate" (Committee for the Protection of Human Participants in Research 1982, 32). After informing potential participants about the nature of the research, researchers typically ask participants to sign a consent form indicating that the participants are informed about the research and agree to participate in it.

3. *Deception and debriefing.* Sometimes the researcher must disguise the purpose of the research in order to obtain valid data. Researchers may deceive participants as to the purpose or nature of a study only if there is no other way to study the problem. When deceit is used, participants should be informed of this deception (debriefed) as soon as possible. Participants should be given a complete and honest description of the study and why deception was necessary.

4. *Protection from harm.* Researchers must protect participants from any physical and psychological harm that might result from participating in a research study. This is both a moral and a legal obligation. It would not be ethical, for example, for a researcher studying drinking and driving behavior to observe an intoxicated individual leaving a bar, getting into the driver's seat of a car, and driving away.

   Researchers are also obligated to respect the privacy rights of research participants. If anonymity is promised, it should be kept. Anonymity is maintained in mail surveys by identifying questionnaires with a number coding system, rather than with the participants' names. When such anonymity is not possible, as is the case with face-to-face interviews, researchers should tell participants that the information they provide will be treated as confidential. Although interviews may be summarized and excerpts quoted in published material, the identity of the individual participants is not revealed. If a research participant experiences either physical or psychological harm as a result of participation in a research study, the researcher is ethically obligated to provide remediation for the harm.

5. *Reporting of research.* Ethical guidelines also govern the reporting of research results. Researchers must make research reports freely available to the public. In these reports, researchers should fully describe all evidence obtained in the study, regardless of whether the evidence supports the researcher's hypothesis. The raw data collected by the researcher should be made available to other researchers who might request it for purposes of analysis. Finally, published research reports should include a description of the sponsorship of the research study, its purpose, and all sources of financial support.

REFERENCES

American Sociological Association. 1984. *Code of Ethics.* Washington, D.C.: Author.

Committee for the Protection of Human Participants in Research. 1982. *Ethical Principles in the Conduct of Research with Human Participants.* Washington, D.C.: American Psychological Association.

Nachmias, David and Chava Nachmias. 1987. *Research Methods in the Social Sciences.* 3rd ed., New York: St. Martin's Press.

Glossary

abortion The removal of an embryo or fetus from a woman's uterus.

absolute poverty The chronic absence of the basic necessities of life including food, clothing, and shelter.

achieved status A status assigned on the basis of some characteristic or behavior over which the individual has some control.

acquaintance rape Rape that is committed by someone known by the victim.

activity theory A theory that emphasizes that the elderly disengage, in part, because they are structurally segregated and isolated with few opportunities to engage in active roles.

affirmative action A series of programs based on the 1964 Civil Rights Act that provide opportunities or other benefits to persons on the basis of their group membership (e.g., race, gender, ethnicity).

age grading The assignment of social roles to given chronological ages.

age pyramid A graph-like presentation that shows the percentage of a population in various age groups.

ageism The belief that age is associated with certain psychological, behavioral, and/or intellectual traits.

alienation The concept used by Karl Marx to describe the condition when workers feel powerless and meaningless as a result of performing repetitive, isolated work tasks. Alienation involves becoming estranged from one's work, the products one creates, other human beings, and/or one's self; also refers to powerlessness and meaninglessness experienced by students in traditional, restrictive educational institutions.

alternative certification programs Programs that permit college graduates, without education degrees, to be certified to teach based on job and/or life experiences.

amalgamation The physical blending of different racial and/or ethnic groups resulting in a new and distinct genetic and cultural population; results from the intermarriage of racial and ethnic groups over generations.

anomie A state of normlessness in which norms and values are weak or unclear; results from rapid social change and is linked to many social problems including crime, drug addiction, and violence.

antabuse A prescribed medication used in the treatment of alcoholism; produces severe nausea when combined with alcohol consumption.

ascribed status A status that society assigns to an individual on the basis of factors over which the individual has no control.

assimilation The process by which minority groups gradually adopt the cultural patterns of the dominant majority group.

automation A type of technology in which self-operated machines accomplish tasks formerly done by workers; develops as a society moves toward industrialization and becomes more concerned with the mass production of goods.

beliefs Definitions and explanations about what is assumed to be true.

bilingual education Educational instruction provided in two languages—the student's native language and another language. In the United States, bilingual education involves teaching individuals in both English and their non-English native language.

biodiversity The variability of living organisms on earth.

bisexuality A sexual orientation that involves cognitive, emotional, and sexual attraction to members of both sexes.

Brady Bill A law that requires a five-day waiting period for handgun purchases so that sellers can screen buyers for criminal records or mental instability.

capitalism An economic system in which private individuals or groups invest capital to produce goods and services, for a profit, in a competitive market.

chemical dependency A condition in which drug use is compulsive, and users are unable to stop because of physical and/or psychological dependency.

child abuse The physical or mental injury, sexual abuse, negligent treatment, or maltreatment of a child under the age of eighteen by a person who is responsible for the child's welfare.

Cold War The state of political tension and military rivalry that existed between the United States and the former Soviet Union from the 1950s through the late 1980s.

colonialism When a racial and/or ethnic group from one society takes over and dominates the racial and/or ethnic group(s) of another society.

coming out Short for "coming out of the closet"; the process in which a person recognizes her or his homosexuality and discloses it to others.

community policing A type of policing in which uniformed police officers patrol and are responsible for certain areas of the city as opposed to simply responding to crimes as they occur.

computer crime Any violation of the law in which a computer is the target or means of criminal activity.

conflict perspective A sociological perspective that views society as comprised of different groups and interests competing for power and resources.

control theory A theory that argues that a strong social bond between a person and society constrains some individuals from violating norms.

convergence hypothesis The argument that capitalist countries will adopt elements of socialism and socialist countries will adopt elements of capitalism; i.e., they will converge.

cooperative learning Learning in which a heterogeneous group of students, of varying abilities, help one another with either individual or group assignments.

crime An act or the omission of an act that is a violation of a federal, state, or local law and for which the state can apply sanctions.

cultural lag A condition in which the material part of the culture changes at a faster rate than the nonmaterial part.

cultural sexism The ways in which the culture of society perpetuates the subordination of individuals based on their sex classification.

cybernation The use of machines that control other machines in the production process; characteristic of postindustrial societies that emphasize service and information professions.

de facto segregation Segregation that is not required by law, but exists "in fact," often as a result of housing and socioeconomic patterns.

de jure segregation Segregation that is required by law.

deconcentration The redistribution of the population from cities to suburbs and surrounding areas.

decriminalization The removal of criminal penalties for a behavior, as in the decriminalization of drug use.

defensible space A neighborhood that is structurally arranged in such a way as to prevent or reduce crime (e.g., adding speed bumps to roads, dividing larger neighborhoods into smaller ones to facilitate community bonding, and closing off selected streets to deter "cruising").

defensive medicine A practice in which health care providers use tests and/or treatments that may be unnecessary in order to guard against malpractice suits; this practice contributes to the high cost of medical care.

deforestation The destruction of the earth's rain forests.

deindustrialization The loss and/or relocation of manufacturing industries.

demographic transition theory A theory that attributes population growth patterns to changes in birth and death rates associated with the process of industrialization. In preindustrial societies, the population remains stable because, although the birth rate is high, the death rate is also high. As a society becomes industrialized, the birth rate remains high, but the death rate declines, causing rapid population growth. In societies with advanced industrialization, the birth rate declines, and this decline, in conjunction with the low death rate, slows population growth.

demography The study of the size, distribution, movement, and composition of human populations.

dependent variable The variable that the researcher wants to explain. See also *independent variable*.

deregulation The reduction of government control of, for example, certain drugs.

desertification The expansion of deserts and the loss of usable land due to the overuse of semi-arid land on the desert margins for animal grazing and obtaining firewood.

deskilling The tendency for workers in a postindustrial society to make fewer decisions and for labor to require less thought.

detente The philosophy of "negotiation rather than confrontation" in reference to relations between the United States and the former Soviet Union; put forth by Henry Kissinger's Declaration of Principles in 1972.

deterrence The use of harm or the threat of harm to prevent unwanted behaviors.

differential association A theory developed by Edwin Sutherland that holds that through interaction with others individuals learn the values, attitudes, techniques, and motives for criminal behavior.

discrimination Differential treatment of individuals based on their group membership.

discriminatory unemployment High unemployment rates among particular social groups such as racial and ethnic minorities and women.

disengagement theory A theory claiming that the elderly disengage from productive social roles in order to relinquish these roles to younger members of society. As this process continues, each new group moves up and replaces another, which, according to disengagement theory, benefits society and all of its members.

diversity training Workplace training programs designed to increase employees' awareness of cultural differences in the workplace and how these differences may affect job performance.

divorce mediation A process in which divorcing couples meet with a neutral third party (mediator) who assists the individuals in resolving such issues as property division, child custody, child support, and spousal support in a way that minimizes conflict and encourages cooperation.

domestic partnership A status that grants legal entitlements such as health insurance benefits and inheritance rights to heterosexual cohabiting couples and homosexual couples.

double jeopardy See *multiple jeopardy*.

doubling time The time it takes for a population to double in size from any base year.

drug abuse The violation of social standards of acceptable drug use resulting in adverse physiological, psychological, and/or social consequences.

economic conversion The reallocation of resources from military forces and defense industries to other sectors of the economy.

endogamy The social norm that influences people to marry within their social group and discourages interracial and interethnic marriages.

enterprise zones Low-income urban areas in which businesses receive tax incentives for locating there with the stipulation that they must hire a certain proportion of local employees. Enterprise zones stimulate the local economy, create jobs for the unemployed, and increase city revenues.

equity principle The belief that those who have more resources in society deserve them because of their greater contributions to society.

ethnicity A shared cultural heritage.

experiment A research method that involves manipulating the independent variable in order to determine how it affects the dependent variable.

familism A value system that encourages family members to put their family's well-being above their individual and personal needs.

family As defined by the U.S. Census Bureau, a group of two or more persons related by birth, marriage, or adoption who reside together. Some family scholars have redefined the family to include nonrelated persons who reside together and who are economically, emotionally, and sexually interdependent (e.g., cohabiting heterosexual or homosexual couples).

feminization of poverty The tendency for women to be poorer than men.

field research A method of research that involves observing and studying social behavior in settings in which it naturally occurs; includes participant observation and nonparticipant observation.

flextime An option in work scheduling that allows employees to begin and end the workday at different times as long as they perform forty hours of work per week.

future shock The state of confusion resulting from rapid scientific and technological changes that challenge traditional values and beliefs.

gateway drug A drug (e.g., marijuana) that is believed to lead to the use of other drugs (such as cocaine and heroin).

gender The social definitions and expectations associated with being male or female.

gene therapy The transplantation of a healthy duplicate gene to replace a defective or missing gene.

genetic engineering The manipulation of an organism's genes in such a way that the natural outcome is altered.

genetic screening The use of genetic maps to detect predispositions to human traits or disease(s).

genocide The systematic annihilation of one racial and/or ethnic group by another.

gentrification The process by which private individuals and/or developers purchase and renovate housing in older neighborhoods; also called "neighborhood revitalization."

gerontophobia Fear or dread of the elderly.

glass ceiling An invisible, socially created barrier that prevents some women and other minorities from being promoted into top corporate positions.

global economy An interconnected network of economic activity that transcends national borders.

greenhouse effect The collection of increasing amounts of chlorofluorocarbons (CFCs), carbon dioxide, methane, and other gases in the atmosphere where they act like the glass in a greenhouse, holding heat from the sun close to the earth and preventing the heat from rising back into space. The greenhouse effect threatens to raise the temperature of the globe by as much as 9.9 degrees Fahrenheit by the year 2040; the resulting heat and drought would cause crop failures, accelerate the extinction of numerous species, and lead to the death of various plants and trees.

guaranteed annual income A guarantee by the government that a poor person's income will not fall below a specified percentage of the country's median income.

guerrilla warfare Warfare in which organized groups oppose domestic or foreign governments and their military forces; often involves small groups of individuals who use camouflage and underground tunnels to hide until they are ready to execute a surprise attack.

hate crimes Acts of violence motivated by prejudice against different racial, ethnic, religious, gender, or sexual orientation groups.

health maintenance organizations (HMOs) Health care organizations that provide complete medical services for a monthly fee.

heterosexism The belief that heterosexuality is the superior sexual orientation; results in prejudice and discrimination against homosexuals and bisexuals.

heterosexuality The predominance of cognitive, emotional, and sexual attraction to persons of the opposite sex.

home schooling The education of children at home instead of in a public or private school; often part of a fundamentalist movement to protect children from perceived non-Christian values in the public schools.

homophobia Negative attitudes toward homosexuality.

homosexuality The predominance of cognitive, emotional, and sexual attraction to persons of the same sex.

household All persons who share occupancy of a housing unit such as a house or an apartment.

human ecology The study of the relationship between populations and their natural environment.

hypothesis A prediction or educated guess about how one variable is related to another variable.

in-vitro fertilization (IVF) The union of an egg and a sperm in an artificial setting such as a laboratory dish.

incapacitation A criminal justice philosophy that views the primary purpose of the criminal justice system as preventing criminal offenders from committing further crimes against the public by putting them in prison.

independent variable The variable that is expected to explain change in the dependent variable.

index offenses Crimes identified by the FBI as the most serious including personal crimes (homicide, rape, robbery, assault) and property crimes (burglary, larceny, car theft, arson).

individual discrimination Discriminatory acts by individuals that are based on prejudicial attitudes.

individualism A value system that stresses the importance of individual happiness. Individualism is viewed as contributing to the divorce rate as spouses leave their marriages to pursue individual goals.

Industrial Revolution The period between the mid-eighteenth and the early nineteenth century when machines and factories became the primary means for producing goods. The Industrial Revolution led to profound social and economic changes.

infant mortality rate The number of deaths of infants under one year of age per 1,000 live births in a calendar year.

infantilizing elders The portrayal of the elderly in the media as childlike in terms of clothes, facial expression, temperament, and activities.

infotech An abbreviation for "information technology"; any technology that carries information.

infowar The utilization of technology to manipulate or attack an enemy's military and civilian infrastructure and information systems.

institution An established and enduring pattern of social relationships. The five traditional social institutions are family, religion, politics, economics, and education. Institutions are the largest elements of social structure.

institutional discrimination Discrimination in which the normal operations and procedures of social institutions result in unequal treatment of minorities.

integration hypothesis A theory that states that the only way to achieve quality education for all racial and ethnic groups is to desegregate the schools.

Internet An international information infrastructure available through many universities, research institutes, government agencies, and businesses; developed in the 1970s as a Defense Department experiment.

job sharing A work option in which two people, often husband and wife, share and are paid for one job.

labeling theory A symbolic interactionist theory that is concerned with the effects of labeling on the definition of a social problem (i.e., a social condition or group is viewed as problematic if it is labeled as such) and with the effects of labeling on the self-concept and behavior of individuals (e.g., the label "juvenile delinquent" may contribute to the development of a self-concept and behavior consistent with the label).

latent functions Consequences that are unintended and often hidden, or unrecognized; e.g., a latent function of education is to provide schools that function as baby-sitters for employed parents.

legalization Making prohibited behavior legal; e.g., legalizing marijuana or prostitution.

lesbian A female homosexual.

life chances A term used by Max Weber to describe the opportunity to obtain all that is valued in society including happiness, health, income, and education.

life expectancy The average number of years that a person born in a given year can expect to live.

lifestyle A distinct subculture associated with a particular social class.

MADD Mothers Against Drunk Driving. A social action group committed to reducing drunk driving.

Malthusian theory Thomas Malthus's theory that states that populations are growing faster than the food supply. Malthus predicted that masses of people were destined to be hungry, and that food shortages would lead to war, disease, and starvation that would eventually slow population growth.

manifest functions Consequences that are intended and commonly recognized; e.g., a manifest function of education is to transmit knowledge and skills to youth.

maternal mortality Deaths that result from complications associated with pregnancy or childbirth.

mechanization The use of tools to accomplish tasks previously done by workers; characteristic of agricultural societies that emphasize the production of raw materials.

Medicaid A jointly funded federal-state-local assistance program designed to provide health care for the poor.

medical-industrial complex Physicians and other health care providers, corporations that provide health goods and services, and insurance companies acting in concert with one another to maximize profits.

medicalization The tendency to define negatively evaluated behaviors and/or conditions as medical problems in need of medical intervention.

Medicare A national public insurance program created by Title XVIII of the Social Security Act of 1965; originally designed to protect people sixty-five years of age and older from the rising costs of health care. In 1972, Medicare was extended to permanently disabled workers and their dependents and persons with end-stage renal disease.

Medigap The difference between Medicare benefits and the actual cost of medical care.

mental disorder A behavioral or psychological syndrome or pattern that occurs in an individual, and that is associated with present distress or disability, or with a significantly increased risk of suffering, death, pain, disability, or loss of freedom.

metropolis From the Greek meaning "Mother City." See also *metropolitan area.*

metropolitan area A central core area containing a large population and any adjacent communities that have a high degree of social and economic integration with the core; a large city and its surrounding suburbs; also called a "metropolis."

micro-society school A simulation of the "real" or nonschool world where students design and run their own democratic, free-market society within the school.

military-industrial complex A term used by Dwight D. Eisenhower to connote the close association between the military and defense industries.

minority A category of people who are denied equal access to positions of power, prestige, and wealth because of their group membership.

modernization theory A theory claiming that as society becomes more technologically advanced, the position of the elderly declines.

morbidity The amount of disease, impairment, and accidents in a population.

multicultural education Education that includes all racial and ethnic groups in the school curriculum and promotes awareness and appreciation for cultural diversity.

multiculturalism A philosophy that argues that the culture of a society should represent and embrace all racial and ethnic groups in that society.

multiple jeopardy The disadvantages associated with being a member of two or more minority groups.

mutually assured destruction (MAD) A perspective that argues that if both sides in a conflict were to lose in a war, neither would initiate war.

neglect A form of abuse involving the failure to provide adequate attention, supervision, nutrition, hygiene, health care, and a safe and clean living environment for a minor child or a dependent elderly individual.

new ageism The belief that the elderly are a burden on the economy and, specifically, on the youth of America.

no-fault divorce A divorce that is granted based on the claim that there are irreconcilable differences within a marriage (as opposed to one spouse being legally at fault for the marital breakup).

norms Socially defined rules of behavior; include folkways, mores, and laws.

nuclear winter The predicted result of a thermonuclear war whereby dust storms and concentrations of particles would block out vital sunlight, lower temperatures in the northern hemisphere, and lead to the death of most living things on earth.

occupational sex segregation The concentration of women in certain occupations and of men in other occupations.

operational definition In research, a definition of a variable that specifies how that variable is to be measured (or was measured) in the research.

organized crime Criminal activity conducted by members of a hierarchically arranged structure devoted primarily to making money through illegal means.

outing Publicly identifying the sexual orientation of homosexuals without their consent.

patriarchal Literally, rule by father; today, connotes rule by males.

patriarchy A tradition in which families are male-dominated.

peace dividend Resources that are diverted from military spending and channeled into private or public investment or consumption, used to reduce the deficit, and/or used to lower taxes.

phased retirement Retirement in which the older worker can withdraw from the workforce gradually.

pink-collar jobs Jobs that offer few benefits, often have low prestige, and are disproportionately held by women.

planned obsolescence The manufacturing of products that are intended to become inoperative or outdated in a fairly short period of time.

pluralism A state in which racial and/or ethnic groups maintain their distinctness, but respect each other and have equal access to social resources.

postindustrialization The shift from an industrial economy dominated by manufacturing jobs to an economy dominated by service-oriented, information-intensive occupations.

post-traumatic stress disorder A set of symptoms that may result from any traumatic experience including crime victimization, war, natural disasters, or abuse.

poverty line An annual dollar amount below which individuals or families are considered officially poor by the government.

prejudice An attitude or judgment, usually negative, about an entire category of people based on their group membership.

primary aging Biological changes associated with aging that are due to physiological variables such as cellular and molecular variation (e.g., gray hair).

primary prevention strategies Family violence prevention strategies that target the general population.

primary work sector The set of work roles in which individuals are involved in the production of raw materials and food goods; develops when a society changes from a hunting and gathering society to an agricultural society.

privatization The use of private services in the public educational system.

public assistance A general term referring to some form of economic support by the government to citizens who meet certain established criteria.

quality circle A type of welfare corporatism in which workers and managers who are responsible for production meet to discuss performance problems and ways to improve morale.

race A category of people who are believed to share distinct physical characteristics that are deemed socially significant.

racism The belief that certain groups of people are innately inferior to other groups of people based on their racial classification. Racism serves to justify discrimination against groups that are perceived as inferior.

regionalization The merging of city and suburban governments to create one government.

rehabilitation A criminal justice philosophy that views the primary purpose of the criminal justice system as changing the criminal offender through such programs as education and job training, individual and group therapy, substance abuse counseling, and behavior modification.

relative poverty The inability of an individual or family to maintain a standard of living considered normal by members of society.

reverse discrimination The unfair treatment of members of the majority group (i.e., white males) that, according to some, results from affirmative action.

role A set of rights, obligations, and expectations associated with a status.

SADD Students Against Drunk Driving; a student social action group committed to reducing drunk driving.

sample In survey research, the portion of the population selected to be questioned.

sanctions Social consequences for conforming to or violating norms. Types of sanctions include positive, negative, formal, and informal.

sandwich generation The generation that has the responsibility of simultaneously caring for their children and their aging parents.

school vouchers Tax credits that are transferred to the public or private school of a parent's choice.

science The process of discovering, explaining, and predicting natural or social phenomena.

secondary aging Biological changes associated with aging that can be attributed to poor diet, lack of exercise, and increased stress.

secondary prevention strategies Prevention strategies that target groups that are thought to be at high risk for family violence.

secondary work sector The set of work roles in which individuals are involved in the production of manufactured goods from raw materials; emerges when a society becomes industrialized.

segregation The physical and social separation of categories of individuals, such as racial or ethnic groups.

self-fulfilling prophecy A concept referring to the tendency for people to act in a manner consistent with the expectations of others.

senescence The biology of aging.

sexism The belief that there are innate psychological, behavioral, and/or intellectual differences between females and males and that these differences connote the superiority of one group and the inferiority of another.

sexual harassment When an employer requires sexual favors in exchange for a promotion, salary increase, or any other employee benefit and/or the existence of a hostile environment that unreasonably interferes with job performance, as in the case of sexually explicit remarks or insults being made to an employee.

sexual orientation The aim or object of an individual's sexual and emotional interests—toward members of the same sex, the opposite sex, or both sexes; also involves issues concerning lifestyle and self-identity.

single-payer system A single tax-financed public insurance program that replaces private insurance companies.

slavery A condition in which one social group treats another group as property to exploit for financial gain.

social class Groups of people who share a similar position or social status within the stratification system.

social group Two or more people who have a common identity, interact, and form a social relationship. Institutions are made up of social groups.

social mobility Movement within the stratification system.

social problem A social condition that a segment of society views as harmful to members of society and in need of remedy.

social stratification The division of people into categories based on their unequal access to resources such as power, prestige, and wealth.

socialism An economic ideology that emphasizes public rather than private ownership. Theoretically, goods and services are equitably distributed according to the needs of the citizens.

sociological imagination A term coined by C. Wright Mills to refer to the ability to see the connections between our personal lives and the social world in which we live.

split-labor market The existence of primary and secondary labor markets. A primary labor market refers to jobs that are stable and economically rewarding and have many benefits; a secondary labor market refers to jobs that offer little pay, no security, few benefits, and little chance for advancement.

state The organization of the central government and government agencies such as the armed forces, police force, and regulatory agencies.

status A position a person occupies within a social group.

stereotypes Oversimplified or exaggerated generalizations about a category of individuals. Stereotypes are either untrue or are gross distortions of reality.

strain theory A theory that argues that when legitimate means of acquiring culturally defined goals are limited by the structure of society, the resulting strain may lead to crime or other deviance.

structural-functionalism A sociological perspective that views society as a system of interconnected parts that work together in harmony to maintain a state of balance and social equilibrium for the whole; focuses on how each part of society influences and is influenced by other parts.

structural sexism The ways in which the organization of society, and specifically its institutions, subordinate individuals and groups based on their sex classification.

structural unemployment Unemployment that results from structural variables such as government and business downsizing, job exportation, automation, a reduction in the number of new and existing businesses, an increase in the number of people looking for jobs, and a recessionary economy where fewer goods are purchased and, therefore, fewer employees are needed.

subcultural theories A set of theories that argue that certain groups or subcultures in society have values and attitudes that are conducive to crime and violence.

subculture The distinctive lifestyles, values, and norms of discrete population segments within a society.

suburbanization The process in which city dwellers move to the suburbs due to concern about the declining quality of life in urban areas.

suburbs The urbanlike areas surrounding central cities.

survey research A method of research that involves eliciting information from respondents through questions; includes interviews (telephone or face-to-face) and written questionnaires.

sustainable development Societal development that meets the needs of current generations without threatening the future of subsequent generations.

symbolic interactionism A sociological perspective that emphasizes that human behavior is influenced by definitions and meanings that are created and maintained through symbolic interaction with others.

technological fix The use of scientific principles and technology to solve social problems.

technology Activities that apply the principles of science and mechanics to the solution of specific problems.

technology-induced diseases Diseases that result from the use of technological devices, products, and/or chemicals.

telecommute A work option in which workers complete all or part of their work at home with the use of information technology.

terrorism The premeditated use or threatened use of violence by an individual or group to gain a political objective.

tertiary prevention strategies Prevention strategies that target families who have experienced family violence.

therapeutic communities Organizations where approximately 35–100 individuals reside for up to fifteen months in order to abstain from drugs, develop marketable skills, and receive counseling.

tracking An educational practice in which students are grouped together on the basis of similar levels of academic achievement and abilities.

triple jeopardy See *multiple jeopardy.*

underclass A persistently poor and socially disadvantaged group that disproportionately experiences joblessness, welfare dependency, involvement in criminal activity, dysfunctional families, and low educational attainment.

underemployment Employment in a job that is underpaid or is not commensurate with one's skills, experience, and/or education, and/or involves working fewer hours than desired.

urban homesteading Programs that encourage individuals and investors to purchase aban-

doned houses at reduced prices in order to bring people back into neighborhoods, reduce the number of vacant homes, and increase the property tax base.

urban population Persons living in cities or towns of 2,500 or more inhabitants.

urban villages Neighborhood communities, within urban settings, that facilitate the formation of intimate and strong social bonds among community members.

urbanism The culture and lifestyle of city dwellers, often characterized by individualistic and cosmopolitan norms, values, and styles of behavior.

urbanization The transformation of a society from a rural to an urban one.

urbanized area One or more locations and their adjacent territories that together have a minimum population of 50,000.

values Social agreements about what is considered good and bad, right and wrong, desirable and undesirable.

variable Any measurable event, characteristic, or property that varies or is subject to change.

victimless crimes Illegal activities, such as prostitution or drug use, that have no complaining party; also called "vice crimes."

virtual reality Computer-generated three-dimensional worlds that change in response to the movements of the head or hand of the individual; a simulated experience of people, places, sounds, and sights.

war Organized armed violence aimed at a social group in pursuit of an objective.

wealthfare system Governmental policies and regulations that economically favor the wealthy.

welfare corporatism A broad term that refers to varying levels of employee involvement in planning and production processes.

white-collar crime Includes both occupational crime, where individuals commit crimes in the course of their employment, and corporate crime, where corporations violate the law in the interest of maximizing profit.

work sectors The division of the labor force into distinct categories (primary, secondary, and tertiary) based on the types of goods/services produced.

Name Index

Kettering, Charles Franklin, 28
Khator, Renu, 458
Kidron, Michael, 307
Kilbourne, Barbara S., 228, 244
Killpack, S., 136, 152
King, Abby C., 45, 46, 47, 61
King, Martin Luther, Jr., 269, 496
King, Rodney, 257
King, Yolanda, 151
Kingsley, Gregory, 171
Kinney, David A., 373, 396
Kinsey, Alfred C., 193–194, 218
Kirschenman, Joleen, 261, 276
Kishor, Sunita, 20, 30
Kissinger, Henry, 488
Kitson, Gay C., 145, 154
Klassen, Albert D., 19, 30, 195, 206, 218
Kleber, Herbert D., 83
Kleg, Milton, 268, 275
Klein, Fred, 192, 218
Klein, Lawrence R., 466, 492
Kleinman, Joel C., 121
Kleinman, Paula Holzman, 86, 90
Kleniewski, Nancy, 354, 366
Klerman, Jacob A., 40, 60
Klerman, Lorraine V., 40, 60
Klingman, Avigdor, 477, 492
Klonoff-Cohen, Sandra H., 81, 90
Kluegel, James R., 275
Knight, Jerry, 264, 275
Knoke, David, 176, 188
Knudsen, Dean, 133, 154
Knutson, John F., 137, 154
Koenig, Dieter, 450, 455–456, 457, 459
Kolata, Gina, 194, 218
Kolland, Franz, 165, 188
Kopelman, Loretta M., 226–227
Korbin, Jill E., 182, 187
Kort, Marcel de, 85, 90
Koss, M. P., 103, 122, 139, 154
Kotlowitz, Alex, 265
Kozol, Jonathan, 264, 352, 365, 372–373,
376, 379, 380, 382, 383, 384, 396
Krackov, Andrew, 219
Kraft, Ronald M., 213, 218
Krieger, Nancy, 52–53, 60
Kriska, Andrea, 45, 46, 47, 61
Krivo, Lauren J., 20, 30
Krohn, Marvin D., 100, 122
Kroner, Tracie, 233, 245
Krueger, Alan, 328, 337
Krug, Ronald S., 136, 154
Krugman, R. D., 133, 154
Krysan, Maria, 264, 275
Kuhn, Anthony, 356, 365
Kuhn, Margaret, 184
Kuhn, Thomas, 408, 427
Kurdek, Lawrence A., 145, 154
Kurz, Kathleen M., 40, 61

Labich, Kenneth, 315, 338
Labouview, Erich W., 81, 91
Laird, Bob, 492
Lamielle, Mary, 445–446, 496, 497
Landau, Elaine, 268, 275
Lang, Eugene, 393
Lang, k d, 211
Lange, Jessica, 168, 238
Langone, John, 259, 262, 276
Lareau, Annette, 381, 396
Larson, Jan, 346, 365
Laub, John H., 100, 123
Lauer, Jeanette C., 146, 154
Lauer, Robert H., 146, 154
Laufer, William S., 85, 89, 95, 121
Laumann, Edward O., 194, 218
Laver, Robert, 79, 90
Lays, Julie, 378, 396
Learner, Harriet G., 237
Lee, F. R., 324, 338
Lee, Philip R., 45, 52, 61
Leigh, Wilhelmina A., 52, 60
Leightdelstein, Ellen Schneider, 81, 90
Leland, John, 496, 497
Lenherr, M., 133, 154
Lenski, Gerard, 307
Lenski, J., 307
Leon, Arthur L., 45, 46, 47, 61
Leonard, K. E., 77, 90
Lesieur, Henry R., 122
Letterman, David, 163
Lever, Janet, 193, 194, 218
Levin, Jack, 168, 187, 267, 268, 276
Levinson, D., 90, 150, 154
Levinson, Marc, 295, 307
Levitt, Eugene E., 19, 30, 195, 206, 218
Levy, Barry S., 60, 204, 217, 307
Levy, Steven, 411, 425, 427
Lewis, Bernard, 473, 492
Lewis, Oscar, 323, 338
Lewis, Robert, 479
Lewis, Shawn D., 226
Lewontin, Richard C., 215, 218
Lichter, Daniel T., 320, 338
Lichter, Linda S., 259, 276
Lichter, Robert S., 276
Liem, G. Ramsey, 294, 307
Liem, Joan H., 294, 307
Light, Ivan, 356, 364
Li Nan, 441, 459
Linden, Eugene, 434, 441, 459
Link, Bruce G., 45, 61
Lippman, Walter, 8
Lipton, Douglas S., 79, 82, 90
Liska, A., 97, 122
Liskowsky, David R., 292, 307
Liu, Melinda, 209, 219
Livermore, Charles, 358, 365
Lloyd, Donald A., 58, 62

Lloyd, S. A., 133, 136, 154
Loeb, Paul, 496, 497
Loeber, Rolf, 87, 91
Logan, John, 111, 121, 167
Long, J. Scott, 228, 244
Long, Peter, 55, 56, 62
Lopez, J. A., 301, 308
Lopez, M. Elena, 397
Lord, George F., 351, 365
Loseke, D. R., 141, 154
Loury, Glenn C., 270, 276
Lowell, James Russell, 314
Lubetkin, Barry, 81
Lukoff, Irving F., 86, 90
Lyons, Barbara, 55, 56, 62

Mabry, Marcus, 269, 276
MacAndrew, C., 78, 90
Macera, Carolina A., 45, 46, 47, 61
MacKinnon, C. E., 233, 245, 412
Macklin, Ruth, 422, 427
Mahmud, Simeen, 437, 439, 459
Maine, Deborah, 39, 40, 60
Makris, Lukas, 181, 188
Malthus, Thomas, 431
Maluso, D., 228, 245
Malveaux, Julianne, 354
Mandela, Nelson, 158, 273
Manis, Jerome G., 20, 30
Marble, Manning, 276
Marcus, Bess H., 45, 46, 47, 61
Marcus, Eric, 192, 207, 218
Marini, Margaret Mooney, 237, 244
Markey, Edward, 476
Markle, Gerald E., 4, 31, 73, 90
Marlow, L., 146, 154
Marsiglio, W., 129, 155
Martin, Clyde E., 218
Martin, Patricia Yancey, 230, 244
Martin, Sally S. Kees, 223, 246
Martindale, Melanie, 244
Marx, Karl, 13, 302, 313–314, 398
Masheter, C., 146, 154
Massey, Douglas S., 264, 276, 354, 364
Massey, James L., 100, 122
Matousek, Jiri, 489–490, 492
Matras, Judah, 162, 163, 174, 184, 188
Mattera, Philip, 418, 427
Mauro, Tony, 271, 276
Mayhew, Patricia, 94, 124
Maynard, Douglas W., 17, 30
Mazur, Allan, 425
McAneny, Leslie, 308
McCammon, Holly, 298, 308
McClelland, Kent, 260, 276
McCormick, John, 103, 108, 123
McCormick, S. J., 424, 427

Subject Index

health costs in, 79, 81
latent functions of policies on, 68
legalization of, 85
marijuana in, 74
narcotics in, 75
psychoactive, 67
psychological theories of, 70
social context of, 64–67
societal consequences of, 77–79, 81
structural-functionalist perspective of, 67–68
symbolic interactionist perspective of, 69
testing for, 80
tobacco in, 71–74
treatment alternatives for, 81–83
understanding, 87–88
use of, in United States, 65–67
as vice crimes, 104–105
Drunk driving as social problem, 16
Dual economy, 289

Ecology, human, 430
Economic consequences of divorce, 145
Economic conversion, 468
Economic costs of crime and violence, 111–112
Economic development
increasing, in curbing population growth, 440
sustainable, 456
Economic development and environmental problems, 450–451
Economic discrimination against children, 170–172
Economic Dislocation and Worker Adjustment Act (EDWAA), 299
Economic inequality
components of, 313–315
global, 313
rectifying, 328–333
in United States, 312–313
Economic institution, 282
Economic Opportunity Act (1964), 330
Economic resources
diversion of, 477–478
redistribution of, 486
Economics
of military spending, 466–469
power of elderly, 184–185
Economic underdevelopment, and population growth, 437–438
Ectasy, 77
Education, 330
achieving improvements in, 333
alternative choices in, 391–392
bilingual, 383–384
computer technology in, 391

conflict perspective of, 372–373
deterioration of, in urban areas, 352
experiences in, and cultural sexism, 233–234
global comparisons of, 368–369
home, 391
impact of poverty on, 325
in improving status of women, 439
inadequacies of facilities and personnel, 379–380
inequalities in attaining, 381–385
interpersonal, 388–389
latent function of, 12
mandatory, 127
manifest function of, 11
micro-society, 389–390
moral, 388–389
multicultural, 269–270
privatization in, 392–393
problems in American system, 375–380
setting national standards in, 390–391
in social context, 368–369
socialization function of, 370
structural-functionalist perspective of, 369–372
and structural sexism, 227–228
symbolic interactionist perspective of, 373, 375
and technological inequality, 420–421
trends and innovations in American, 388–393
understanding crisis in, 393–394
vouchers in, 391
Educational Amendments Act (1963) in reducing gender inequity, 242
Educational discrimination, 262–263
Education Amendments (1972), 384
Eighteenth Amendment, 70
Elder abuse, 134
Elderhood, 164
Elderly
activism by, 182–185
economic power of, 184–185
and health care reform, 185
health issues for, 178
increases in number of, 173–175
lack of employment for, 176
living arrangements for, 180–181
myths and facts about, 169
political power of, 184
poverty for, 177
problems of, 175–182
quality of life for, 178–180
treatment of, 165
victimization and abuse for, 182
Electronic redlining, 421
EMIT, 80

Employee stock ownership plans, 303
Employment
and income discrimination, 261–262
and job training programs, 330
lack of, for elderly, 176
status variations in poverty by, 320, 322
Encryption, 419
Endogamy, 252
Energy, alternative sources of, 454
Engineering, genetic, 413
Enterprise zones, 361
Environment
destruction of, 479–482
understanding, 456–457
Environmentalist groups, 452–453
Environmental problems
limited solutions and limited gains, 451–456
pollution as, 44, 442, 444, 446–449
social causes of, 450–451
Equal Employment Opportunity Commission (EEOC), 231
Equal Pay Act (1963)
and structural sexism, 231
in reducing gender inequity, 242
Equal Rights Amendment (ERA), 240–241
Equity principle, 335
Ethnic cleansing, 473
Ethnicity. *See also* Race and ethnic relations
and affluence, 316
impact on health, 51–52, 57
social meaning of, 250
Experiments in social problems research, 22
Exxon Valdez oil spill, 449

Face-to-face interviews, 23
Fair Standards Labor Act (1938), 170–172
Families, 126, 147–148. *See also* Divorce; Unmarried and teenage parenthood
in attaining education, 381–383
blended, 128
children as economic asset to, 438
conflict perspective of, 130–131
effects of drug use and abuse on, 78
as factor in domestic violence and abuse, 139
social context of, 126–129
as social group, 5–6
strengthening postdivorce, 146
structural changes in, and poverty, 322
structural-functionalist perspective of, 130

National Rifle Association (NRA), 118–119
National Science and Technology Council (NSTC), 424
National security, threats of, 479–482
Natural resources
    depletion of, 435, 450
    global conflict over, 472
Neglect, 132
Neighborhood watch programs, 114
Neo-Nazis, 268
Netherlands, drug use in, 64
New ageism, 177
New Orleans
    crime in, 350, 357
    urban decoy in, 357–358
New poor, 322
Newspapers, gender stereotypes in, 235
New York City, 343
    crime in, 350, 351
    growth rate of, 342–343
    inadequacy of housing in, 354
    mass transit in, 353
    privatization of education in, 393
    services in, 352
Nicotine, 71
Nixon, Richard, drug policy under, 68
No-fault divorce, 144
Nonfamily households, 128–129
Non-Marxist conflict theories of social problems, 14–15
Nonparticipant observation research, 24
Nonverbal symbolic abuse, 132
Normlessness and alienation, 290
Norms as cultural element, 7–8
Norplant, 414
Nuclear fission, 416–417
Nuclear Nonproliferation Treaty, 489–490
Nuclear waste, disposal of, 447–448
Nuclear Waste Fund, 448
Nuclear Waste Policy Act (1982), 448
Nuclear winter, 482
Nursing homes, 181
Nutrition and population growth, 434–435

Occupational crime, 105
Occupational prestige rankings, 314
Occupational Safety and Health Administration (OSHA), 299
Occupational sex segregation, 229
Office of Technology Assessment, 424
Official statistics on crime, 95–96
Older Women's League, 183–184
Operational definition, 20

Opium, conflict perspective on, 68
Organization for Economic Cooperation and Development (OECD), 293
Organized crime, 105
Osaka-Kobe-Kyoto, Japan, growth rate of, 343
Outing, 211–212
Overt discrimination, 260
Ozone layer, depletion of, 442

Parent abuse, 133
Parental involvement in education, 381–382
"Parenting After Divorce," 146
Participant observation research, 24
Partner abuse, effects of, on children, 136
Patriarchy, 131
PCB, 449
Peace dividend, 467–468
Pell grants, 330
Perspective, 10. See also specific
Pesticides, 448–449
Peyote, 75
Phased retirement, 177
Philadelphia, 343
Phobia
    geronto, 168
    homo, 200–201
Phoenix House, 82
Physical and mental health problems, social correlates of
    ethnicity, 51–52, 57
    gender, 52–53, 57
    marital status, 53
    race, 51–52, 57
    social class, 50–51, 57
Pink-collar jobs, 230
Planned obsolescence, 451
Planned Parenthood of Southeastern Pennsylvania v. Casey, 415
Plessy v. Ferguson, 251
Pluralism, 252
Policing, community, 351
Political discrimination, 266
Political power of elderly, 184
Political strategies
    in combating race and ethnic problems, 270
    in reducing gender inequity, 242
Politics
    in post-Cold War era, 484–486
    and structural sexism, 231
Pollution
    air, 442, 444
    indoor air, 445–446
    land, 444, 446–449

water, 449–450
Population
    metropolitan, 345
    understanding, 456–457
    United States, 431
    urban, 342–343, 344
    world, 431
Population density, urban crowding and high, 435–436
Population growth
    social context of, 430–434
    social problems related to unrestrained, 434–436
    strategies for limiting, 438–442
    structural and cultural influences on, 436–438
    theories of, 431–434
    and water shortages, 435
Portland Progress Associates, 359
Post-Cold War era
    internal conflict in, 483
    politics in, 484–486
Postindustrialization, 282–283
Post-traumatic stress disorder, 477
    and domestic violence, 136
Poverty
    absolute, 318
    and crime, 357–358
    cultural explanations of, 323
    definitions and measurement of, 318–319
    demographic variations in, 319–320
    in domestic violence and abuse, 139
    for elderly, 177
    failure of United States programs on, 331–333
    and gender role socialization, 237
    individual consequences of, 323–325
    influence on health care, 41–42
    international responses to, 333
    relative, 318
    for single mothers and children, 148
    social context of, 312–315
    societal consequences of, 325
    structural explanations of, 322–323
    and technology, 420–421
    understanding, 334–336
    urban, 356–358
    variations by employment status, 320, 322
Poverty cycle, 335
Poverty index, 318–319
Poverty line, 318
Power, 313–314
Powerlessness and alienation, 290
Pregnancy Discrimination Act (1978) in reducing gender inequity, 242
Prejudice, 158
    definition of, 258